AF574623

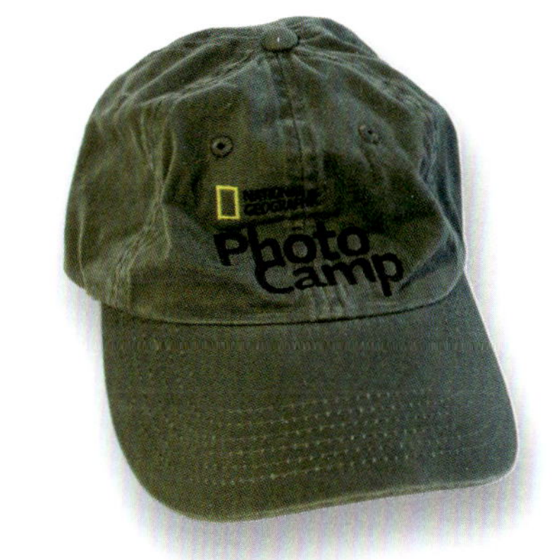

Photo Camp Stories

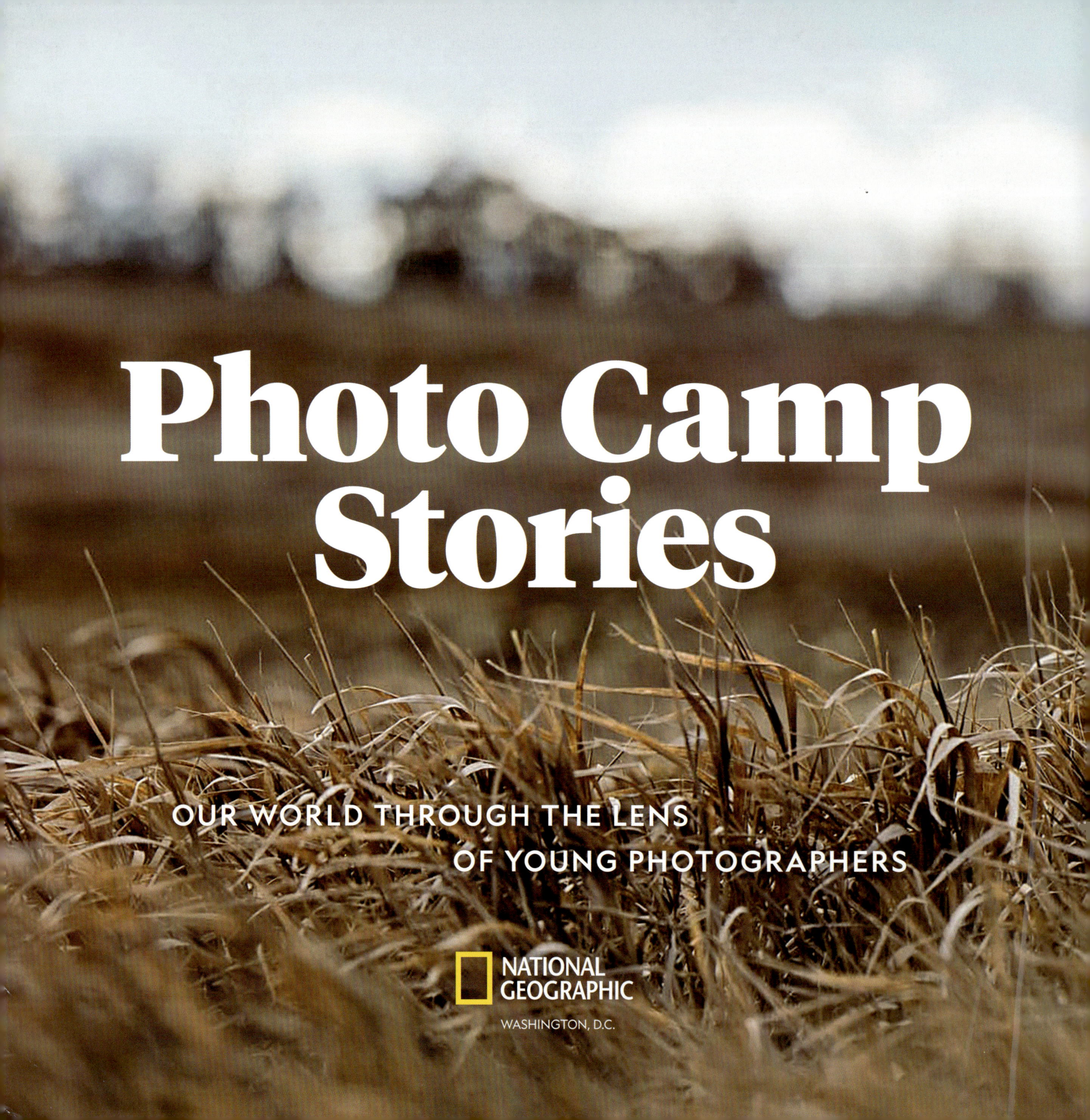

Photo Camp Stories

OUR WORLD THROUGH THE LENS OF YOUNG PHOTOGRAPHERS

NATIONAL GEOGRAPHIC
WASHINGTON, D.C.

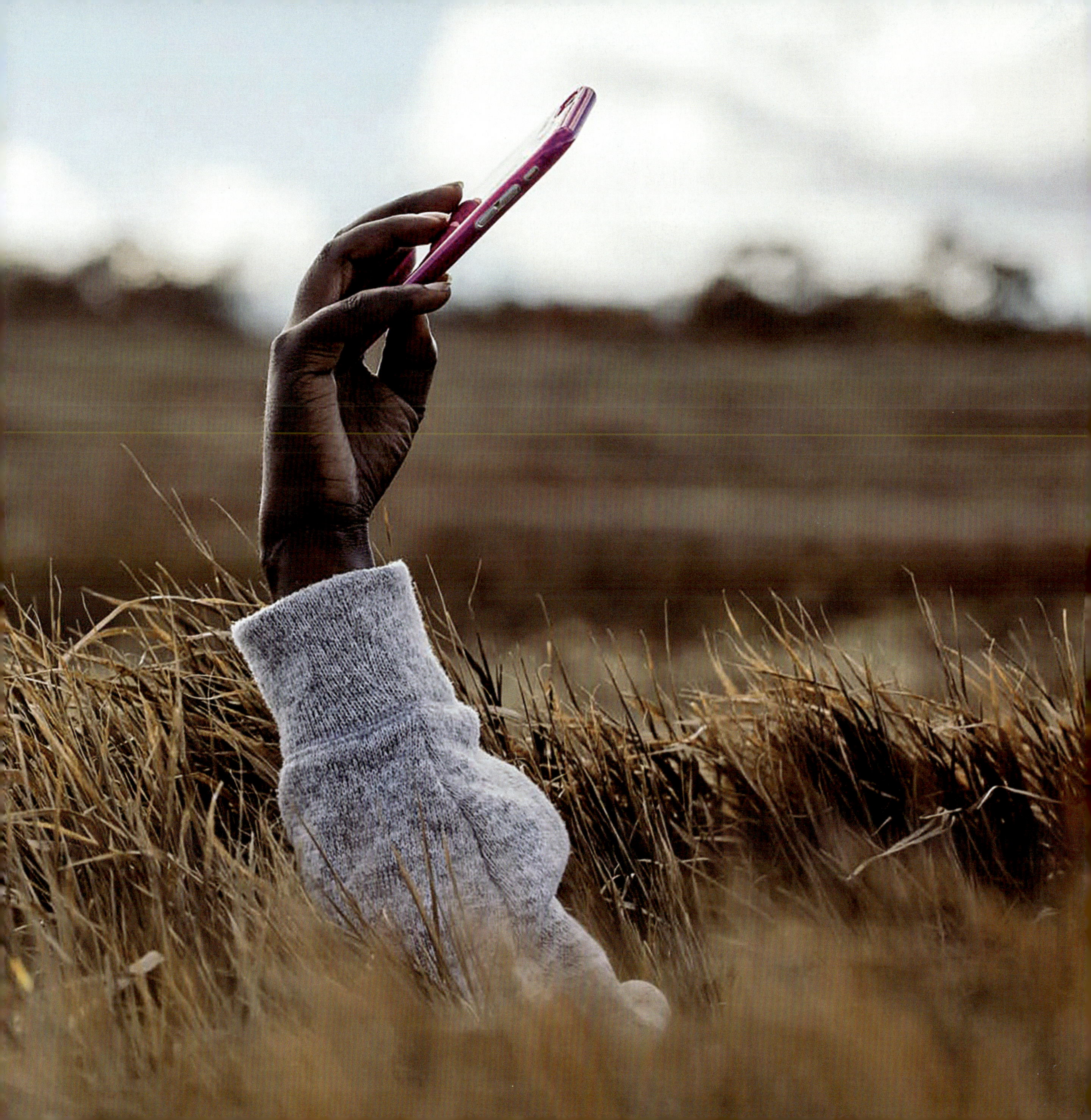

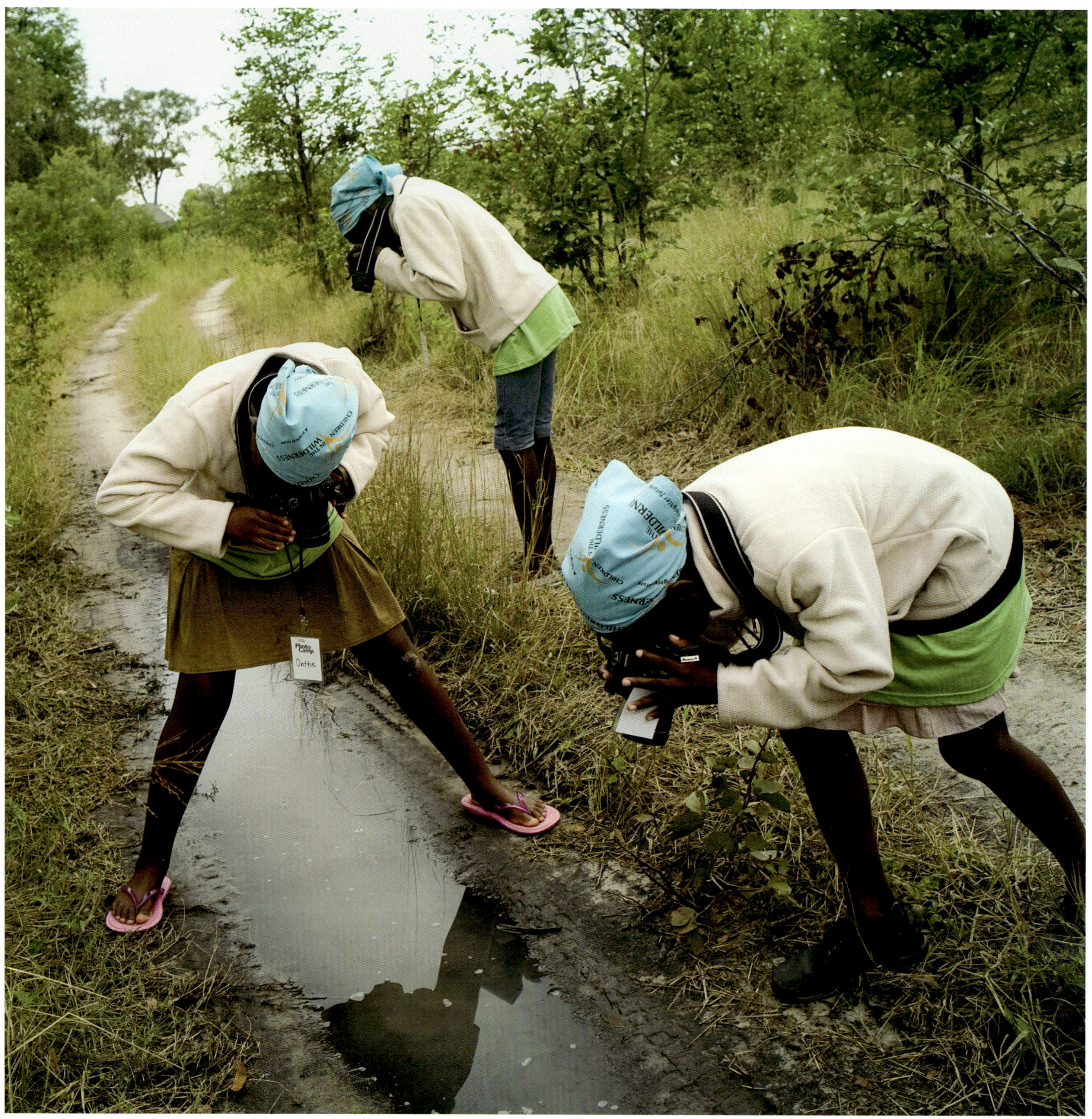
CHILDREN IN THE WILDERNESS
Photo Camp
Onttie

LYNN JOHNSON, PHOTO CAMP STAFF / BOTSWANA 2009 PREVIOUS PAGES: RONAN DONOVAN, PHOTO CAMP STAFF / VIRGINIA, U.S.A. 2016

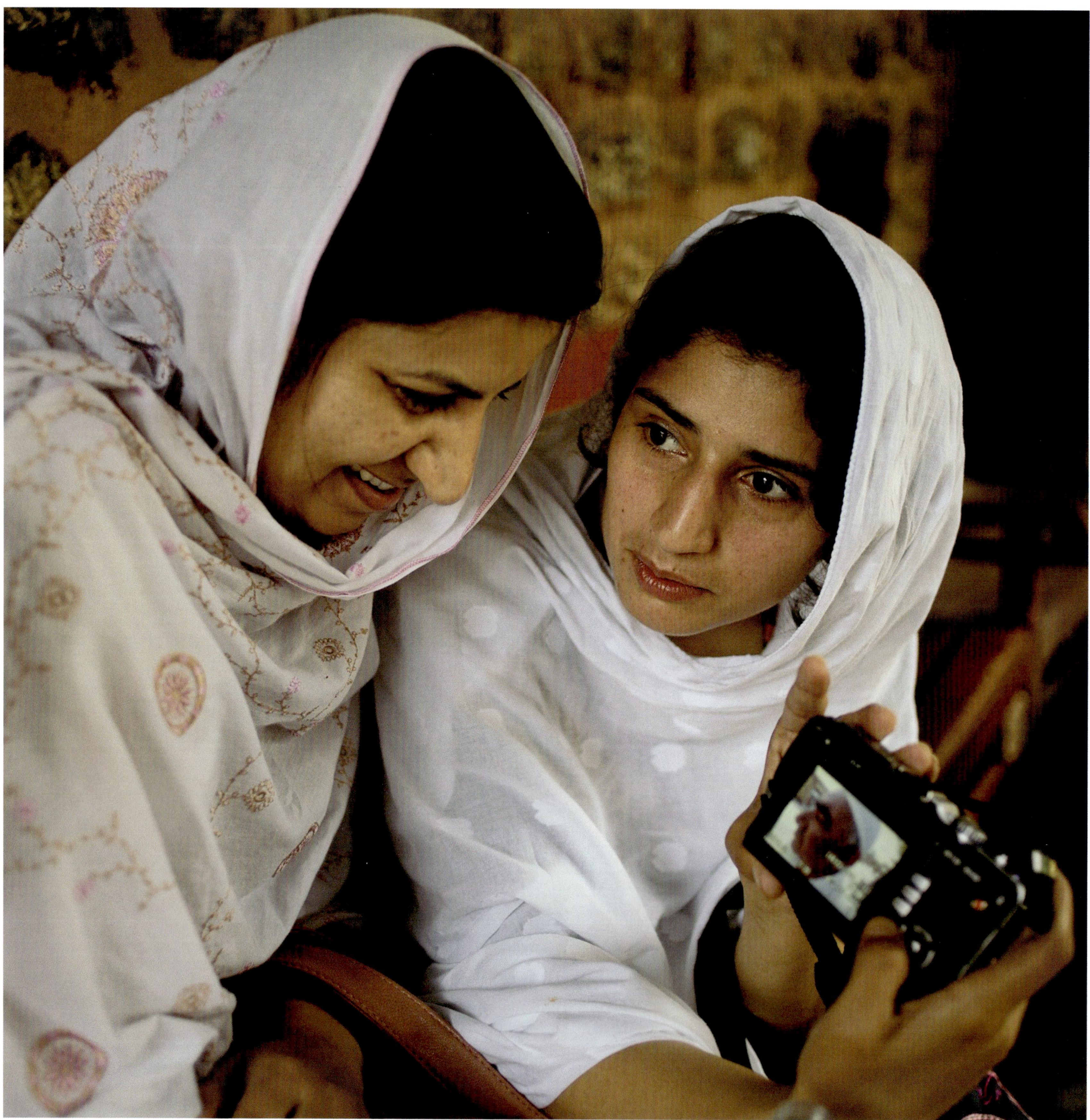

The Power of Youth

I WAS A 23-YEAR-OLD INTERN AT NATIONAL GEOGRAPHIC, and I remember being asked if I'd like to spend a week as a teaching assistant at a relatively new initiative called Photo Camp. That lucky assignment had me stomping through Washington, D.C., and learning about photography, about teaching, about seeing, and about empathy. The students in that camp remain in my memory 18 years later. Their stories, the images they made, and their presence remain a part of me, as do the camps I've been able to attend since then.

Nothing can prepare you for a Photo Camp. It's one part photojournalism school, one part summer (or winter) camp, one part community engagement—and it's all brilliantly orchestrated by Kirsten Elstner, its founder and director. I've had the opportunity to work with many of the world's leading visual storytellers as part of my role at National Geographic, often in far-flung locations—and yes, I've learned a great deal from them. But I can say, without hesitation, that I've learned the most from Photo Camp students—Sartre, whom I met in Shenandoah National Park in Virginia; Olive, whom I met in Rwanda; and so many others. The vivid sparks they brought to their work glowed ever brighter through the week I spent with them.

Through the inspired guidance of master National Geographic photographers, these students have brought us stories of their families and friendships. And in observing them, I learned something that has always stayed with me: These images and voices of youth have real power—and if we listen to them, the world will be better for it.

Since my first exposure in 2005, Photo Camp has worked with thousands of students around the world, supporting them to illuminate stories of their own communities and realize the power of their own voices. I hope you'll take a moment to immerse yourself in their words and images, to learn from the experiences of 20 years of young people around the world.

—**KAITLIN YARNALL,** CHIEF STORYTELLING OFFICER, NATIONAL GEOGRAPHIC SOCIETY

AMY TOENSING, PHOTO CAMP STAFF / PAKISTAN 2012

The Heart of Photo Camp

EVERYONE HAS A STORY, but not all of us are encouraged to tell it. What would a young person seeking refuge in Jordan or a girl who has lost her parents in India or a child from a Native American reservation in South Dakota have to say if the world stopped to listen?

The answers to these questions are contained in these pages. Over the past 20 years, thousands of young people at National Geographic Photo Camps have been guided by photographers eager to share their knowledge, but just as eager to learn and to be inspired in return. I've come to believe that there's no doubt: Stories can change lives.

RECENTLY, I RECEIVED one of those text messages that remind me of the importance of the journey I've traveled since 2003 as director of National Geographic Photo Camp. Kurena Singh, a young woman I met on a program in Banbasa, India, wrote to tell me that she's now planning a career in hotel management and dreams of attending graduate school. A shy 18-year-old, Kurena barely spoke during the workshop I was running in the spring of 2018 at an orphanage in northeastern India. Her story began there, as a child abandoned at the mission's gate because she was a girl.

Though she was small and quiet, Kurena had a fierceness in her eyes, as if she had seen too much and was always on high alert. But soon, we connected over cameras and essays as she worked on creating a series of self-portraits and writings about her life. Kurena started opening up, telling me about her early years sitting alone at the playground, wondering if her mom would return for her. The more I listened, the more she dropped her guard.

Most of the time, this is all it takes. At Photo Camp, I ask young people to tell me their stories, and I give them my full attention in return. In my experience, this is something many of us need: to have our stories matter to someone, even to just one person. This is the goal of the Photo Camp program: to inspire youth to see the power of their own voice and to understand the world through their eyes.

It's a surprising concept at first to most of our participants: the idea that our stories have the power to bind us, challenge us, connect us to one another as we recognize our own struggles and triumphs in the life of someone else. It tells us we are not alone. And when this happens, our hearts open, our minds expand, and the world grows a little bit closer.

In 2019, Kurena joined a second Photo Camp in another part of India. There, she met kids from similar backgrounds who encouraged her to go to college. She blossomed during a 2020 virtual Photo Camp alongside youth from 13 countries, including Cuba, Bhutan, Ethiopia, Nigeria, Ireland, and the United

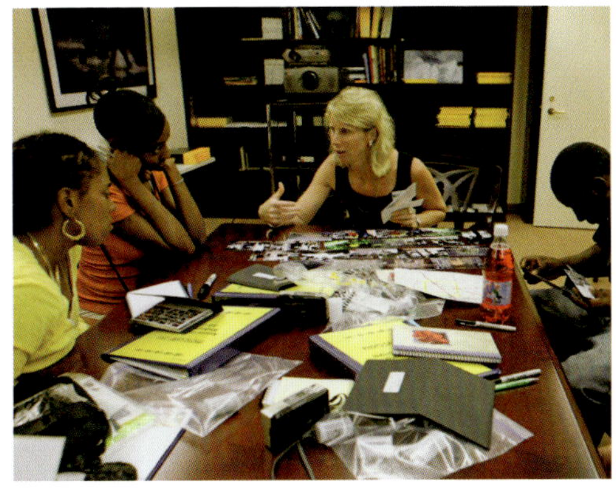

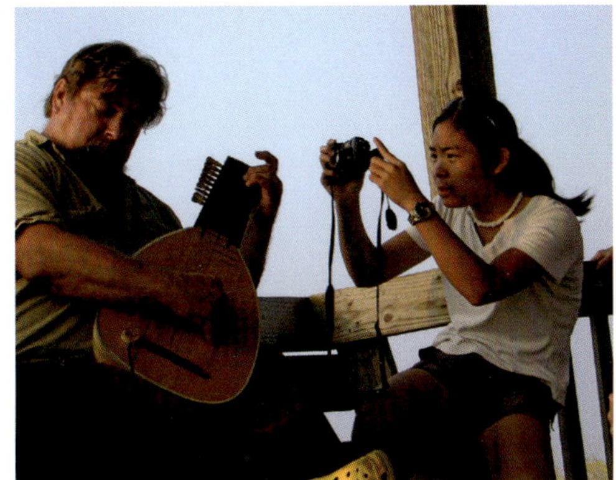

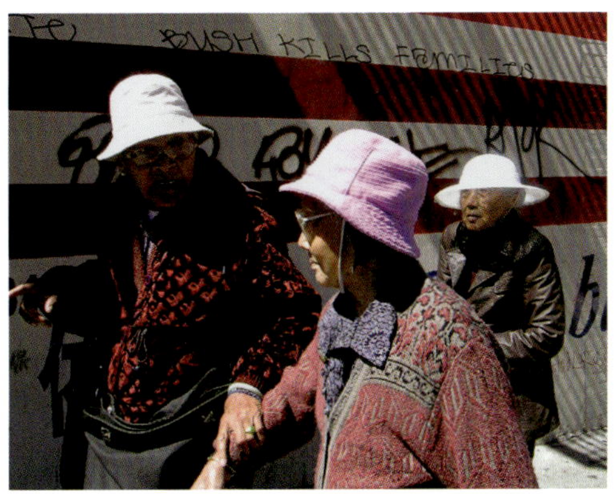

Two Decades of Accomplishments

2003

Photo Camp was born in 2003 as a weekly summer photography workshop for interns at the National Geographic Society. The program was modeled on *National Geographic* magazine's ZipUSA series, and the participants fanned out through the neighborhood immediately around headquarters to take their photographs.

2004

The program grew in 2004, expanding to New York, San Francisco, coastal Georgia, and the Channel Islands of California and building partnerships with such organizations as the International Center of Photography and the Office of National Marine Sanctuaries at the National Oceanic and Atmospheric Administration (NOAA).

2005

The program expanded further in 2005, partnering with universities and newspapers such as the *Miami Herald* and the University of Miami, Minnesota State, the *San Francisco Chronicle*, and the *New York Times*.

States. Together, the group created a shared story of life around the globe during the early days of the COVID-19-pandemic-induced lockdowns. They made self-portraits, many centered on a hand touching the glass windows that separated them from the outside world.

Kurena's self-portrait was accompanied by a caption, next to intricate drawings of places she loved. "My home and your home are probably very different," she wrote. "I live in a place that you would call an orphanage. To me, it is just my home." Kurena photographed her "sister" Reeva and wrote her a letter to accompany the images. "We may not be sisters by blood, but we are always sisters by heart."

KURENA'S STORY IS WHAT I HAD ENVISIONED when I first dreamed up the idea of Photo Camp in the difficult days following September 11, 2001. I was working as a freelance photographer for the *New York Times* and other publications, and I saw how the world reacted to the tragedy with empathy and a desire for unity. Inspired, I wanted to create something in my life that would reject division and add to humanity's sense of global connection.

I was drawn to young people as the future stewards of our complex world and wanted to design a program that focused on their perspectives. Working with other photographers, I created an organization

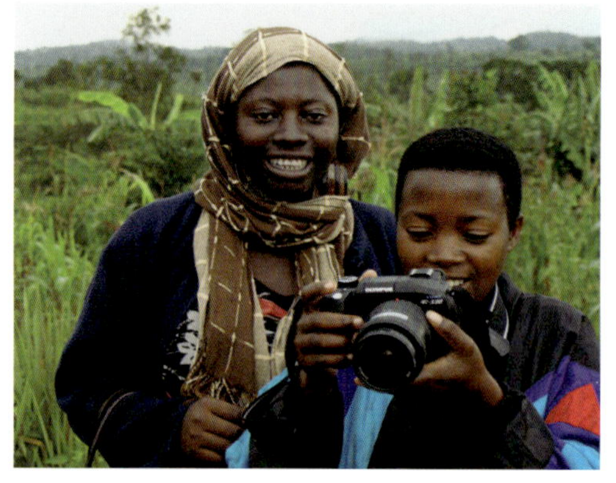

2006

Photo Camp's expansion to international locations began in 2006, as the program traveled to Uganda in partnership with the International Medical Corps. Photo Camp's partners bolster its ability to connect with and understand the communities where it works. The program's post-Hurricane Katrina camp, which also took place at this time, marked the first time students' written and spoken words were used to describe their stories alongside their photographs.

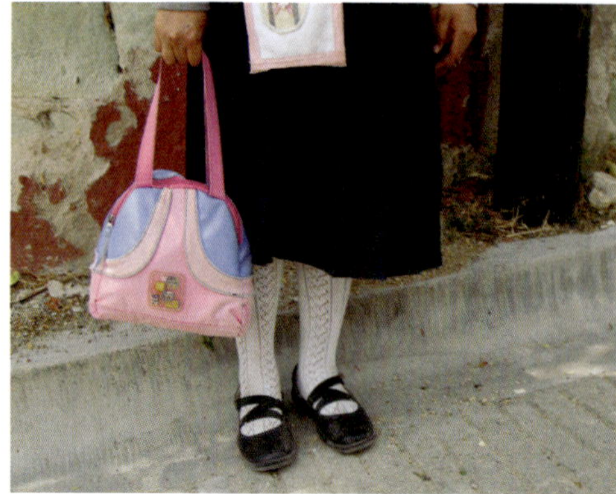

2007

In 2007, Photo Camp began connecting its programs thematically, and the stories students shared this year described their experiences as displaced youth. It began its second international program, with youth in Oaxaca, Mexico, exploring their experiences with the immigration of family members to the United States. It also began partnerships with such organizations as Newcomers High School in Queens, New York, and the Refugee Youth Project in Baltimore, Maryland.

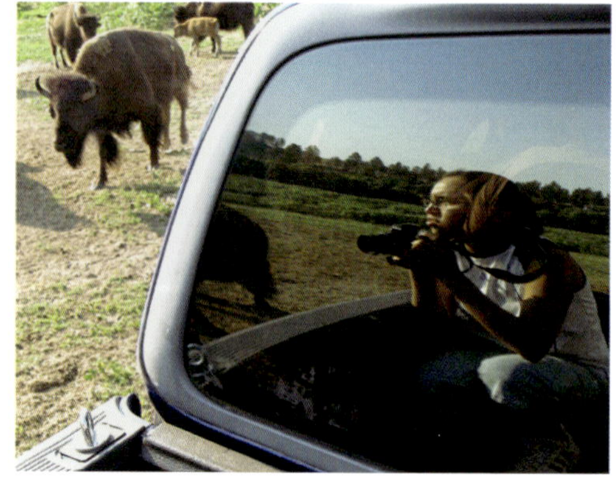

2008

In 2008, the program's theme was students' connection to nature. Photo Camp worked with youth on Tangier Island and the Appalachian Trail in Virginia, as well as the Pine Ridge Reservation in South Dakota. It traveled to Costa Rica and India, gathering young people's perspectives on environmental issues in their communities.

called VisionWorkshops. We began by teaching storytelling skills to youth struggling with addiction at the juvenile drug treatment court in my hometown of Annapolis, Maryland. We provided cameras, journals, and encouragement for them to describe the world from their point of view. Two years later, I brought the concept to photographers and editors at the National Geographic Society, and the Photo Camp program was born.

Since that first workshop in 2003, we've run more than 125 Photo Camps in 35 countries. The premise is simple: Over the course of a week, we gather 20 young people from diverse backgrounds and often little experience or opportunity to share their ideas through photography. We work with local partners to understand the needs of the community and trust them to find the young people who would benefit most from the program. Photo Camp fosters a deep sense of community, which continues after the workshops have ended.

Some of our students have never held a camera in their hands. Our team of National Geographic photographers sets out to inspire and mentor these youth. We guide them as they learn to use the tools of photography, teaching the basics of composition, color, perspective, balance, and light. The camera unlocks their creativity.

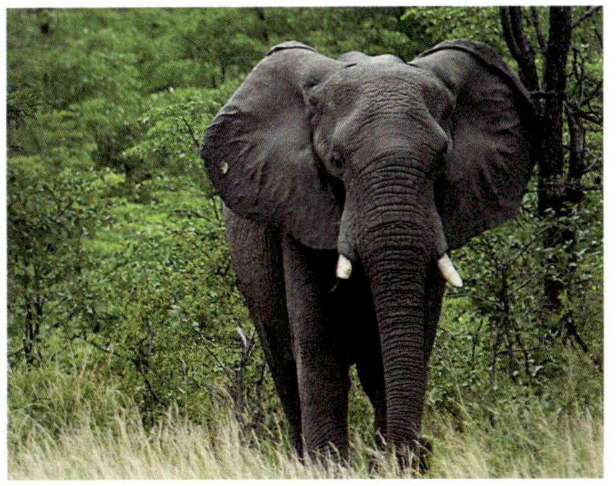

2009

In 2009, Photo Camp focused on ocean conservation and other environmental concerns of young people around the world. It strengthened partnerships with such organizations as Children in the Wilderness in Botswana and the SuAnne Big Crow Boys and Girls Club in South Dakota.

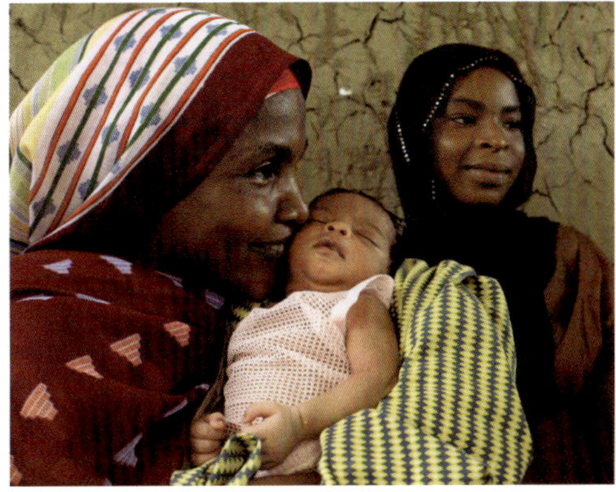

2010

The year 2010 brought new collaborations with Internews and USAID. Highlights included a three-camp series for young storytellers from diverse backgrounds in N'Djamena, Chad, and themes related to water conservation in Barbados and Florida.

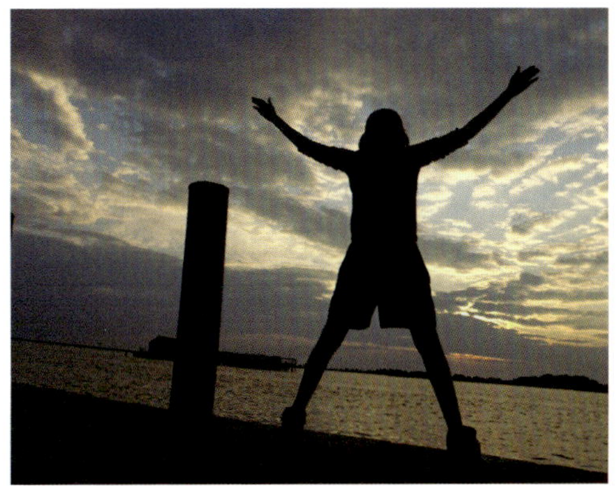

2011

Photo Camp's 2011 program included partnerships with the Chesapeake Bay Foundation and NOAA for a series of workshops exploring youth perspectives on sea level rise on Smith Island in Virginia and the Channel Islands of California.

Twenty years later, each time I sit with a young person at a Photo Camp anywhere in the world looking at the images they've made and listening to their stories, I can see that hope goes hand in hand with a deep longing for connection. As Abigael, a student at several camps we've held in partnership with the Refugee Youth Project in Baltimore, Maryland, says about the workshop process, "I see now that my story is important. That it can inspire others."

Abigael escaped from a difficult life in the Democratic Republic of the Congo, eventually landing in Baltimore as a teenager. She joined several Photo Camps over the years, teaching me and others about grace and perseverance through the artistic spirit of her work. Before each assignment, she closed her eyes and took a deep breath, as if gathering her creativity for the task ahead.

I trekked a portion of the Appalachian Trail with Abigael alongside students from Yemen, Ethiopia, Myanmar, and Eritrea. She photographed a path through wet fall leaves, brilliant orange at sunrise, as she recalled in her notebook the journeys of her childhood in Africa. Her assignment partner was Naum Khan Lun, a young poet from Myanmar. They shared a huge umbrella as they walked and made portraits of one another. In that process, they discovered that they had a common bond: Both yearned for grandmothers back home, whom they could no longer see. But they could describe them, and they

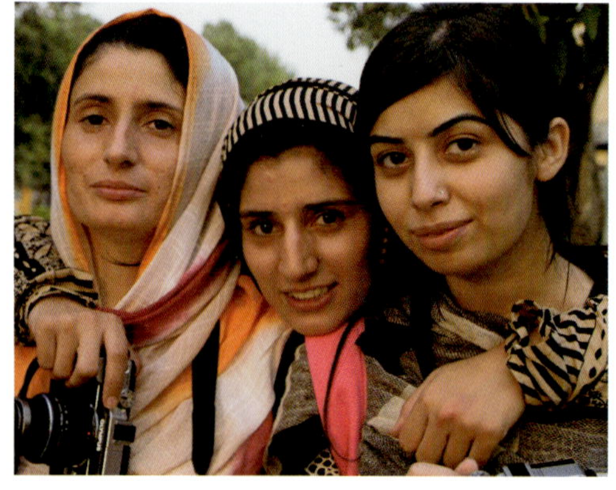

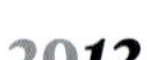

2012

In 2012, Photo Camp developed a series of workshops exploring themes of youth leadership and cross-cultural understanding in Pakistan, Haiti, the Bahamas, and Baltimore. A highlight was our program in Doha, Qatar, featuring an exchange between Brazilian and Qatari youth using photography to find common ground.

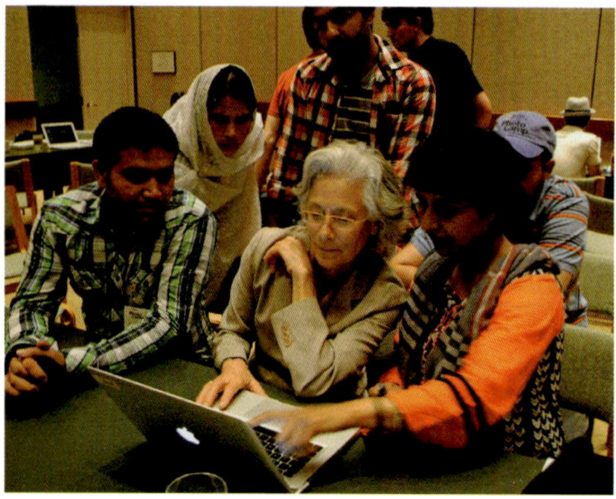

2013

In 2013, Photo Camp continued its theme of cross-cultural understanding with a master class based at National Geographic headquarters in Washington, D.C., and an exhibition of student work at the United States Institute for Peace.

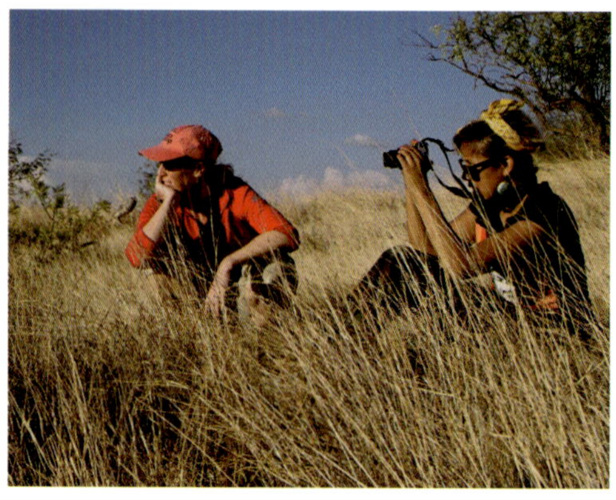

2014

A high point in 2014 was the Photo Camp that took place in Juba, South Sudan, the world's newest internationally recognized country at that time. We also learned about students' experiences in the U.S./Mexico border community of Arivaca, Arizona, and partnered again with Internews to explore health-related journalism reflecting 30 years of HIV in Kenya.

painted pictures for each other. That experience led me to create an assignment series: Write a letter to your ancestors and make a photograph to represent them. Write a letter to the future. I've used this approach at many Photo Camps since then.

When I read these letters, I feel like I'm peering into the collective hopes and challenges of a generation who understands that we're all far more connected than we are divided. Everyone involved in Photo Camps, myself included, is gifted with revelations.

We often hear that young people are more comfortable communicating online through social media than they are in person, face-to-face. But what I've seen in my encounters with youth around the globe is just the opposite: an ache, a search for in-person connection with other human beings. That doesn't mean that they see a nondigital future, or a world where iPhones and the internet have no relevance. But maybe they also see a world where an experience like Photo Camp—people sitting around the campfire of photography—can make a real difference in the way we live our lives and see our futures together.

In 2017, we worked in several European cities with young people who had fled conflict in the Middle East and North Africa, where they no longer felt safe. Half of our students were a part of that influx of new people seeking refuge far from home; the other half were Greek and Norwegian youth. As

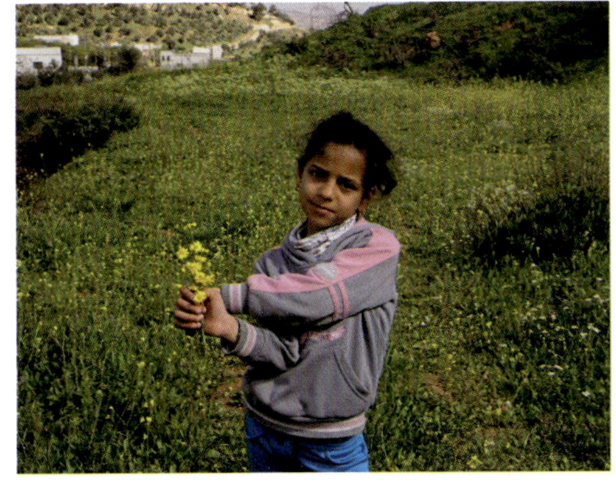

2015

In 2015, Photo Camp explored the world through the eyes of Syrian youth displaced from their homes and living in Jordan. It traveled to Sarajevo on the 20-year anniversary of the Dayton Accords, which set a framework for peace in Bosnia and Herzegovina, to chronicle the stories of its youth. The Photo Camp in Kharkiv, Ukraine, that year explored a similar theme, highlighting students dealing with disrupted lives.

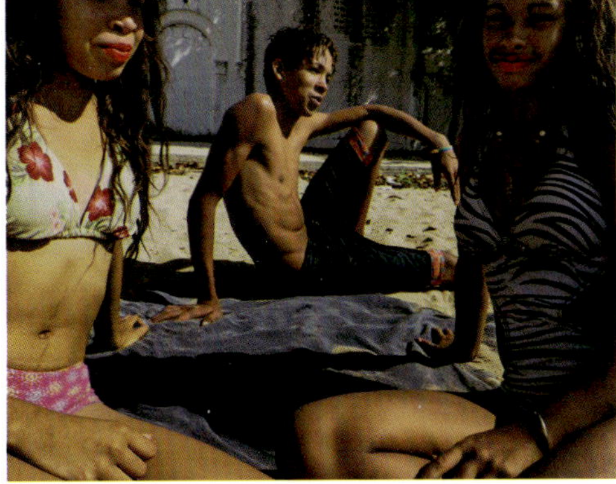

2016

Highlights from the 2016 Photo Camp included a workshop in Havana to learn through students' words and photos what life was like in the fleeting days of normalized Cuba-United States relations. The program also worked with displaced youth from around the world at a workshop based in Shenandoah National Park in Virginia, and another in Volcanoes National Park in Rwanda.

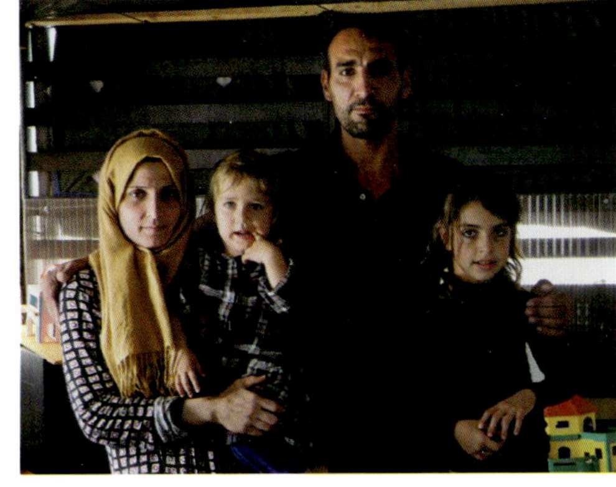

2017

In 2017, Photo Camp partnered with the Nobel Peace Center and the Norwegian Red Cross. From Oslo to Athens, we used the bonding capacity of a photography workshop to connect young people. Newly arrived refugees from Afghanistan, Syria, and Iran paired up with Norwegian and Greek youth, making portraits and powerful connections. Their work was displayed at an outdoor exhibition at the Nobel Peace Center in Oslo.

part of the workshop, students visited each other's homes and spaces that were meaningful to them.

Raouf was from Syria, and he partnered with Athens native Alexandra. They photographed each other, shared stories, and did what so many in our workshops do: They began a conversation, starting the process of understanding what someone else's life is like. That's a powerful ingredient of the Photo Camp magic. Raouf and Alexandra made portraits and learned about each other's backgrounds. Through photography, Alexandra learned the reasons why an 18-year-old would leave his homeland to travel alone on a dangerous journey across the Mediterranean to a place he'd never seen.

This is the heart of Photo Camp. It's a journey that begins on Day One of each workshop, when a group of people with seemingly nothing in common look one another in the eye and begin to create a shared story together. That act of creation culminates in an exhibit of student work shown on the final day. This process takes honest communication and learning the techniques of a journalist: Interview. Listen. Make a portrait. Write. Edit. Listen some more. From the outside, it can look like creative chaos. But in the end, students talk about their experience joining the "Photo Camp family" at the final show—and we all understand that it's been worthwhile.

During an assignment in Trondheim, Norway, 18-year-old Zabih set out to photograph his new

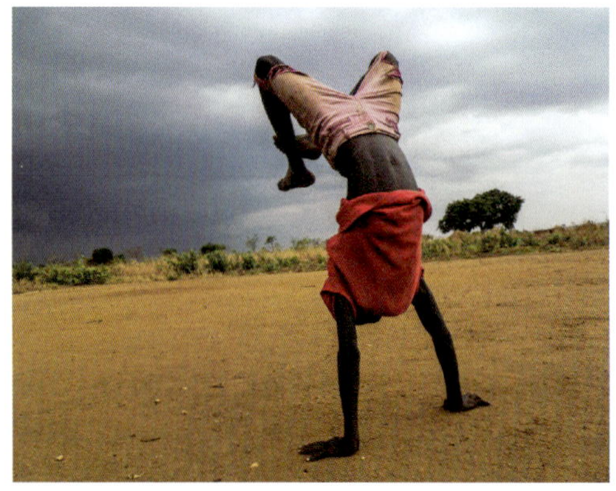

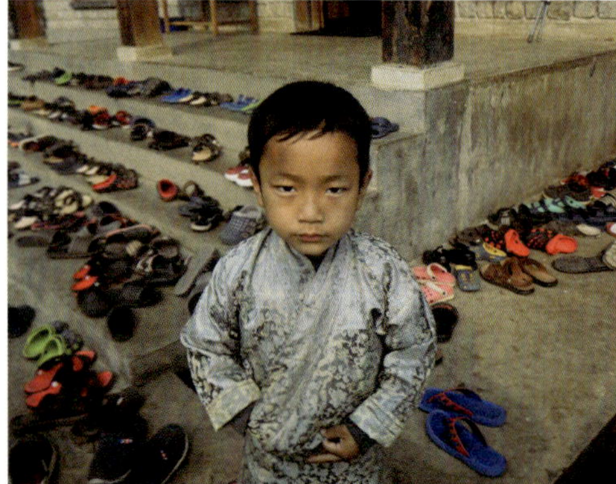

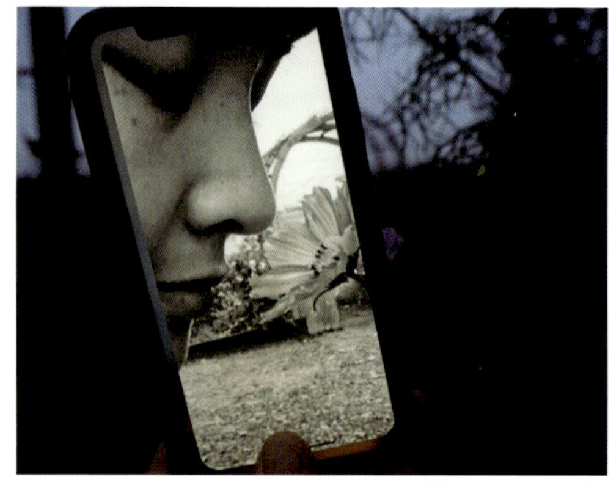

2018

Photo Camp's 2018 partnership with writer Paul Salopek and the Out of Eden Walk took the program across India, learning about the lives of youth in three cities along Salopek's route. Workshops also took place in Quinhagak, Alaska—featuring youth from the Yup'ik community—Myanmar, Moldova, and the BidiBidi Refugee Settlement in Uganda, weaving together important stories of youth from a global perspective.

2019

In 2019, Photo Camp met in one of the world's newest democracies, Bhutan. A Photo Camp in Brazil documented the journeys of young Venezuelans living in the Boa Vista UN Refugee Agency camp. The year culminated in a retrospective exhibition at the Kennedy Center in Washington, D.C. A group of master class students and alumni told the story of the Photo Camp family during a World Refugee Day event at the opening of the exhibition.

2020

The last in-person Photo Camp before the COVID-19 lockdown was on Costa Rica's Osa Peninsula in February 2020. That spring, the program became virtual, with a June workshop that brought together young people from 13 countries to describe life during a global pandemic. Later that year, storytellers from Indigenous communities worldwide gathered to share stories of their lives, common hopes for the future, and connection to the environment.

home and write about his journey. He was navigating the Norwegian school system, where he felt misunderstood by his teachers and classmates. Through a combination of words and pictures, he wanted to explain why he had left his family to seek a new life in a snowy country far from home:

> *The children of my country are just thinking of their futures, and how they didn't have a future there and it was not safe. I went from Afghanistan to Pakistan to Iran—walking, running, through the mountains. I went to Turkey, and then paid smugglers to take me by boat across the Mediterranean.*
>
> *You don't have a choice. You must go on this boat.*
>
> *You are making one life—one future—so you turn your face forward to the future.*
>
> *It was dark, and we could only see one light. The boat was crashing onto the cliffs. We were all helping each other. At that moment it didn't matter which country you were from; you just helped each other. This is what unity is.*

In his words I see a new spark of community, a vision of what can still be created in our world.

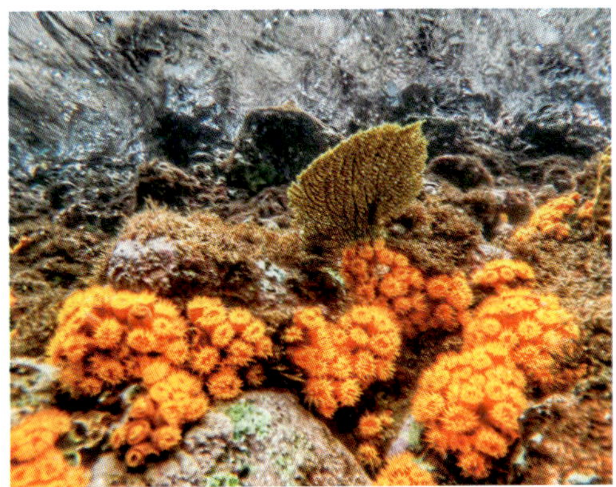

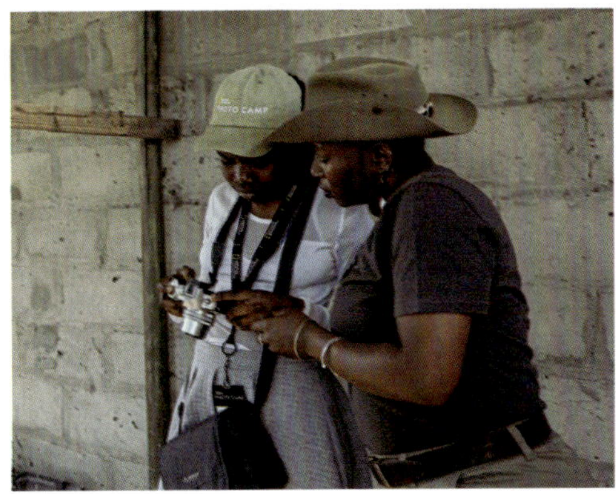

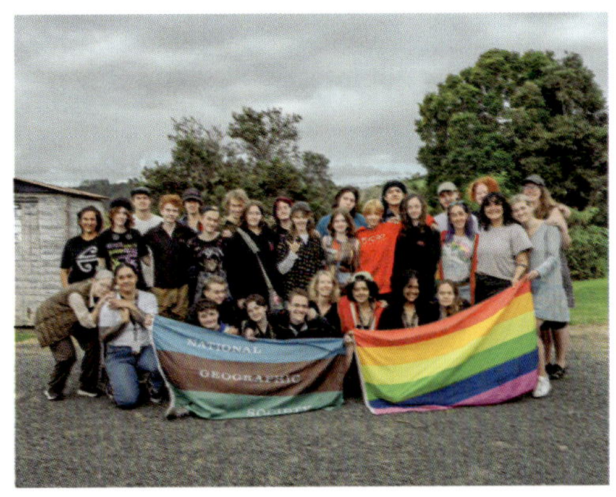

2021

Virtual Photo Camps continued in 2021, featuring the work of youth from diverse communities across the United States for the "Democracy in Action" project and that of global youth for the "Ocean Connections" project.

2022

In 2022, Photo Camp partnered with NGS Explorers and photographers to develop a series of workshops focused on ways that water connects us across the planet. From Tara Roberts's Diving With a Purpose program in the Florida Keys to the Okavango Delta in Botswana to schools in Oregon, Colorado, and the Chesapeake Bay region, these camps explored youth perspectives around water.

2023

For its 20th anniversary year, Photo Camp helped youth use storytelling to explore the ways humanity is connected to help move past the issues that divide us. Early in the year, the program worked with Rainbow Youth in Northland, New Zealand, and Pasifika youth in Auckland, New Zealand.

I've now collected piles of notebooks from those early days. As I read through them, I find that they almost always start with a note to remember special moments gathered from 20 years of listening.

I remember Akhil. On the last day of a Photo Camp in India in 2019, he stood up to say all of our names, after he had had such a hard time using his voice all week. He lived in an orphanage in Rishikesh, and he worked on his photography very intently during the workshop. I knew he had struggled in his young life based on our conversations; I believe he saw his world now in new ways. We walked together in the evenings after class, and he told me about his favorite books. The last evening, he stopped along the banks of the Ganges River, turned to me, and said, "Thank you for listening to me."

And Kurena? She is now in her third year of undergraduate studies at a top university in northern India. She's one of the first teens from the orphanage to attend college. She wants to pursue a graduate degree, but also travel and help others in whatever ways possible. She knows that her story is important.

All people, but especially young people, want to be heard. They want to be seen. This is something that Photo Camp can do.

I believe that this is a generation with something to say. And the world should be listening.

—**KIRSTEN ELSTNER,** FOUNDER AND DIRECTOR, NATIONAL GEOGRAPHIC PHOTO CAMP

By the Numbers

Photos Made

2,500,000

Camps

144

Students

3,000

Number of Student Countries

44

Faculty

92

Number of Faculty Countries

21

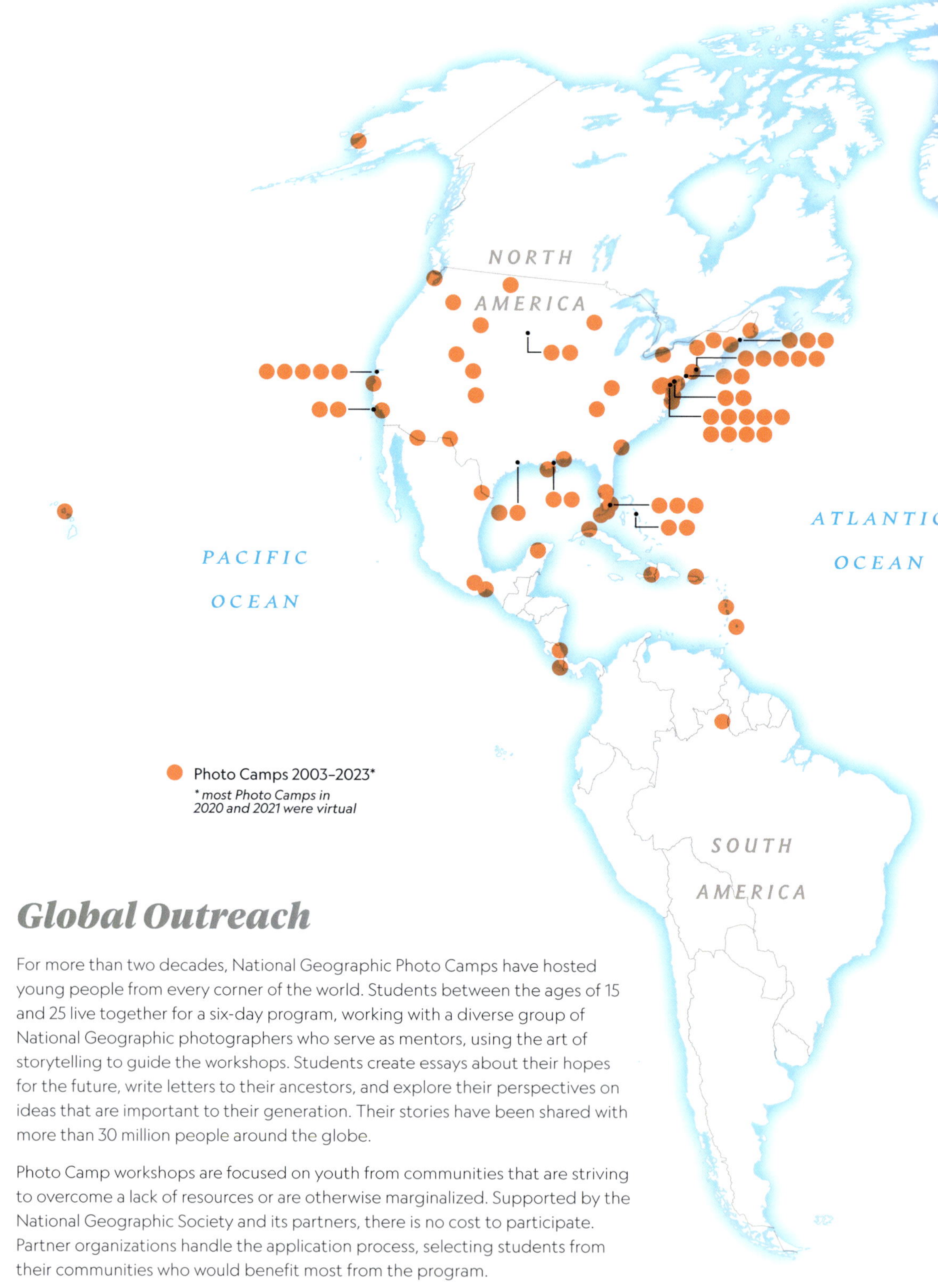

Global Outreach

For more than two decades, National Geographic Photo Camps have hosted young people from every corner of the world. Students between the ages of 15 and 25 live together for a six-day program, working with a diverse group of National Geographic photographers who serve as mentors, using the art of storytelling to guide the workshops. Students create essays about their hopes for the future, write letters to their ancestors, and explore their perspectives on ideas that are important to their generation. Their stories have been shared with more than 30 million people around the globe.

Photo Camp workshops are focused on youth from communities that are striving to overcome a lack of resources or are otherwise marginalized. Supported by the National Geographic Society and its partners, there is no cost to participate. Partner organizations handle the application process, selecting students from their communities who would benefit most from the program.

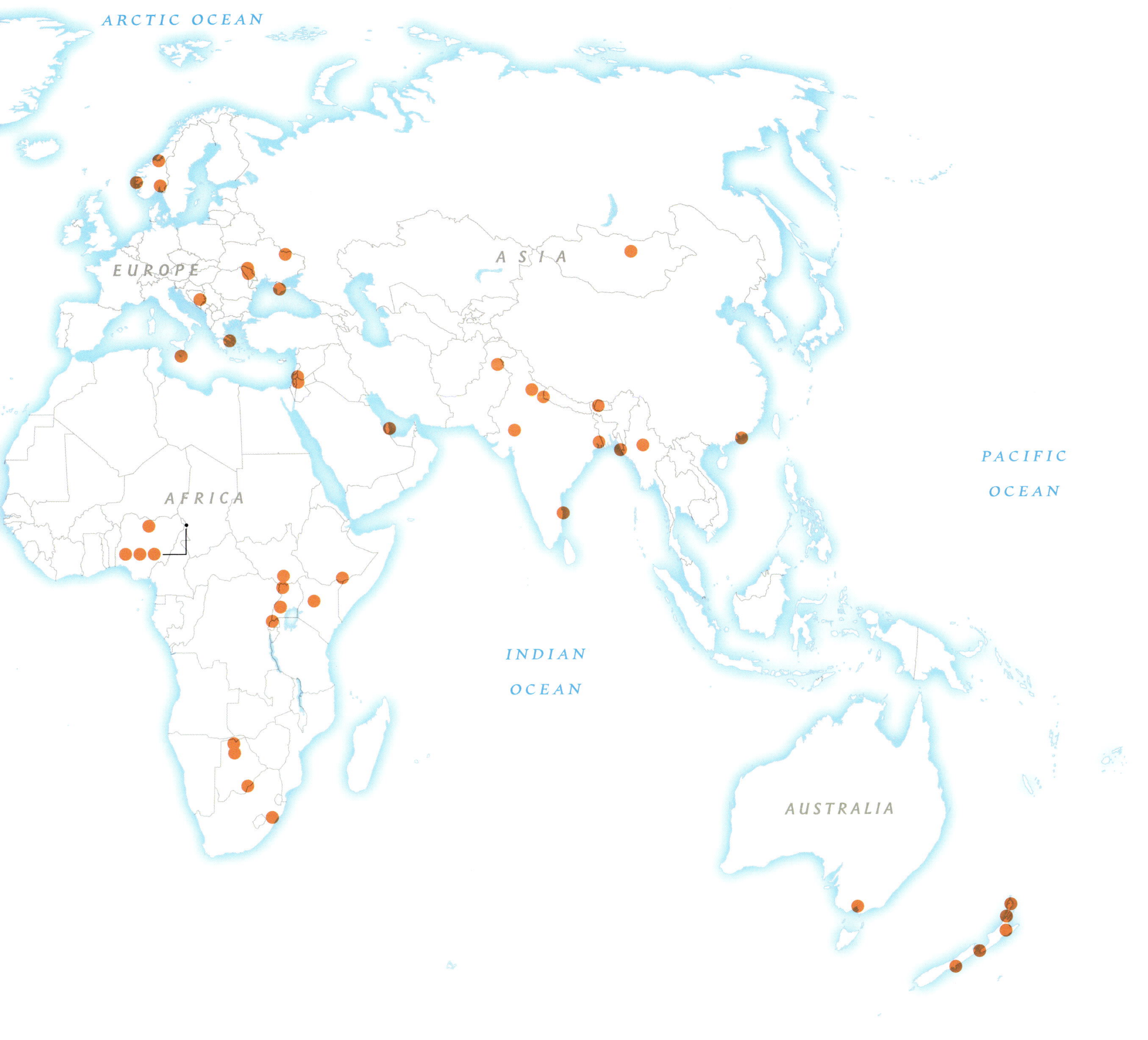
ARCTIC OCEAN
EUROPE
ASIA
AFRICA
PACIFIC OCEAN
INDIAN OCEAN
AUSTRALIA

CHAPTER 1

Community

"Through the lens I can recognize that we, as human beings, are attached to one another and nature. We are all connected and depend on one another."

—BULLEN CHOL, SOUTH SUDAN 2014

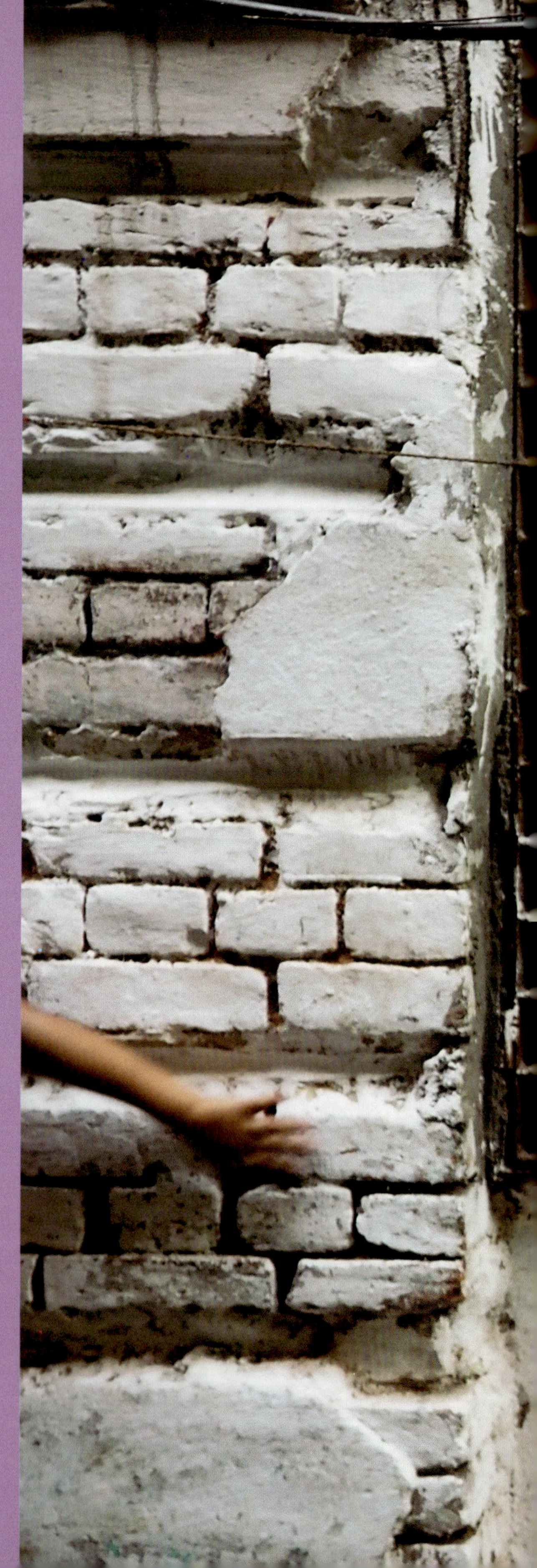

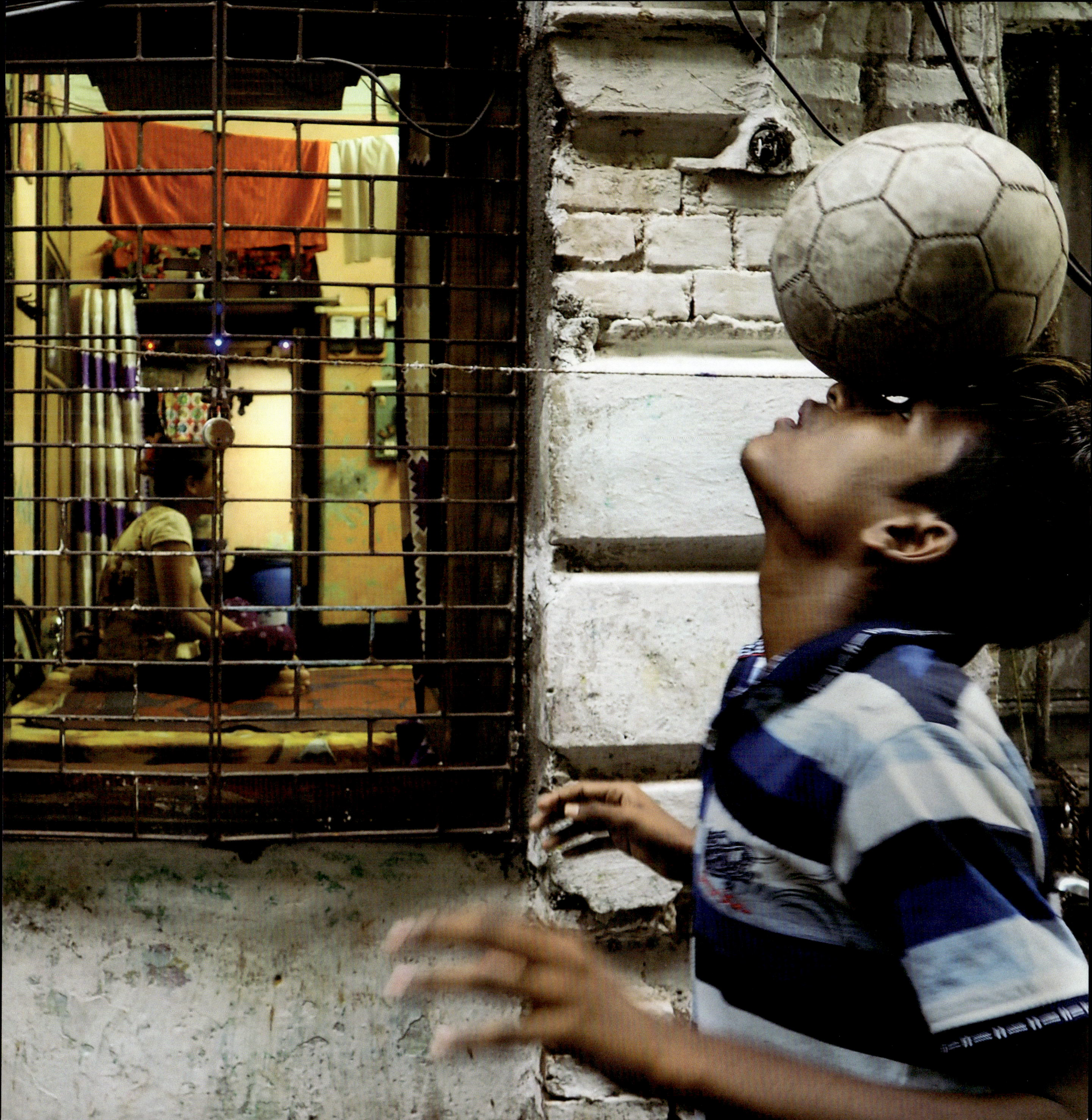

Something Bigger

THE GOAL OF EVERY PHOTO CAMP is building a tight circle of students, teachers, and staff. But rarely does the camaraderie come as quickly as it did at a January 2023 Photo Camp for LGBTQ youth in New Zealand. "They say that they have never felt more like family than they have in this place," noted National Geographic photographer Lynn Johnson, a mentor at this workshop in the Bay of Islands, on the east coast of North Island.

"When you talked about your story or shared your struggles in any manner, everyone was very receptive," recalled student Cam Ryans. "It felt like you could just be yourself no matter what." The group grew so close that Cam admits that going back to his old life felt like a letdown. "I feel that I left my home behind when I left Photo Camp," he said. But through social media, he continues to garner support and encouragement from the mentors and friends he made at the program.

What seems to happen naturally at each workshop in fact requires forethought. "The most important thing to consider when trying to build a true community of photographers is to understand the Photo Camp participants' backgrounds," Johnson said of the camp's objectives. At every camp, director Kirsten Elstner takes time around the campfire to tell the students that they are part of something bigger: a Photo Camp family of storytellers and photographers now spanning 20 years. It's a powerful message to youth who often feel alienated and alone.

Nevertheless, there can be barriers to creating solidarity. As a result, it's sometimes necessary to peel away layers of suspicion, as students from Bahrain, Egypt, Jordan, Saudi Arabia, and the United States learned at the Ocean for Life program in 2009. Brought together to observe and learn about the ocean life around California's Monterey Bay, they began with a shared interest in marine biology—but not much else. The students harbored stereotypes about each other, but the camp offered the opportunity to counteract the stereotypes and build sincere relationships across differences.

But student Erie French had a particular concern: He was the only Black student in the group. "Imagine the weight of negative stereotypes I am carrying," the 16-year-old commented. Nonetheless, he felt the group came a long way over the course of the workshop and that "interconnectedness was revealed through all the different cultures represented." Ahmed El Awadly, from Egypt, agreed: "Meeting people from other cultures has taught me to know more about the world. It's taught me to connect with other people, and how to share emotions."

Prejudice—even enmity—was discussed openly at a 2018 Photo Camp in Moldova before any bonding could begin. The Moldovan, Russian, and Roma youth assembled were wary of each other; they

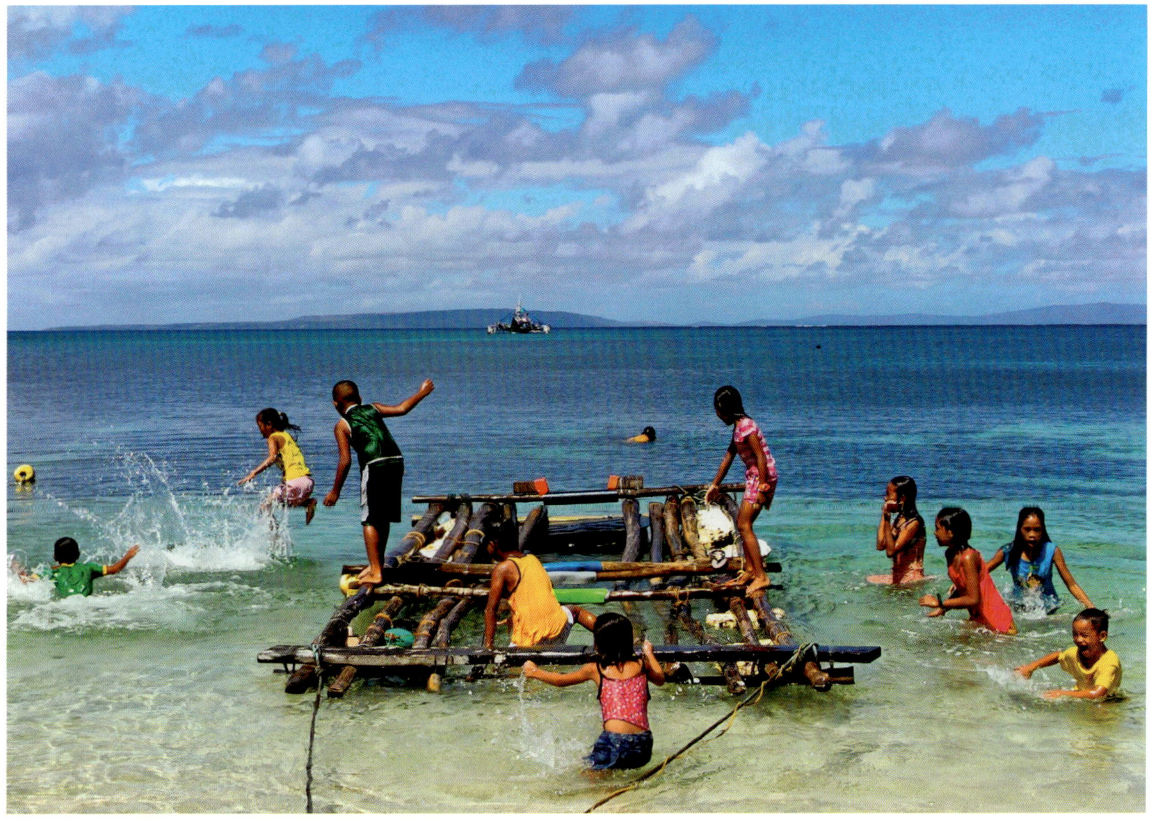

ABOVE: **RACELLE RESCODADO / PHILIPPINES 2021** PREVIOUS PAGES: **VAGMI PATHAK / INDIA 2018**

spoke different languages and nursed some long-standing grudges. Those from Roma communities were understandably distressed by some bigoted descriptions of their ethnic group, made openly in their presence. "We spent a lot of time talking about small interactions that would come up in the workshops," photographer-mentor Dominic Bracco recalled. "These would manifest as microaggressions, or sometimes more serious comments that were offensive."

But when the students began photographing each other's communities, the hostility began to recede. And as the students explored neighborhoods they would have avoided in the past, their perspectives were widened to other cultures.

Graves in the Roma cemetery, piled with baskets of fruit for the deceased to enjoy at Easter, proved a powerful subject. After the session, students and teachers broke bread together and drank homemade plum juice. Bracco is honest about the challenges of creating a community. When it came time for the students to part, Bracco said: "They were friends. Mostly."

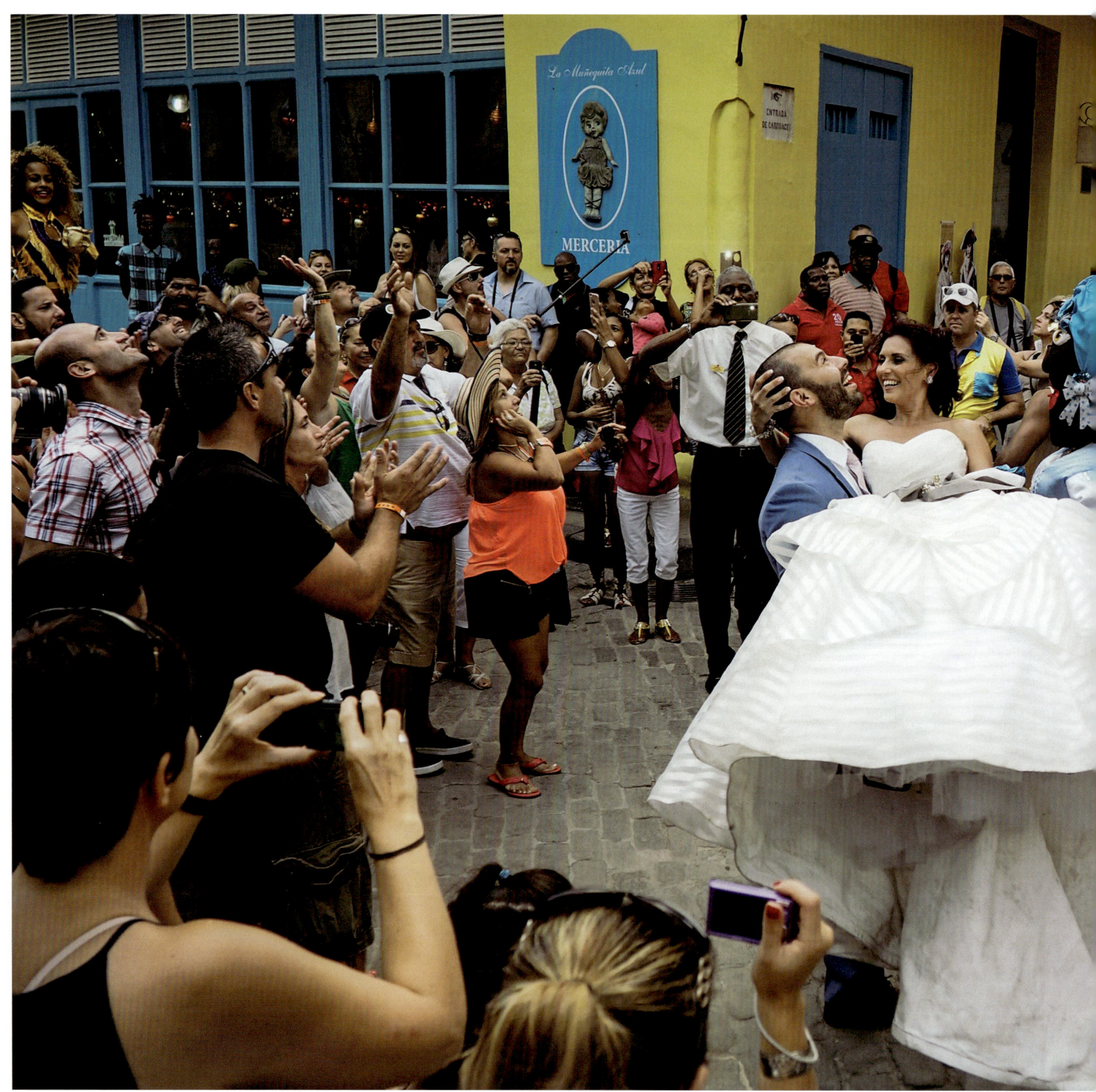
La Muñequita Azul
MERCERIA
ENTRADA

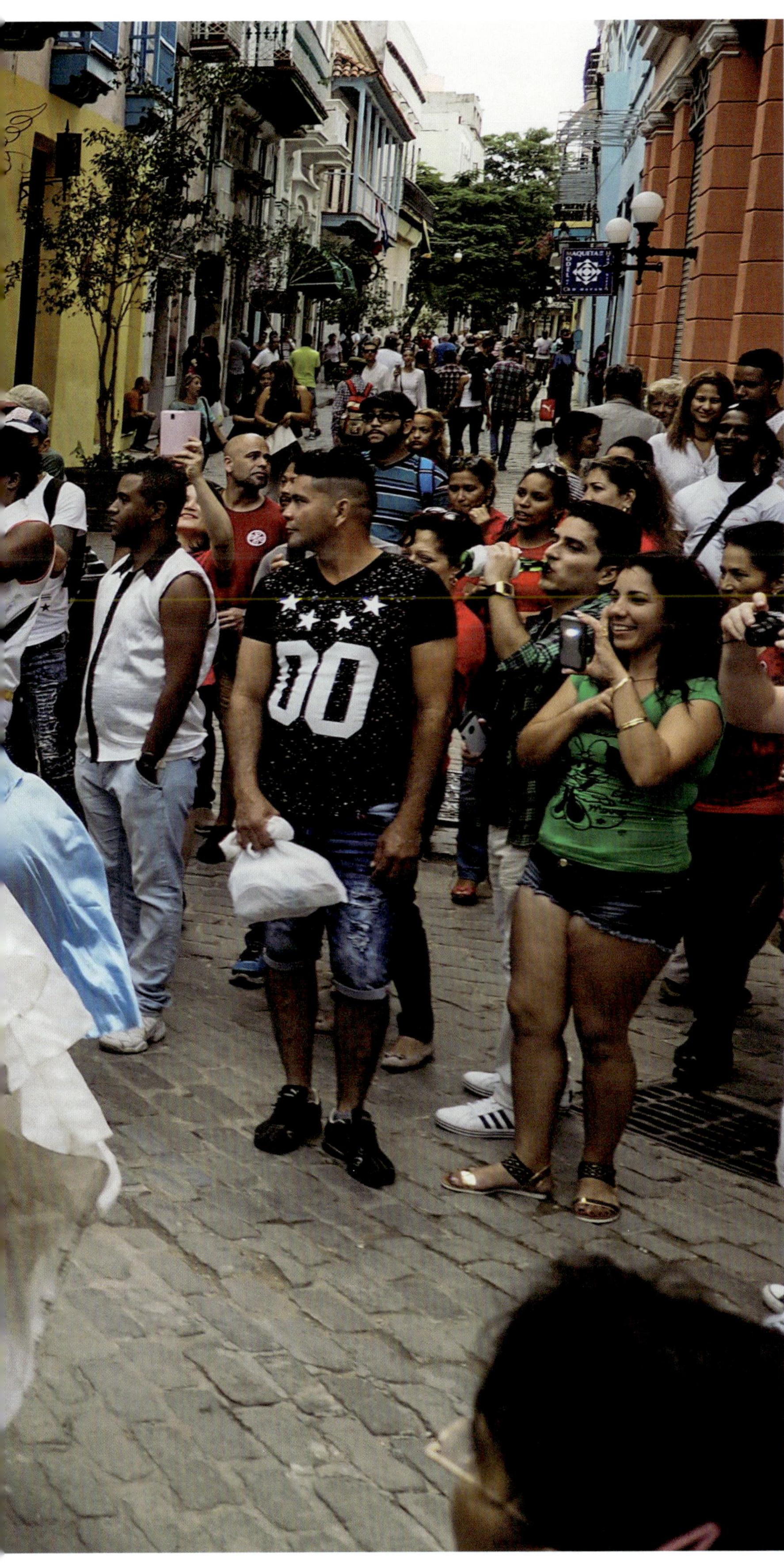

"People from my generation are fearless, intrepid, and we have added these elements to the new Cuba. We are the future. I see my country as a big family; in the end it's my homeland, and I'll love it just the way it is."

—ANDRA DELFÍN DE LEÓN, CUBA 2016

AMALIA CASTILLO SILES / CUBA 2016

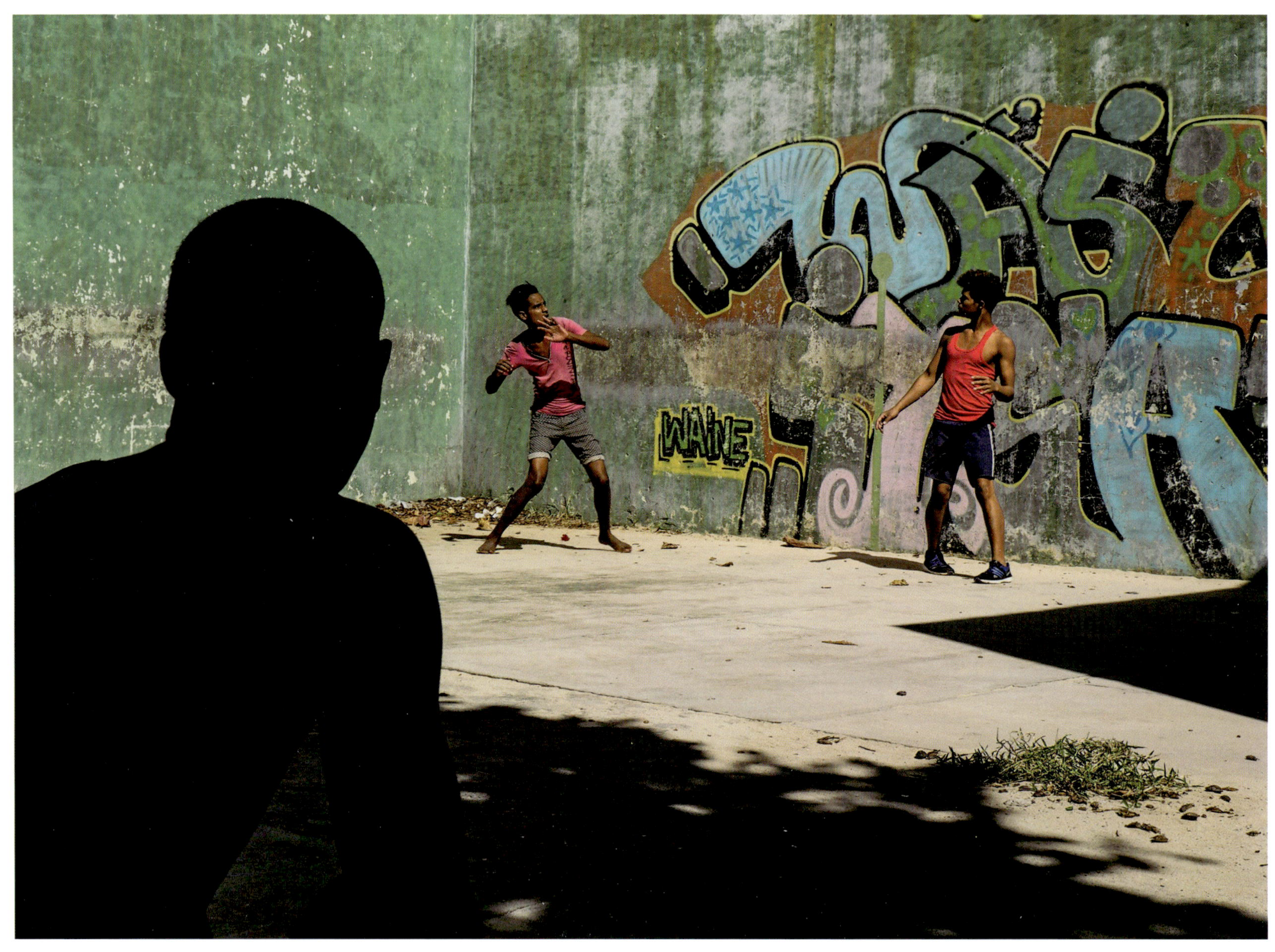

ALEJANDRO DIAZ SANCHEZ / CUBA 2016

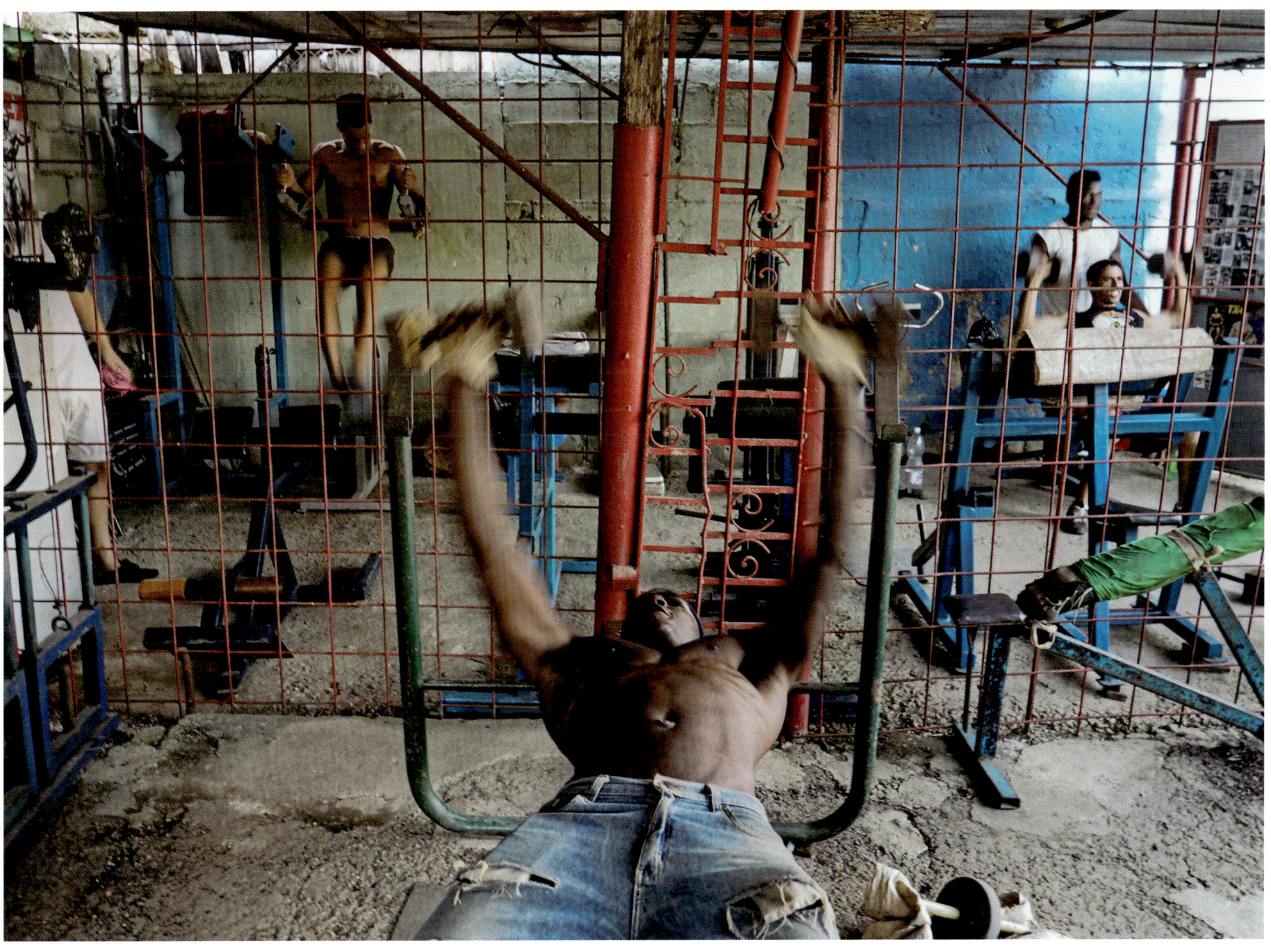

DARIEL GODOY GONZALES / CUBA 2016

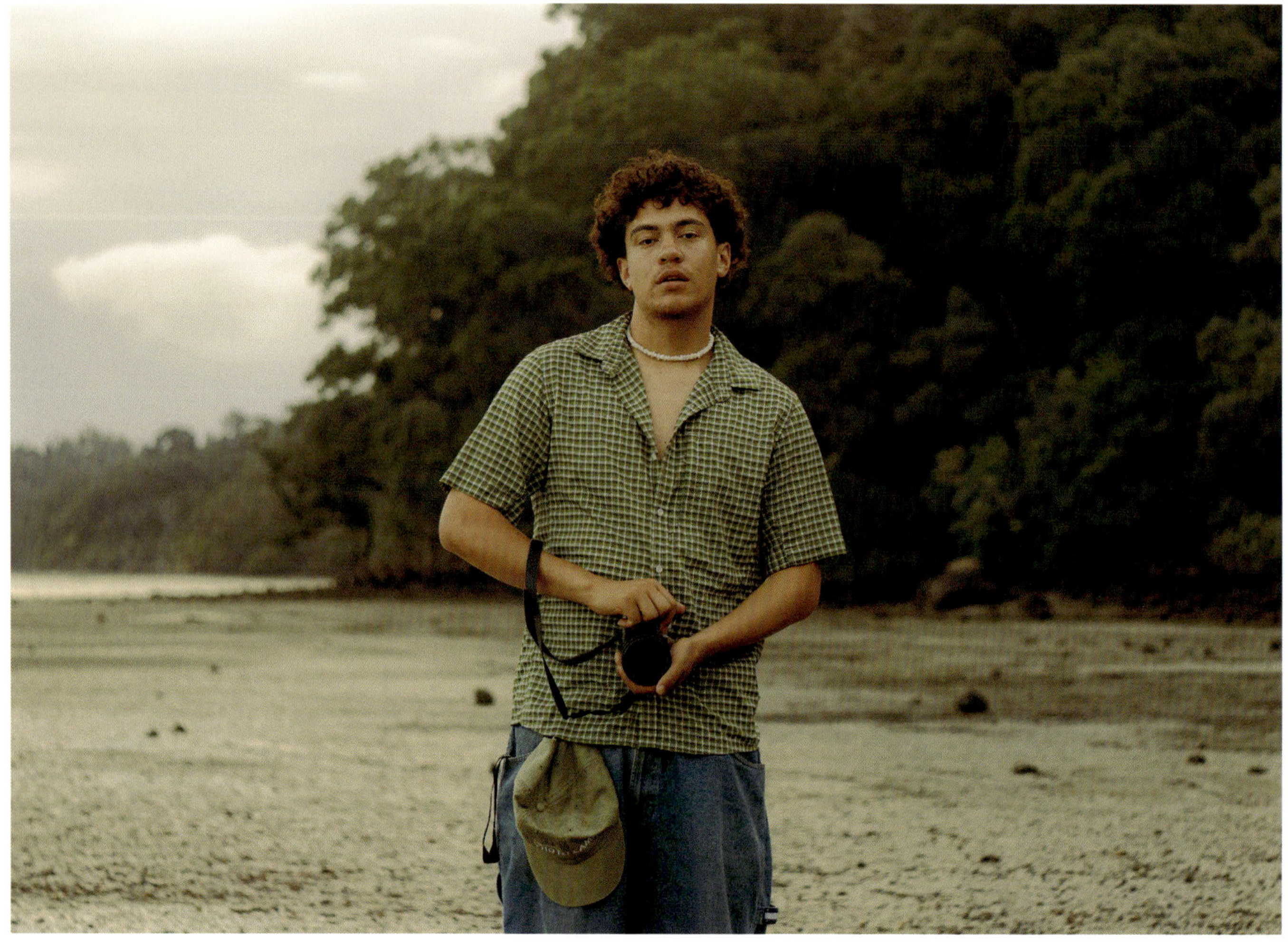

ABOVE: **JAZMIN TAINUI MIHI PAGET-KNEBEL / NEW ZEALAND 2023**
OPPOSITE: **SHALIA POHAIKEALOHAIKAPILIMAKAMAE HENDERSON / HAWAII, U.S.A. 2021**

Assignment: Write a letter to your ancestors.

"I am the person you once were, from the land and the barefoot hearty. I have a dream for my people who were once your people ... I am a free spirit because of the sacrifices you made. Your names speak power to me and give me the strength to make your sacrifices worth it."

—NGAWARI TAMANI-FRANSEN, AUCKLAND, NEW ZEALAND 2023

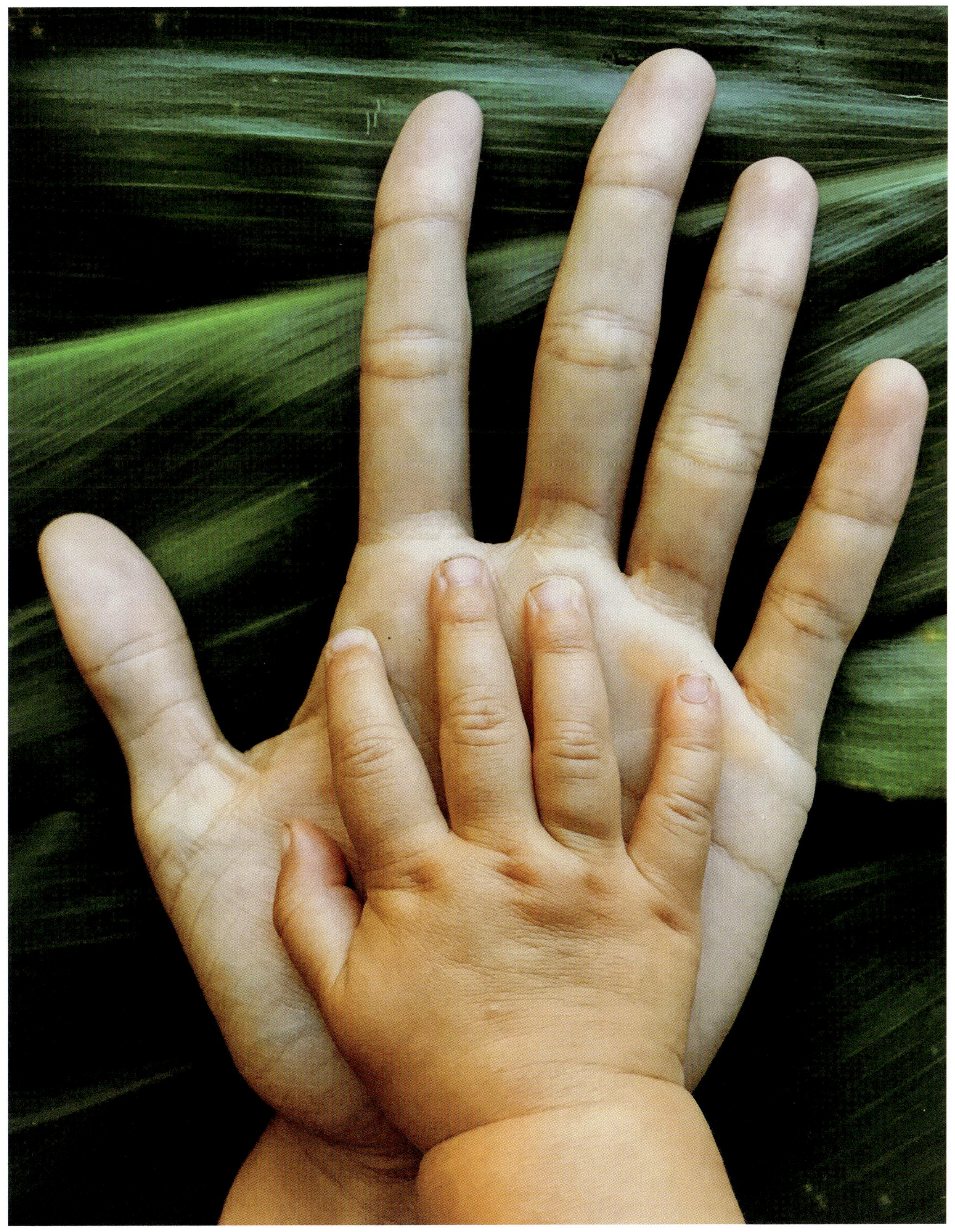

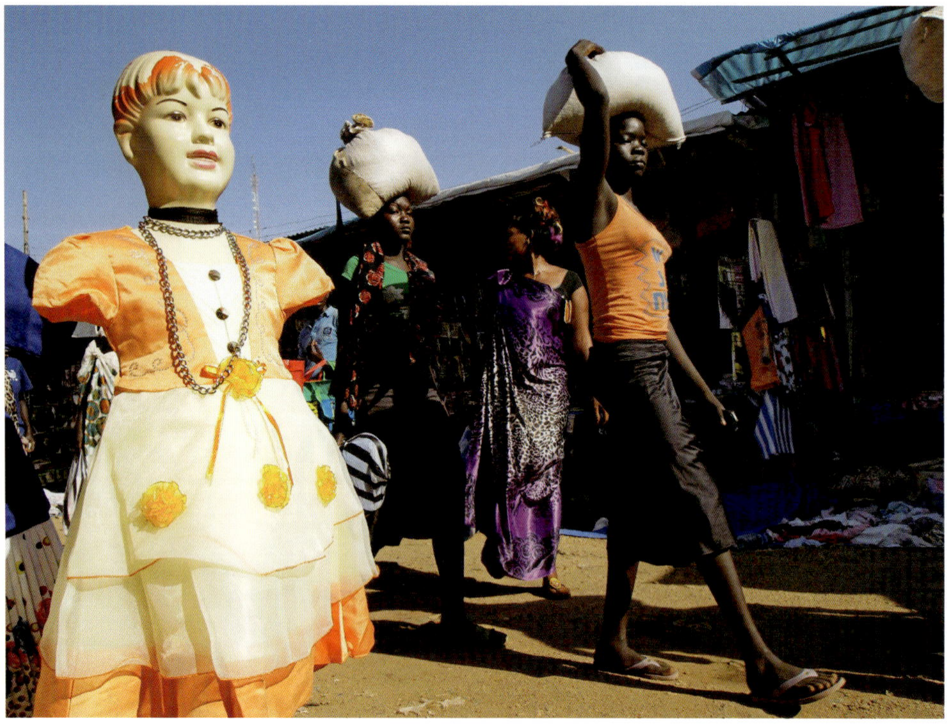

ABOVE: **STELLA PONI GAUDENSIO / SOUTH SUDAN 2014**
RIGHT: **SUZAN SILVESTRO BONA MUSA / SOUTH SUDAN 2014**

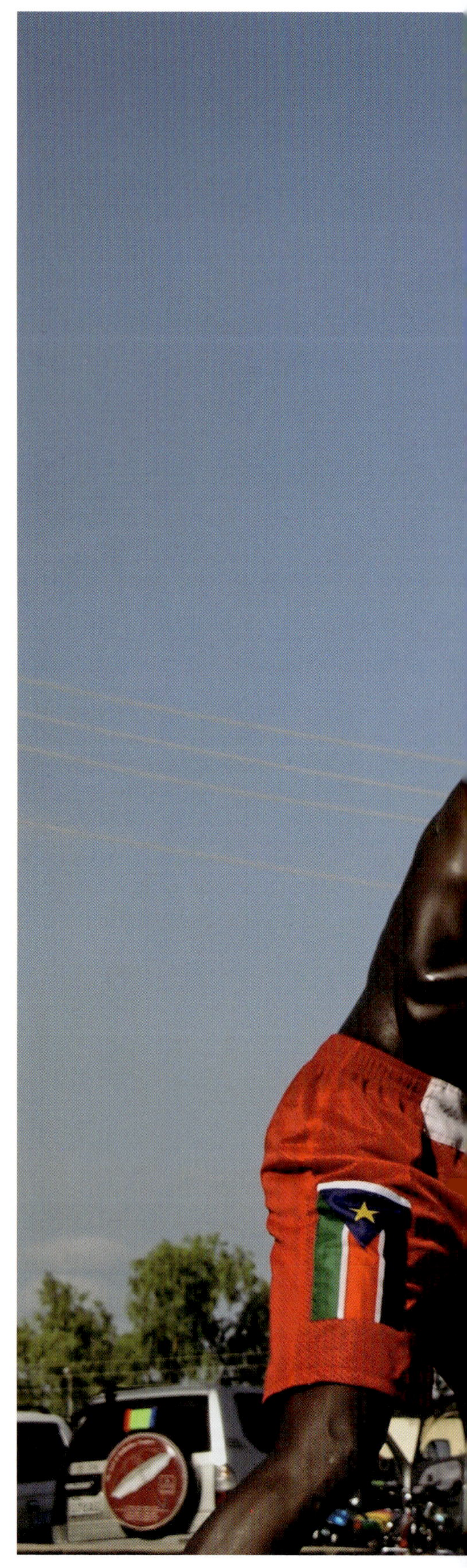

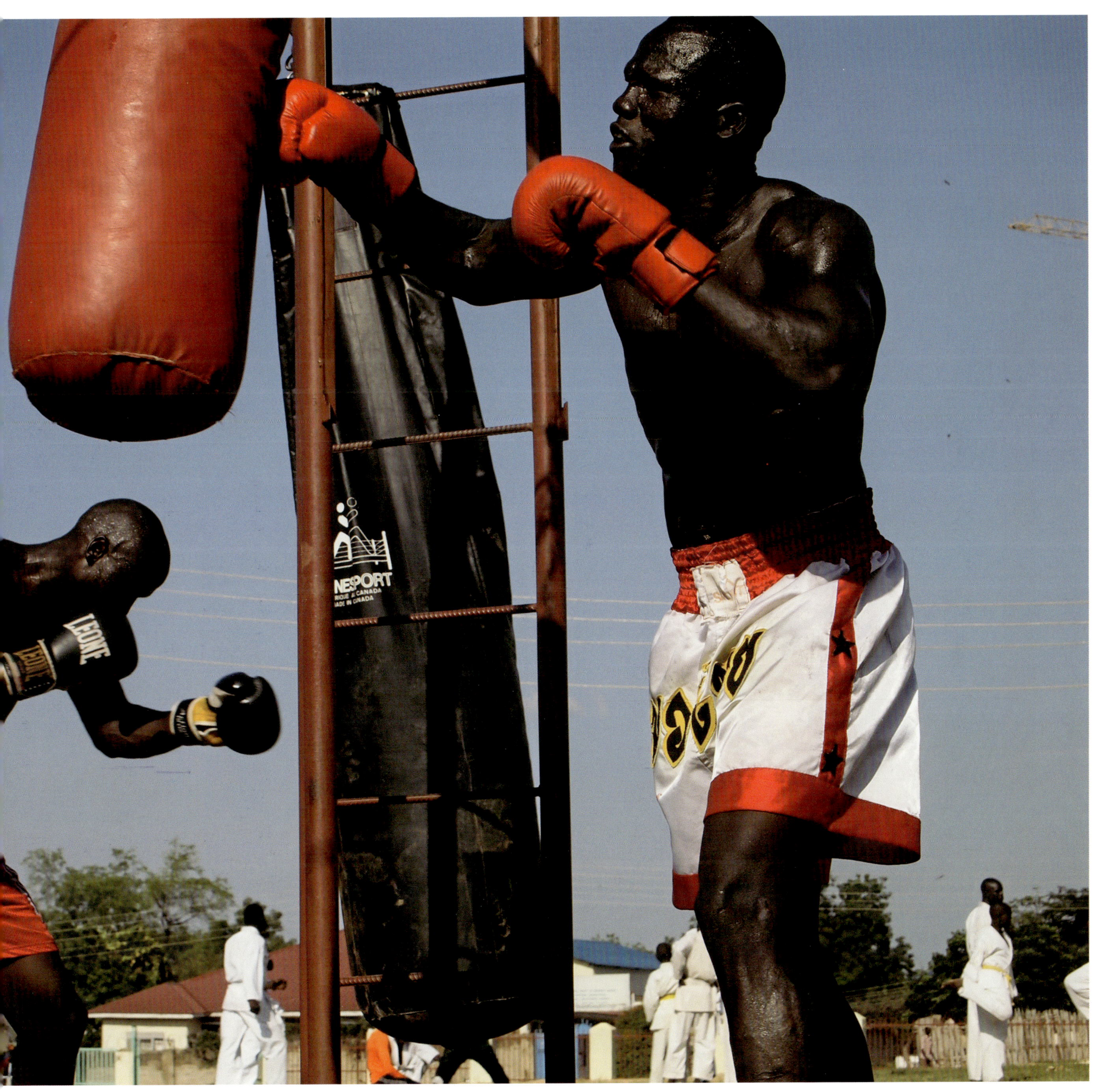
LEONE
NESPORT

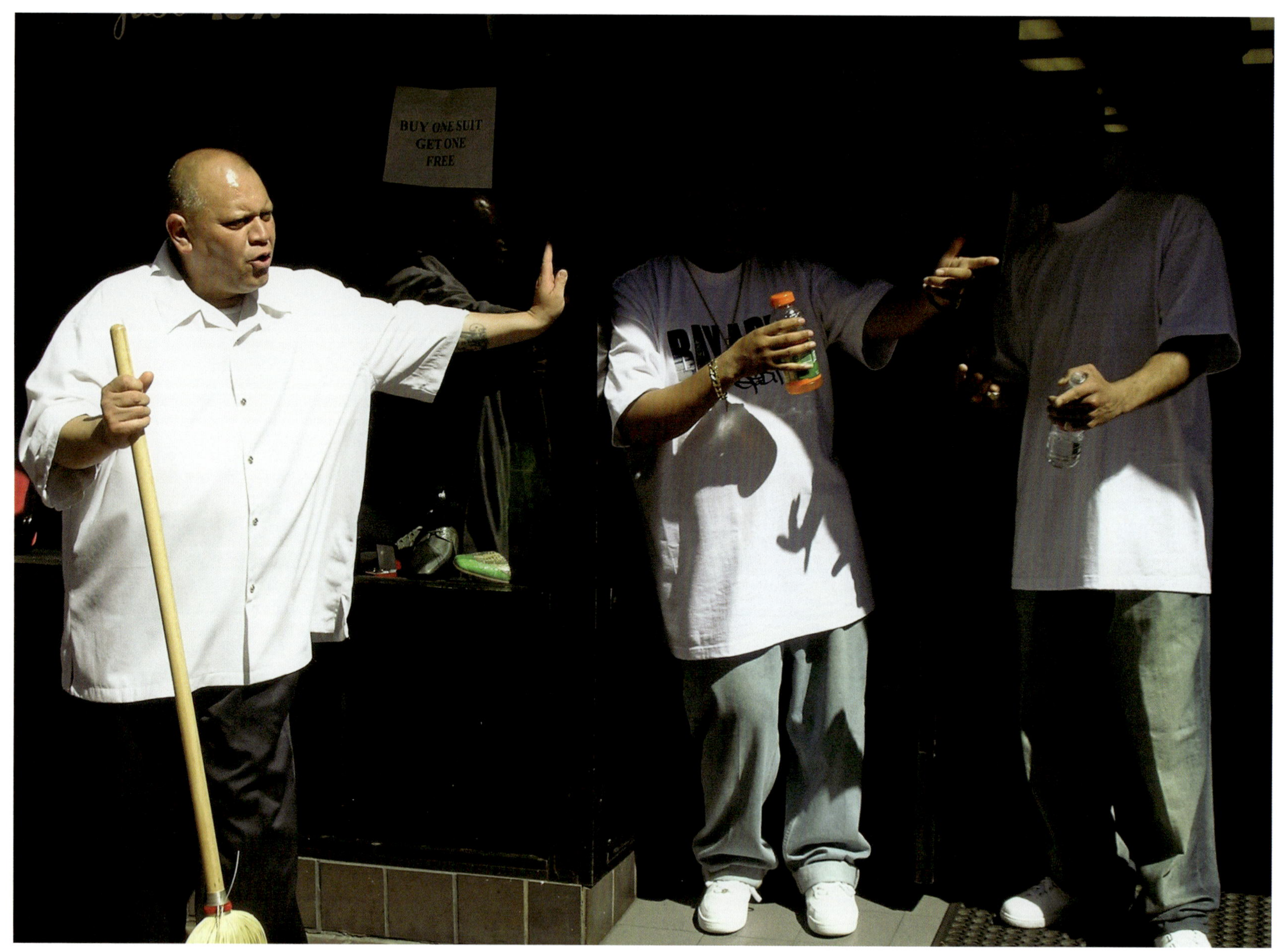

BETHANY CASTRO / CALIFORNIA, U.S.A. 2006

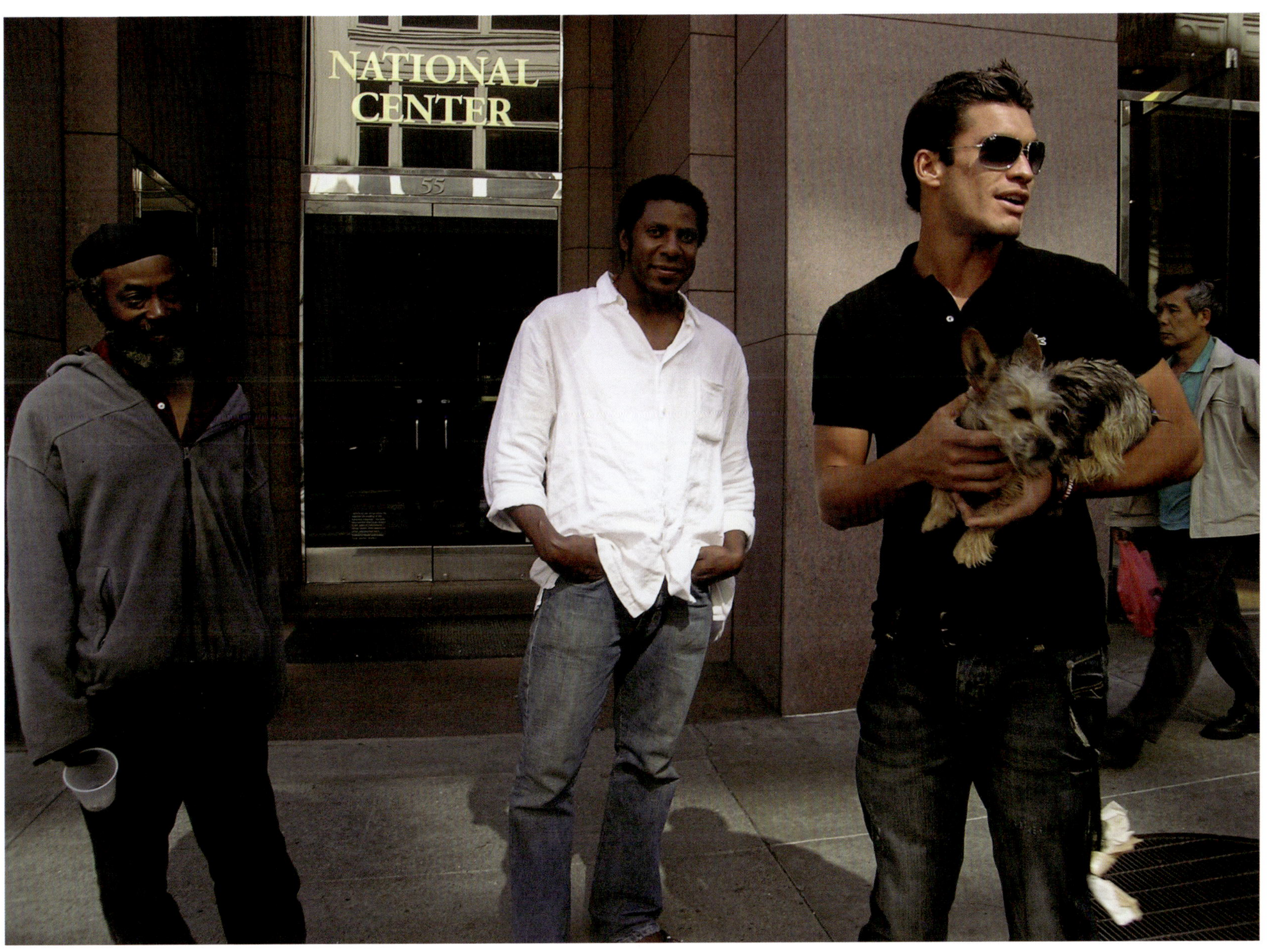

DOMINIQUE MCFARLAND / CALIFORNIA, U.S.A. 2006

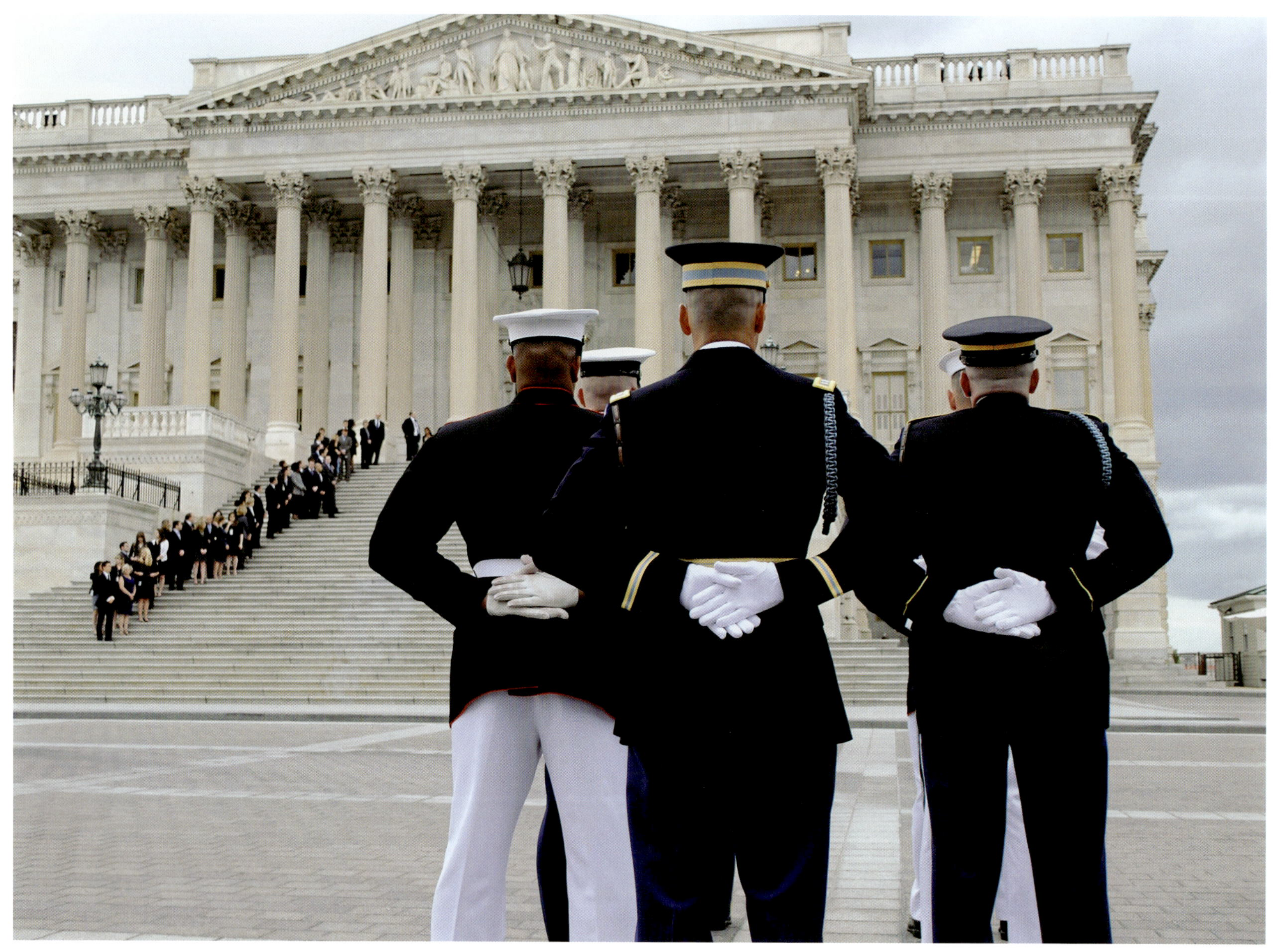

HUMA GUL / WASHINGTON, D.C., U.S.A. 2013

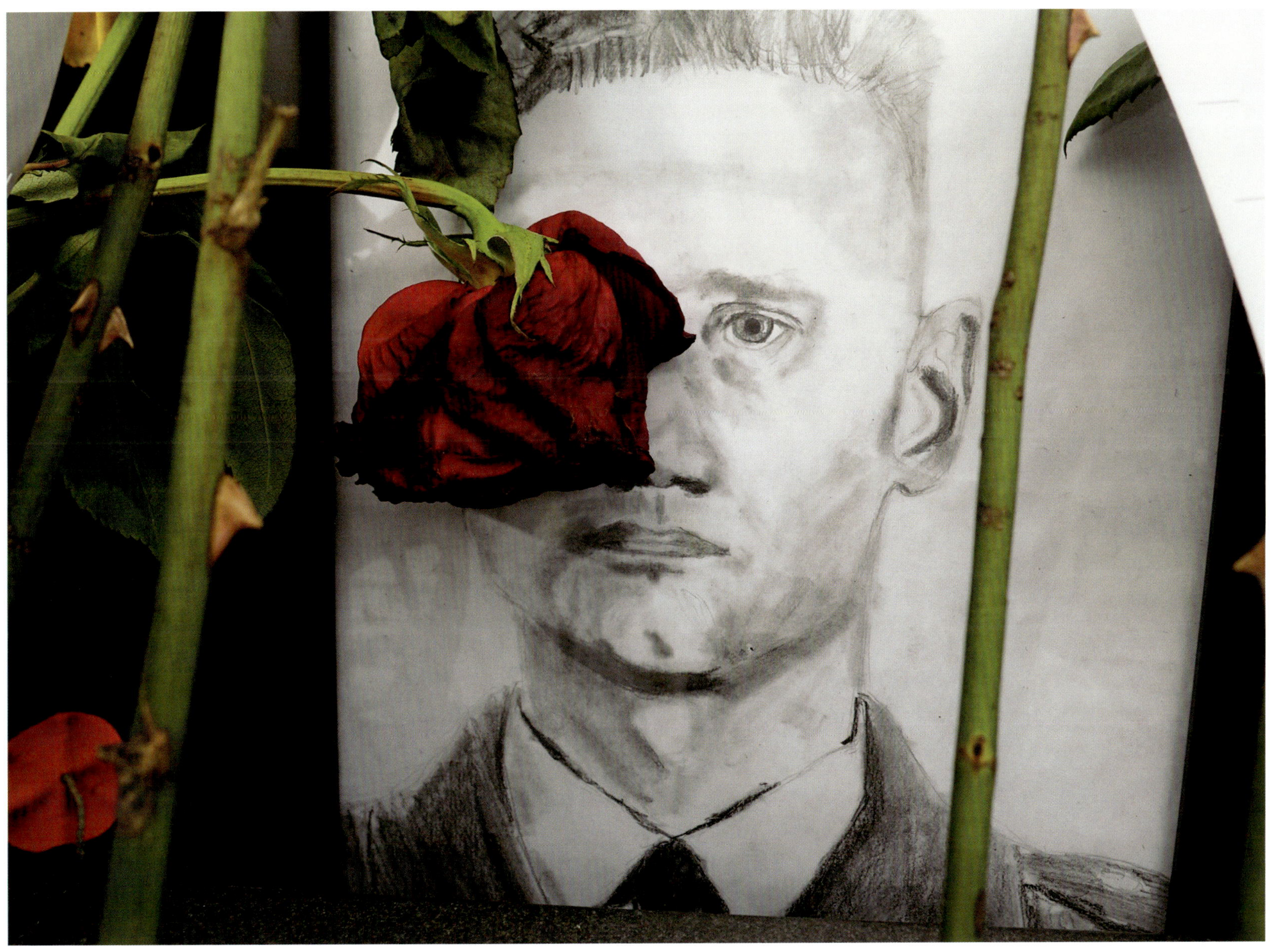

YASMIN MOHAMED / WASHINGTON, D.C., U.S.A., MASTER CLASS 2019

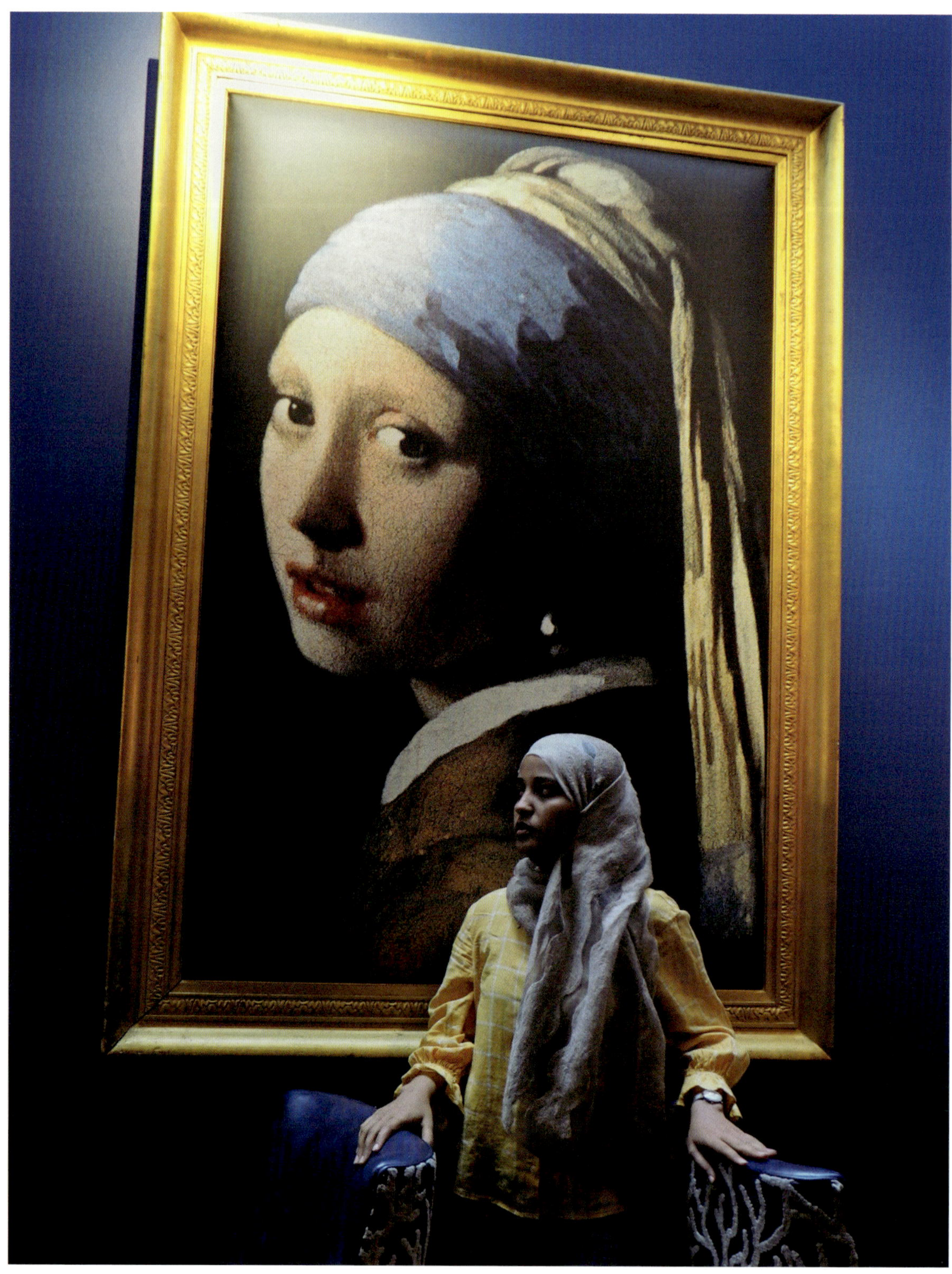

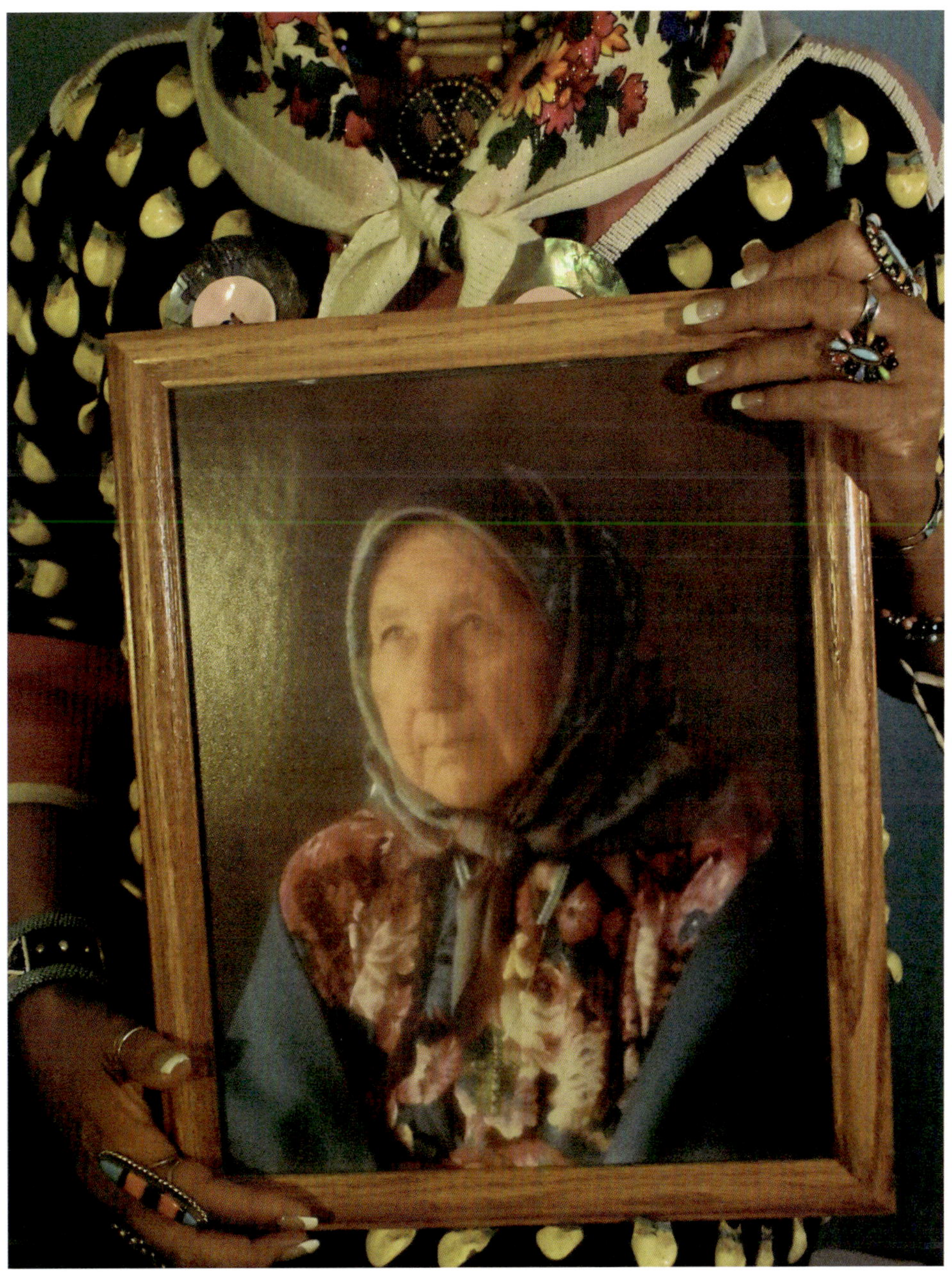

ABOVE: **JORDYNN PAZ / MONTANA, U.S.A. 2020**
OPPOSITE: **MAKDA TESFEMARIAM / WASHINGTON, D.C., U.S.A., MASTER CLASS 2019**

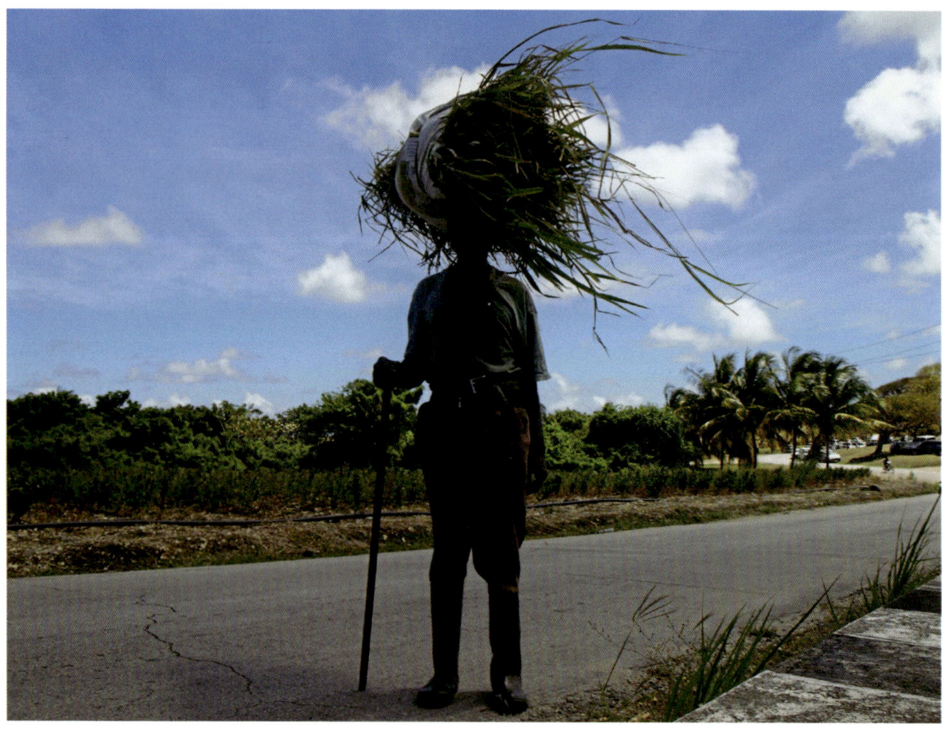

ABOVE: **TYREL HEADLEY / BARBADOS 2010** RIGHT: **CLEMENT FORDE / BARBADOS 2010**

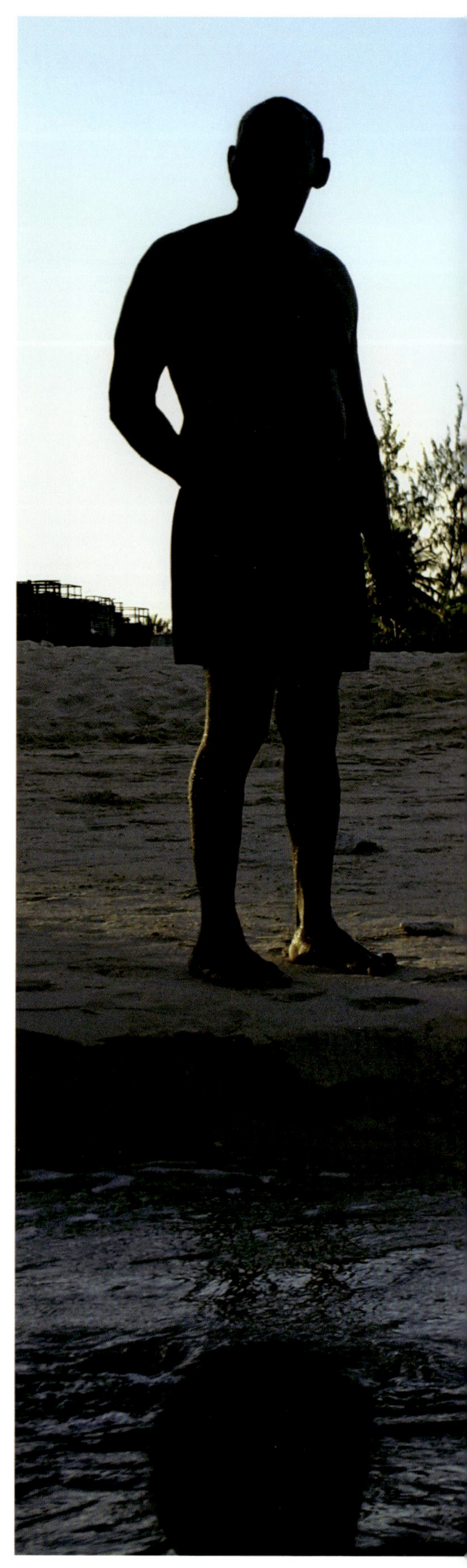

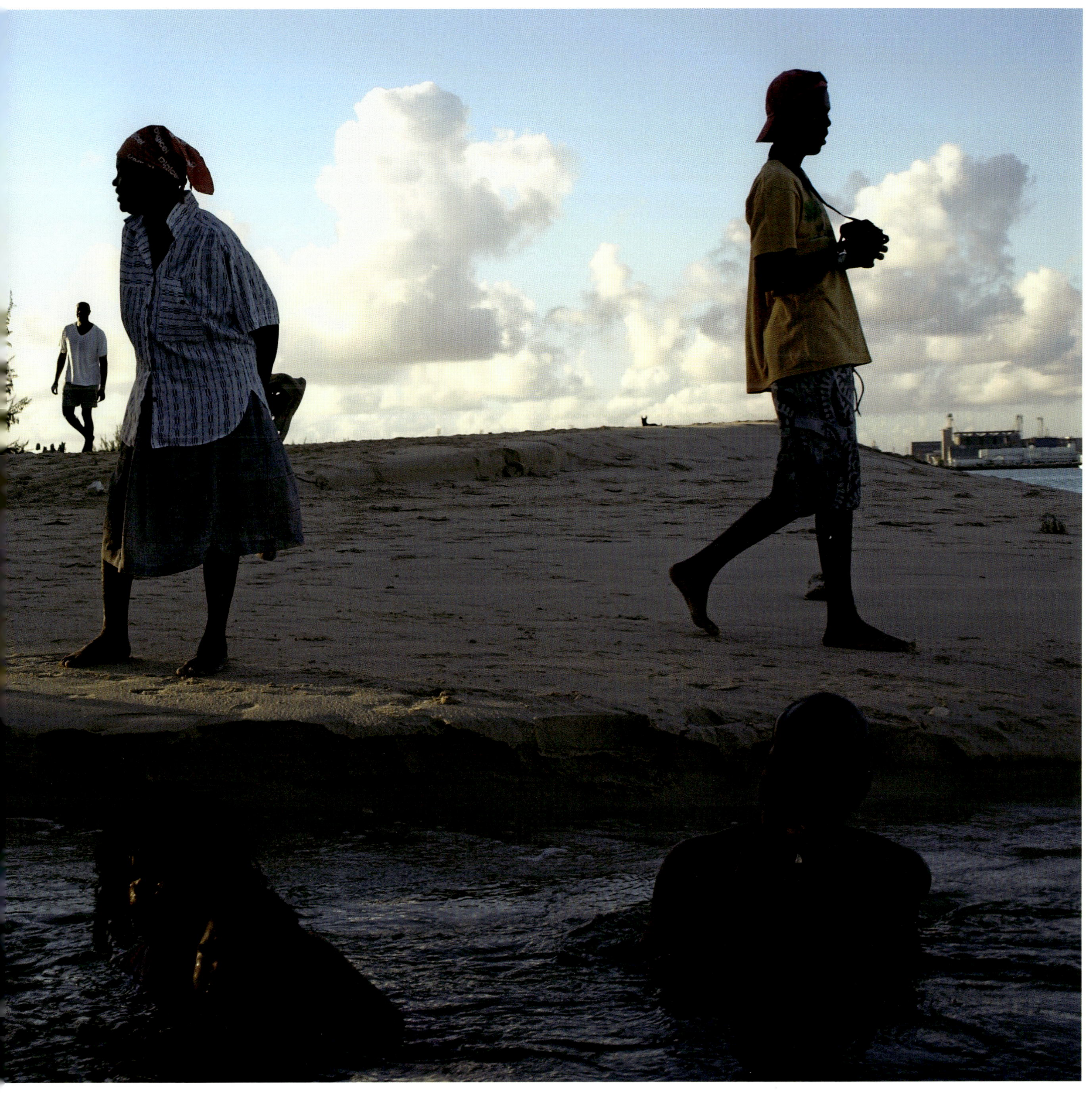

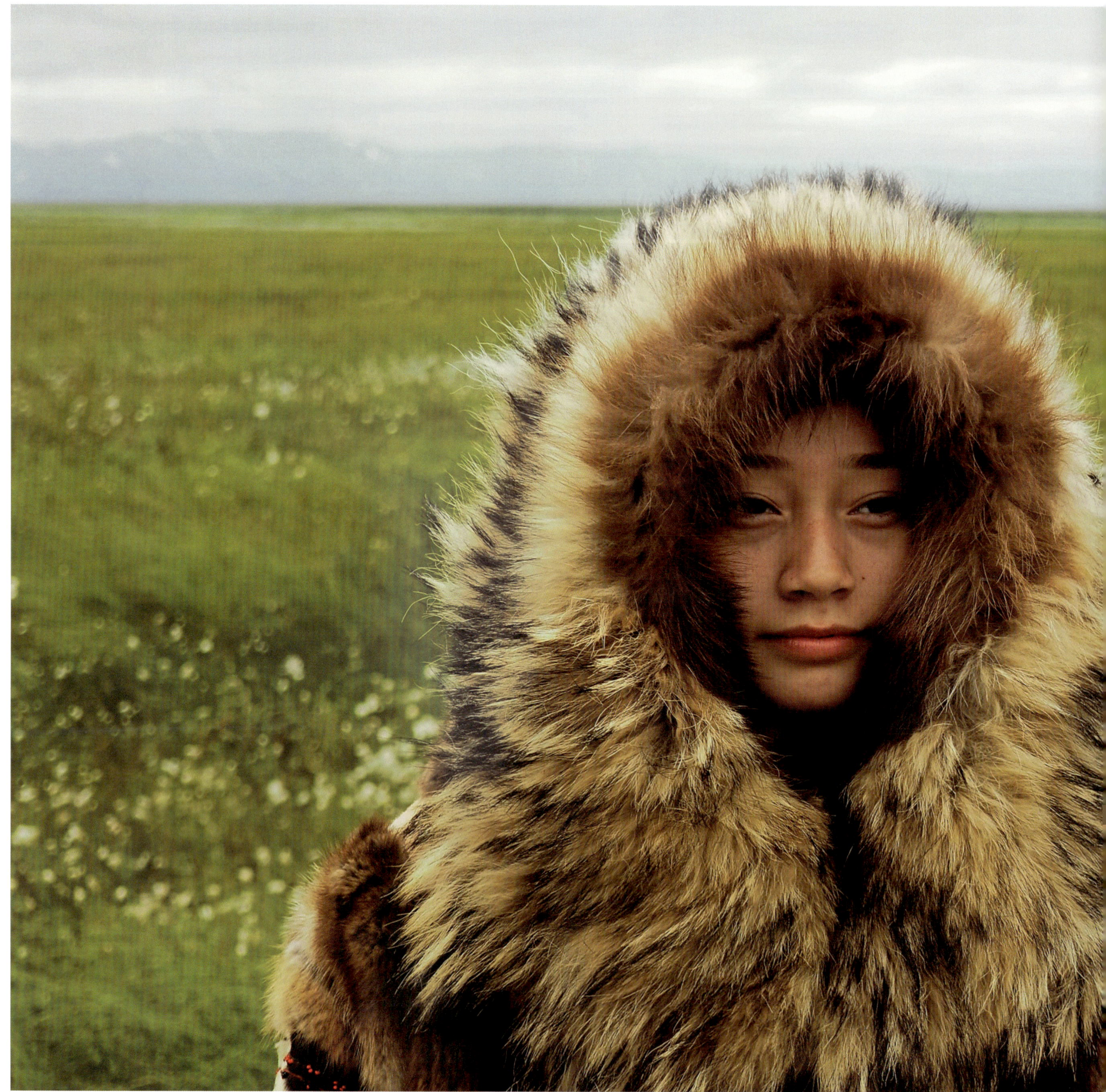

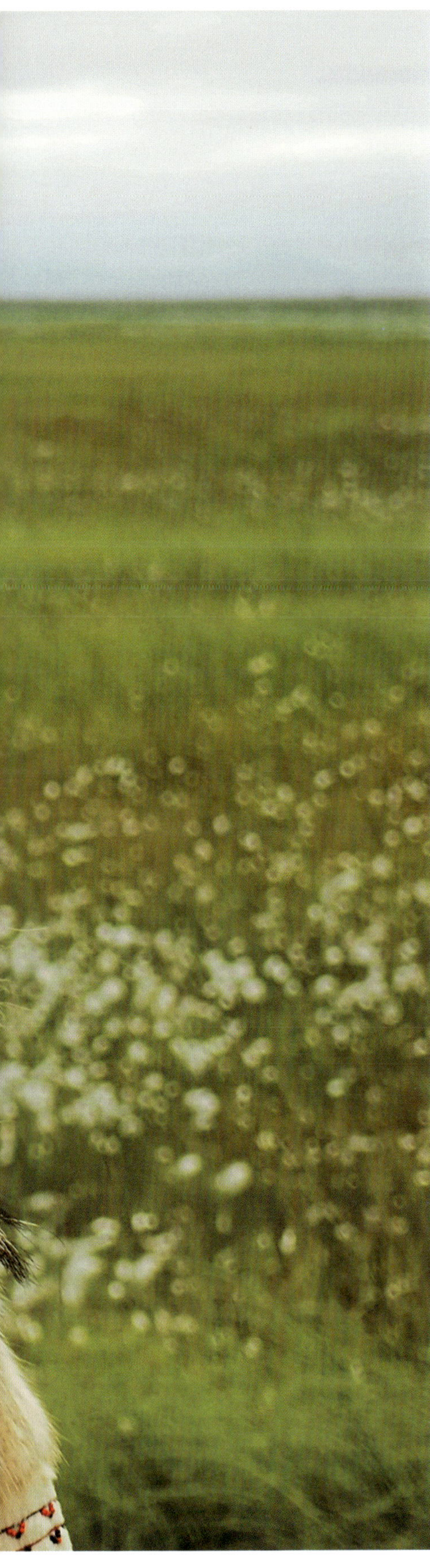

"I think a Yup'ik is a lost loved one, reborn as a guide for the soul they brought from the spirit world. To be Yup'ik means to be whole; you are not seen as 'half Yup'ik,' or a 'quarter Yup'ik.' In the same way, you are loved completely. Being Yup'ik means preserving love for your family members, preserving memories, and preserving stories. My hopes for the future are for the younger generations to carry on tradition and continue what our ancestors started: to love one another."

—RAE ANN TIRIUN, ALASKA, U.S.A. 2018

SHAWN JONES / ALASKA, U.S.A. 2018

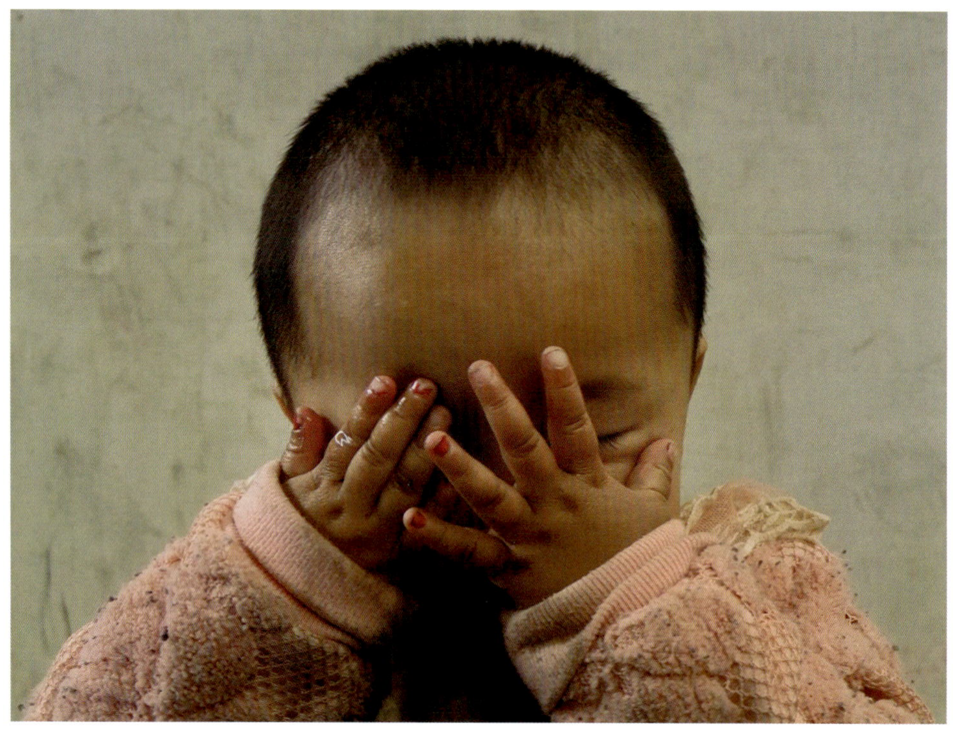

ABOVE: **LISHA SUBBA / BHUTAN 2019** RIGHT: **SANGAY THINLEY TENZING / BHUTAN 2019**

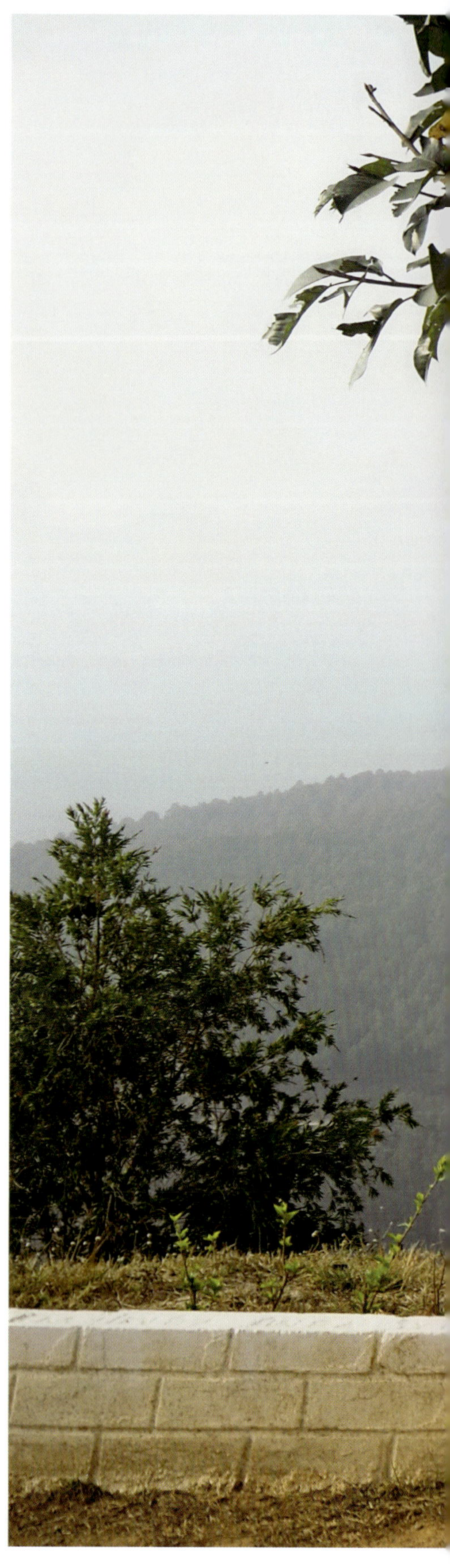

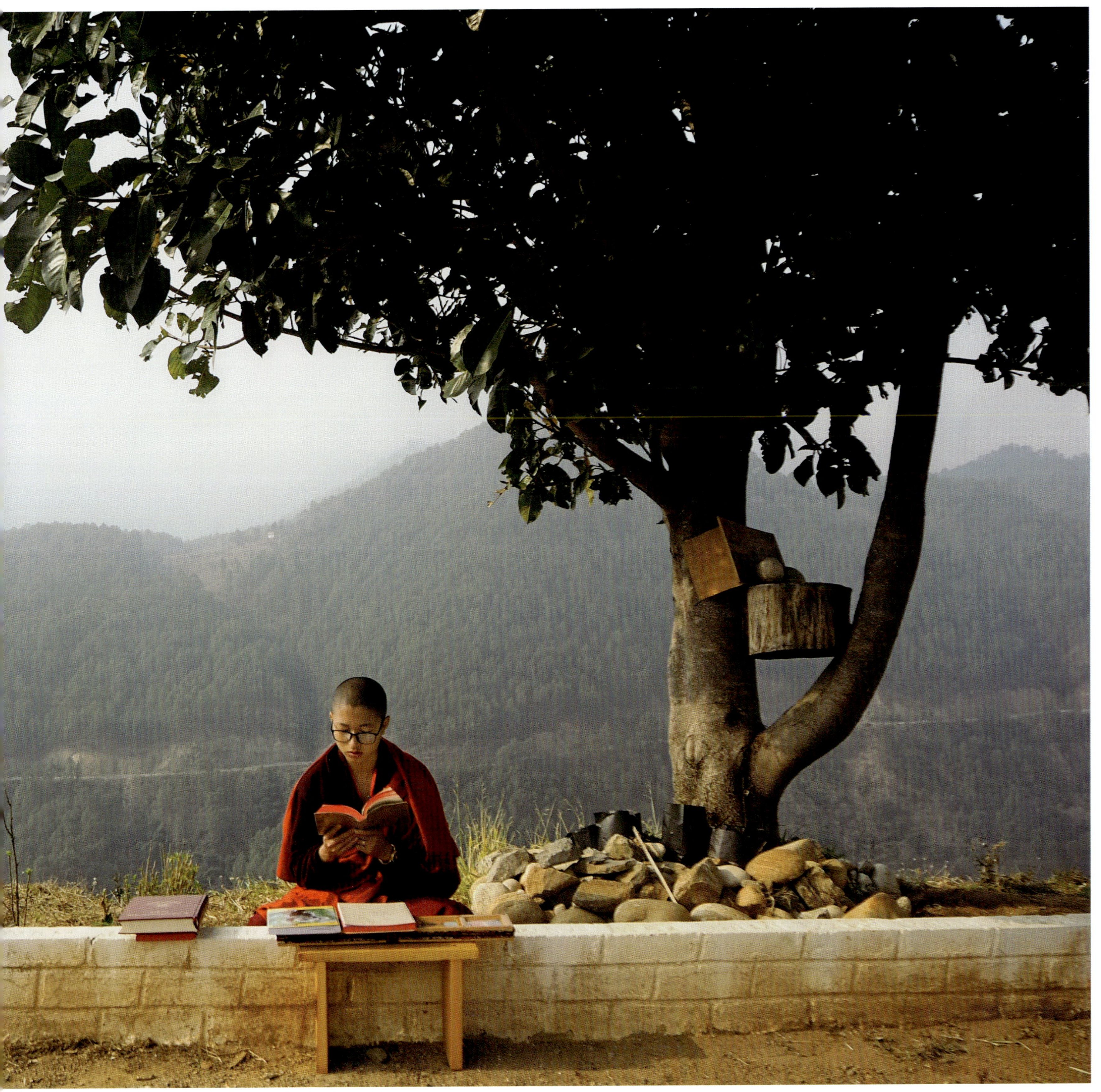

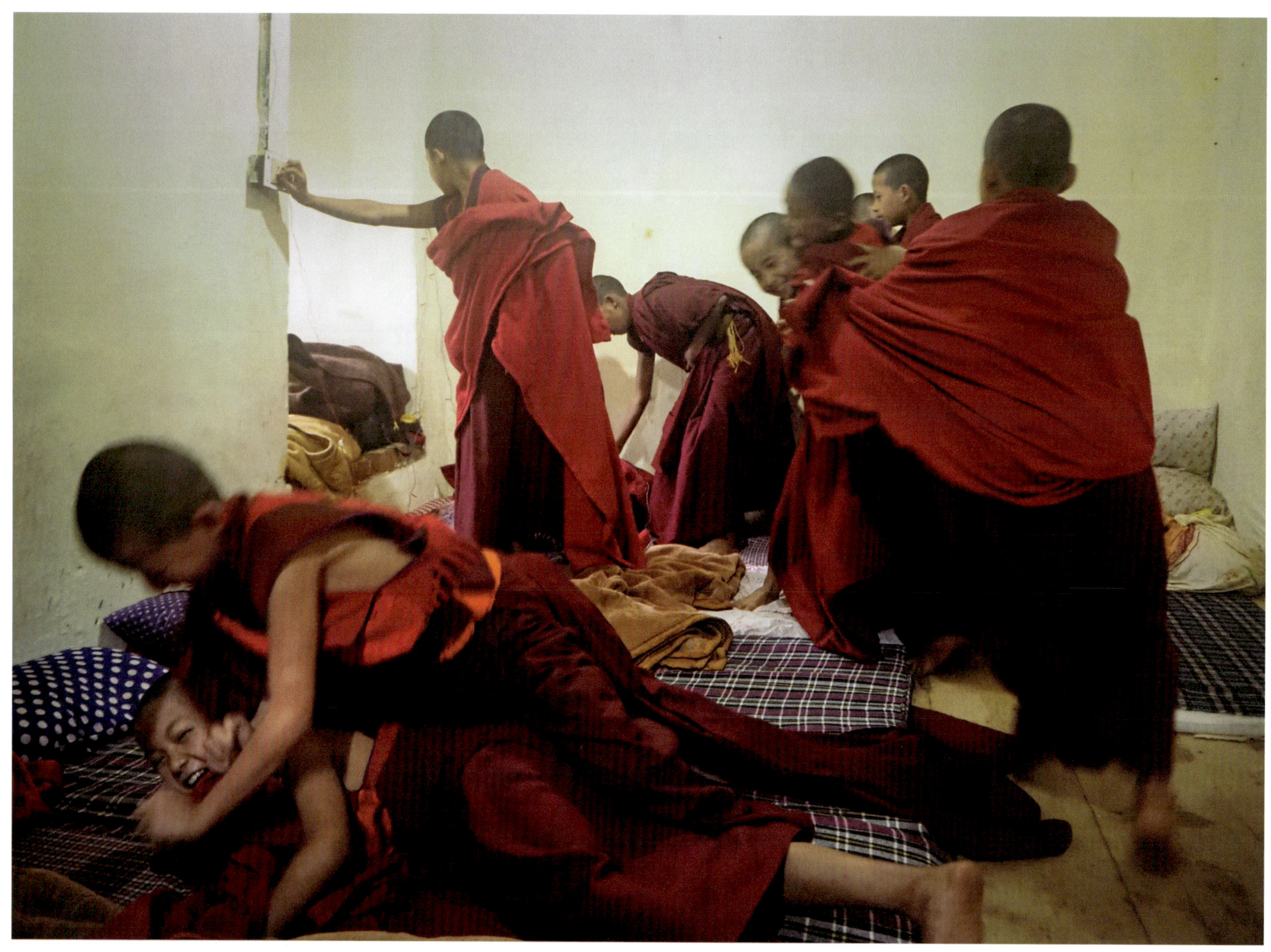

JIGME GYELTSHEN / BHUTAN 2019

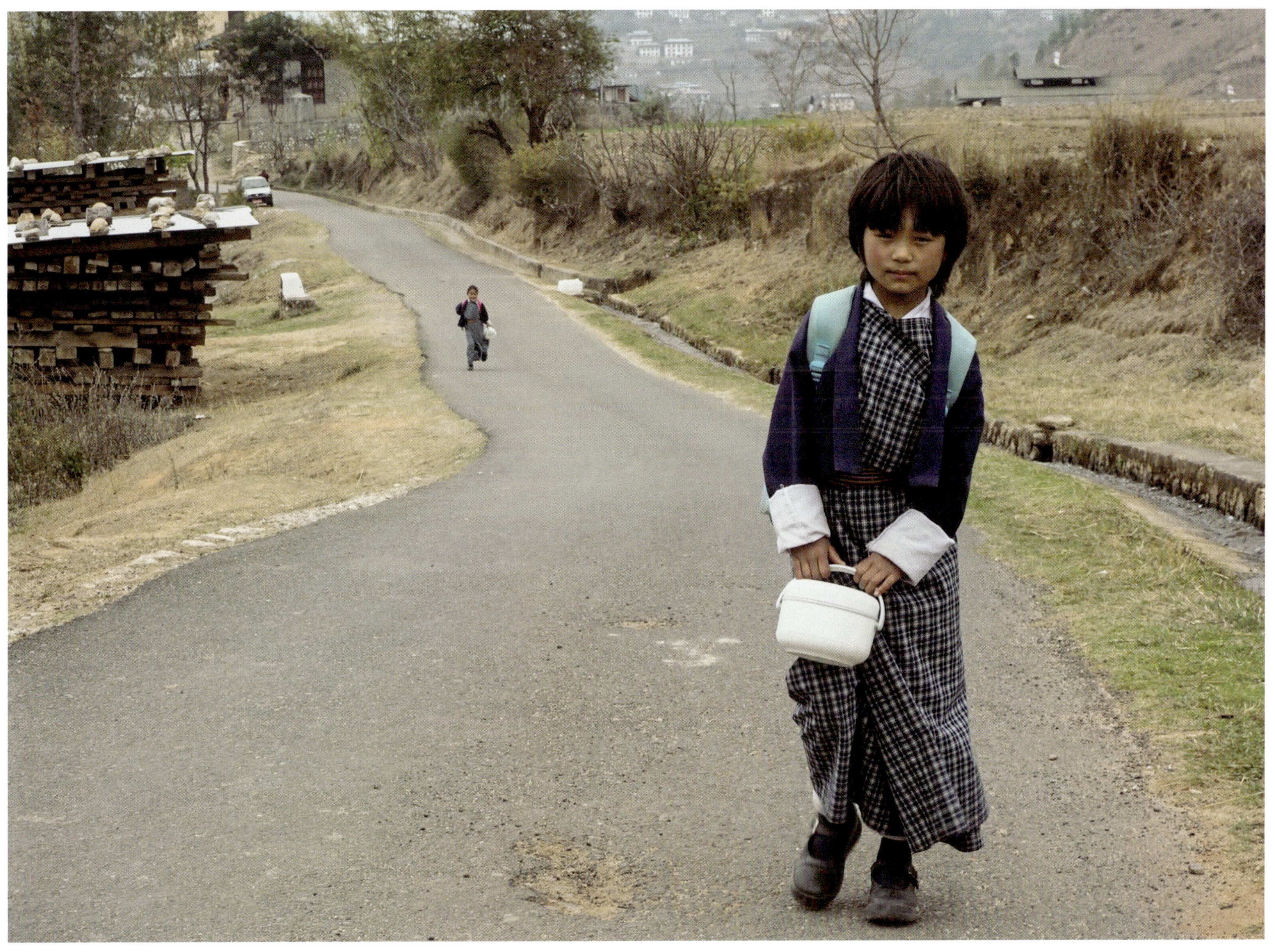

CHOKI WANGMO / BHUTAN 2019

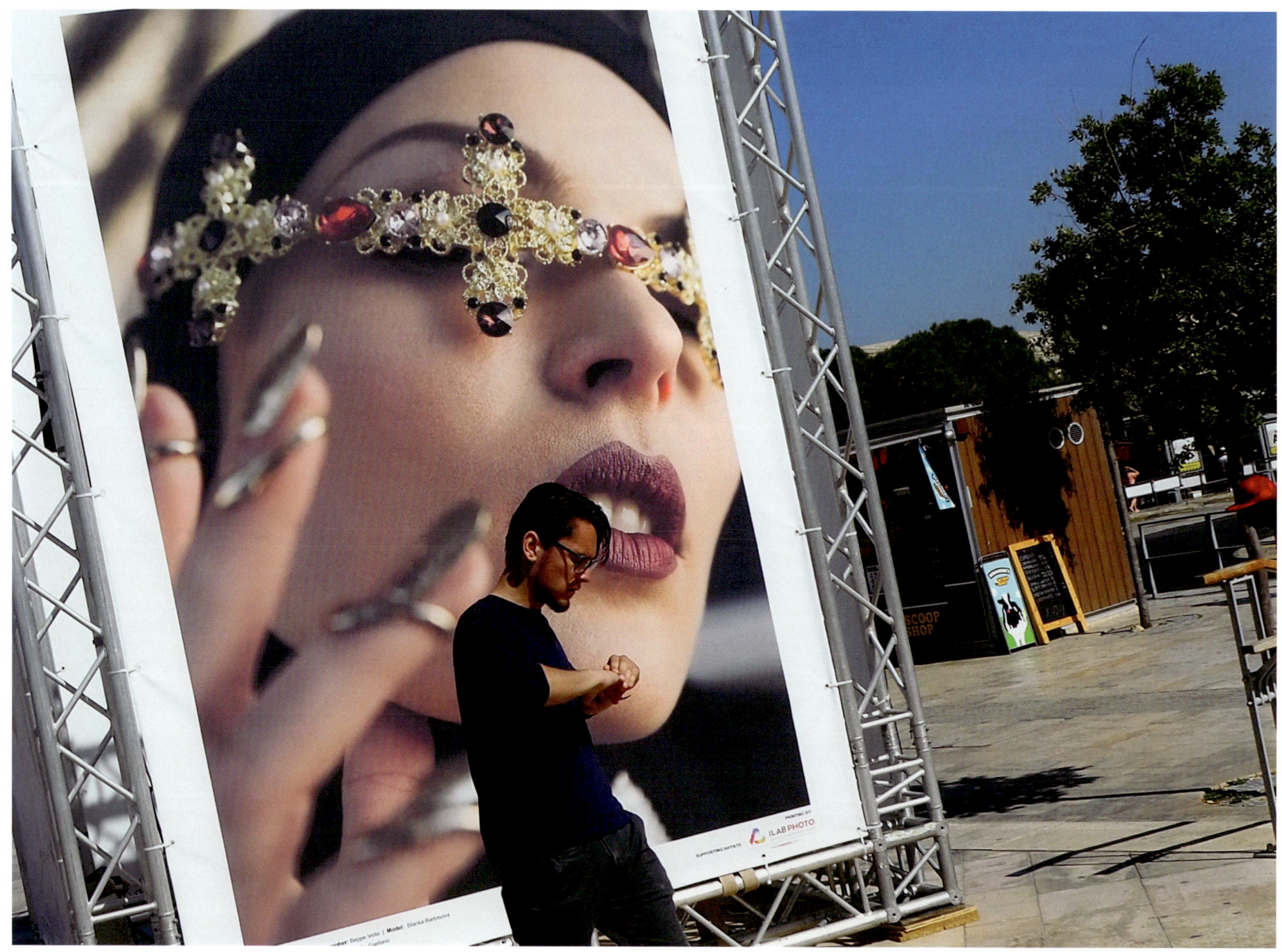

AHMAD OBAID / MALTA 2019

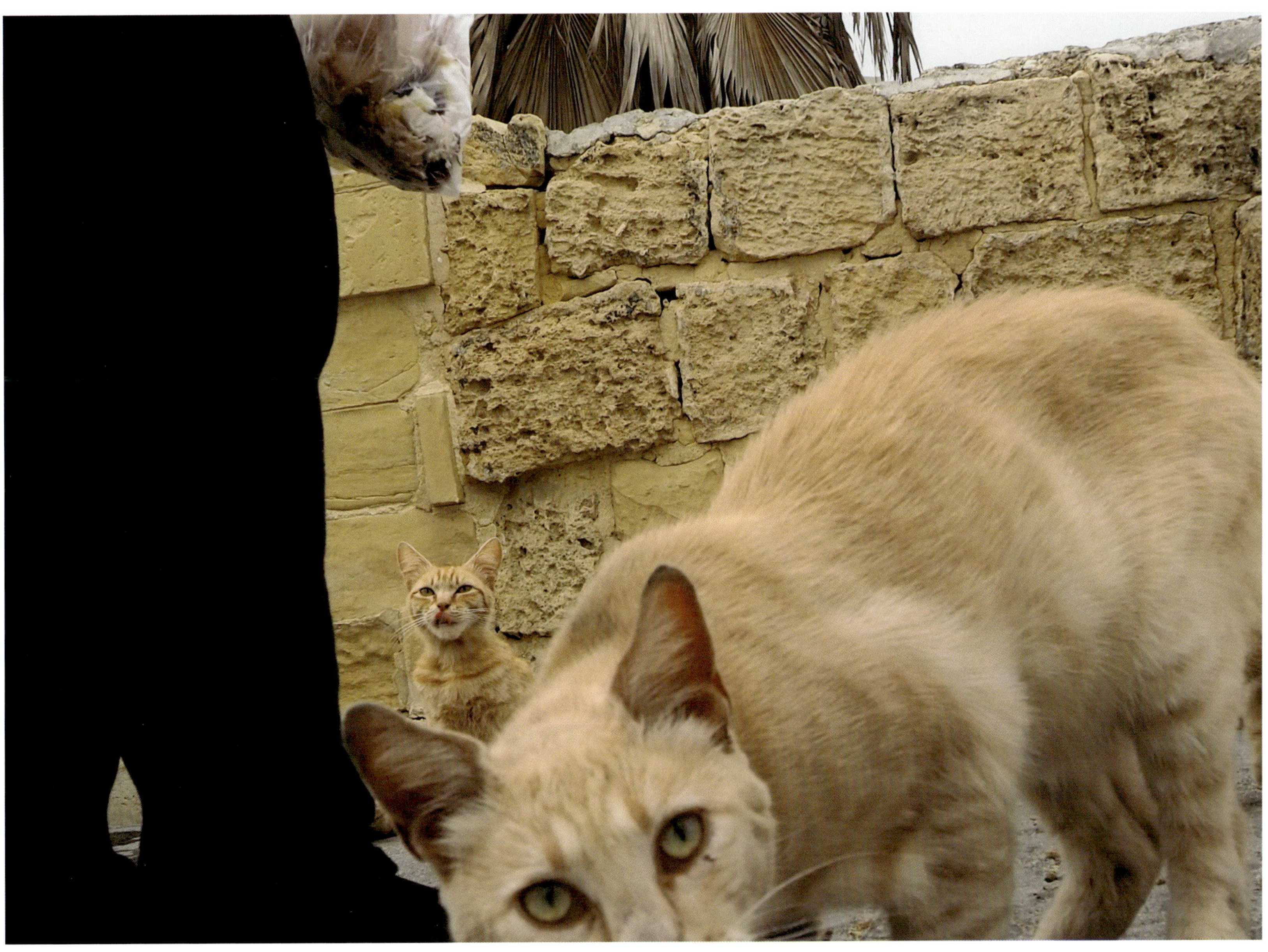

AHMAD OBAID / MALTA 2019

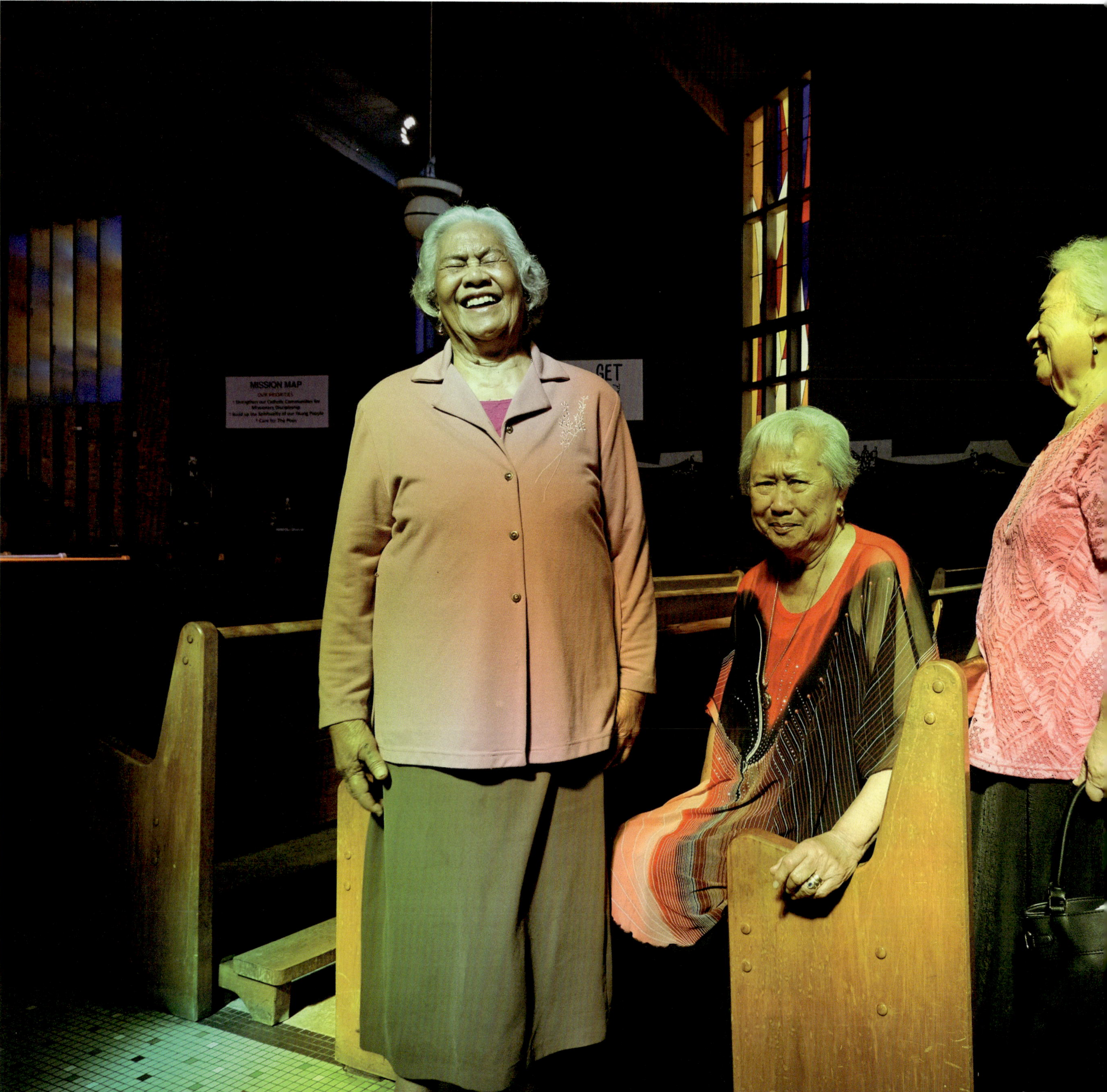
MISSION MAP
GET

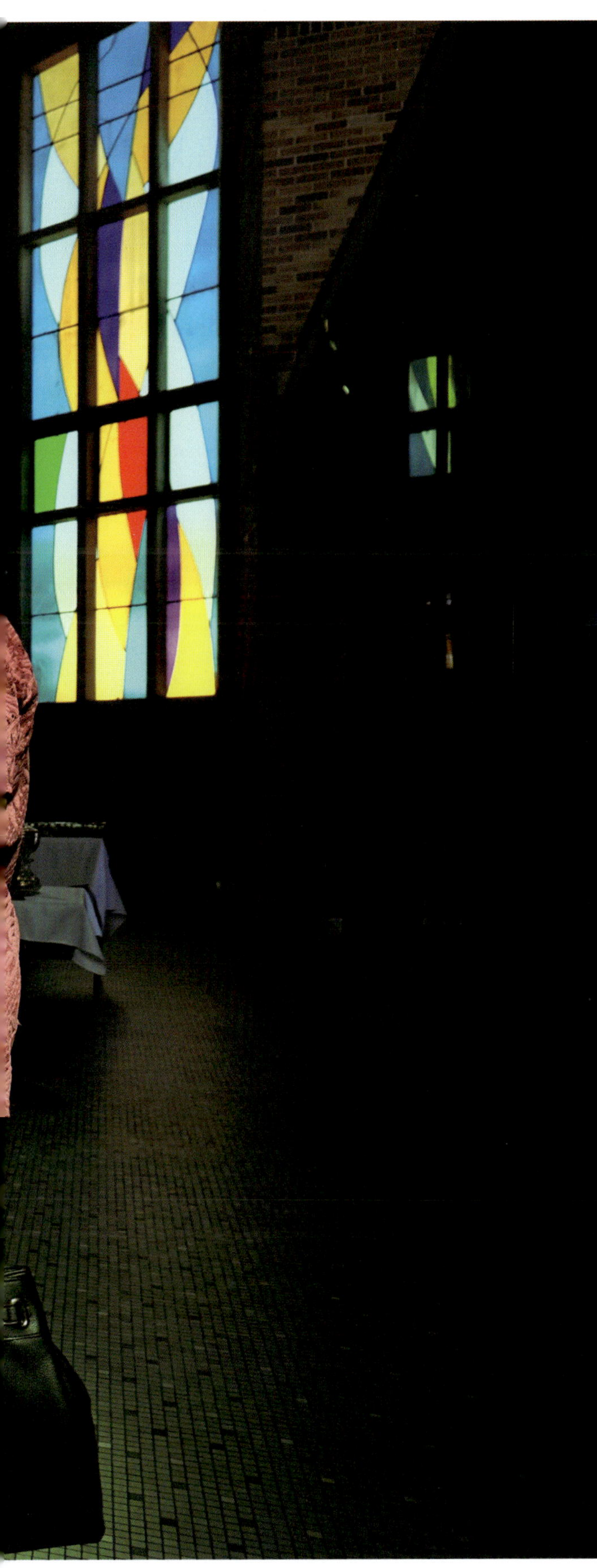

> ***"Our community is like a treasure. We all treat each other like family, and we take care of each other."***
>
> —ALIAH SEMMENS, MURUPARA, NEW ZEALAND 2019

TEUILA VA'AELUA / NEW ZEALAND 2023

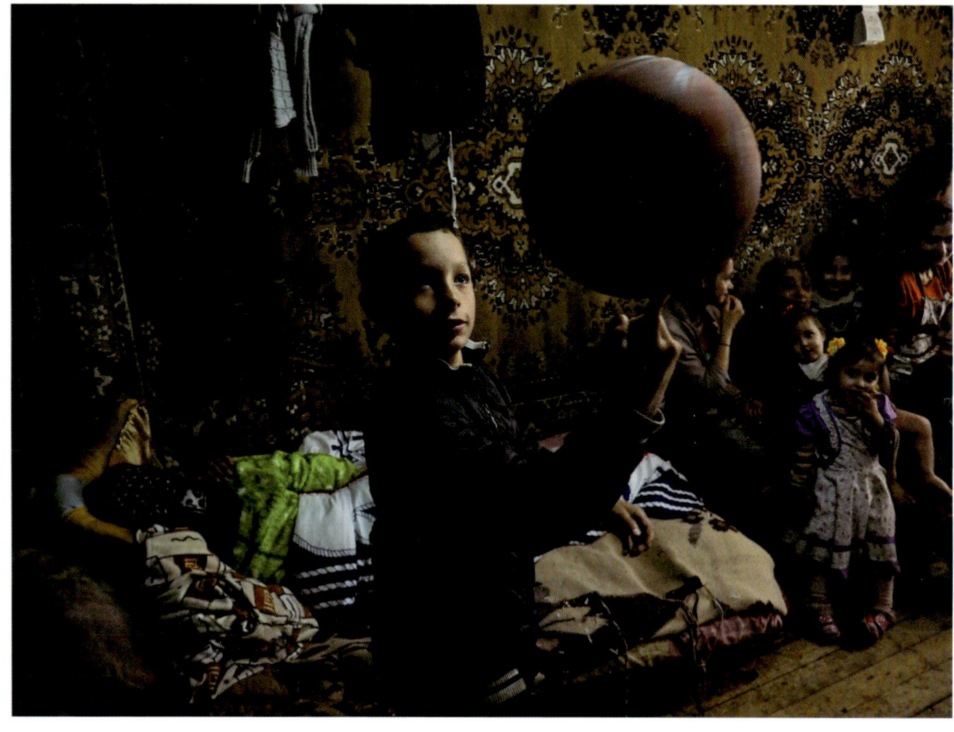

ABOVE: **ALEXANDRU COSTIN / MOLDOVA 2018** RIGHT: **LIUBOVI TABUNȘCIC / MOLDOVA 2018**

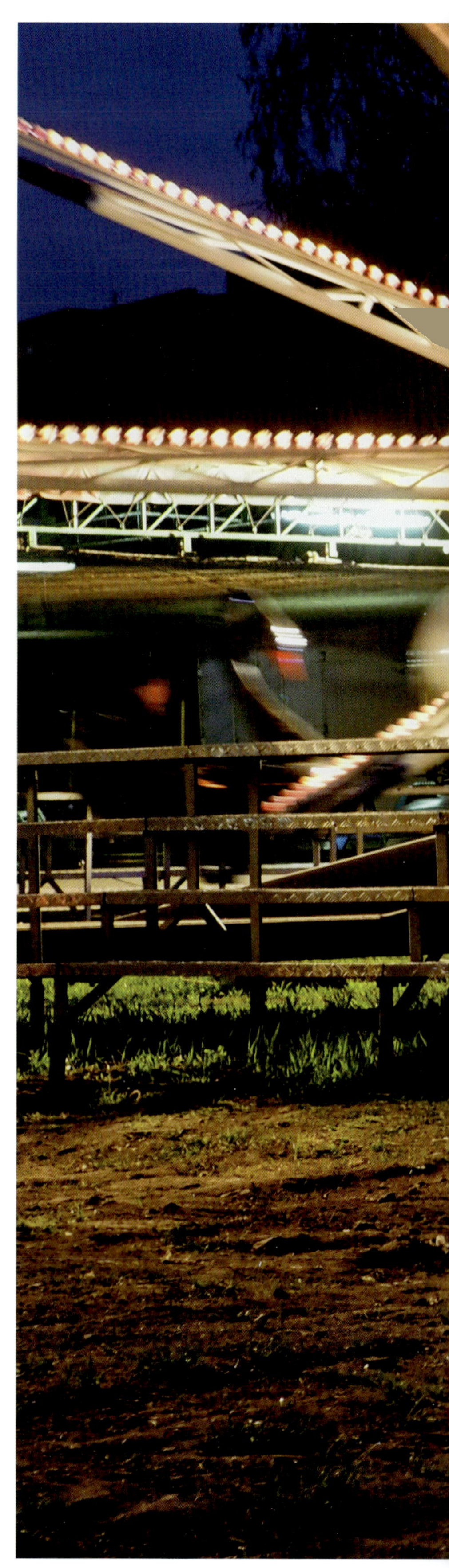

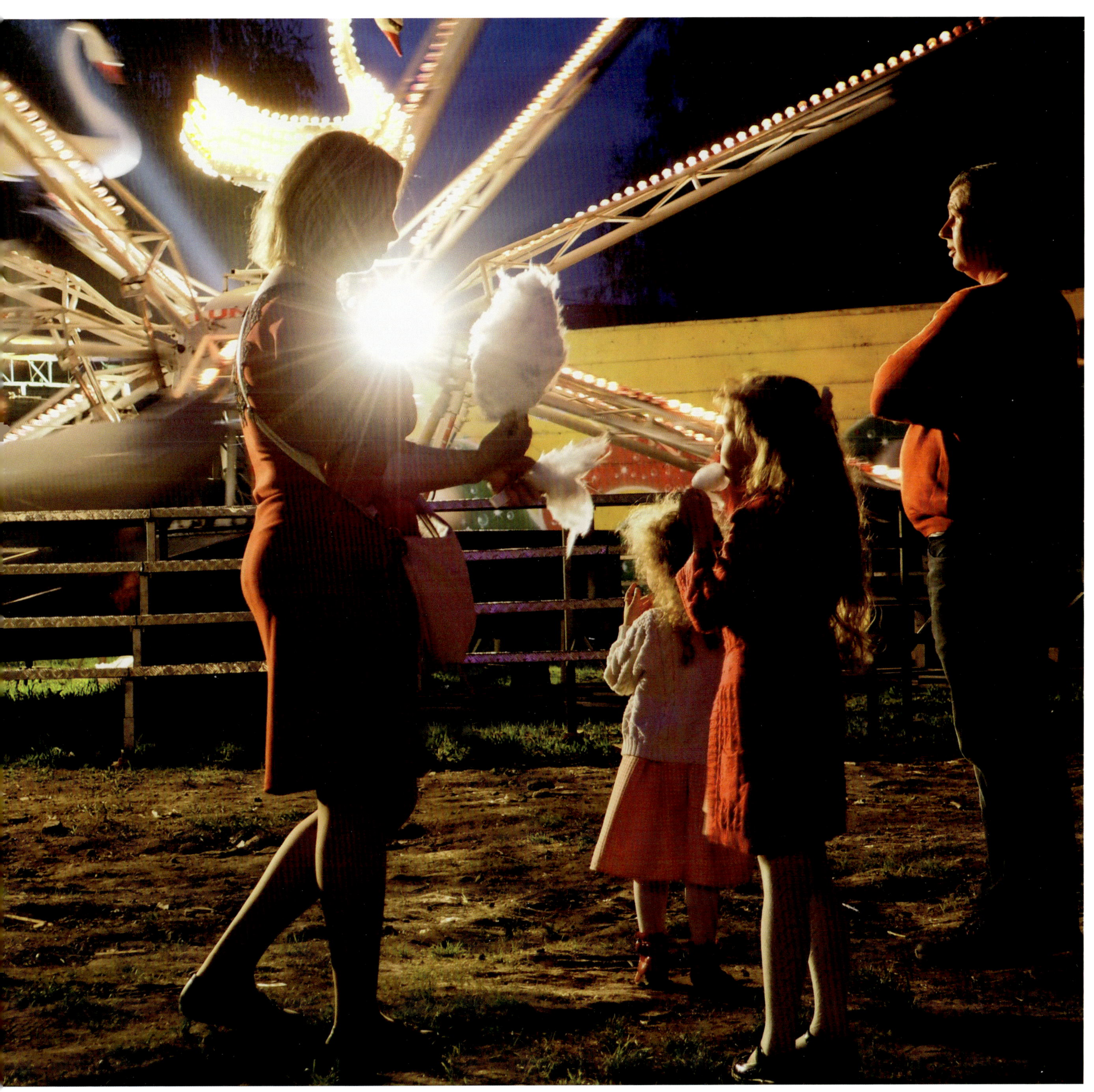

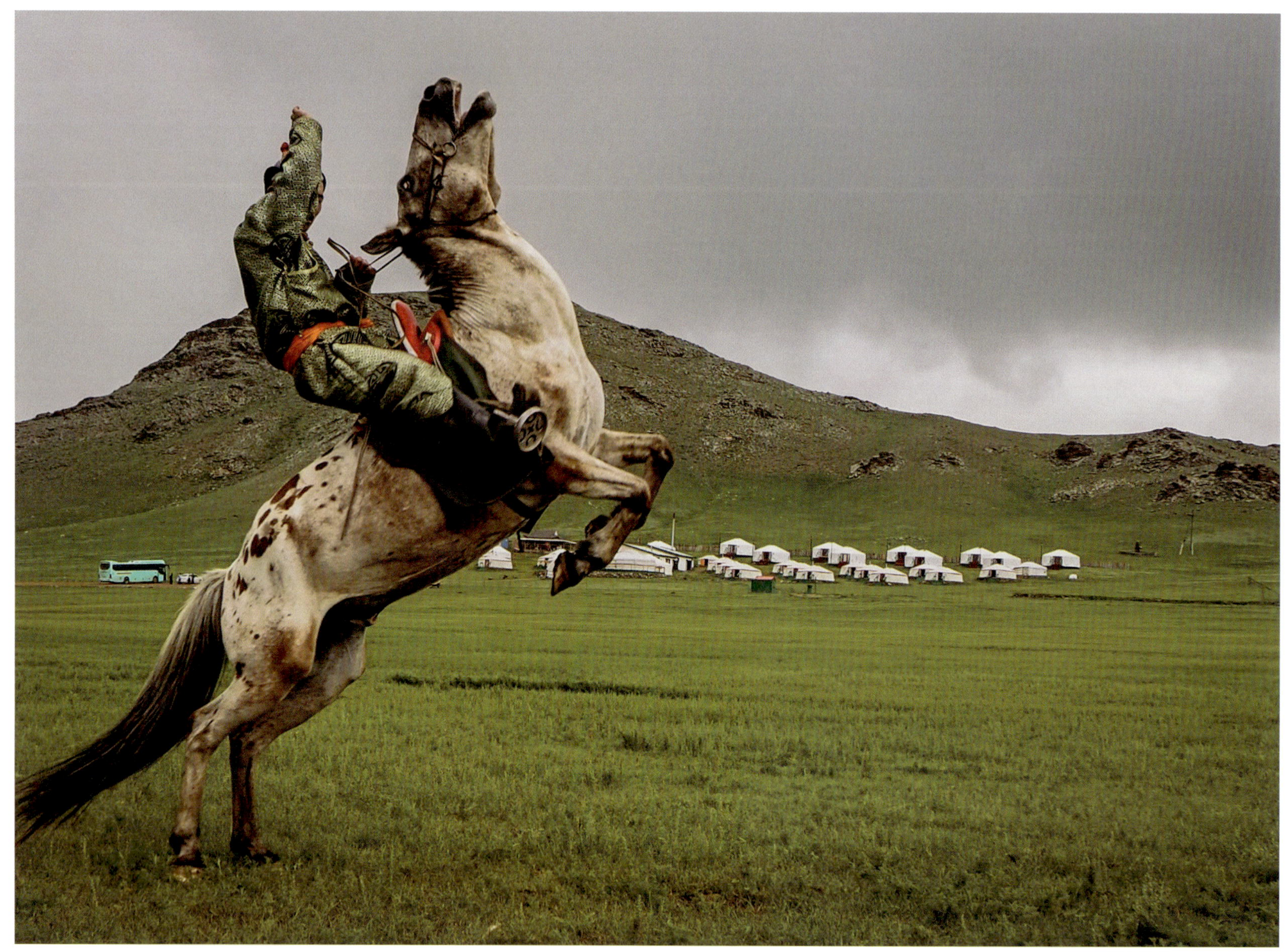

TS. BAYASGALAN / MONGOLIA 2019

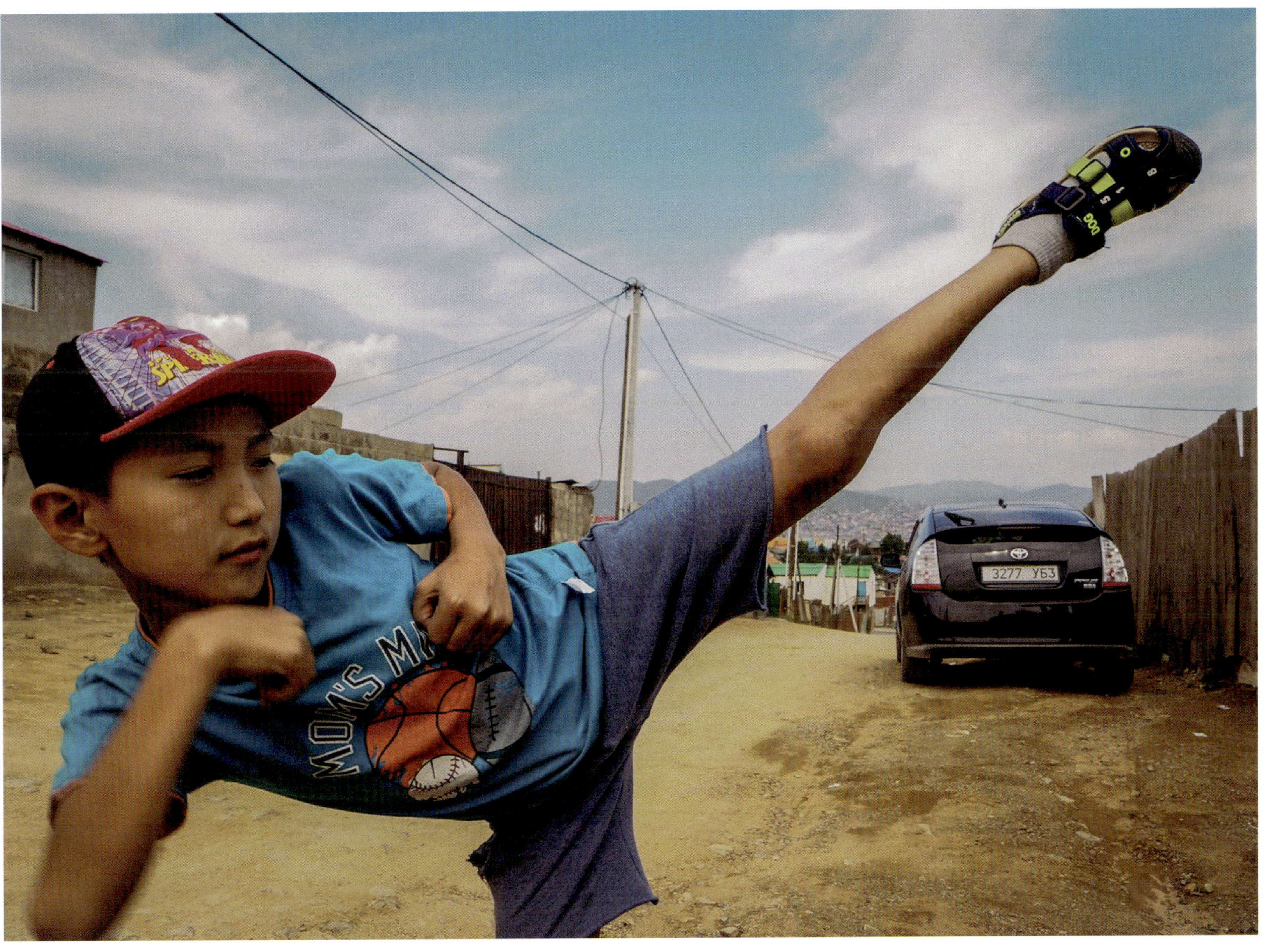

M. UYANGA / MONGOLIA 2019

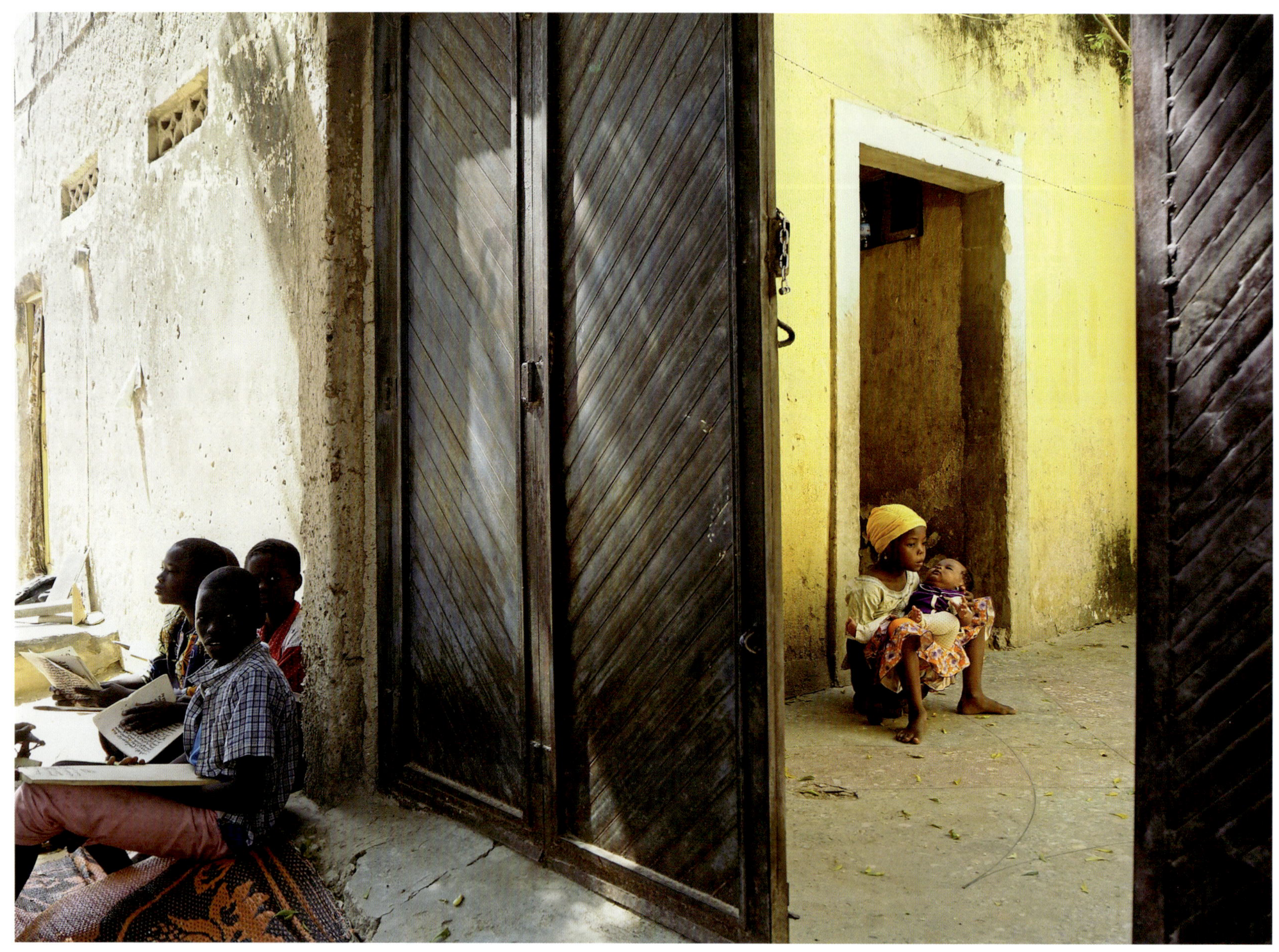

ADAMU MARYAM NDAMUDI / NIGERIA 2019

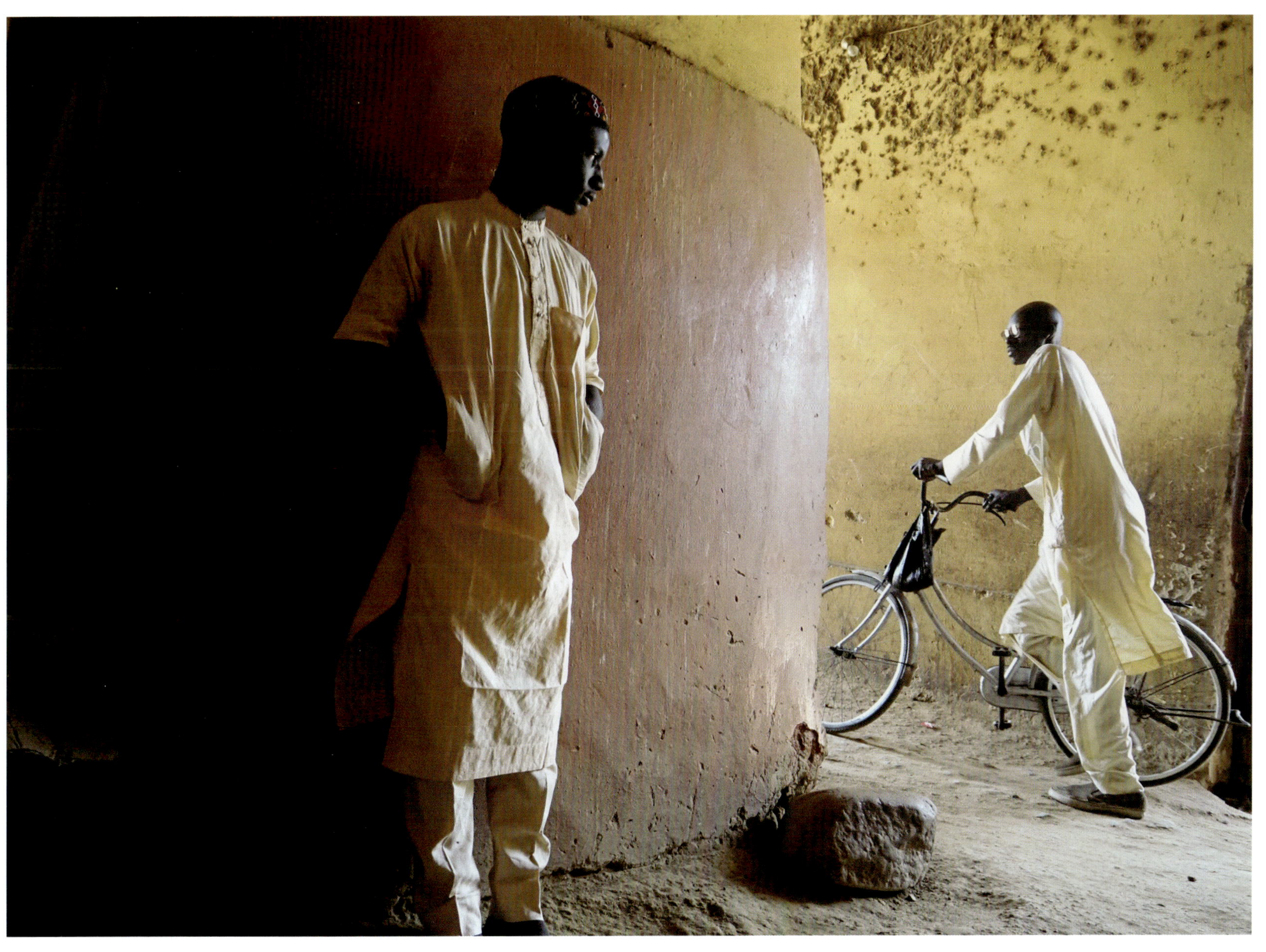

REGINA OJUNOGWA ALFA / NIGERIA 2019

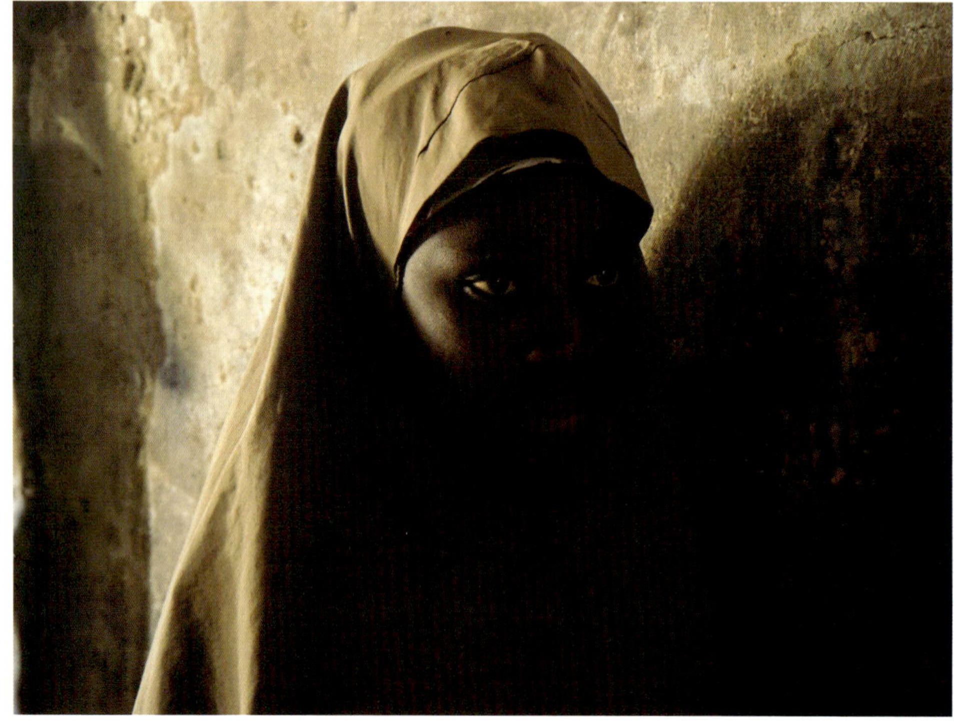

ABOVE: **REGINA OJUNOGWA ALFA / NIGERIA 2019** RIGHT: **SIMON PETER / NIGERIA 2019**

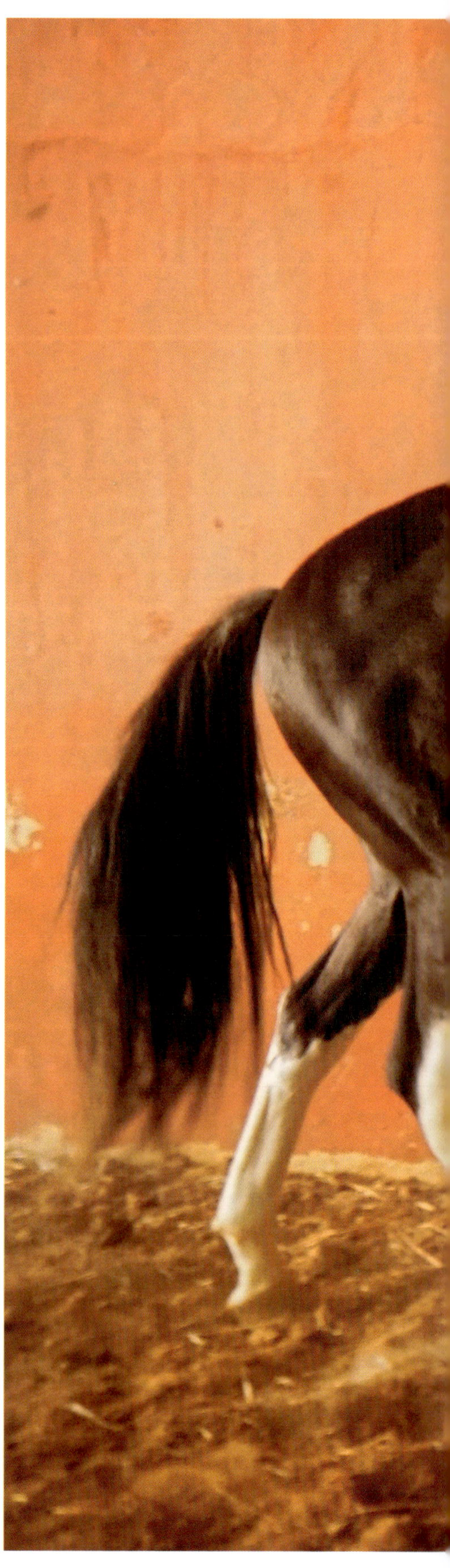

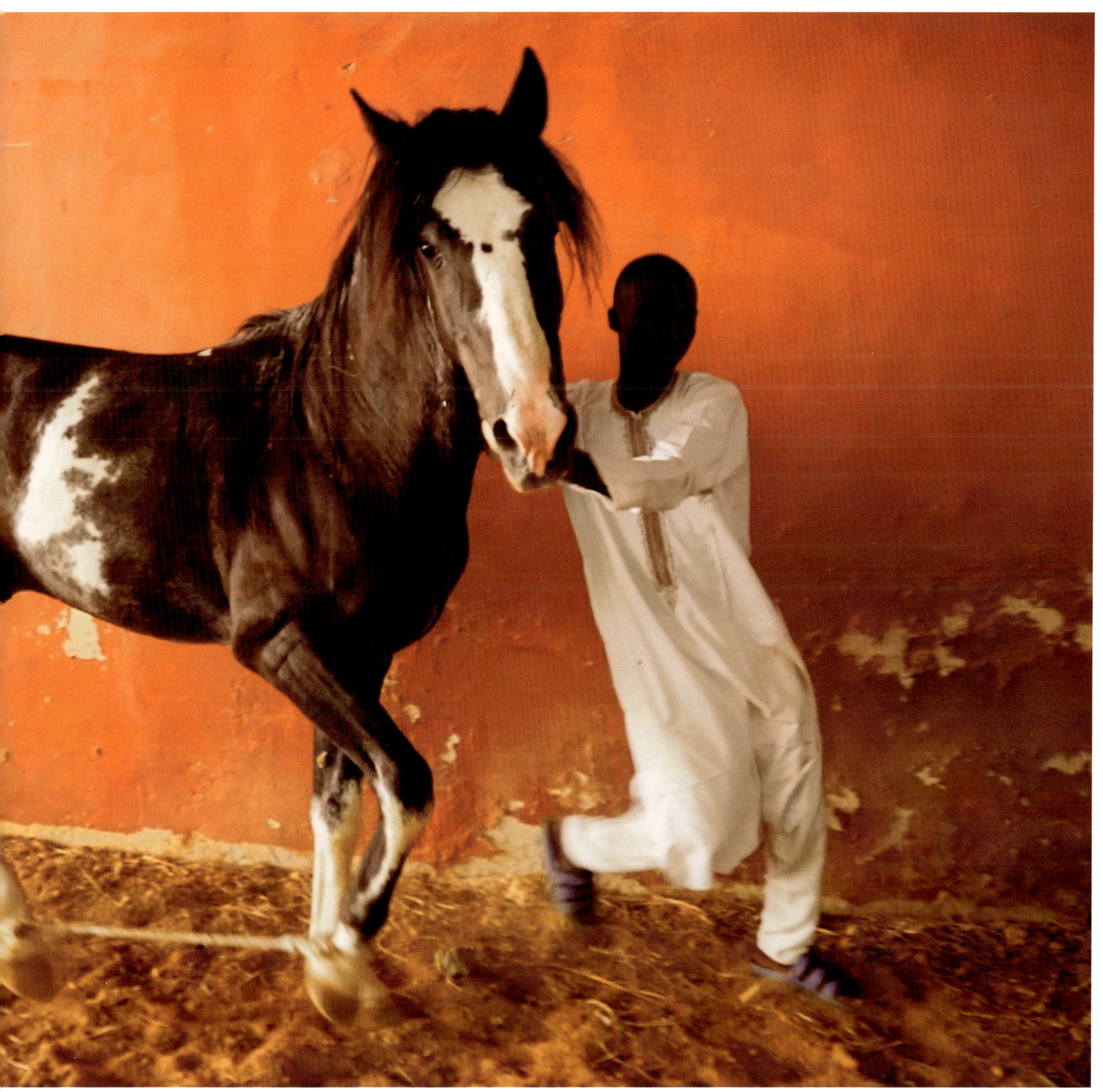

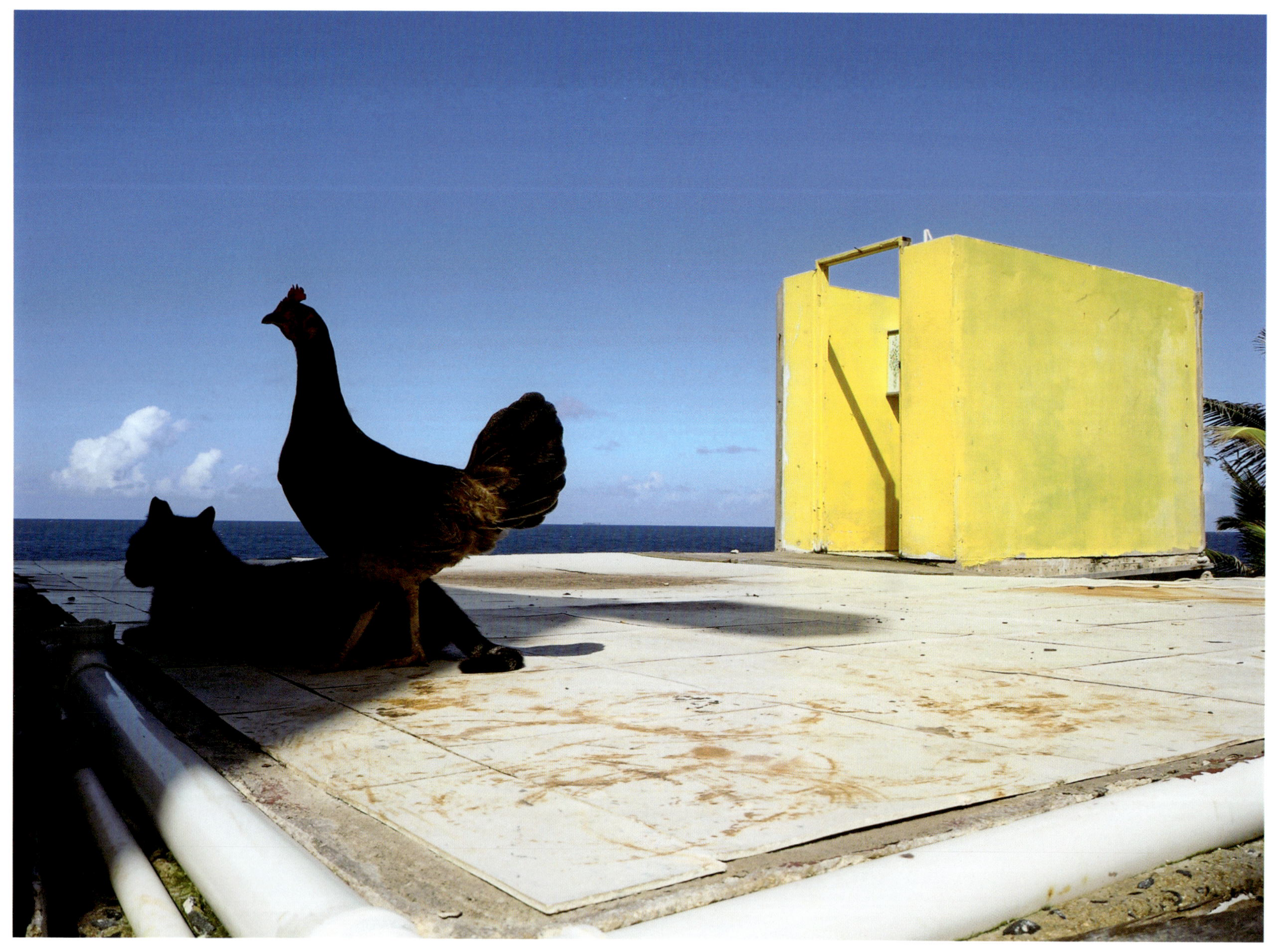

MARANGELI MELENDEZ MORALES / PUERTO RICO 2018

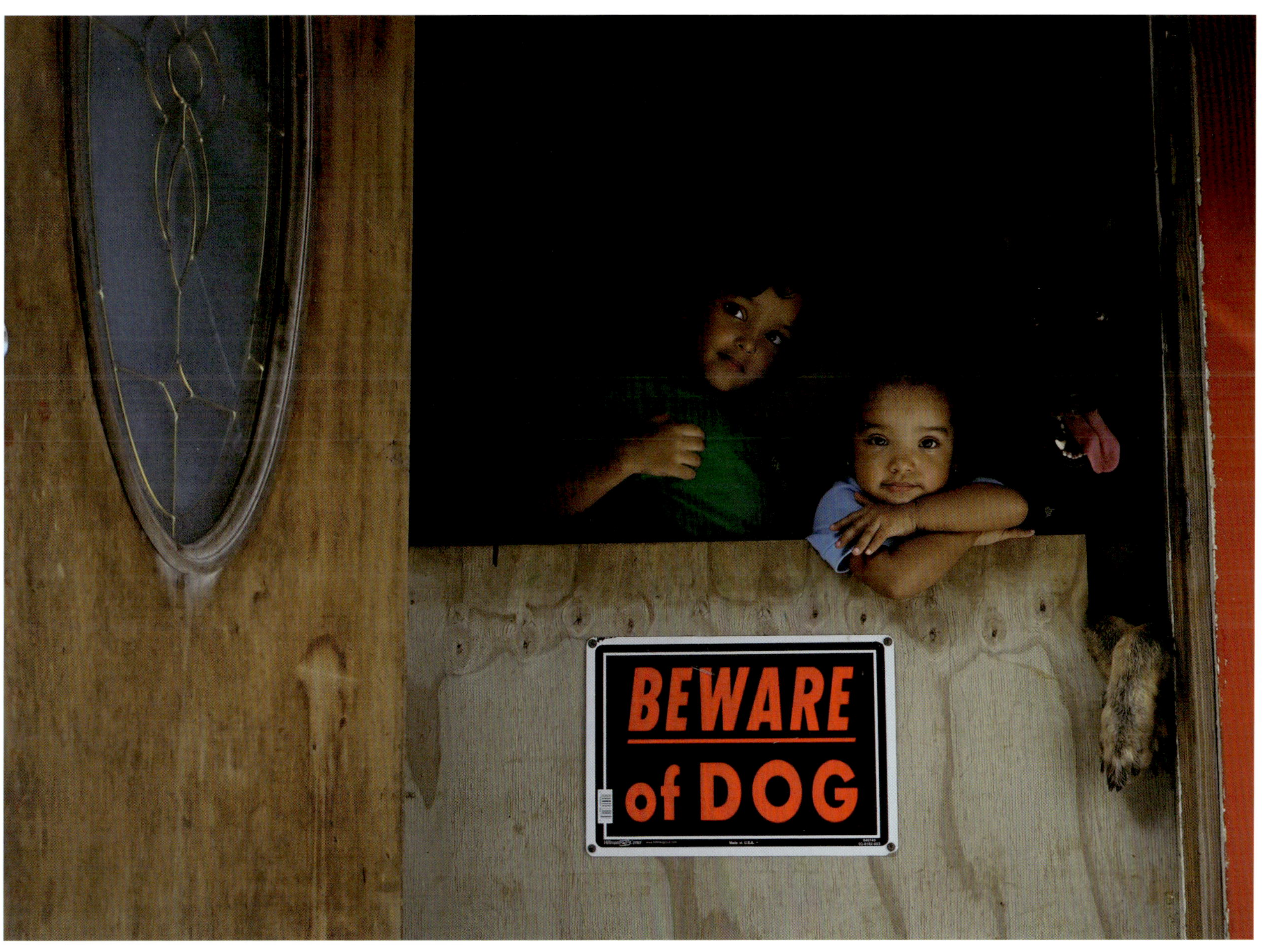

JAN ROLON / PUERTO RICO 2018

Camp Profile
Chad 2010

"I AM VERY SATISFIED WITH THIS TRAINING because it has made me into a complete person. Photography awakened many things in me. Photographic language gives me more of everything to continue my fight to transform society and be the spokesperson for those who don't have a voice."

These words from Mbaihornom Godivah speak volumes about the aspirations of the diverse group of men and women—Christians and Muslims, representing both rural and urban areas—who gathered in Chad's capital city, N'Djamena, for a Photo Camp to explore the themes of community, leadership, and diversity. At the time, Chad was experiencing a welcome but uneasy peace after five years of civil war, so this Photo Camp was one of the first opportunities this group of students had to mingle and listen to each other during the new period of stability. "Before going to the training," Hawa Hgarnim Adoum wrote, "when I learned there would be people from the countryside and there would be a mix of boys and girls, I thought that would be very difficult." But in the end, Hawa was in full agreement with a view expressed by another participant, Amine Souleyman Tidjani, who pledged to "practice what I learned here."

"We came from different regions with different cultures, languages, beliefs, and spent a week together without any problem," Amine observed. "We shared and learned a lot from each other. I thought it couldn't be like that, but we made it. It is those things you won't ever forget."

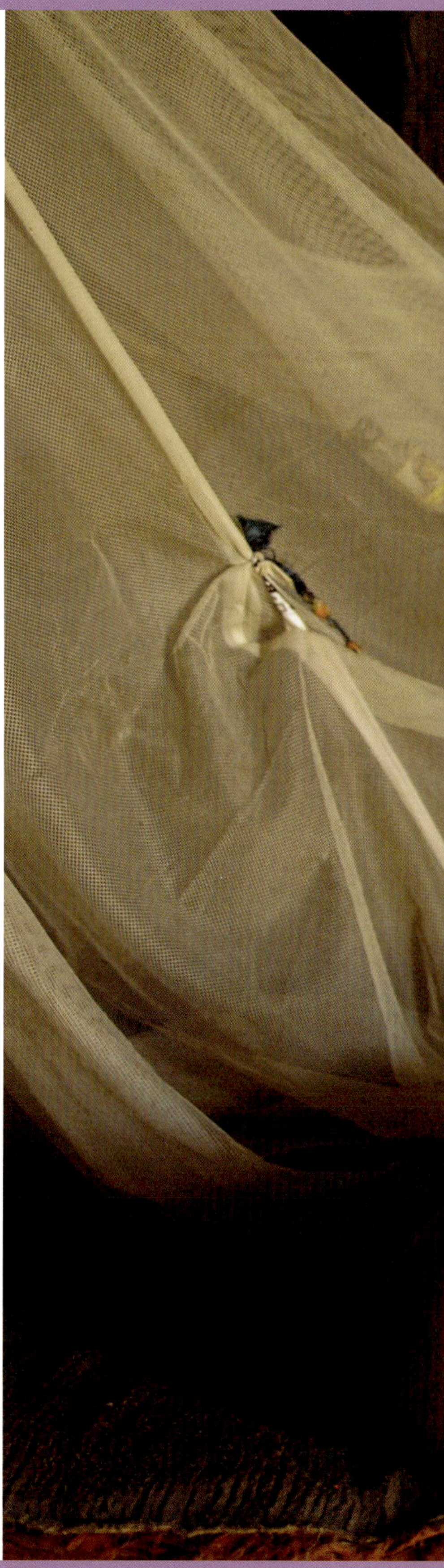

MAHAMOUD ALI AHMAT BELLO / CHAD 2010

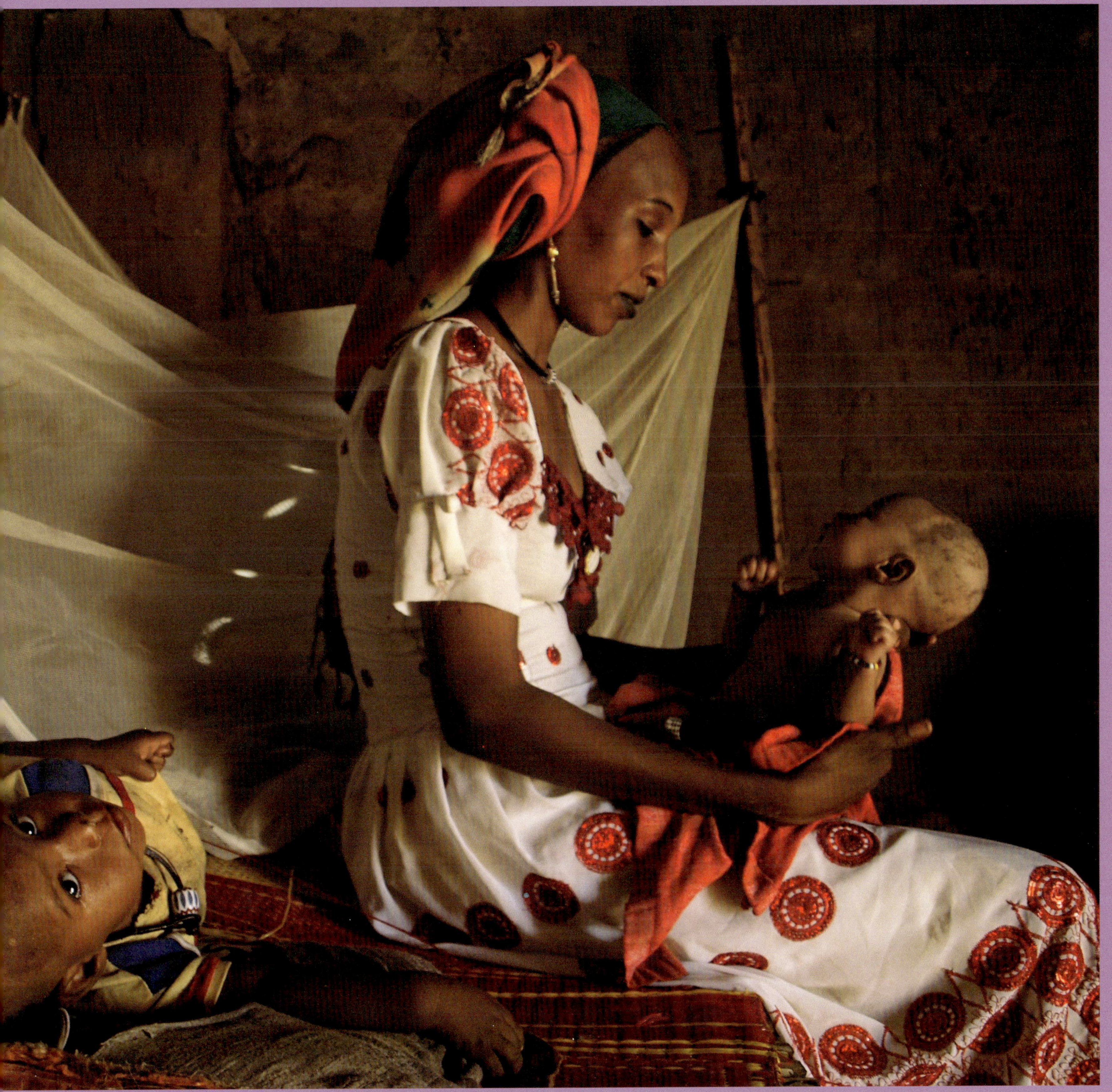

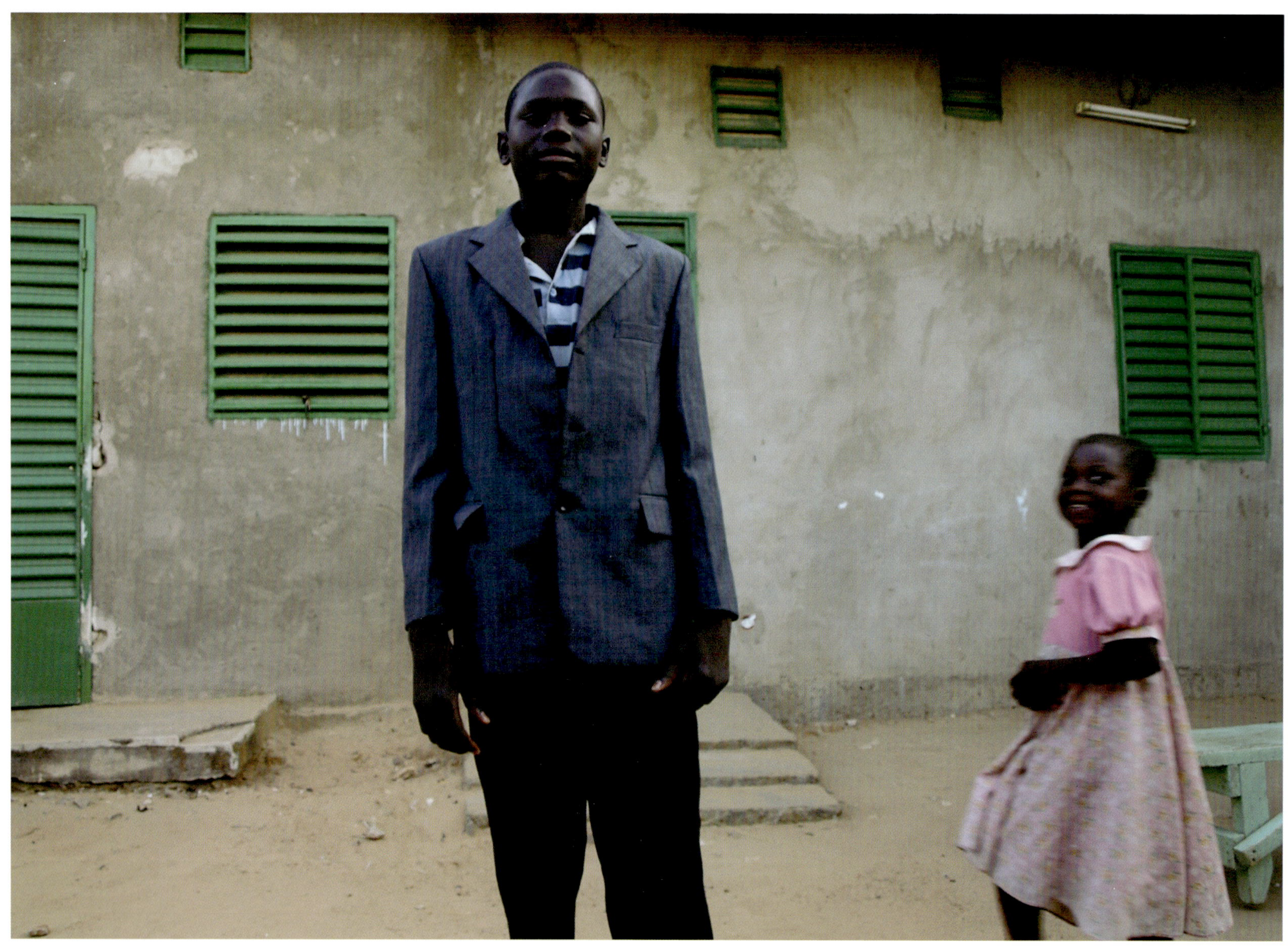

ABOVE: **DILAH SYLVAIN / CHAD 2010** OPPOSITE: **HOUDA HAMAT / CHAD 2010**

"We are the sons of nomadic herders. Our tradition has influenced us. We live in the Sahara, sons of the sun."

—MAHAMAT DADY ALLAHI, CHAD 2010

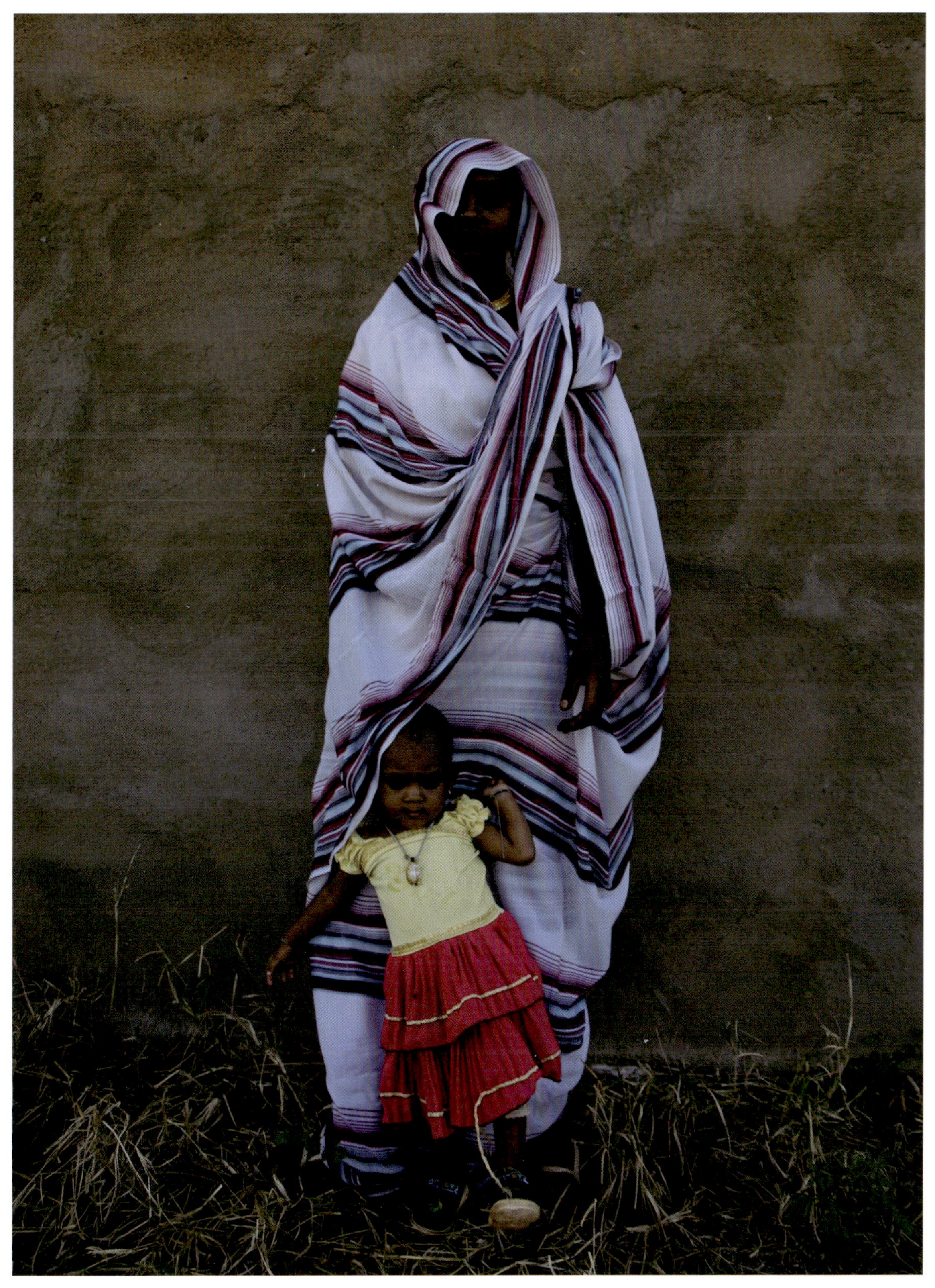

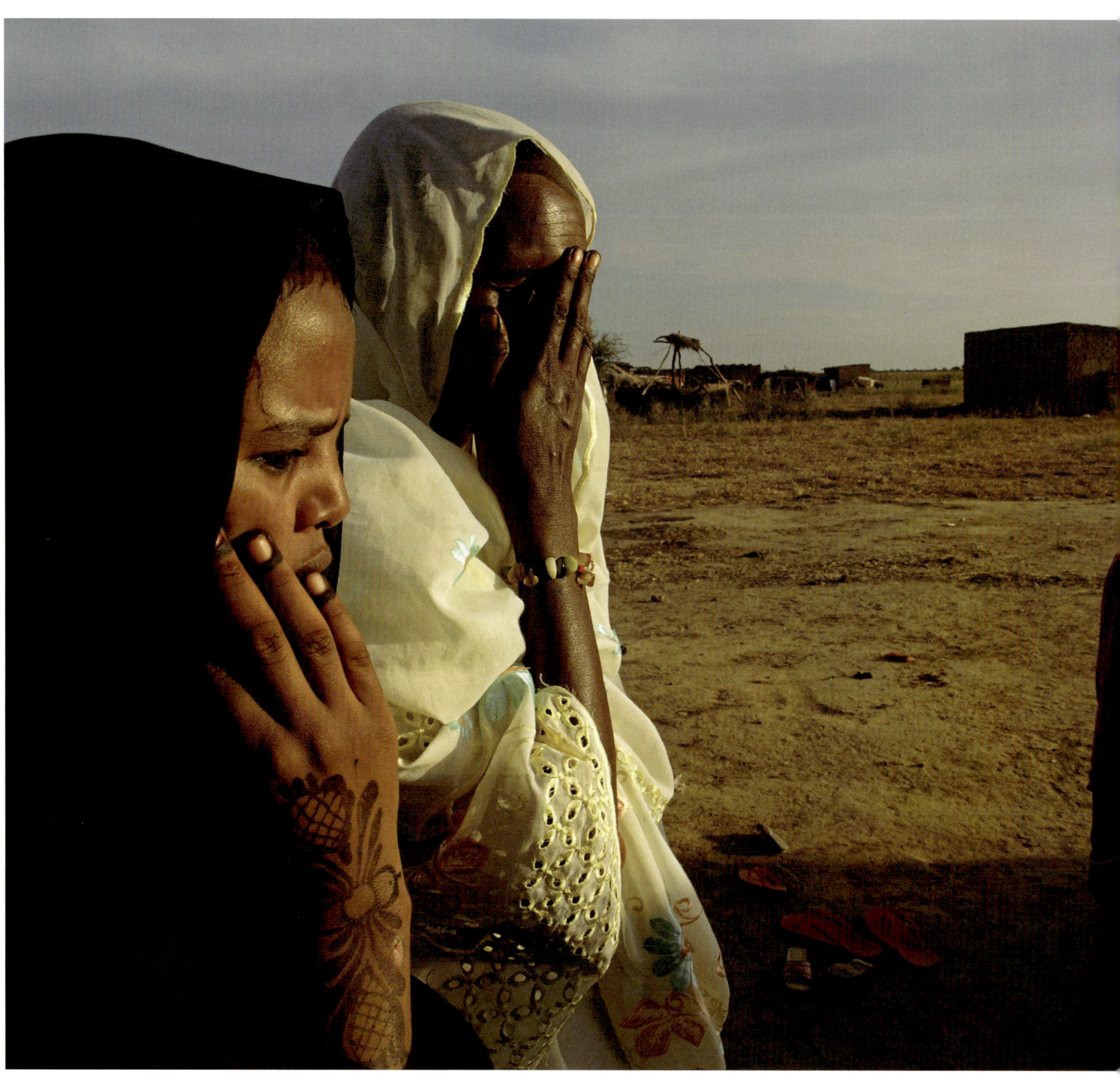

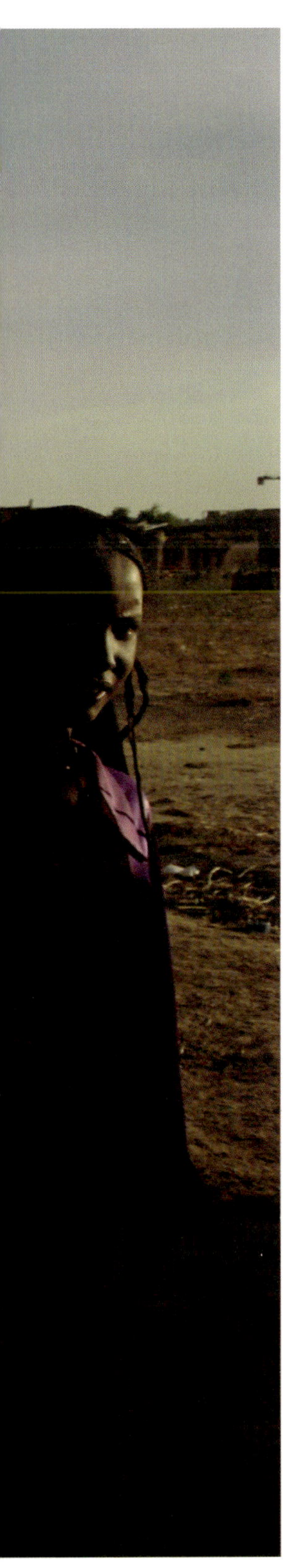

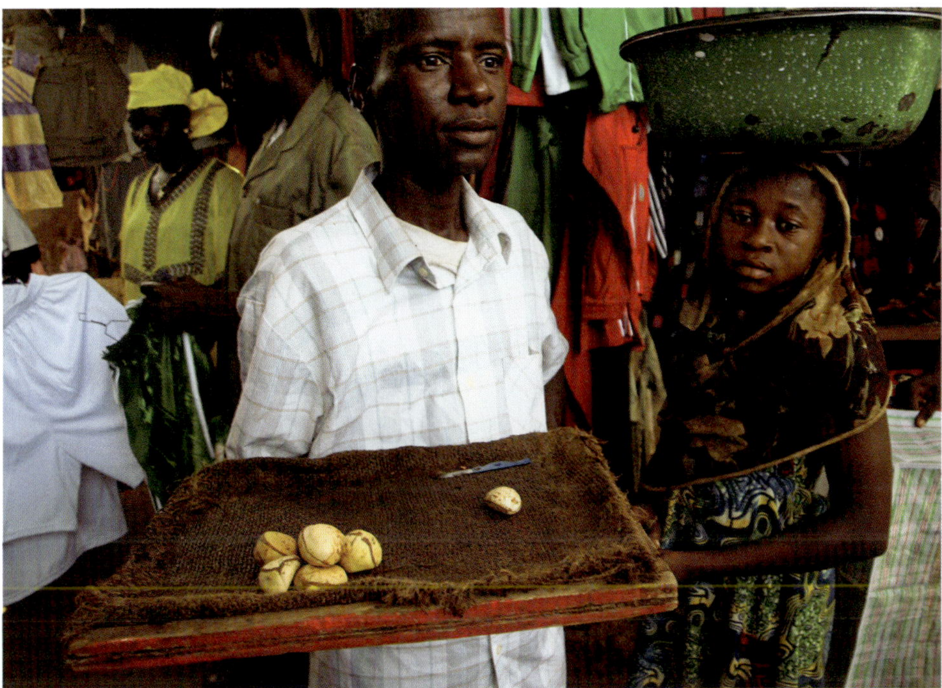

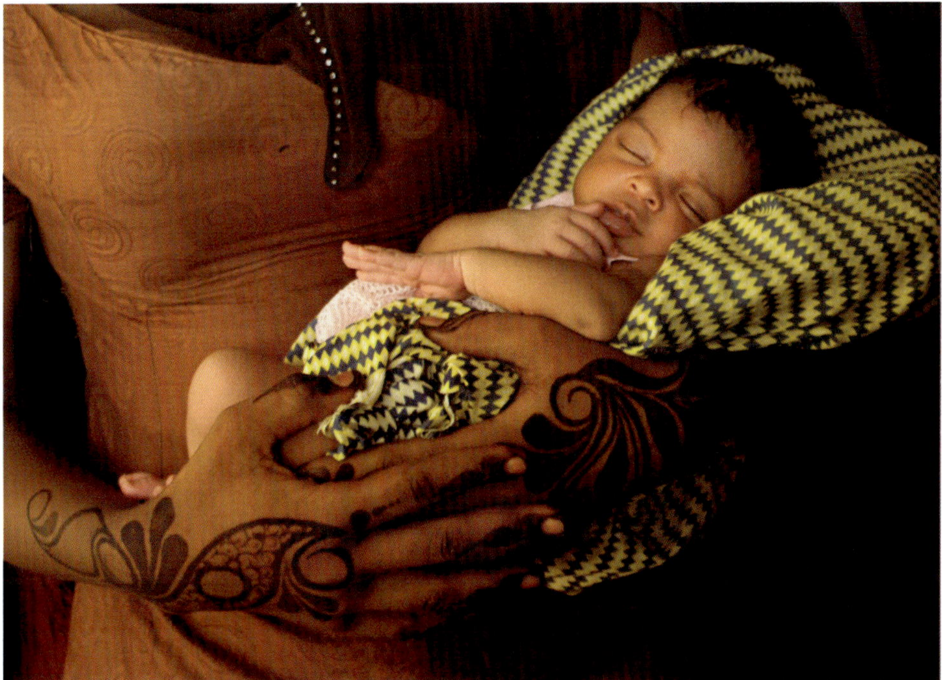

TOP: **ALI YOUNOUSS ALI / CHAD 2010** ABOVE: **BABA HASSAN ADOUM / CHAD 2010**
LEFT: **AHMAT ADAM MAHAMAT / CHAD 2010**

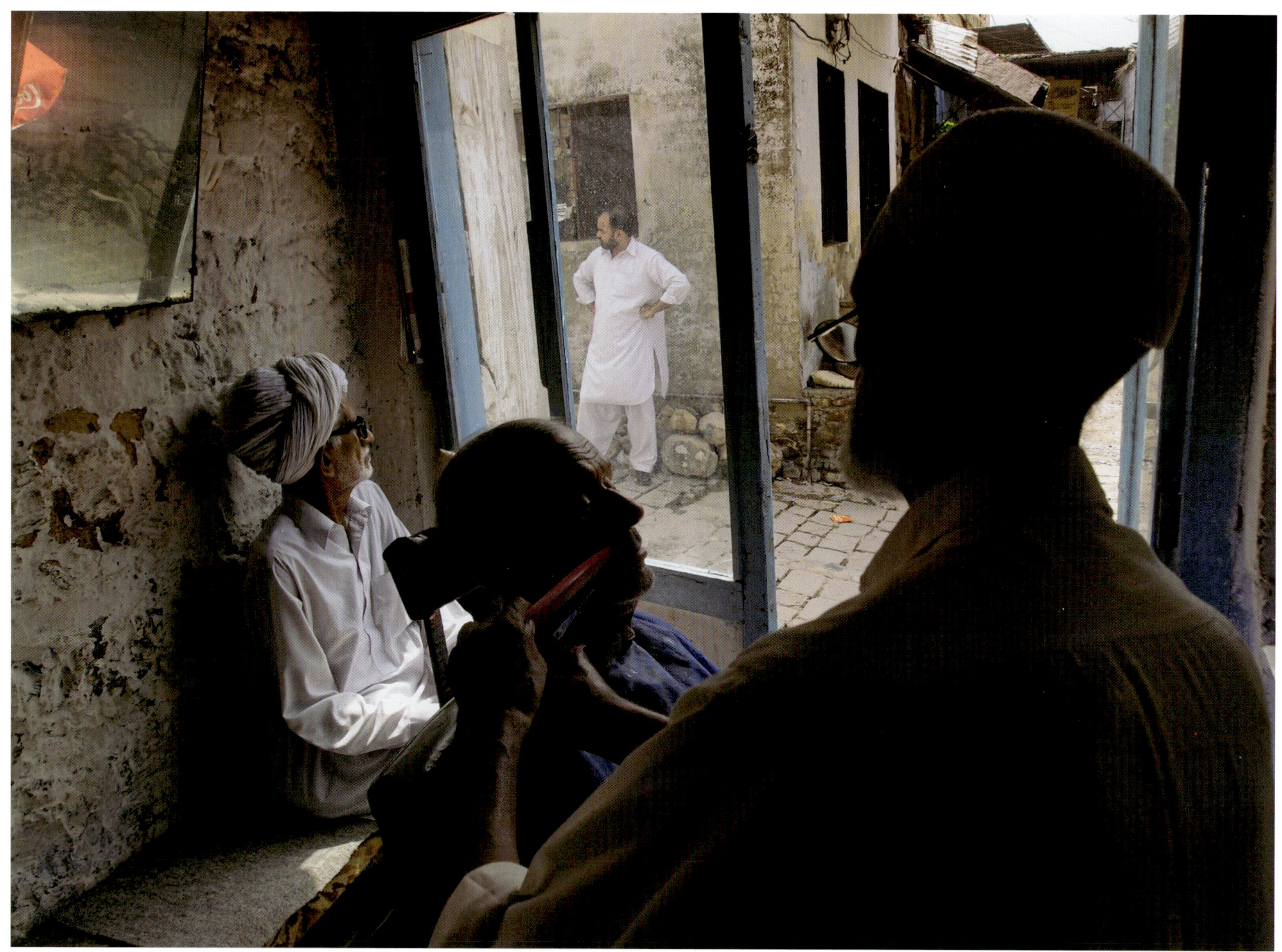

SEEMA GUL / PAKISTAN 2012

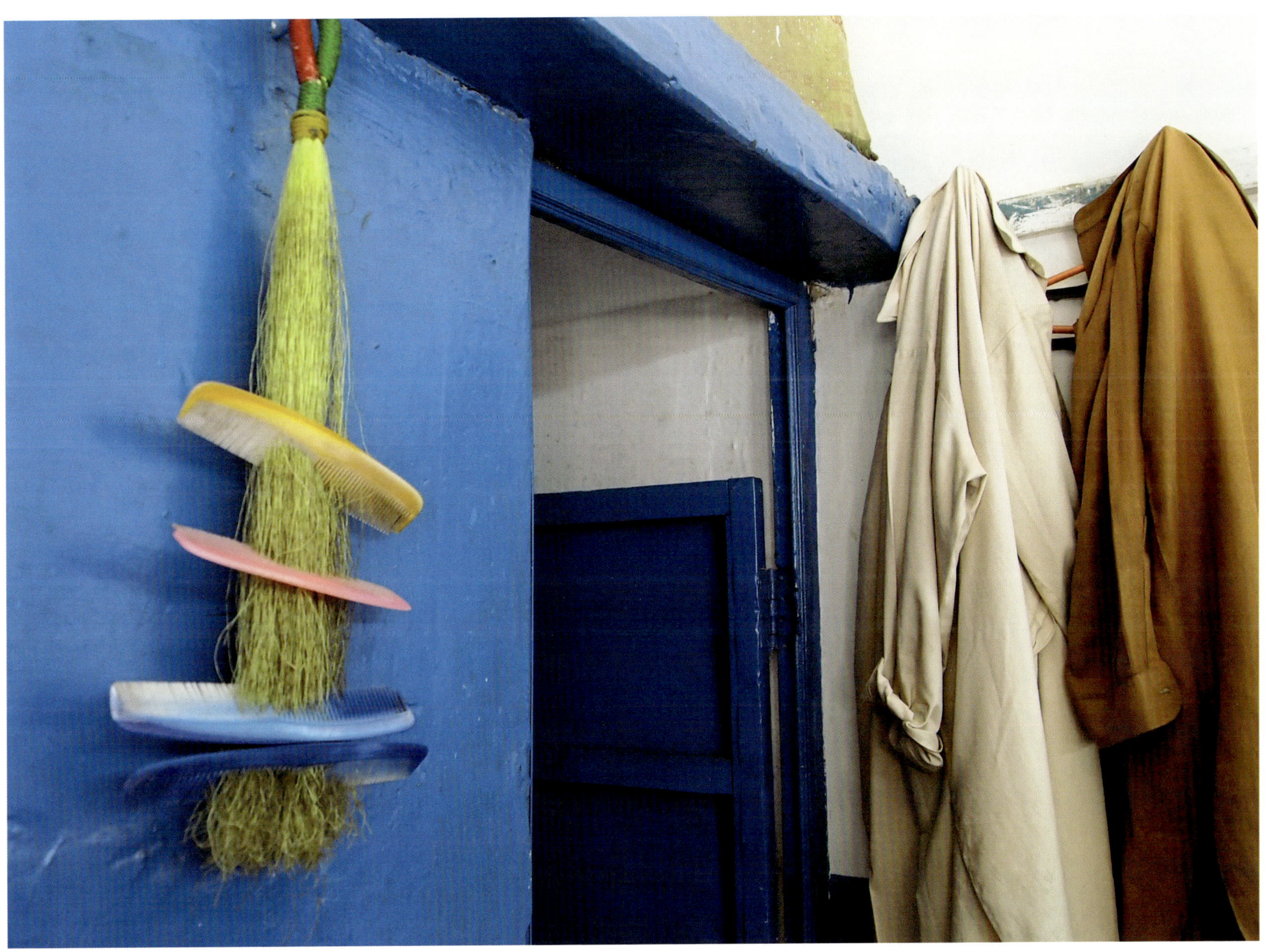

AZMATULLAH KHAN / PAKISTAN 2012

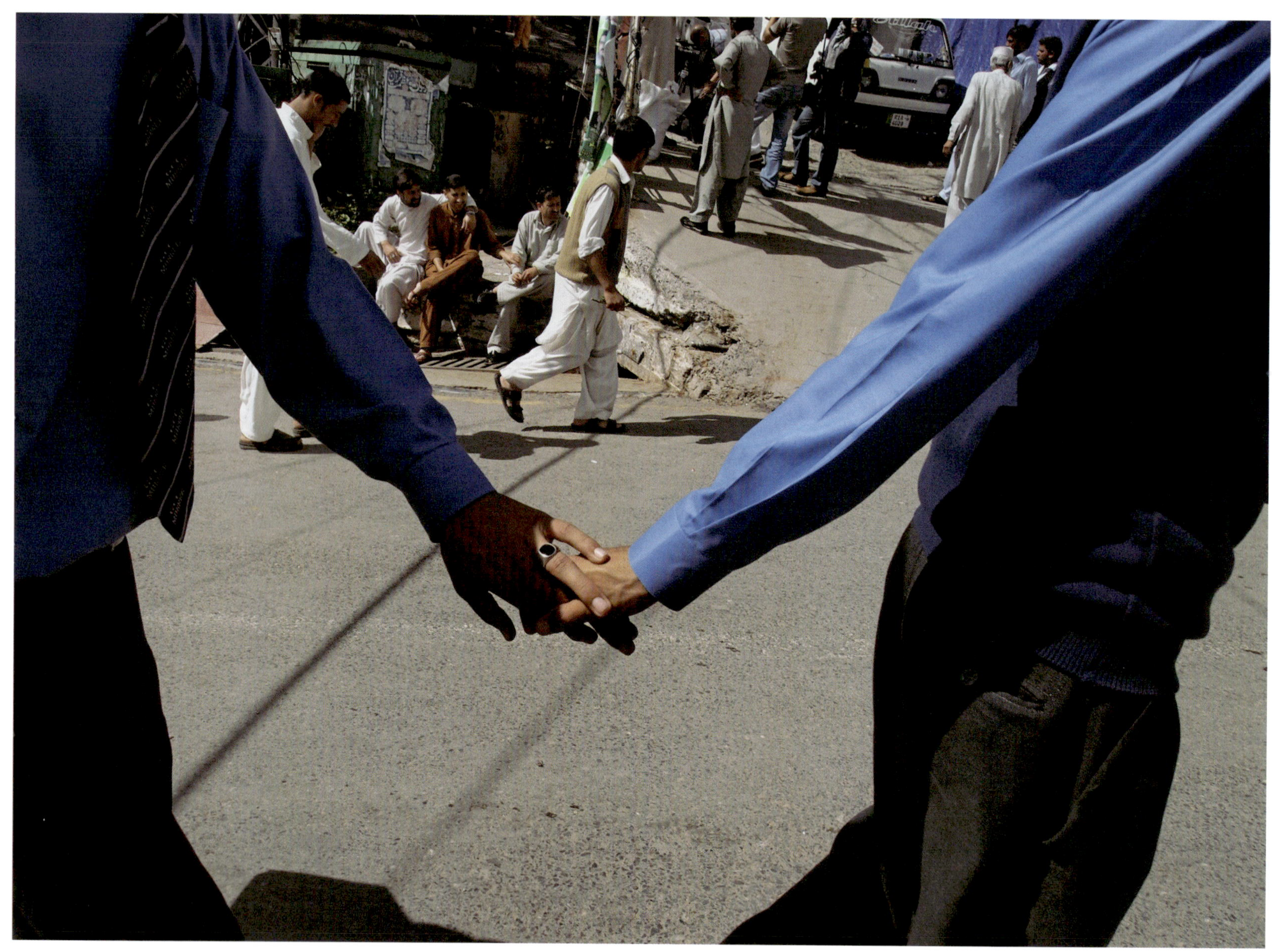

FARYAL MOHMAND / PAKISTAN 2012

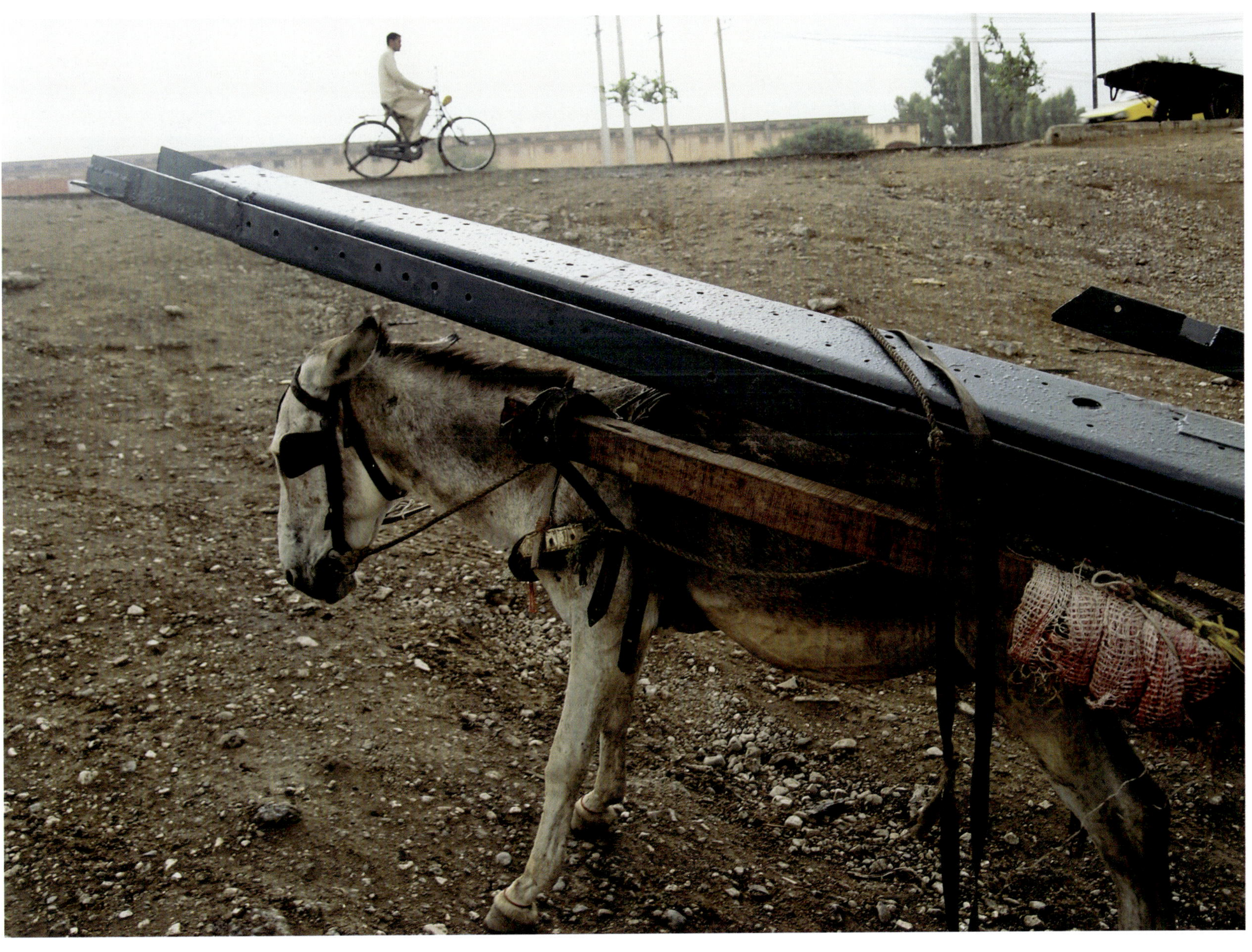

HANIFULLAH JAN / PAKISTAN 2012

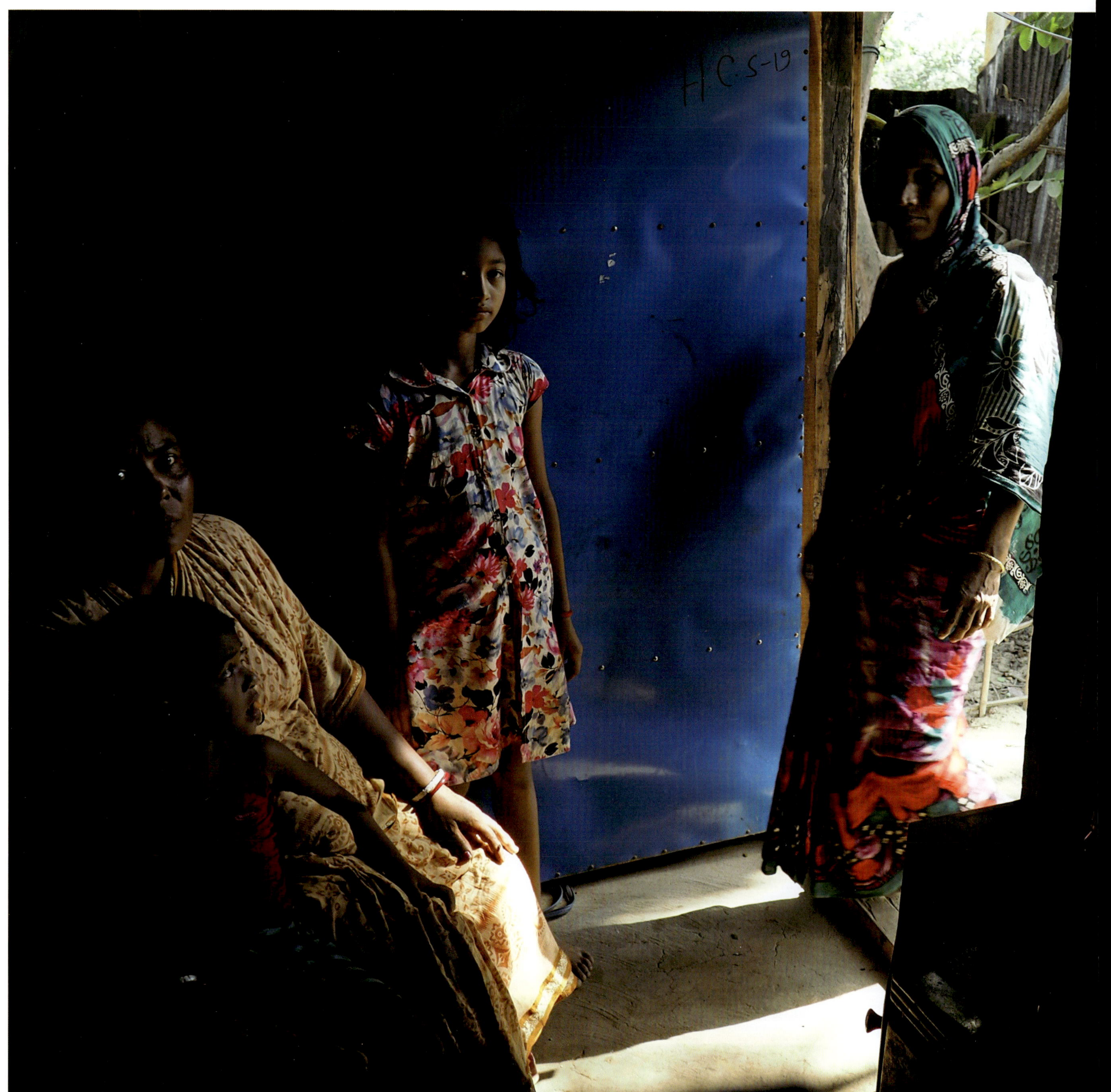

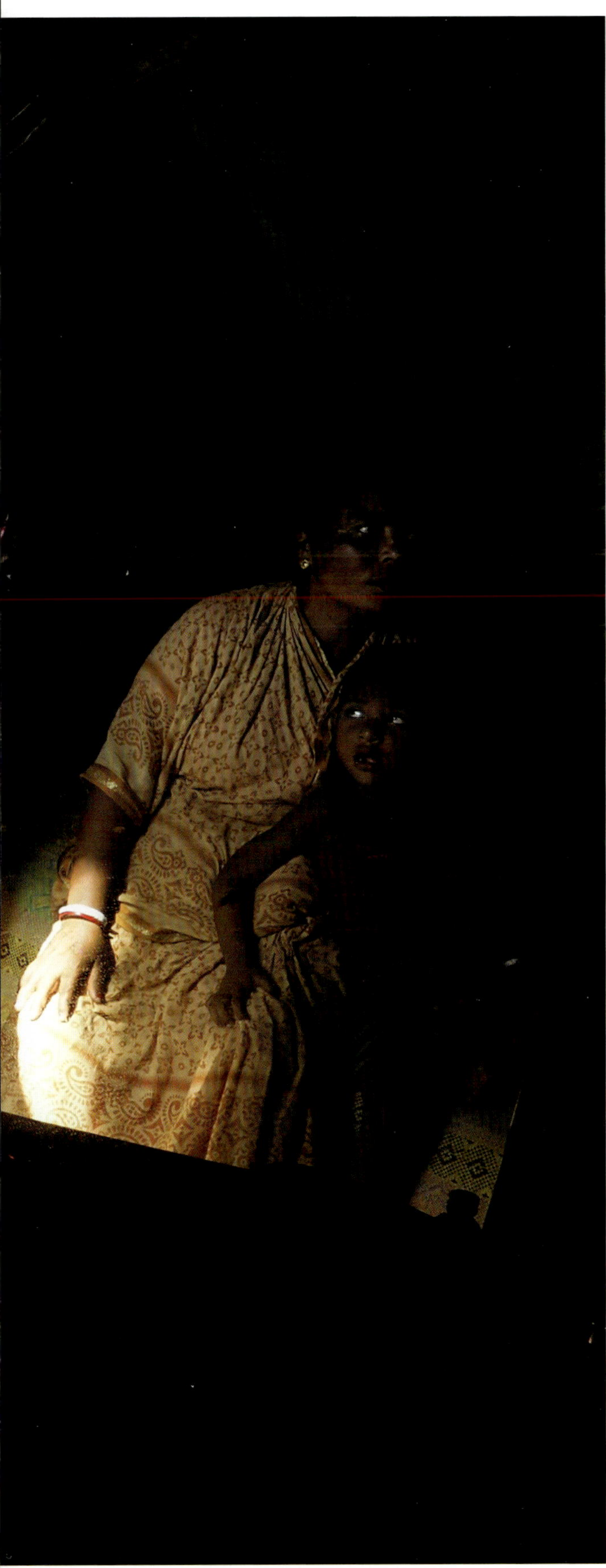

> ***"I was born in Thailand in a refugee camp called Umpiem Mai. But what is home? Deep within my heart, I will always remember that special home country I was born in. I hope that we can all remember where we come from."***
>
> —DOE KPAW SO PAW, UTICA, NEW YORK, U.S.A. 2019

MOHAMMED RUBEL / BANGLADESH 2019

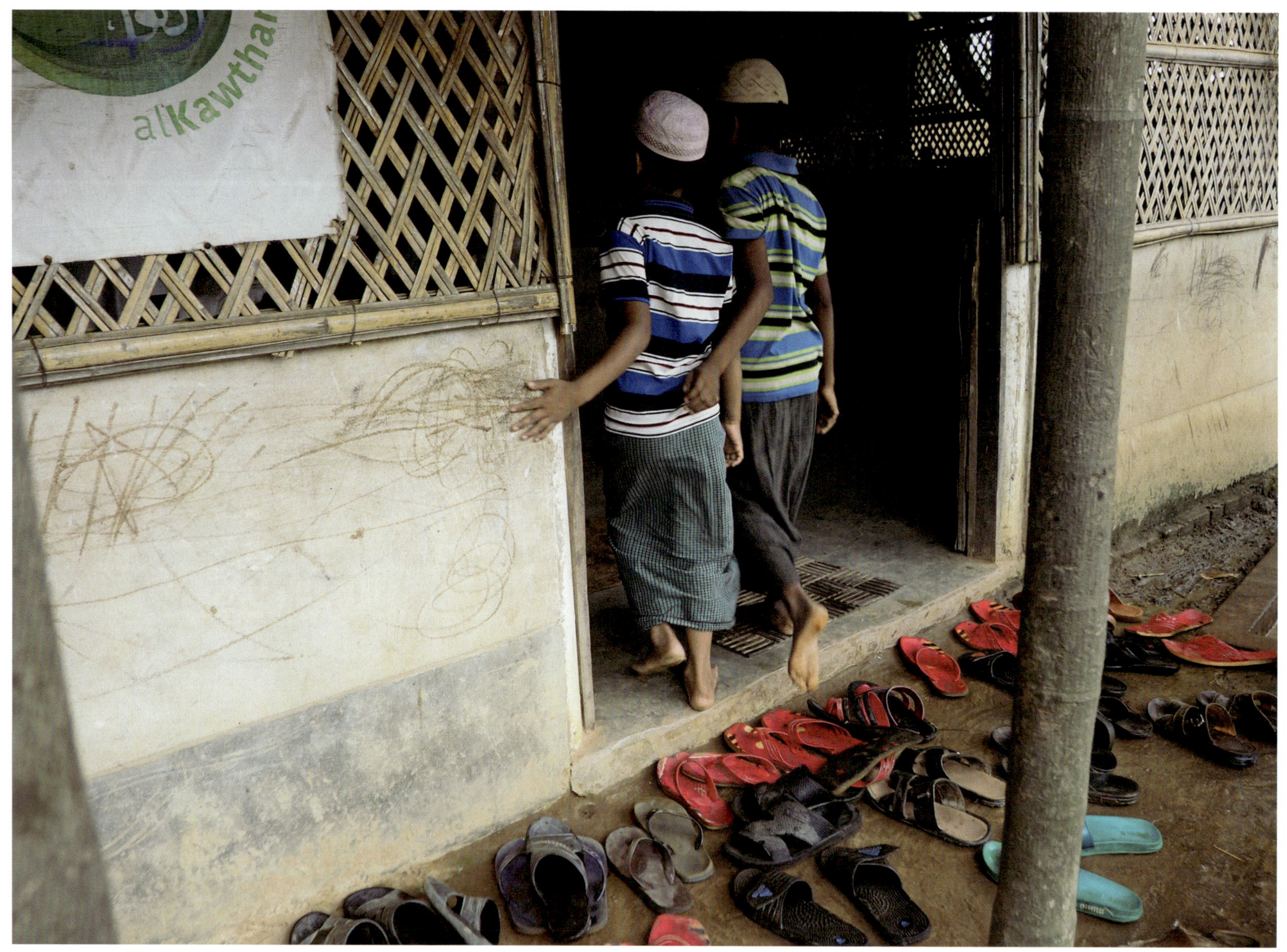

MOHAMMED AMIN / BANGLADESH 2019

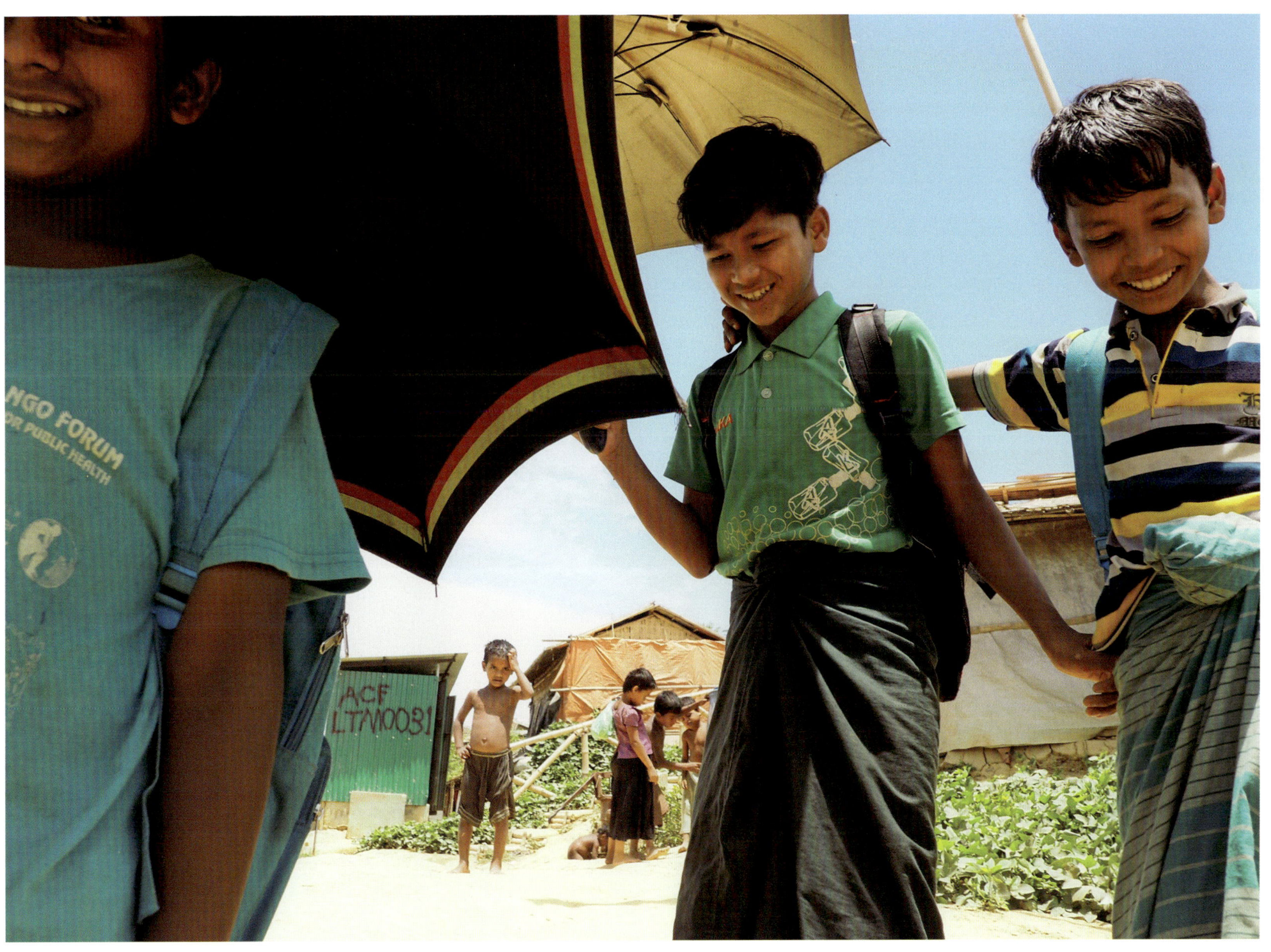

MOHAMMED AMIN / BANGLADESH 2019

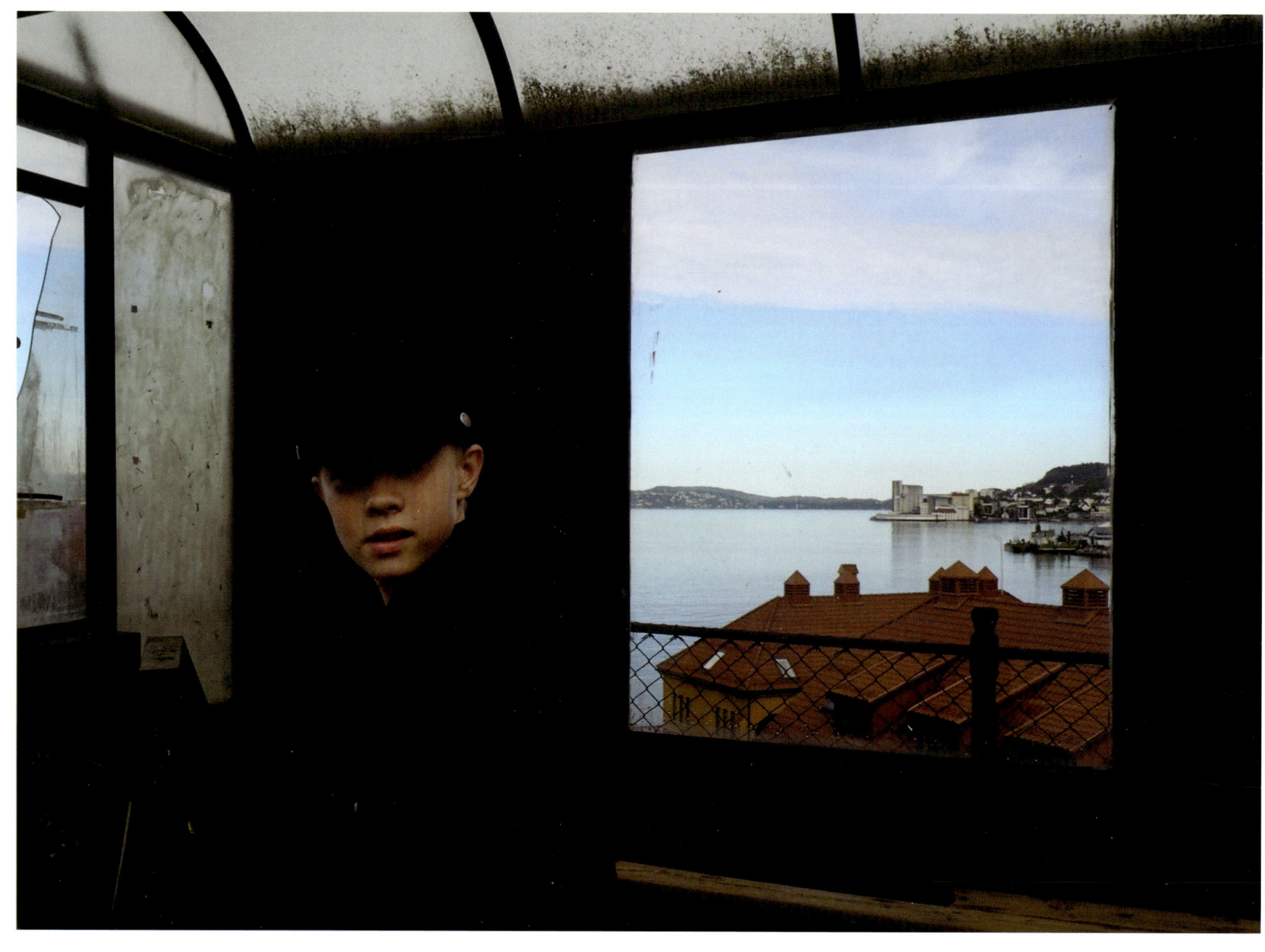

ABOVE: **FENET YERGALEM TADESSE / NORWAY 2017** OPPOSITE TOP: **SOFIE EGIDIUS HELLE / NORWAY 2017** OPPOSITE BOTTOM: **AMIR ALI ZARE / NORWAY 2017**

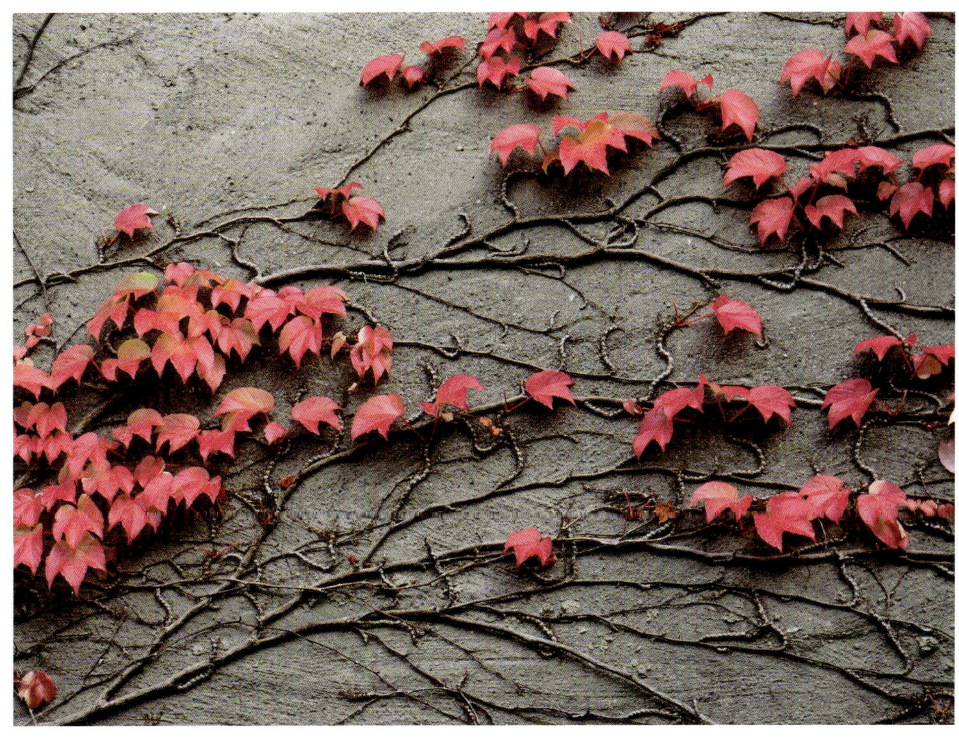

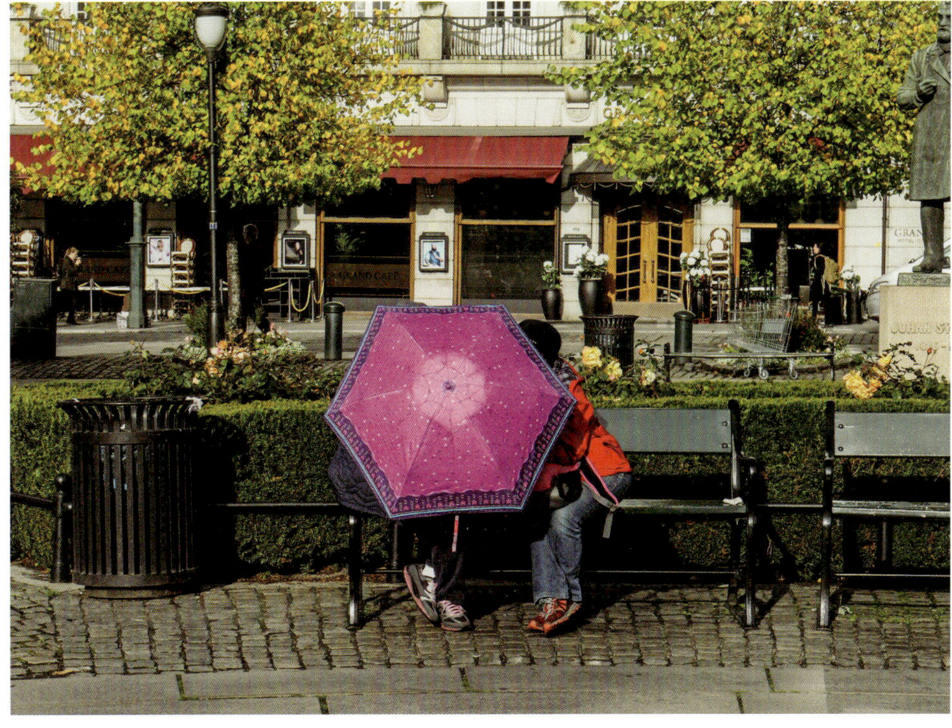

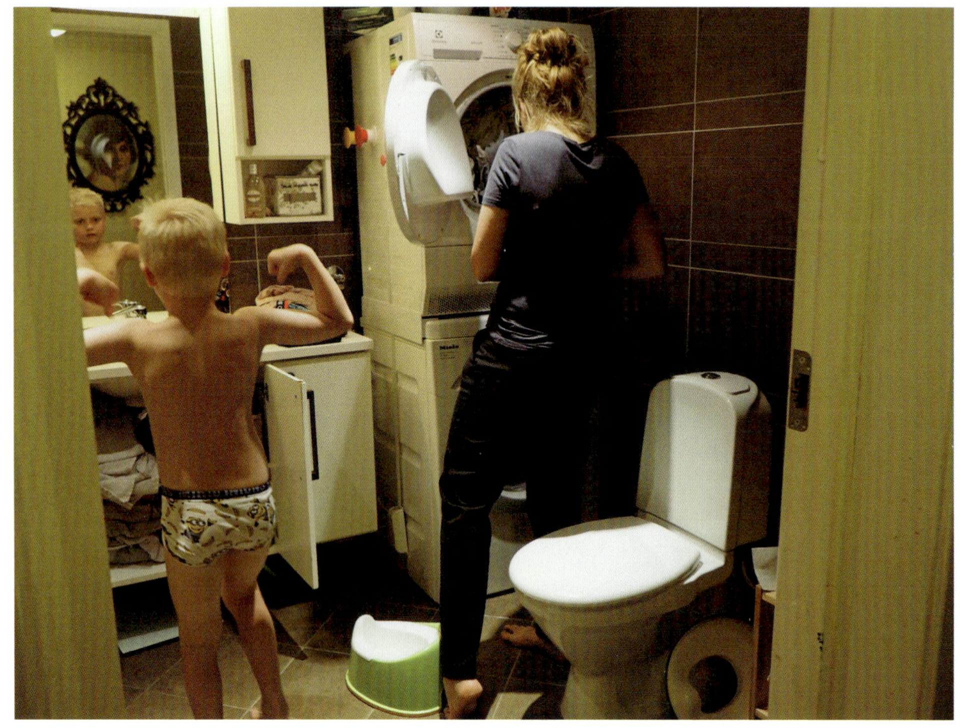

ABOVE: **YOLA KEENLYSIDE / NORWAY 2017** RIGHT: **MASHA PAUNOV / NORWAY 2017**

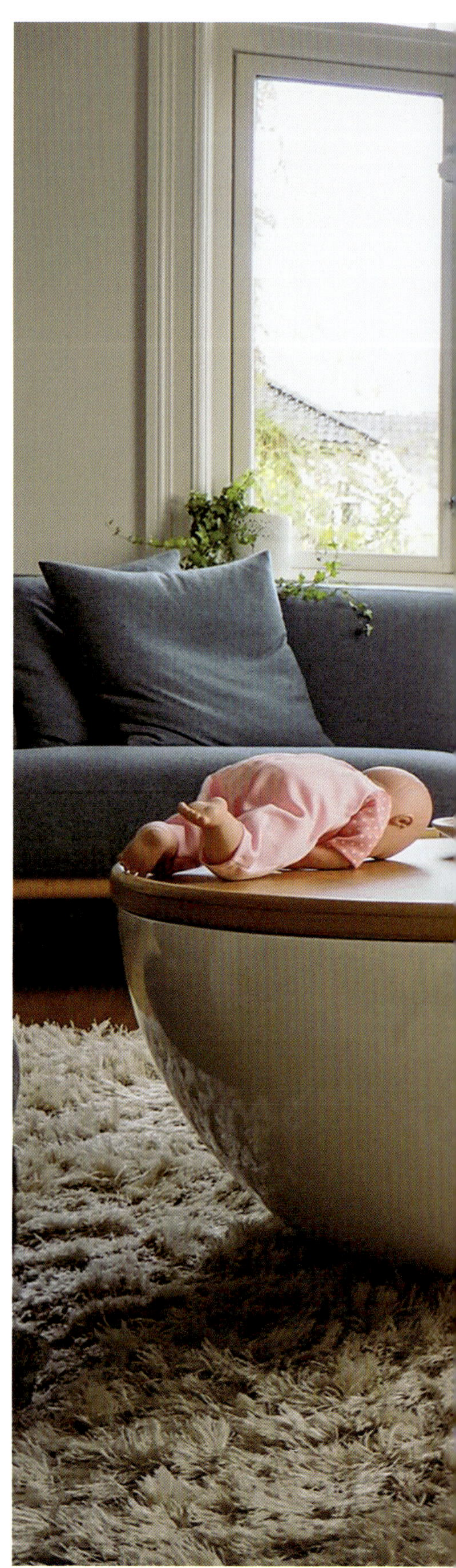

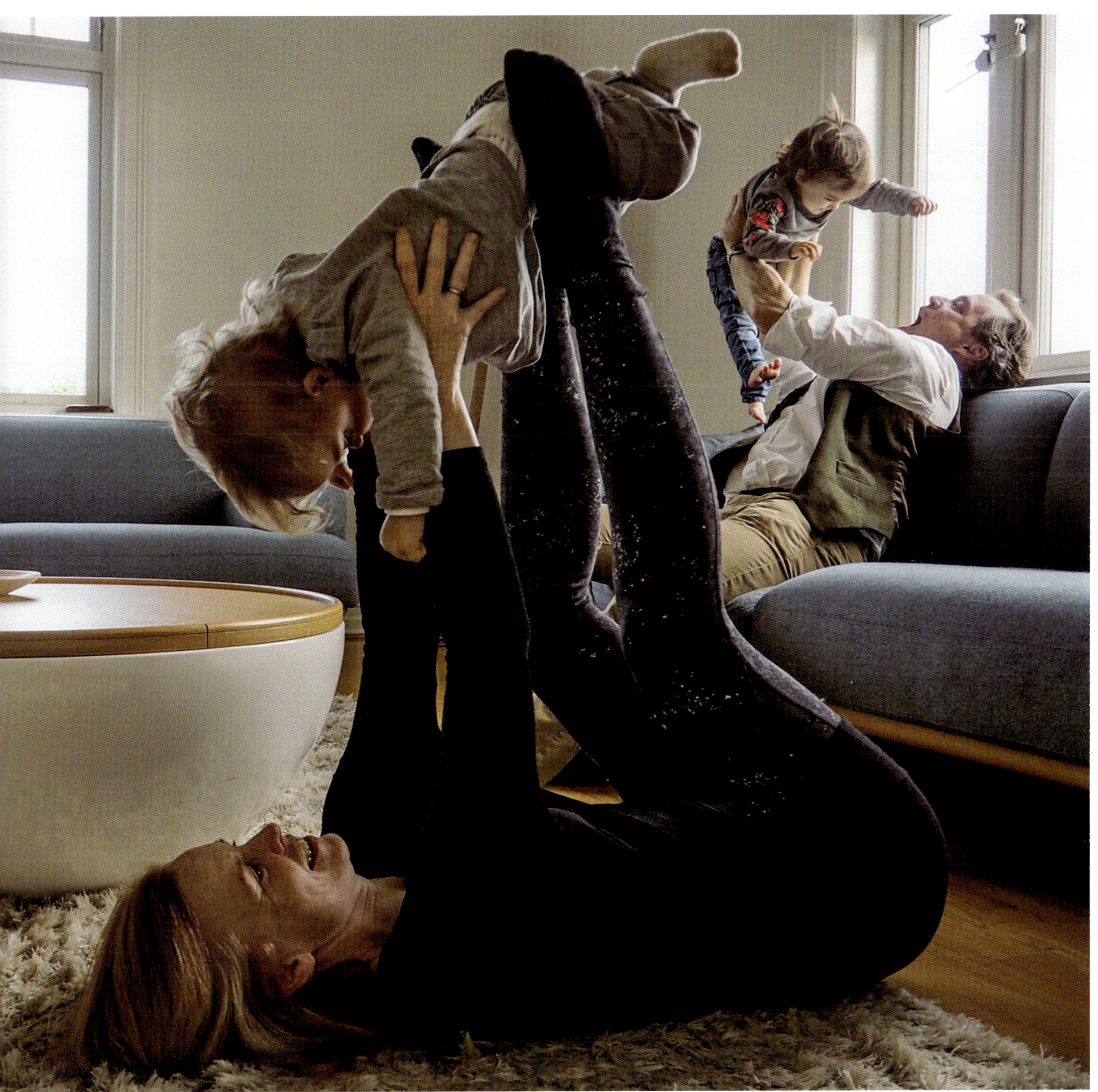

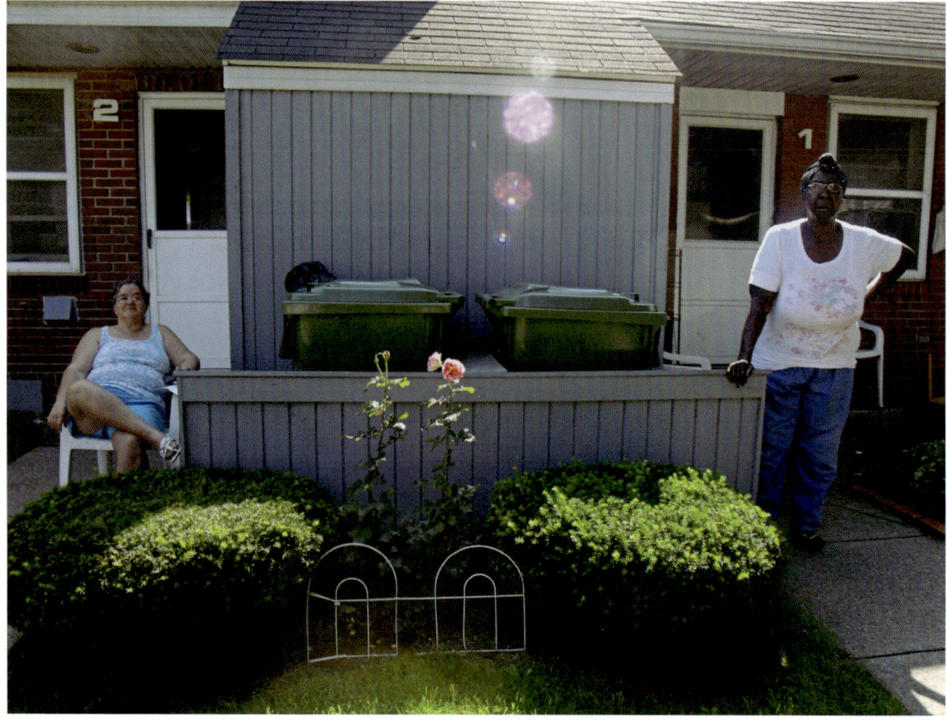

ABOVE: **HALIMO CHIRAMBO / PENNSYLVANIA, U.S.A. 2007**
RIGHT: **JANET NIEDENBERGER / PENNSYLVANIA, U.S.A. 2007**

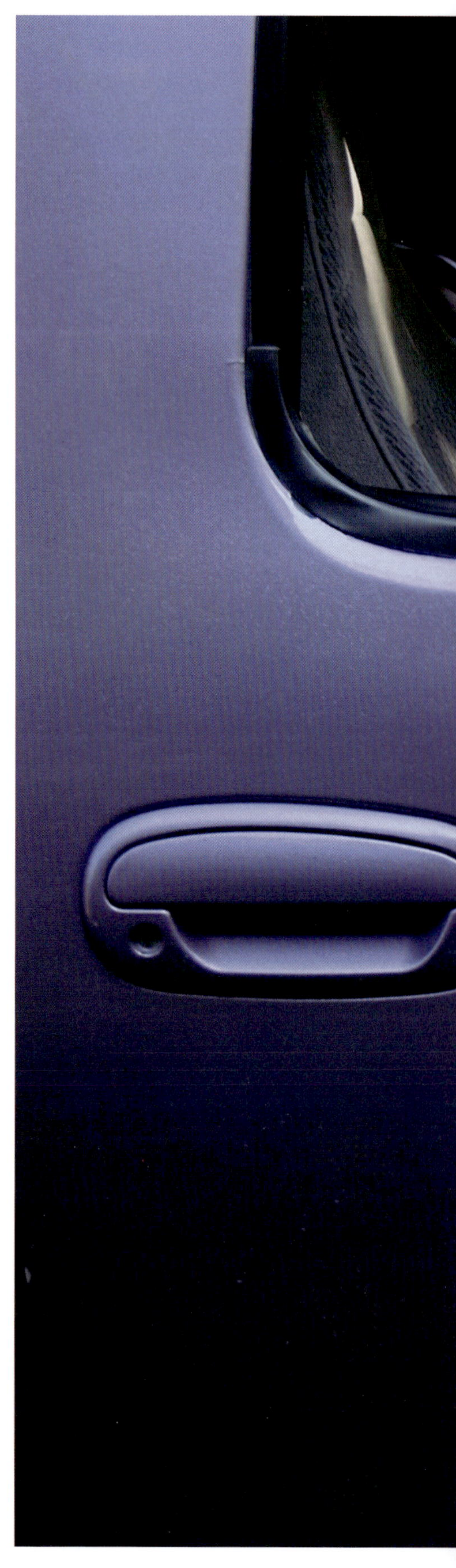

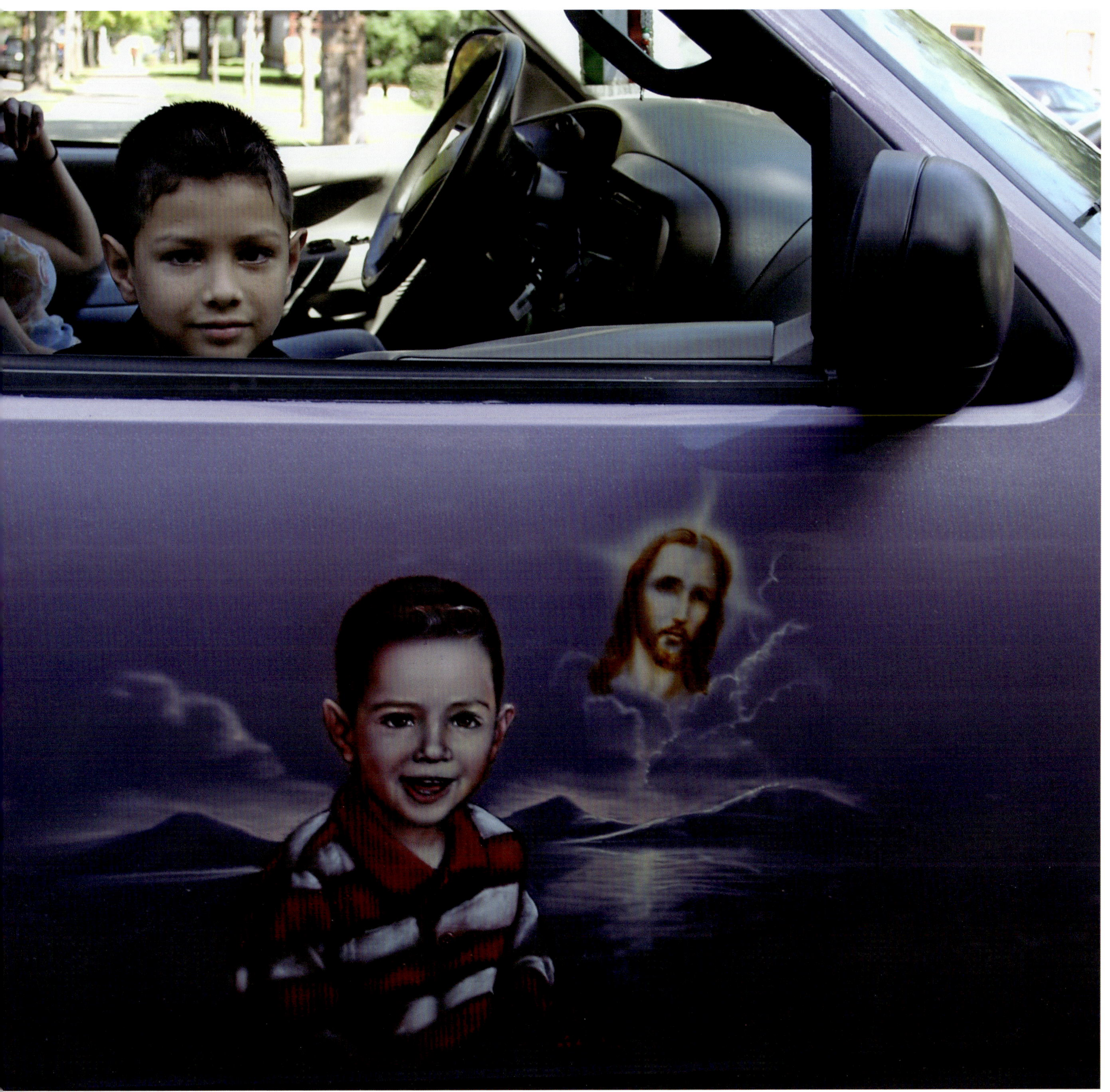

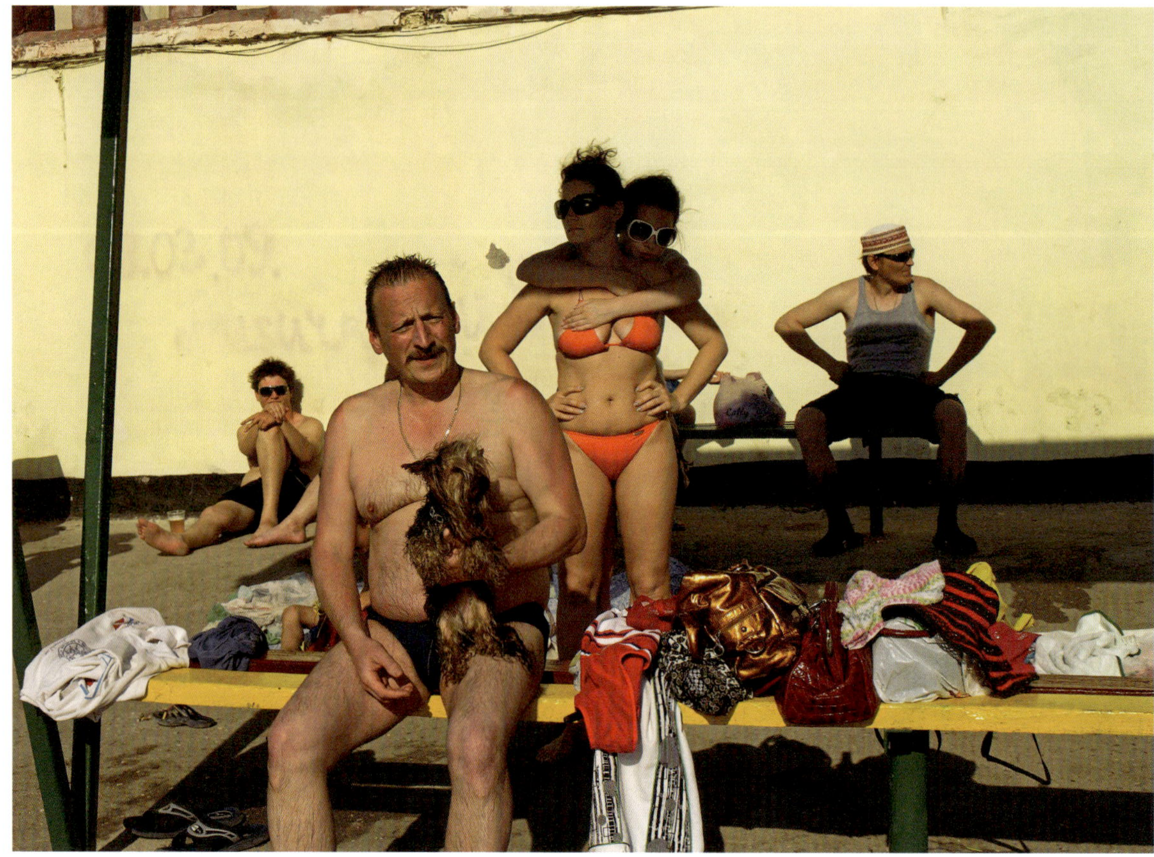

DILYARA DJEMILEVA / CRIMEA 2010

> ***"I had a chance to see the most beautiful spring on Earth—the Crimean spring. Without any politics involved, just trees in blossom, the blue sea, and the wind that blew my way."***
>
> —PETR SMIRNOV, UKRAINE 2015

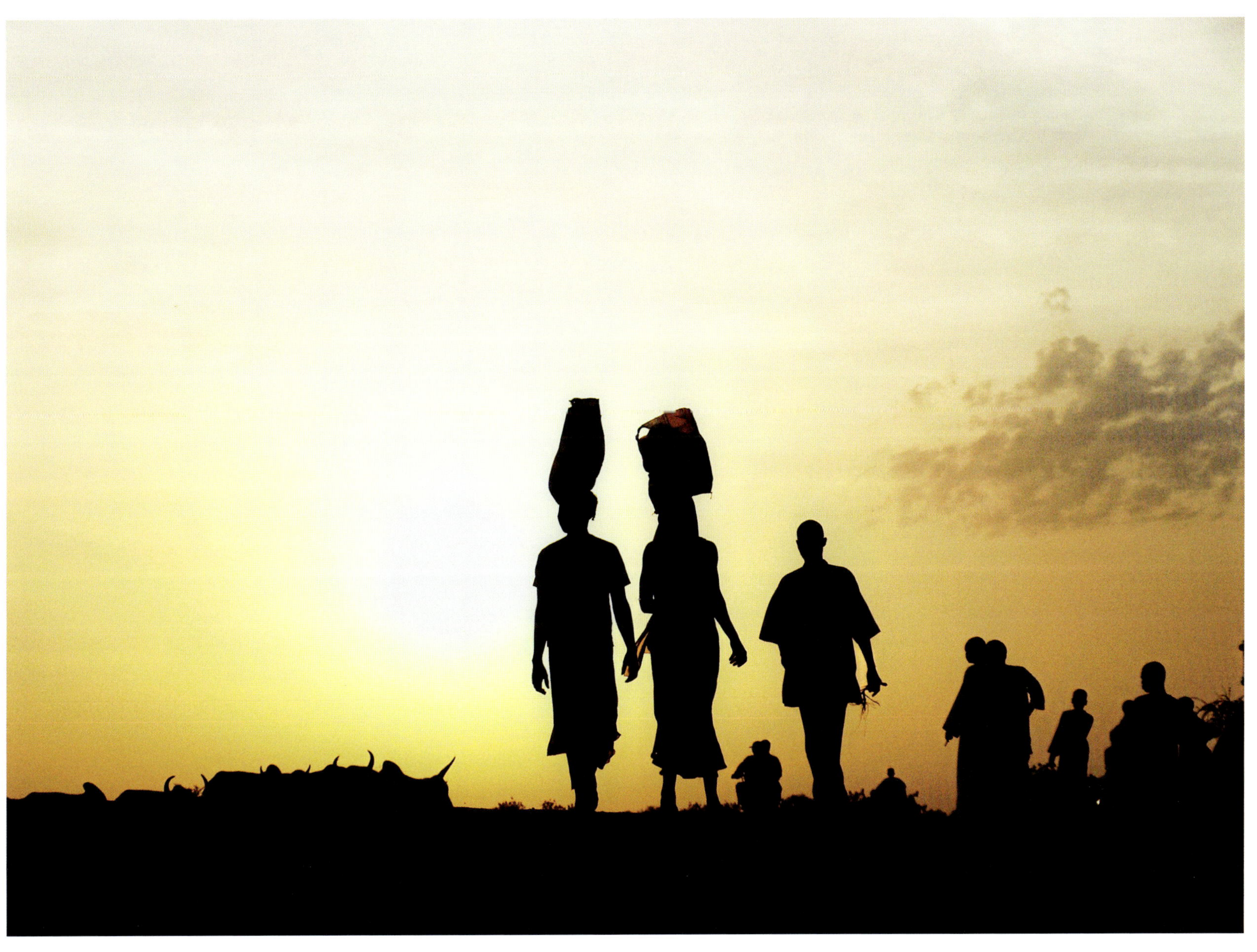

OUMAR MAHAMAT OUMAR / CHAD 2010

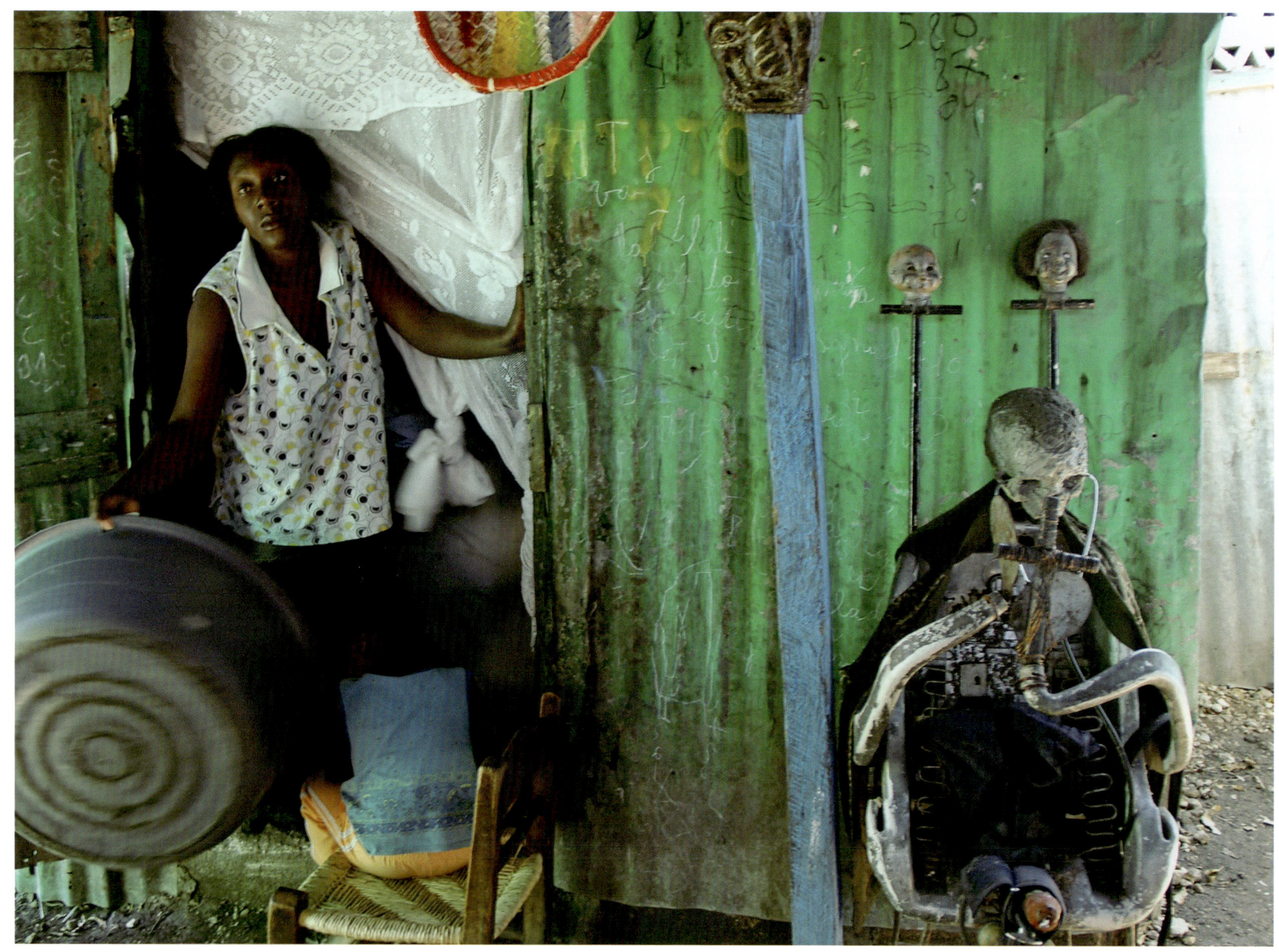

MARCO SALEM BERRY FILS / HAITI 2012

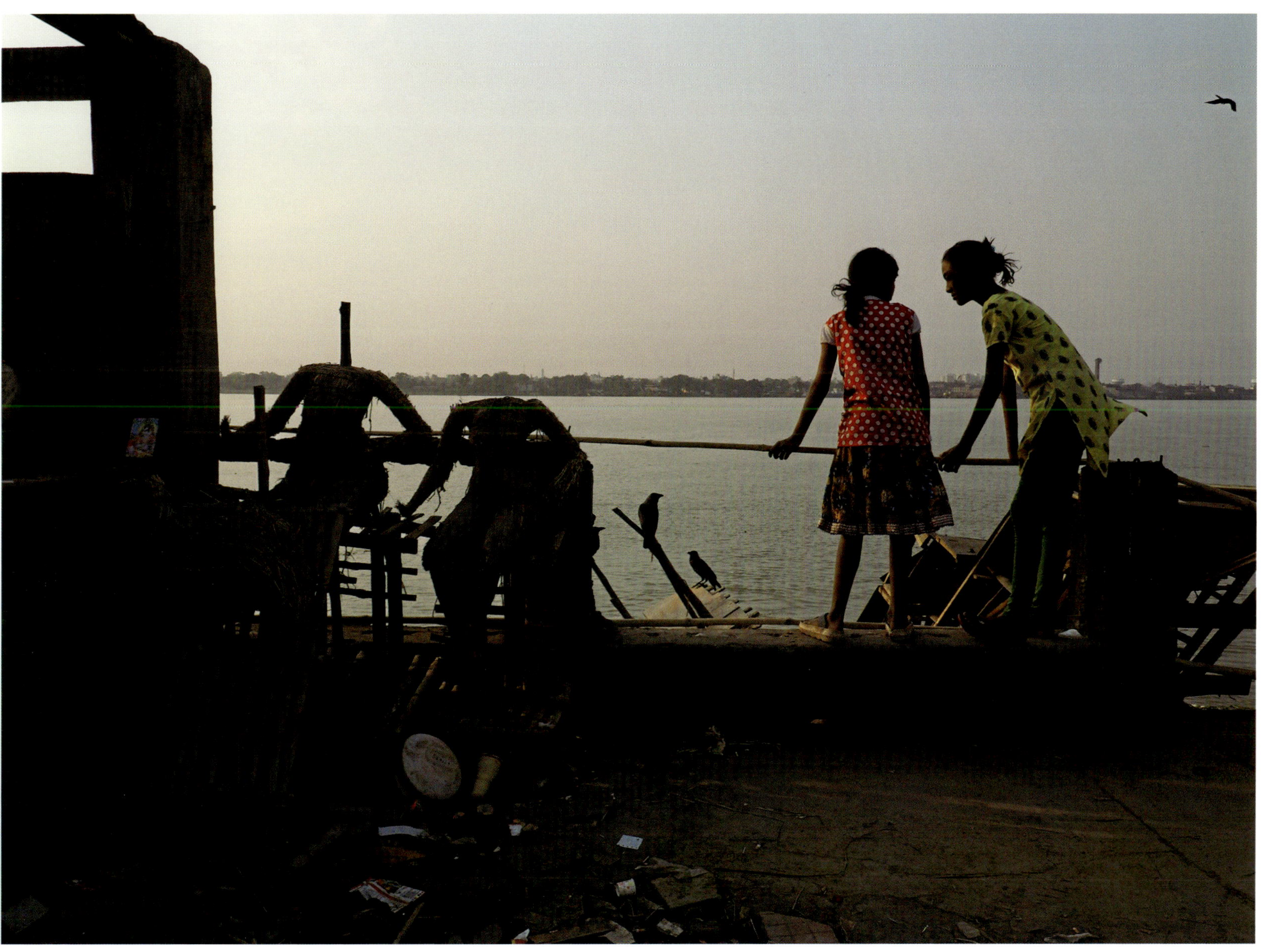

RANITA ROY / INDIA 2018

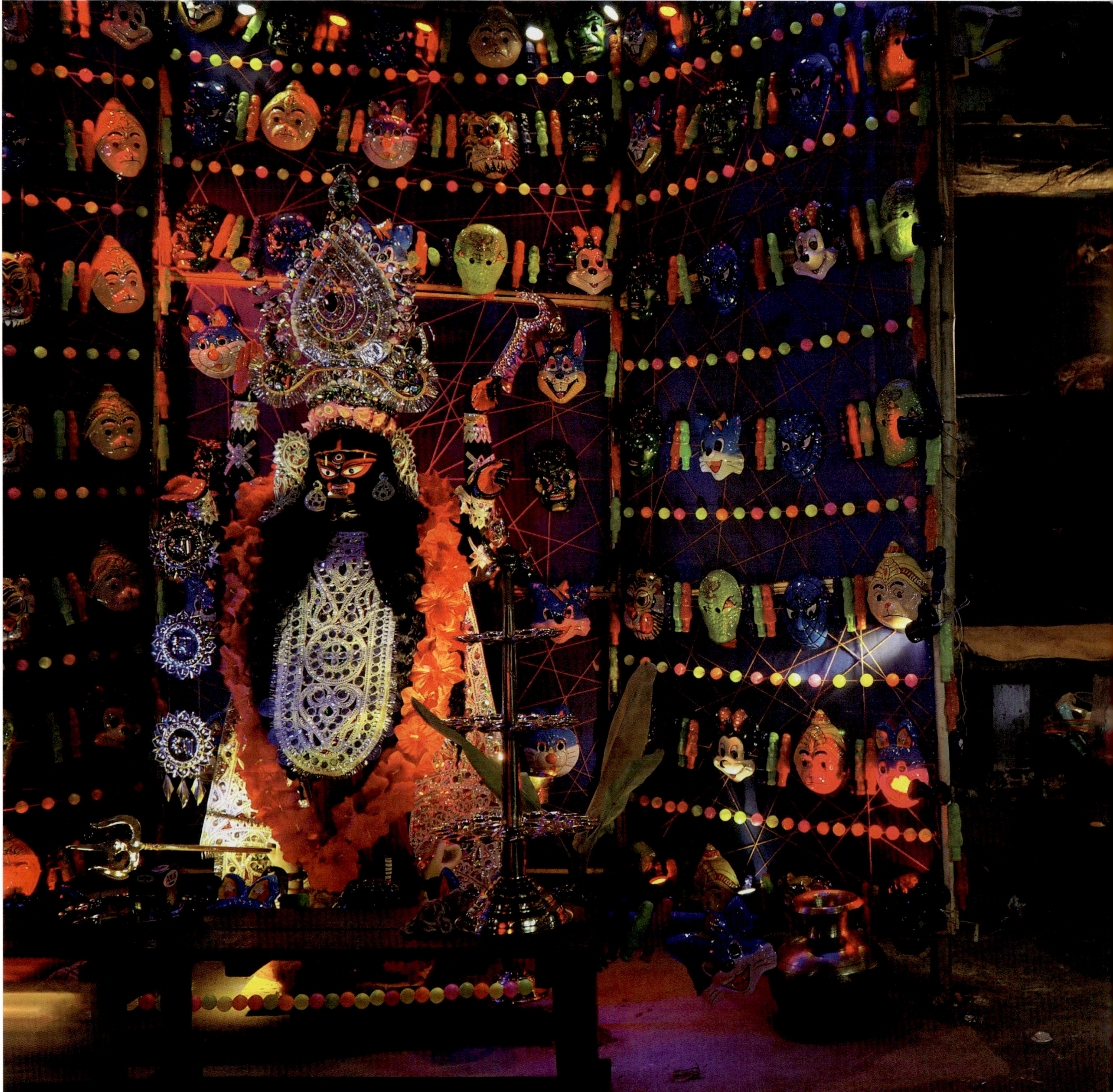

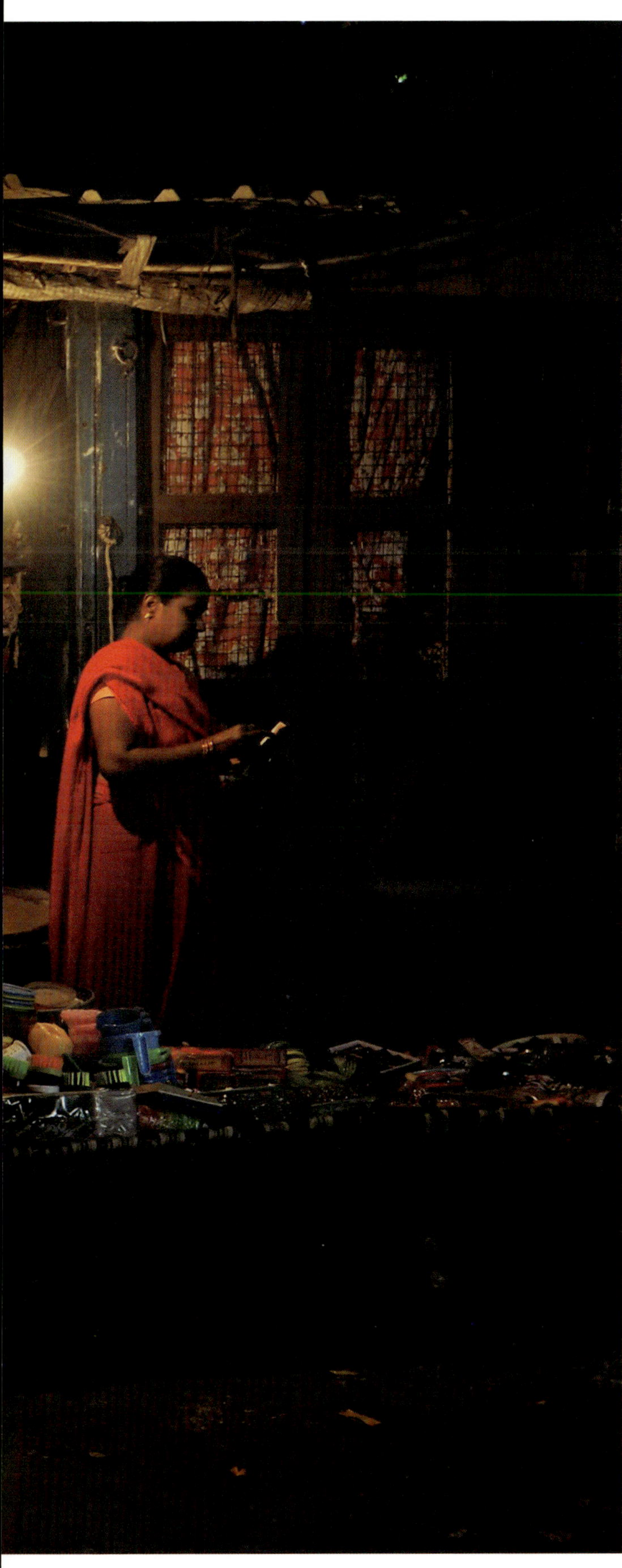

> ***"We came from different regions with different cultures, languages, beliefs, and spent a week together without any problem. We shared and learned a lot from each other. I thought it couldn't be like that, but we made it. It is those things you won't ever forget."***
>
> —AMINE SOULEYMAN TIDJANI, CHAD 2010

RANITA ROY / INDIA 2018

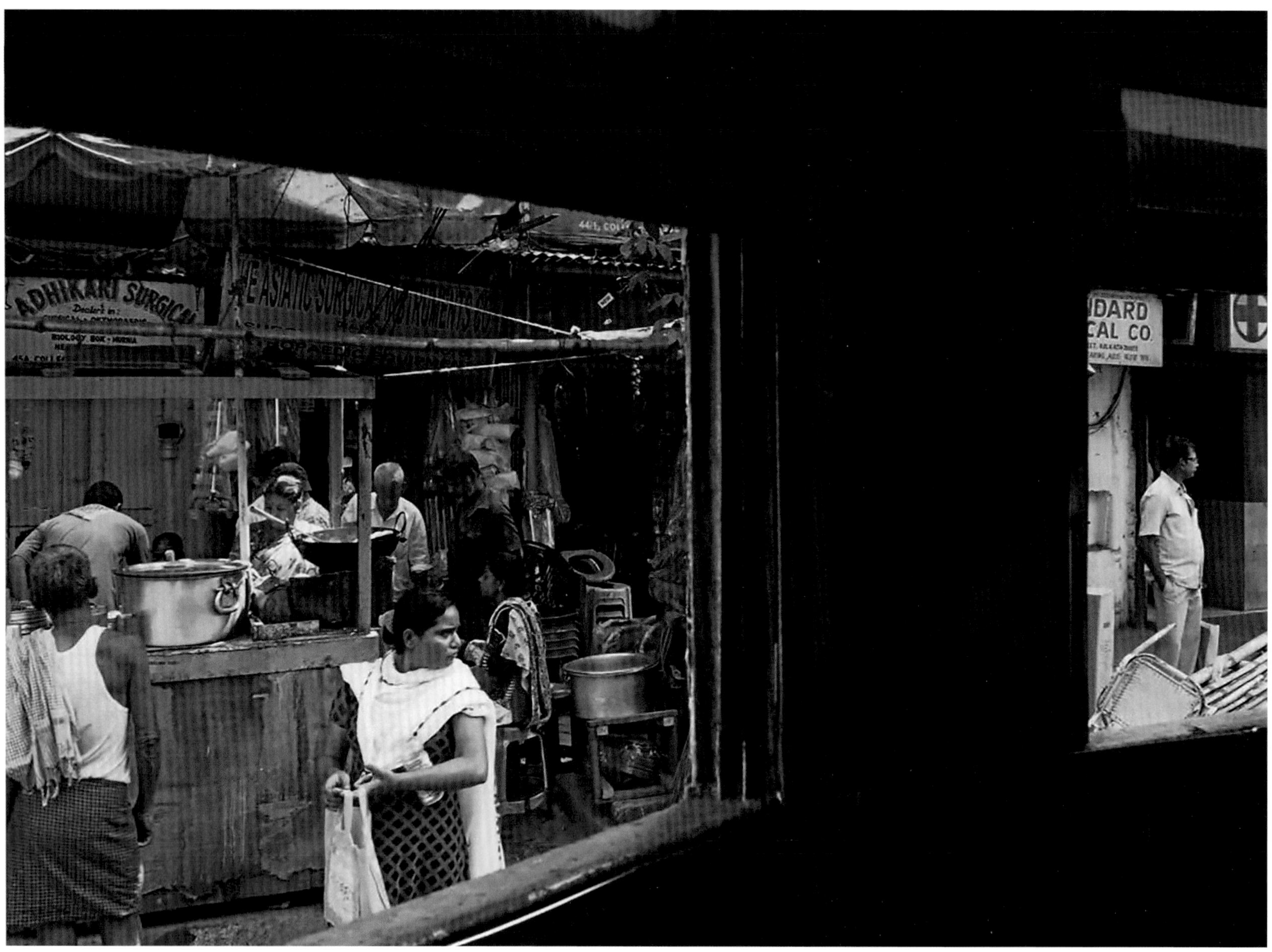

SOHEL AHMED / INDIA 2018

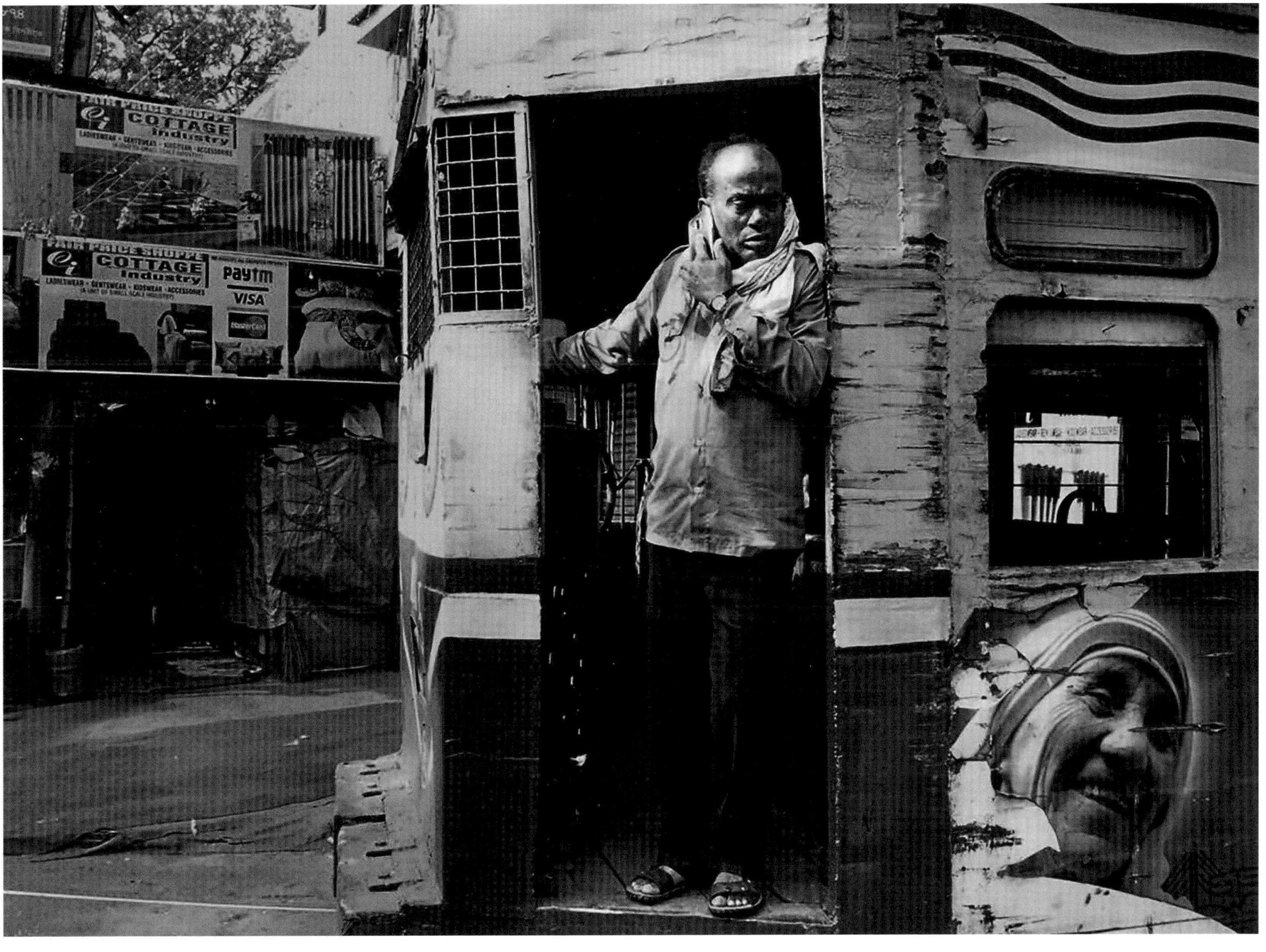

SOHEL AHMED / INDIA 2018

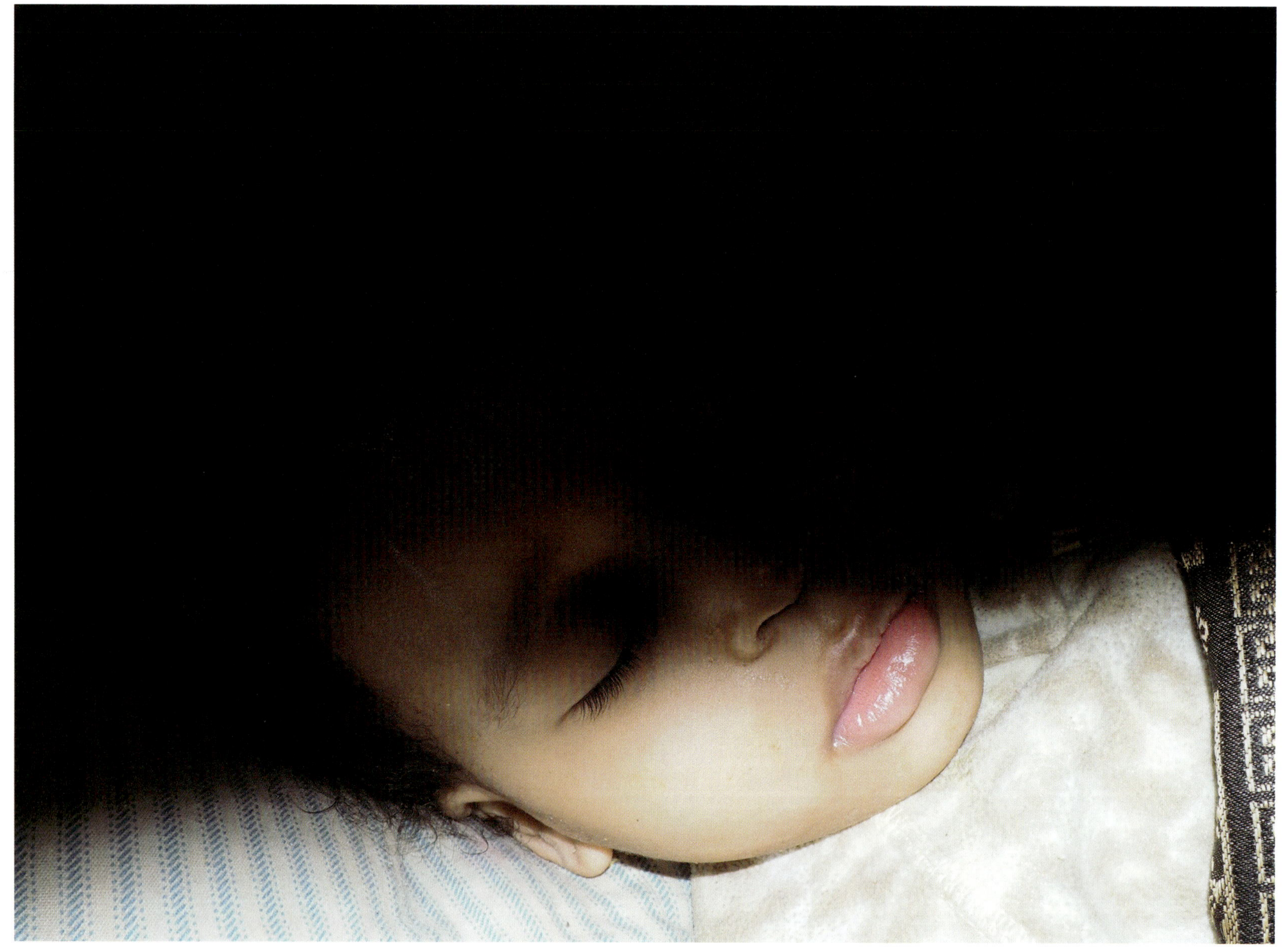

IMRAN ISMAIL / NEW YORK, U.S.A. 2019

"What I want people to know about my family, and about so many other immigrant families, is that they often suffer in silence."

—DAYANA HUDSON, WASHINGTON, D.C., U.S.A. 2018

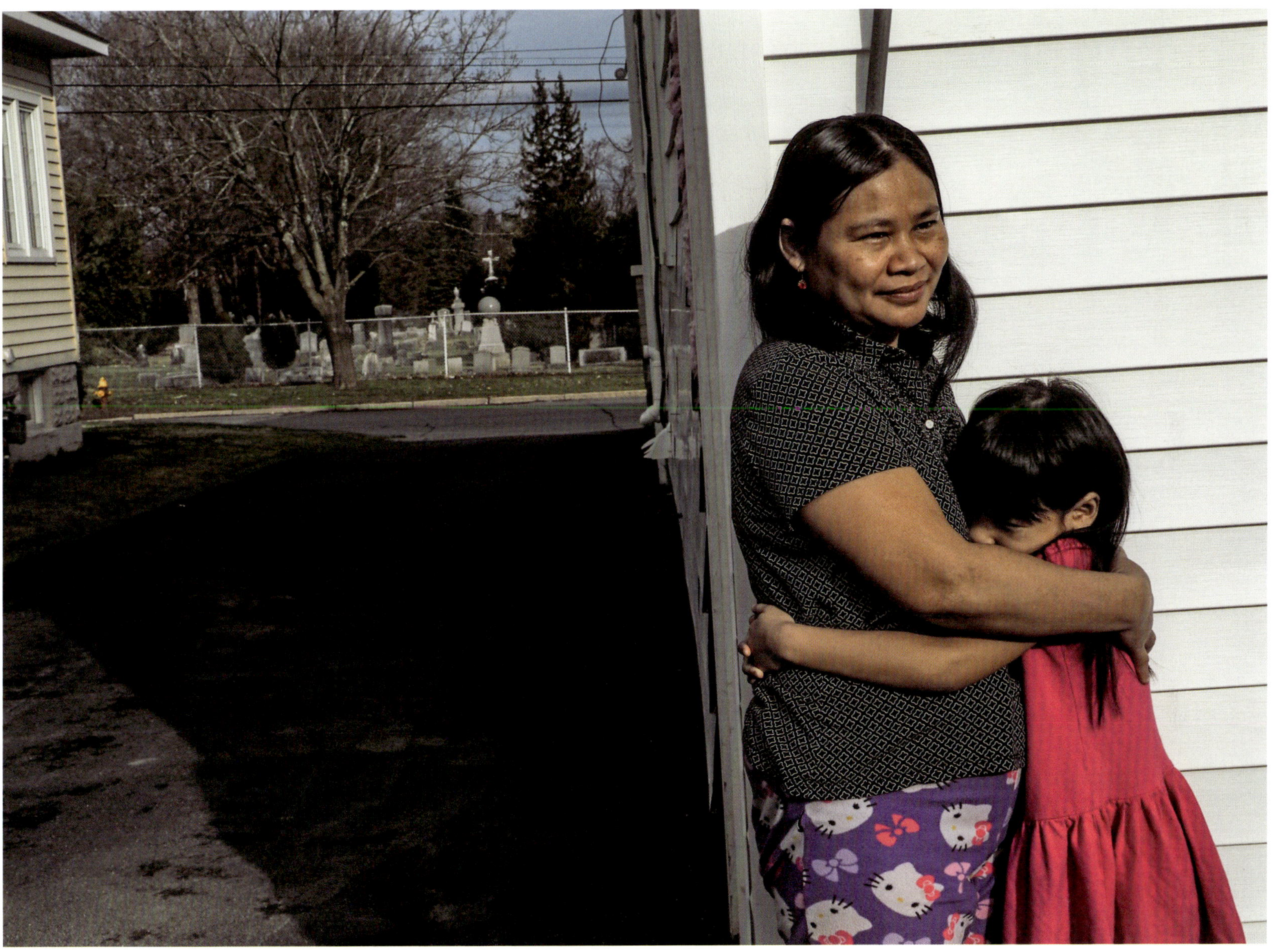

KLAW MOO PAW / NEW YORK, U.S.A. 2019

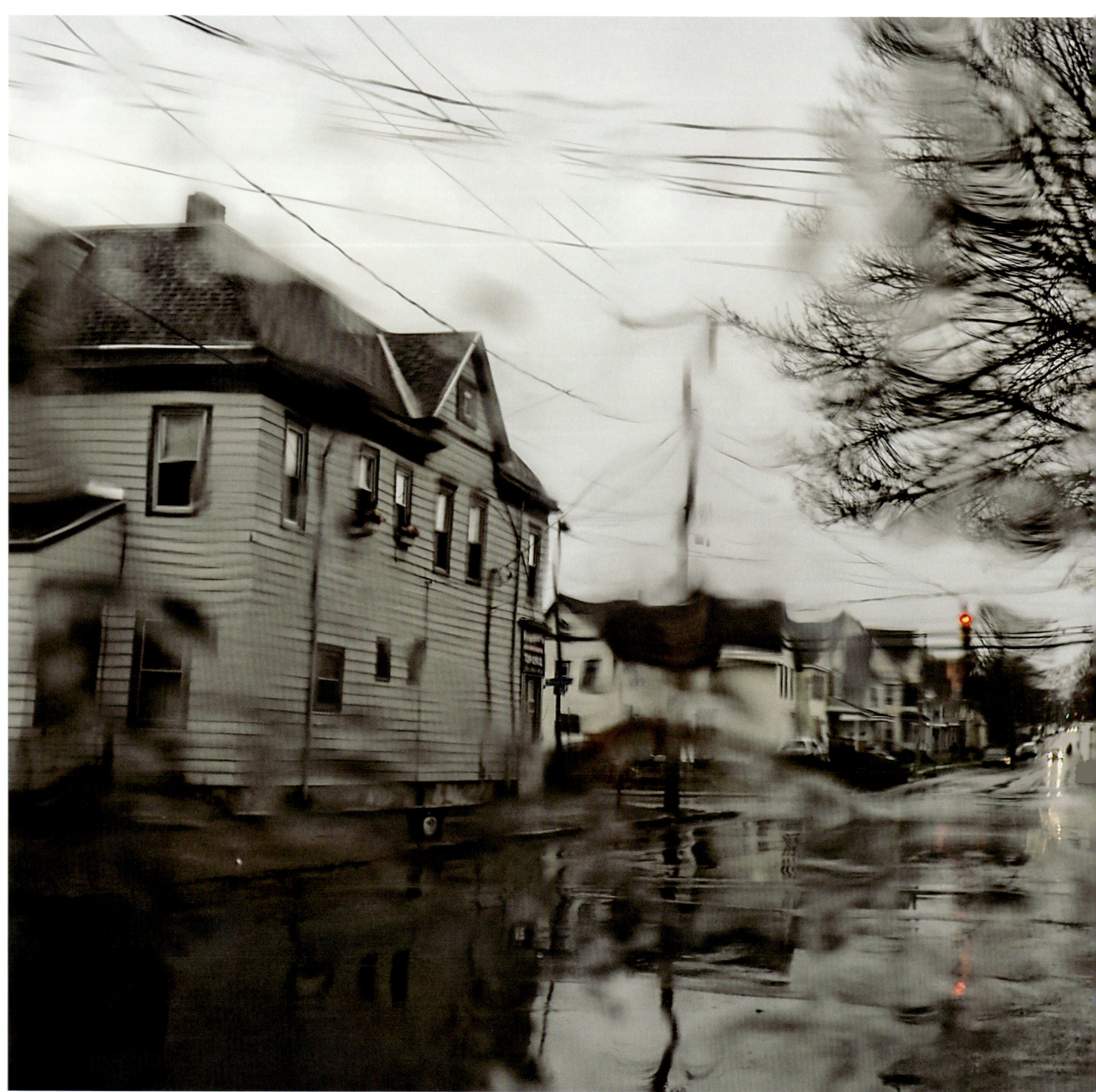

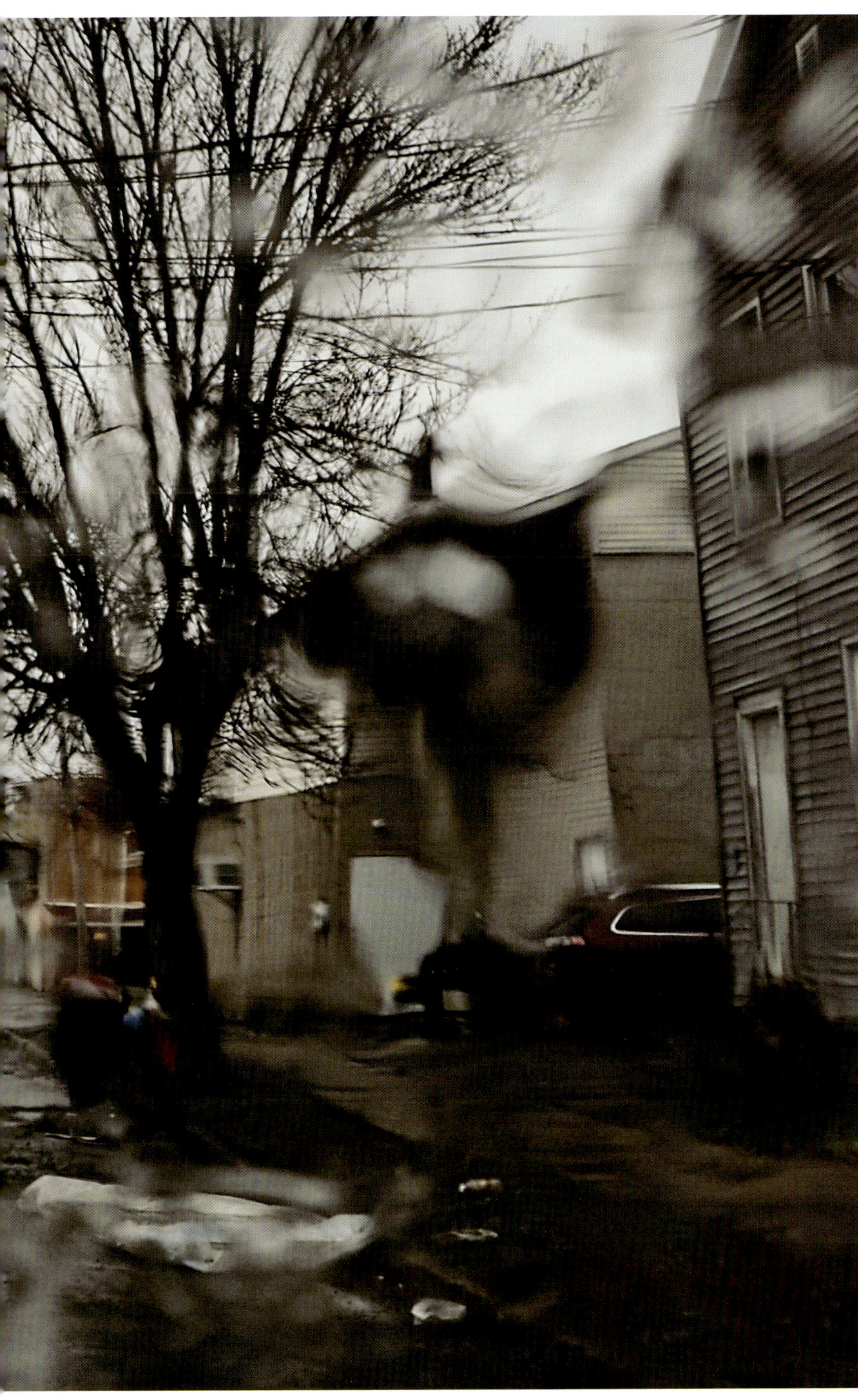

HANEEN ALSAAD / NEW YORK, U.S.A. 2019

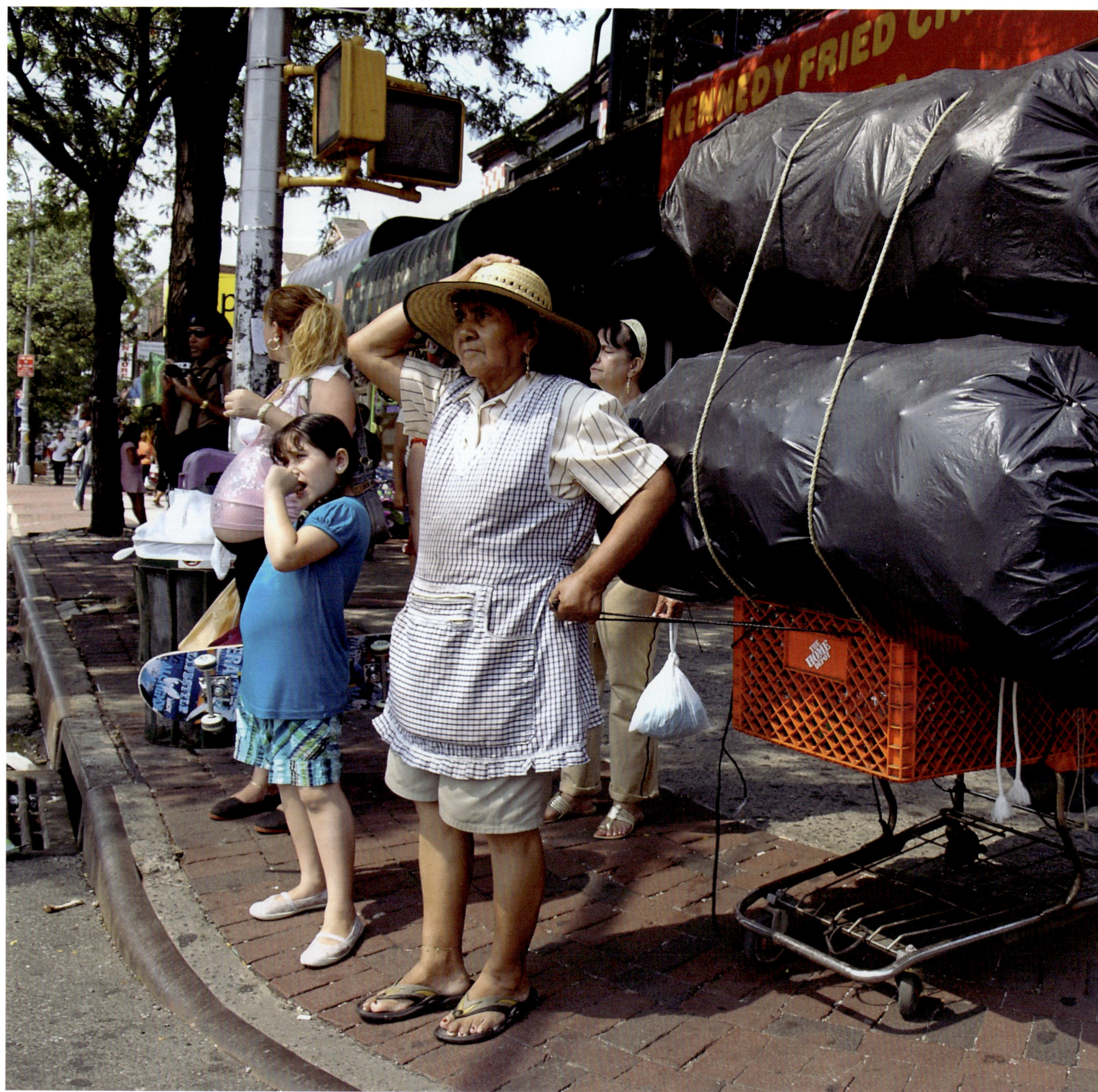
KENNEDY FRIED

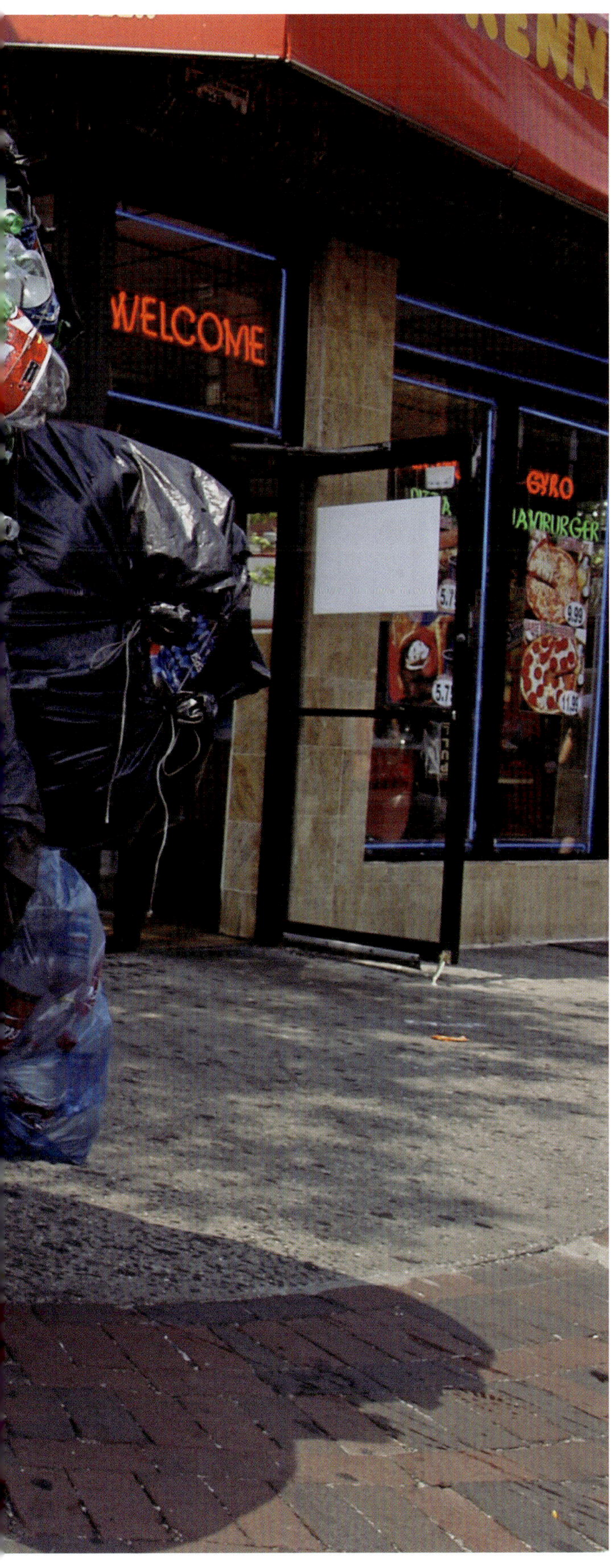

"Everyone seems to believe that refugees are creating riots and problems for society. But I think that it depends on how society treats them, and how it sees them.

Being a refugee is not what we chose to be. My journey has not been easy. I was someone who only had one pair of shoes for a year, who would fix broken shoes to wear again for another year.

Living here is a blessing for me and my family. Never give up, and try to get up every time people make you fall. Never think that you are alone, because there might be someone who is actually stepping on the same journey with you. Be positive and kind to everyone because they'll realize one day that you are actually a human, not just a refugee.

Never give up."

—CING LIAN KIM, SHENANDOAH NATIONAL PARK, VIRGINIA, U.S.A. 2016

BYRON GUINANZACA / NEW YORK, U.S.A. 2007

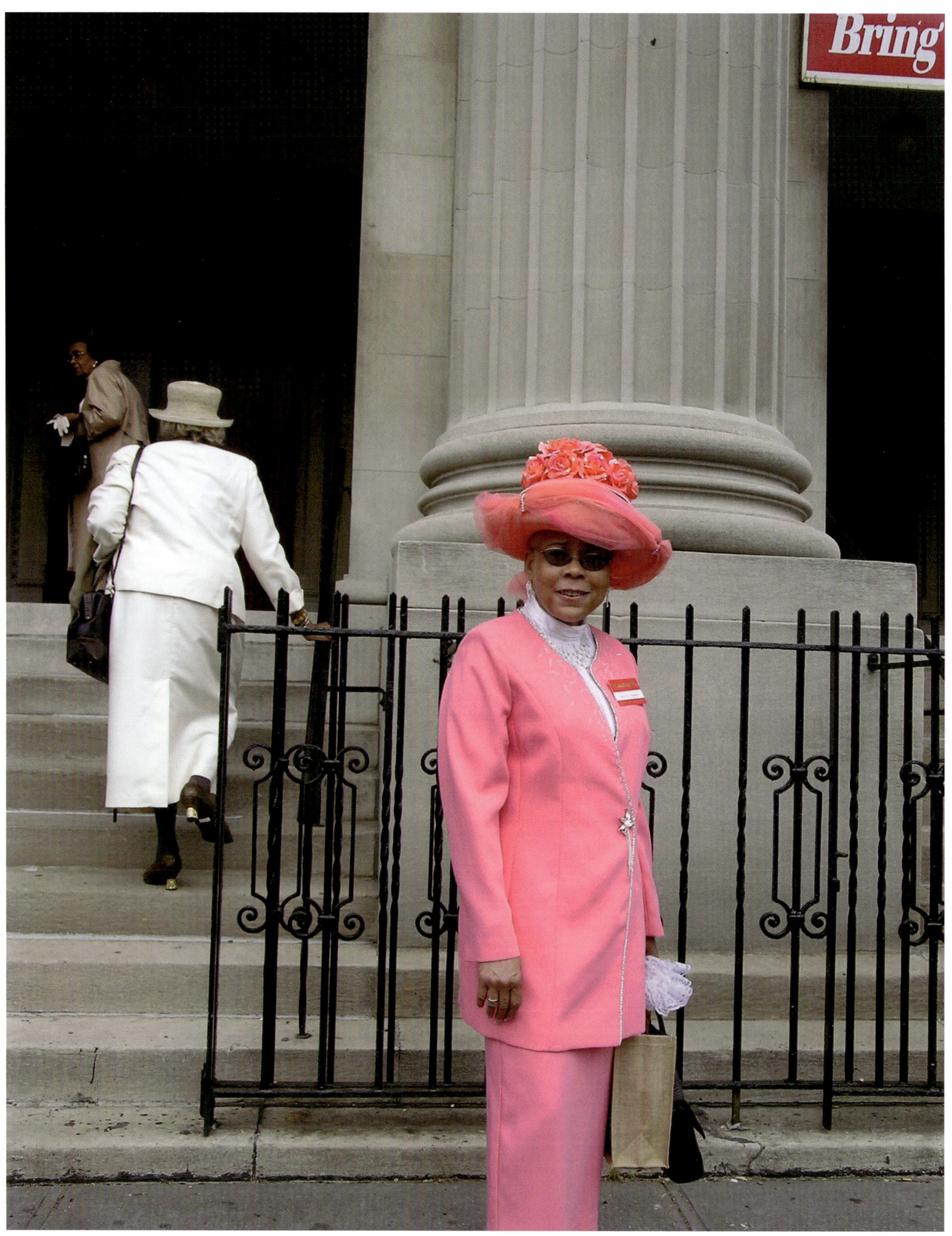
Bring

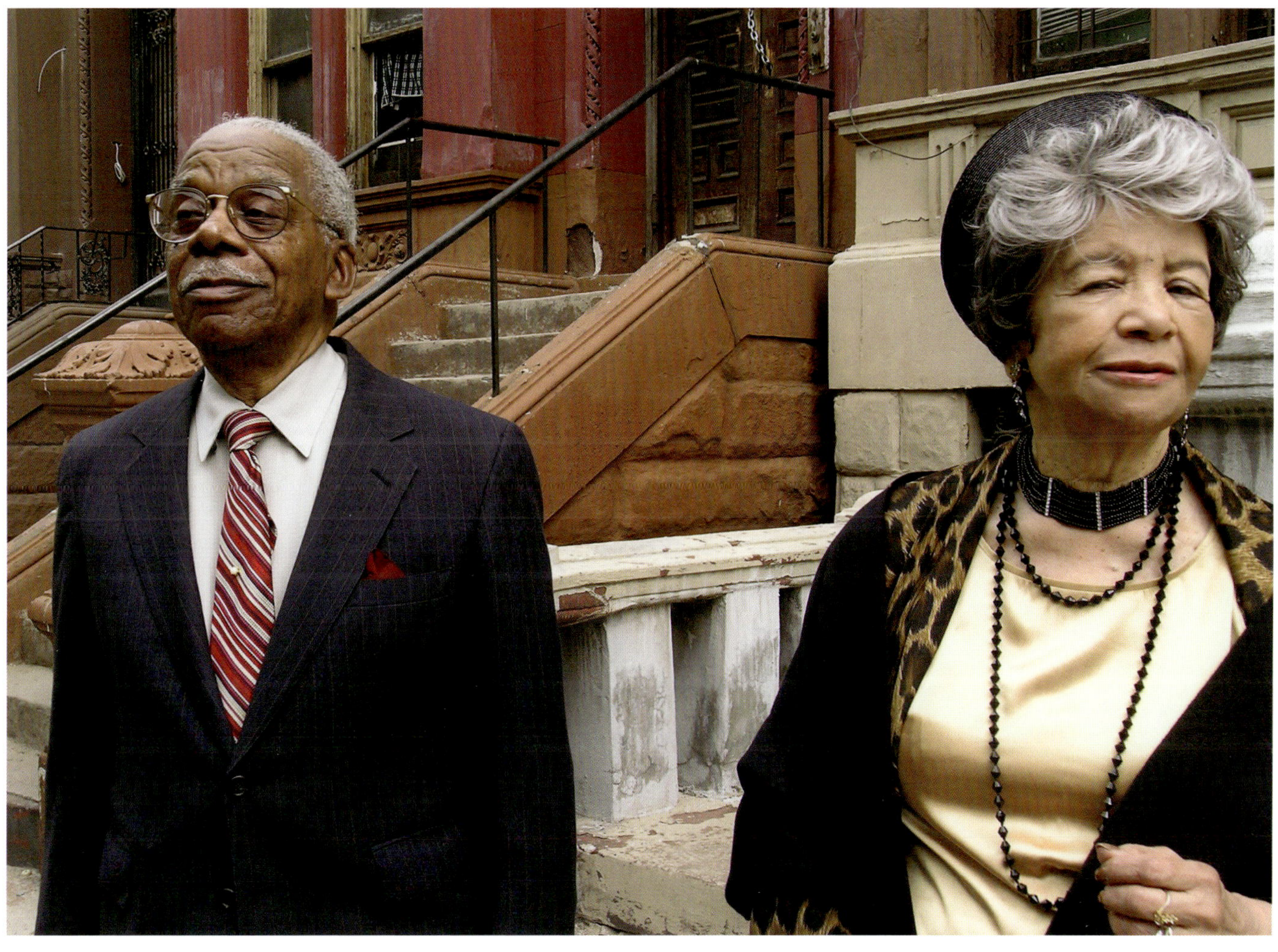

ABOVE: **TIFFANY WILLIAMS / NEW YORK, U.S.A. 2005** OPPOSITE: **YINAURI RODRIGUEZ / NEW YORK, U.S.A. 2005**

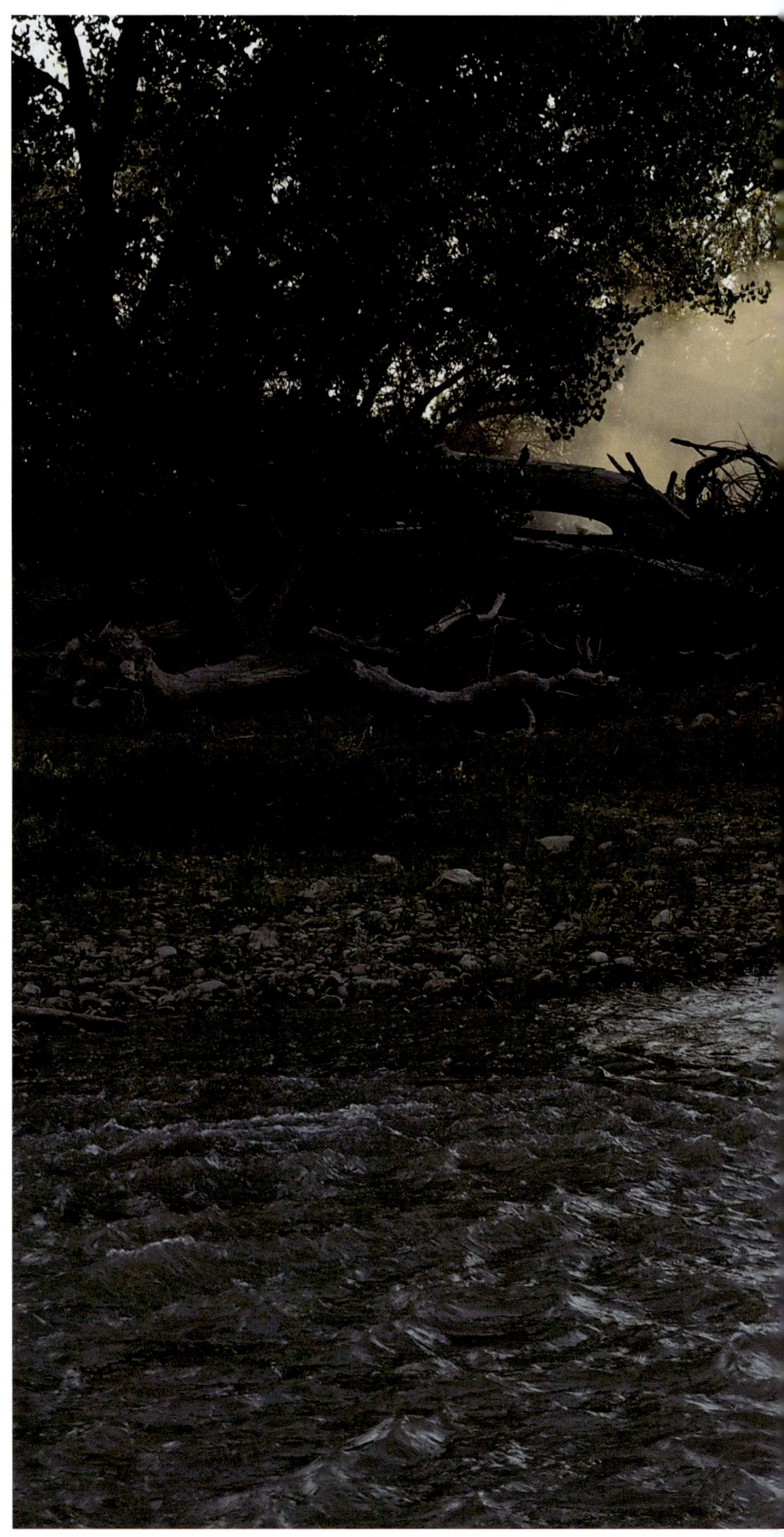

NAKIA SPOTTED HORSE / MONTANA, U.S.A. 2016

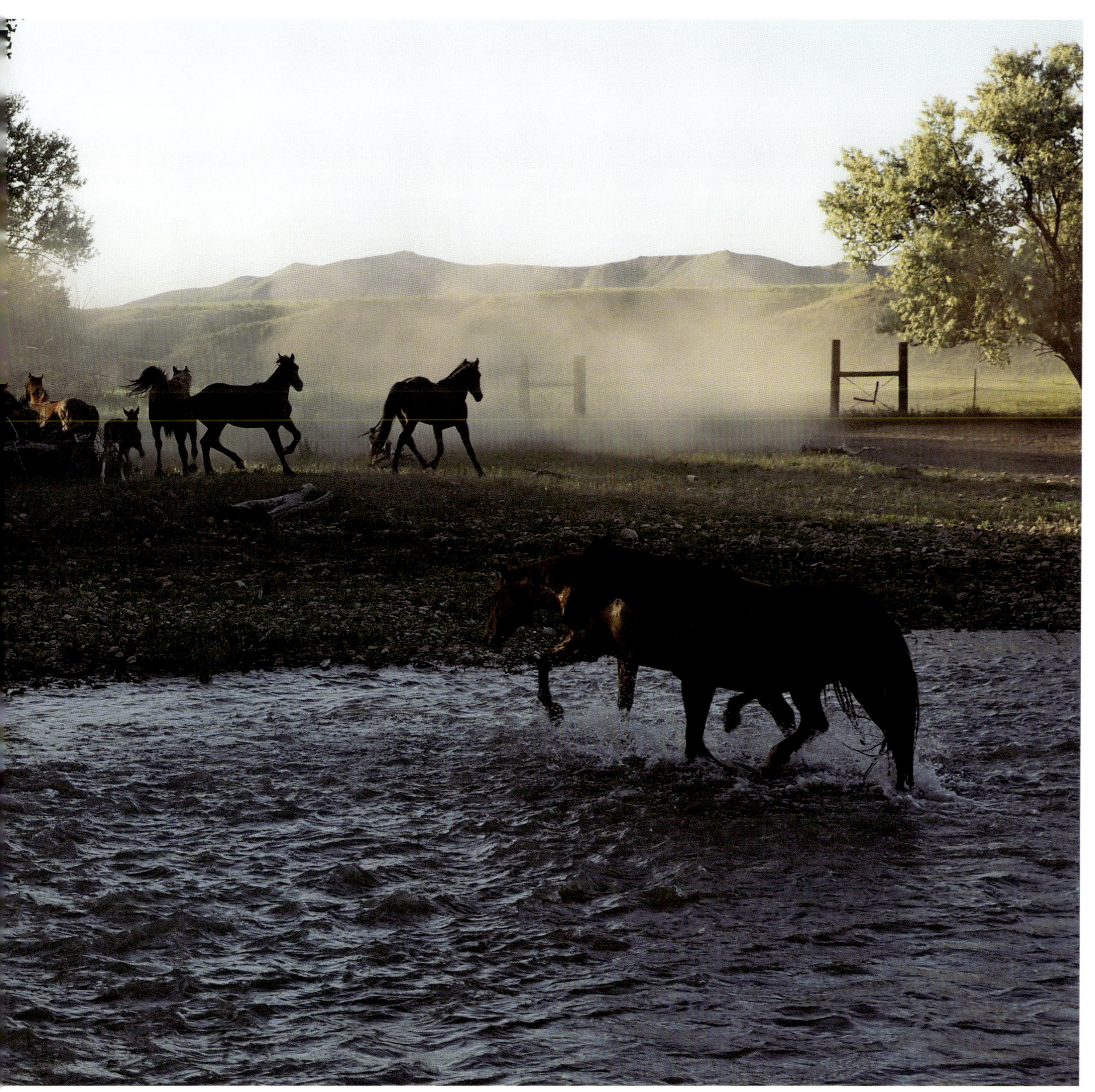

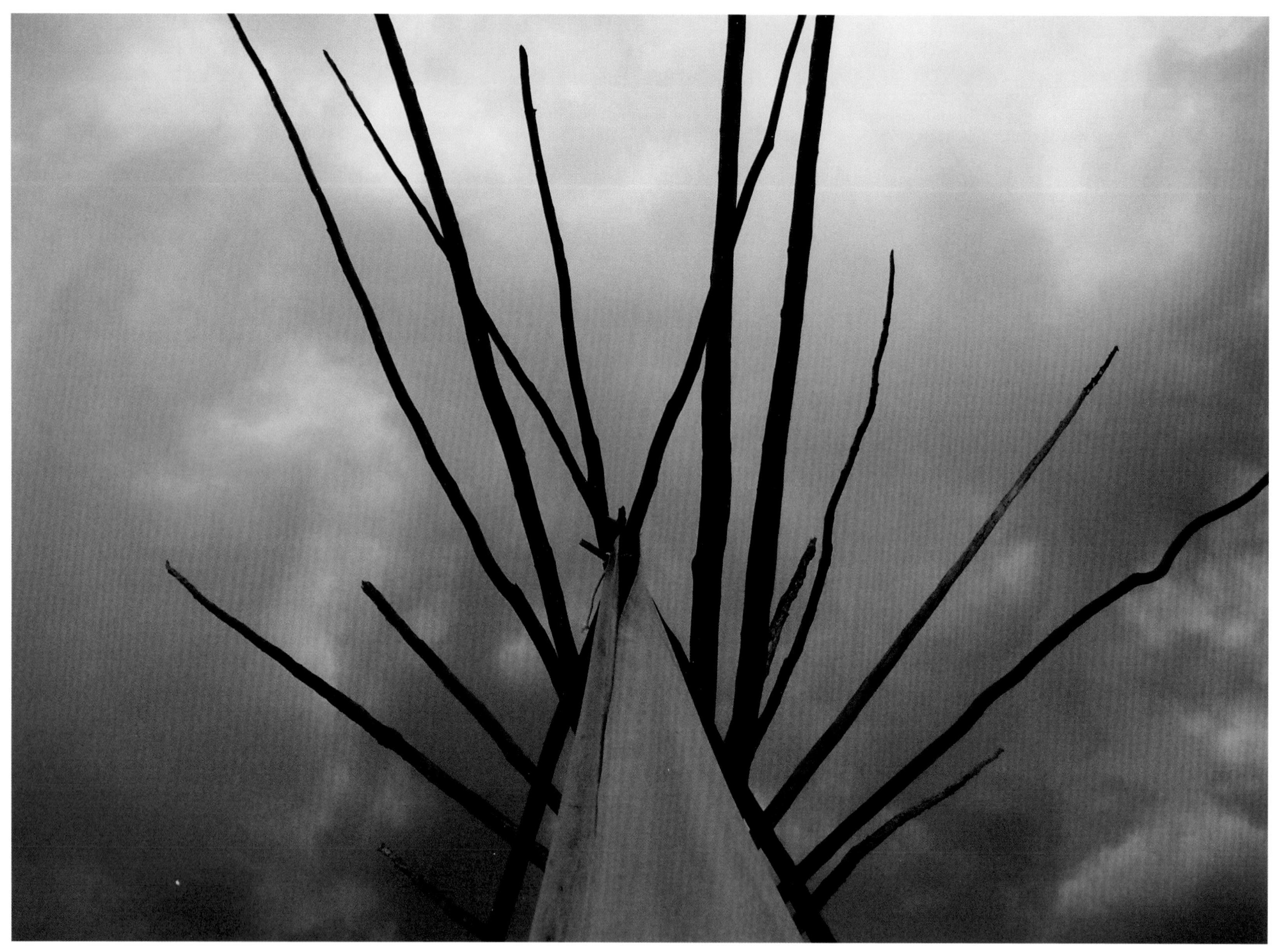

EMILY NOT AFRAID / MONTANA, U.S.A. 2016

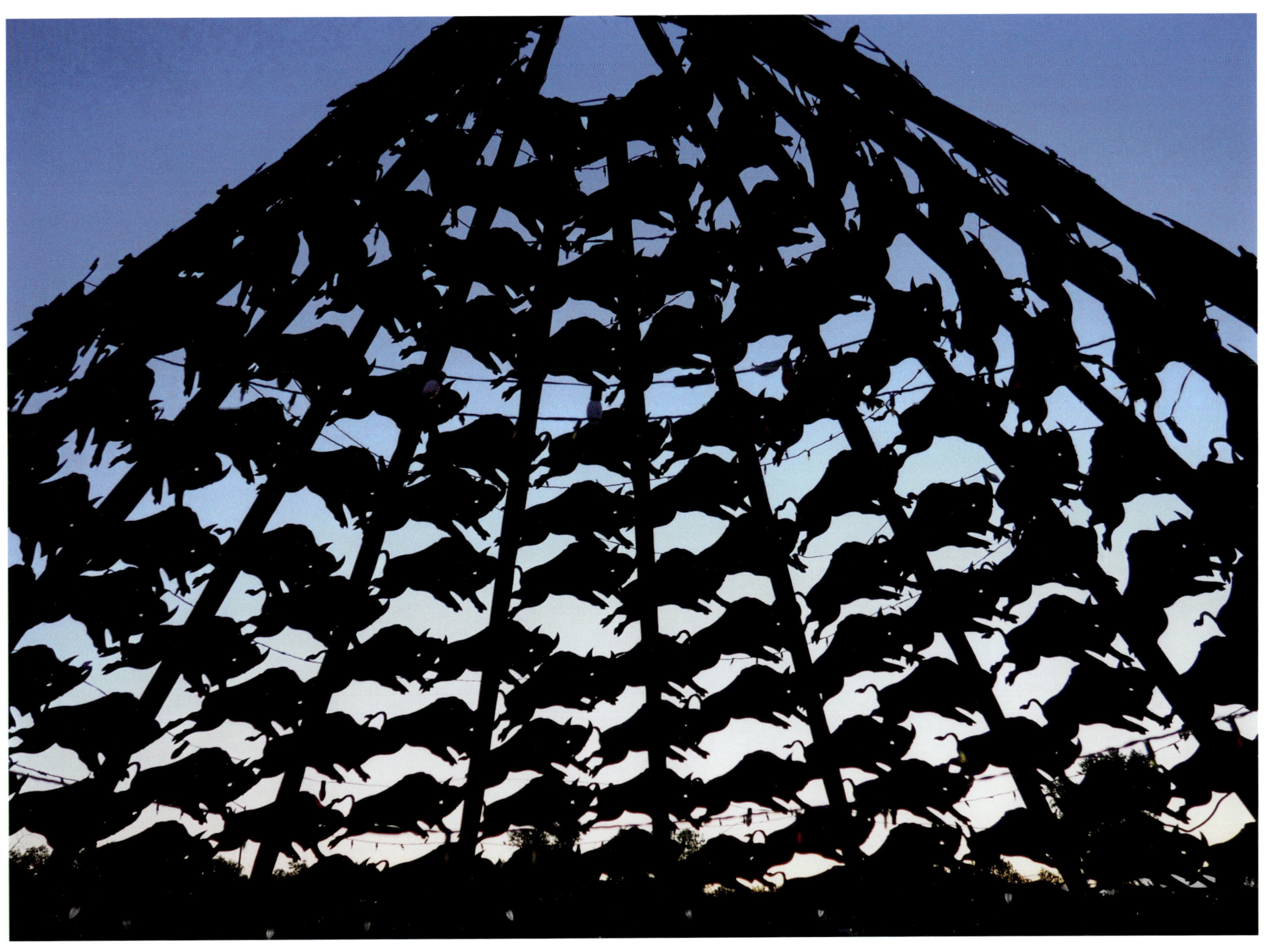

CHRISJYNN NOT AFRAID / MONTANA, U.S.A. 2016

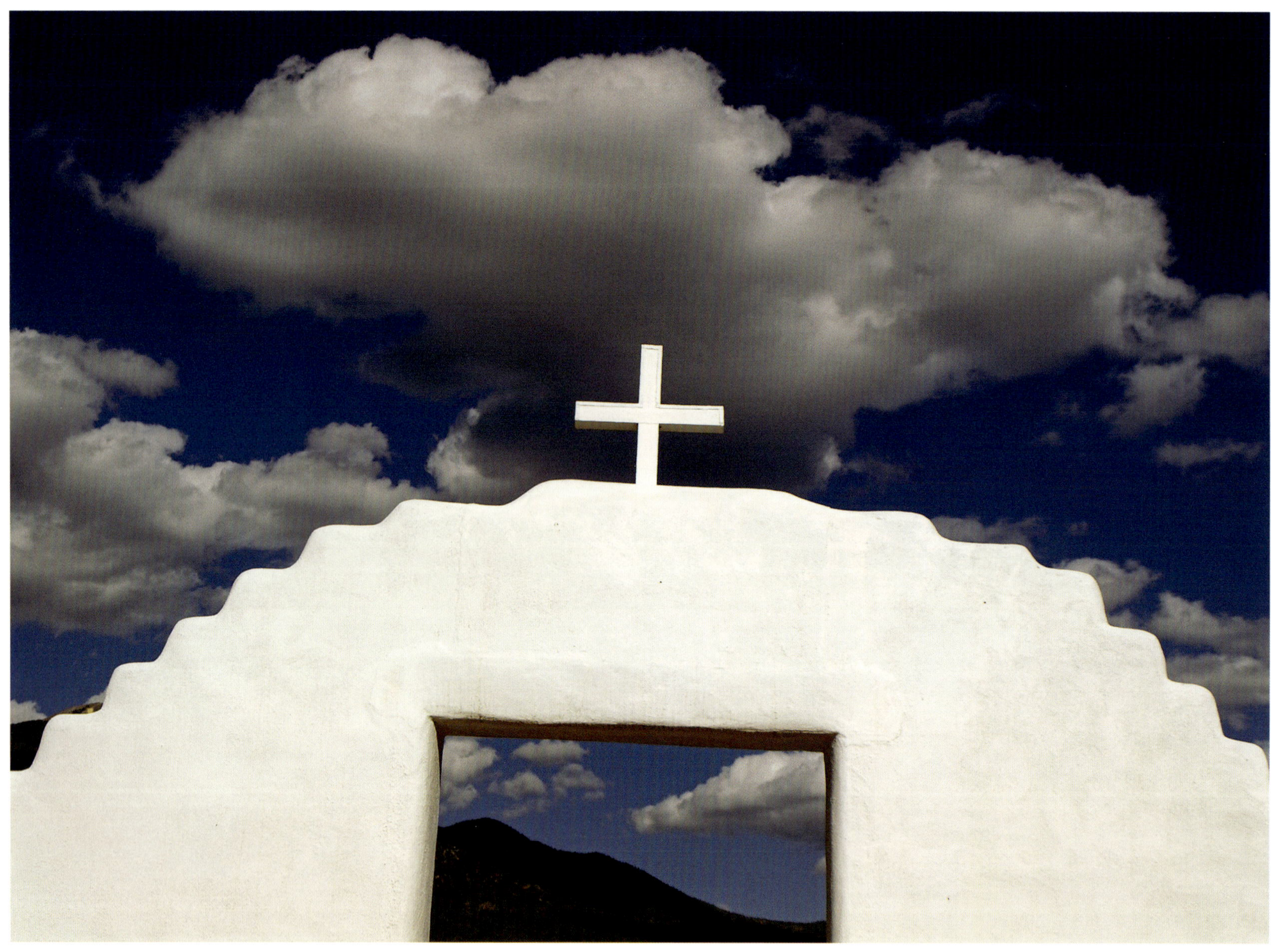

JESSICA ESCH / NEW MEXICO, U.S.A. 2008

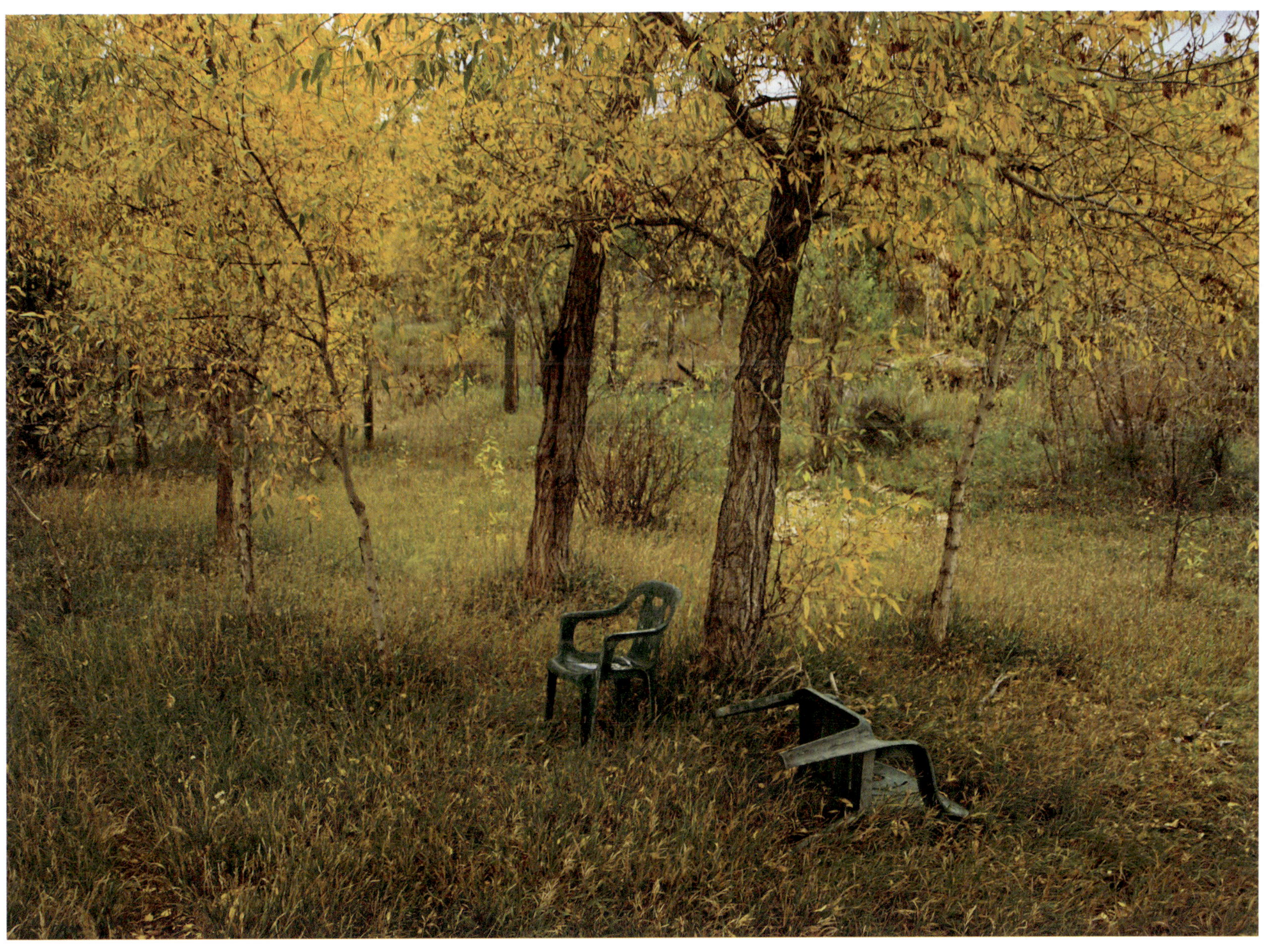

EMMA MCCOLLAM / NEW MEXICO, U.S.A. 2008

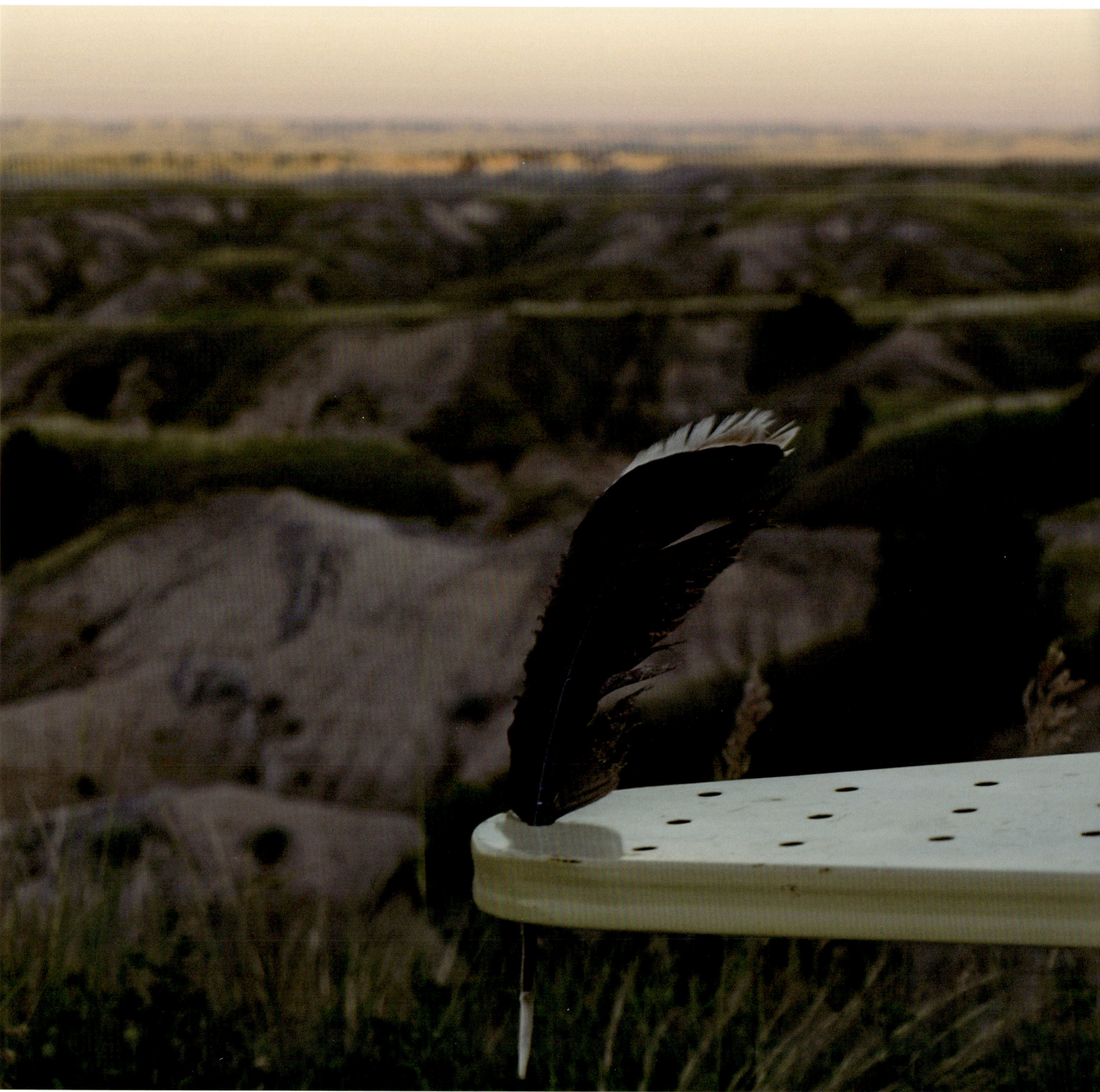

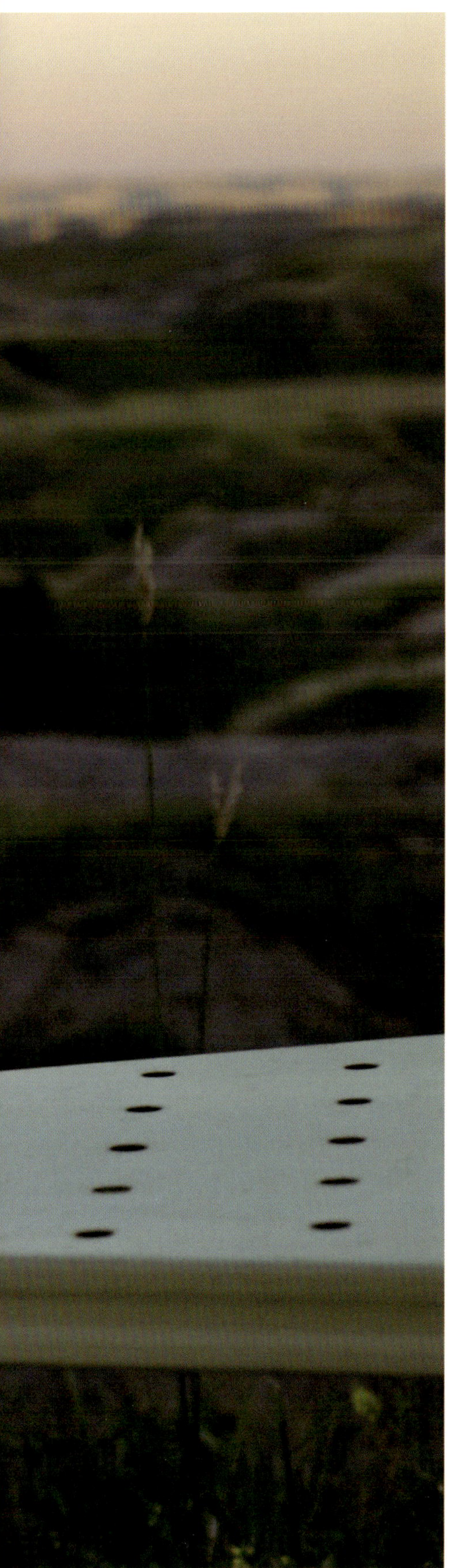

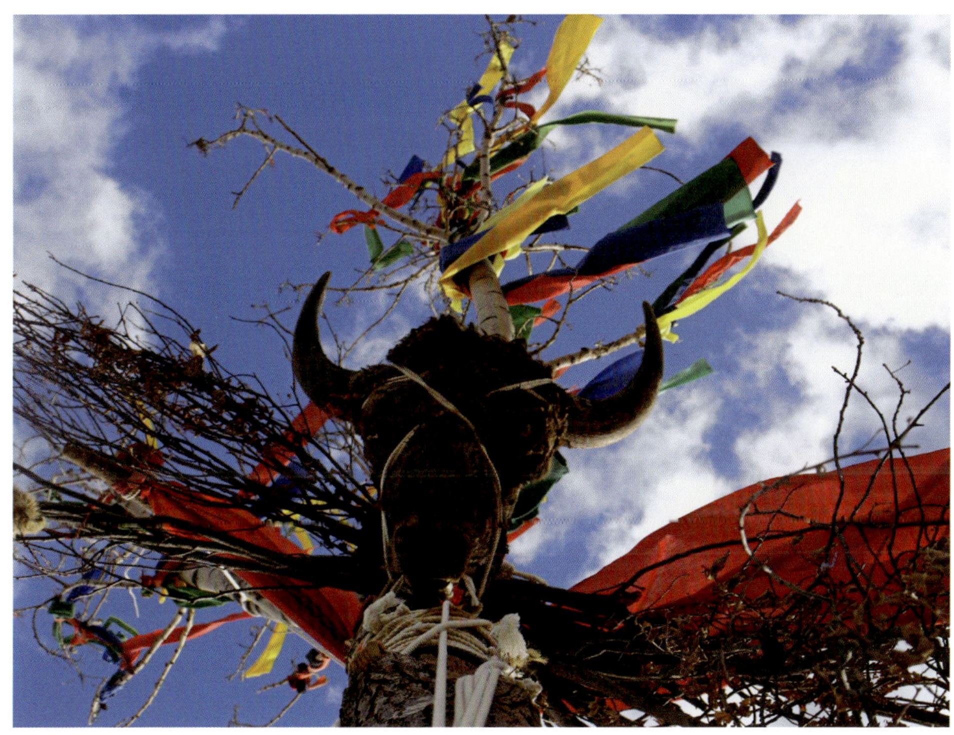

ABOVE: **BRAD LITTLE MOON / SOUTH DAKOTA, U.S.A. 2009**
LEFT: **ANISSA MARTIN / SOUTH DAKOTA, U.S.A. 2008**

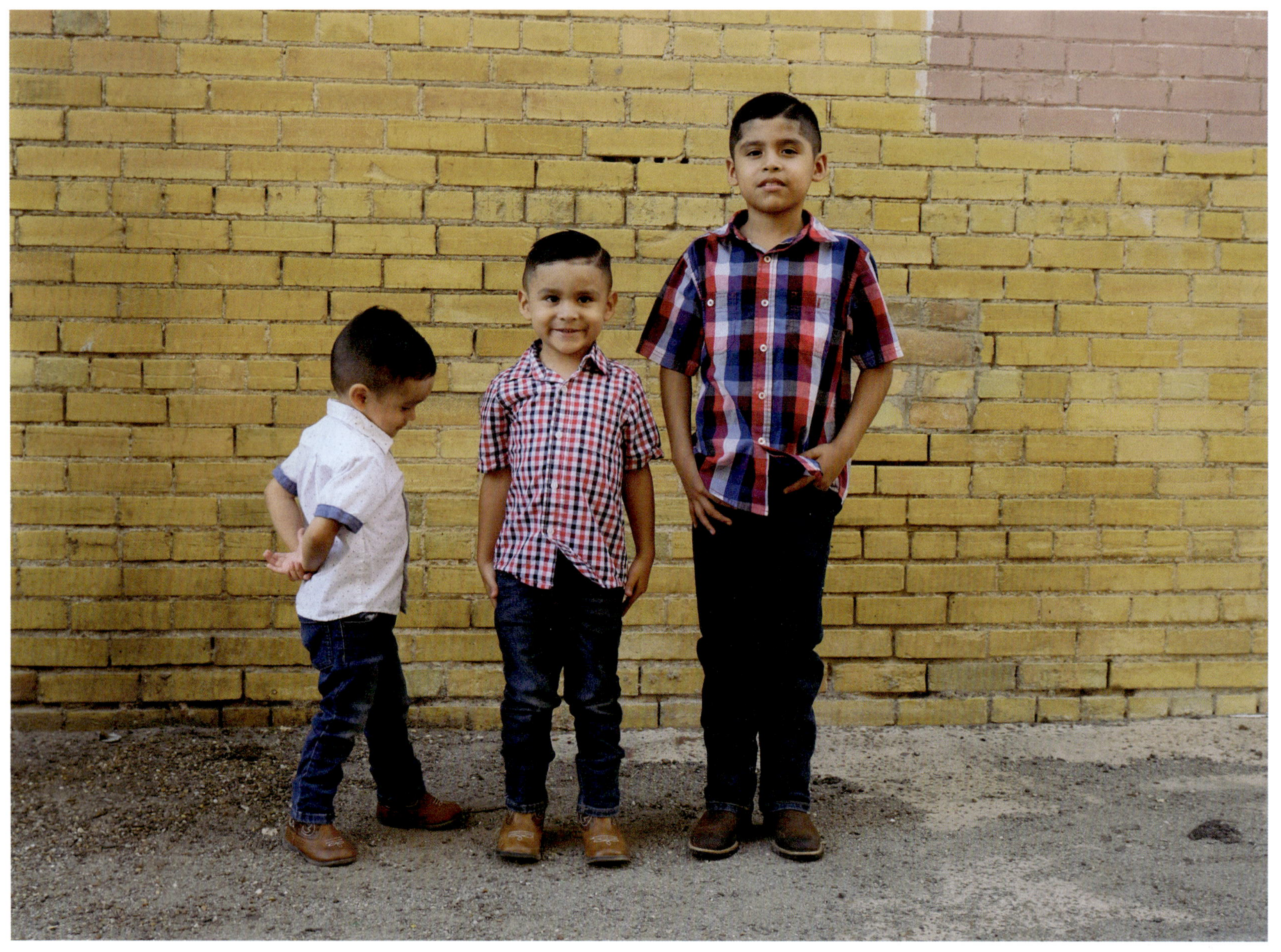

CYNTHIA VASQUEZ / TEXAS, U.S.A. 2023

> ***"The Rio Grande is a river that weaves a path through generations. It is the pride of double tongue,* de dos lenguas; *a dream for children to have no boundary.* Sin frontera."**
>
> —MARIA RUIZ, BROWNSVILLE, TEXAS, U.S.A. 2023

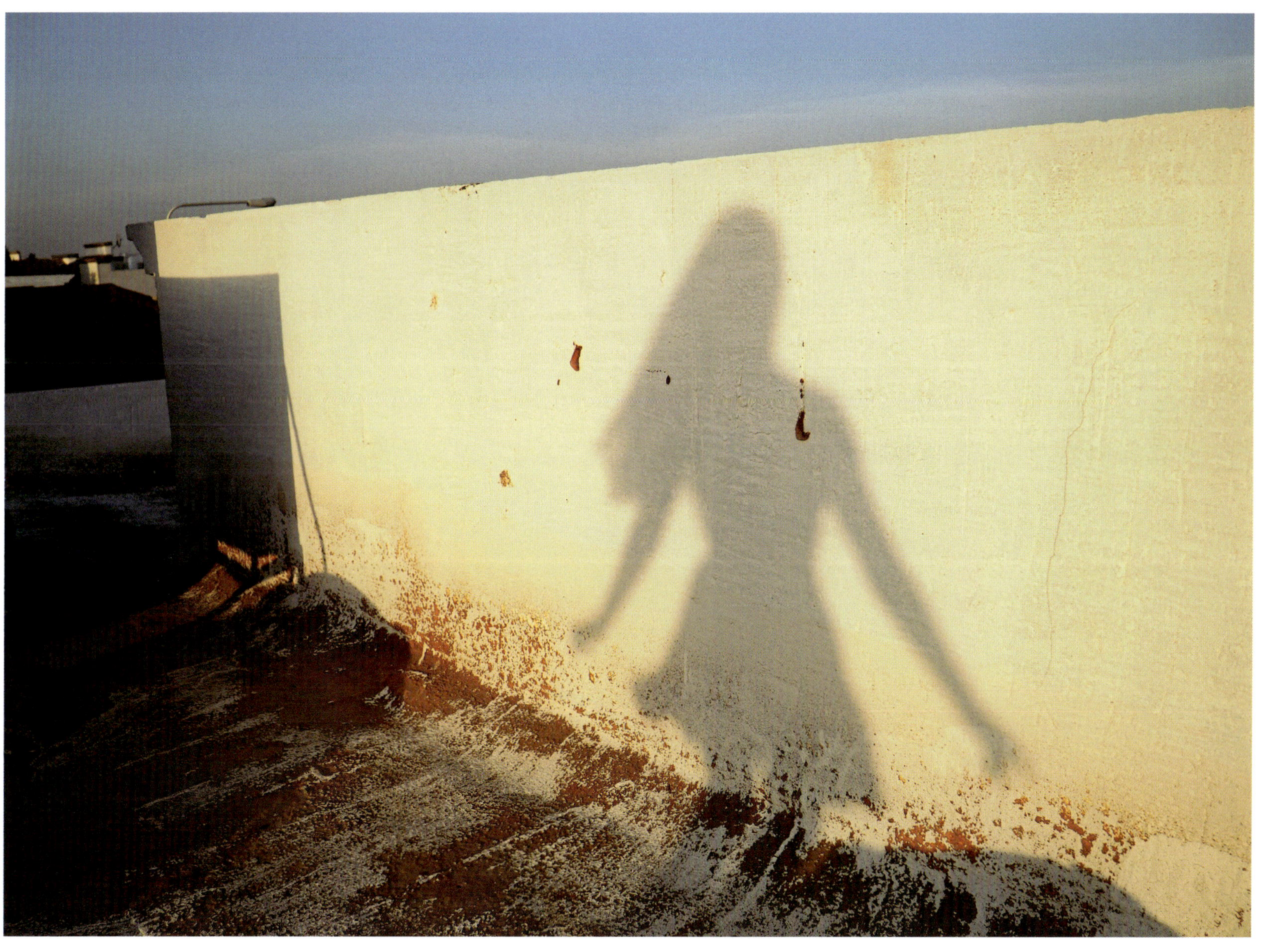

DANIELA DE ANDA / MEXICO 2017

"Living on this border is for people full of hope. I'm proud that despite having gone through very hard times, we continue standing, improving the border that is our home."

—ANDREA LÓPEZ, JUÁREZ, MEXICO 2017

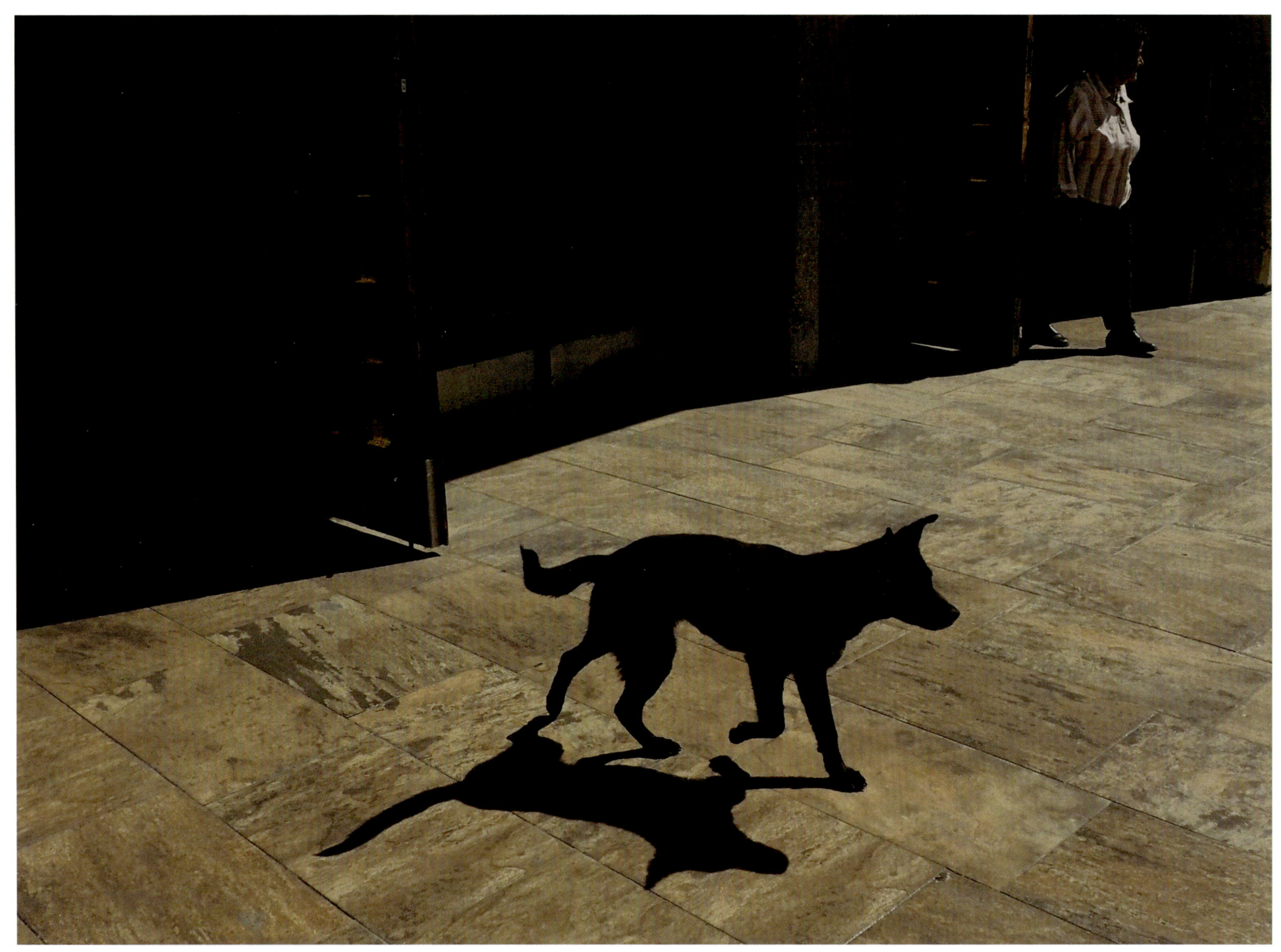

ANDREA LOPEZ / MEXICO 2017

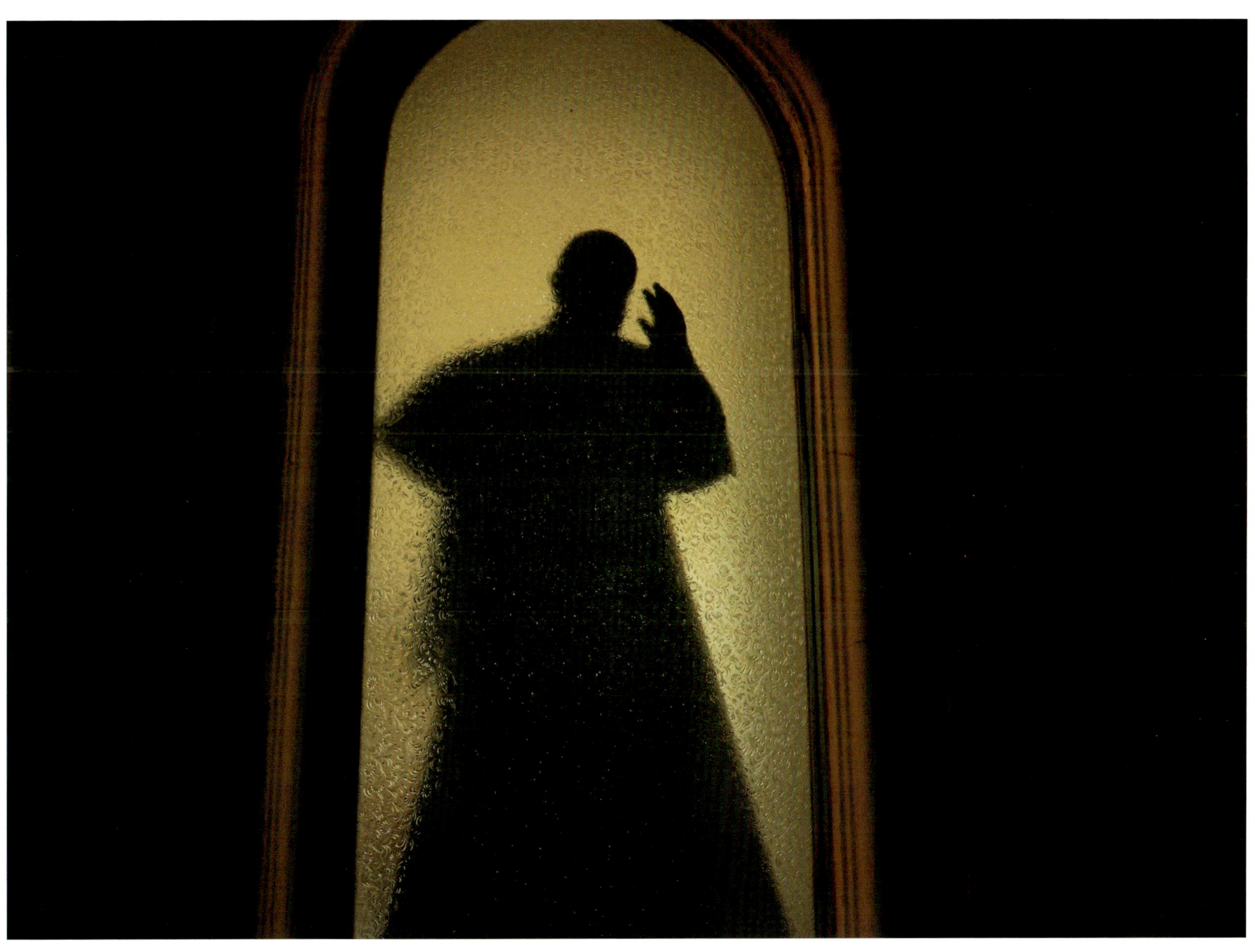

DANIELA DE ANDA / MEXICO 2017

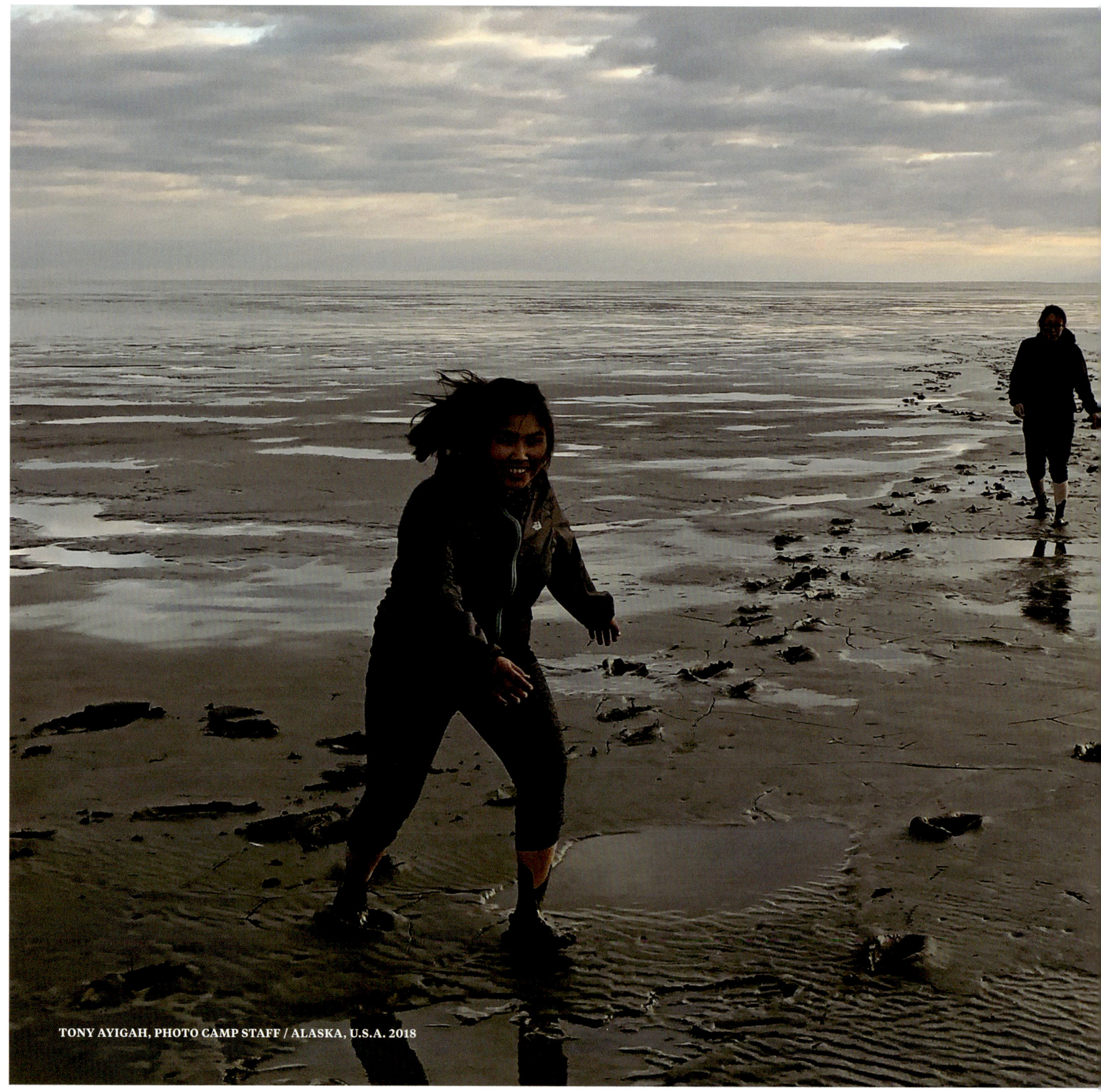

TONY AYIGAH, PHOTO CAMP STAFF / ALASKA, U.S.A. 2018

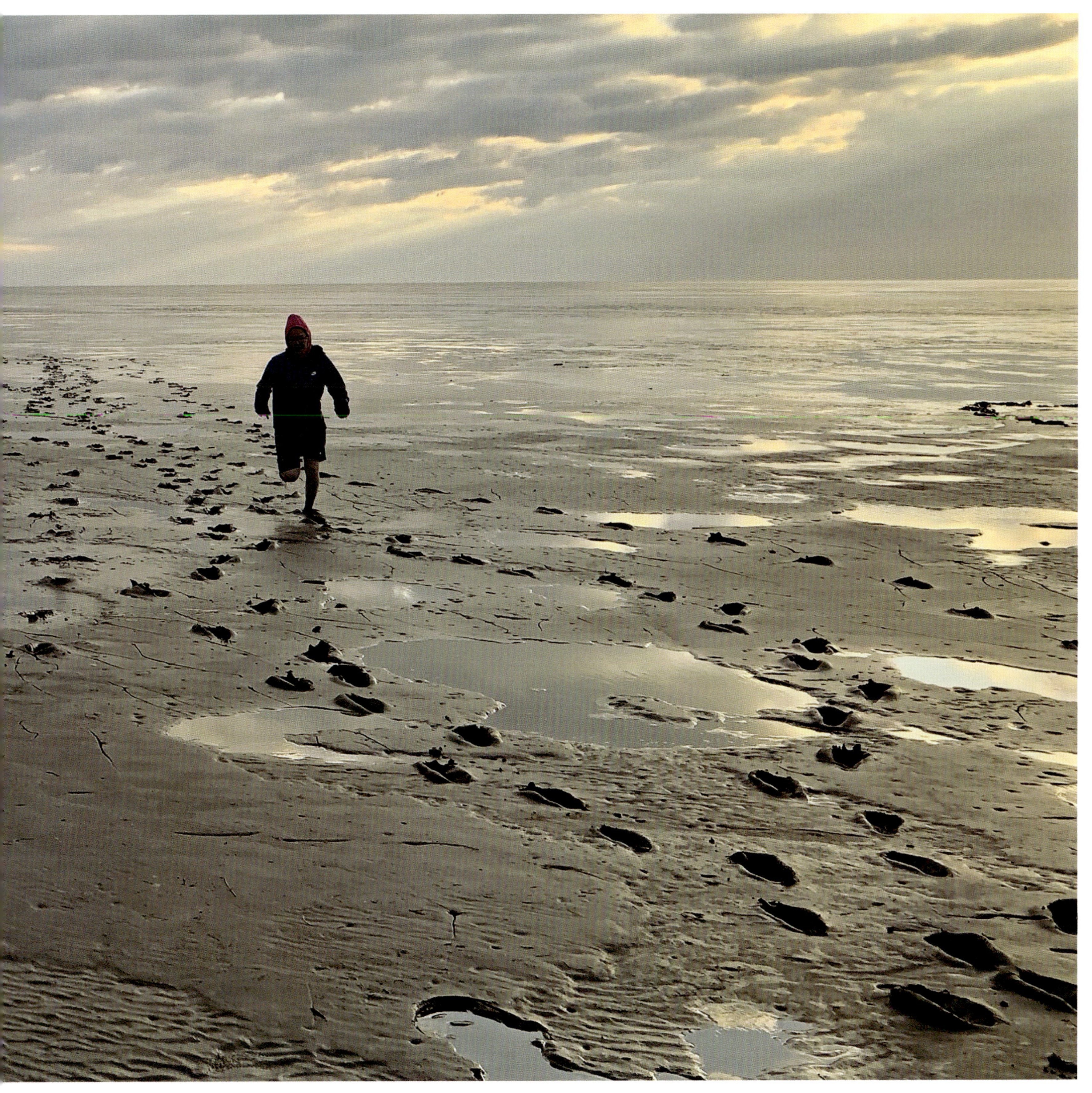

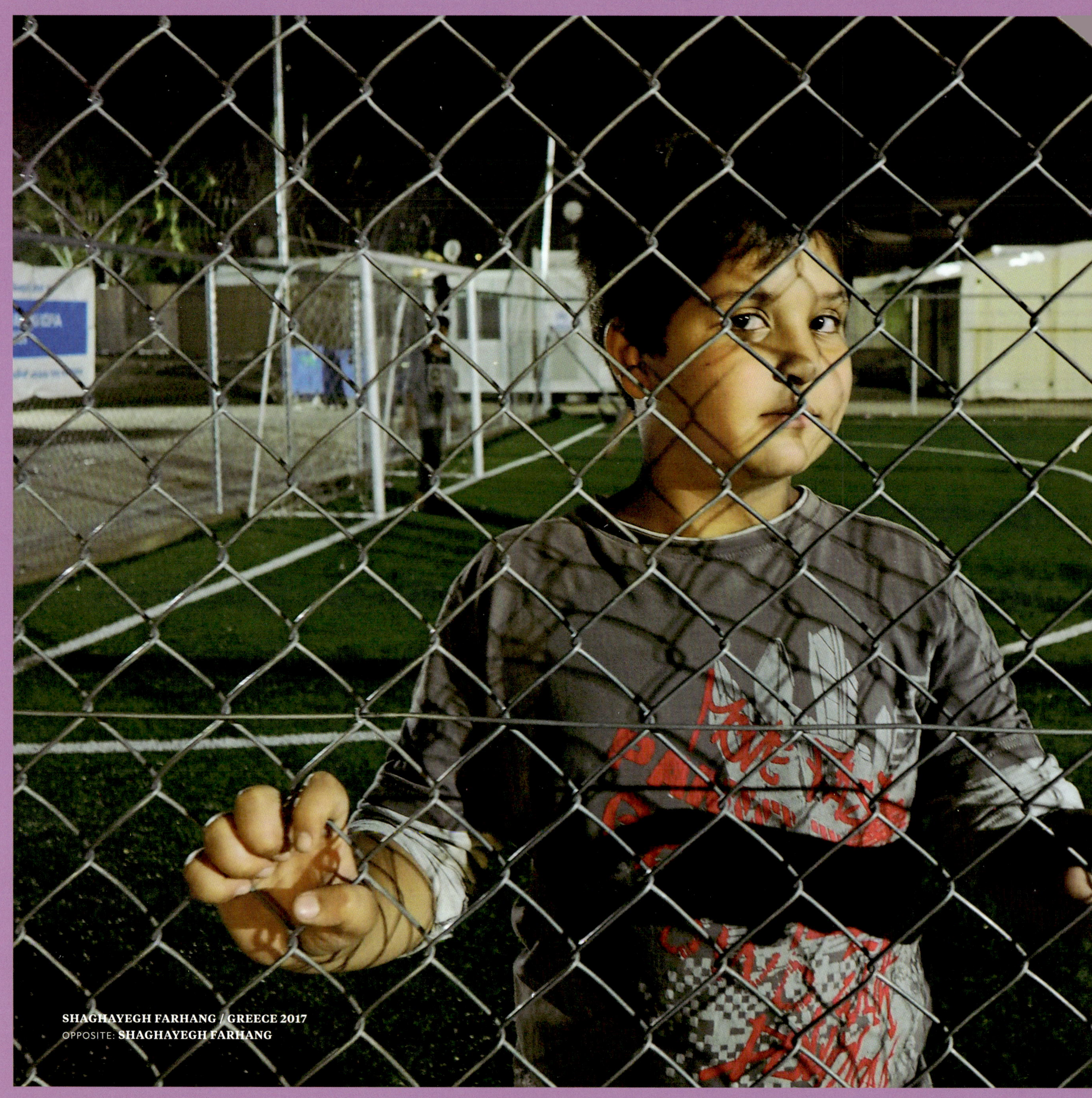

SHAGHAYEGH FARHANG / GREECE 2017
OPPOSITE: SHAGHAYEGH FARHANG

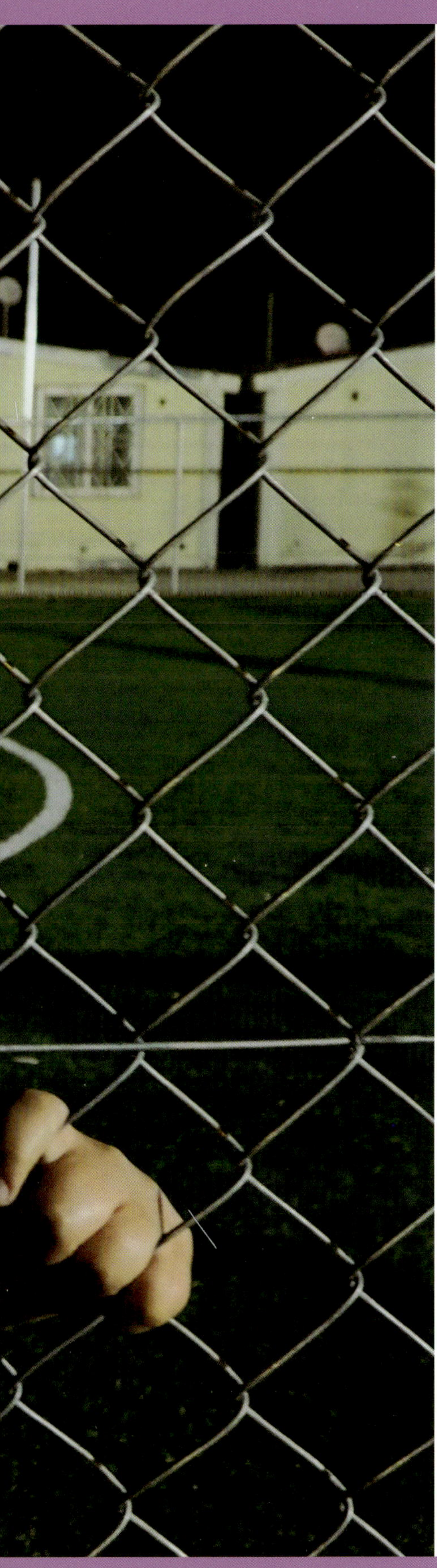

The Camera Speaks
Shaghayegh Farhang

GROWING UP, SHAGHAYEGH FARHANG LOVED hiking in Iran's majestic mountain ranges, where she felt free and alive. But there was only so much time she could spend away from ground-level reality. As innocuous as her job as a wedding photographer might appear, she risked sanctions by taking pictures of men and women together, of women without head scarves, perhaps even drinking alcohol. She was arrested several times. "I had a good family who forgave me," she said. Her father understood she could not stay in Iran, and as difficult as it was to leave the country she loves, Shaghayegh, her mother, and siblings left, reaching a refugee camp in Greece in 2016.

A year later, at the age of 23, she attended her first Photo Camp. She could barely speak English, and photography felt like the only avenue through which she could communicate. Today, Shaghayegh is a Farsi-to-English translator at the Pournara refugee camp on the outskirts of the Cypriot capital of Nicosia. One self-portrait, which she often uses on her social media accounts, shows a young woman in partial profile, reminiscent of Frida Kahlo, with penciled eyebrows and lacy leaves surrounding her face. "I was trying to teach my friend about framing a picture," she explained.

While Shaghayegh is comfortable in her new home, her identity remains Iranian. When she sees the courageous women and men in her country fighting the regime, she pledges to return if her home country becomes free.

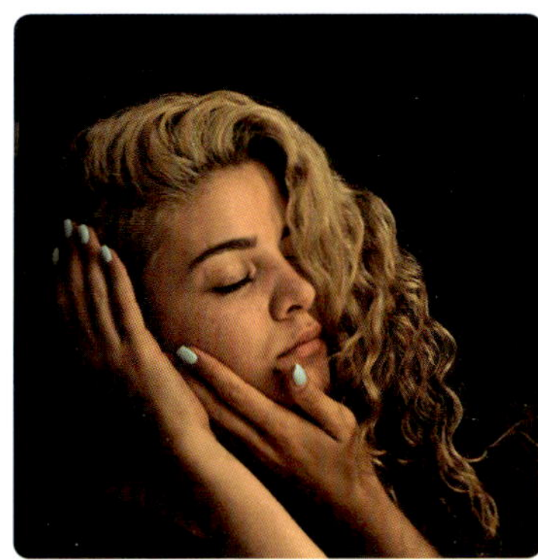

Shaghayegh Farhang started taking photographs in her native land of Iran. In 2016, she sought refuge in Greece and now works as a Farsi-to-English translator in a Cypriot refugee camp.

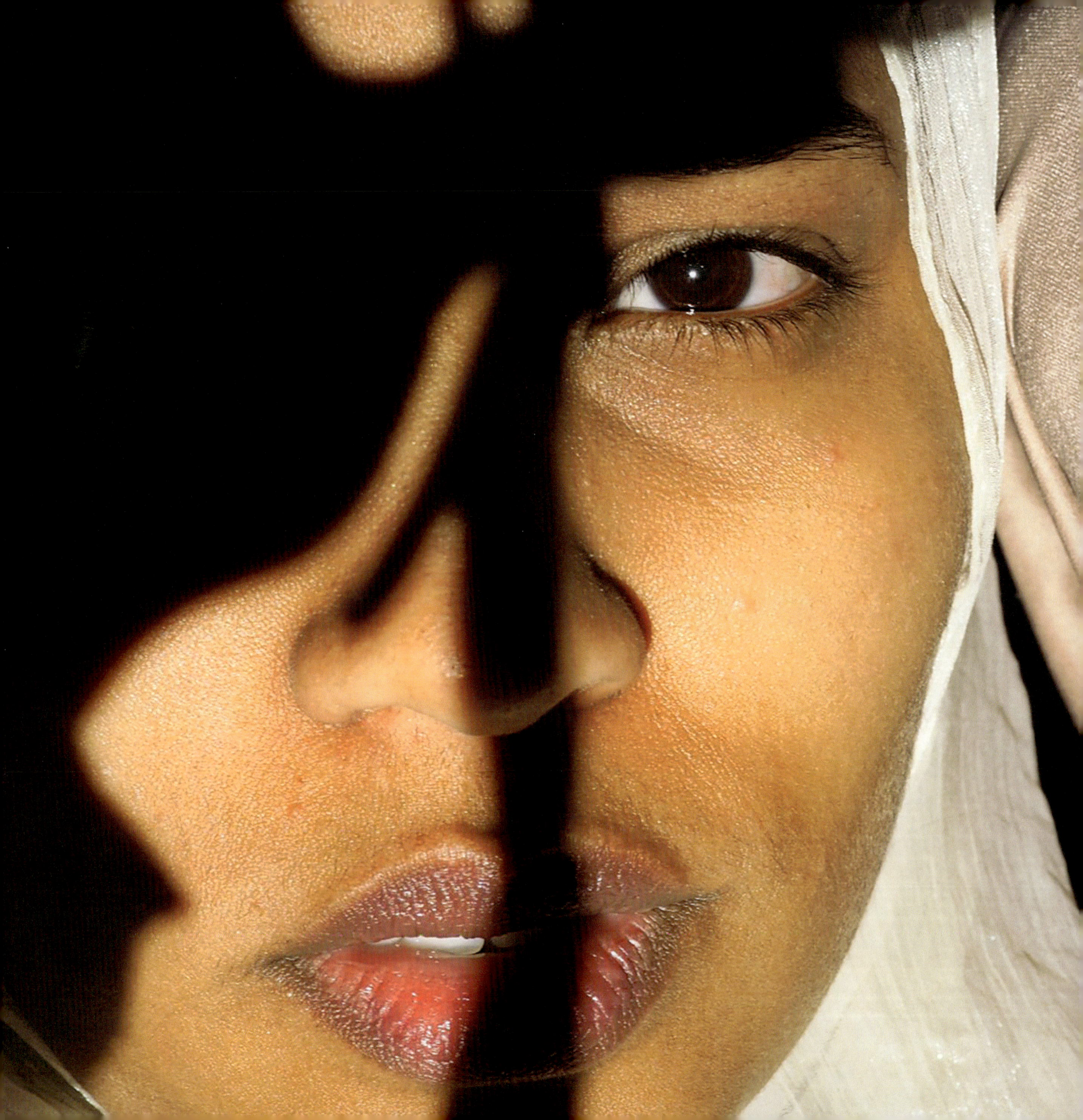

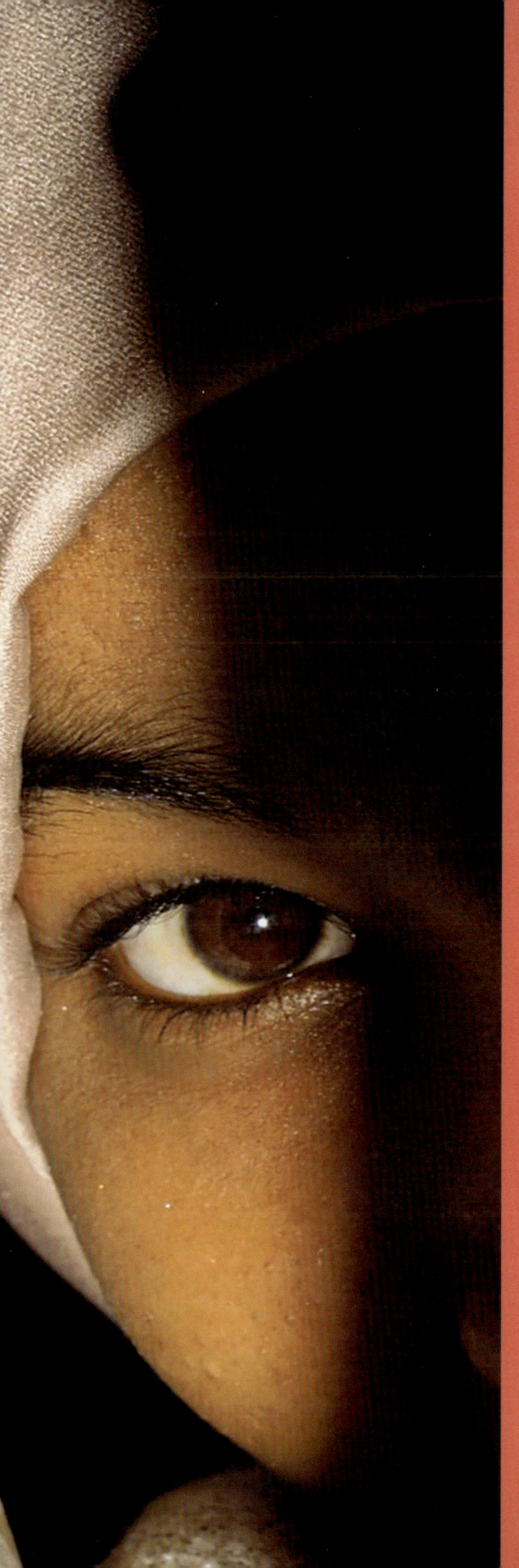

CHAPTER 2

Identity

"When I moved here, I changed. I think about things that I never thought about before, like going to university and becoming a nurse. I'm ready for these opportunities."

—MARWA RAMADAN, NORWAY 2017

Unlocking Memories

MANY PHOTO CAMP STUDENTS RECALL indelible moments from their past: sleeping on a forest floor with dwindling supplies, fleeing arrest, being caught in cross fire, walking through an airline gate and leaving their sobbing family behind. And they show their mettle. "I never thought that I would live in a tent, but that's alright," wrote 15-year-old Anwar Al Sayed, who left her home in Syria behind, during an assignment on the second day of Photo Camp in 2015. "I never thought I would not listen to my English teacher—who I love so much in Syria—but that's alright. I never thought I would not breathe the smells of Syrian fields in the summer night, but that's alright. But to whom it may concern, please ... stop war, and let me go back to my past life."

Since its inception in 2003, the Photo Camp program has welcomed close to a thousand refuge-seeking students into its sessions, often working with young survivors of conflict and disaster worldwide as they learn to use photography and writing to make sense of their experiences. Their self-portraits are telling, often revealing a sharp determination in their eyes and a maturity forged in circumstances sometimes beyond their control. One student captured both journey and hardship in a photograph of half-disintegrated rough-hewn leather shoes, with the wearer's toes jutting out the front.

Photo Camp staff tread softly, but they encourage the students to speak candidly—and few hold back. "I risked losing the most precious thing I have—my life—to get the freedom I have now," said Elias Abood at a 2017 Photo Camp in Greece. "I faced death to reach it. My trip to freedom was really scary."

Venturing out to take pictures can be therapeutic. Amy Toensing, a photographer who has worked with the Photo Camp program since it was launched, said that photography helps realize the goal of using storytelling to open youth to the world around them. She explains that when students are out photographing, their attention is fully absorbed in what they are doing. "It's similar to mindfulness; you are in the moment," Toensing said. Though the students are taught about lighting and shutter speeds, technical exercises are secondary to self-expression. "It's healthy for your brain when you are dealing with trauma, anxiety, or just life to exercise an appreciation and awareness of what's around you," she added.

Program director Kirsten Elstner, who leads Photo Camp's writing workshops, tackles difficult subjects through assignments that may sound simple but can unlock every manner of emotion. In response to the question "What is home?" some students share reminiscences of a grandmother

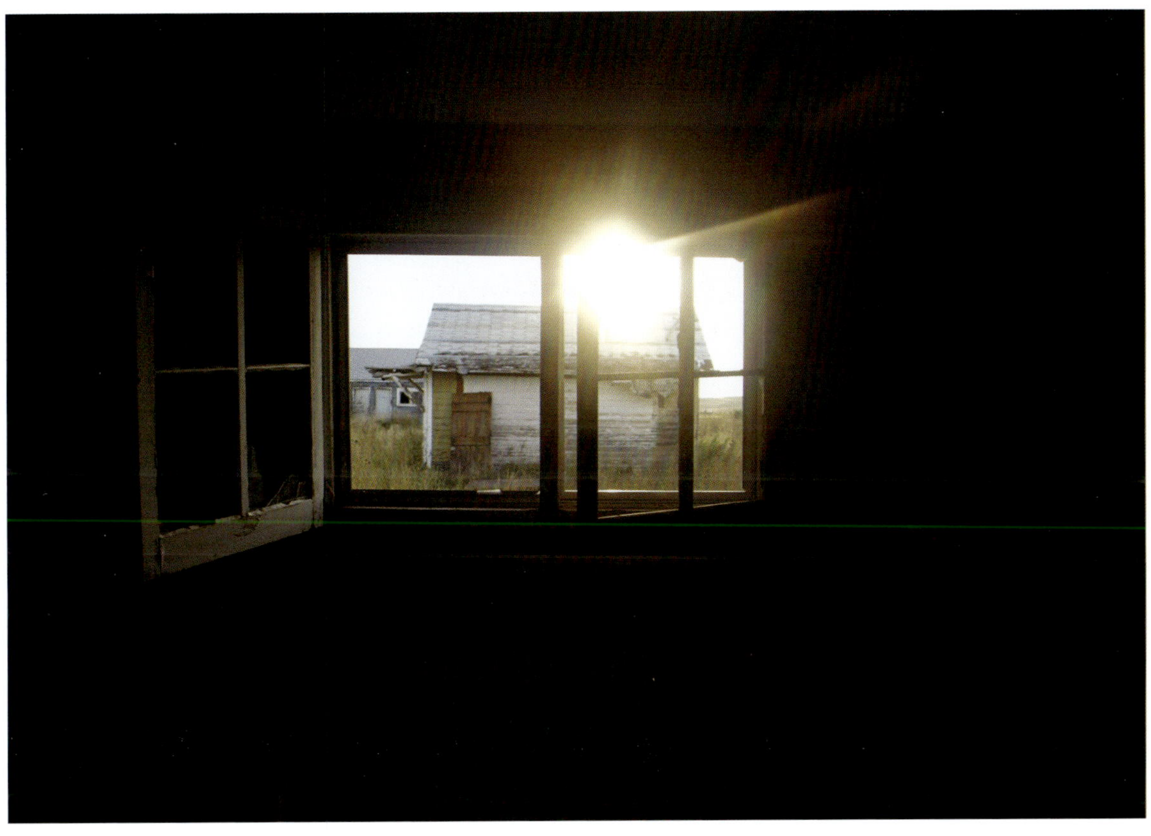

ABOVE: **TANEESHA GOOD LANCE / SOUTH DAKOTA, U.S.A. 2009** PREVIOUS PAGES: **YASMIN MOHAMED / NORWAY 2017**

preparing dinner in a long-lost kitchen, or longingly recount other stories from the past. But others rebuff nostalgia. "For me, Utica means home: a place where I feel safe, a place where I can never be lost," Photo Camp student Wav Yan Aun wrote of her family's resettlement in upstate New York. "In Burma [Myanmar], my grandmother's house was burned down, and my family fled to Thailand. A home is where you build your life, not necessarily where you were born."

At the 2022 Chesapeake Bay Photo Camp—a program for a diverse group of youth from the Annapolis area—the students were asked to write an essay on water, the theme of the camp. Most wrote about environmental issues, but student Jennifer Guillen, 20, associated water with her family's journey from El Salvador. She explained that her long trek never had a negative connotation for her, even in the face of danger. She was in search of her dreams—never mind that it involved crossing the Rio Grande. "The river is small, but with the fear I felt, it seemed huge," she wrote. "When I got to the other side of the river I felt relief, until I saw someone almost die in front of me." Now, every time she smells a brackish mixture of water, fish, and mud, "it reminds me of that dark and silent night" when she crossed into a new life.

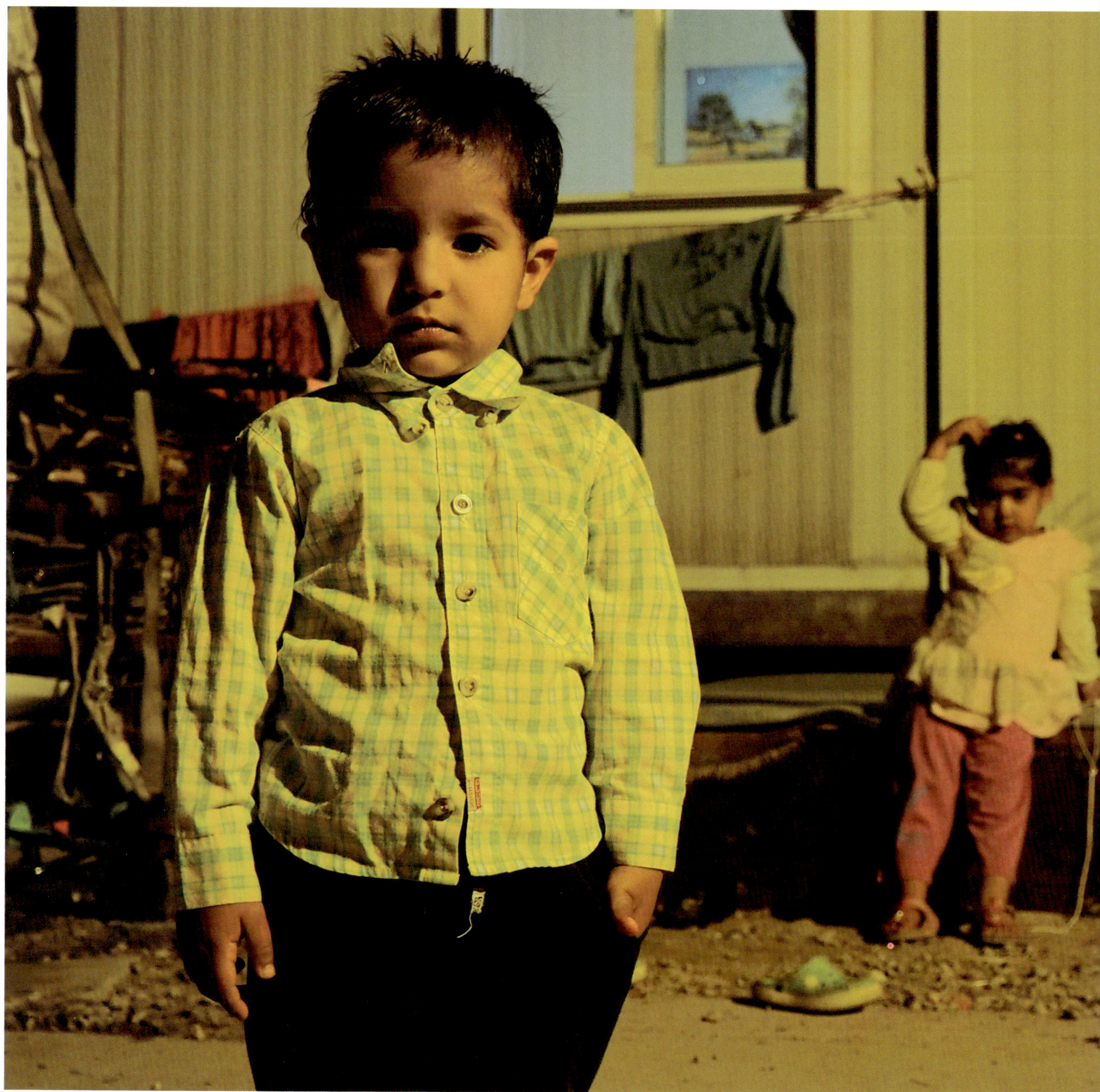

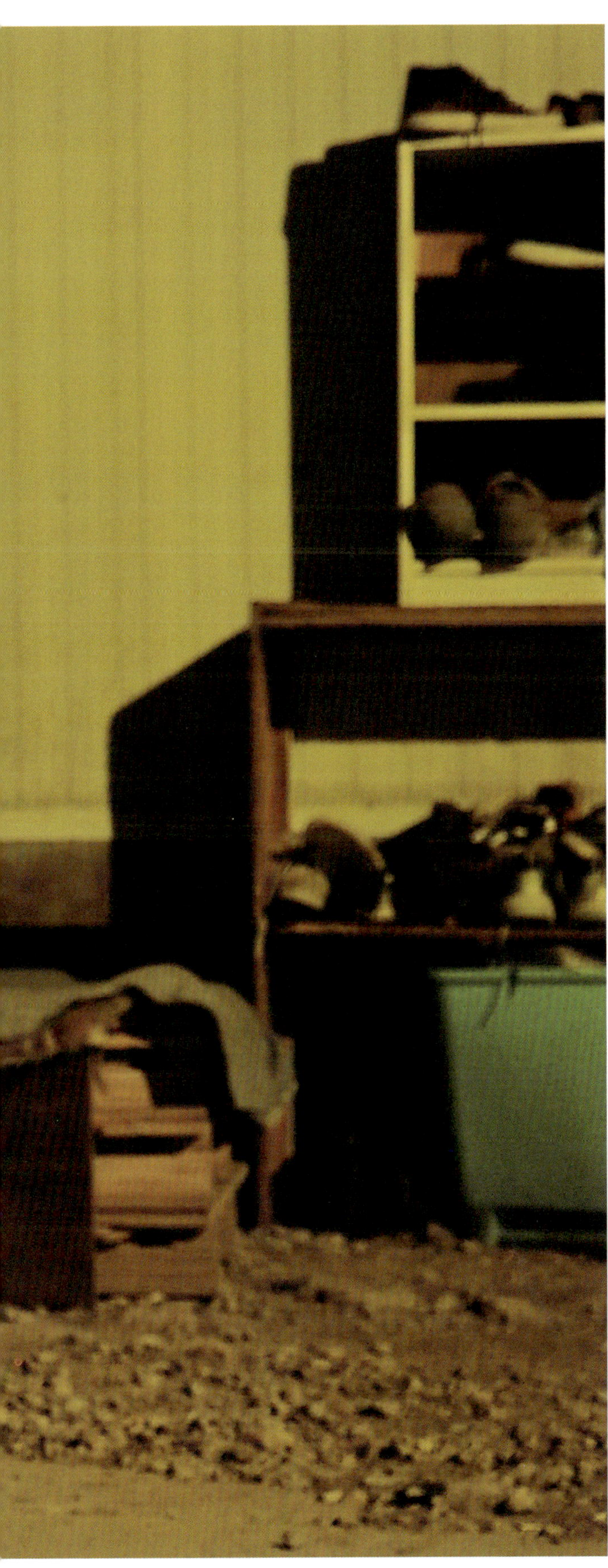

"I'm from Afghanistan. Here I have freedom, but I don't have my family. Not having my mother and father, it's hard to think of where I am as home, because I don't have someone to tell what's in my heart."

—ZABIHULLAH HASSANI, NORWAY 2017

SHAGHAYEGH FARHANG / GREECE 2017

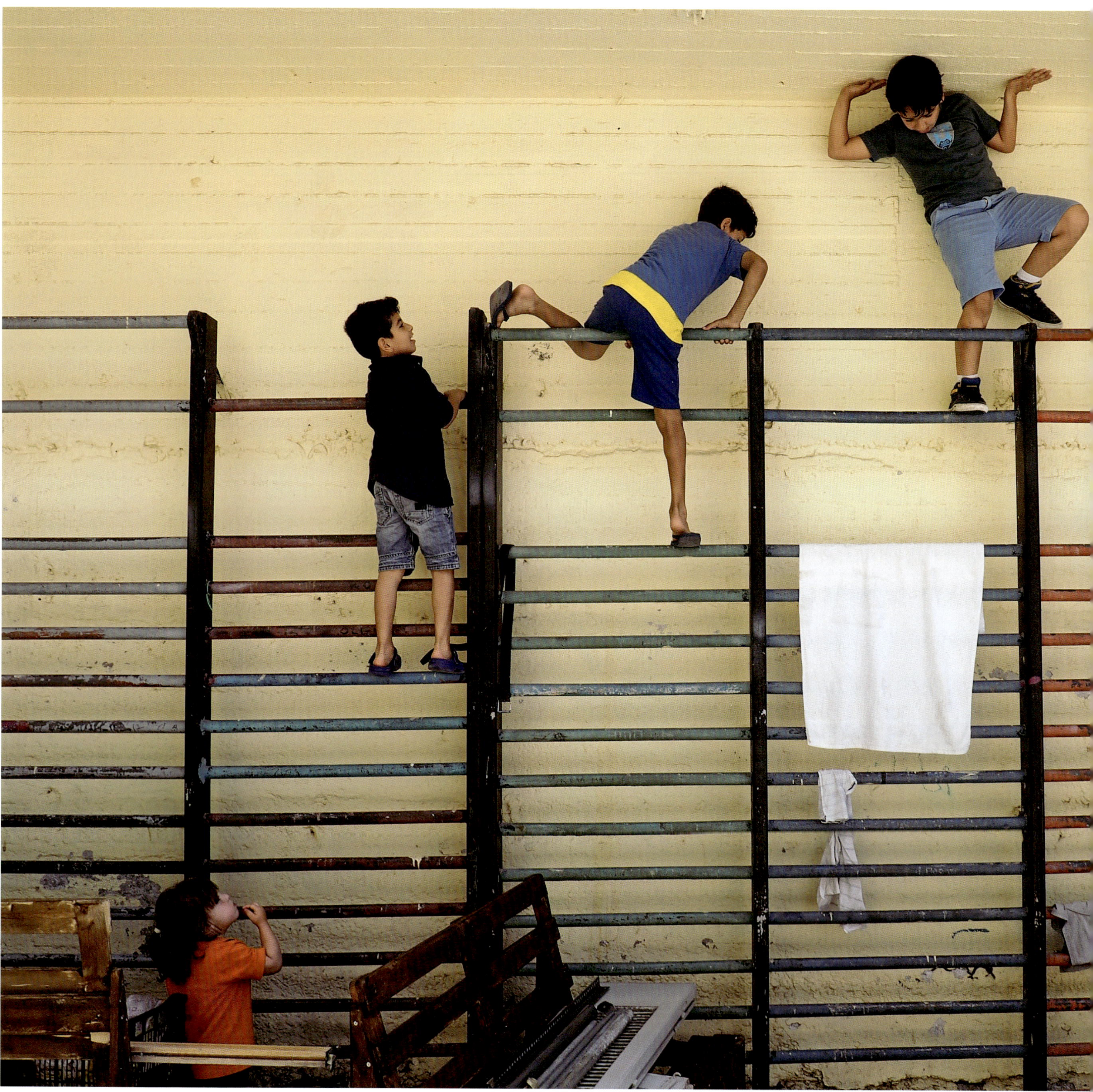

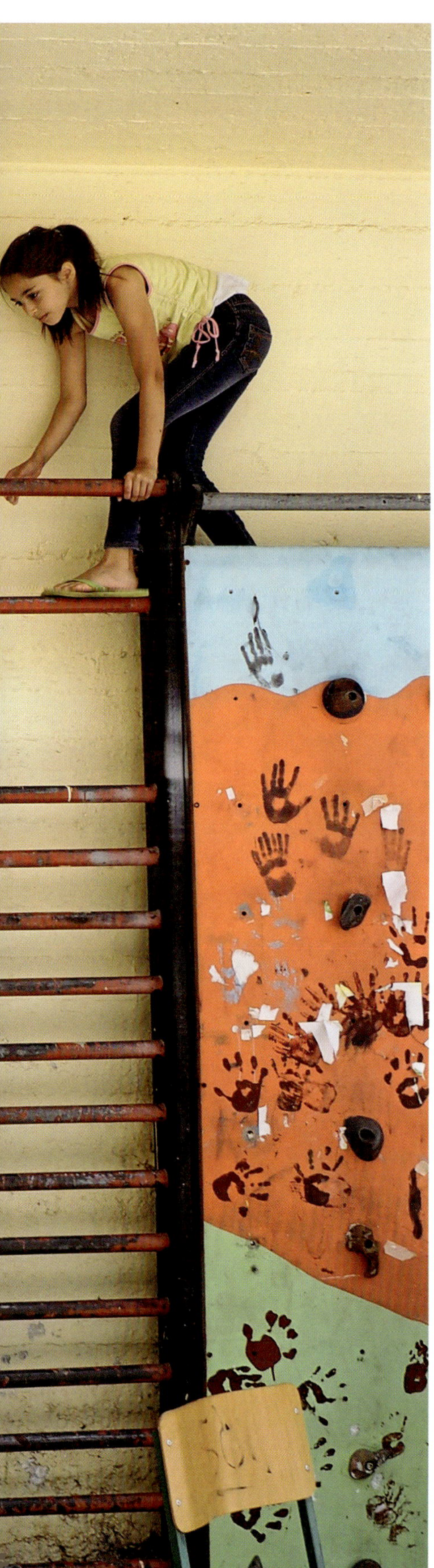

"Freedom means everywhere is my home."

—FOA AHMADI, GREECE 2017

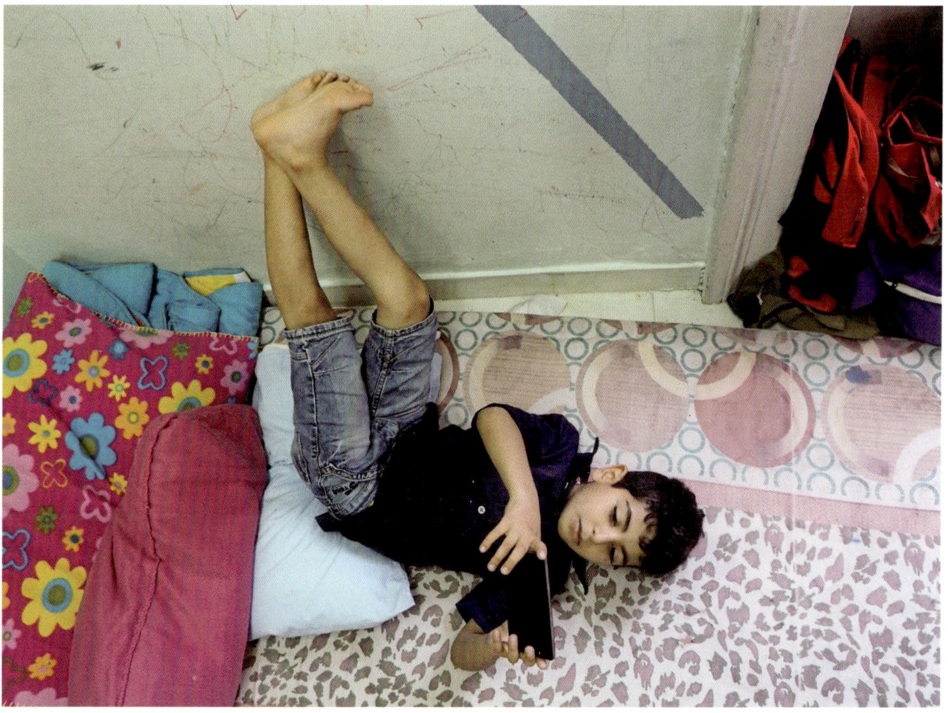

ABOVE: **ELIZA GKRITSI / GREECE 2017** LEFT: **BENJAMIN DALTON / GREECE 2017**

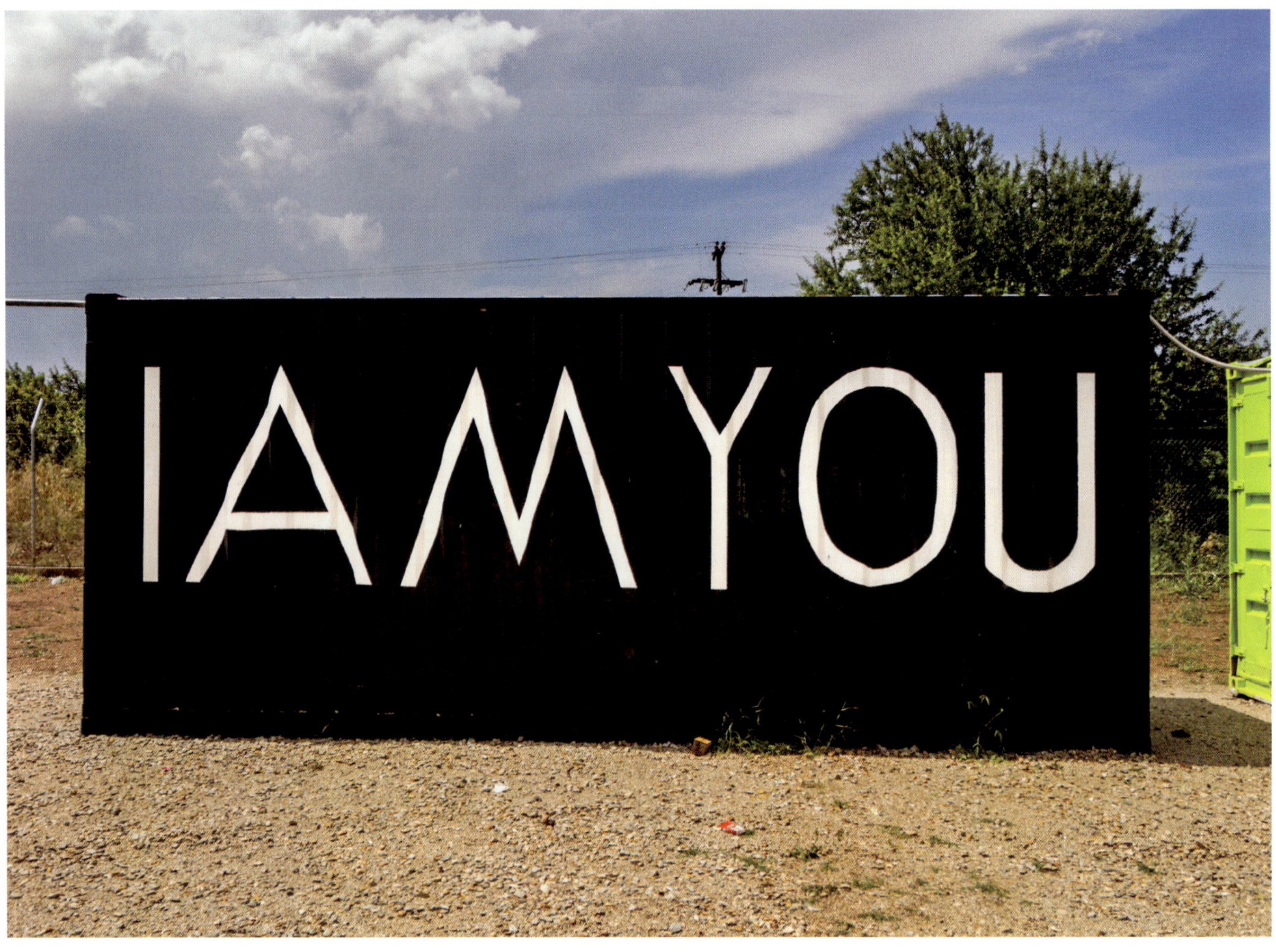

ABOVE: **FARAMARZ AHMADI / GREECE 2017** OPPOSITE: **RADWAN DIRAR / GREECE 2017**

"Freedom means safety, education, and having a legal status. It means dignity, having a decent life, having a job. I risked losing the most precious thing I have—my life—to get the freedom I have now. I faced death to reach it. My trip to freedom was really scary."

—ELIAS ABOOD, GREECE 2017

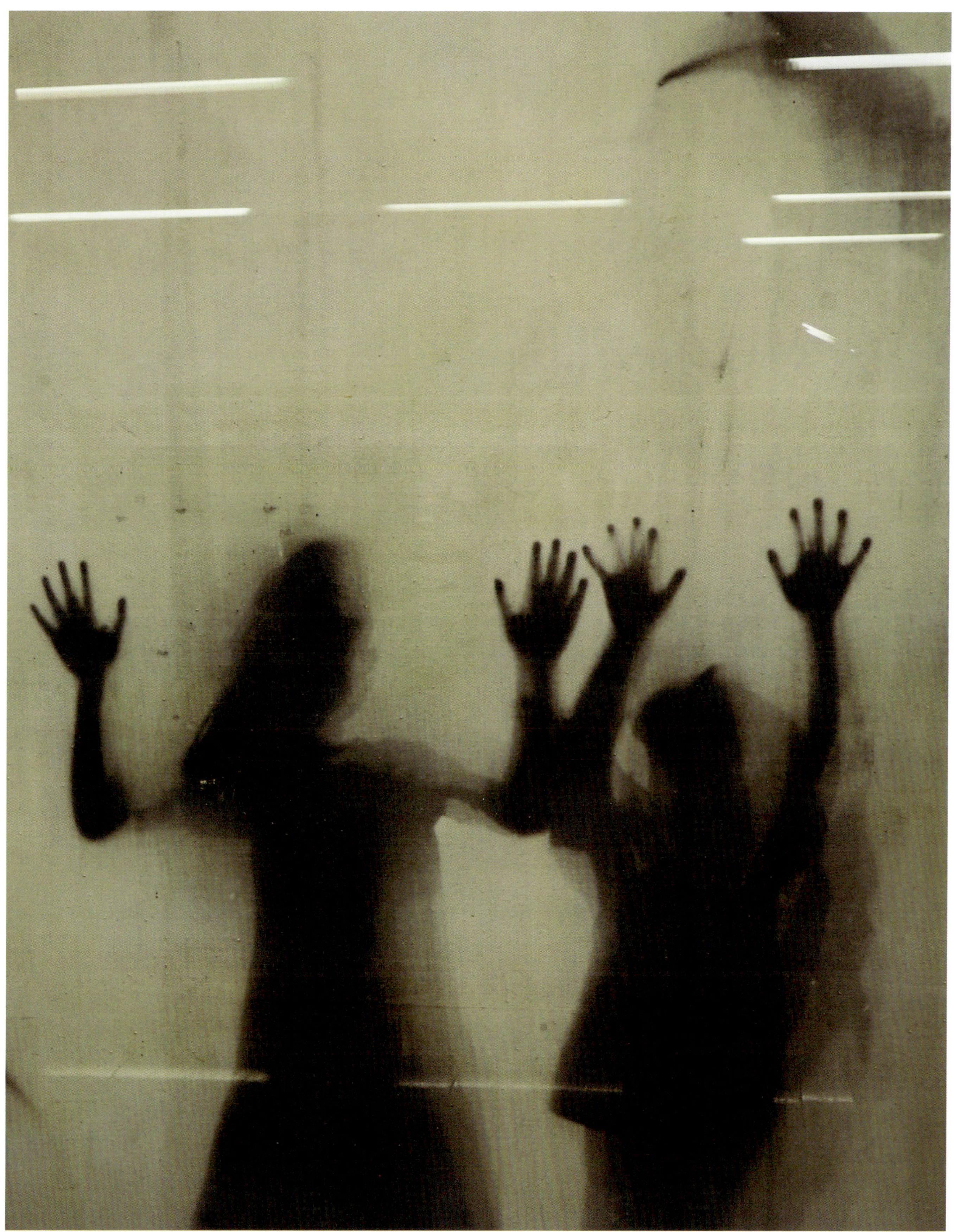

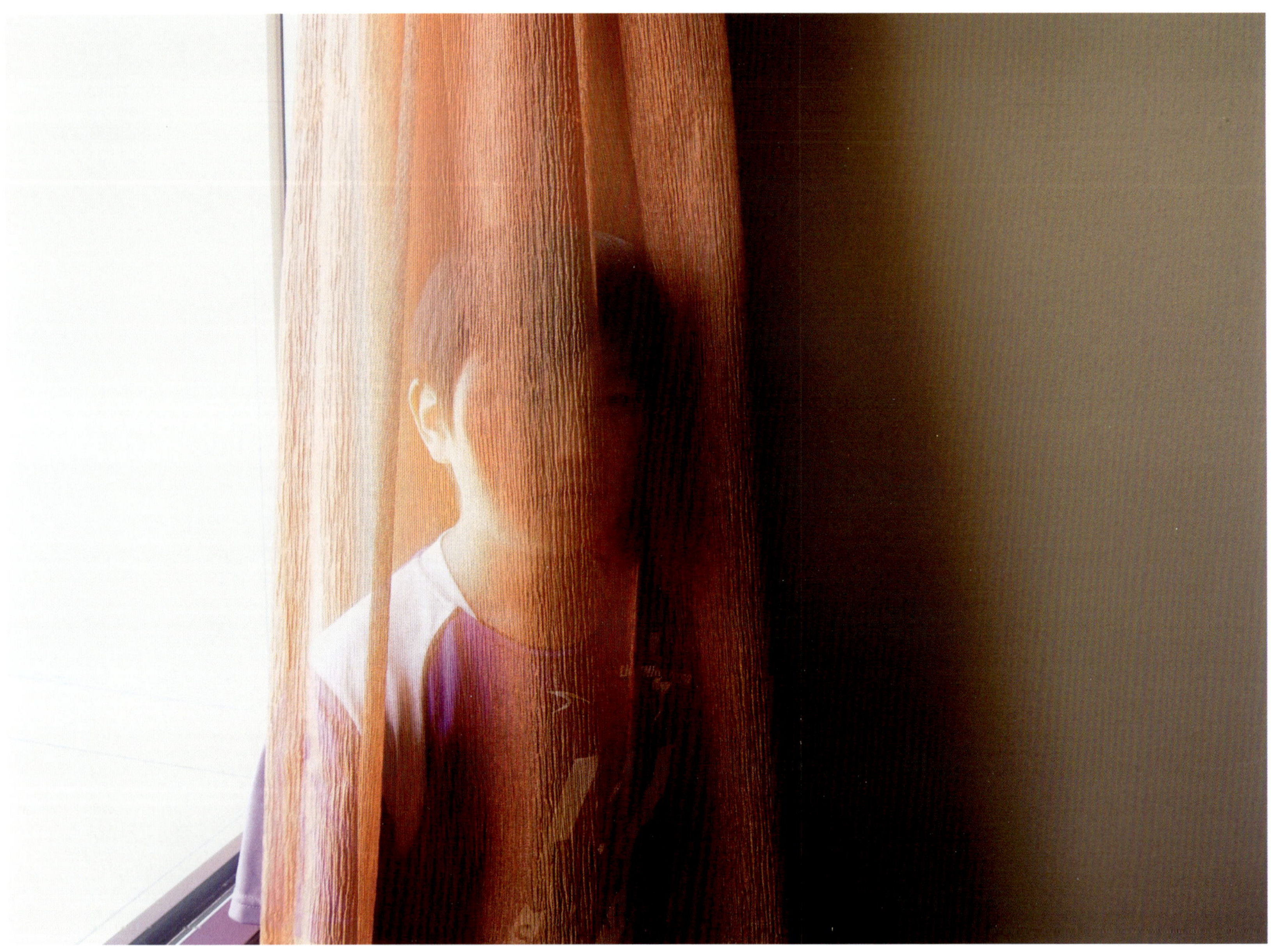

ZAMILAN MUNKHJARGAL / WASHINGTON, D.C., U.S.A. 2018

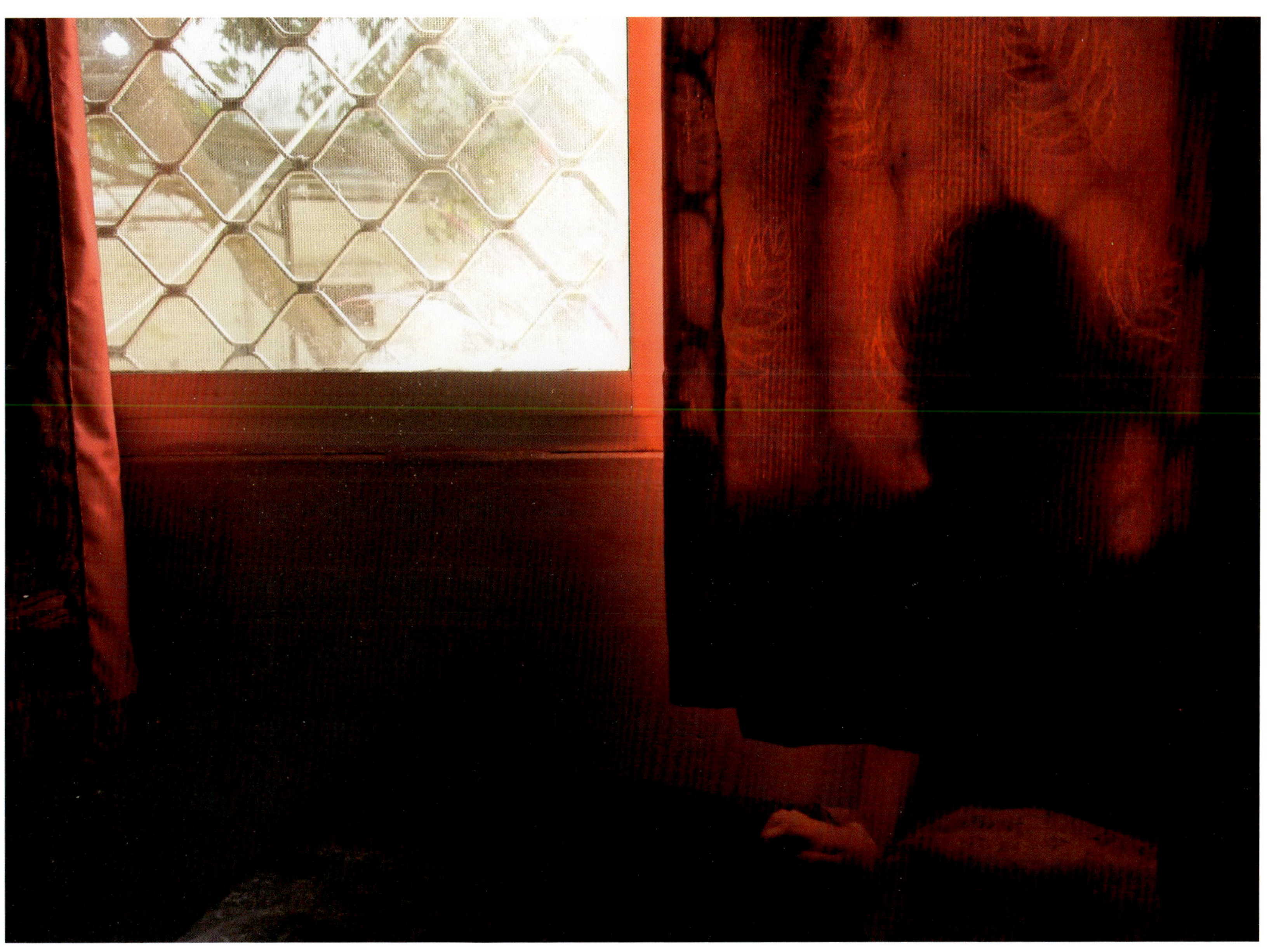

CATHERINE LAL / INDIA 2018

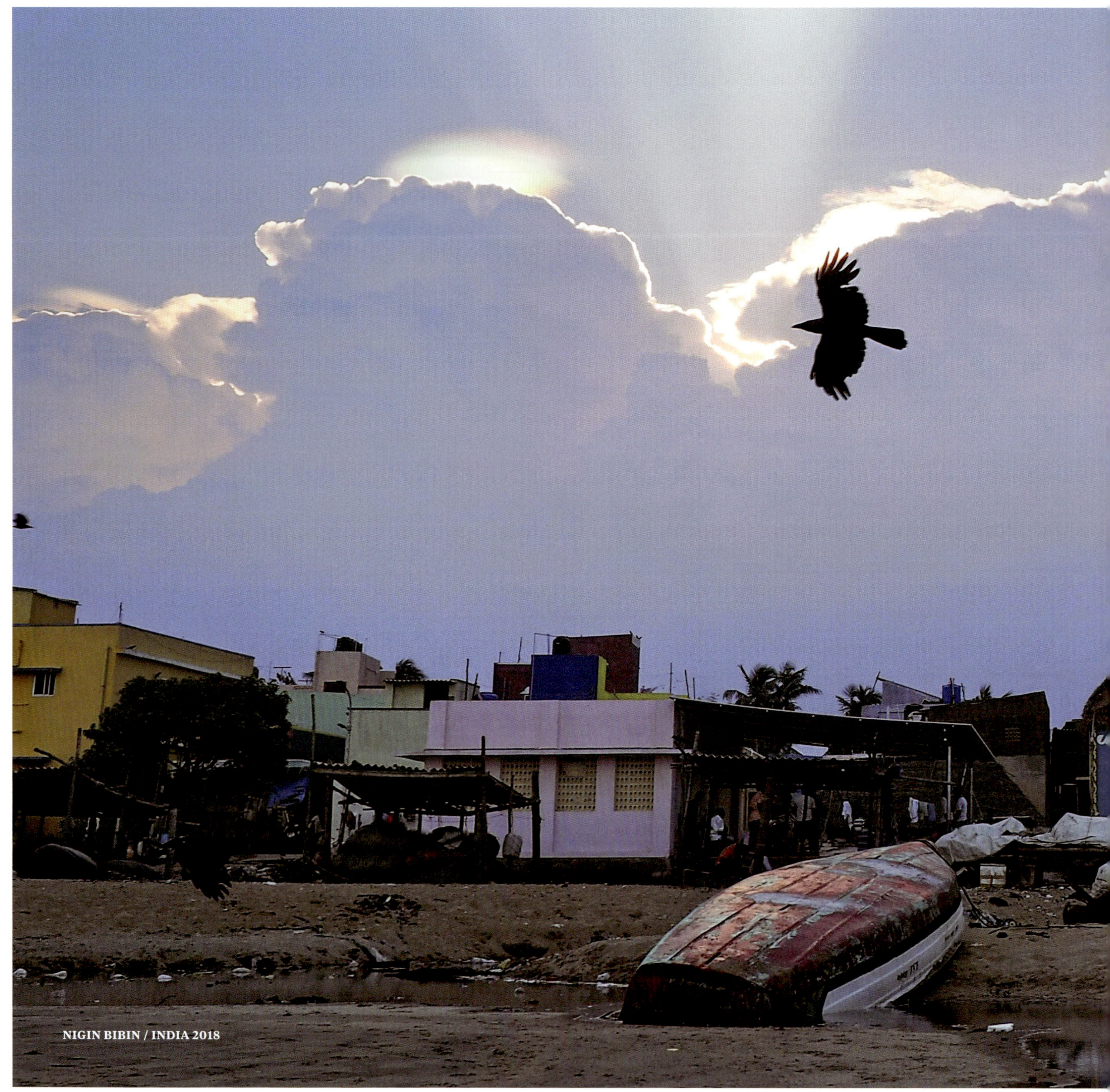

NIGIN BIBIN / INDIA 2018

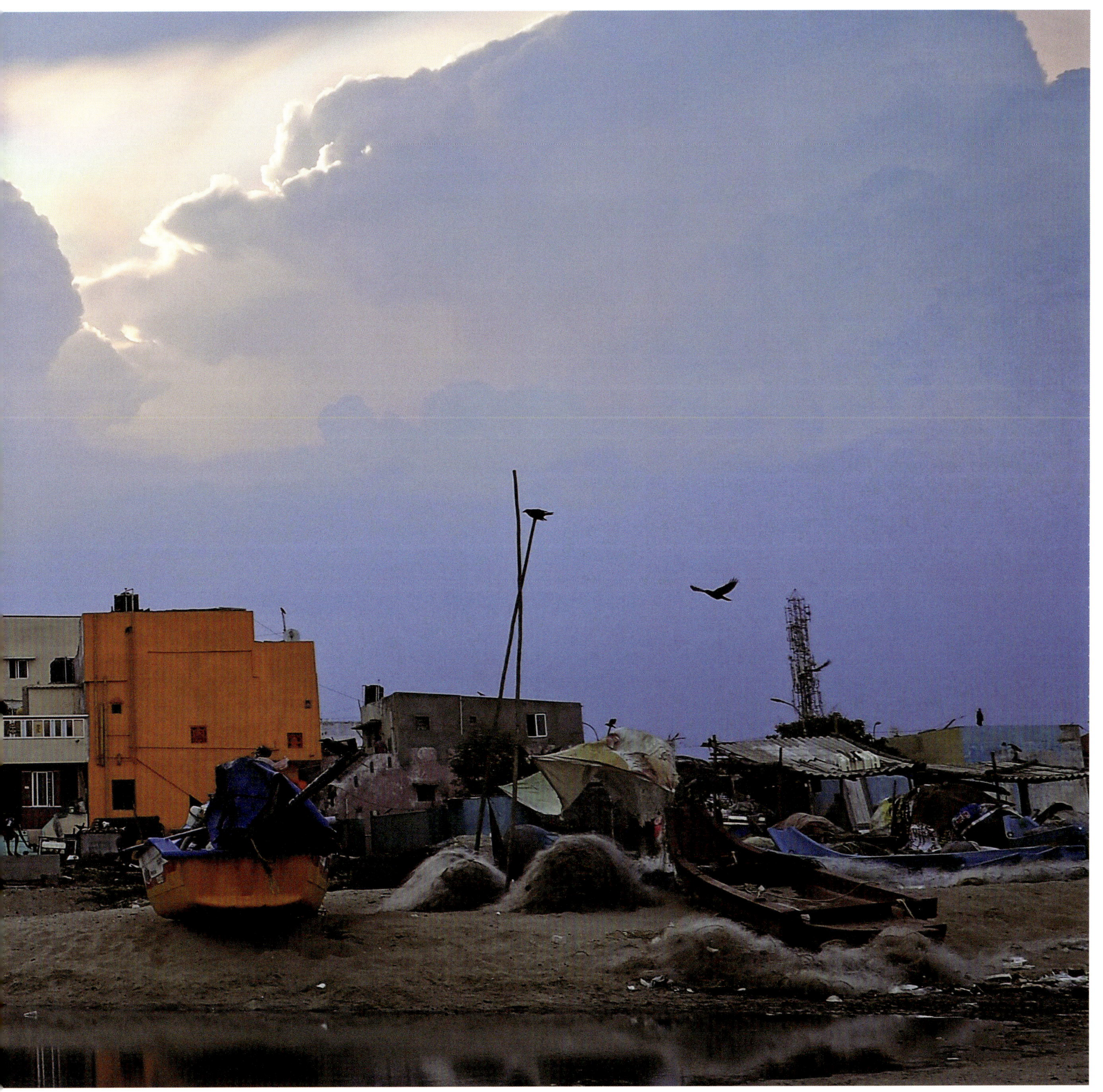

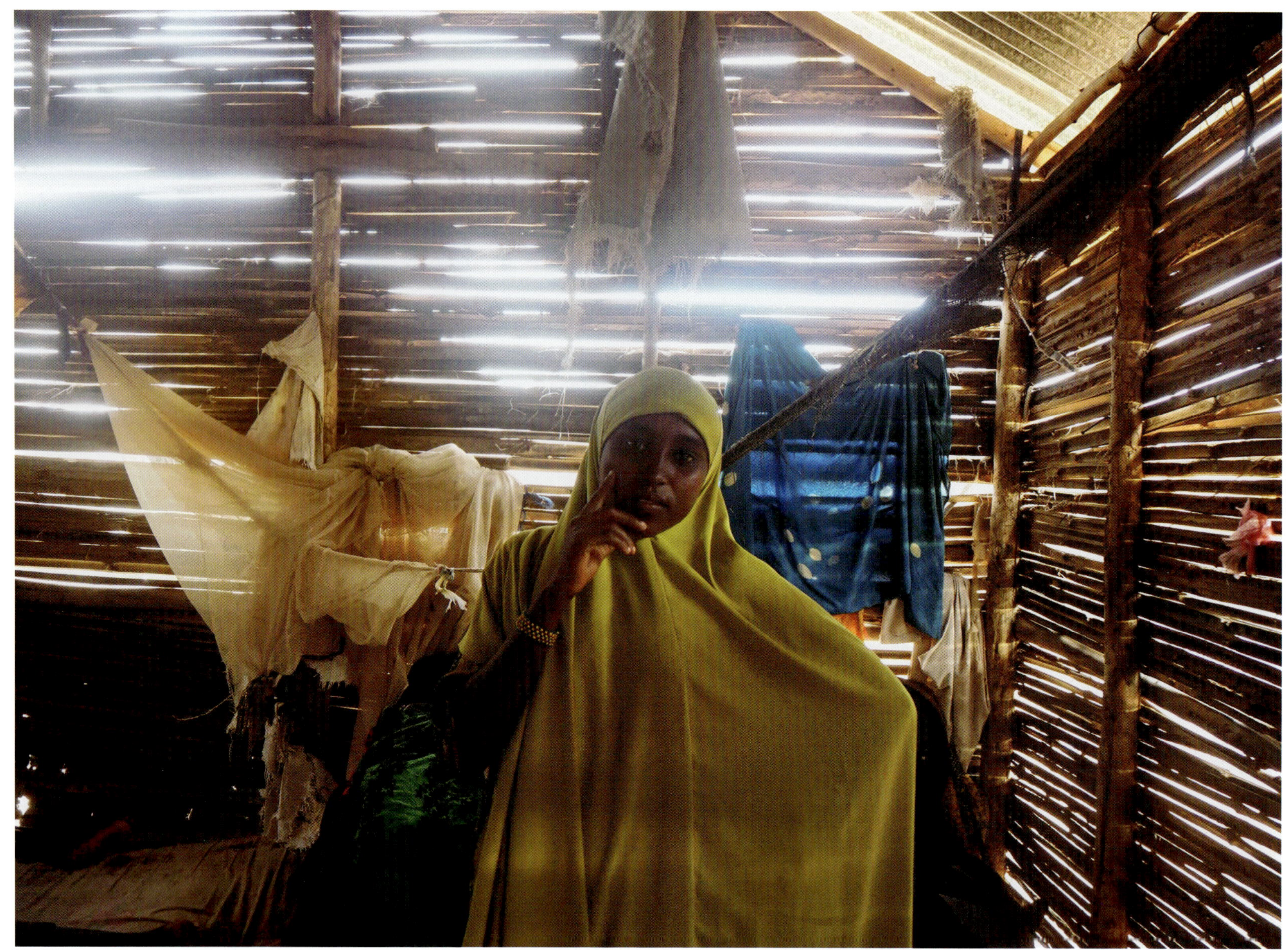

HIBO ABDIKADIR / ETHIOPIA 2019

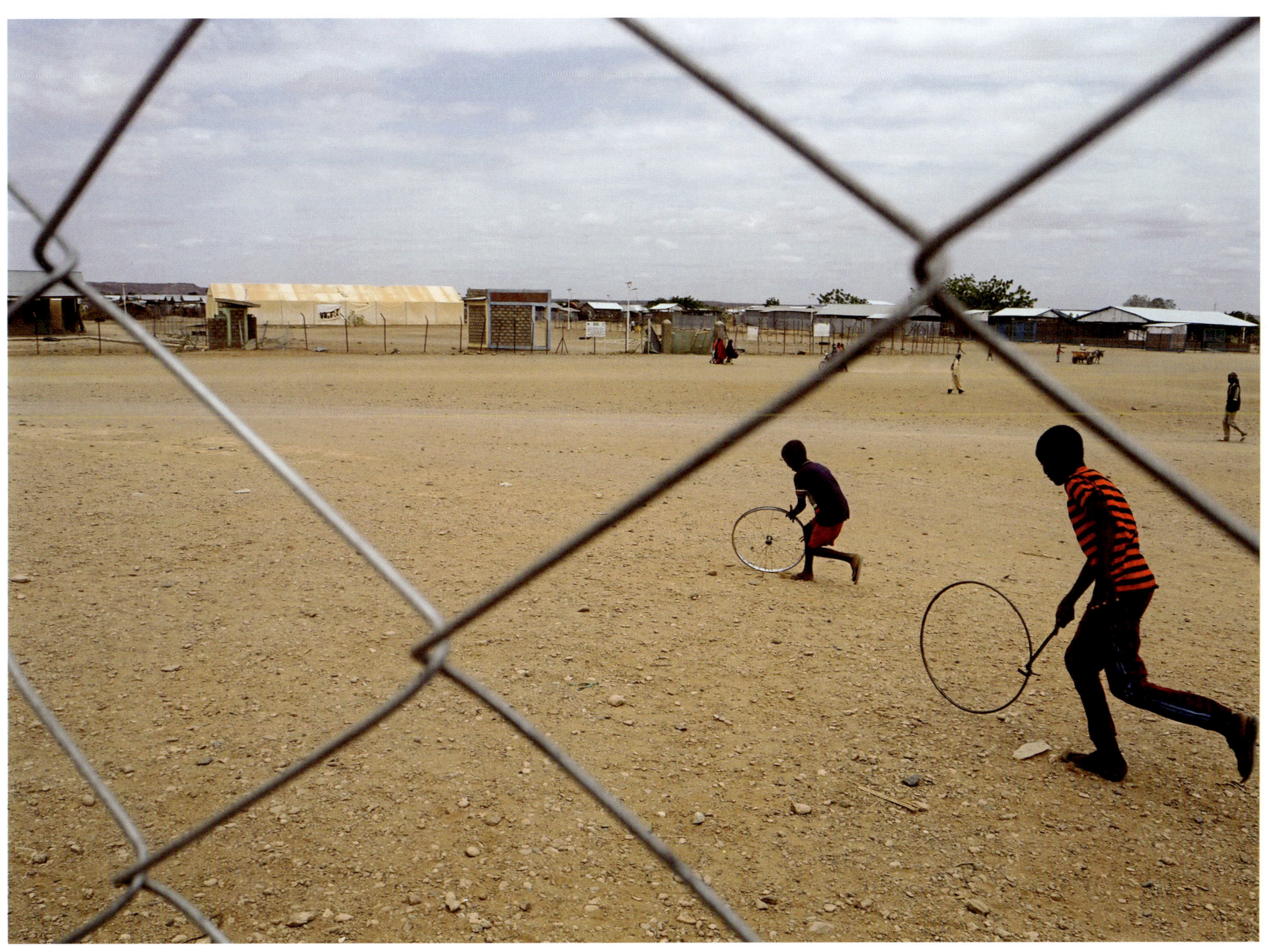

HASAN ADAN / ETHIOPIA 2019

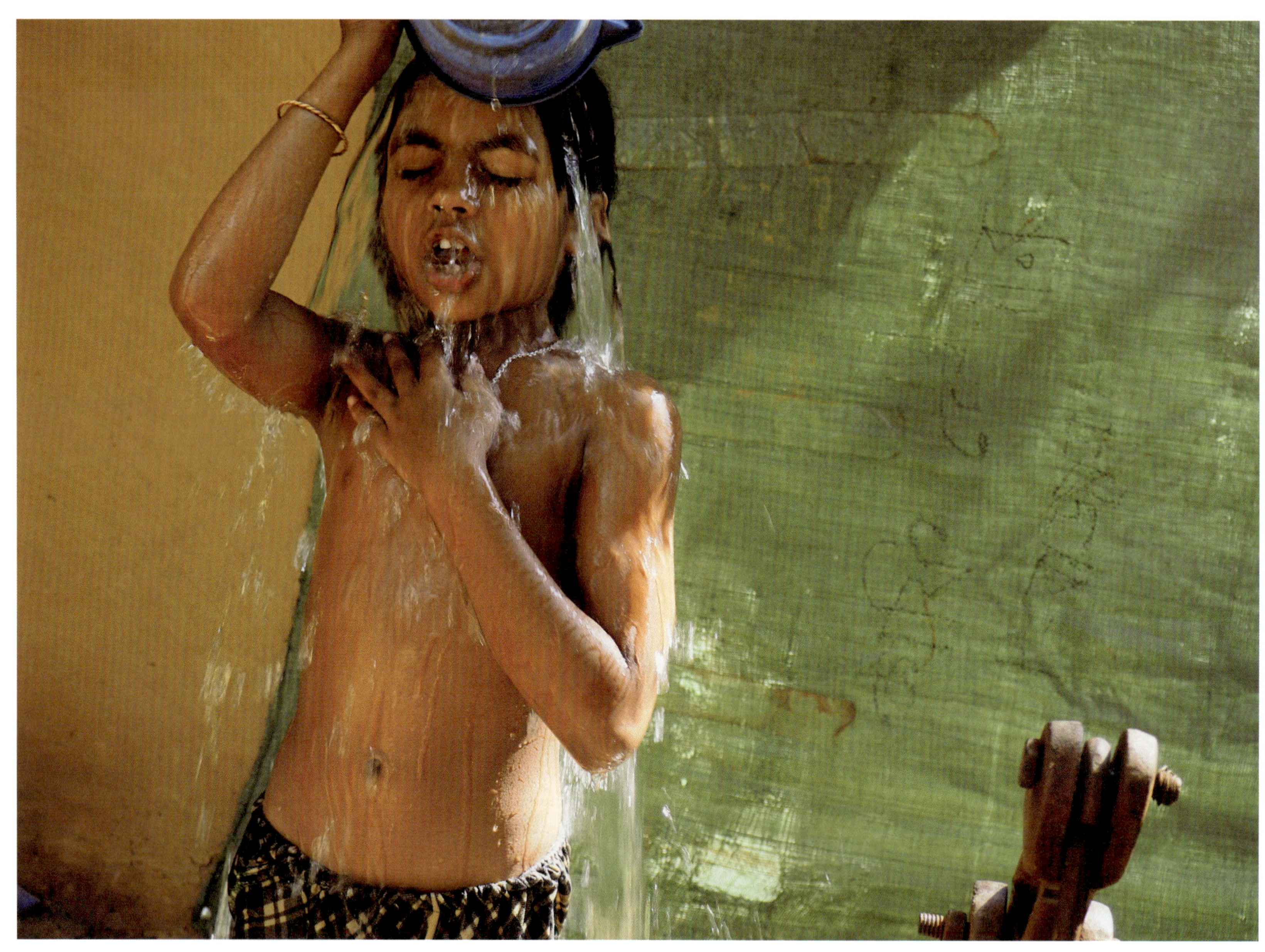

PAPIYA SHABNAM KEYA / BANGLADESH 2019

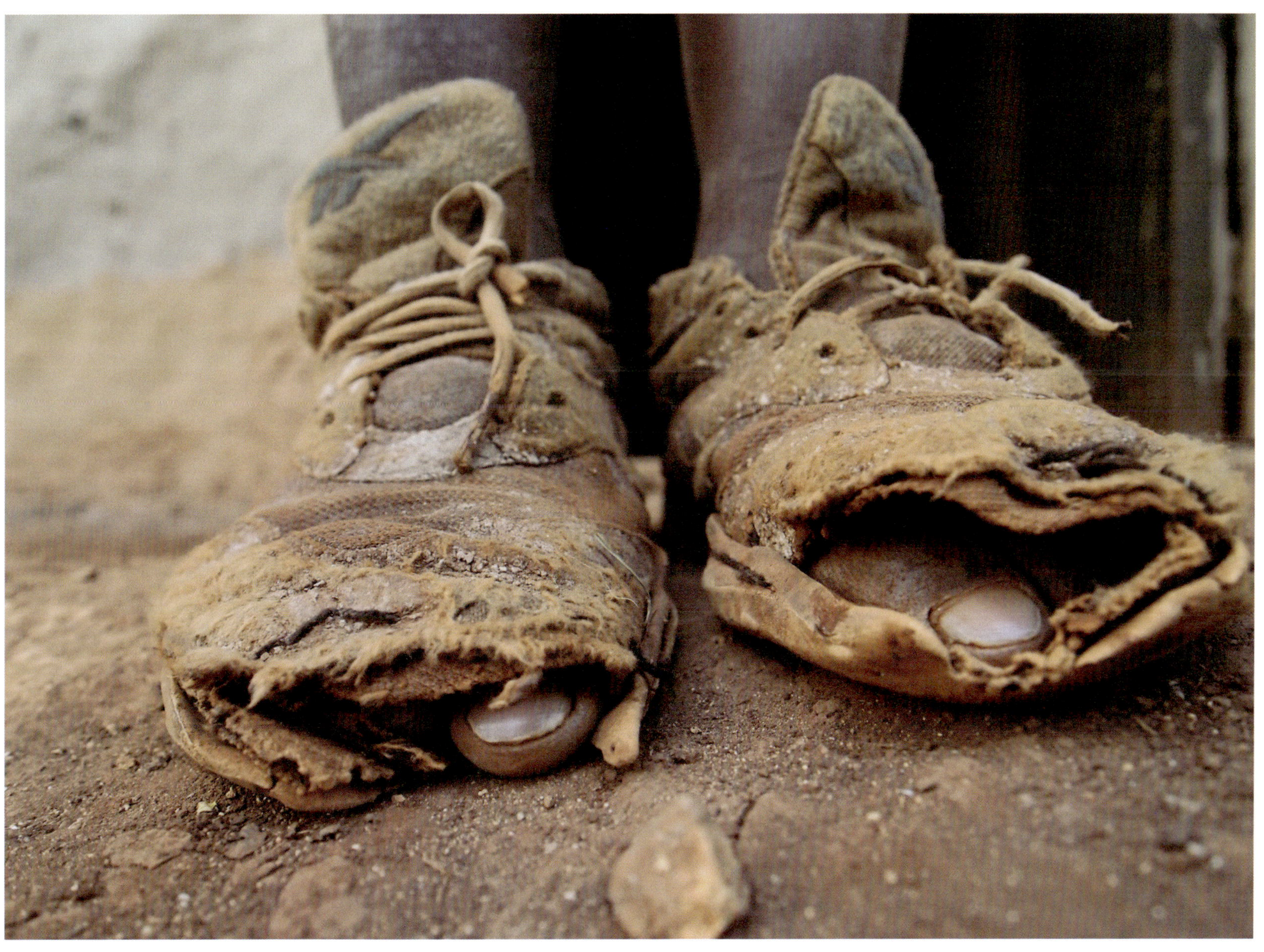

AGATHA NGOTHO / KENYA 2014

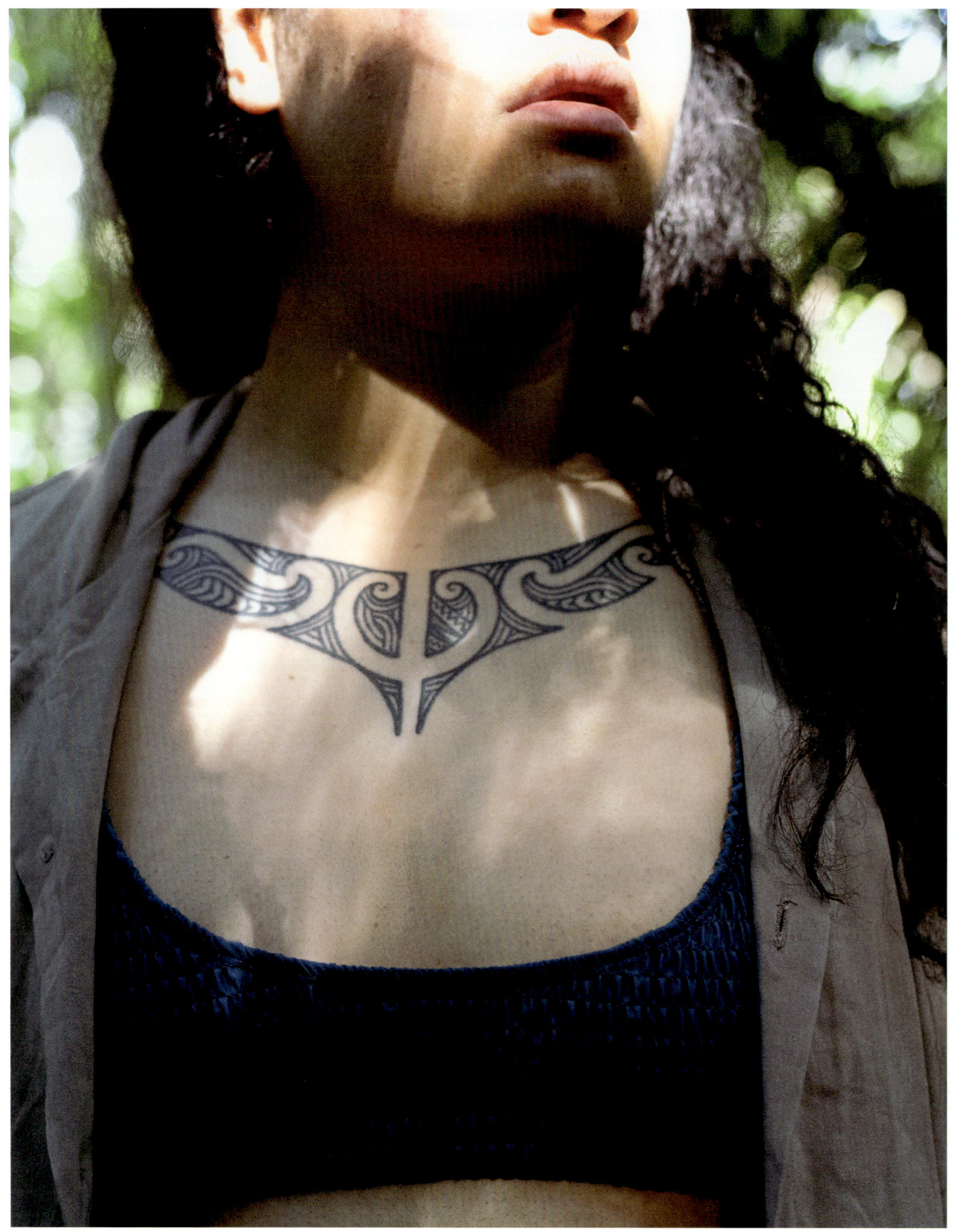

"My hair is a feature carried down from my Māori and Samoan* tīpuna *[ancestors] that I was ashamed of as a young teenager. My nose and lips, my skin and my* tā moko *[traditional Māori tattoos] represent my* whakapapa *[genealogy].

Growing up in a mainstream education and disconnected from my culture, I was always trying to hide [who I was] from those who surrounded me. I was fortunate to reconnect with my language and culture. The things that I was too ashamed to show others are now parts of me that I put at the forefront of my identity."

—TE AHO JORDAN, MURUPARA, NEW ZEALAND 2019

TE AHO JORDAN / NEW ZEALAND 2019

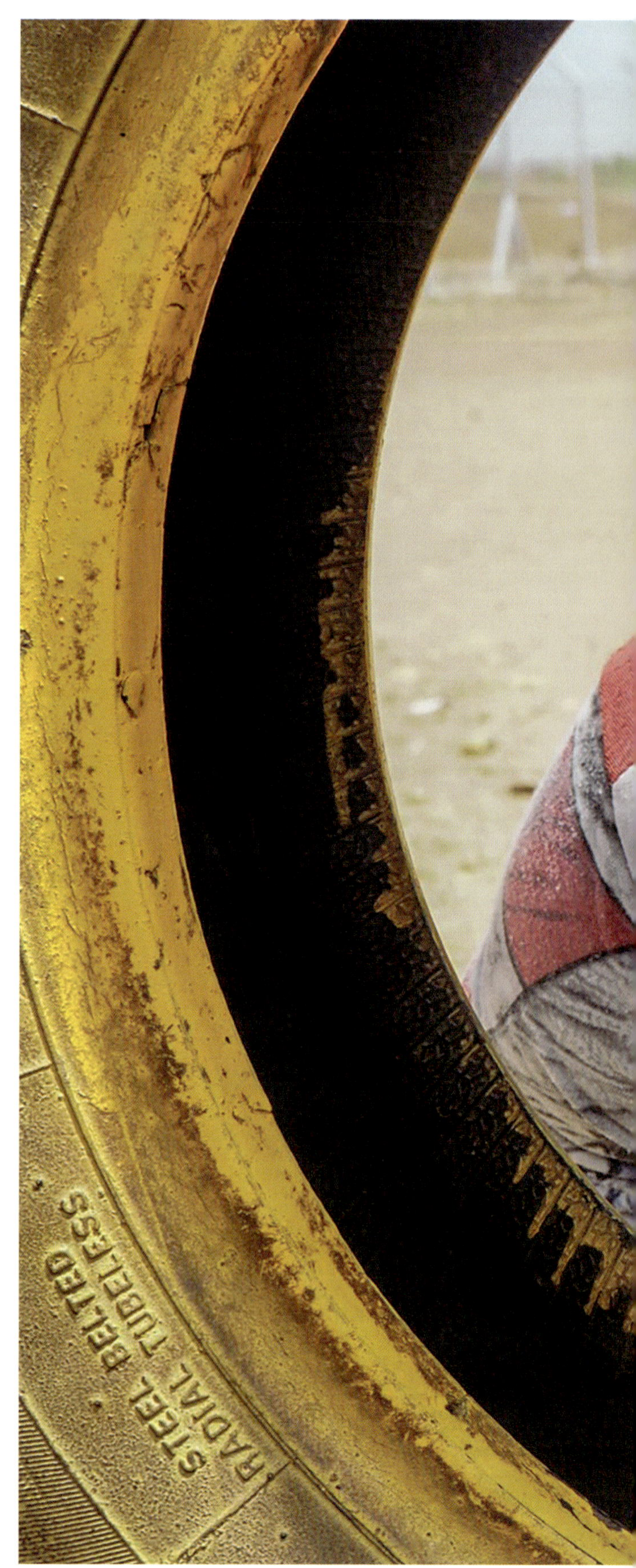

FLORA MERCY JAMES / UGANDA 2018

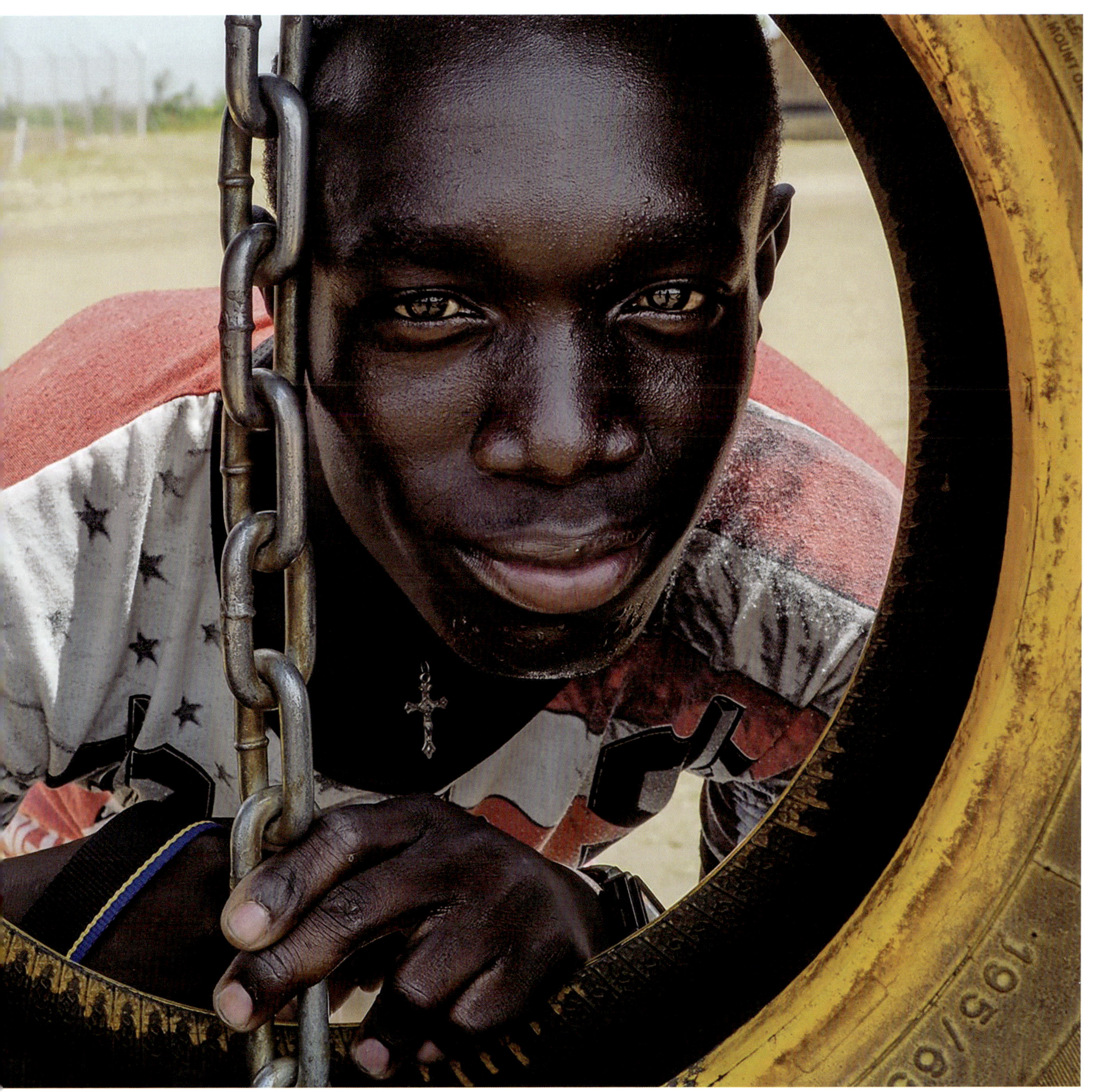

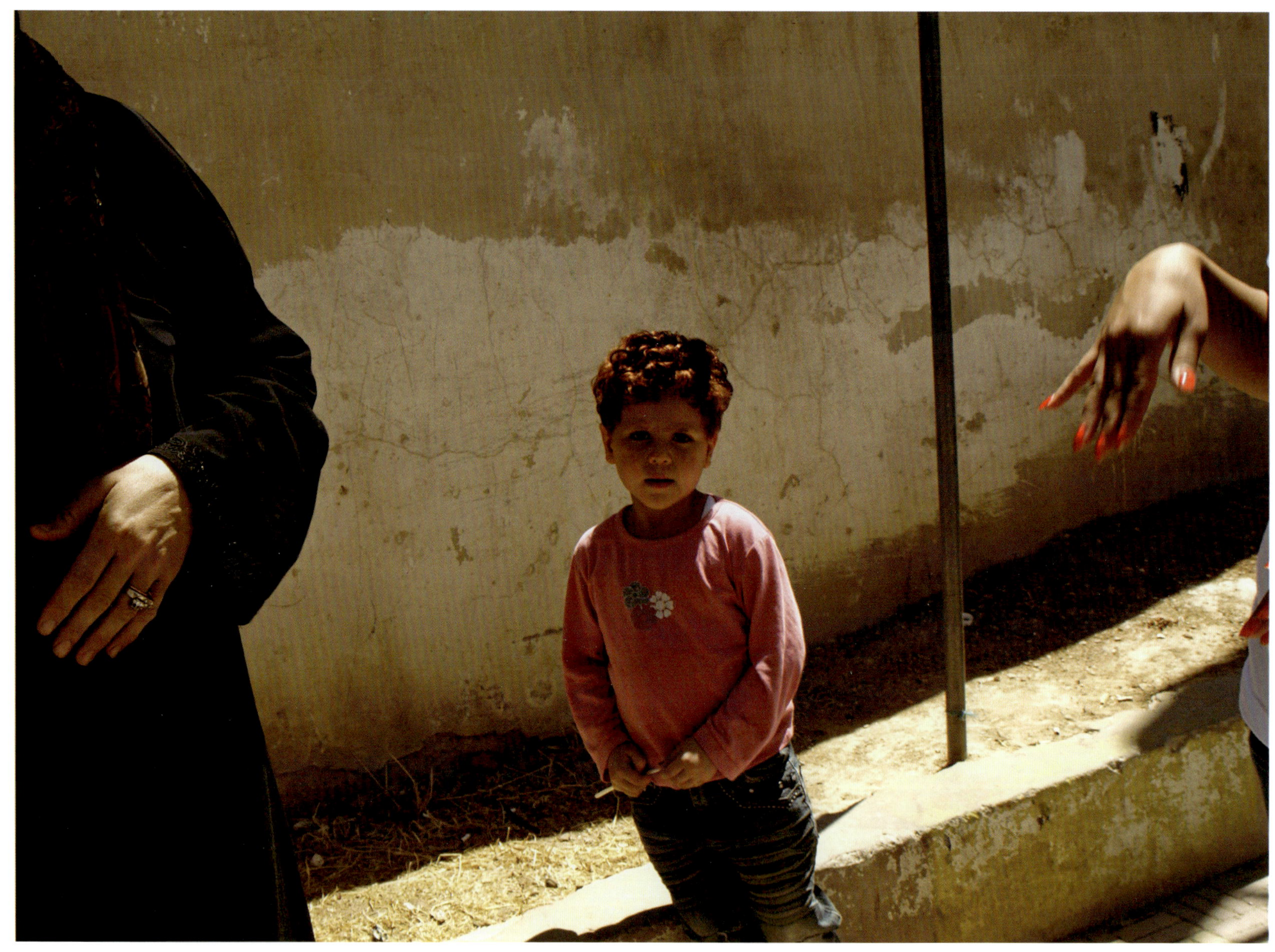

ZUBAIDA NABEEL / JORDAN 2009

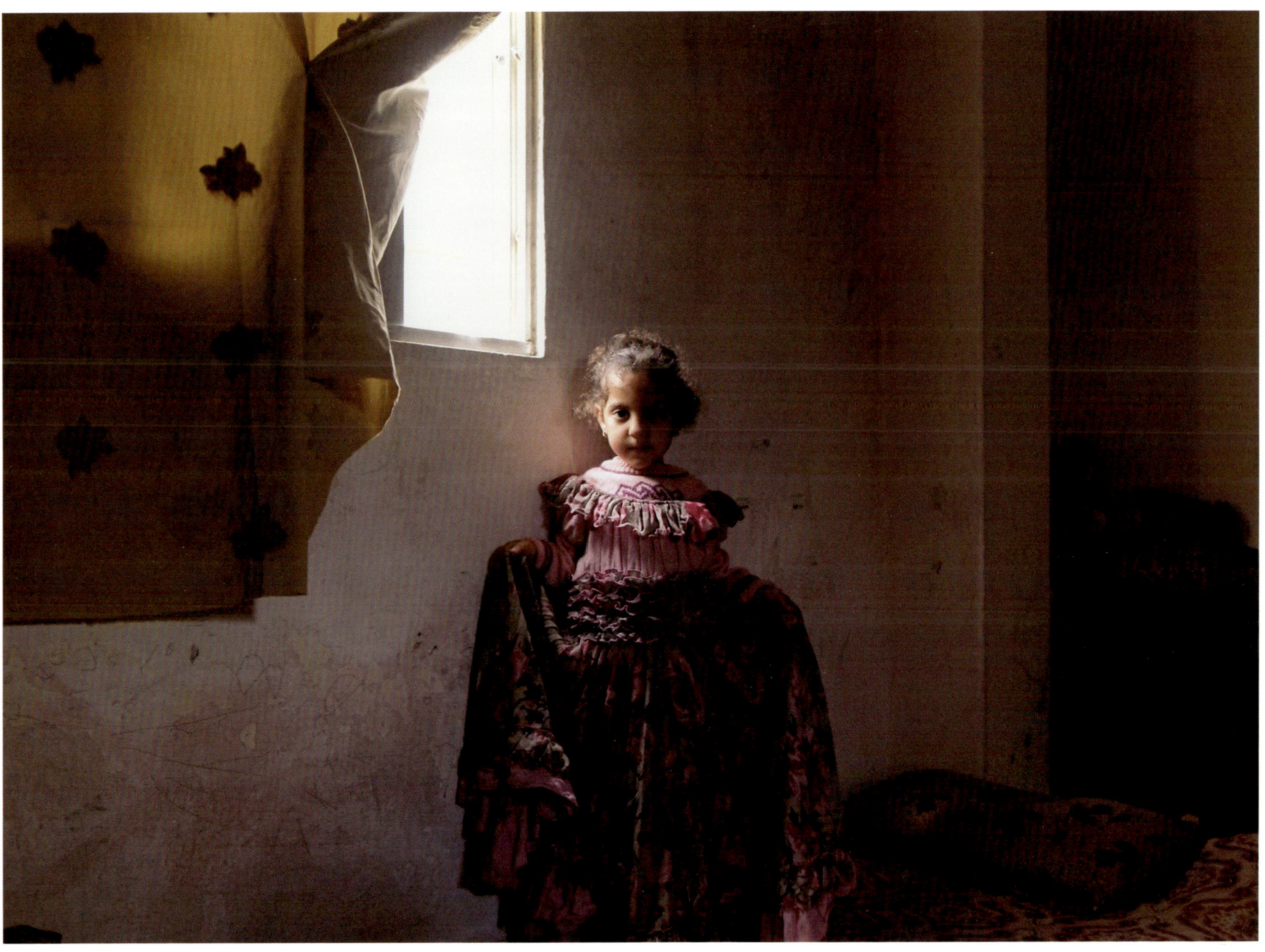

OMAR AL ZOUBI / JORDAN 2009

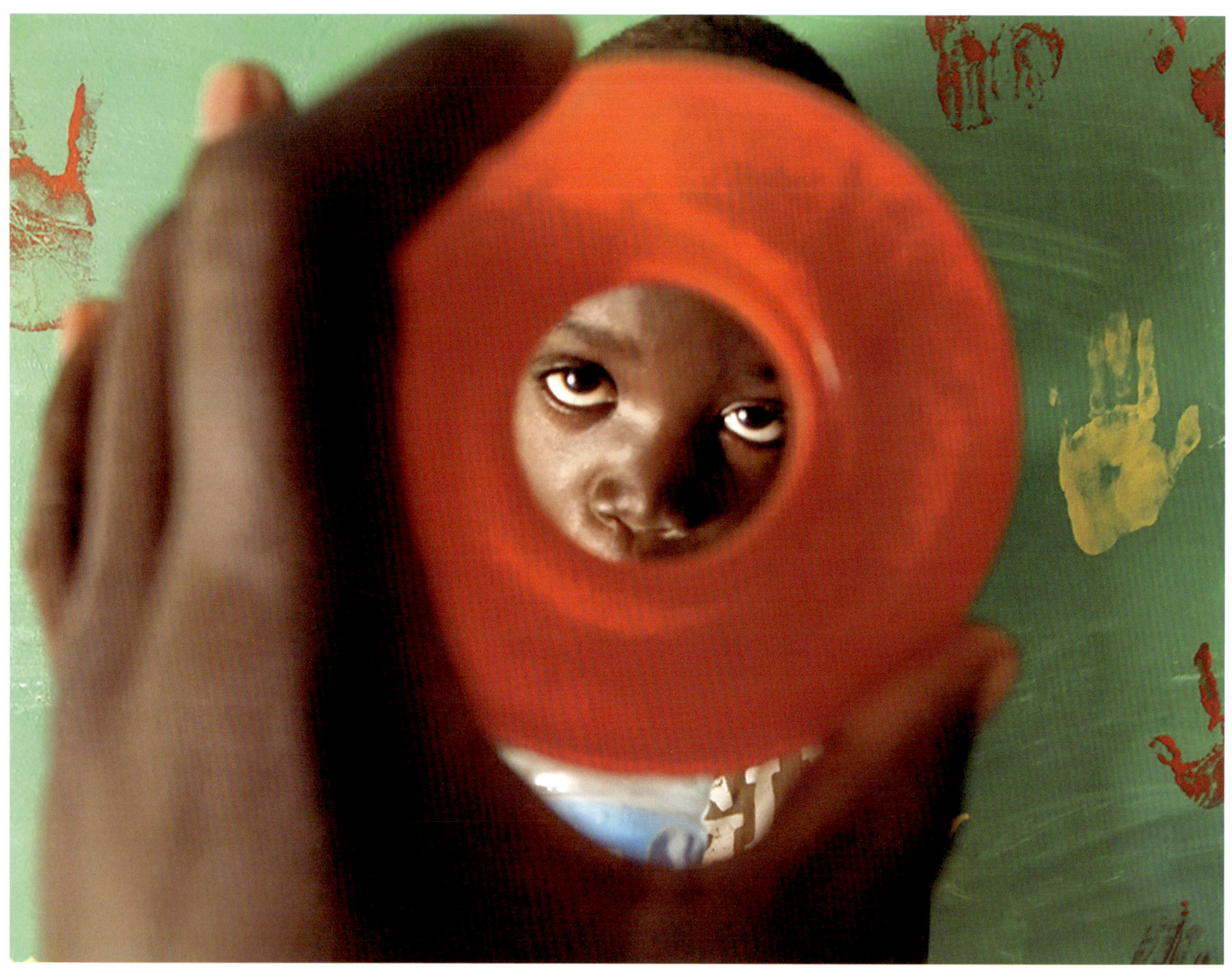

AZMAT ULLAH / SOUTH SUDAN 2014

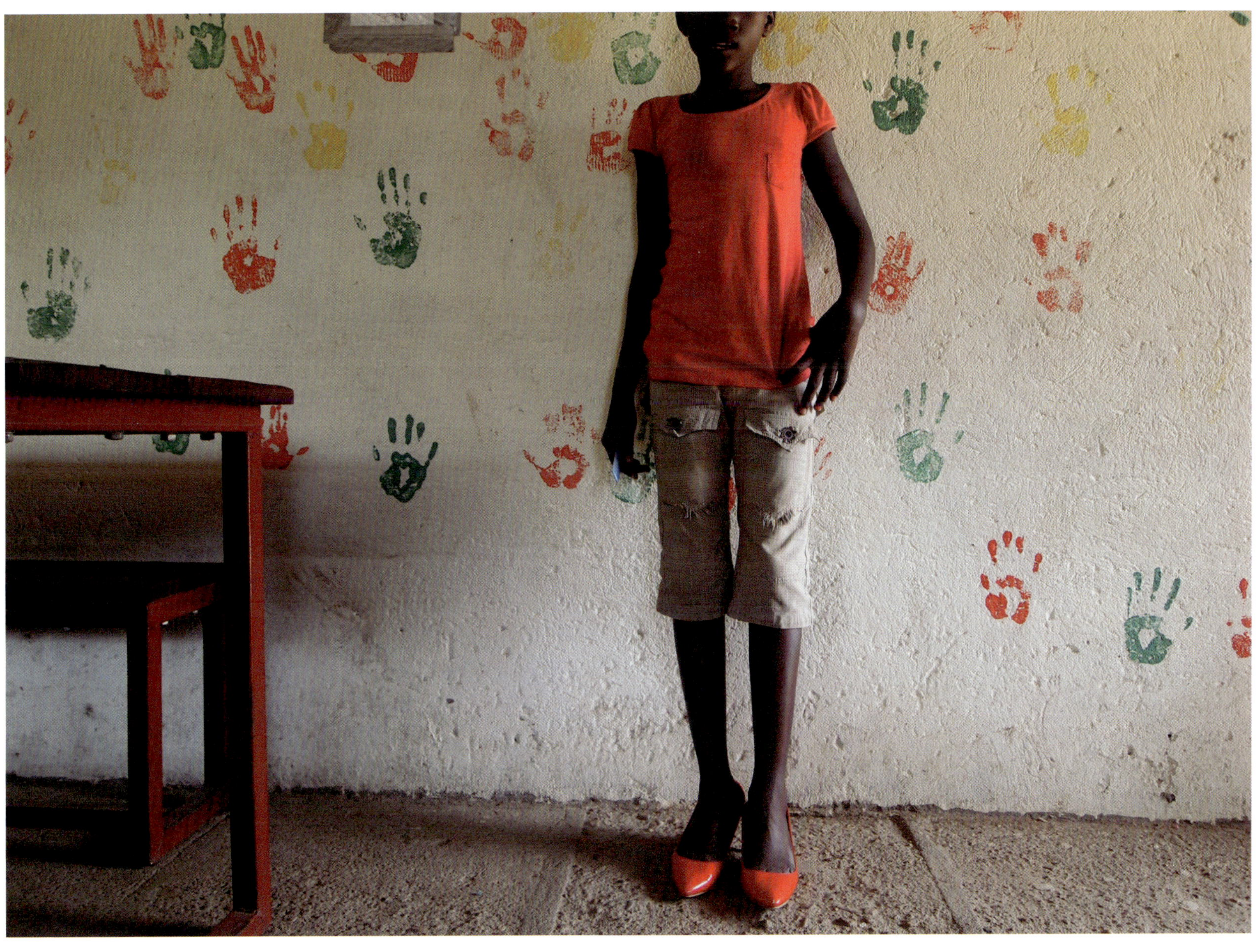

DOTJANG AGANY AWER / SOUTH SUDAN 2014

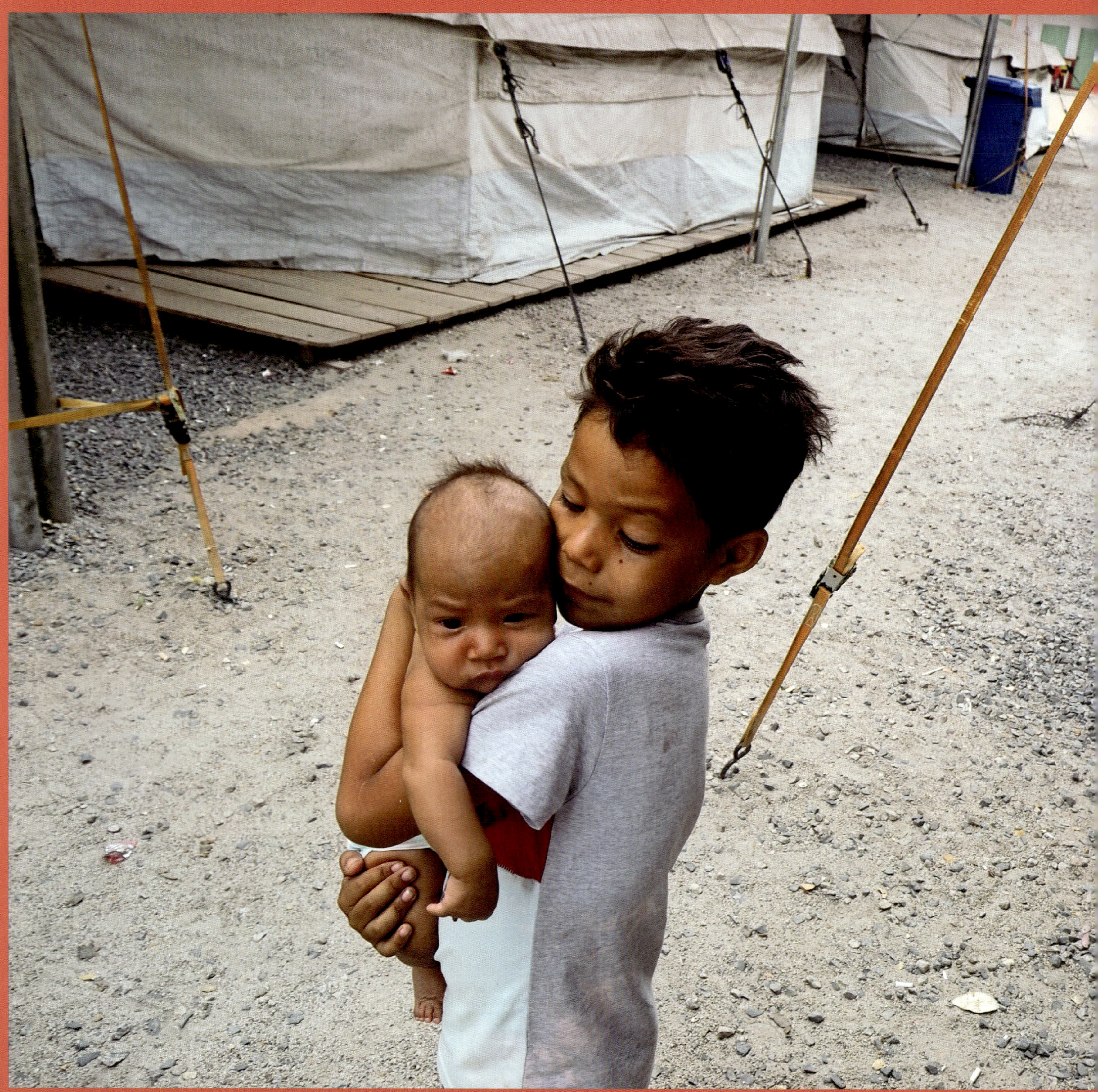

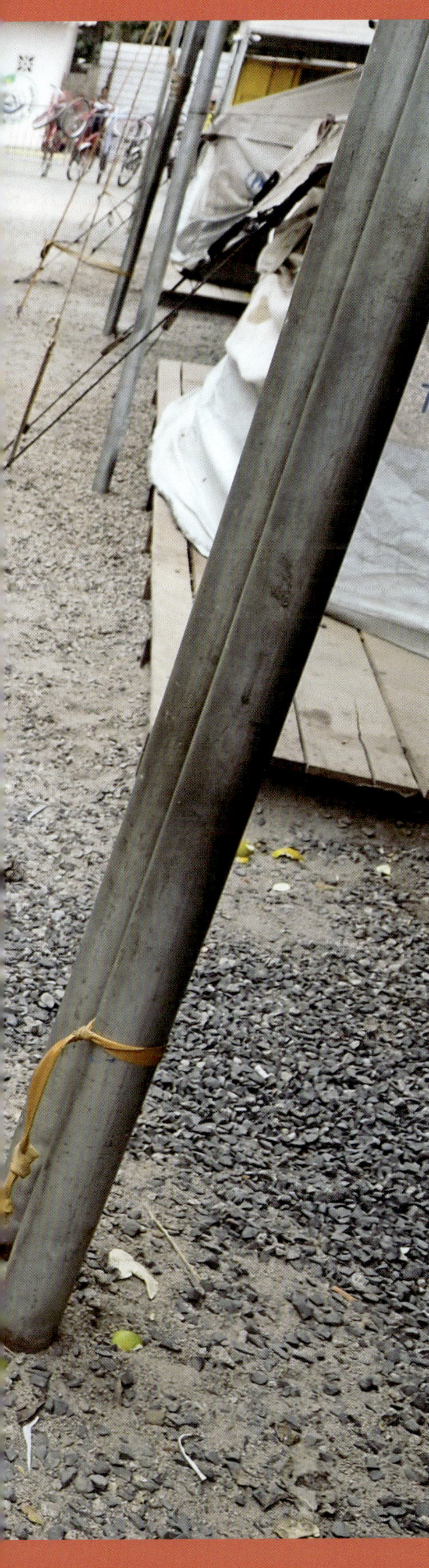

Camp Profile
Brazil 2019

THEY FLED THROUGH THE AMAZON RAINFOREST ON FOOT, counting the miles from their homes in Venezuela to the Brazilian refugee camp of Boa Vista. They left behind a country in political turmoil and economic collapse, with some, like Marco Antonio Rizalez, running from persecution. "When I turned 20, after hiding in order not to be arrested and disappeared by the government, I decided to travel to Brazil," he said. "I came here to save my life."

When they arrived at Photo Camp, students like Marco had a chance to put aside anything that might be happening in their lives and focus on photography and writing. The participants spent five days exploring the world around them as the curious young people they were. Mentor Luján Agusti, recalling the students' excitement swimming in a river, says Photo Camp gave the young people who had experienced displacement a reminder that their lives would be normal again someday. The students' photographic work portrays the camp as a place of makeshift harmony: boys playing soccer as the sun goes down, a woman with her baby on a hammock. Katiuska Del Valle Prado Garcia captured the group's enthusiasm when she wrote, "I have loved having a camera in my hands and being able to hear and photograph my Venezuelan brothers who are in the same situation as me, living in a shelter, waiting for the will of God to change our lives."

KATIUSKA DEL VALLE PRADO GARCIA / BRAZIL 2019

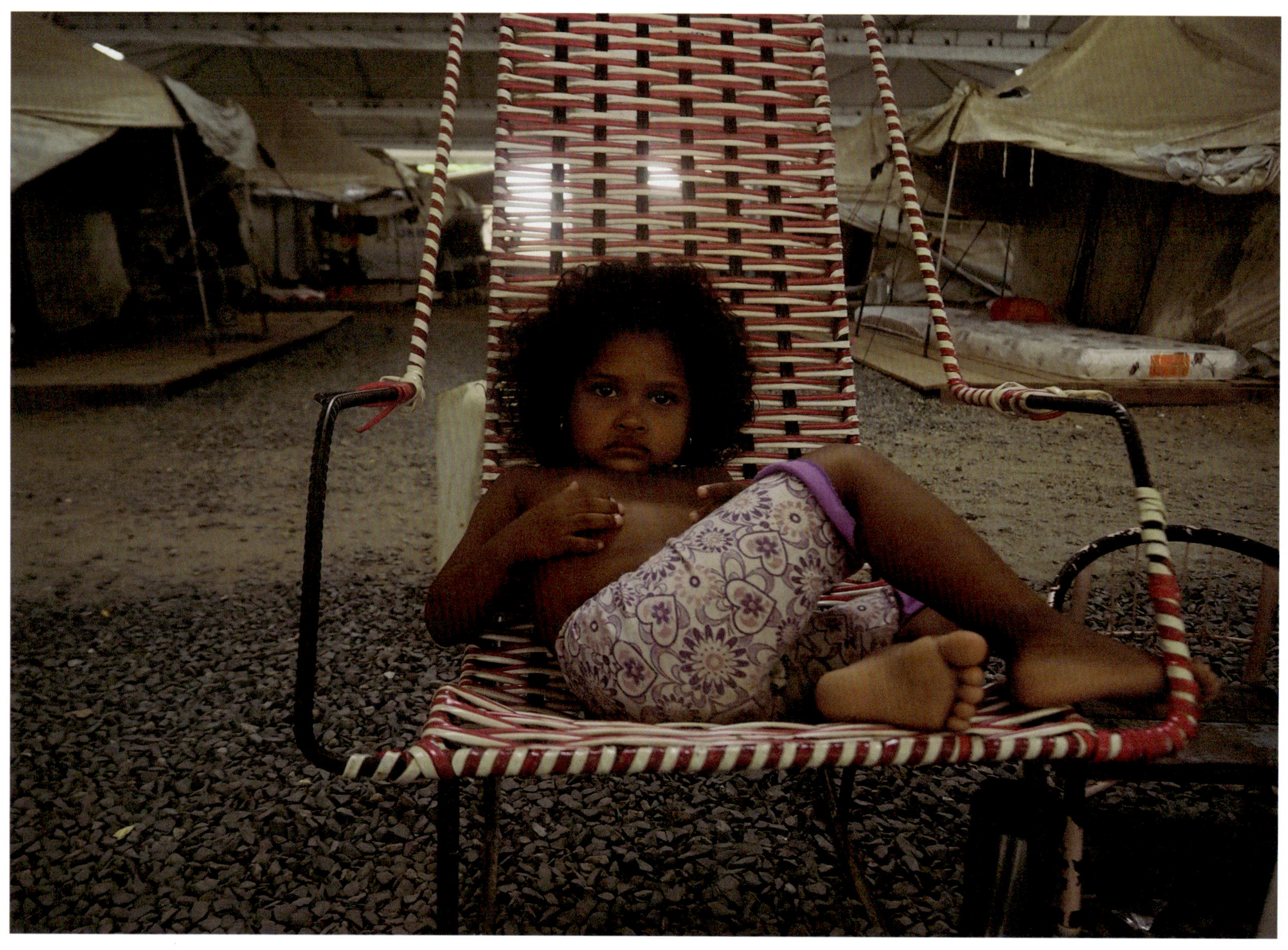

JHORLENIS JINETH DE LA TRINIDAD / BRAZIL 2019

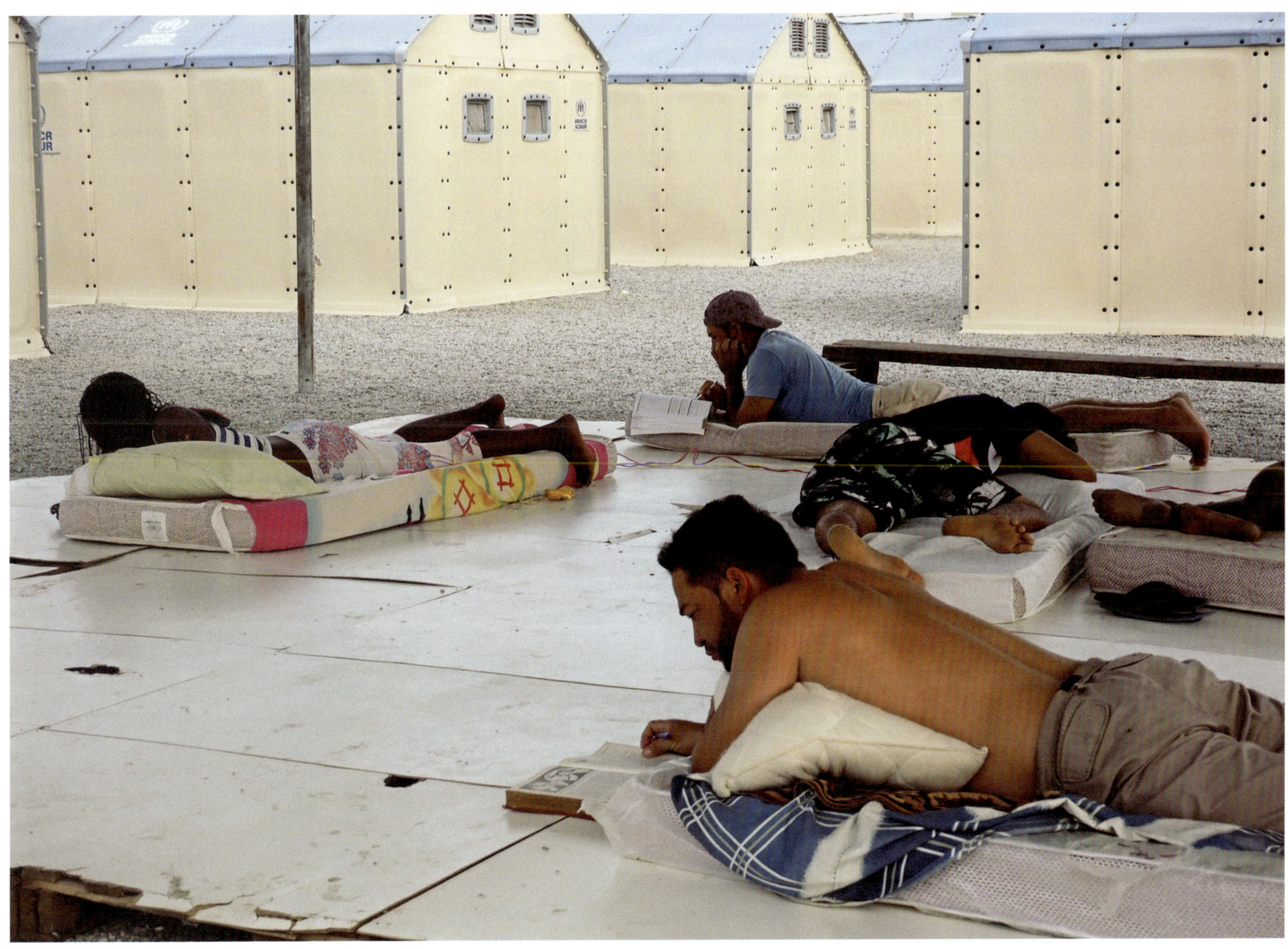

BRAYAN CARMONA / BRAZIL 2019

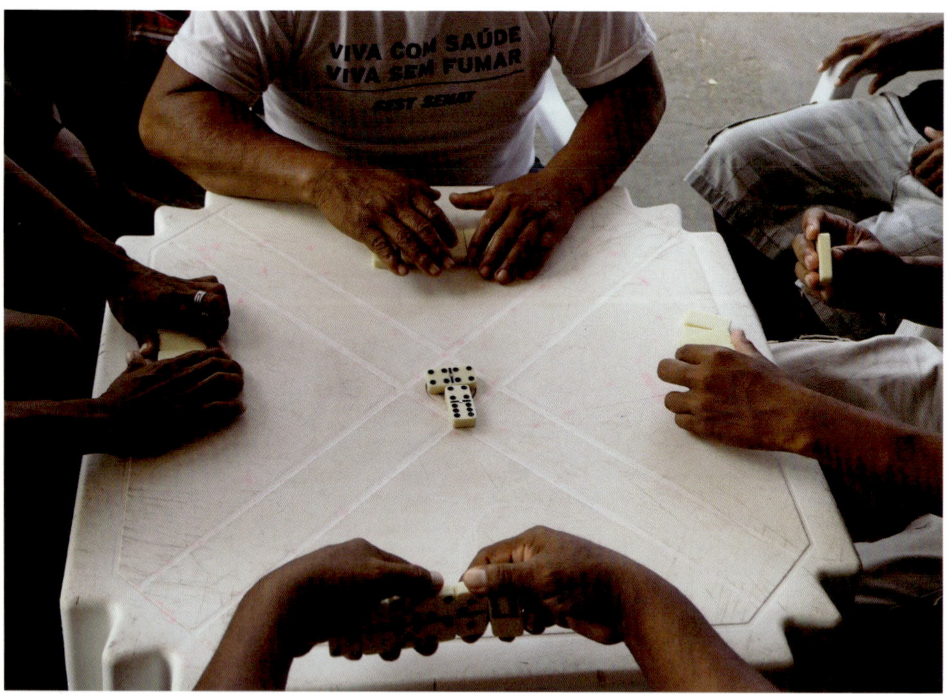

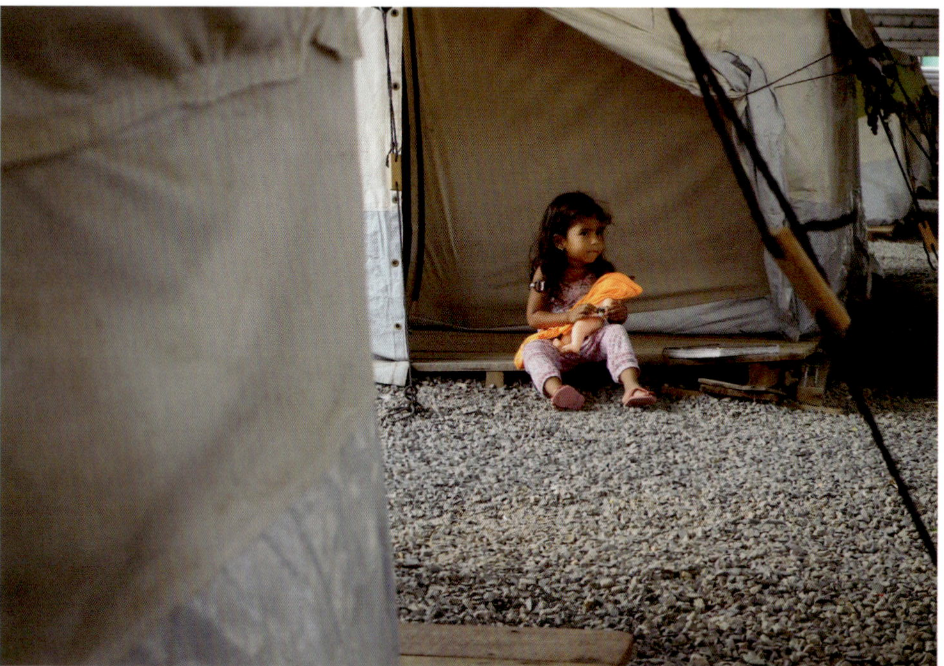

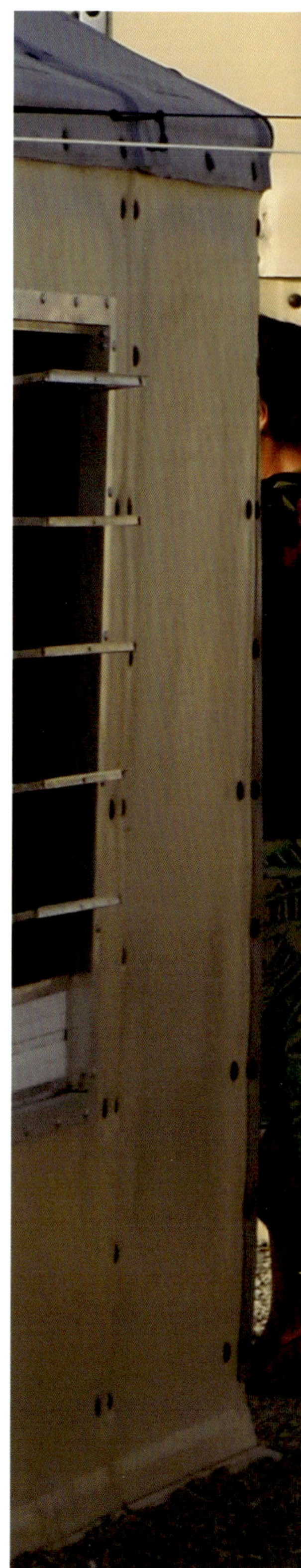

TOP: **GENANGELY PINERO / BRAZIL 2019** ABOVE: **ADRIAN ANTONIO MARTINEZ DANIELDS / BRAZIL 2019** RIGHT: **MARCO ANTONIO RIZALEZ LOPEZ / BRAZIL 2019**

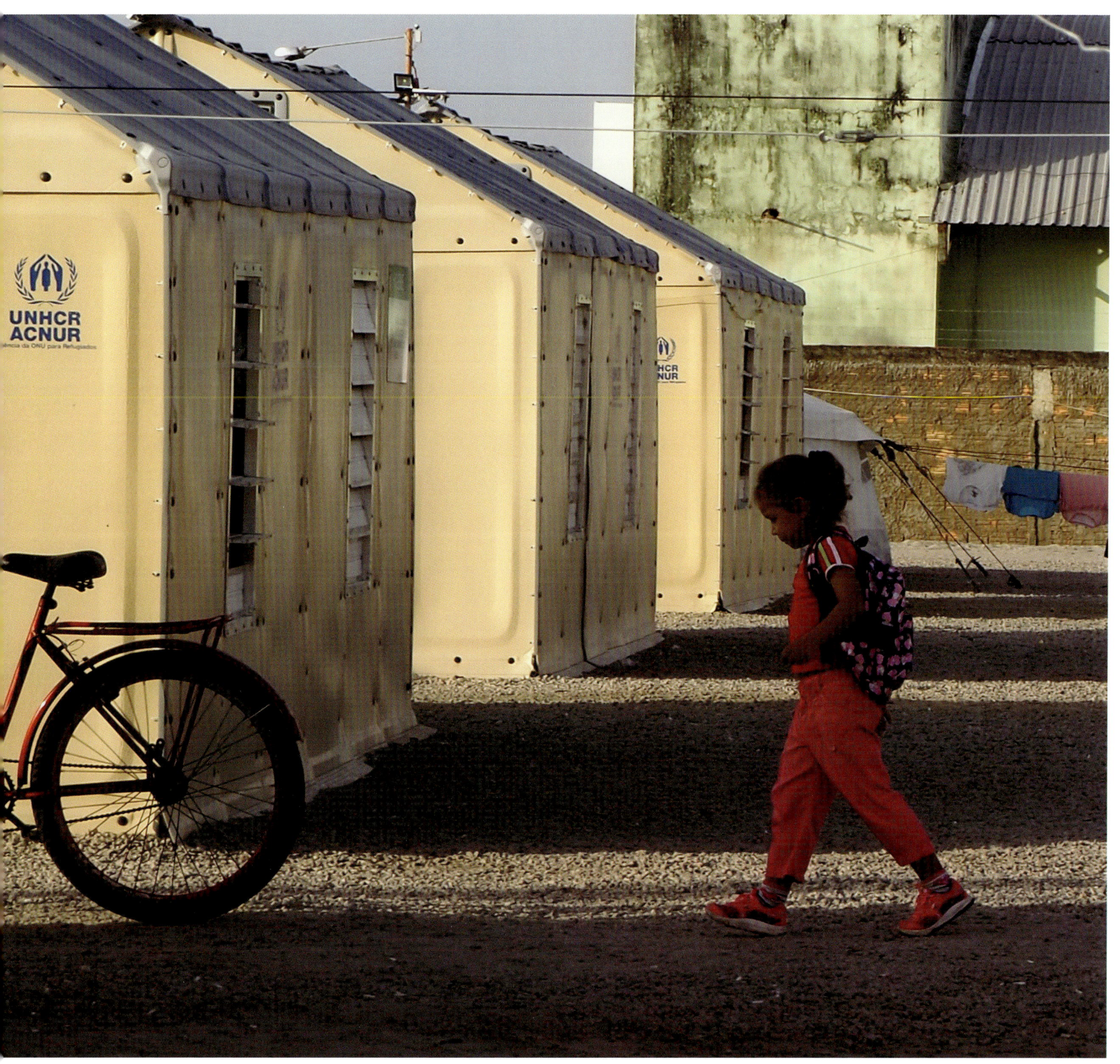
UNHCR
ACNUR

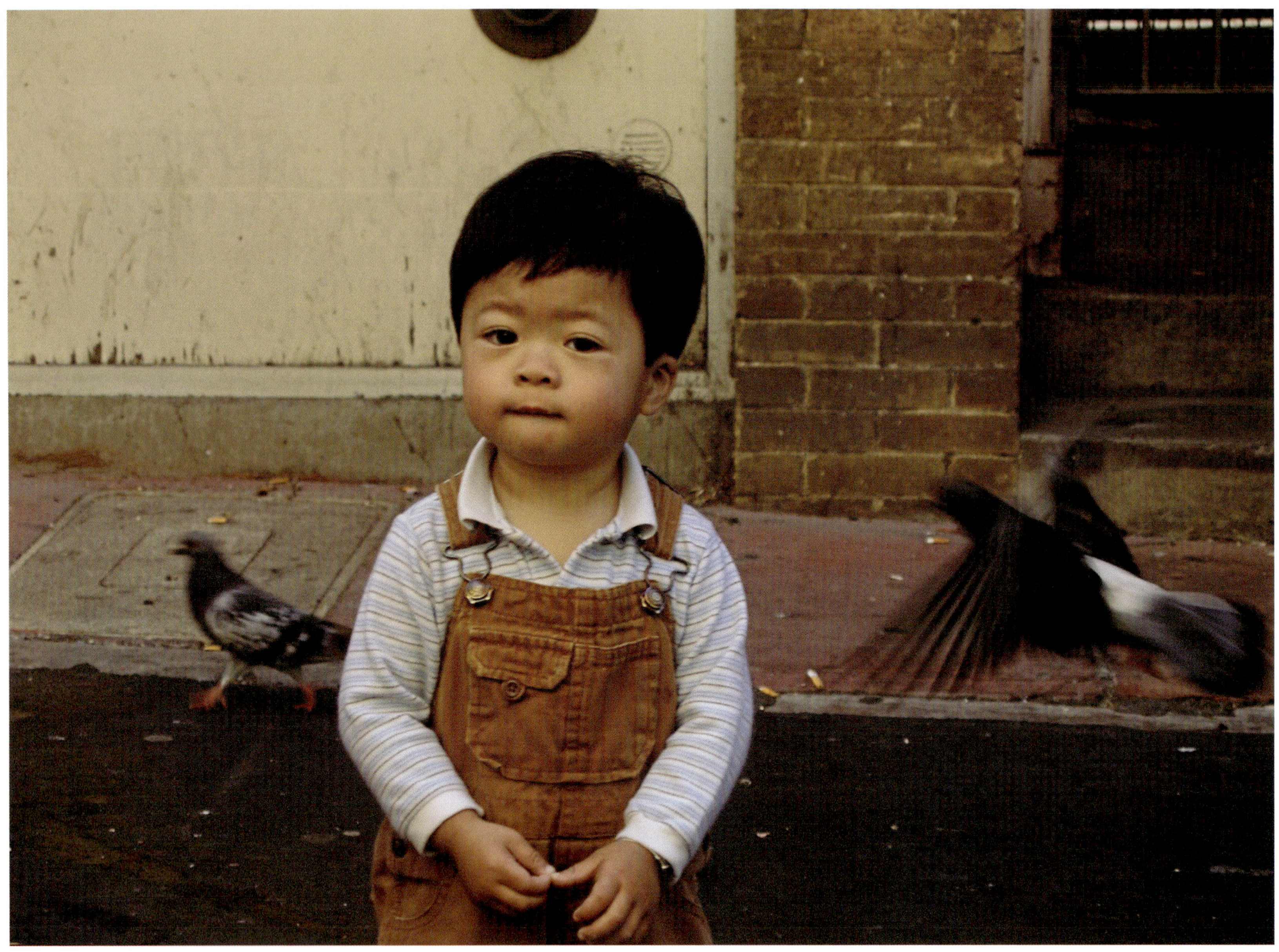

QIAOWEI QUEENIE YU / CALIFORNIA, U.S.A. 2007

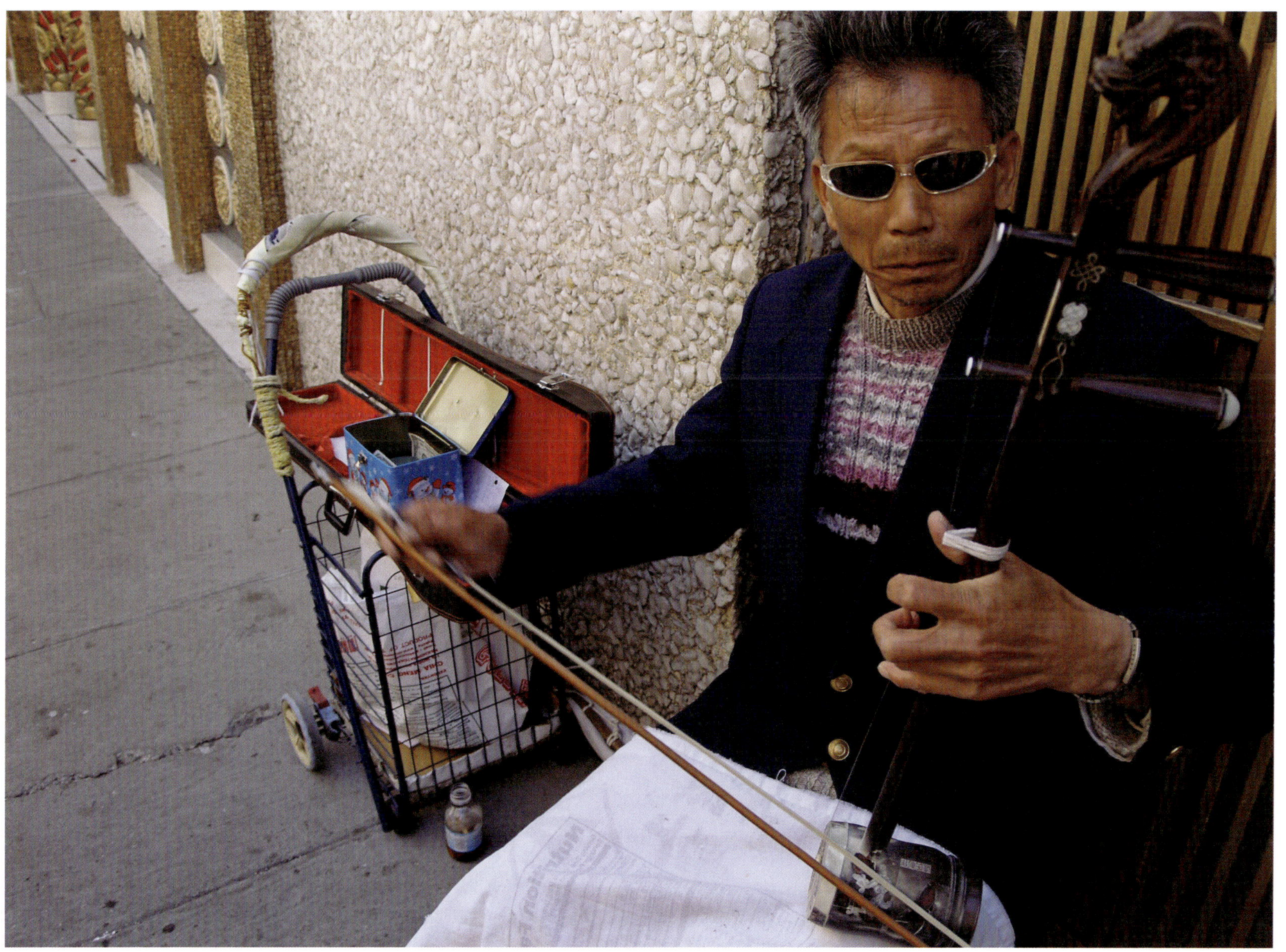

AMY LIU / CALIFORNIA, U.S.A. 2007

NEW YORK, U.S.A.

In 2007, Photo Camp partnered with Newcomers High School in Queens, New York, to create a welcoming and supportive learning environment for immigrant multilingual learners and their families. Students had recently arrived in the United States from six countries and were asked to share their stories through self-portraits, photographs of their communities, and essays about their memories and hopes for the future.

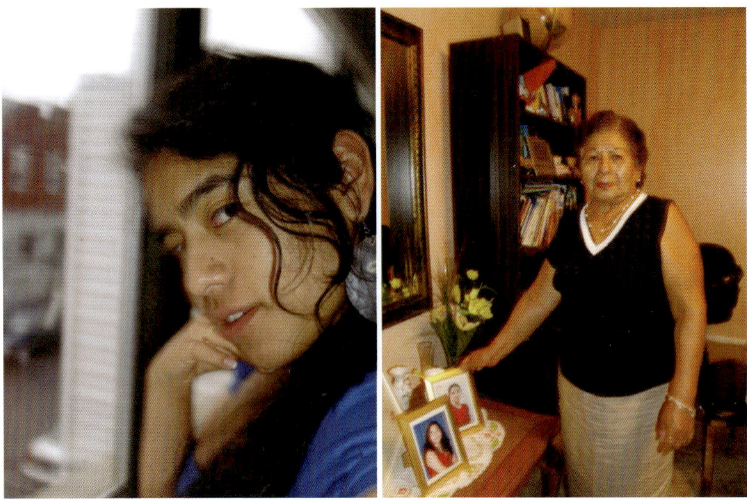

"I remember my native country, Peru—its nature, its coast, its mountains, its jungles. I also remember my lived experiences, my happy childhood, each Sunday in the park, my lovely friends and family. I dream about finishing my high school successfully, going to college, completing my major, and seeing myself as a professional. I want to do everything I can to save lives; simply, I want to be a good doctor."

—SUSAN FLORES

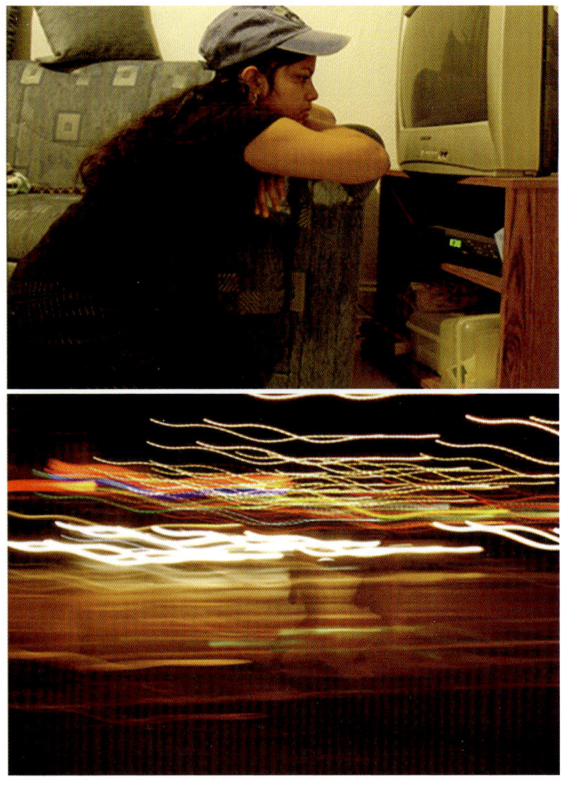

"I remember when I first started photography. I never thought I would be any good, [but now] I dream about becoming a professional photographer. Then my life will have real meaning. I hope that one day, through pictures, I can show people the real face of the world."

—TOWID ARA

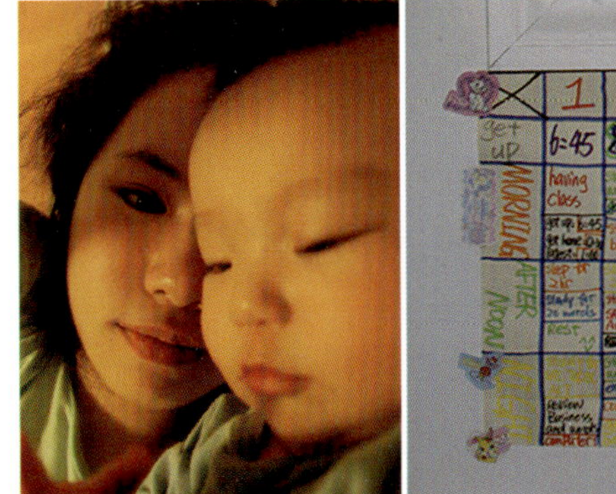

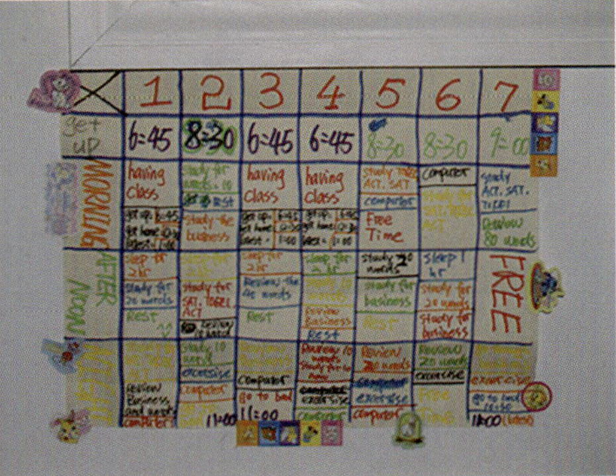

"As I grew up, so many people told me that knowledge is power. In order to be strong, I am eager to absorb knowledge like a sponge."

—YIYANG LI

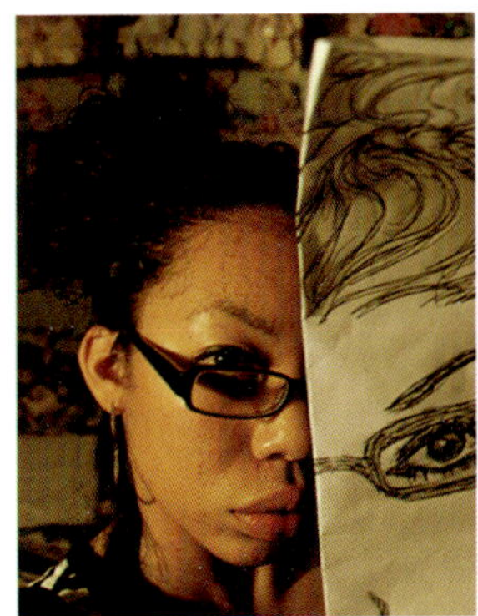

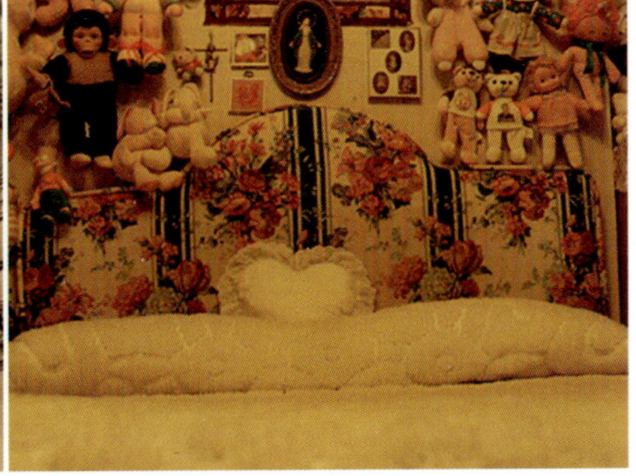

"I dream about a life where I don't have to worry about material things. I hope that the time comes when humans will realize that there's no need for war."

—ARISA WILSON

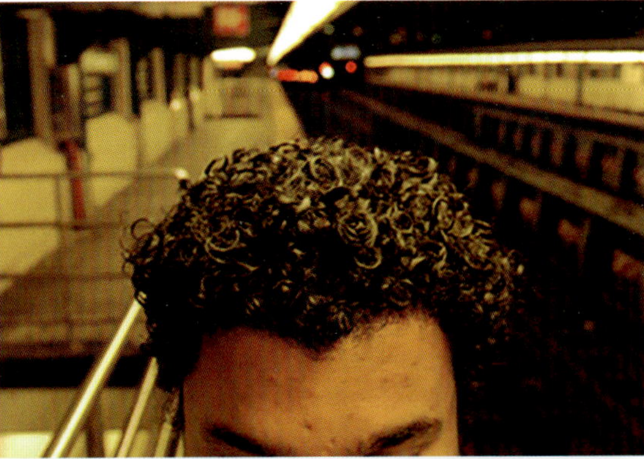

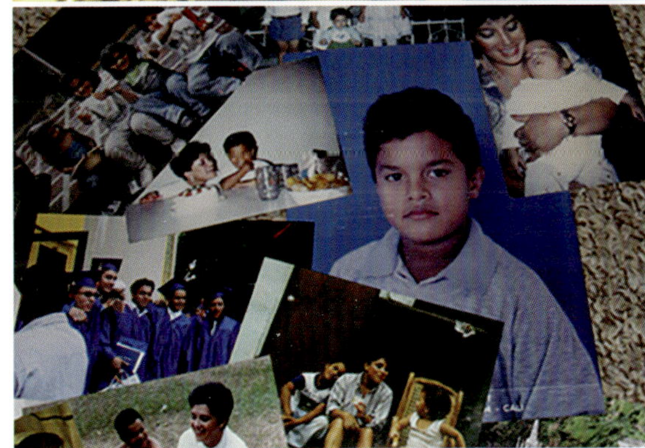

"The thing I remember the most is when my mother didn't have to work six or seven days a week. I hope [someday] to have a stable job, so that my mother does not have to work, and [has] time to paint and enjoy her life."

—YILMAN PINEDA

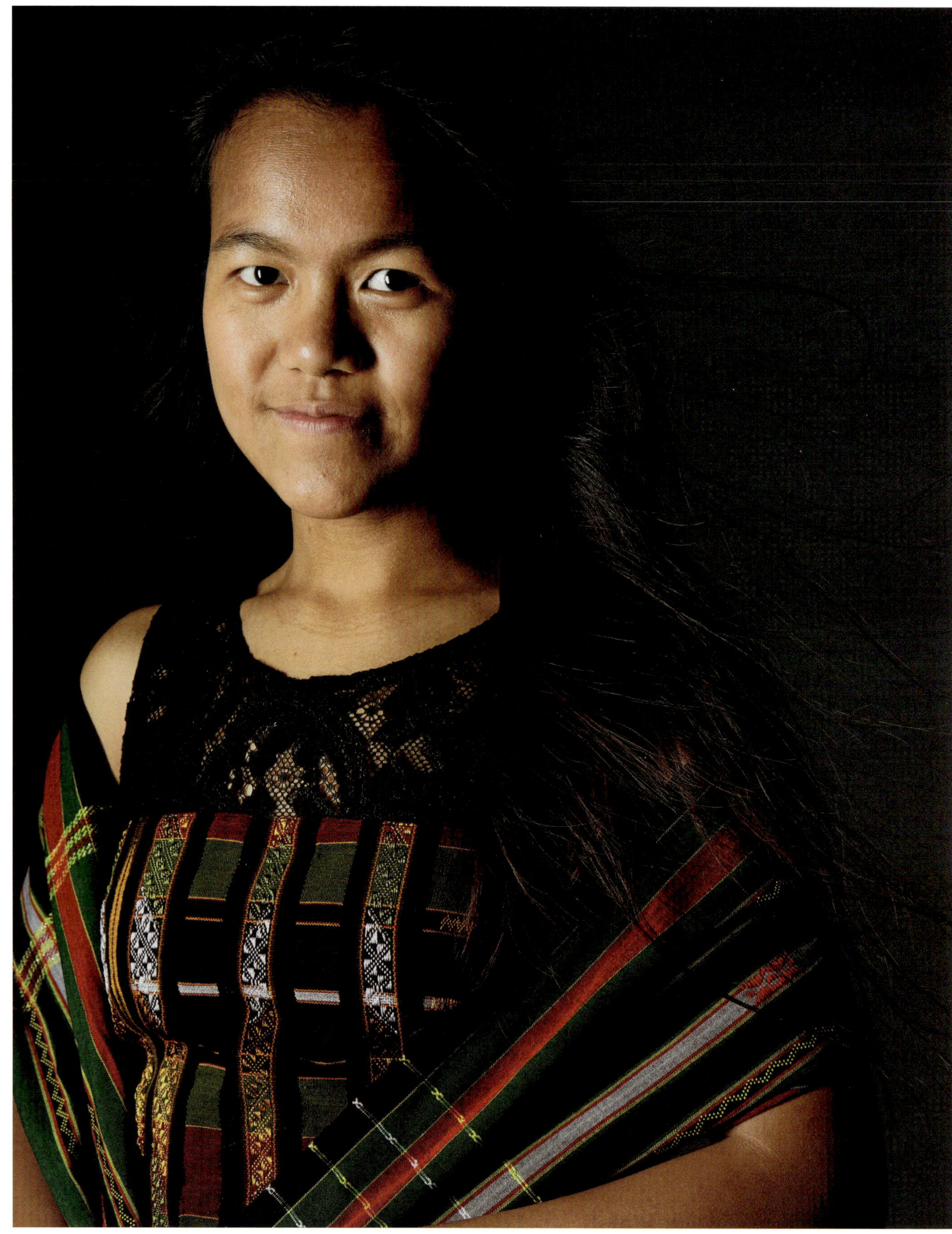

"Everyone has their own story.
So, who am I?

A girl living without a parent
Please understand my silence.
Not fluent in English
Please comfort me well.
Leaving my own country
Please sense my bitterness
Hiding my feelings behind a mask.

I remembered mom's expression
The feeling of leaving her child.
Still envision her tears when she looked away.
Further apart little by little while waving
Looking back as far as I can
Until she disappears in the air.

Today I will move forward.

Message to the world:
My mask is off.
Don't underestimate me.
Because my journey is just starting now."

—NAUM KHAN LUN, SHENANDOAH NATIONAL PARK, VIRGINIA, U.S.A. 2016;
WASHINGTON, D.C., U.S.A., MASTER CLASS 2019

NAUM KHAN LUN / WASHINGTON, D.C., U.S.A., MASTER CLASS 2019

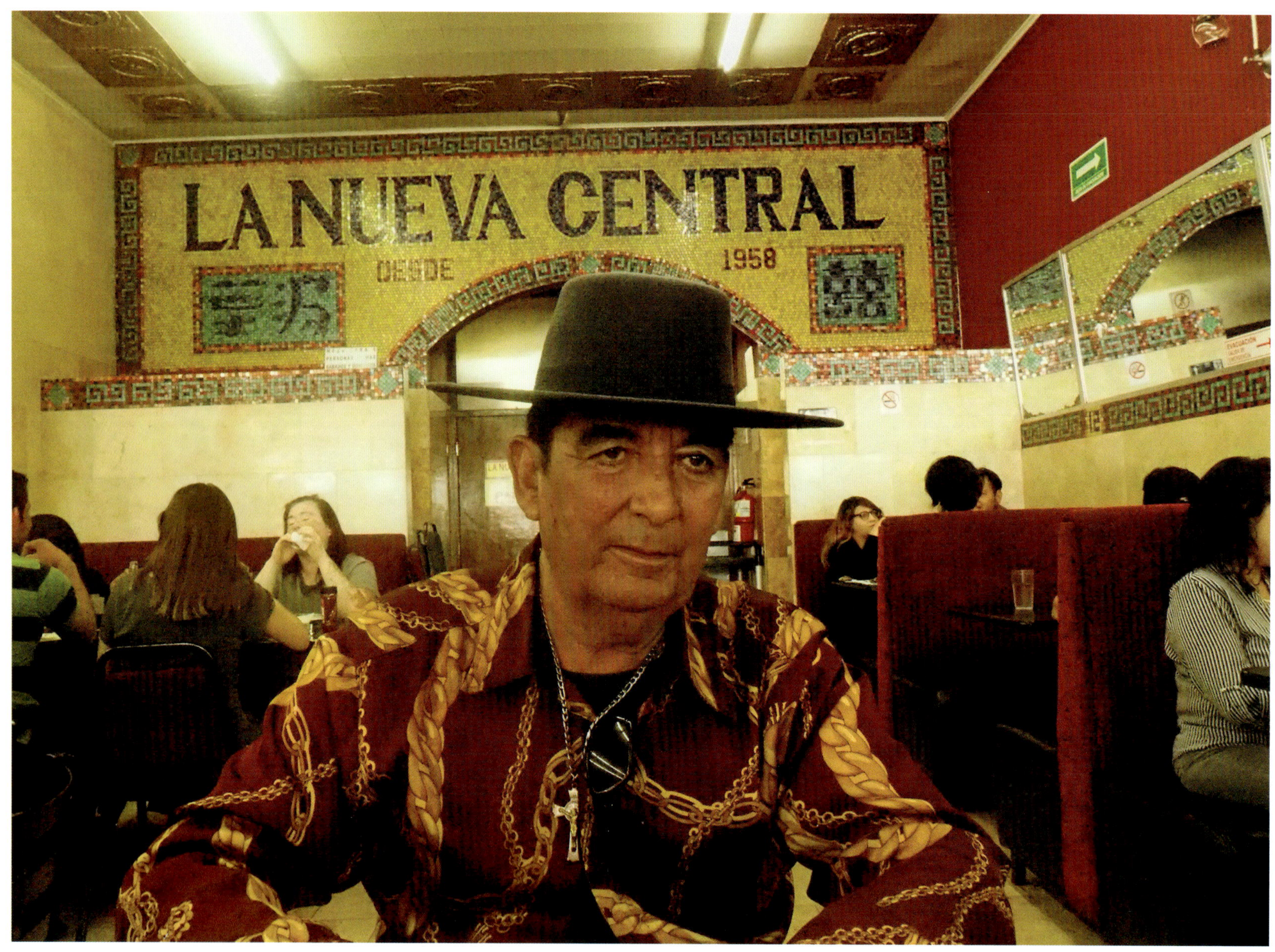

EDGAR VALENCIA / MEXICO 2017

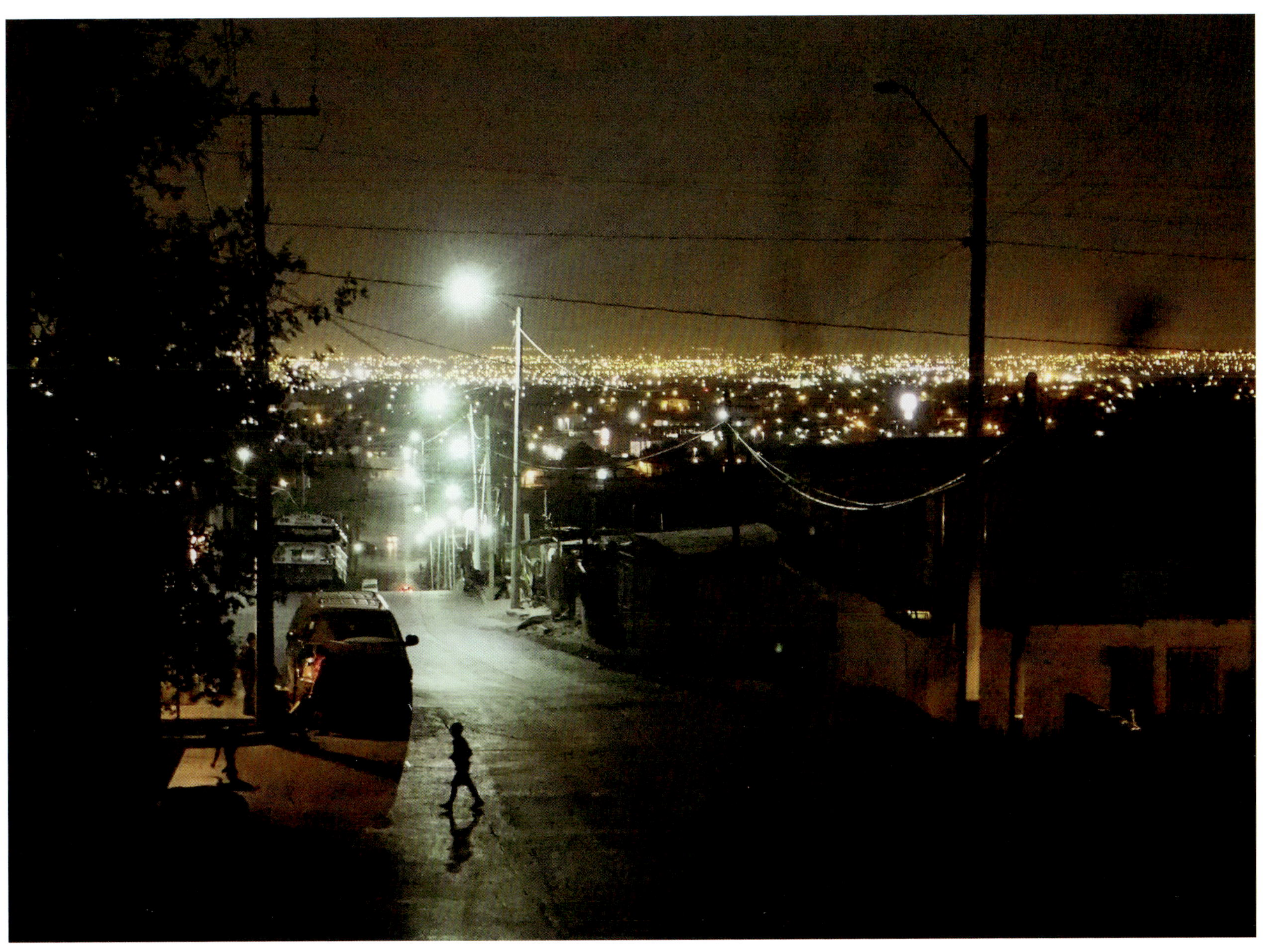

GUADALUPE LUNA / MEXICO 2017

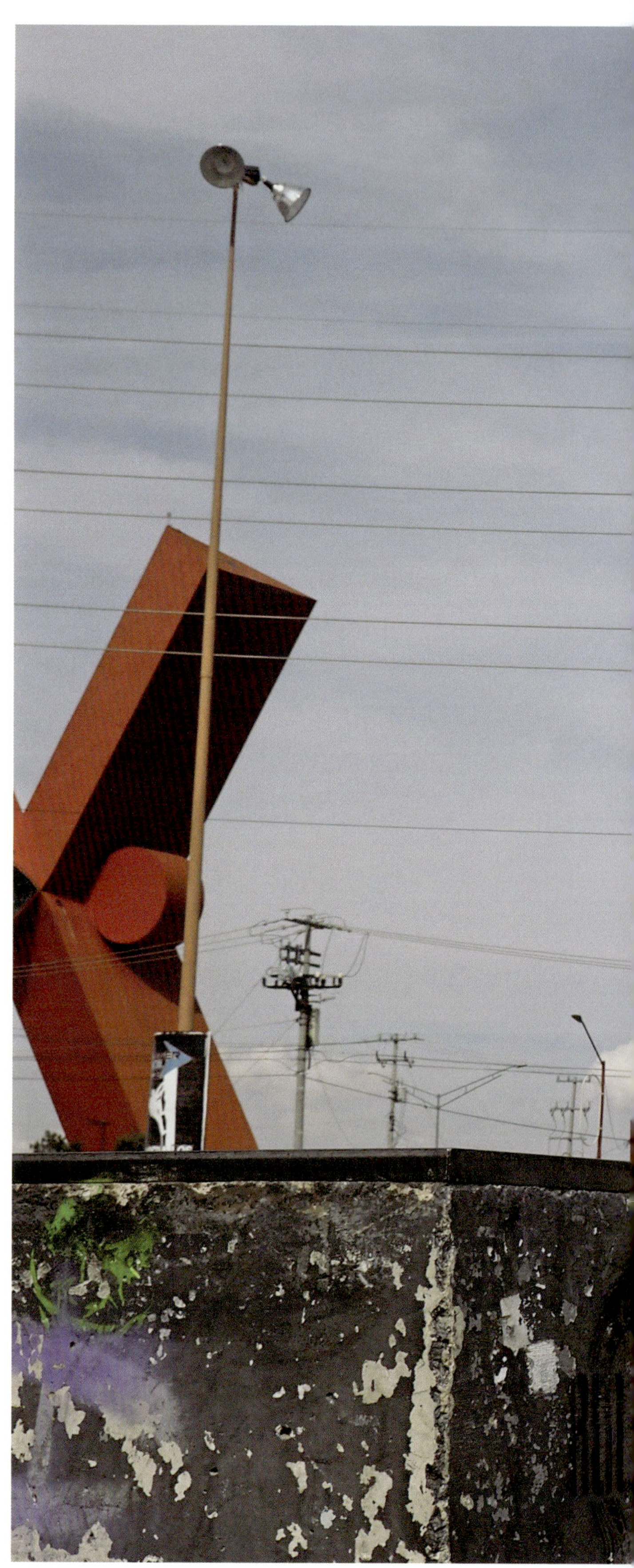

MIGUEL ROMERO / MEXICO 2017

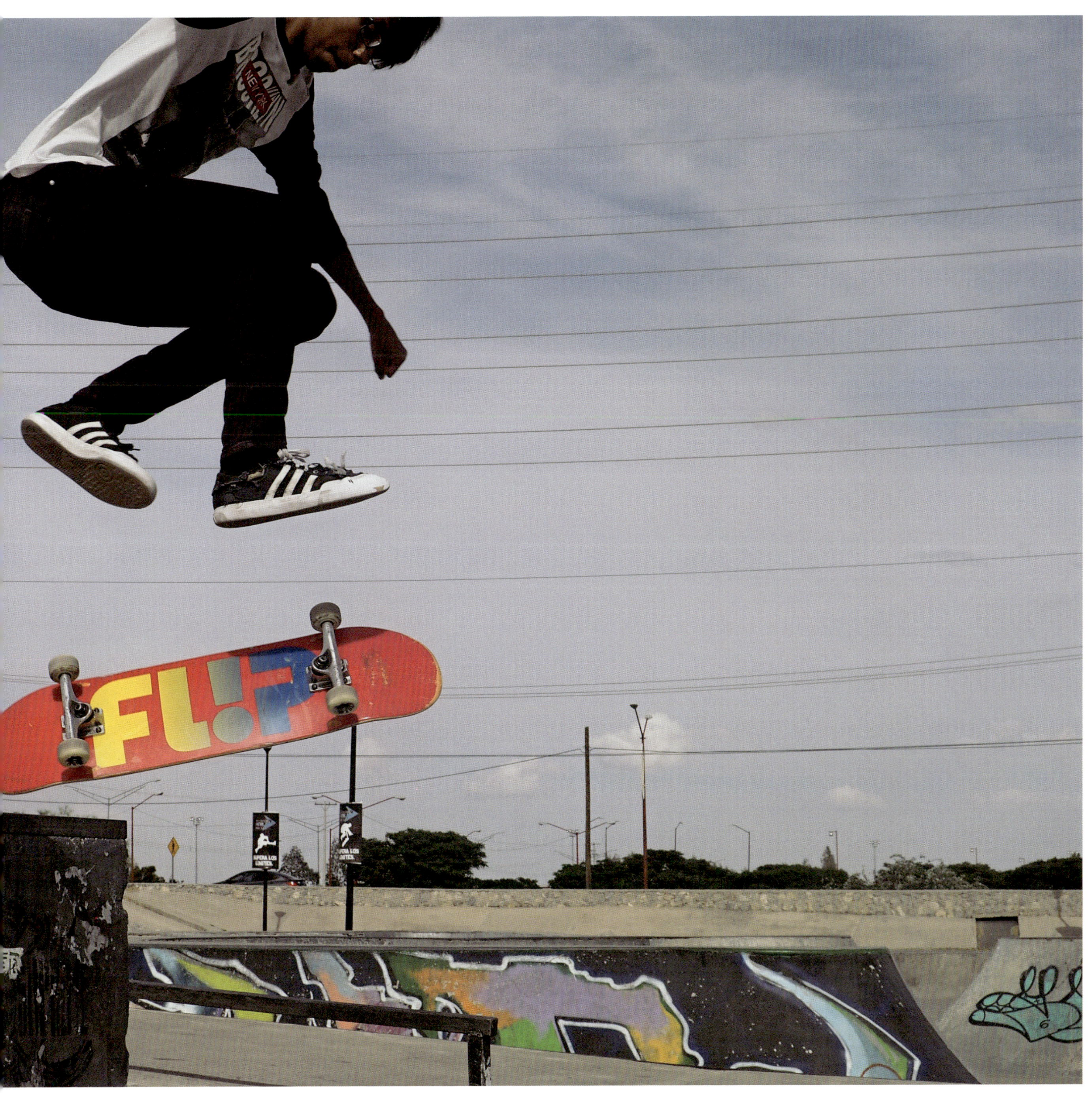
FL!P

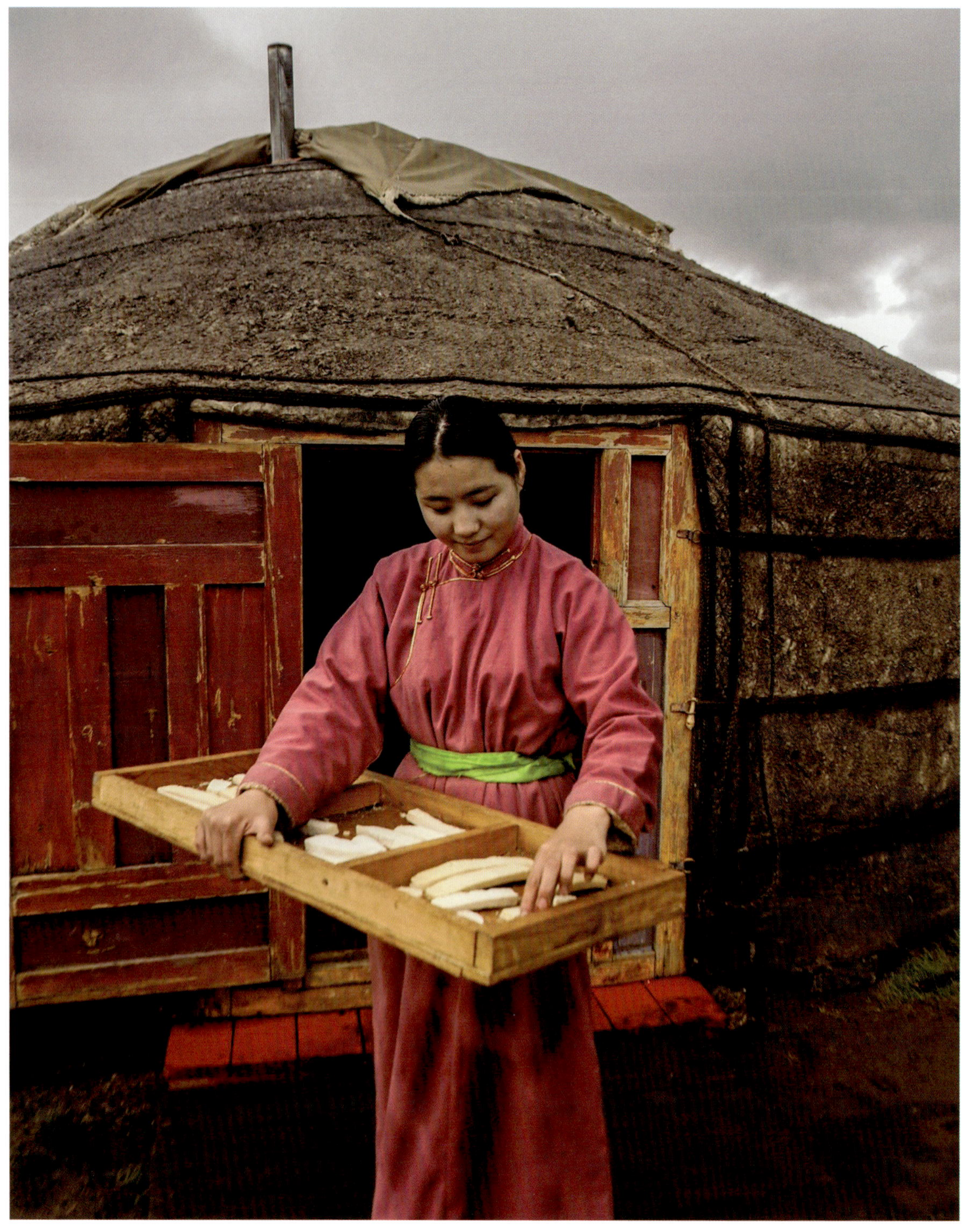

ABOVE: **B. MONKH-ORGIL / MONGOLIA 2019** OPPOSITE TOP: **M. UELEN / MONGOLIA 2019**
OPPOSITE BOTTOM: **B. MONKH-ORGIL / MONGOLIA 2019**

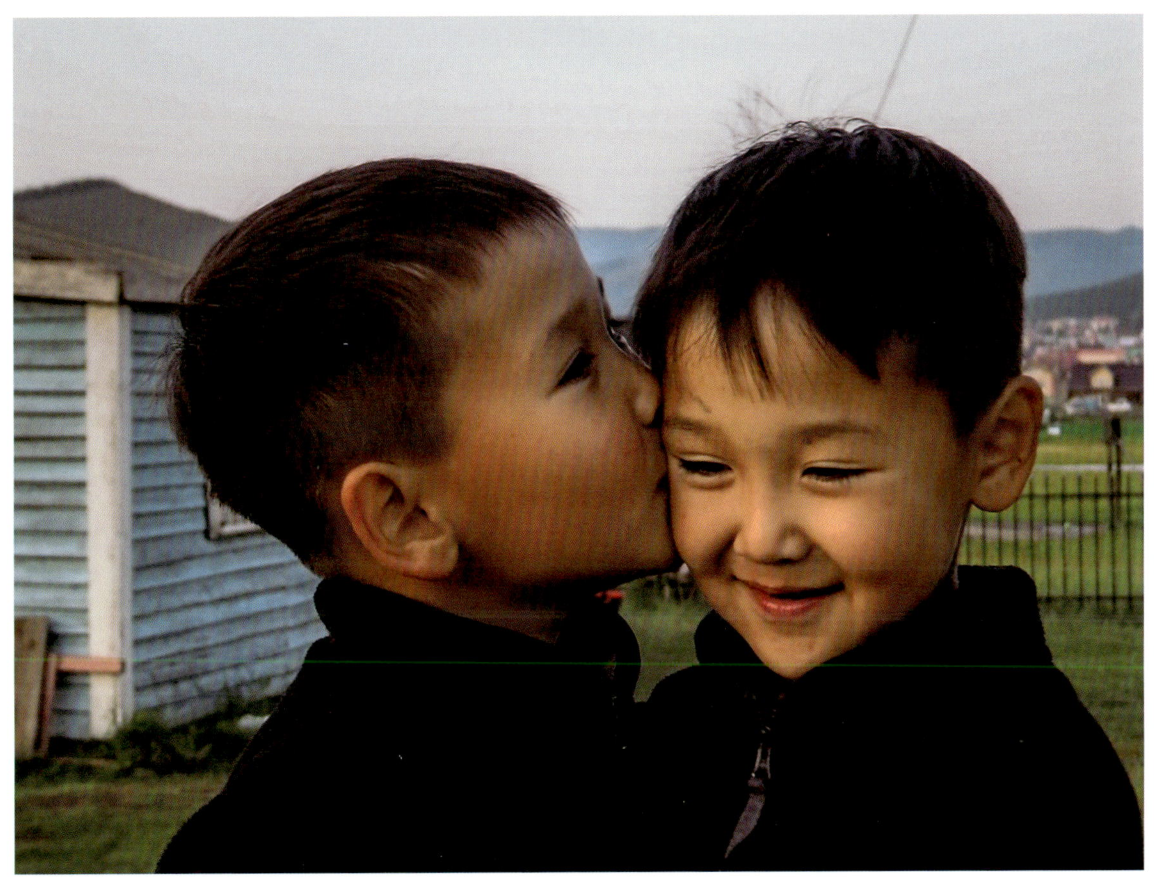

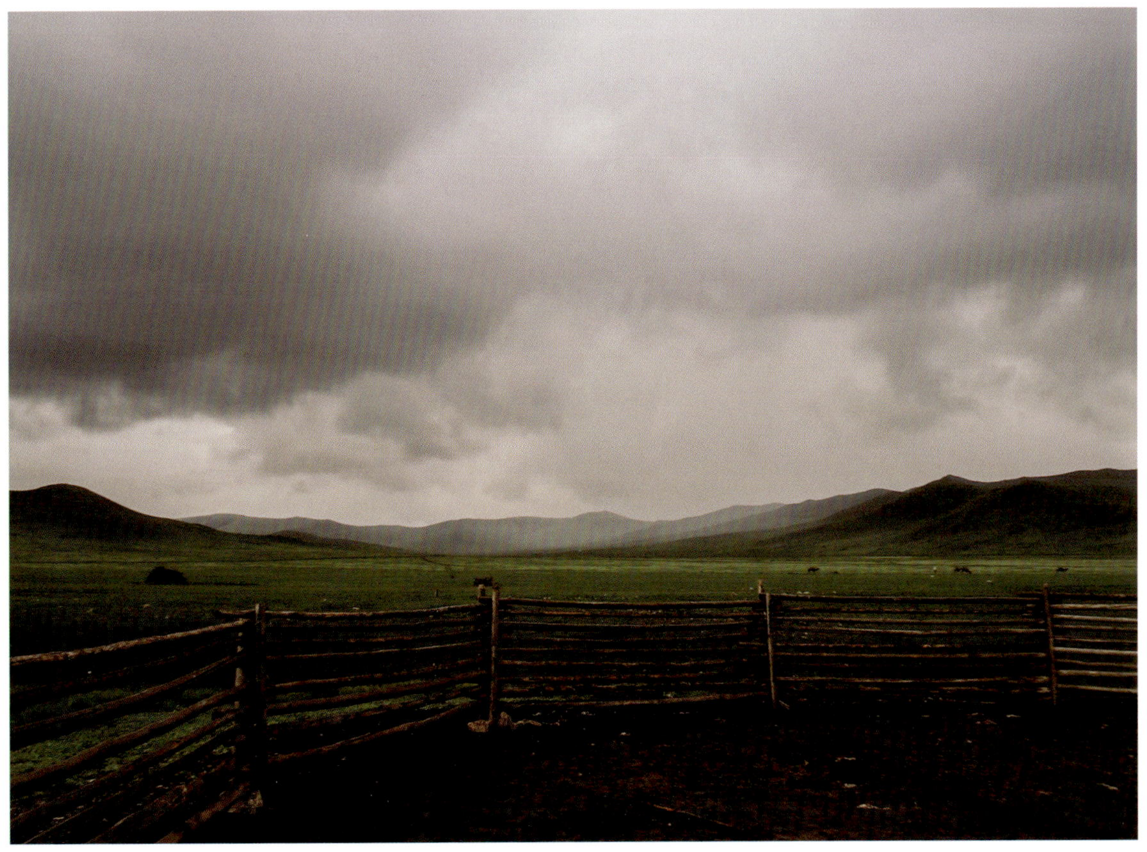

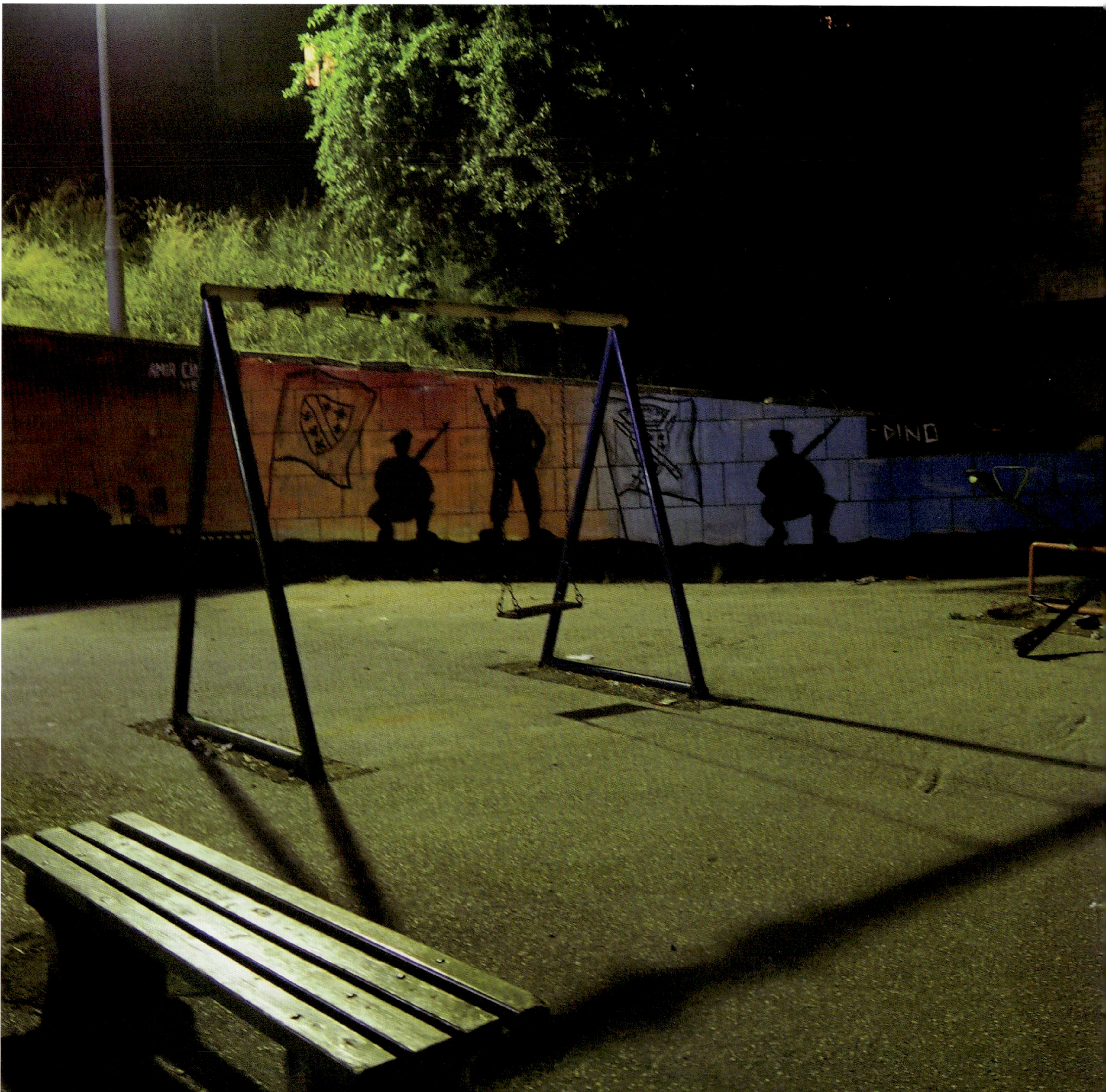
DINO

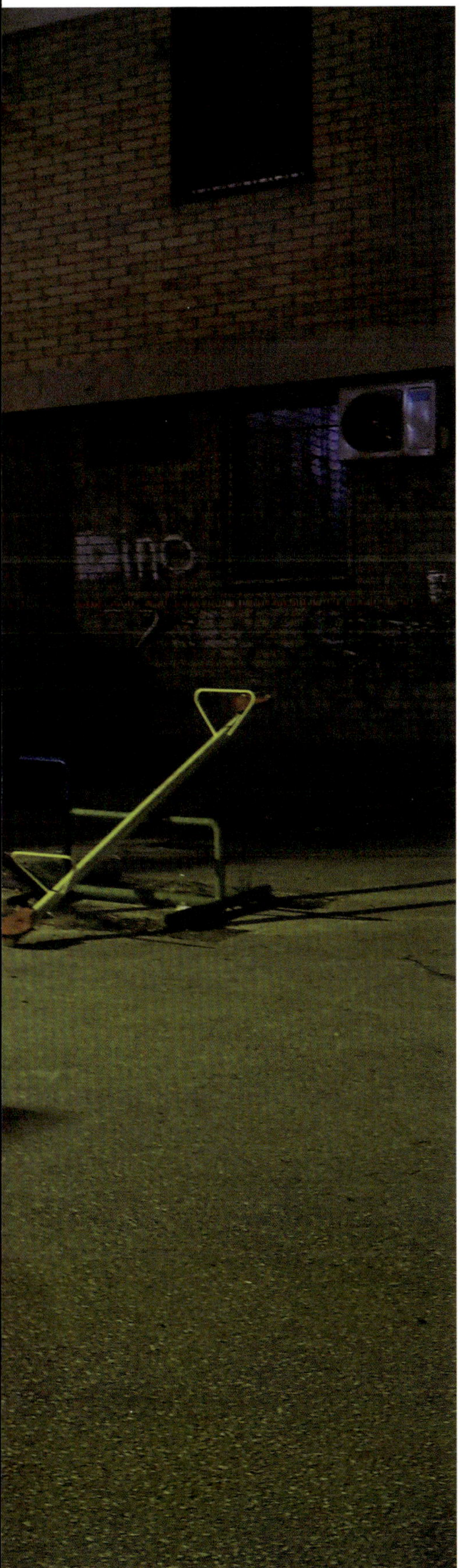

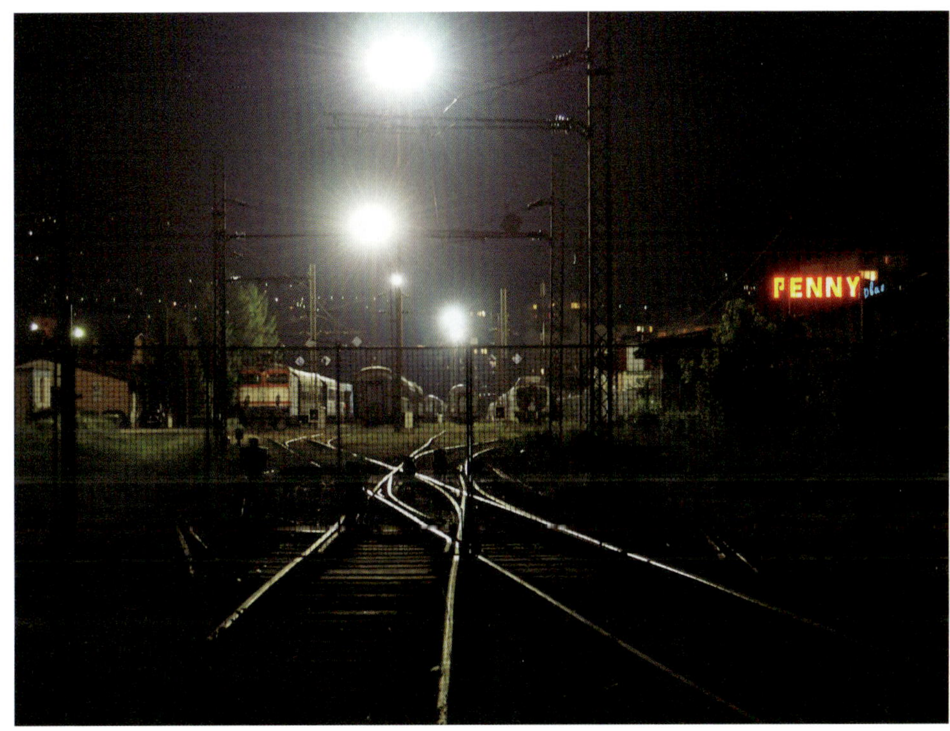

ABOVE: **BESIM BOJADZIJA / BOSNIA AND HERZEGOVINA 2015**
LEFT: **BESIM BOJADZIJA / BOSNIA AND HERZEGOVINA 2015**

"When armed people from the neighboring state were capturing my homeland peninsula, I was there. Grandpa was yelling at me, telling me I knew nothing about this life. And I just wanted to cry because my dear and beloved country, whose independence is only one year older than me, was not there anymore."

—LIDIYA IVANOVA, UKRAINE 2015

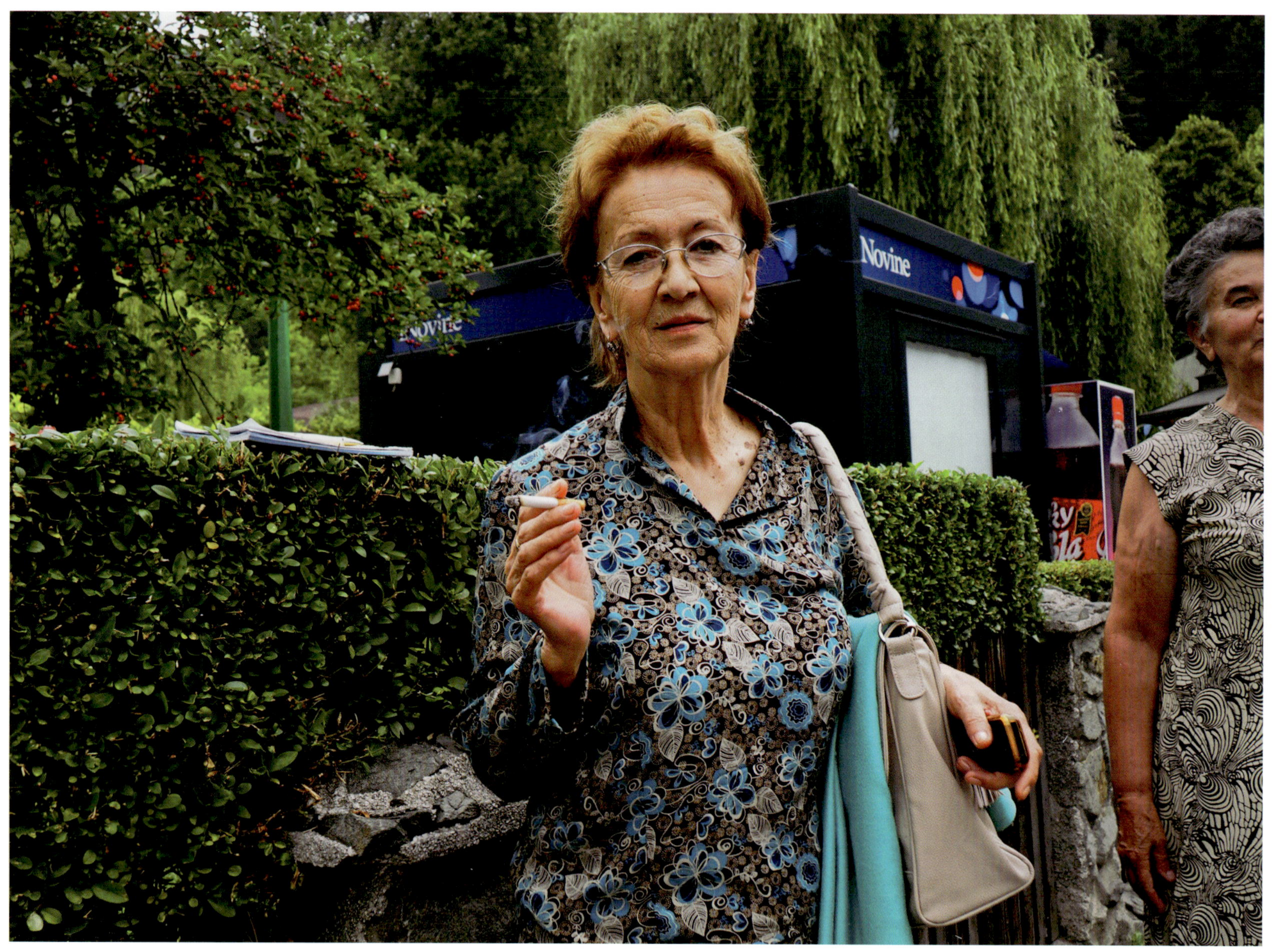

DARIA CORLUKA / BOSNIA AND HERZEGOVINA 2015

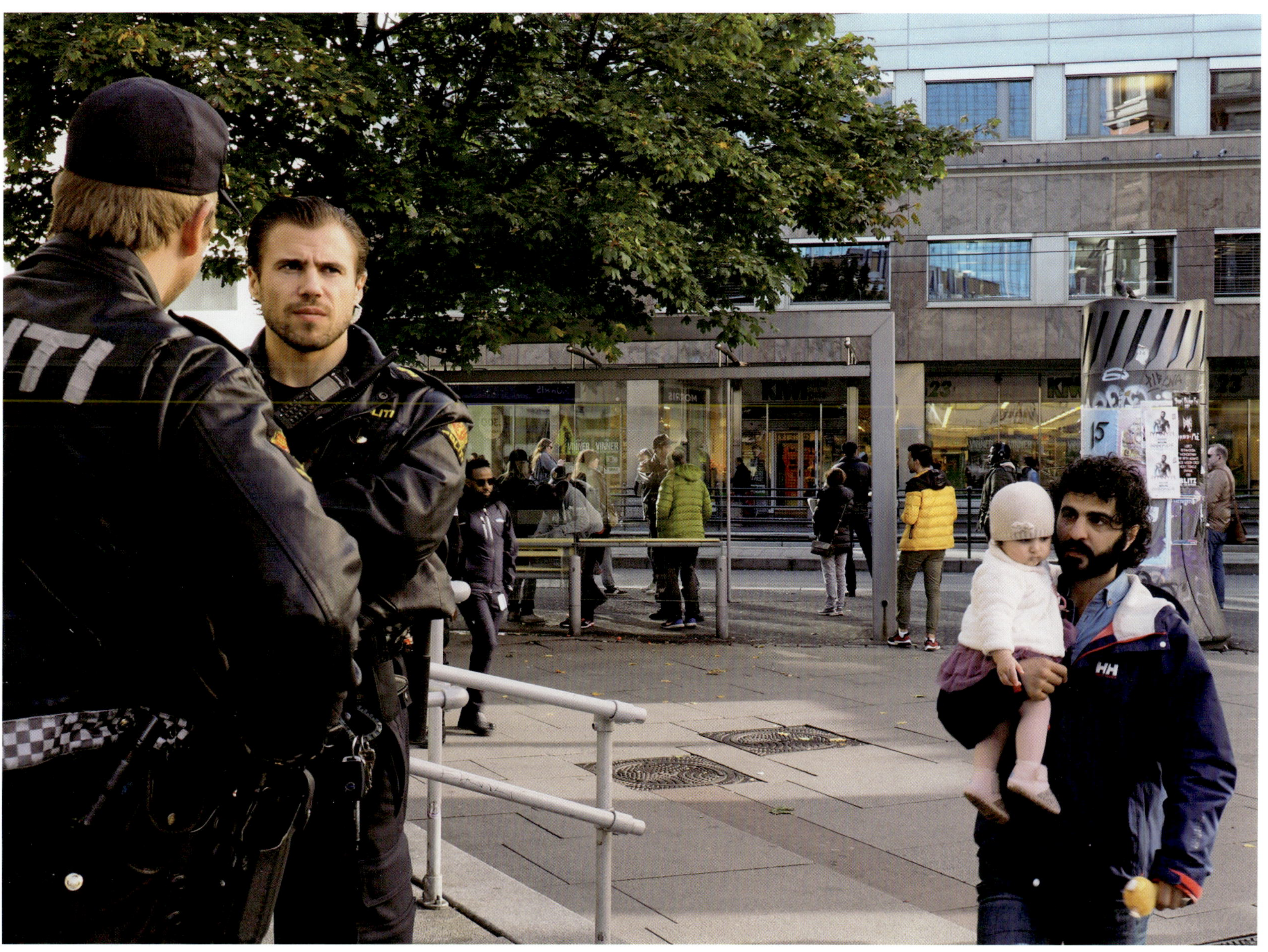

ALI KHALIFA / BOSNIA AND HERZEGOVINA 2015

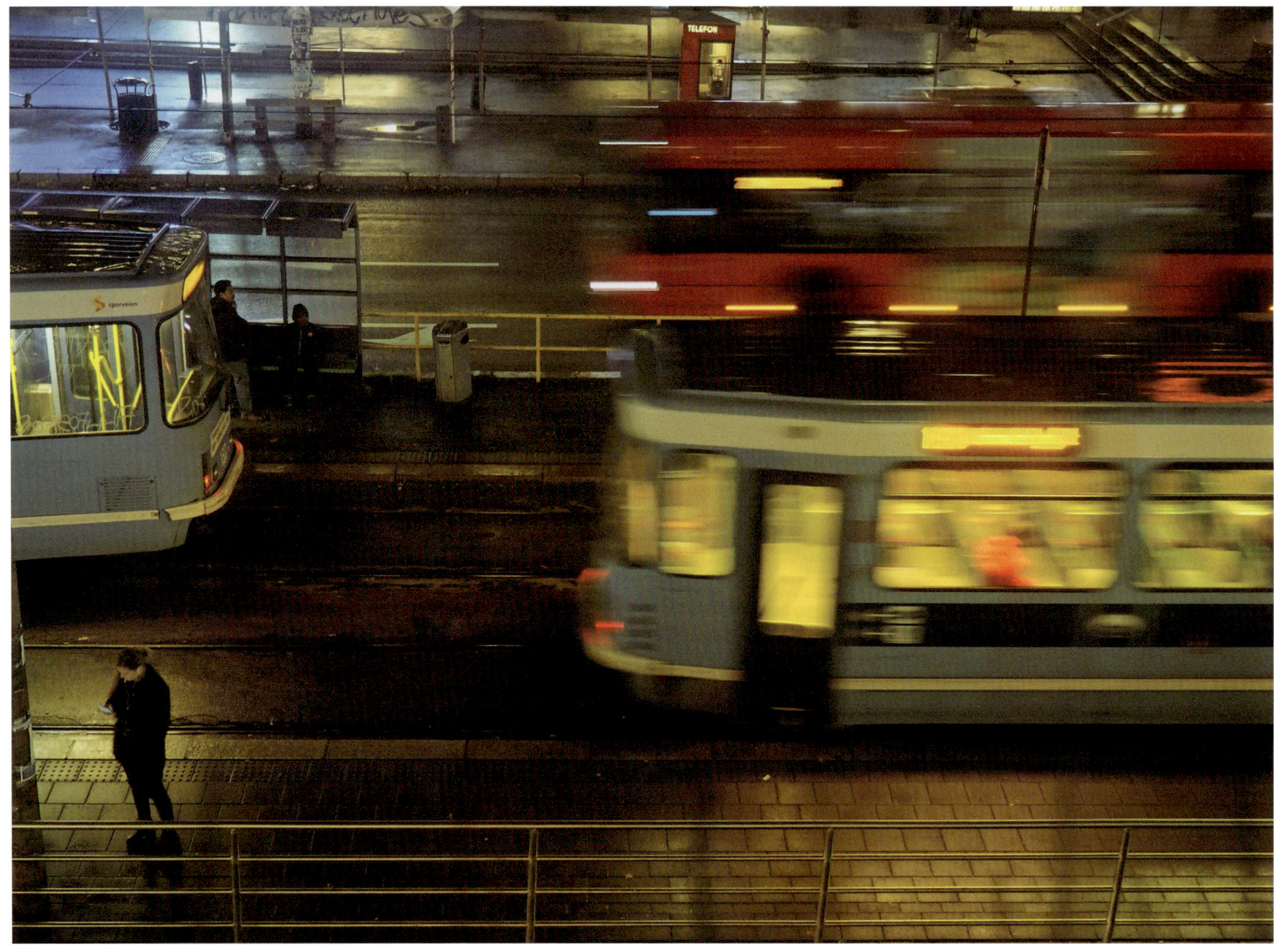

GLADDY ANNE PLATON / NORWAY 2017

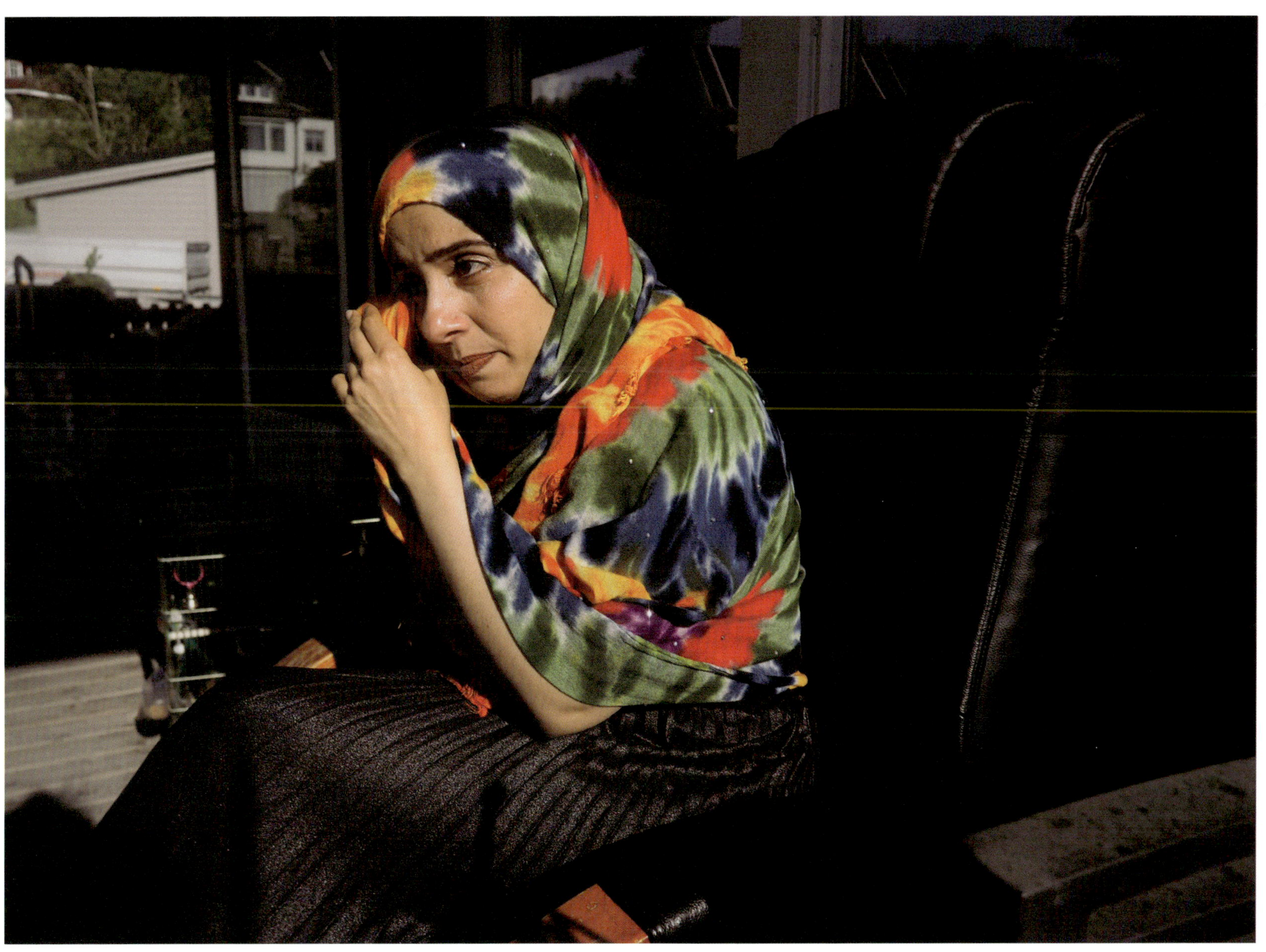

DINA AL MAKHRAMI / NORWAY 2017

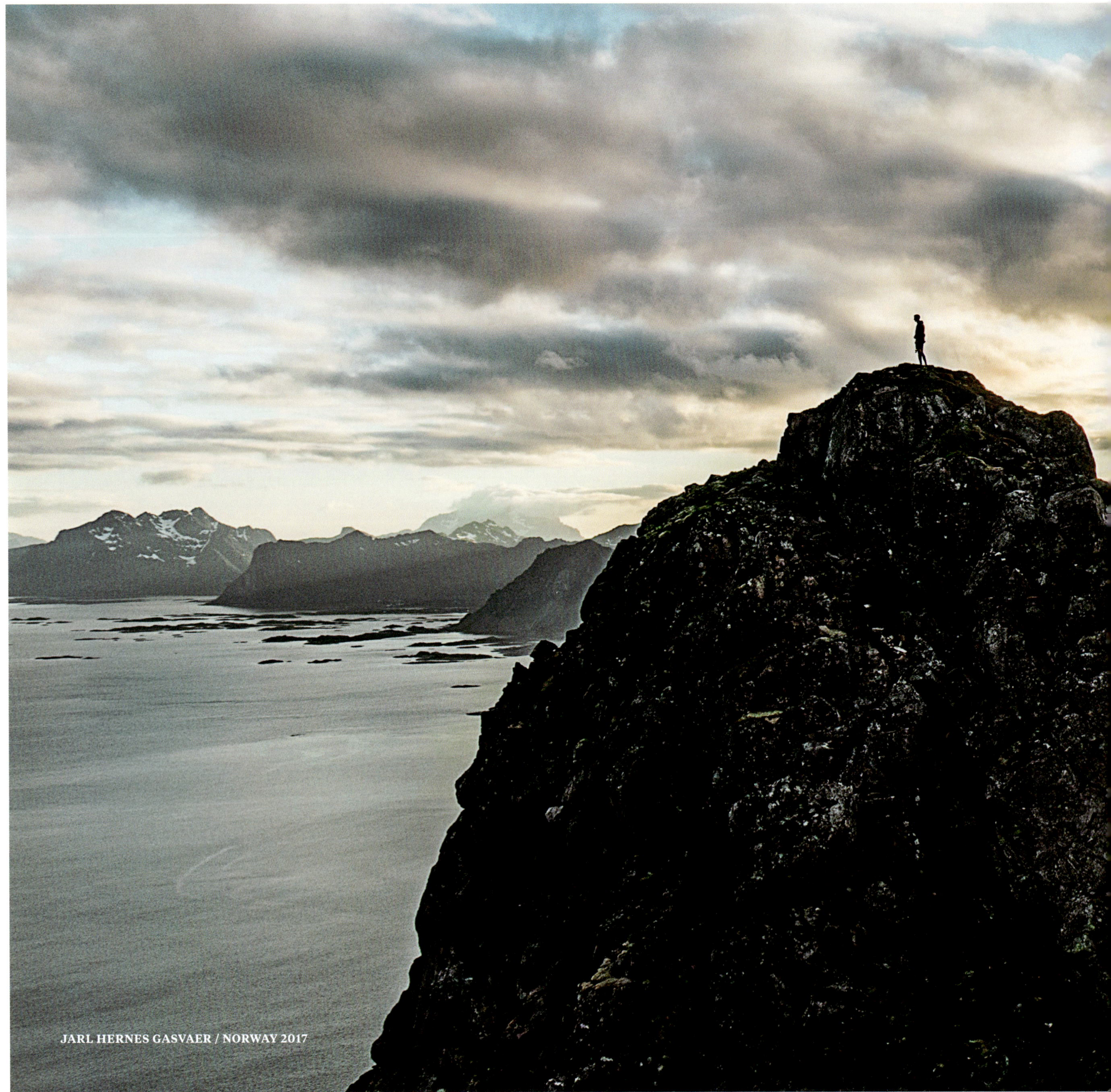

JARL HERNES GASVAER / NORWAY 2017

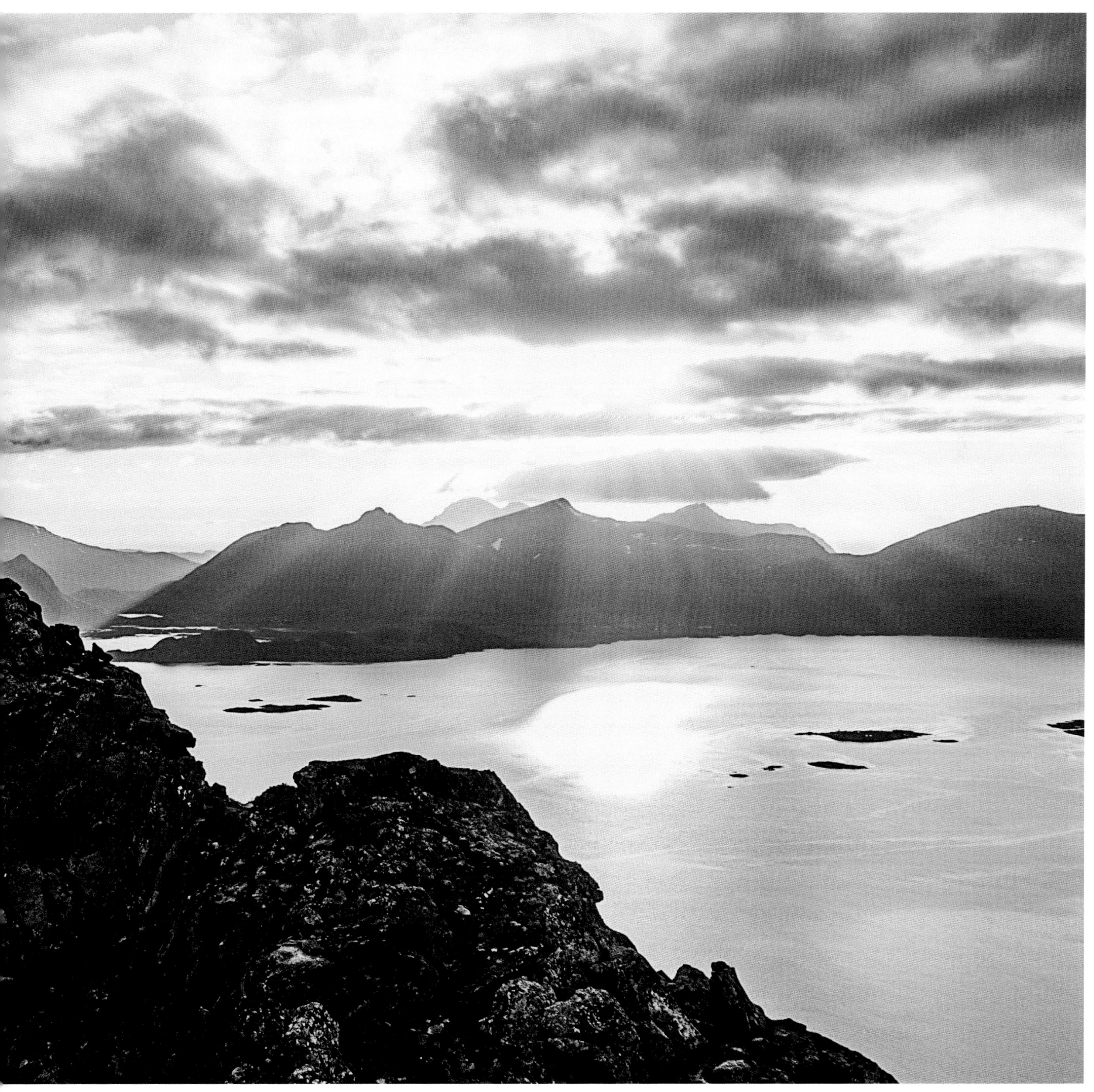

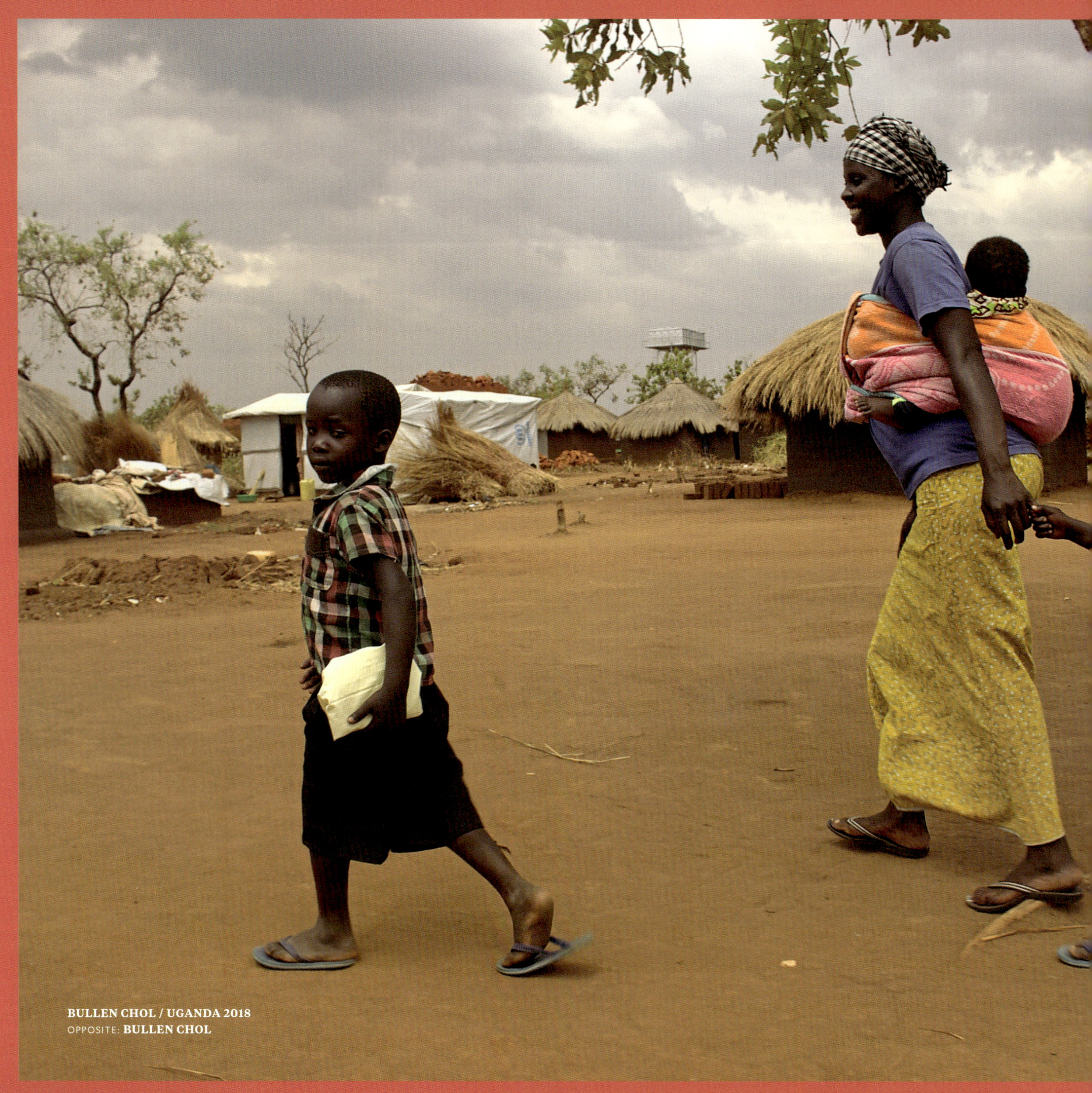

BULLEN CHOL / UGANDA 2018
OPPOSITE: **BULLEN CHOL**

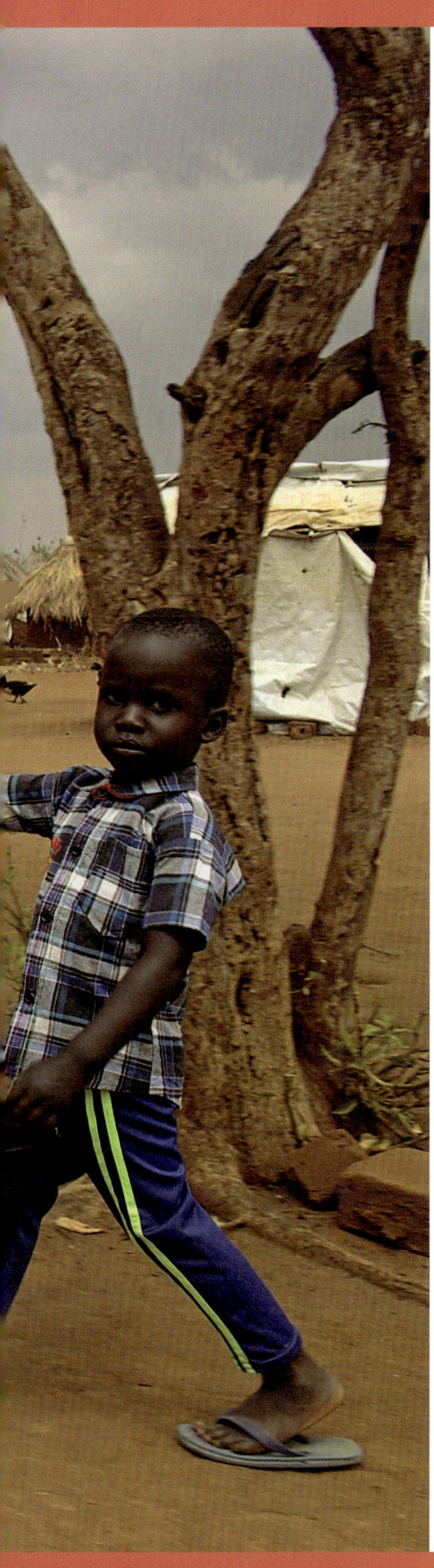

Believing in Africa

Bullen Chol

AS A CHILD FROM SOUTHERN SUDAN, Bullen Chol and his family were continuously on the run as they sought refuge outside their home country. At a 2014 Photo Camp, the then 25-year-old Bullen recalled seeing animals feeding on human remains and other horrors of long war. "[During] the moves I took across the valleys, deserts, rivers and bushes ... dreams were fading away at every single moment," he wrote.

By the time Bullen wrote those words, he had returned to his home region, the freshly minted country of South Sudan. During six days of Photo Camp in 2014 in the capital city of Juba, photography became his passion. After the camp was over, Bullen wanted to continue photographing, but he had no camera. So, he would borrow one, insert his SD card to take a few photos, return the camera, then later find another to borrow. One photo he took with a borrowed camera won a UNESCO photography competition. The prize: a digital camera.

In the nine years since the Photo Camp, he has worked as a professional photographer. In 2020, a UN agriculture program hired him as a digital media associate. "It pays the bills," he said with a laugh.

Photography still drives Bullen, as is clear from his frequently updated Instagram feed. Now a teacher, he dreams of seeing a new generation of African photographers tell the story of the continent. "Someone from the outside doesn't know that there is more than their perspective can give," he said in a recent telephone interview. "Intimacy takes time. If you are part of the situation, you document it the way it is."

Bullen Chol is a photographer and filmmaker living in Juba, South Sudan. He describes himself as "dedicated to documenting the social, cultural, and political issues that define our times."

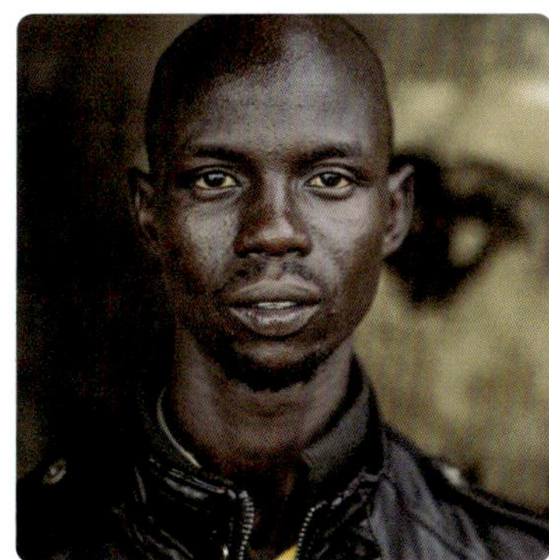

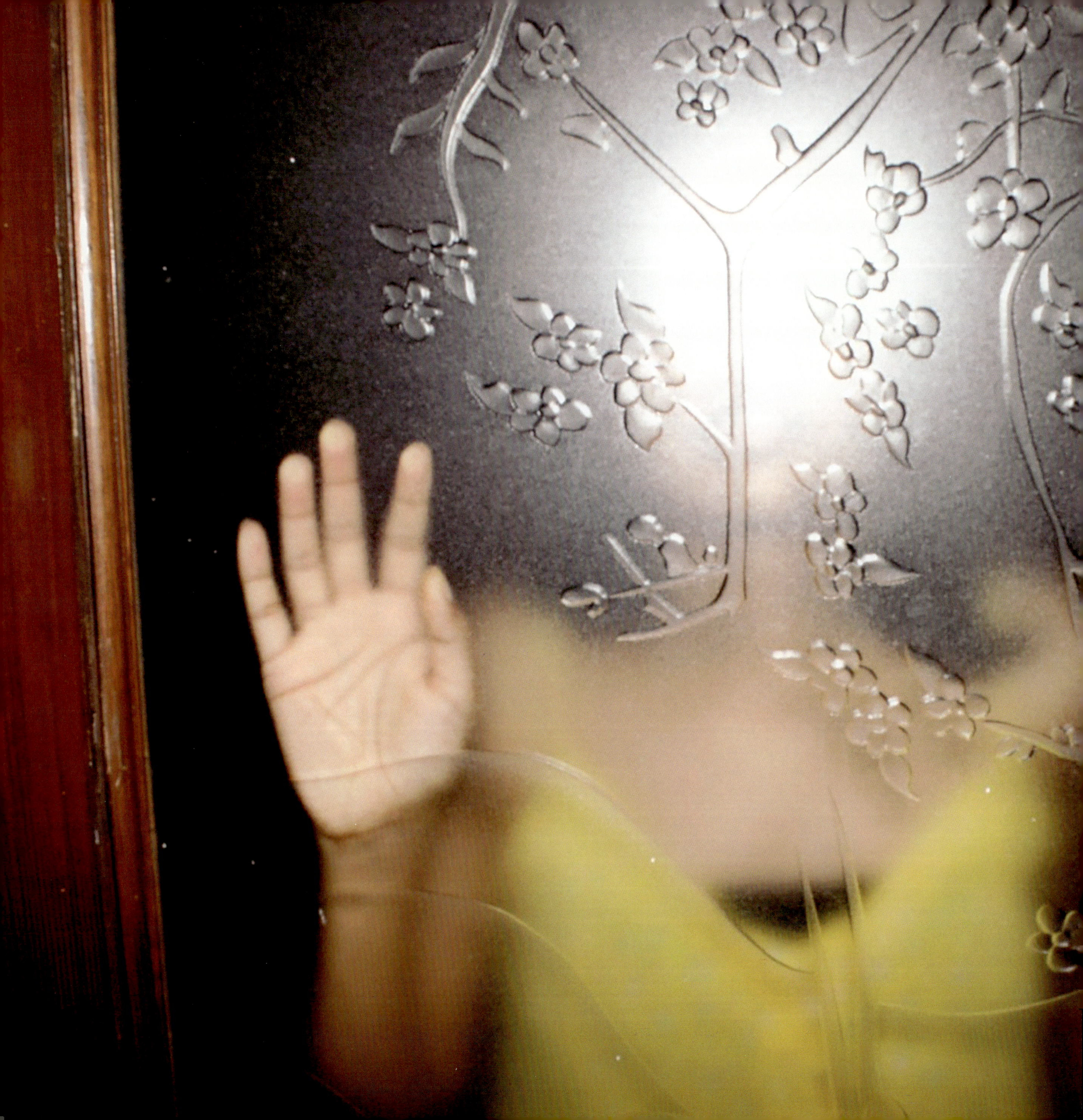

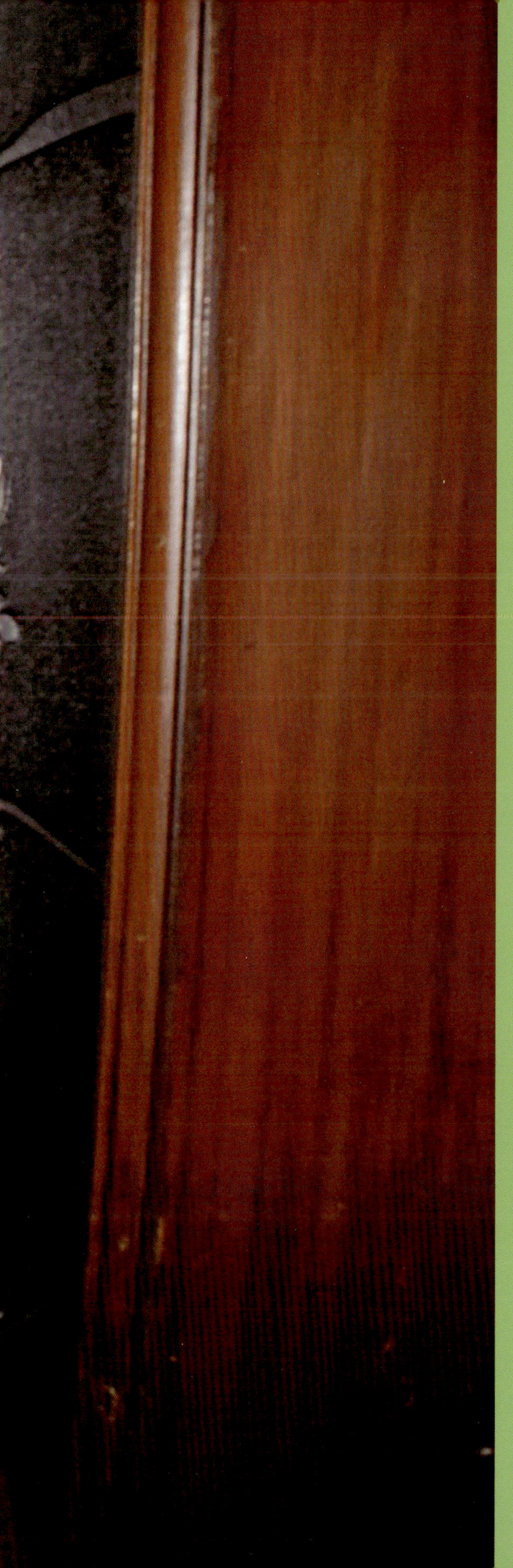

CHAPTER 3

Growth

"I didn't really talk much about the future. But after the workshop, I can confidently say I want to be a writer."

—CATHY LAL, INDIA 2018

Being Seen

TAKE A MOMENT TO VIEW THE WORLD through the eyes of a teenager living in an orphanage in Banbasa, India—an orphanage that exists to give refuge to children abandoned by their families. You would be forgiven for feeling rejected, especially if you were given up for the sole fact of being a girl. Still, you count yourself as lucky; life at the Good Shepherd Agricultural Mission is wholesome. You help grow and cook the food that everyone at the mission eats. You study at the mission school. Your story is characteristic of many of the 80 children living there. In 2018, you and some 20 other girls and boys are invited to take part in a program called National Geographic Photo Camp. You are told it is something very special; you think you have heard of it, but you are not sure.

In one of the very first exercises, each member of the group is asked to create a portrait and describe themselves. "A lot of these students were not used to people—especially teachers—asking for their opinions or perspectives," Kirsten Elstner recalled. "This is a delicate process that takes some layers of trust building to succeed."

Each camp is tailored to the backgrounds of its students; at Banbasa, one-on-one assignments were emphasized as a way for individual students to gain confidence through meeting with a teacher. But at every camp, a premium is placed on helping the students feel seen as people with something to say and give to society.

Elstner saw the change in the young people at camp. "When you make a self-portrait and someone asks you to not only write about your strengths or your gift to the world, and then someone sits down and listens to you when you are shy or feel inadequate, it's a huge self-discovery," she said. The following year, Malaika Vaz, a photographer who mentored at an orphanage in Rishikesh, was inspired by the way the students came up with the idea of visiting the local landfill to document how tourism has created an overwhelming trash problem. Images of children jumping off mountains of garbage "shine a light on the common humanity" and underscore that "unbridled joy is possible in those difficult circumstances," she noted.

Vaz observed that photography can offer a protective "shield to tell your story and a kind of hammer to smash the wall you have created for yourself." This simultaneous process, she explained, "allows a lot of students to begin to figure out what makes them feel alive."

Several of the young women at the Banbasa workshop came to realize that further schooling was their goal, and they became the first of their cohort to pursue higher education. One of the Rishikesh girls, too, decided to go on to college. Elstner said it is no coincidence they were alumni of Photo Camp.

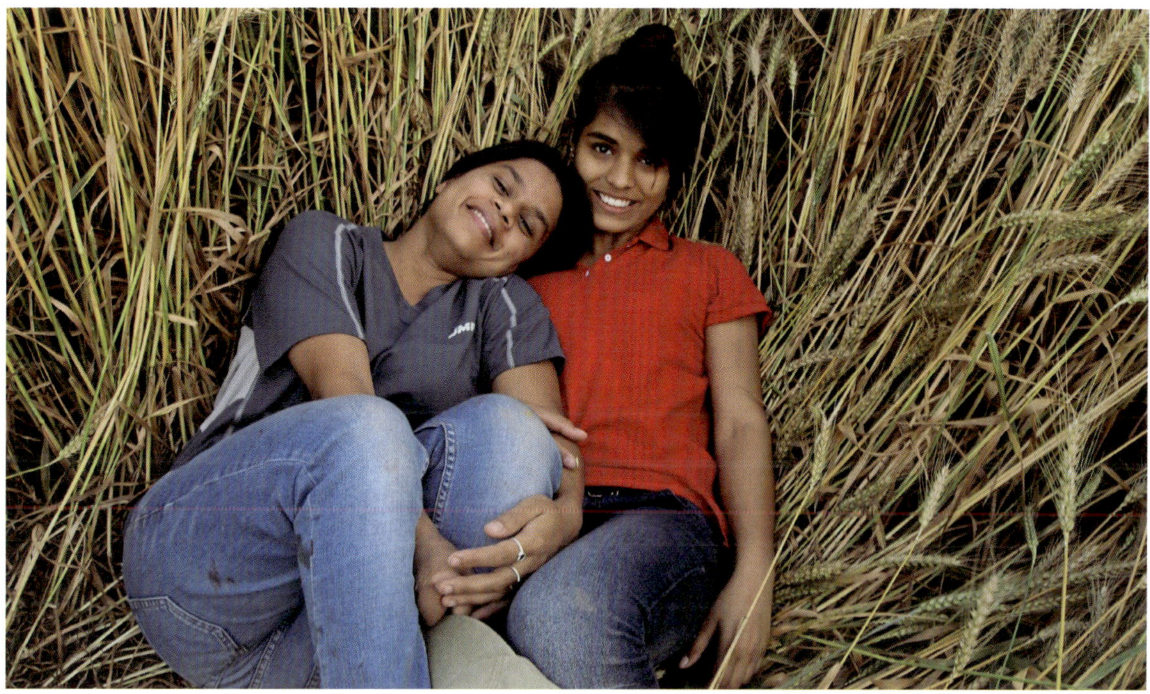

ABOVE: **GORDON RAM / INDIA 2018** PREVIOUS PAGES: **VAGMI PATHAK / INDIA 2020**

Like many other girls at the Banbasa Photo Camp, Cathy Lal thought her story was insignificant, of no consequence to others. She was dropped off at the orphanage gates when she was four months old; later, when she was 13, she had an accident working with farming equipment and severed four of her fingers.

Writer-journalist Paul Salopek mentored Cathy and the other students during the camp. He started off by telling them about his own remarkable journey; his visit to Banbasa was a stop on his Out of Eden Walk, which retraces our ancestors' global migration. Photo Camp "is a process of helping [students] discover their own originality through drafts of work," Salopek recalled. "Then, you take whatever storytelling they produce and help them recognize what they have done in it that's good."

Cathy was a quick study, and Salopek, seeing her eagerness to learn, worked intensely with her. "She was absolutely serious about her craft," he said. "She turned in four drafts, working as hard on her essays as I do on my own pieces. But more than that, she had powerful stories to tell—rich, nuanced, personal stories."

Cathy herself recognized how much she grew from the experience: "I knew for the first time I was good at something. The best part of the workshop was that [Paul] believed in me. He took me so seriously that I thought: I really have something in me."

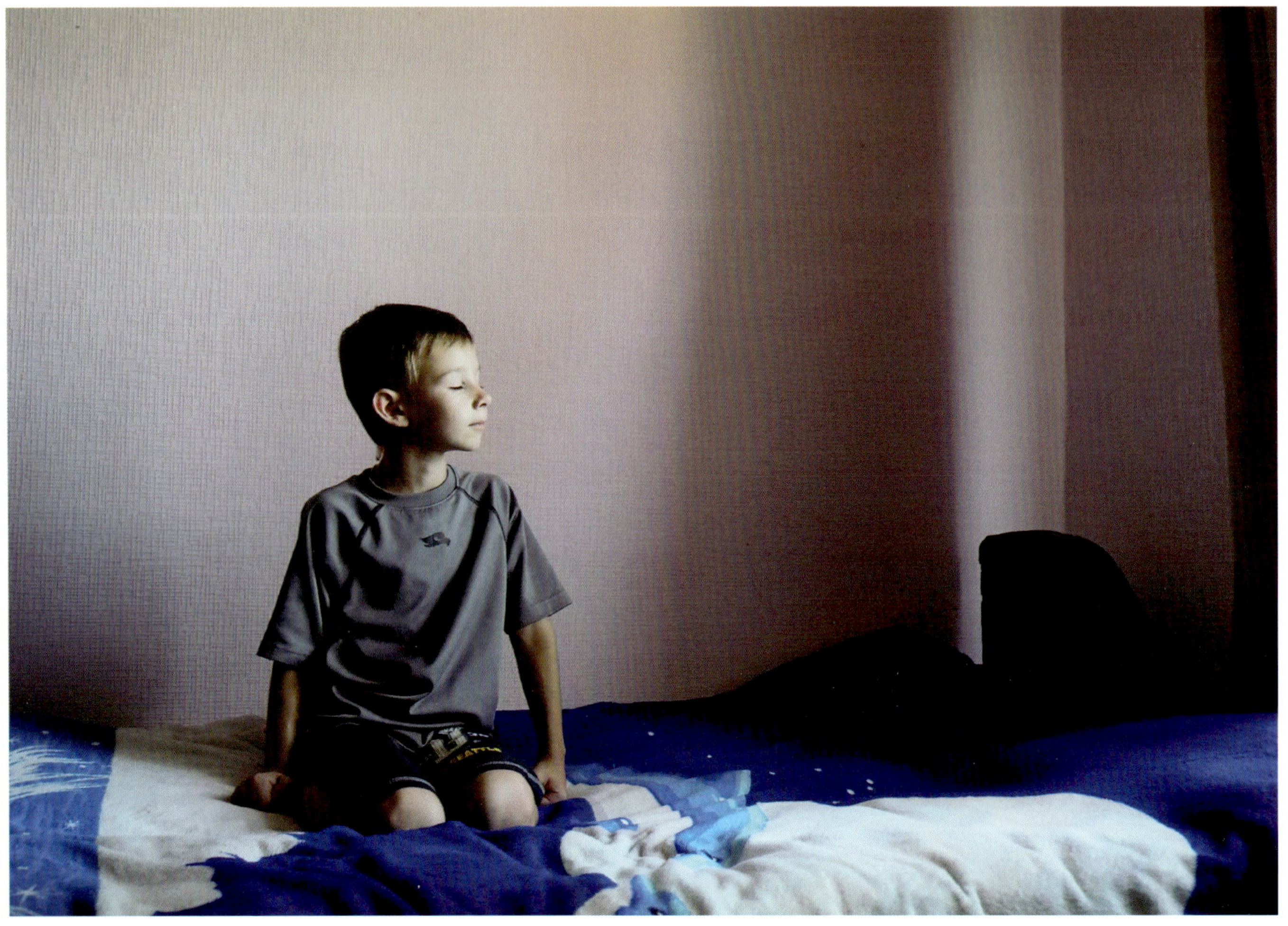

ABOVE: **ANASTASIA RADKOVA / UKRAINE 2015** OPPOSITE: **ELIZABETH GODAR / CALIFORNIA, U.S.A. 2009**

"My story is not actually about my physical relocation. It is about transformation of me as a human being, as a person. And I want to show it in my photos.

We don't need pity. We're just trying to move on ... The war took practically everything from me, but it gave me the opportunity to find myself."

—OLENA BILOUS, UKRAINE 2015

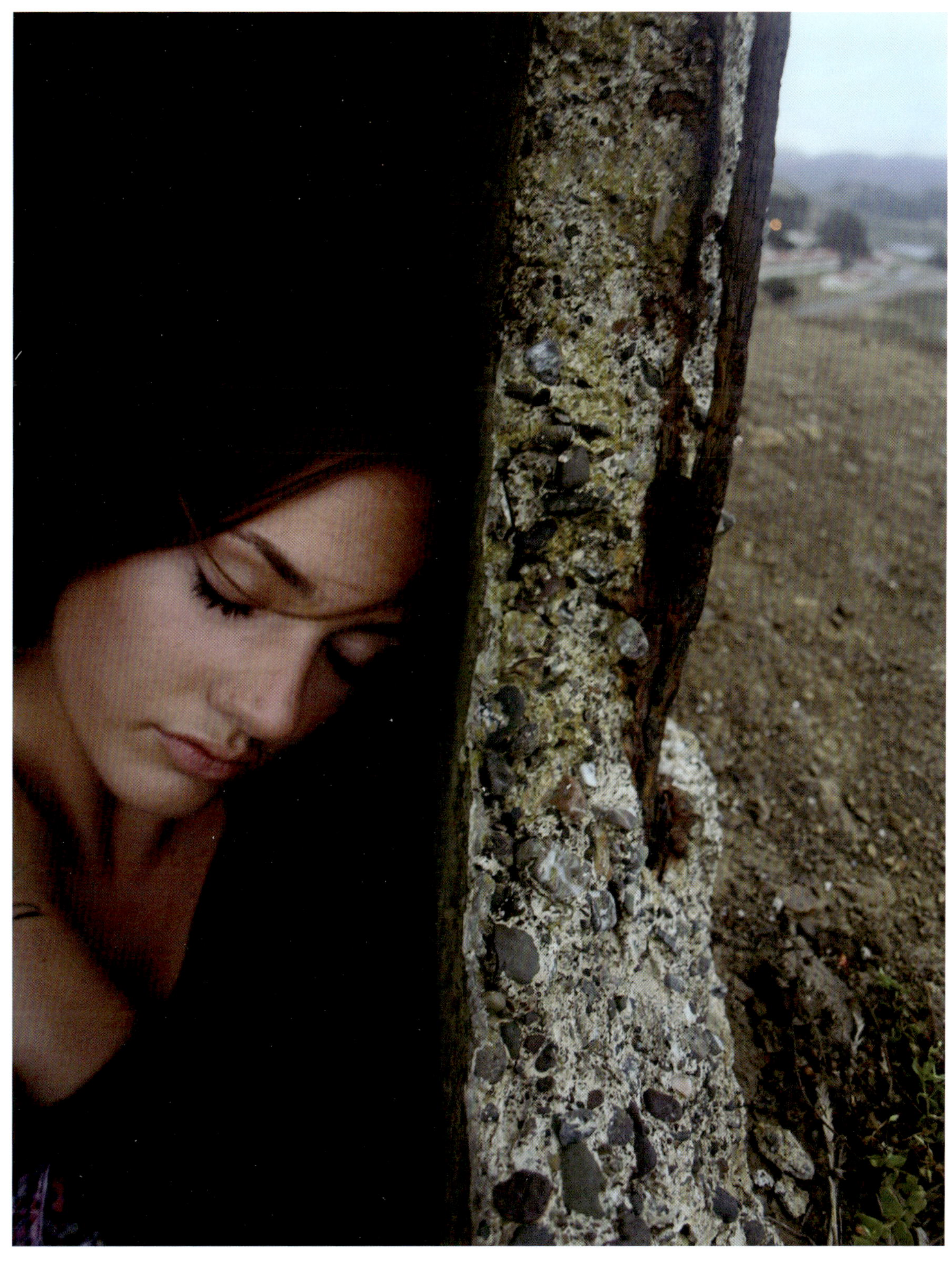

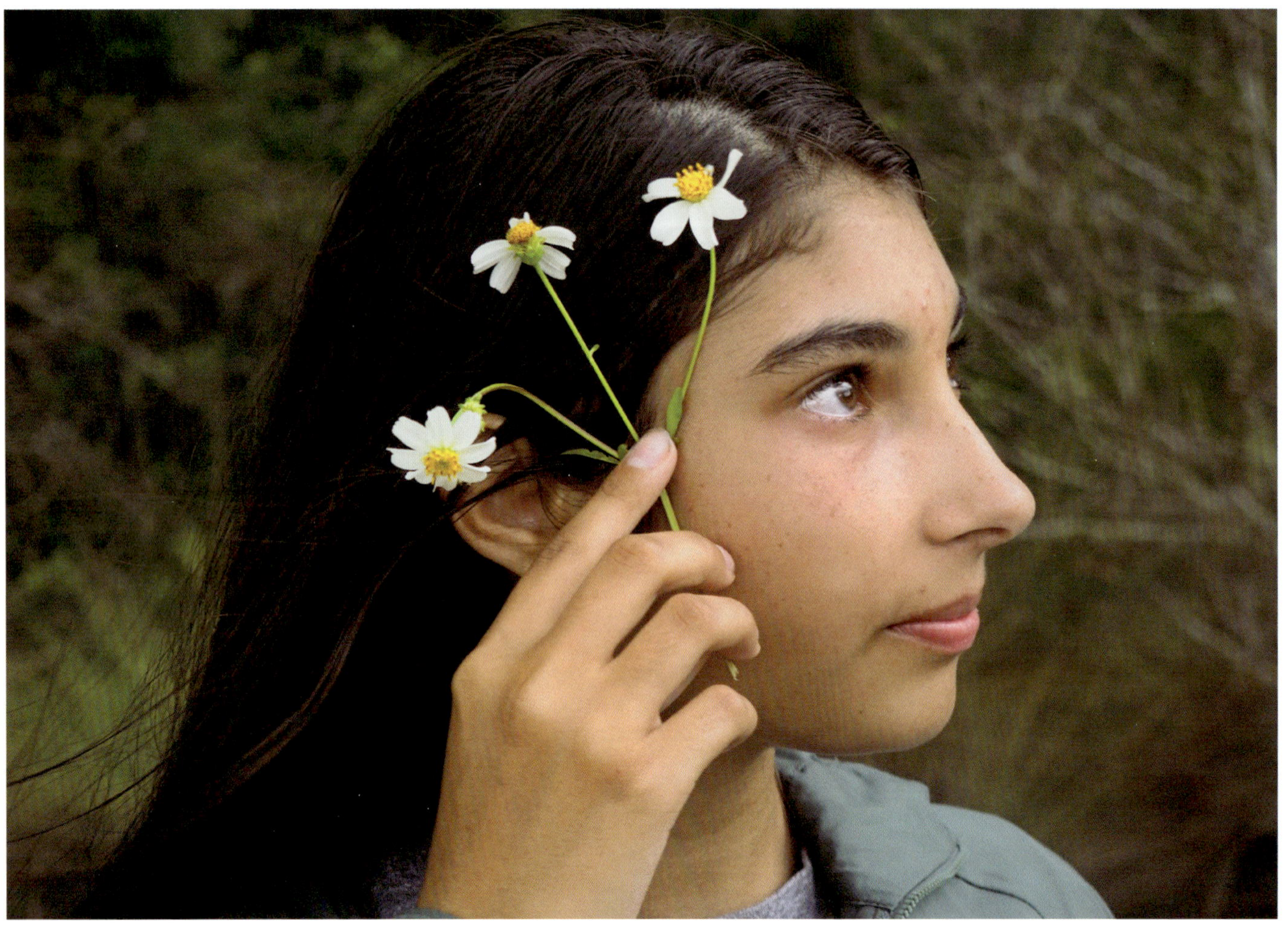

ABOVE: **ISABEL GUERRA / FLORIDA, U.S.A. 2022** OPPOSITE: **KIRSTEN ELSTNER, PHOTO CAMP STAFF / FLORIDA, U.S.A. 2022**

"For the Miccosukee
We are born and raised in the water.
For the Miccosukee
We can't even eat the fish from the Everglades,
We can't even drink the water that surrounds us.
For the Miccosukee
I want to be the person who changes this."

—CARMELLO SHENANDOAH, EVERGLADES, FLORIDA, U.S.A. 2022

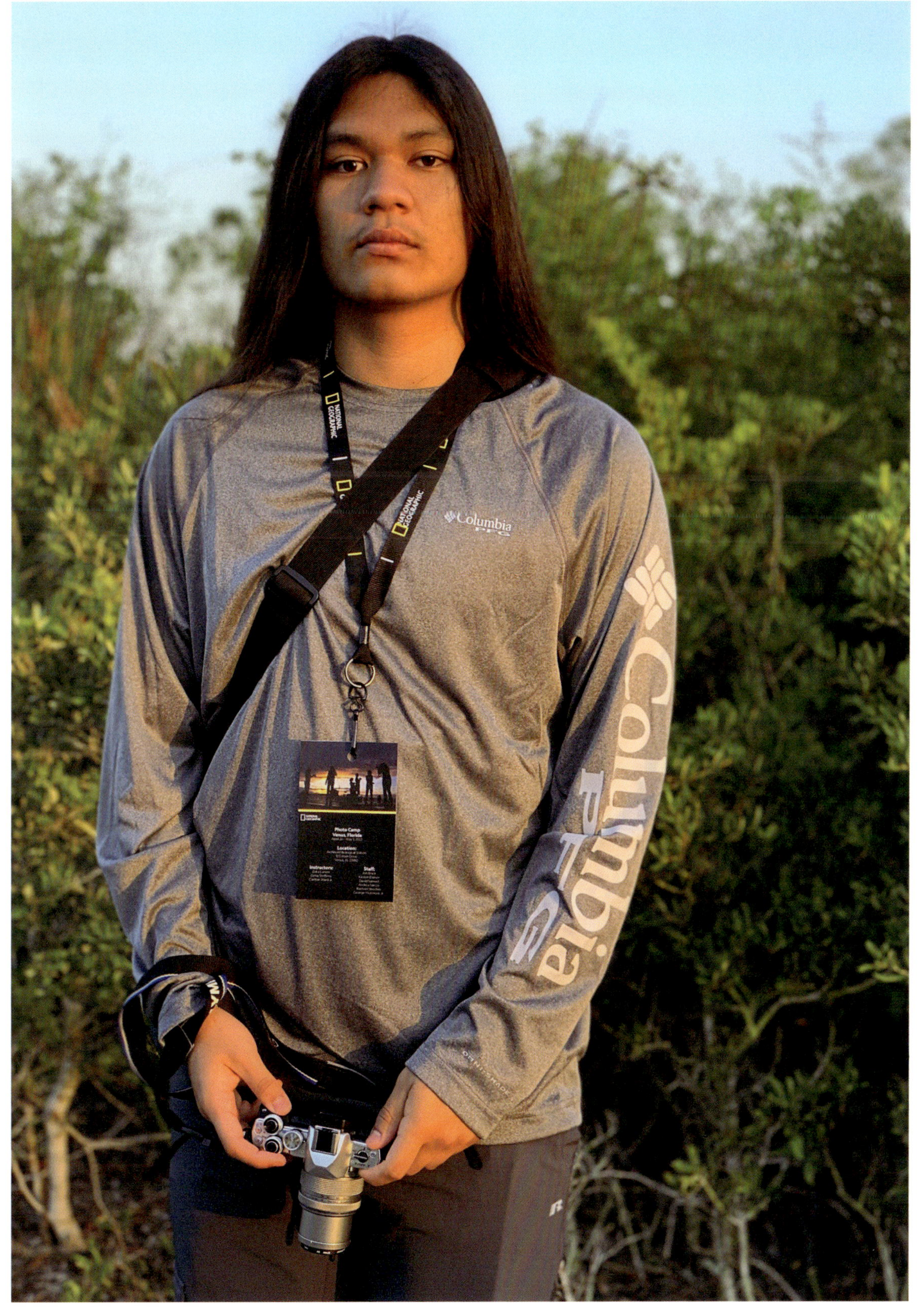
Columbia
PFG
Columbia
PFG

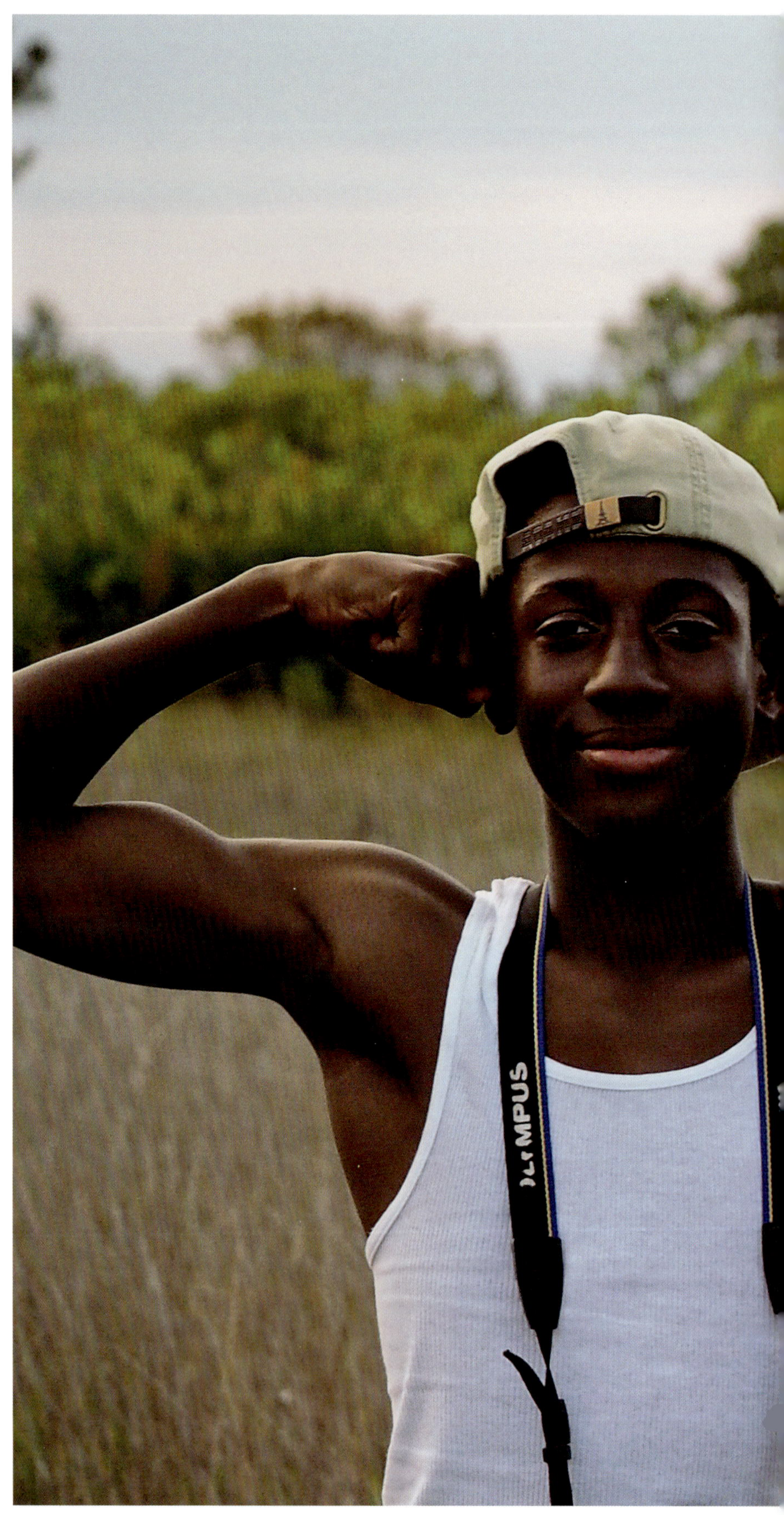

JORDYN WASHINGTON / FLORIDA, U.S.A. 2022

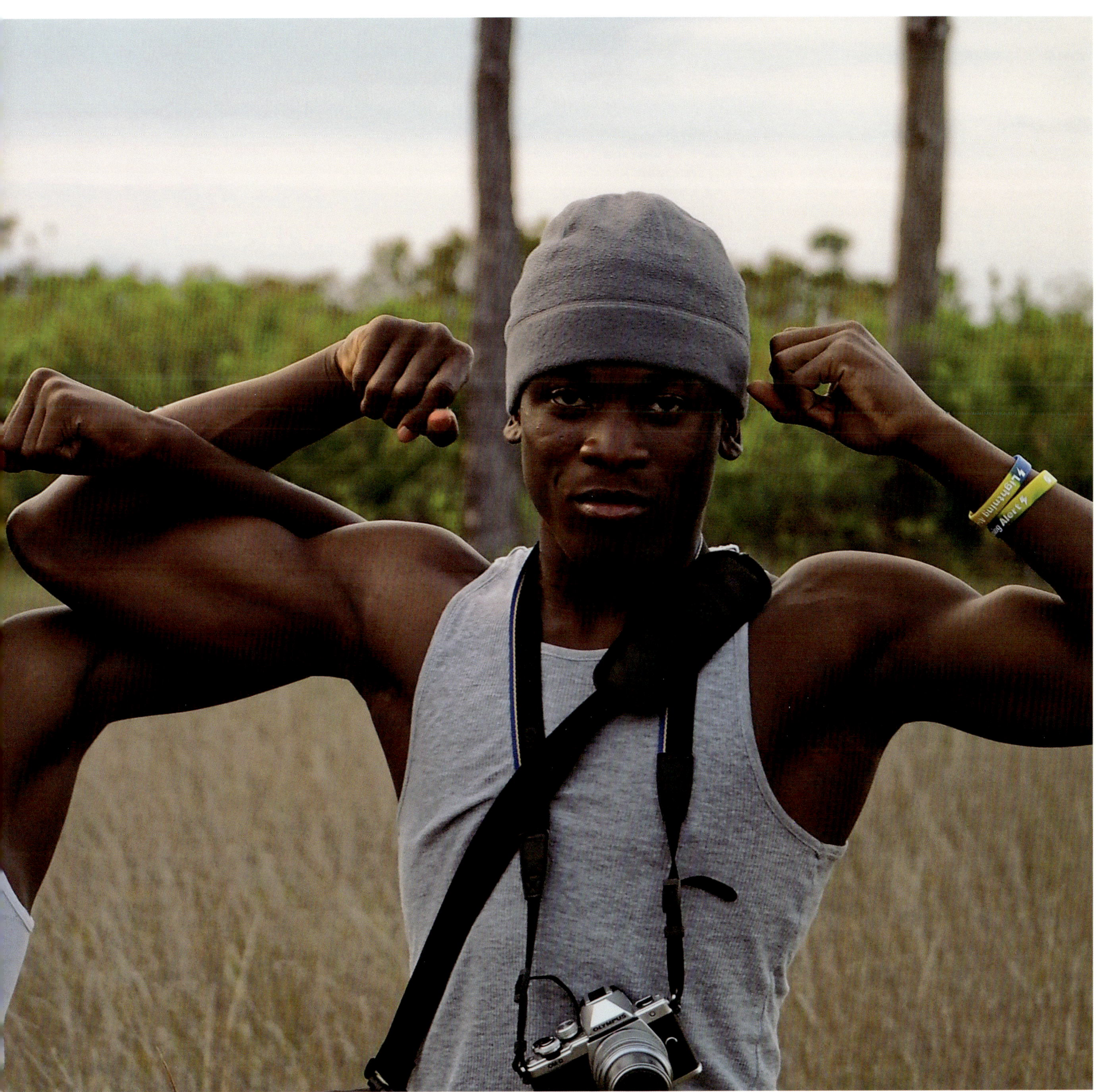
OLYMPUS

> ***"I went to places I never thought would be interesting and beautiful:*** **my** ***neighborhood,*** **my** ***friends, and*** **my** ***family."***
>
> —ANONYMOUS, STUDENT EVALUATION, LITTLE HAVANA, MIAMI, FLORIDA, U.S.A. 2008

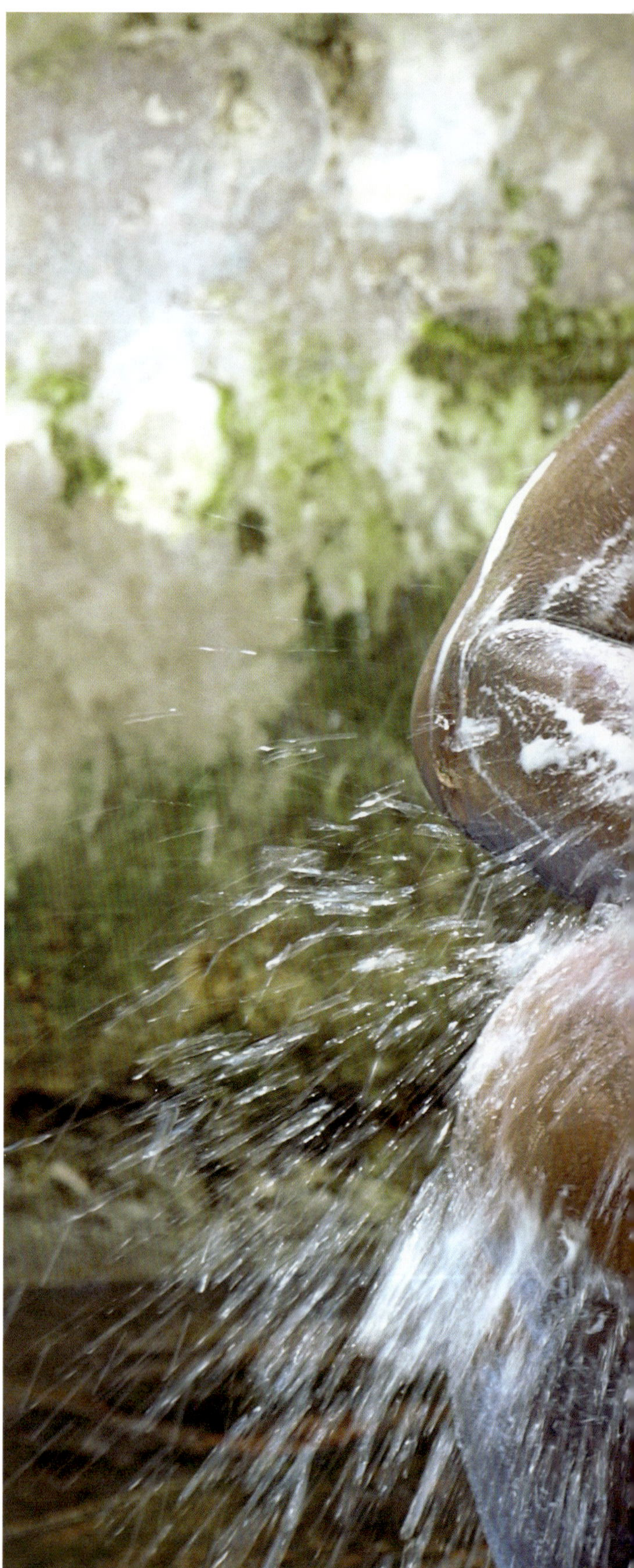

DOMINIQUE BONNETT / BARBADOS 2010

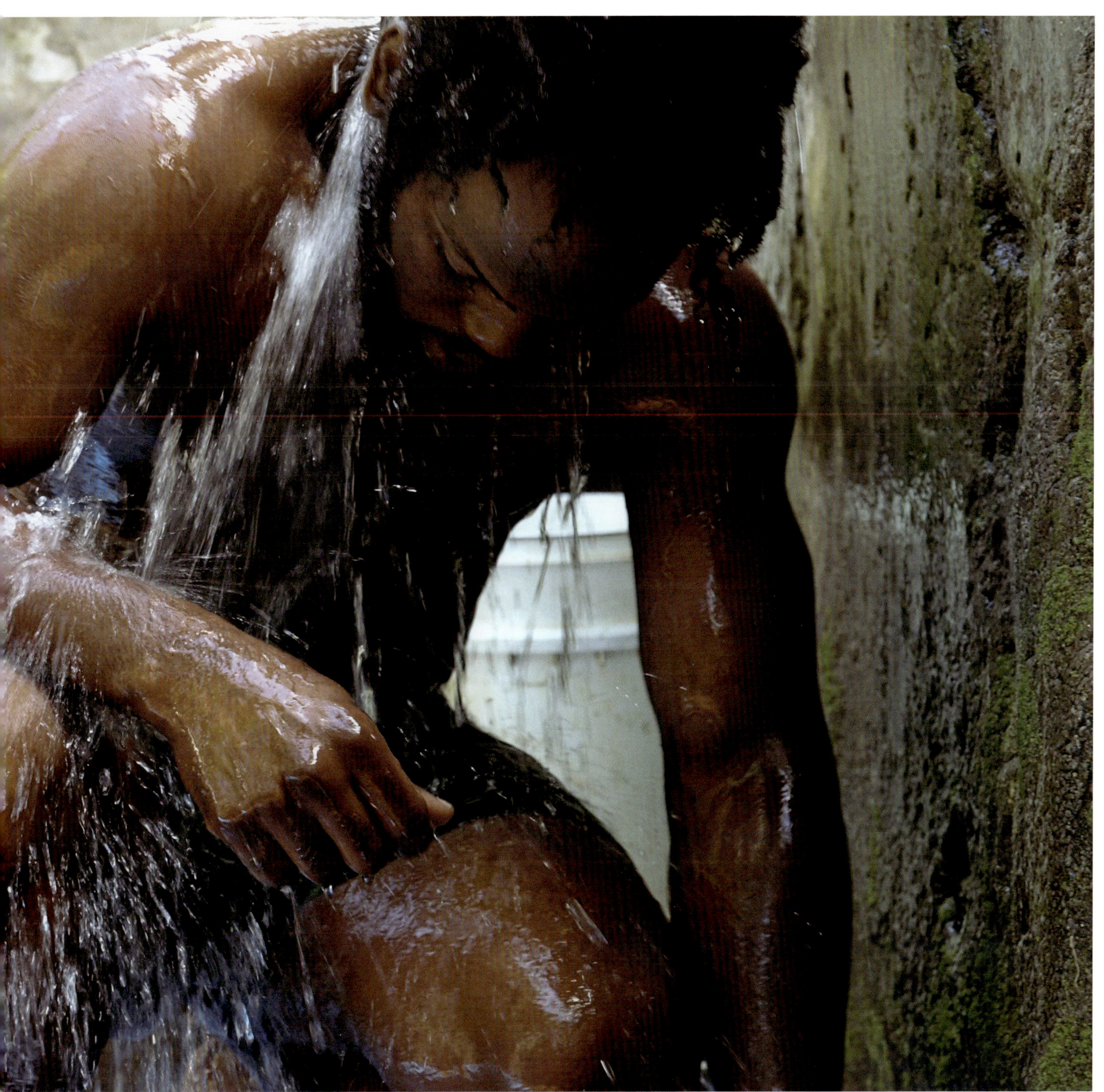

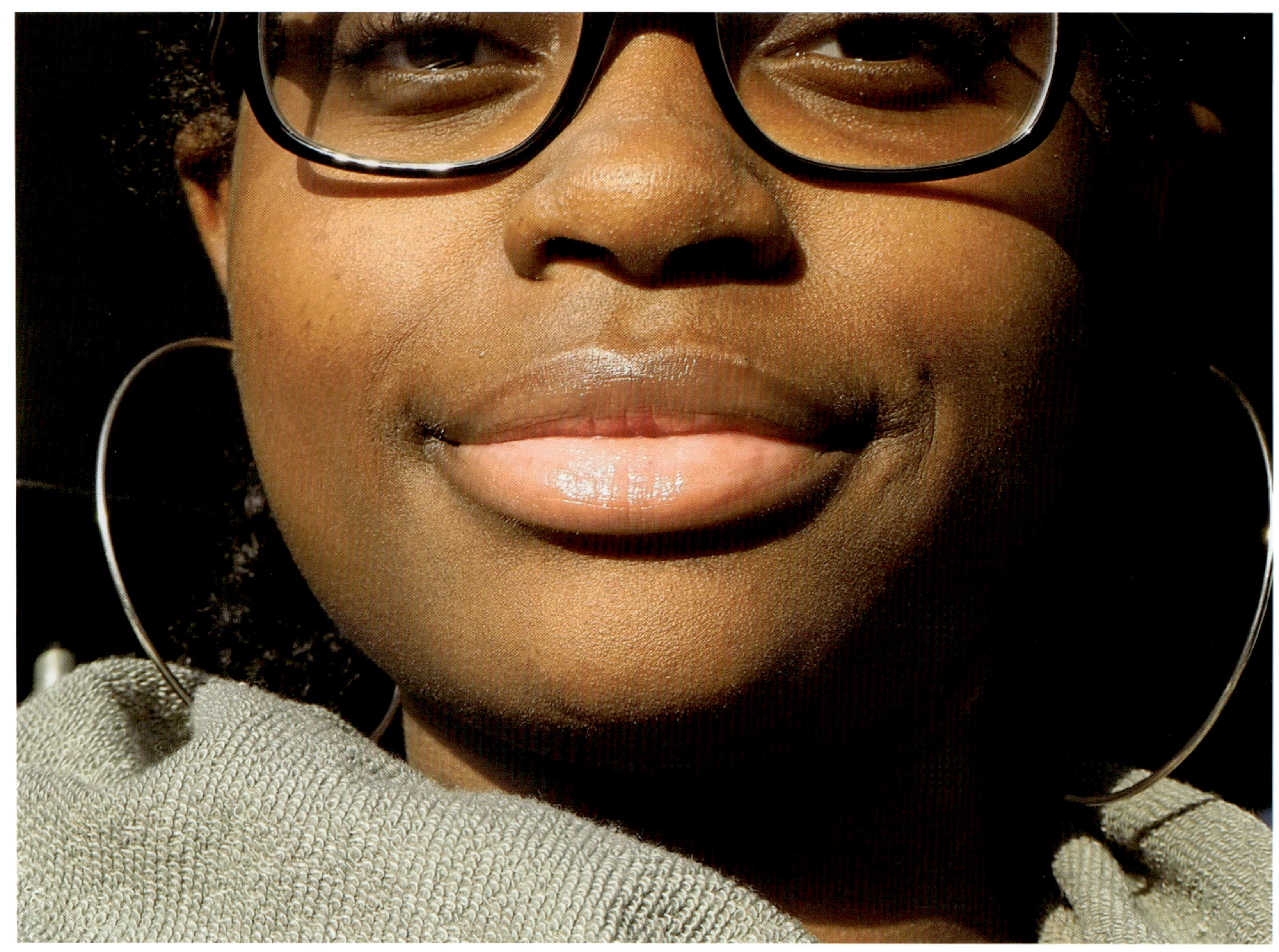

NIJHAE WYNN / NEW JERSEY, U.S.A. 2018

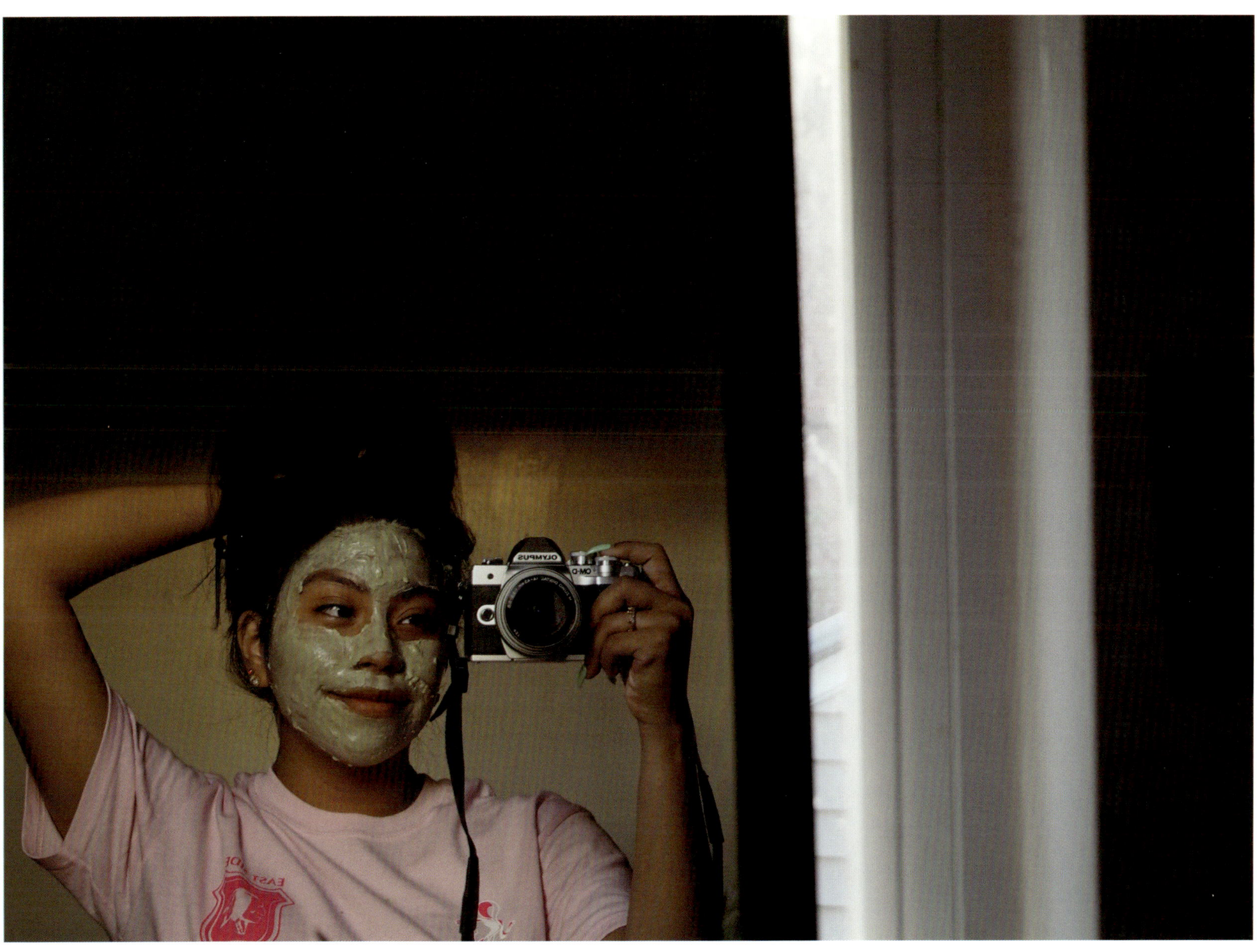

AMERICA NAVARRETE / NEW JERSEY, U.S.A. 2018

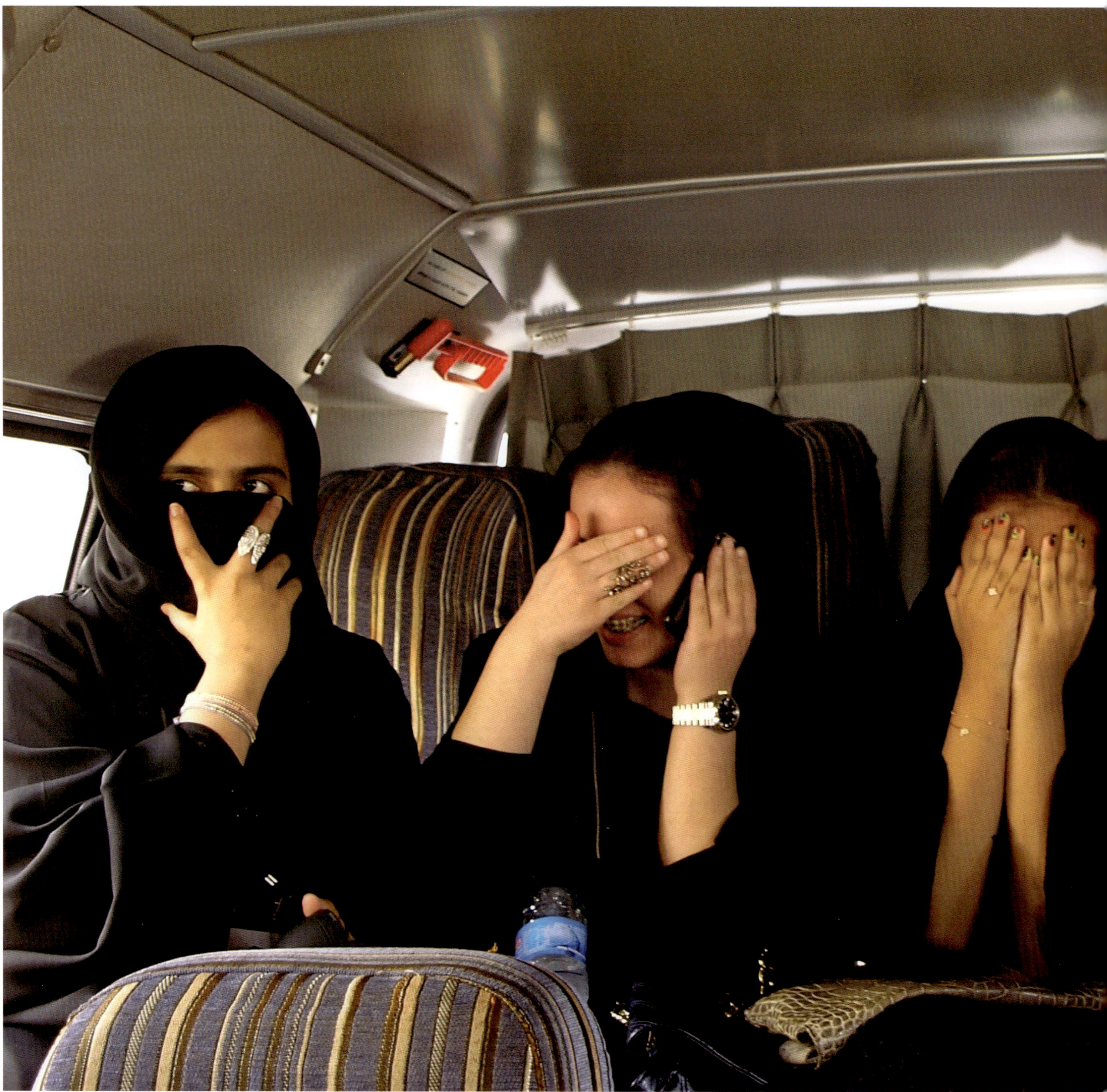

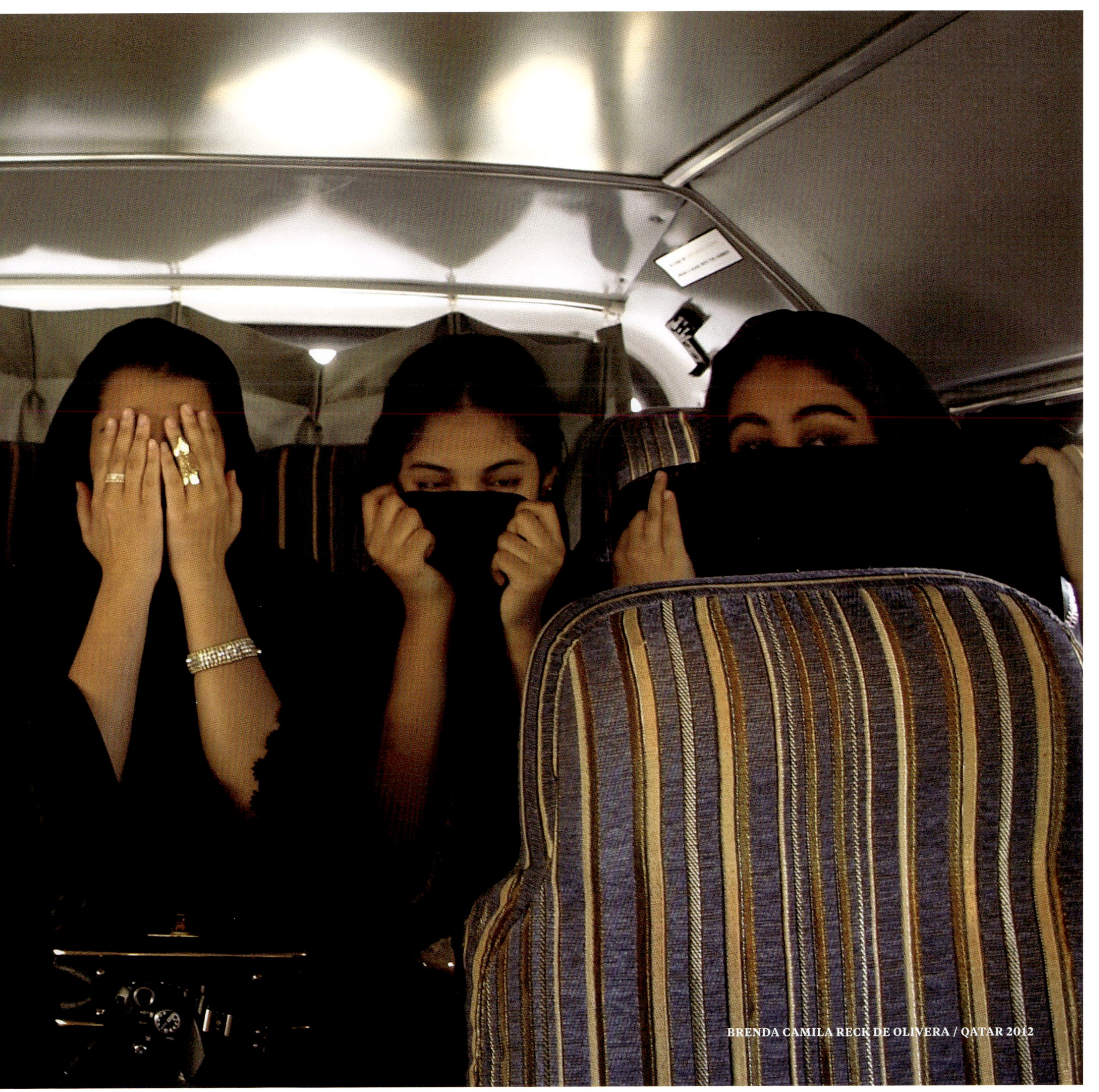
BRENDA CAMILA RECK DE OLIVERA / QATAR 2012

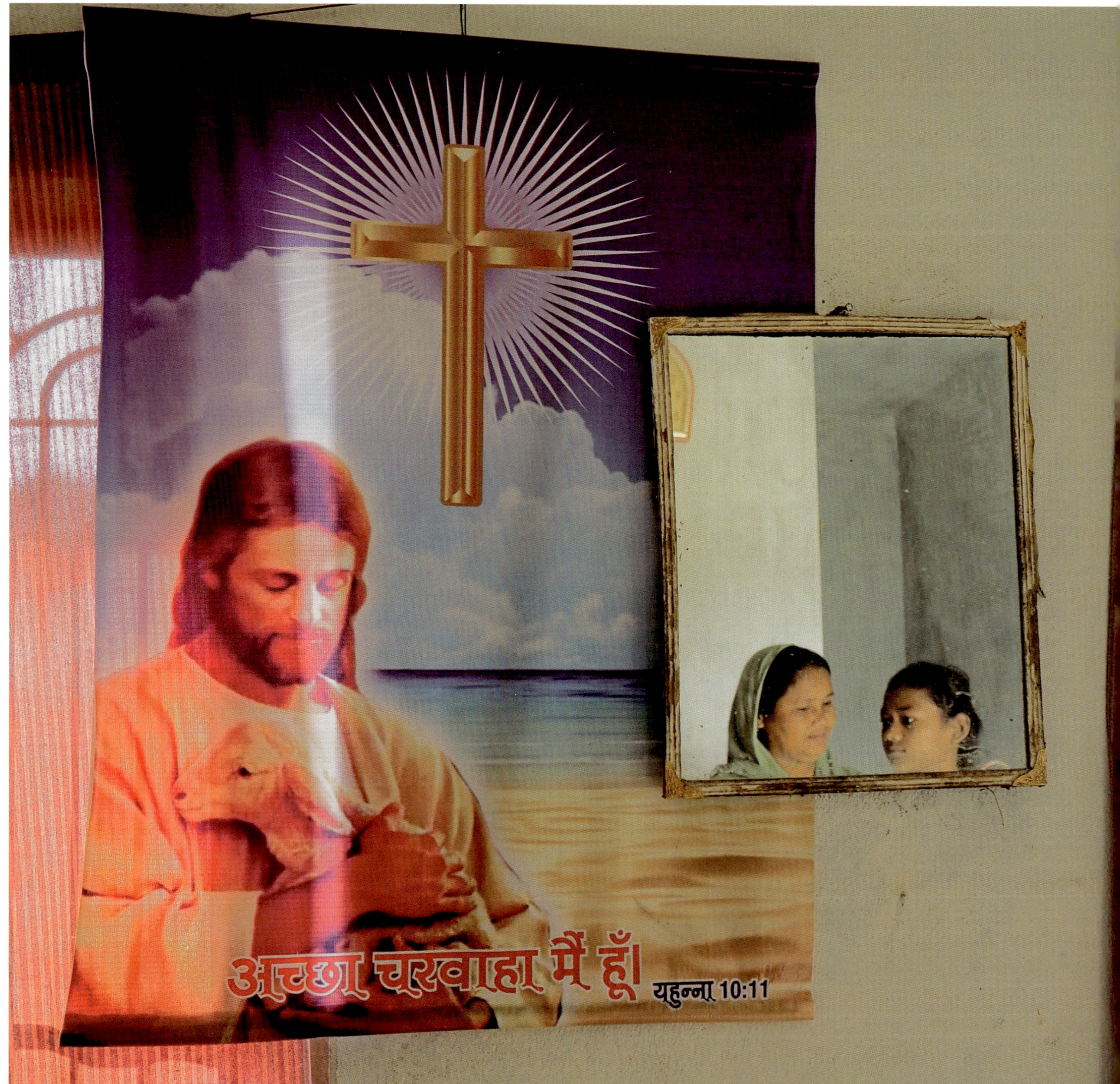
अच्छा चरवाहा मैं हूँ।
यहुन्ना 10:11

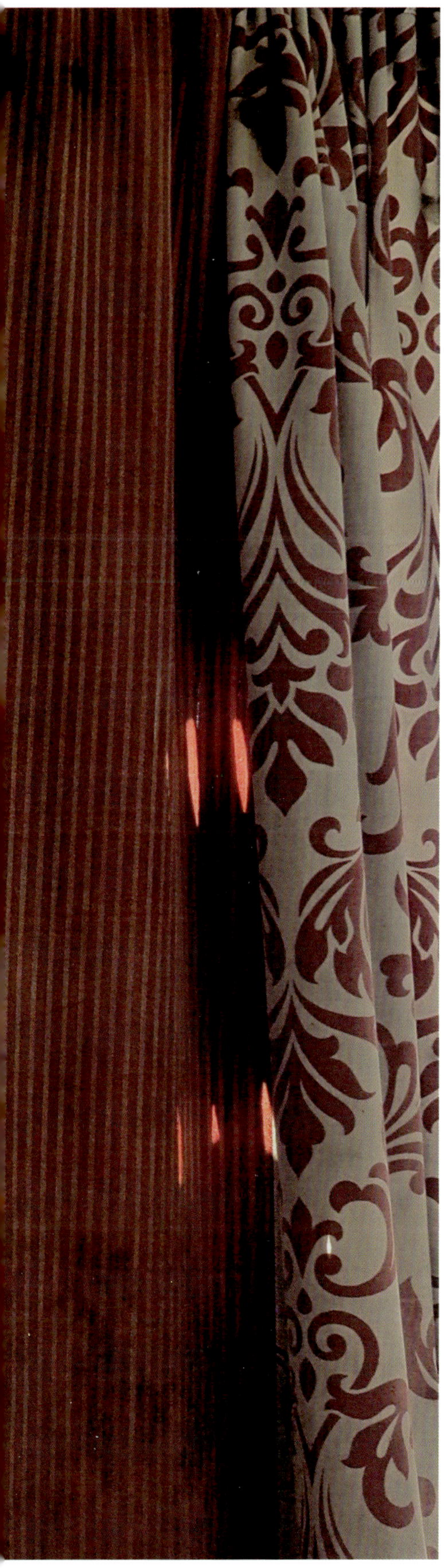

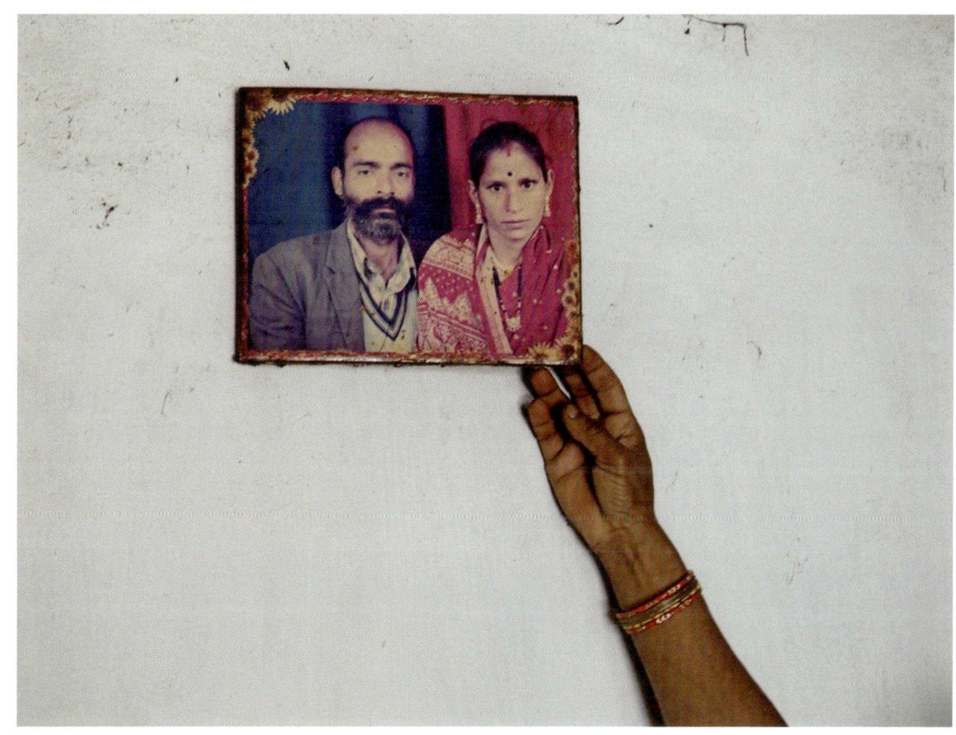

ABOVE: **CLIFFORD CHAND / INDIA 2018** LEFT: **SEEMA BAHADUR / INDIA 2018**

Photo Camp has worked with youth from the Good Shepherd Agricultural Mission in Banbasa, India, on several programs over the years. The artwork on this page was created by Sonia Singh for her first assignment in 2018. Each student was asked to design their own project and to share their stories. Sonia chose to create drawings and poetry, matching them to photographs she made over the course of the week. "My gift to the world," she wrote, "is that I am joyful."

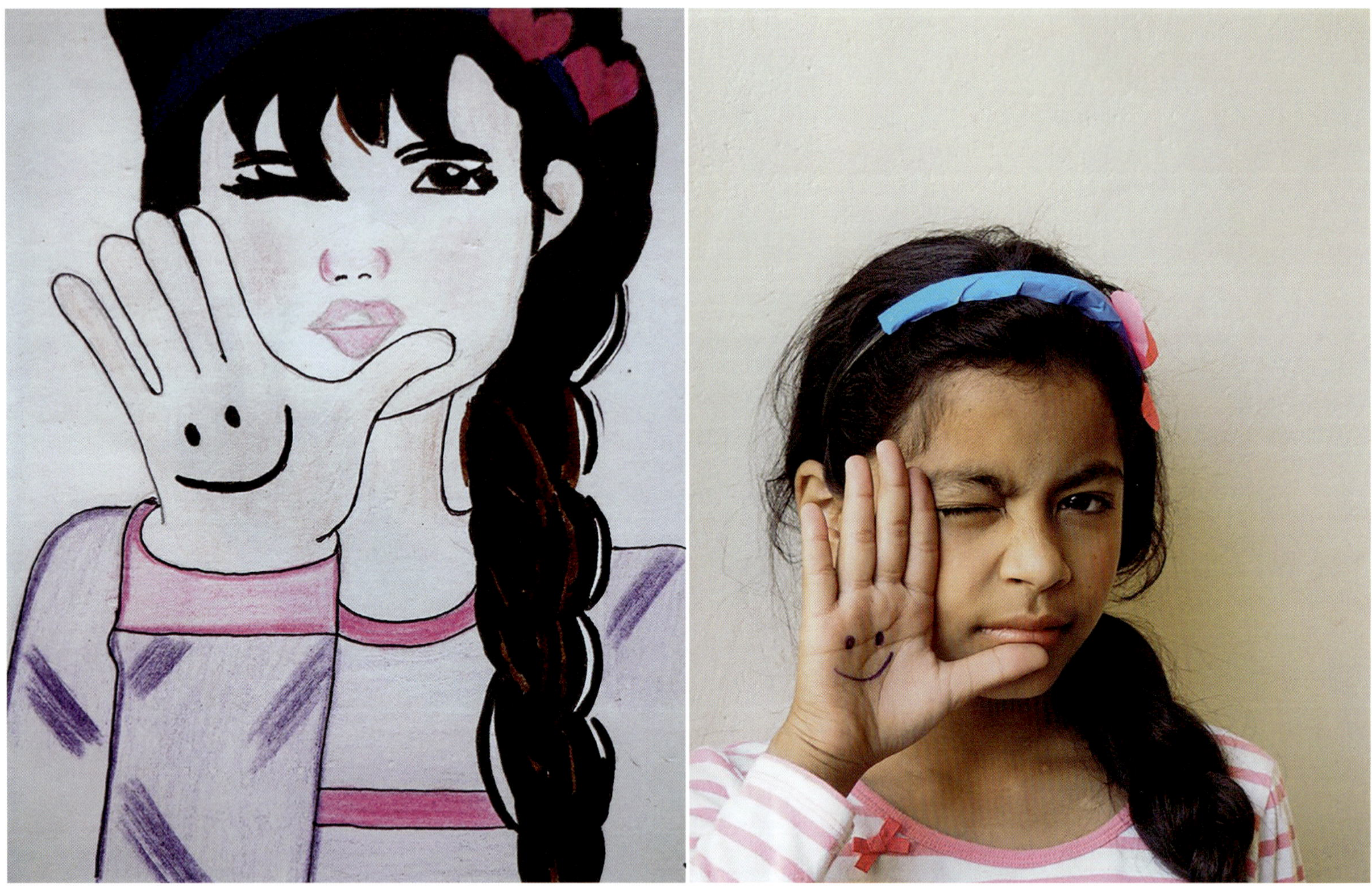

SONIA SINGH / INDIA 2018

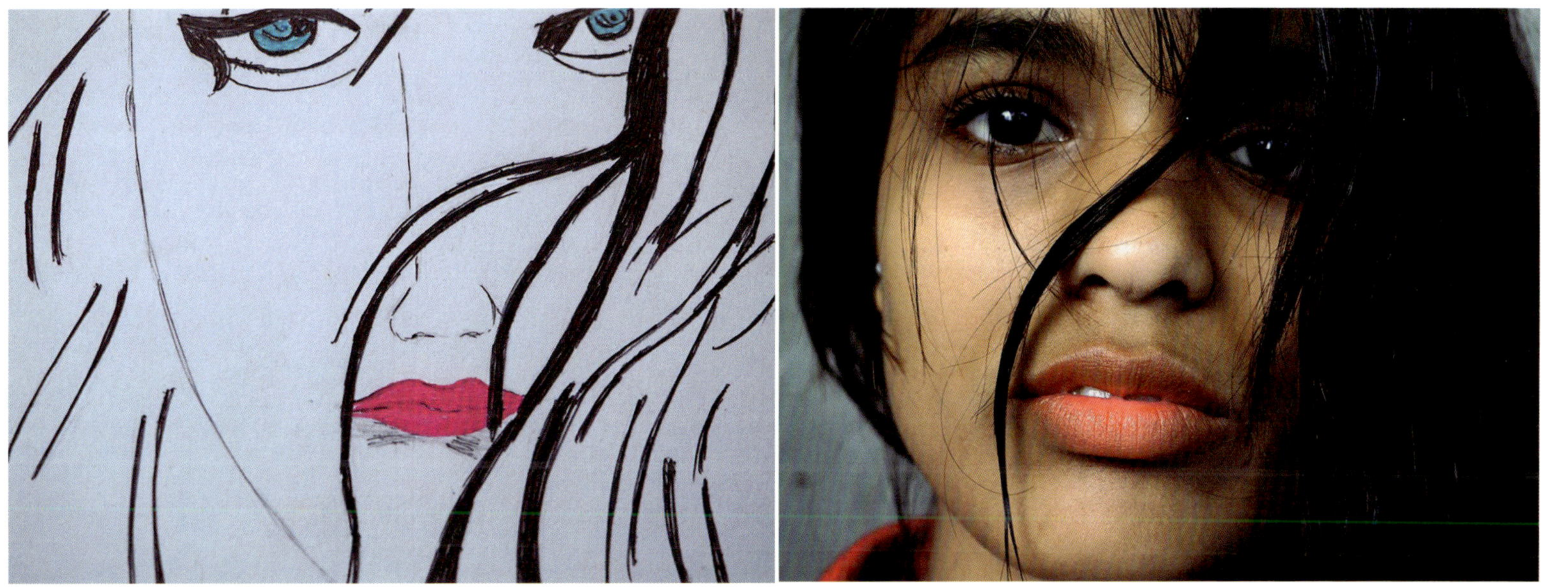

SONIA SINGH / INDIA 2018

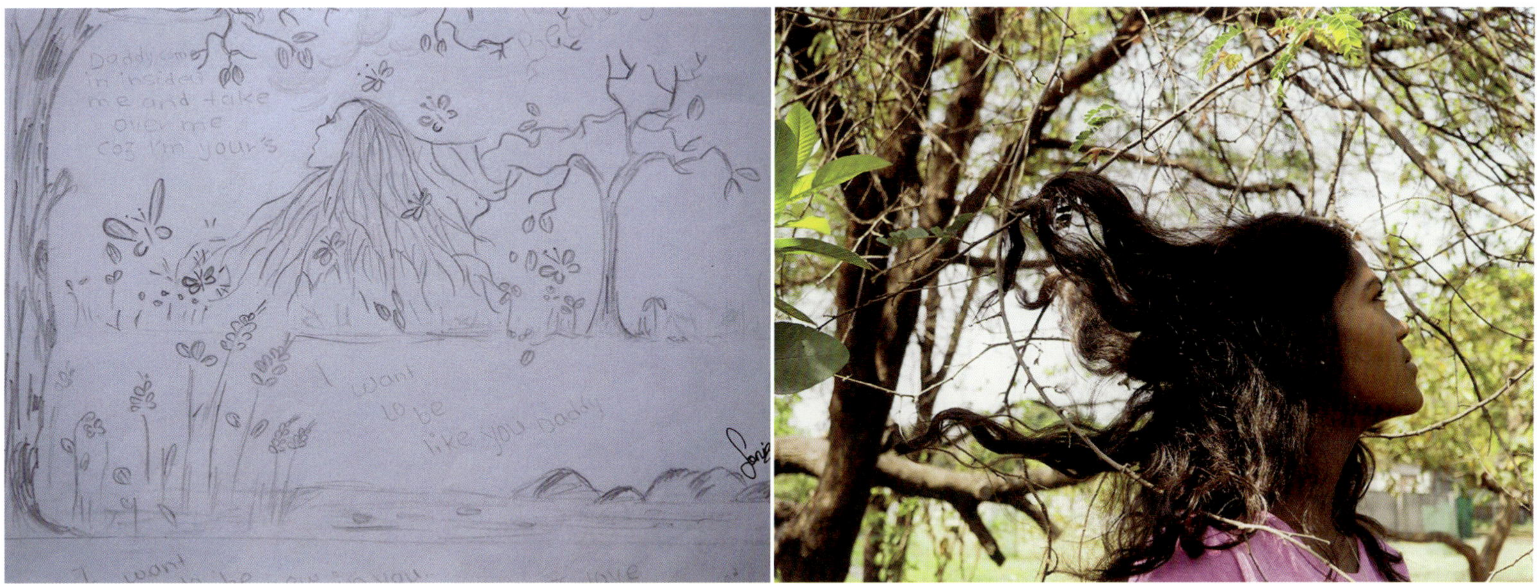

SONIA SINGH / INDIA 2018

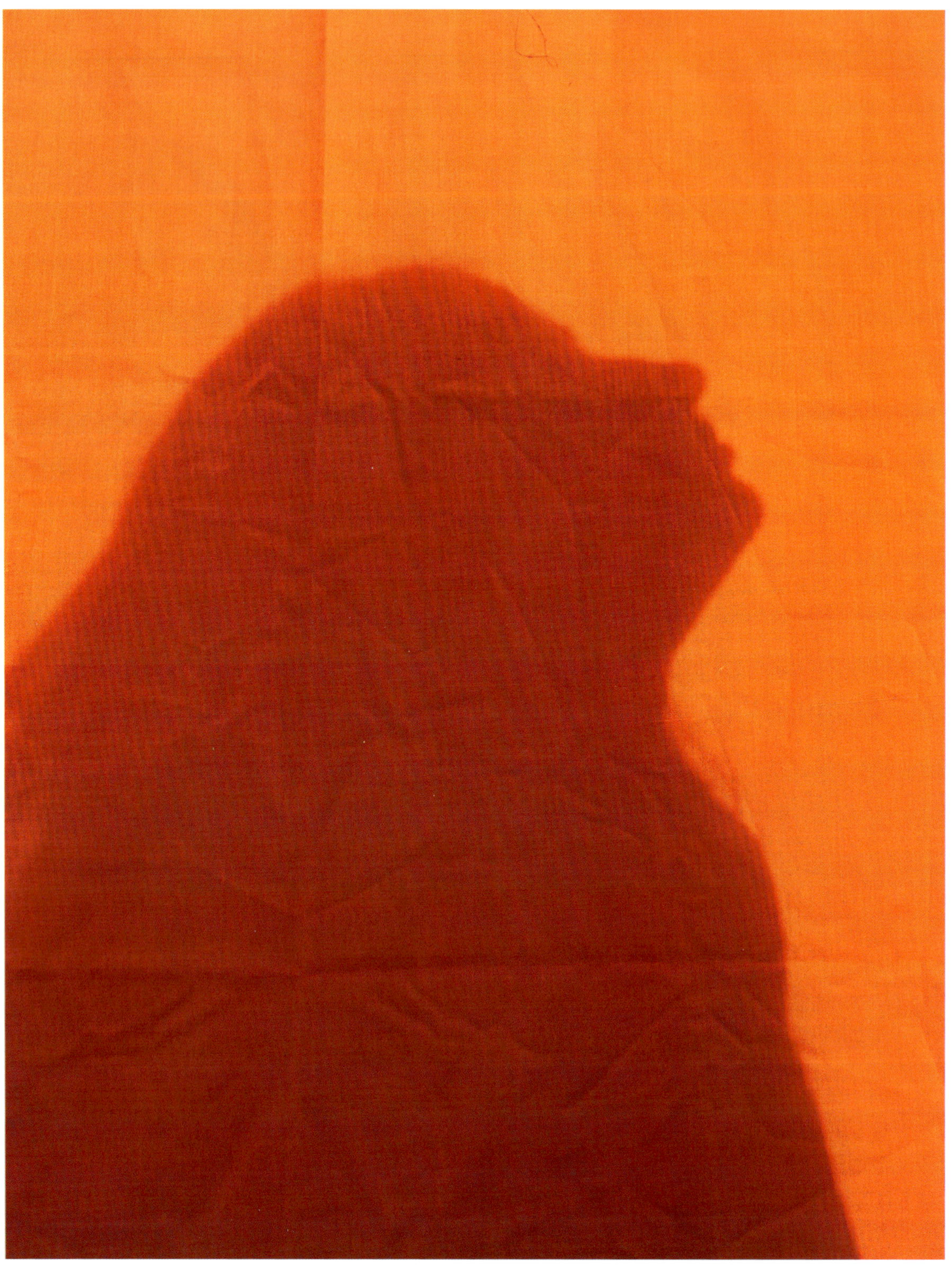

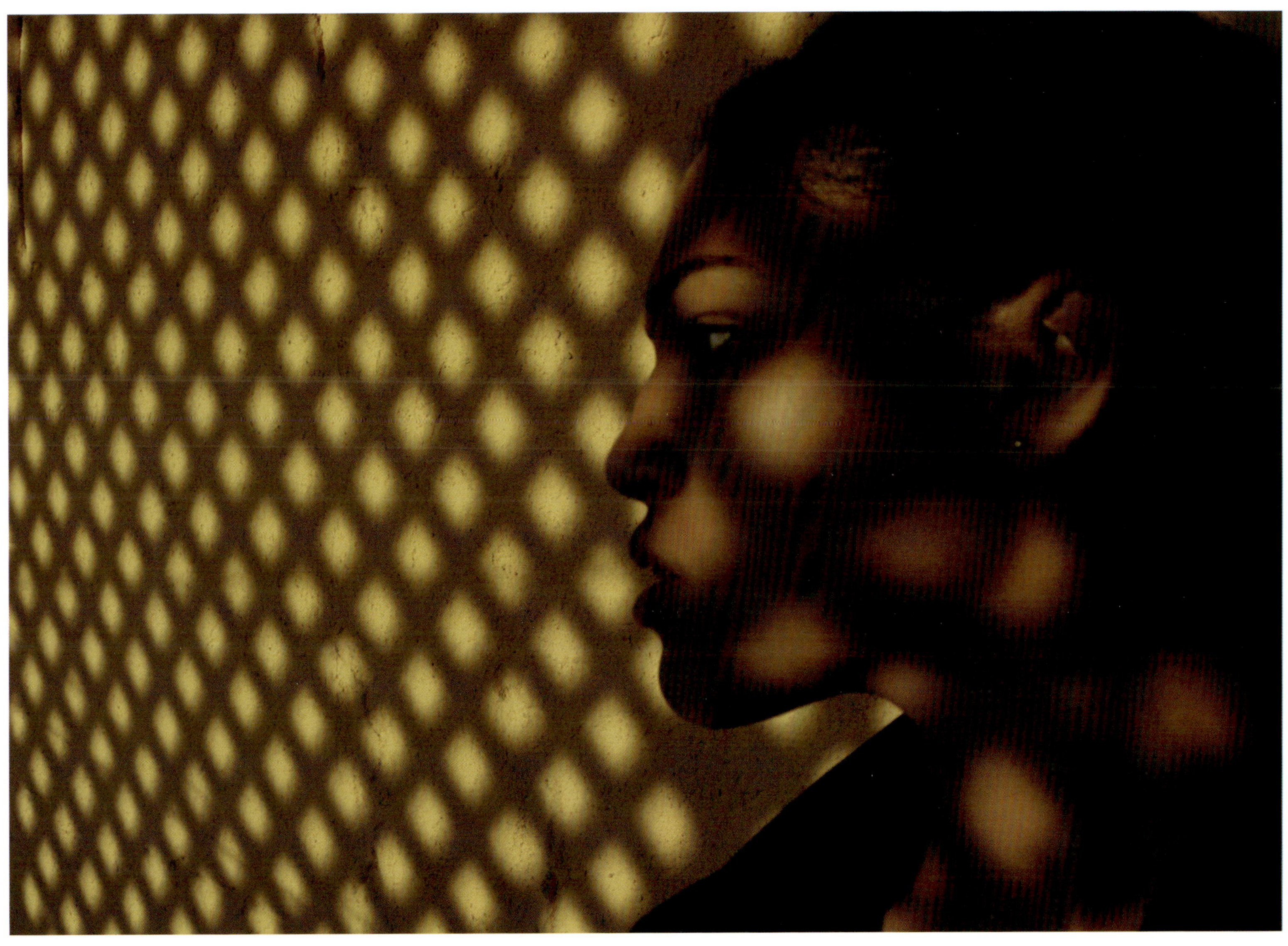

ABOVE: **MELANIE GRANT / BARBADOS 2010** OPPOSITE: **SONIA SINGH / INDIA 2018**

Camp Profile
Virtual Camps 2020 and 2021

AFTER COVID-19 HIT, THE PHOTO CAMP TEAM felt restless. After all, the outbreak forced the closure of a program that had run continuously for 17 years. Then the group came up with a solution that would allow camps to operate over the course of the pandemic.

Virtual Photo Camp was born in 2020 with the mission of using photography to make the difficult days of isolation less confining. It used to its advantage one of the best features of remote communication: Through Zoom and other online platforms, students from every corner of the world were able to see each other, swap stories, and show their photographs. The immediacy of their images—hands pressed against shuttered windows, self-portraits in confined spaces—speaks to the frustrations experienced by many people, perhaps especially adolescents.

Camp participant Alana Daly Mulligan expressed the feelings of millions when she wrote, "Here in Ireland during the pandemic, life is simultaneously boring but also terrifying. I miss hugging more than anything." In an imaginary letter to his parents, Sartre Ndebaneza, wrote a stirring phrase from his adopted city of Baltimore: "The world seems to be tilted away from happiness."

From June 2020 to October 2021, four camps were conducted. In each, the students were encouraged to respond to such questions as "What is democracy?" Student Rayan Abdulahi Mohamed, writing from home in Syracuse, New York, was frank: "As a minority Black Muslim ... am I even welcome in this country?" Laura Johnson, from Long Beach, California, imagined successful democracy as when the "collective voice of the people is loud enough to enact lasting, positive change for the greater good."

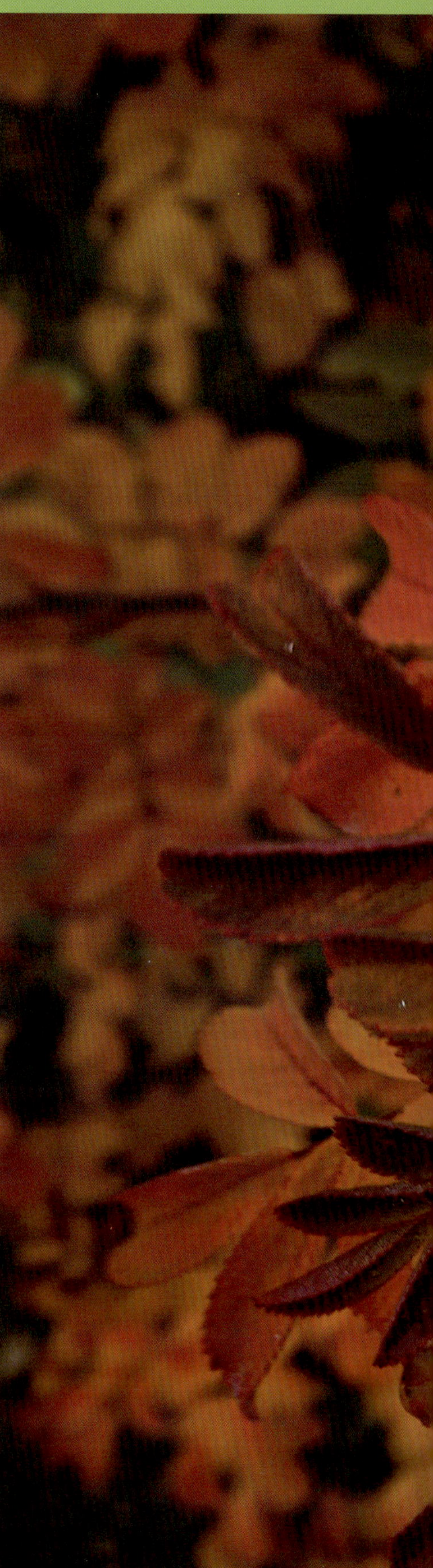

NASTASIA CAOLE / ALASKA, U.S.A. 2020

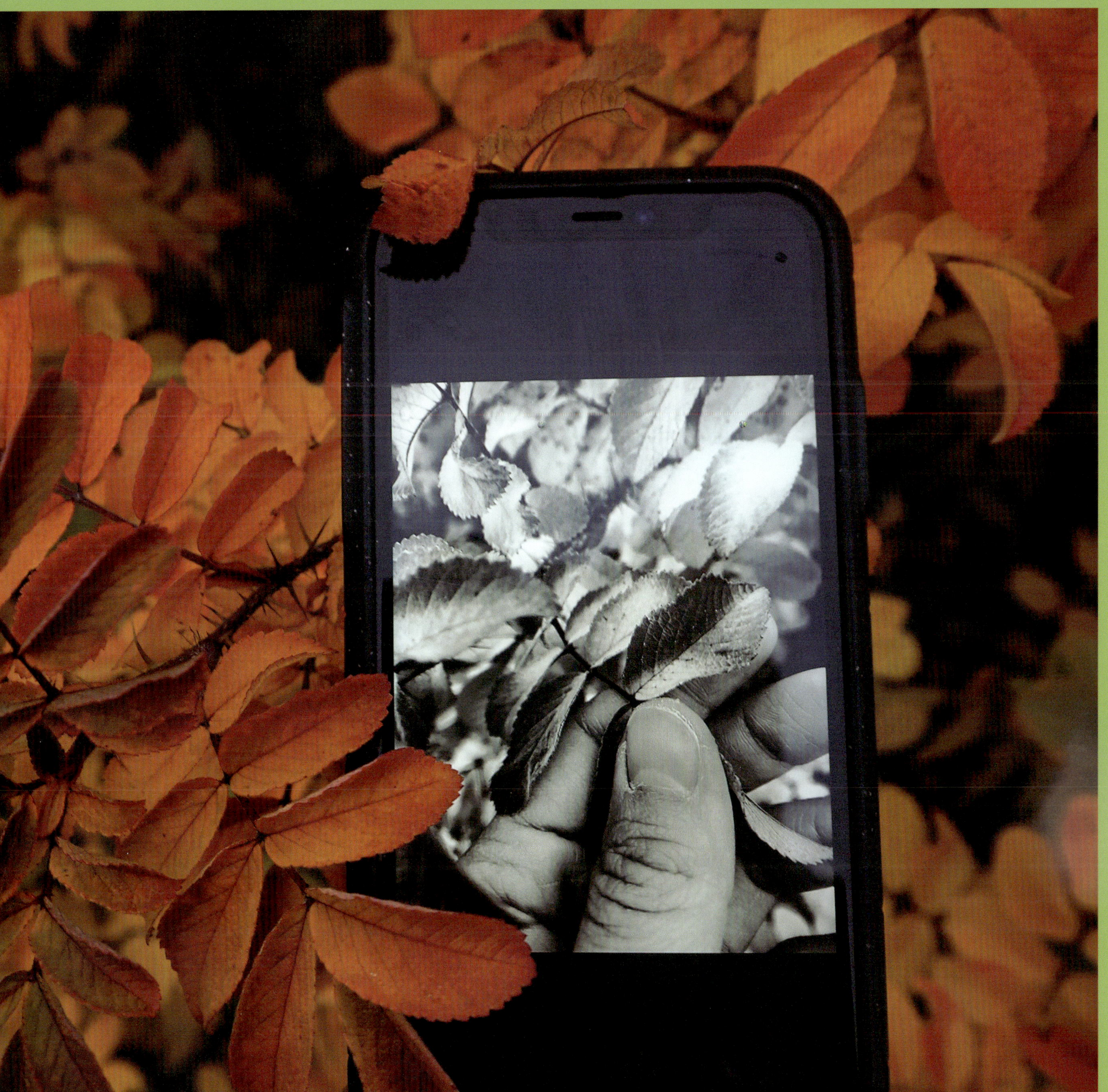

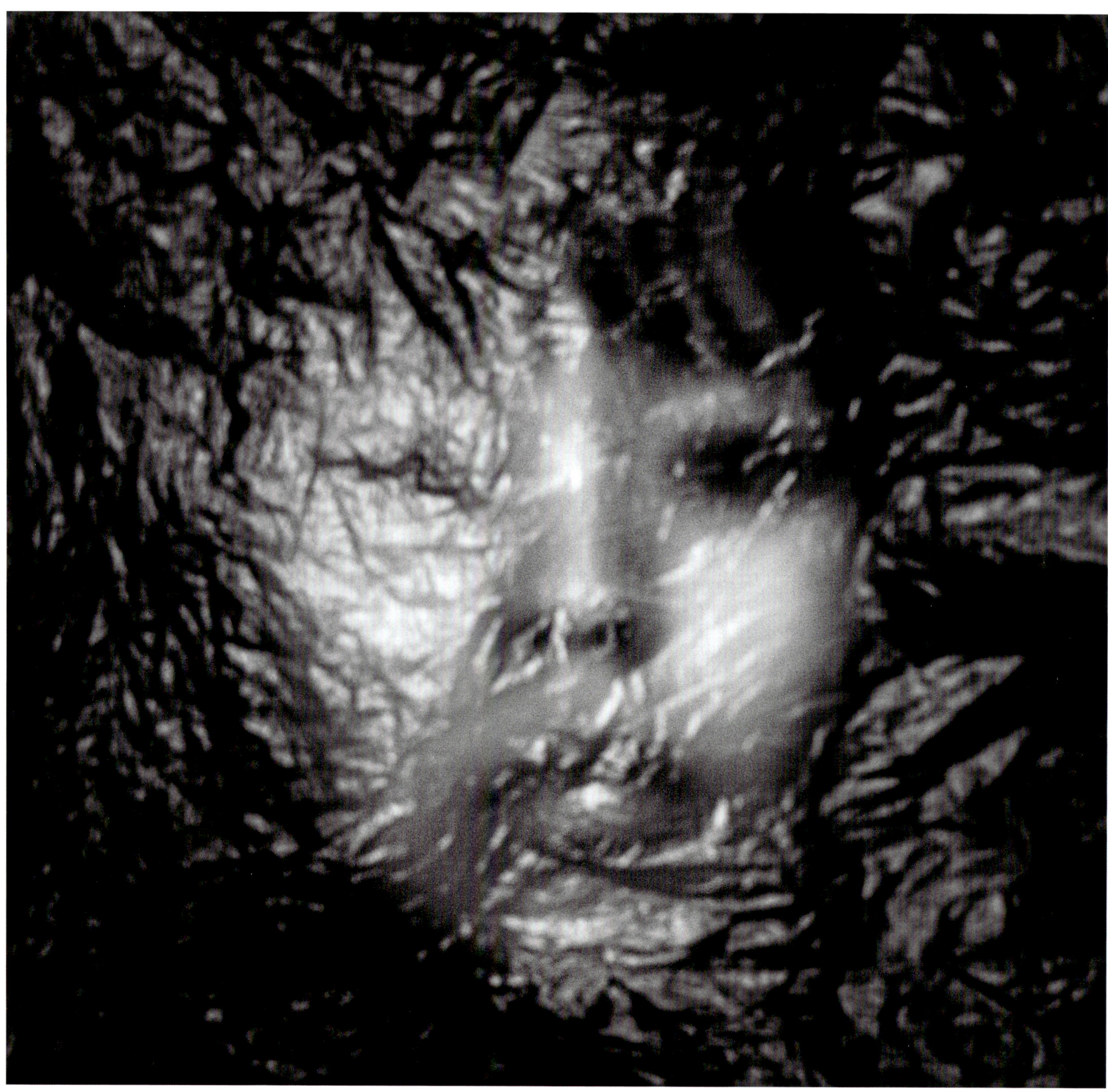

OPPOSITE: **SHARON GONZALES / PERU 2020**

RIGHT: **GABRIELLA NICOLE BÁEZ REYES / PUERTO RICO 2021**

BELOW LEFT: **NASTASIA CAOLE / ALASKA, U.S.A. 2020**

BELOW RIGHT: **MARYAM BADR / TEXAS, U.S.A. 2020**

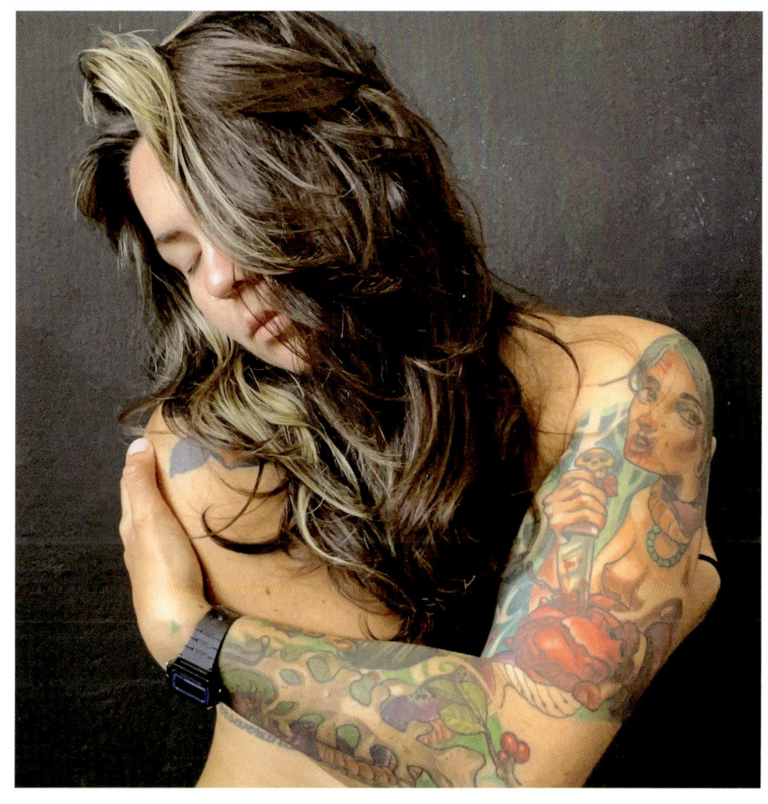

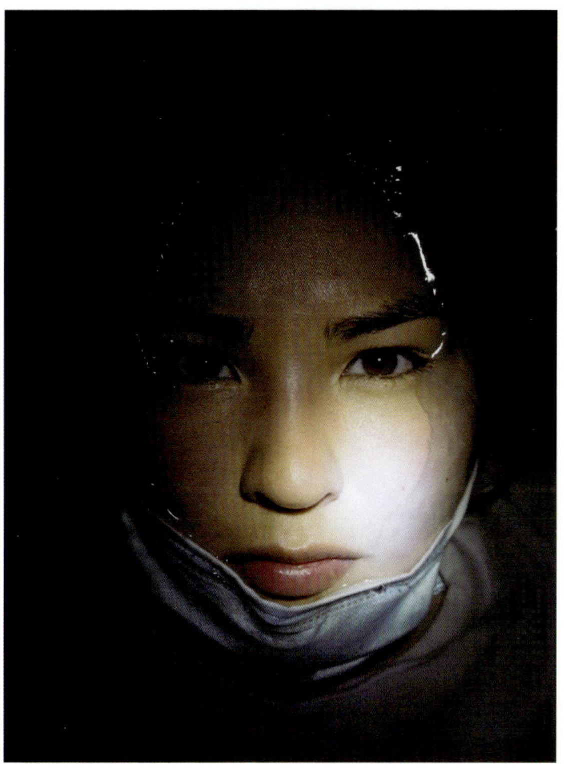

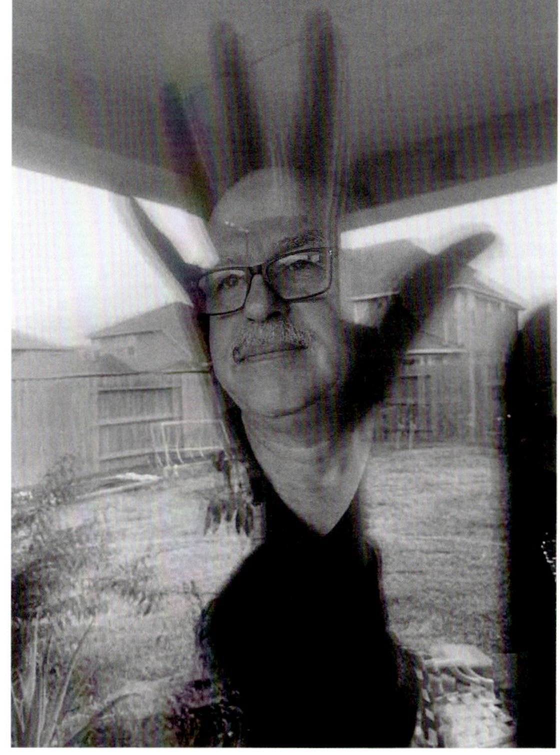

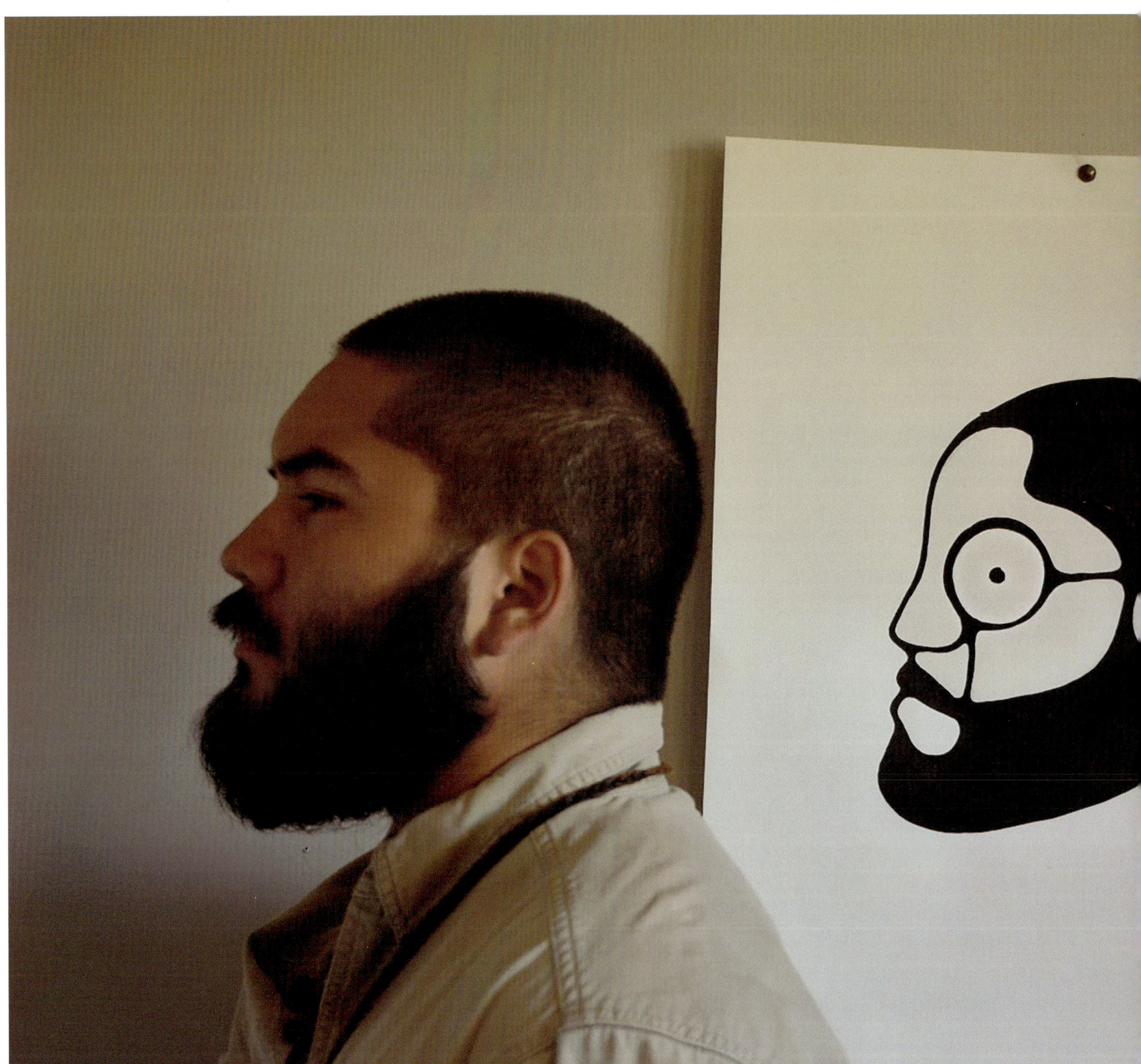

"As an Anishnaabe, Onyota'aka man, I've heard a few teachings surrounding men growin' their hair out long. I've been taught that it's an extension of our spirit, and that the closer it is to the ground, the more connected we are to creation. Being a native kid growin' up in an urban environment without another Indigenous person in sight, my long hair served to be one of my only connections to my culture and pride for the majority of my childhood.

My braid by the age of 18 was essentially a physical representation of the entirety of my life: every moment of happiness and joy, and every moment of loneliness and traumatization. So when I stood there in the mirror a few weeks ago with a pocketknife in hand, and dead set on cutting my hair off with it, I took a moment to look at myself.

What I saw was a father, a man, an artist, and a guy who just wanted to be better than who he was up until that moment."

—TEHATSISTAHAWI KENNEDY, ONTARIO, CANADA,
VIRTUAL PHOTO CAMP EARTH STORIES 2020

TEHATSISTAHAWI KENNEDY / CANADA 2020

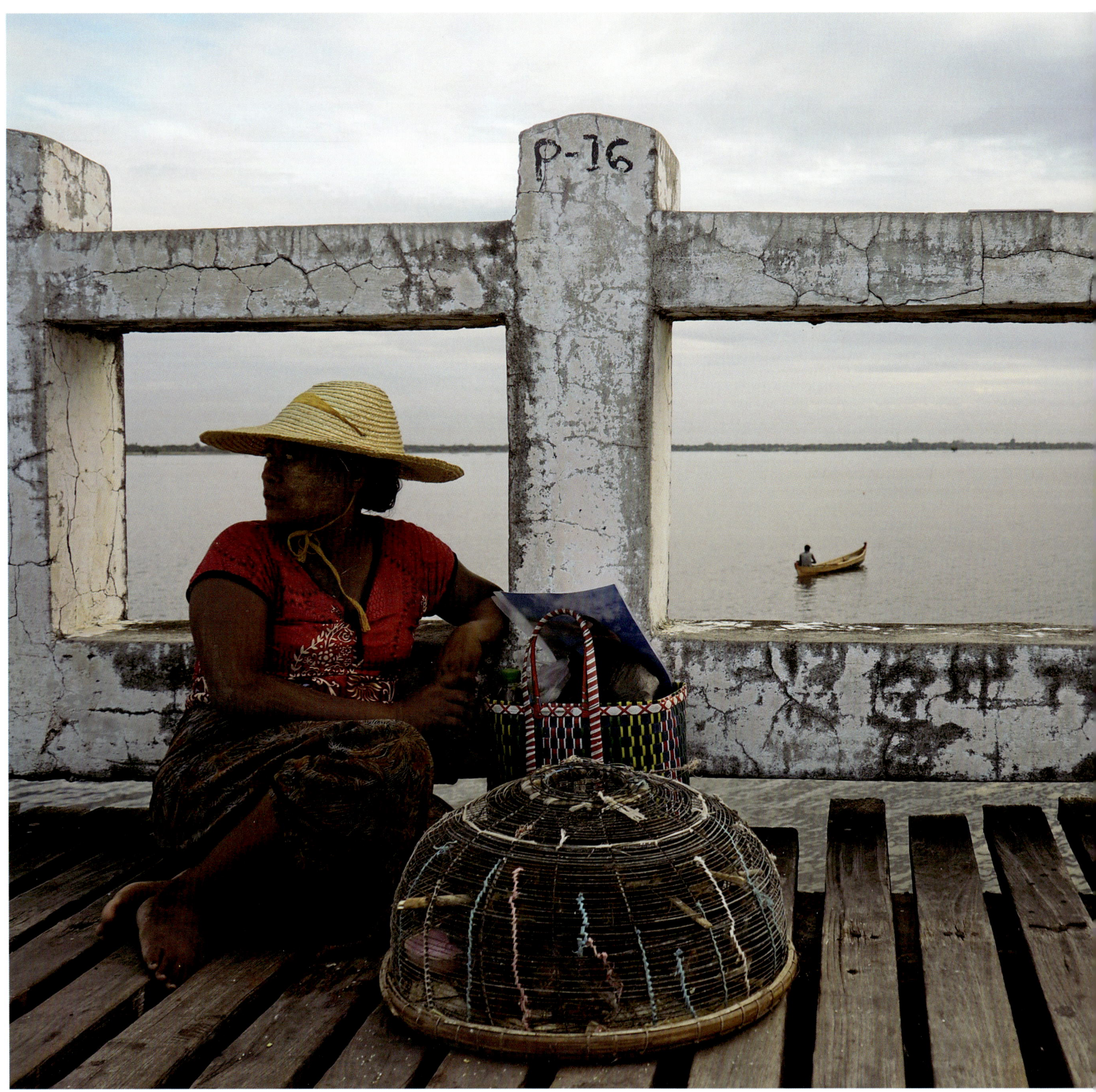
P-16

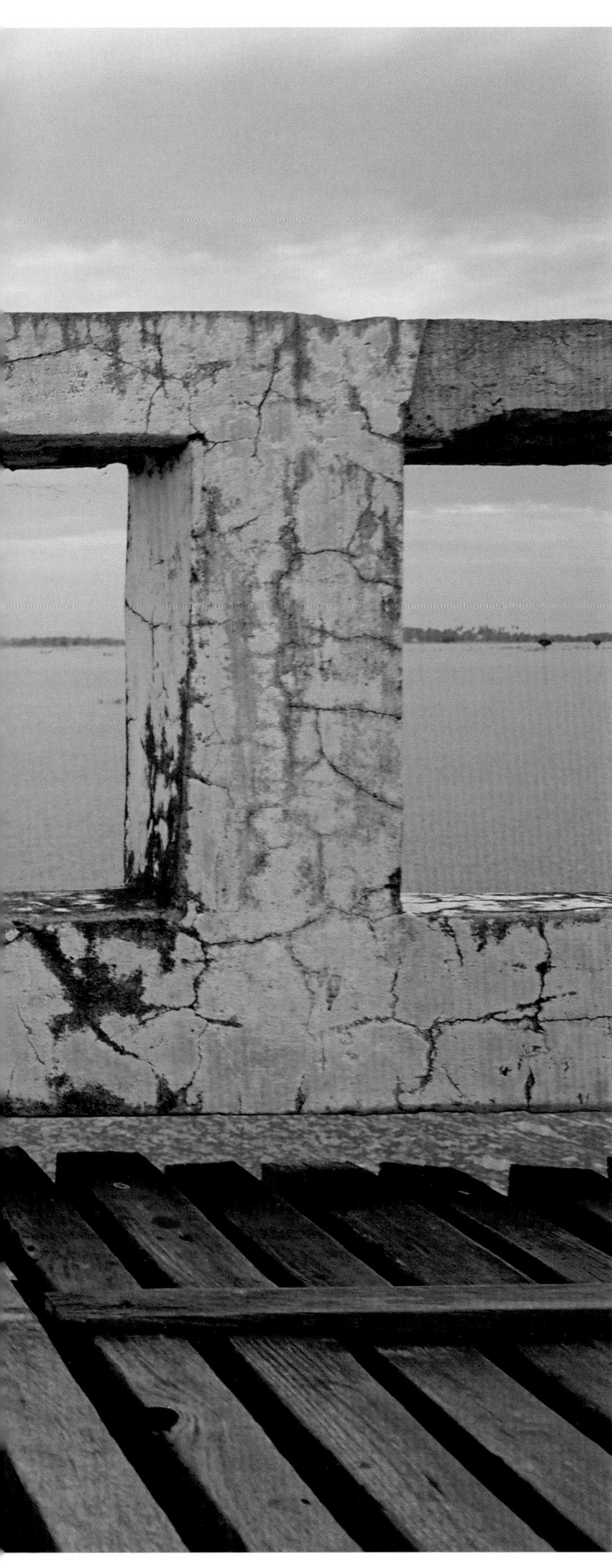

AYE MYAT MON / MYANMAR 2018

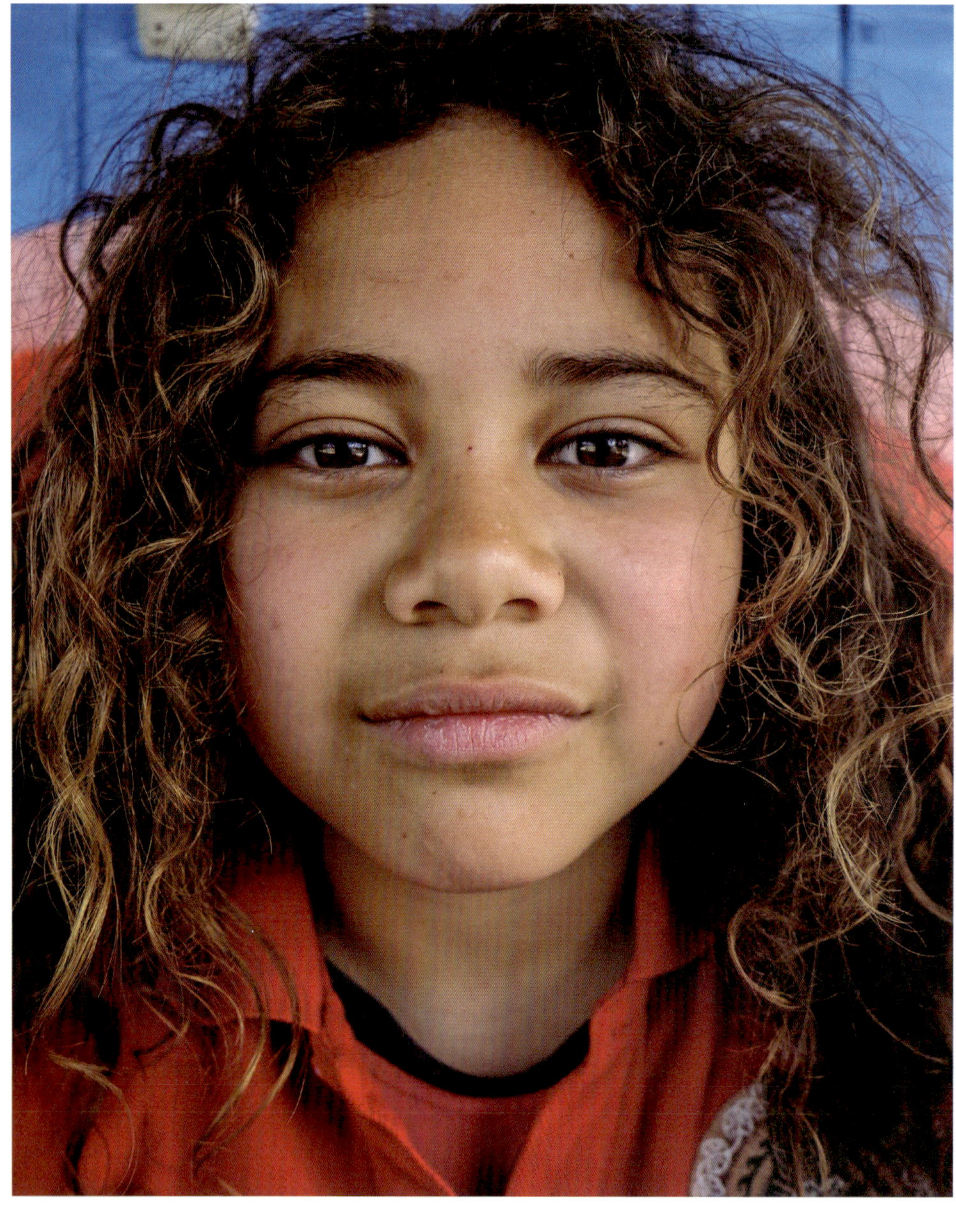

ABOVE: **SHONITA WIKAIRE / NEW ZEALAND 2019**
OPPOSITE: **ANASTASIA HUIARANGI / NEW ZEALAND 2019**

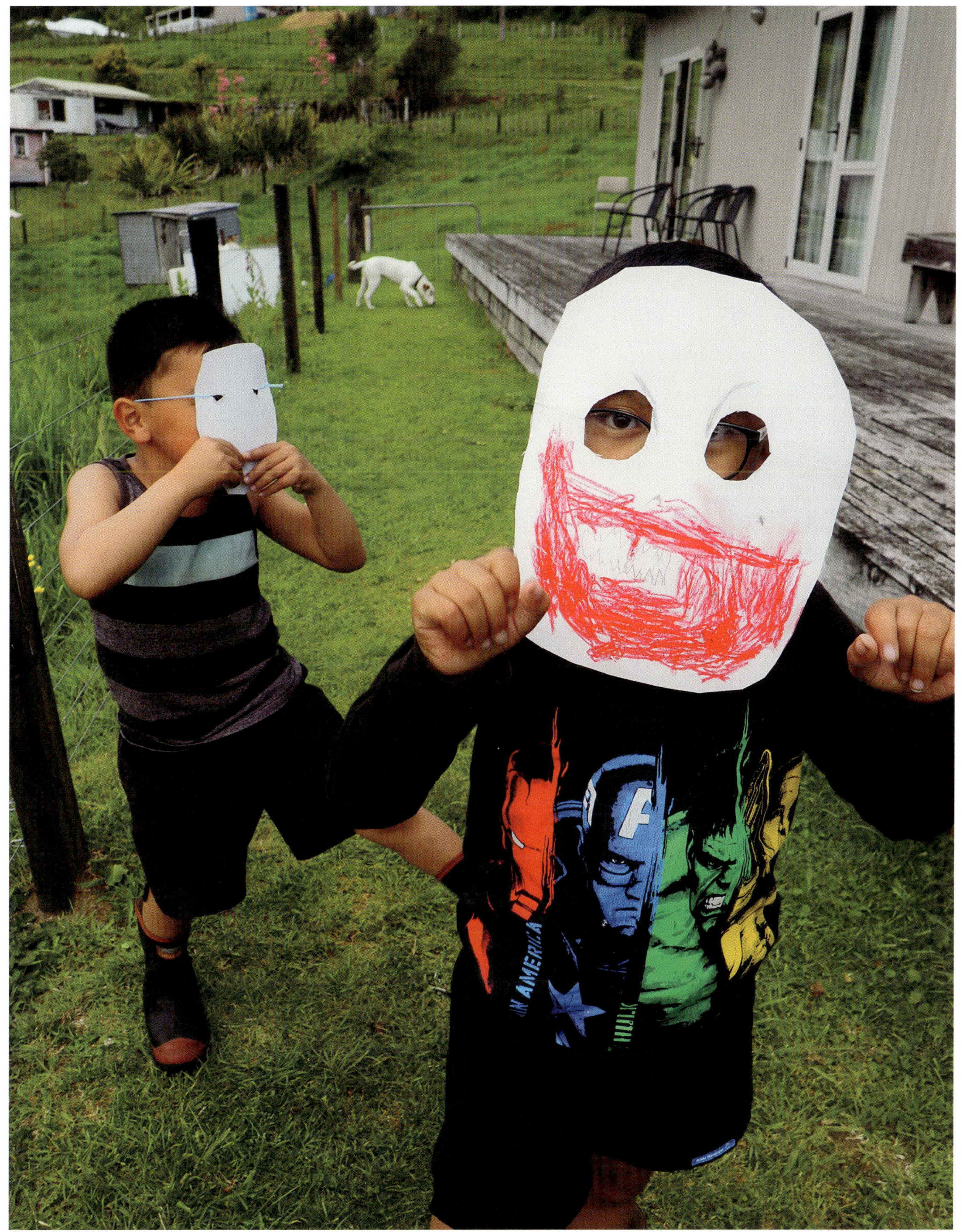

N AMERICA
HULK

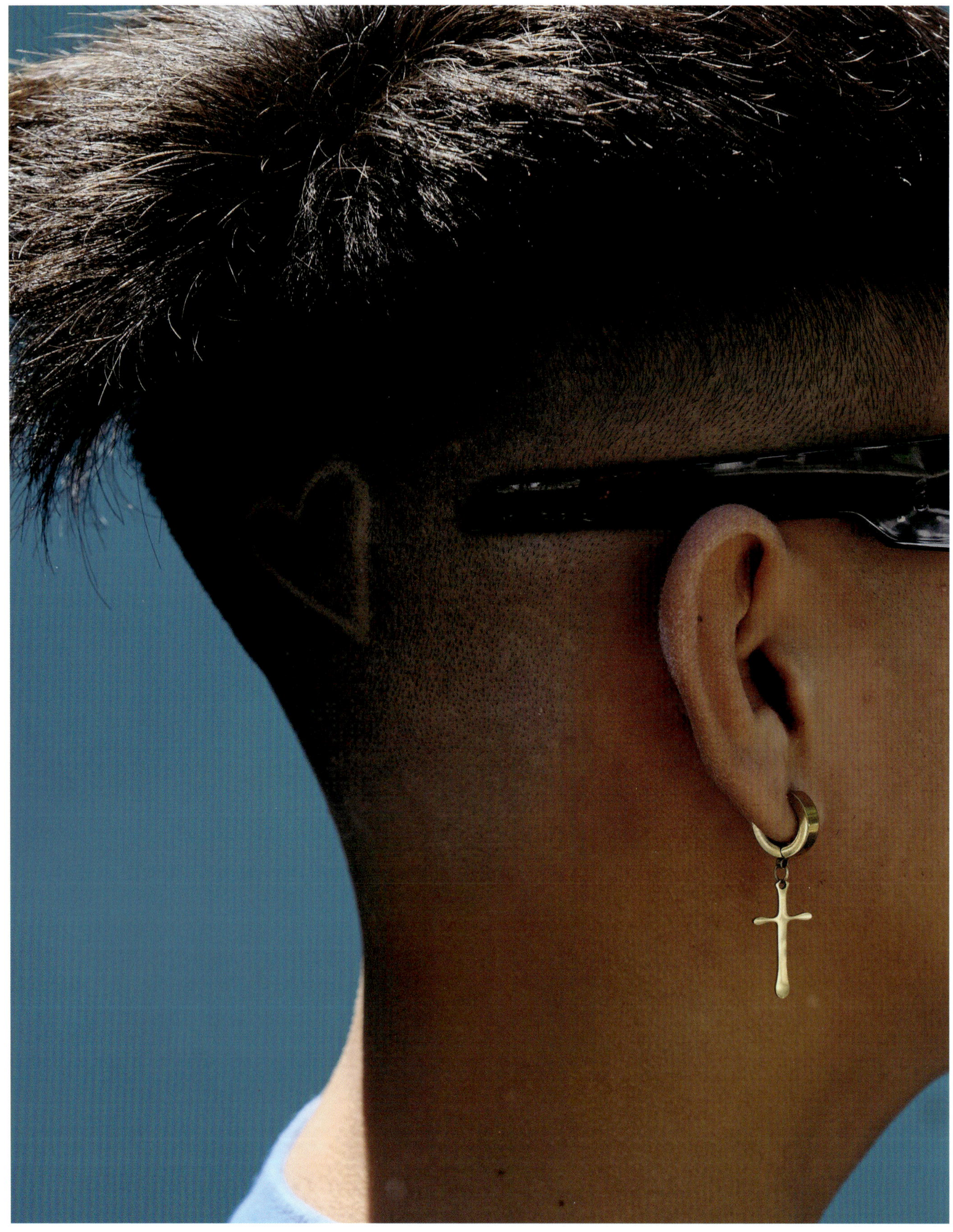

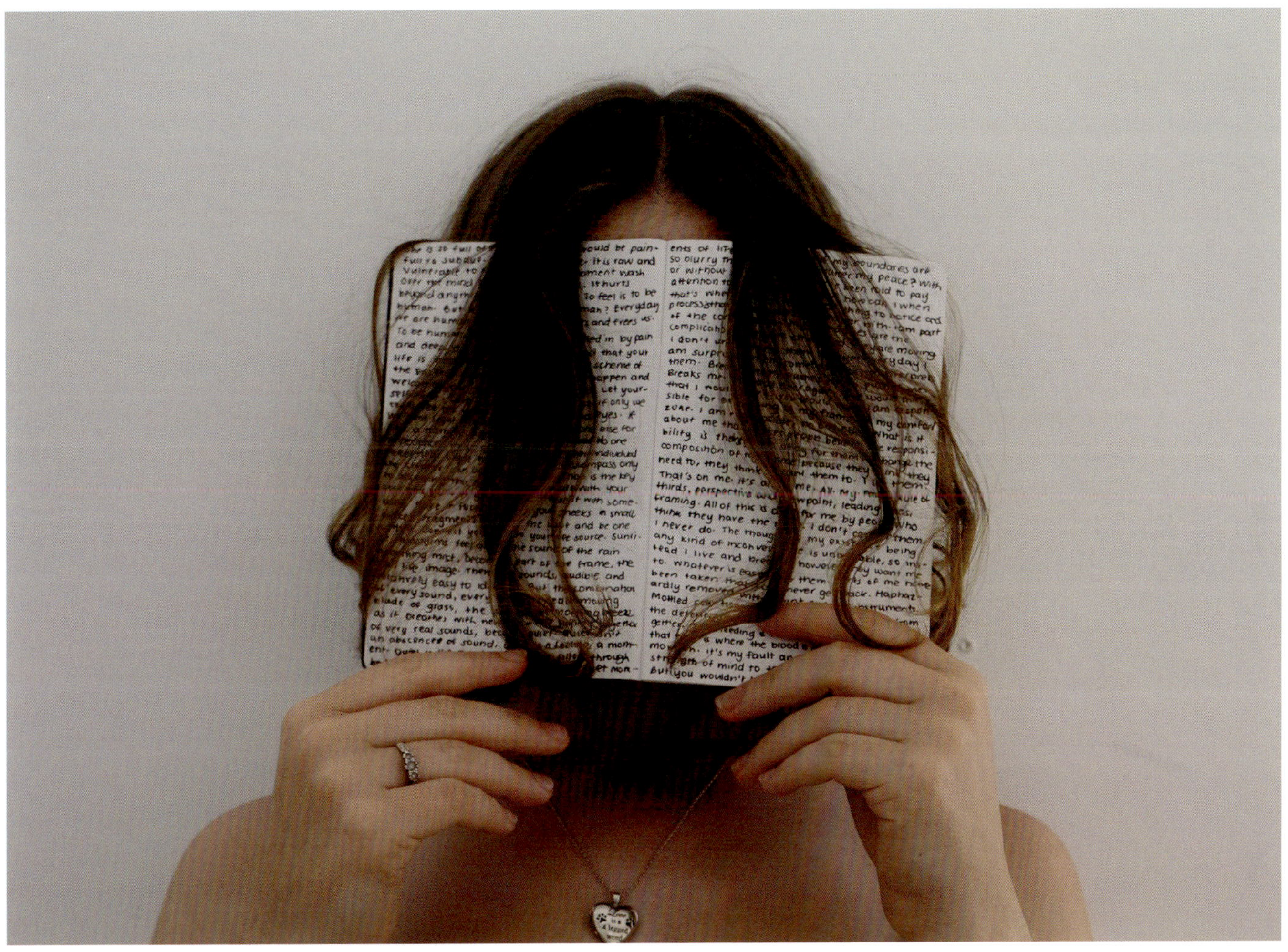

ABOVE: **HELENA NEWMAN / NEW ZEALAND 2023** OPPOSITE: **TAVAKE KAMANA / NEW ZEALAND 2023**

> ***"It's a complicated thing to try and describe the mind of a being that constantly changes. My spirit tries to free itself progressively, searching my roots, in the complexity of my memories."***
>
> —SHARON GONZALES, PERU, VIRTUAL PHOTO CAMP EARTH STORIES 2020

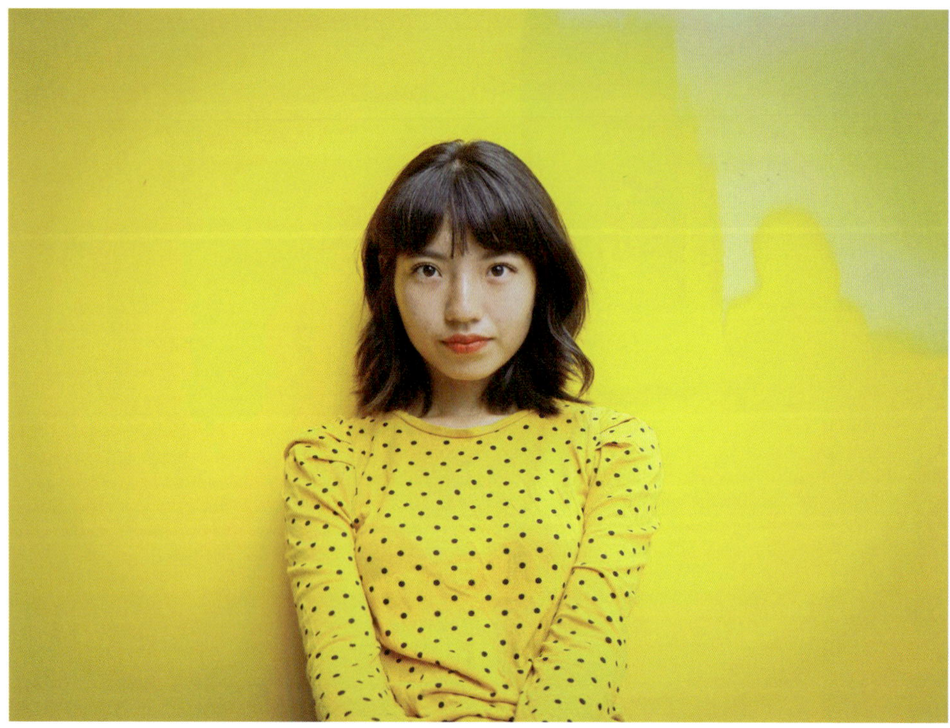

ABOVE: **O. AMGALAN / MONGOLIA 2019** RIGHT: **B. TELMEN / MONGOLIA 2019**

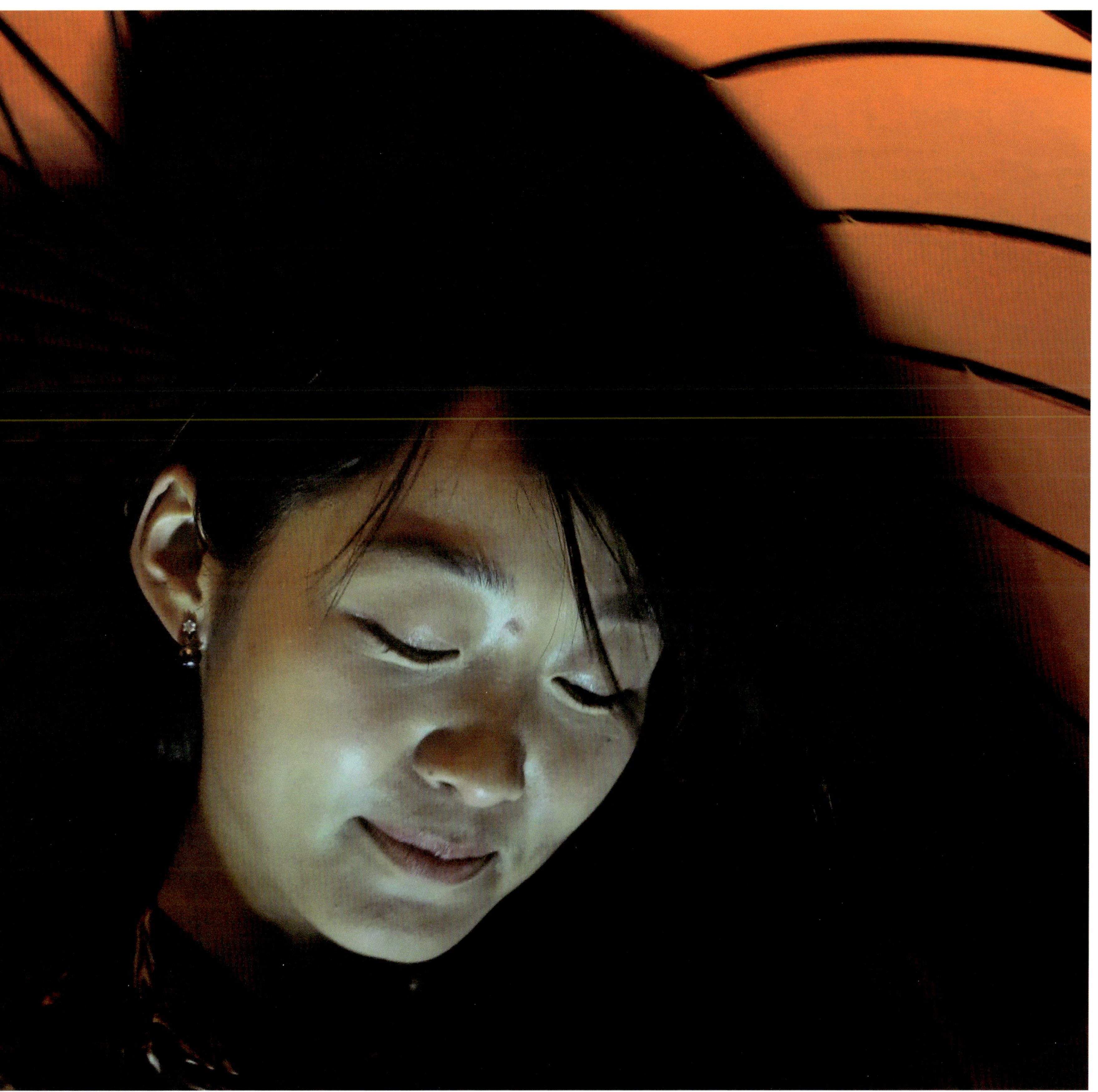

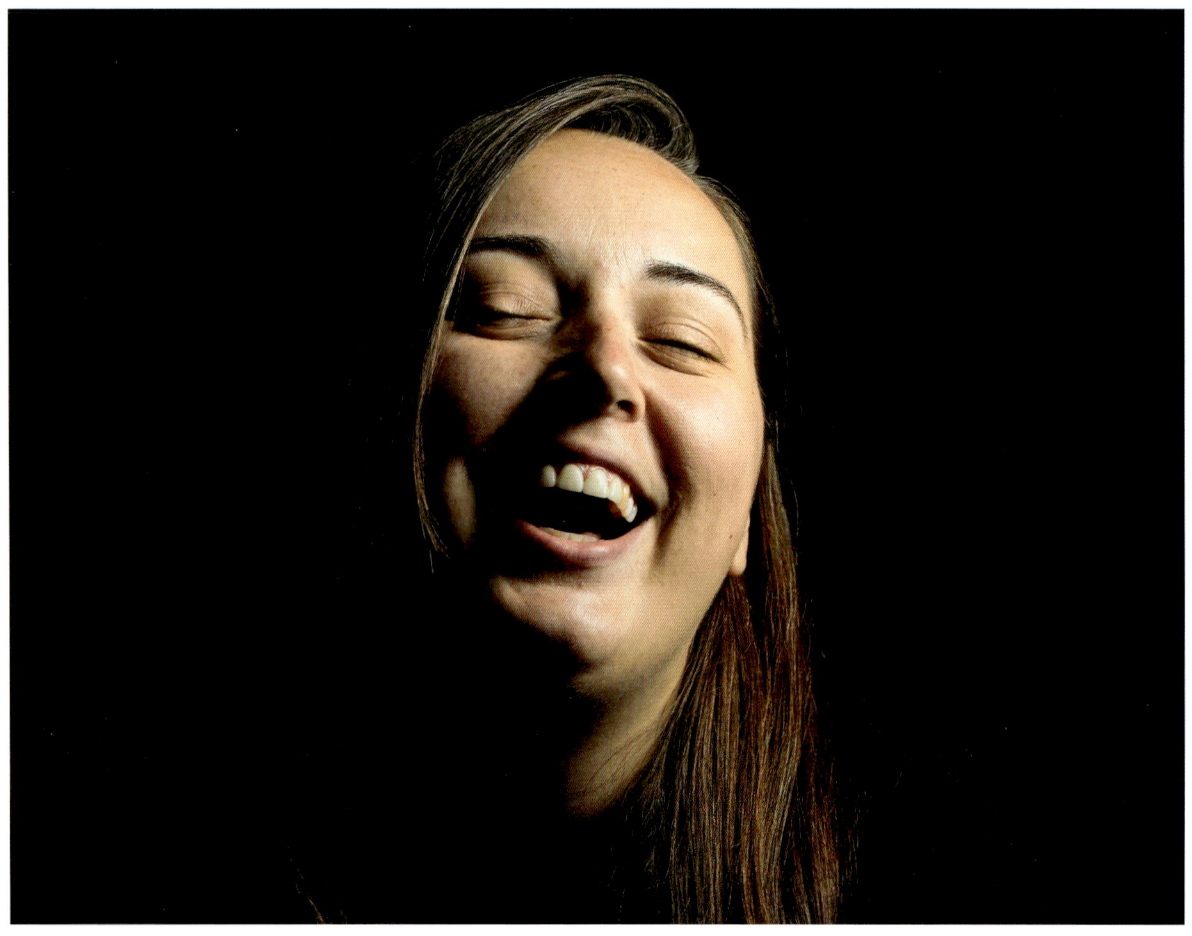

LEFT TO RIGHT: **HANEEN ALSAAD, YONAS FISHAYE, DOE KPAW SO PAW / WASHINGTON, D.C., U.S.A., MASTER CLASS 2019**

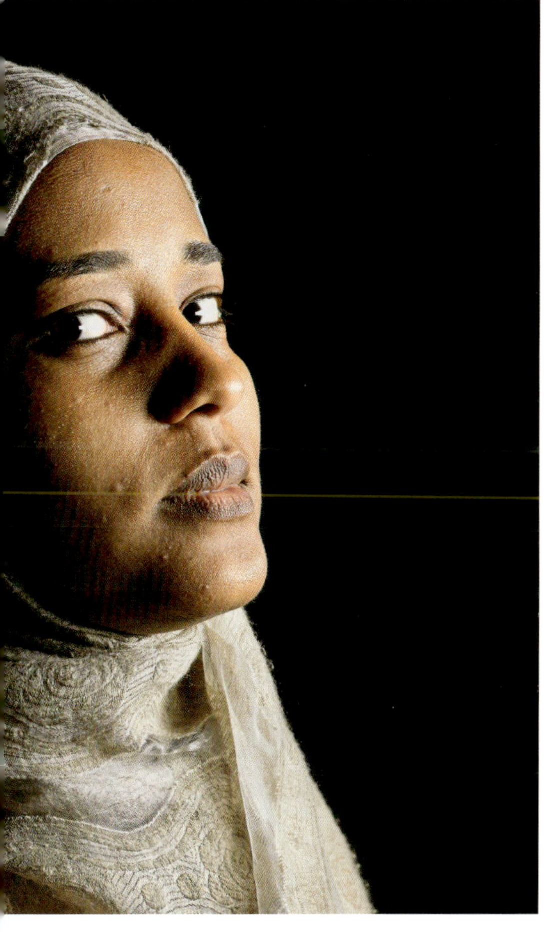

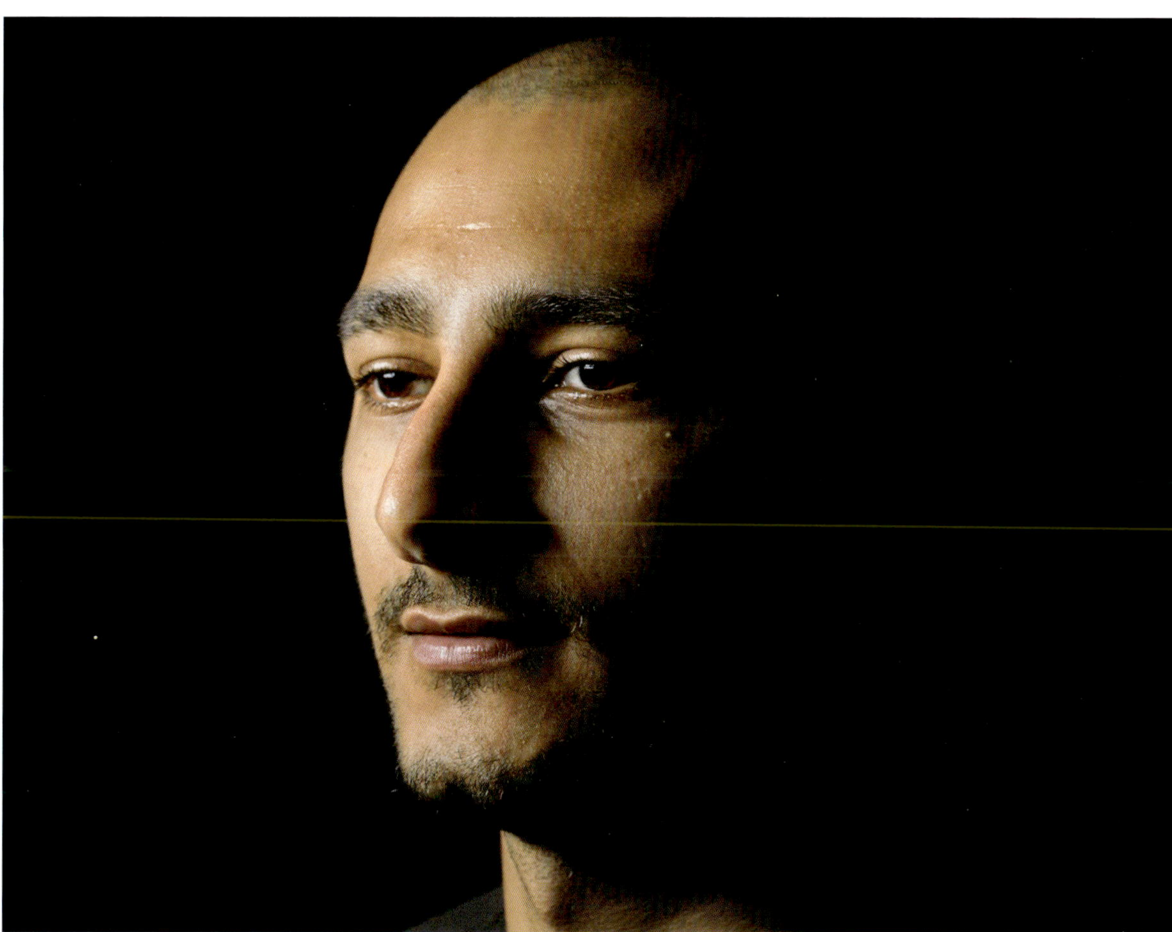

"I woke up to a heavy monsoon rain pattering on my rooftop. I started my spiritual practice as I always start my day: with positivity and optimism and prayers to give me hope to go on despite the tiring times of COVID-19.

I made prayers for the world—the battle the world is fighting with human-created sorrows. As I felt the rain seeping through my skin, I walked in my kitchen garden. The pandemic had taught me the importance of growing my own food."

—CHOKI WANGMO, BHUTAN, VIRTUAL PHOTO CAMP GLOBAL CONNECTIONS 2020

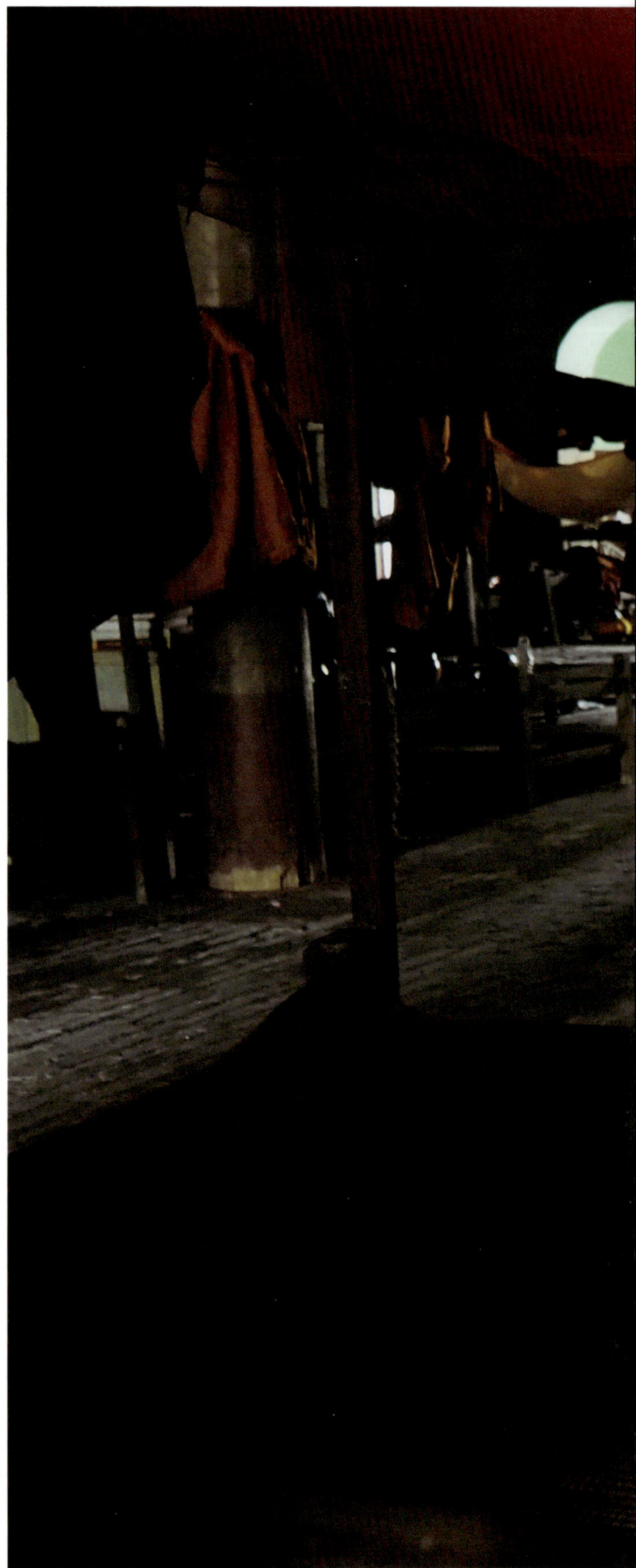

SALAI SANG SIN MANG / MYANMAR 2018

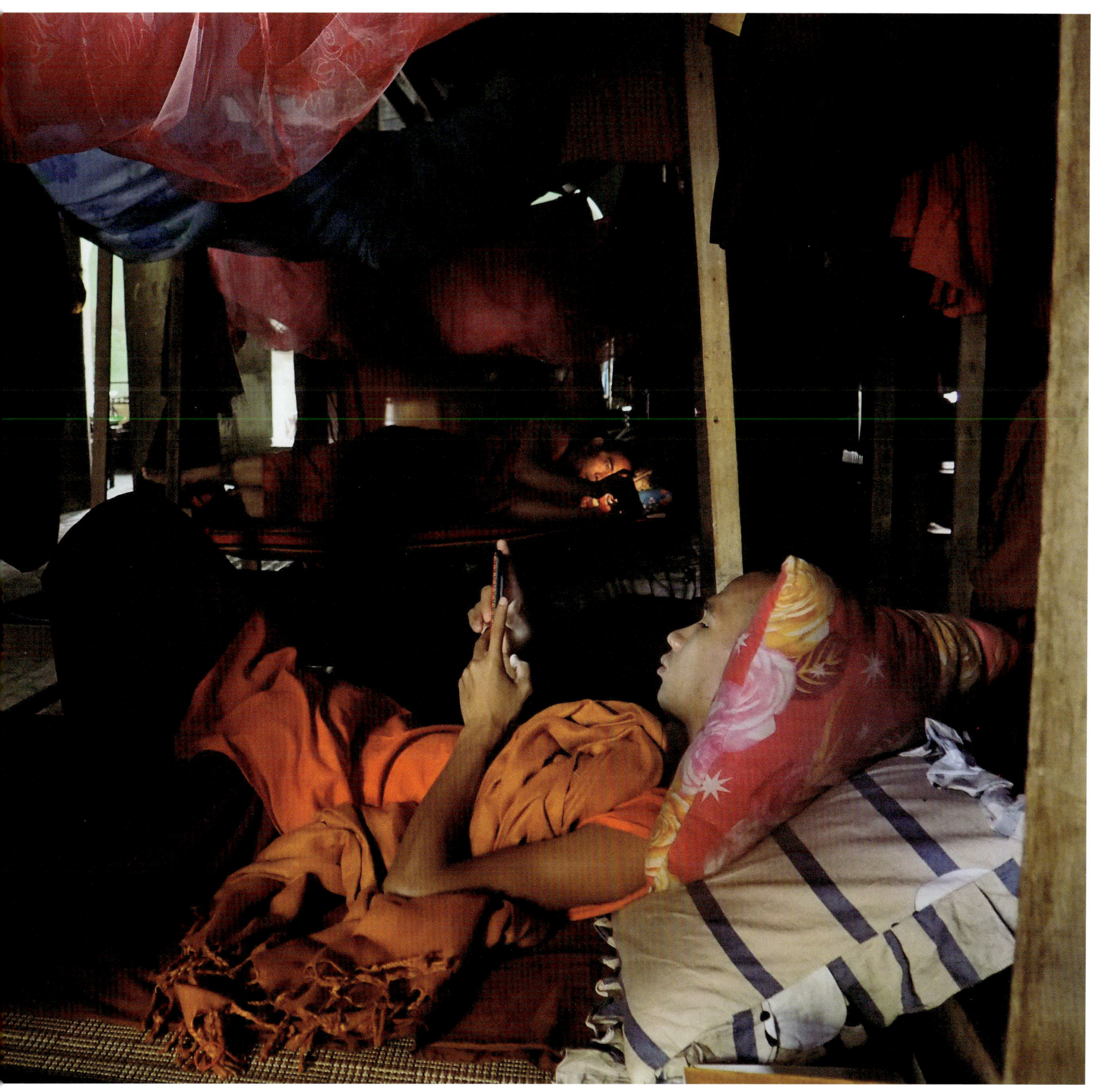

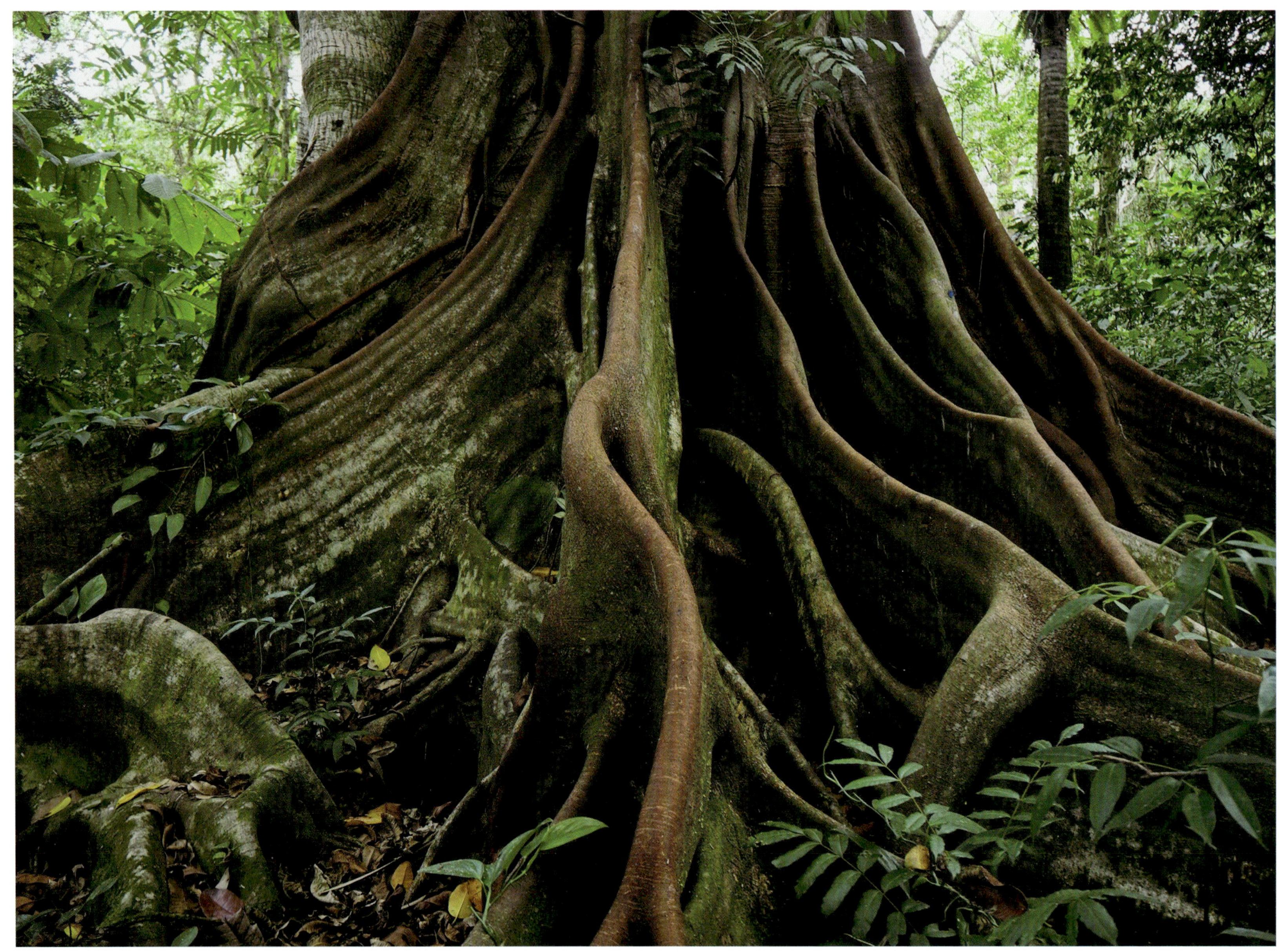

NANCY LÓPEZ / COSTA RICA 2020

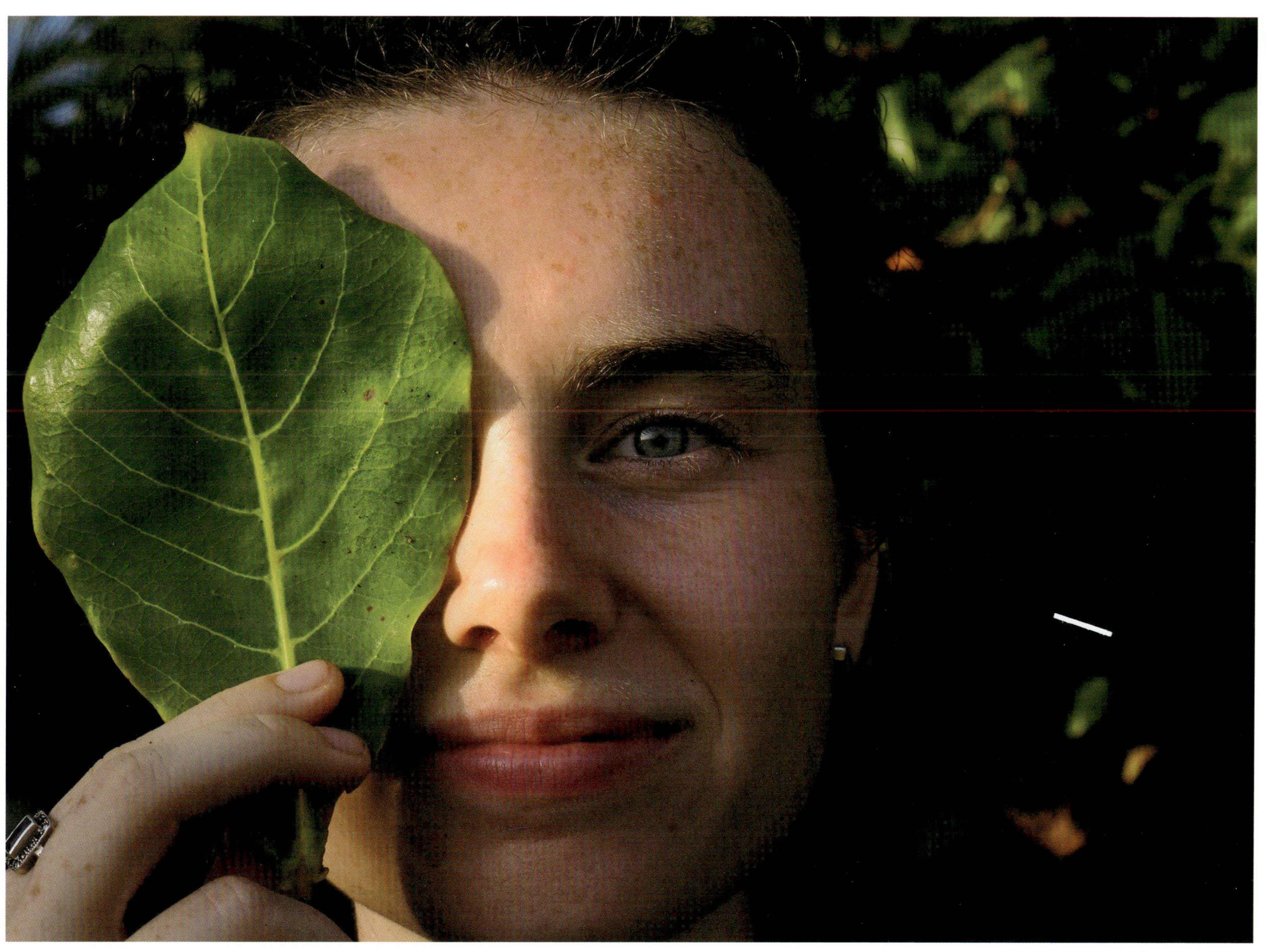

DIEGO ARMANDO COTO GONZALEZ / COSTA RICA 2020

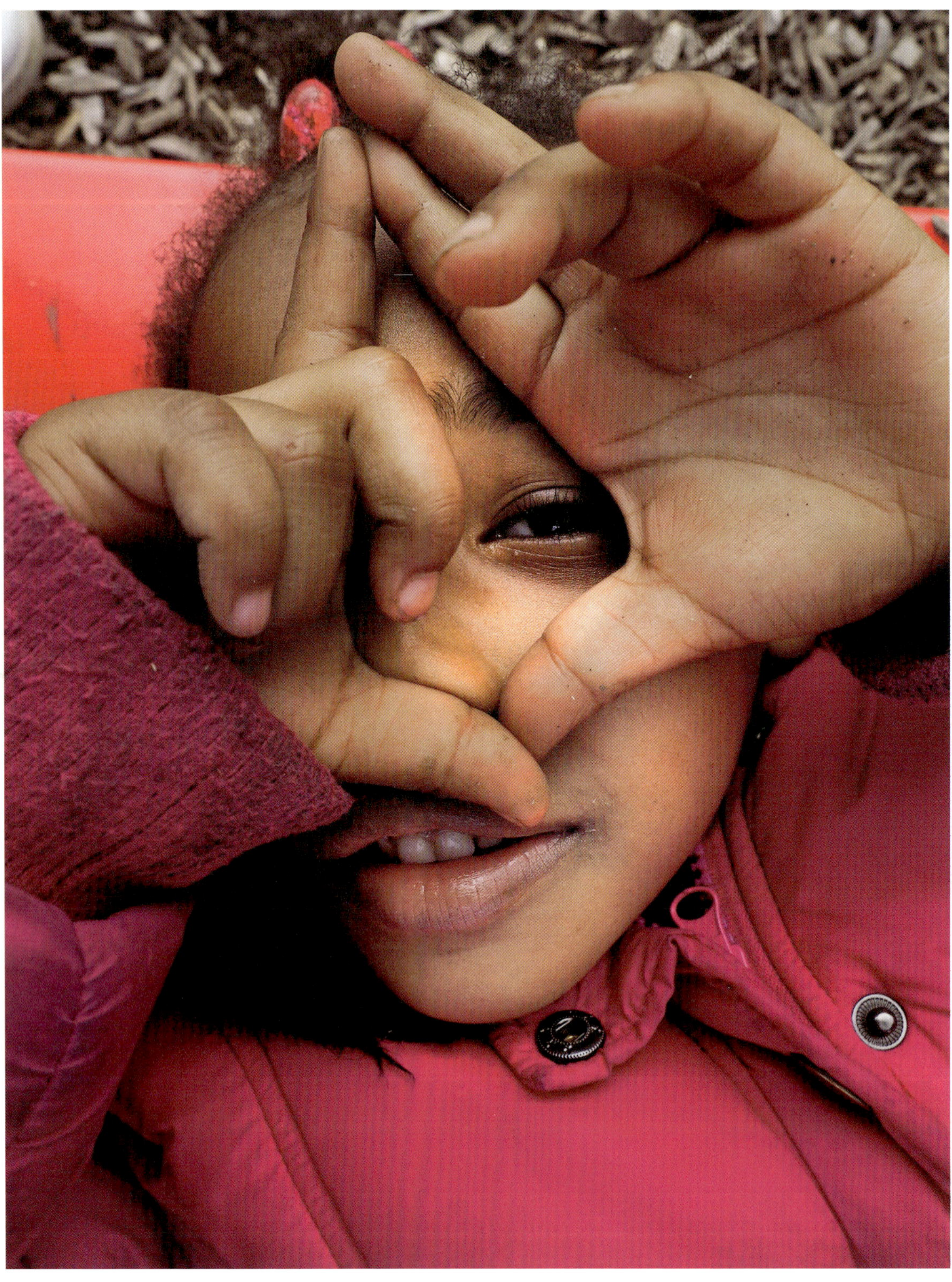

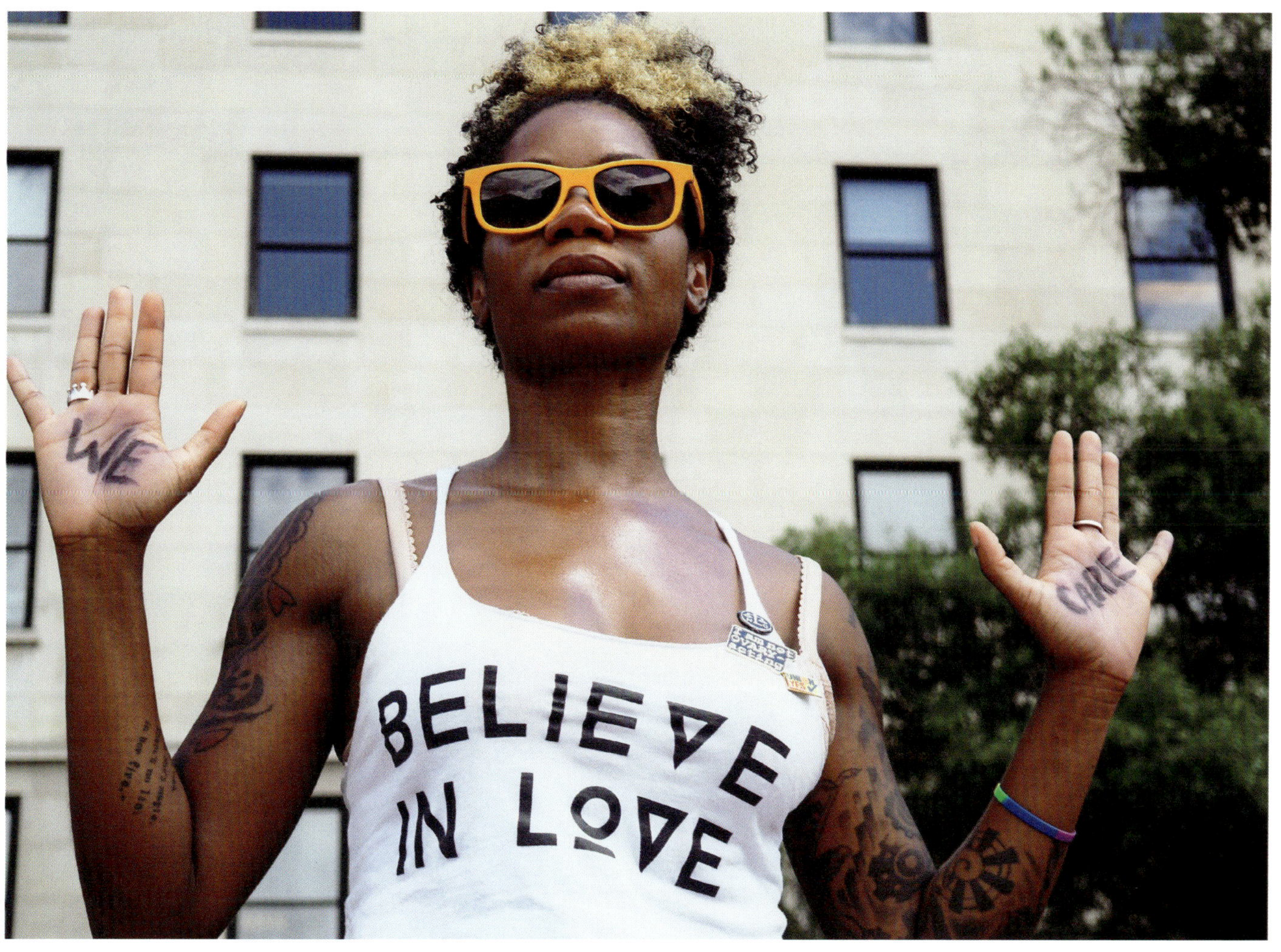

ABOVE: **OLA OSMAN / WASHINGTON, D.C., U.S.A. 2018** OPPOSITE: **MEE RA DA / NEW YORK, U.S.A. 2019**

"I'm prepared to find the American Dream. I'm prepared to make a difference in this world. This I owe to the difficulties I've encountered over the years, and to the people who helped me overcome them."

—JACOB AMARO, NEW JERSEY, U.S.A., VIRTUAL PHOTO CAMP DEMOCRACY 2021

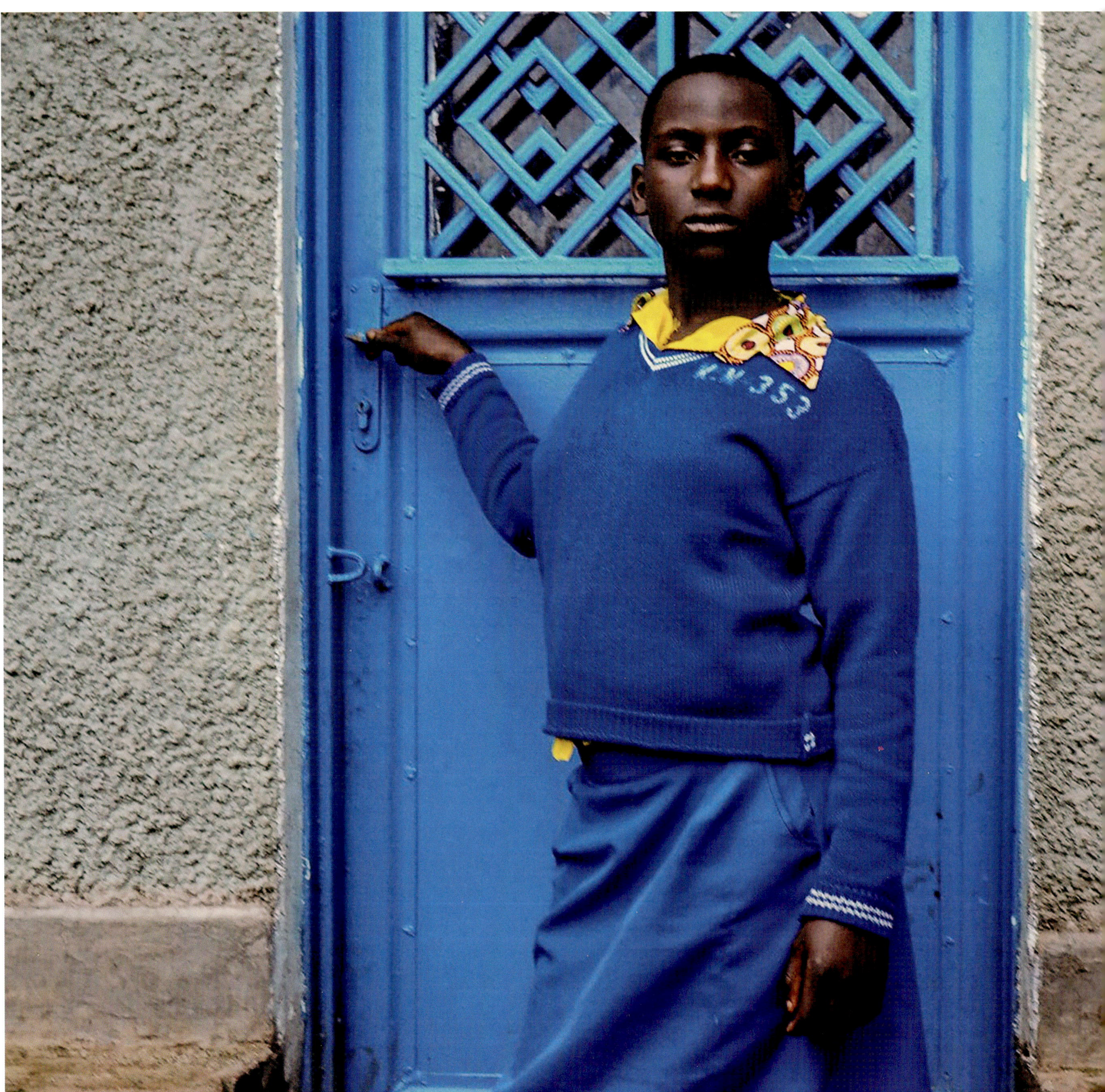

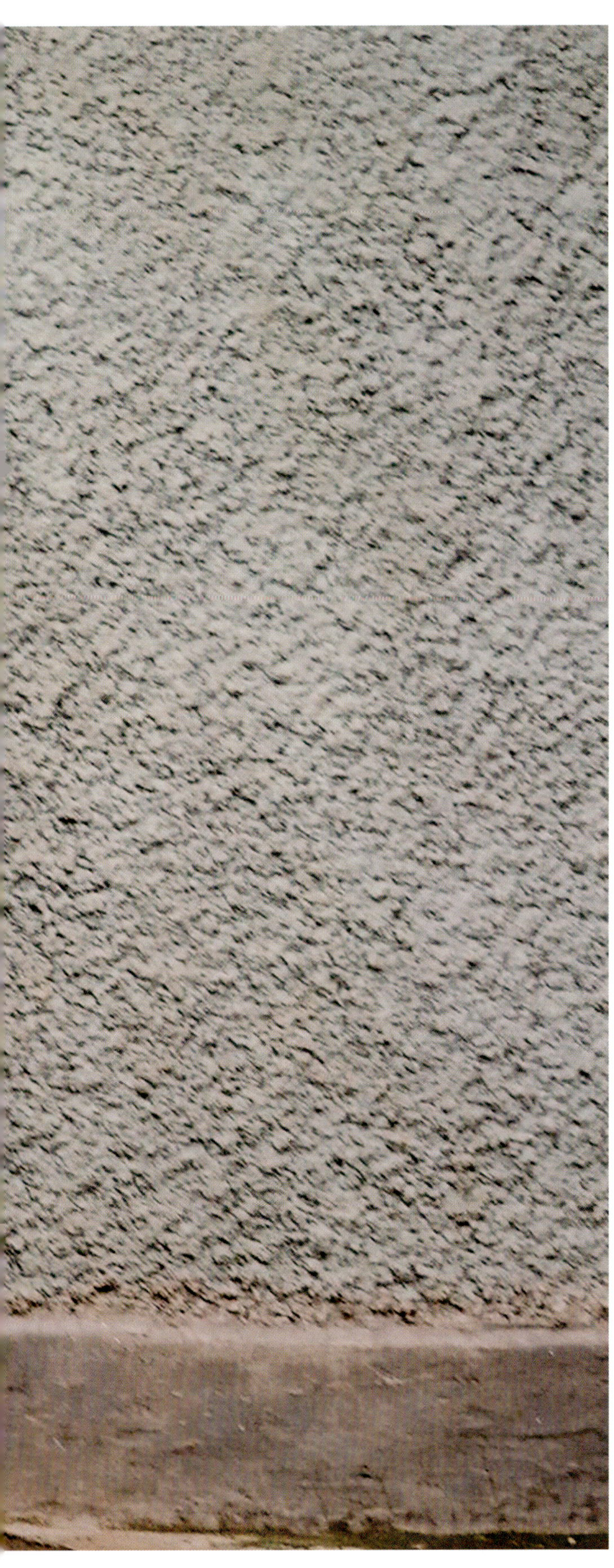

JOSELYNE UWASE / RWANDA 2016

LOUISIANA, U.S.A.

The year 2006 was a turning point in the nascent Photo Camp program. As the previous year's devastation from Hurricane Katrina continued to disrupt the lives of so many in the city, including its youth, we reached out to partners in New Orleans, asking teachers in the community how our storytelling process could help young people make sense of their experiences. For the first time, we began including students' writing alongside their photographs to provide context as they explored and shared their experiences.

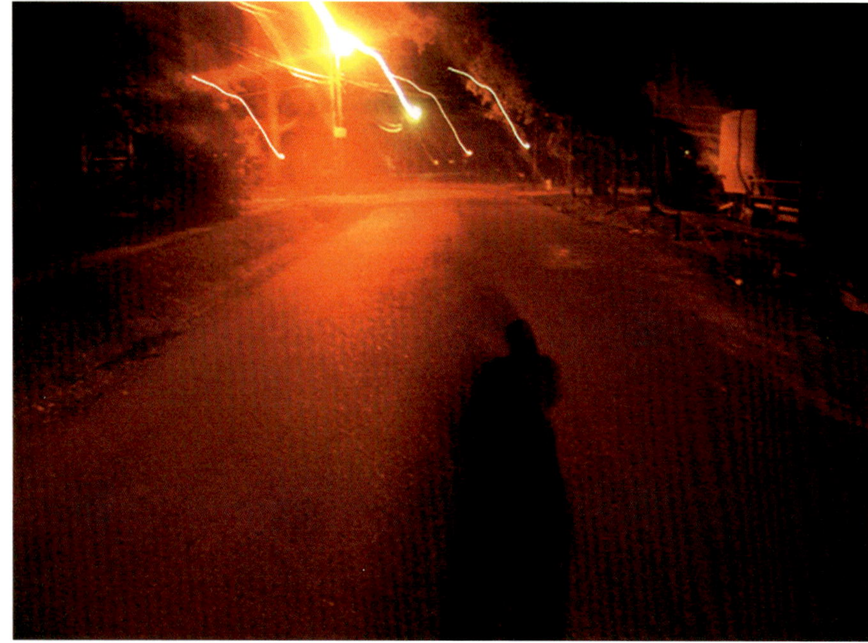

"I miss believing that the hurricane will always just miss New Orleans. I don't miss going from house to house, full of people I didn't know, and sharing a bed with two other people.

I can't wait to forget the fear of not knowing what will happen next.

I can't wait to forget my tears."

—VICTORIA CHESTER

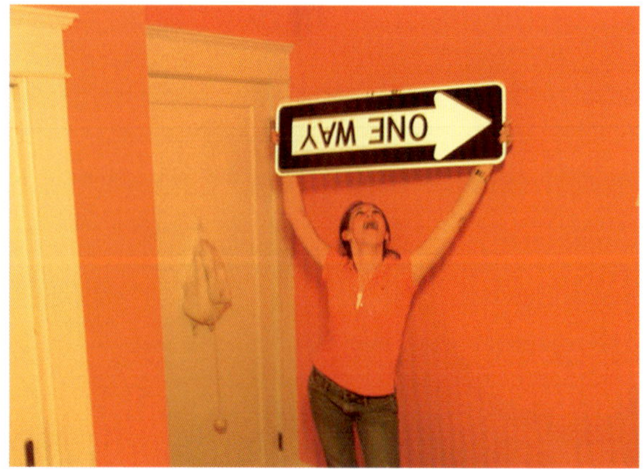

"I remember opening the door to my house and looking at my childhood: scattered, molded, and destroyed on the floor."

—HANNAH DEFELICE

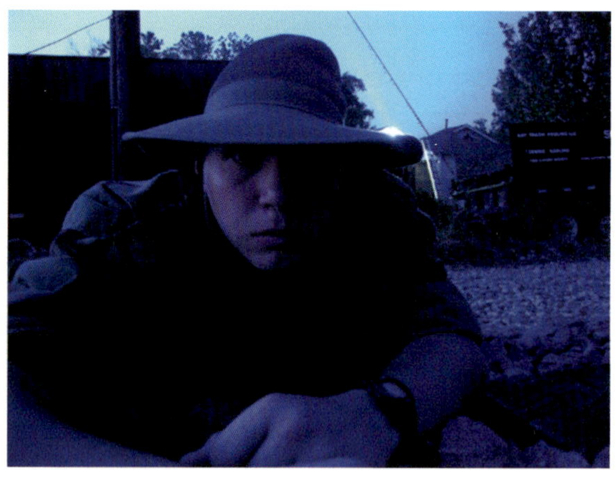

"I remember first coming back to New Orleans, to a place where I once lived. The silence was deafening."

—TYLER SCIFES

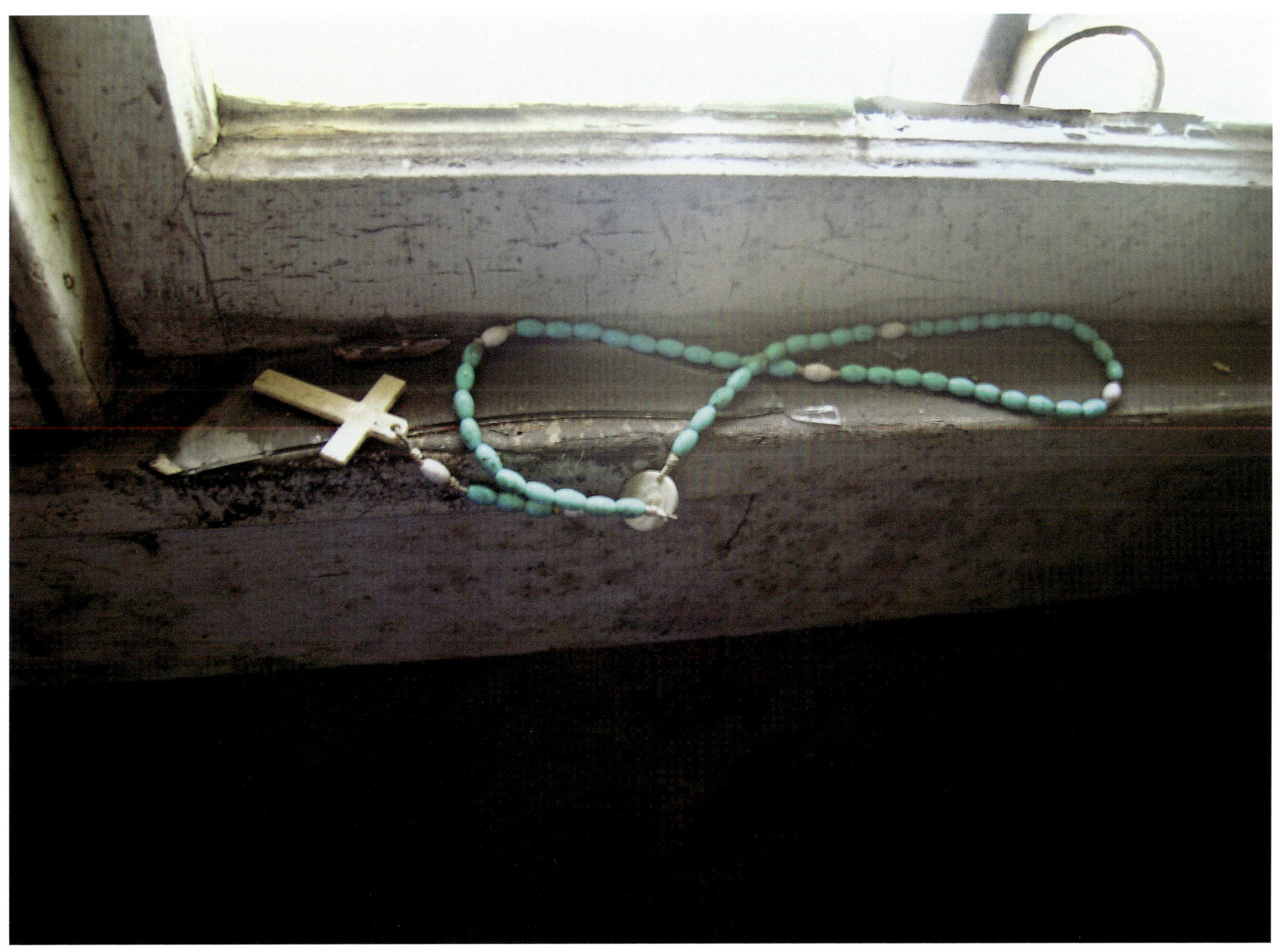

"I remember the noise of Katrina—the singing of the wind made you stay awake to listen to her ... I remember the hours when walking through five feet of water was better than 12.

Ever since we got rescued, I don't think I've ever been so appreciative in my life. To go from so much, to nothing, to a miracle is beautiful."

—JANNAE ASHLEY PACK

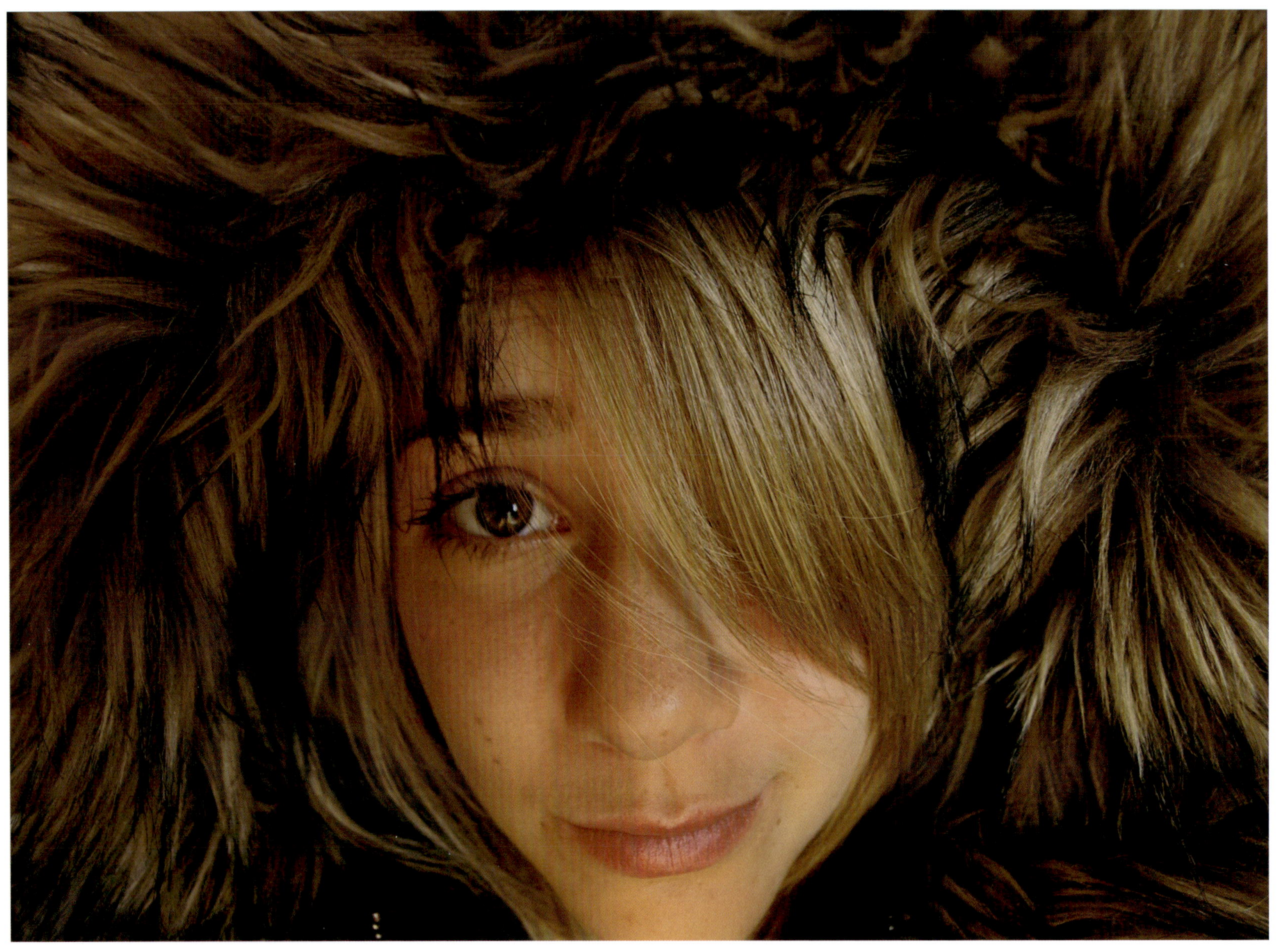

BRITTANY COOPER / MAINE, U.S.A. 2008

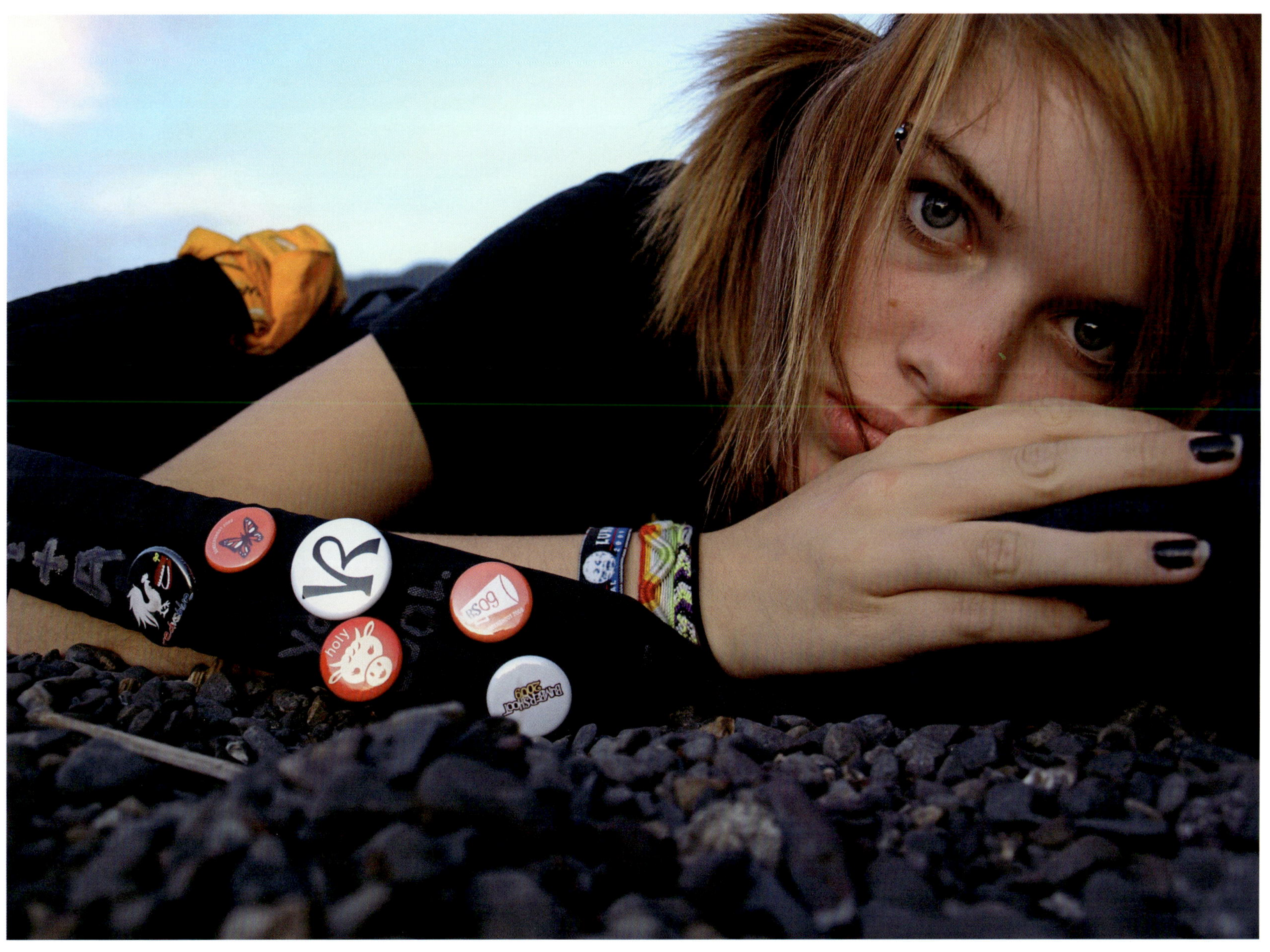

NIKITA MIGHELL / WASHINGTON, U.S.A. 2009

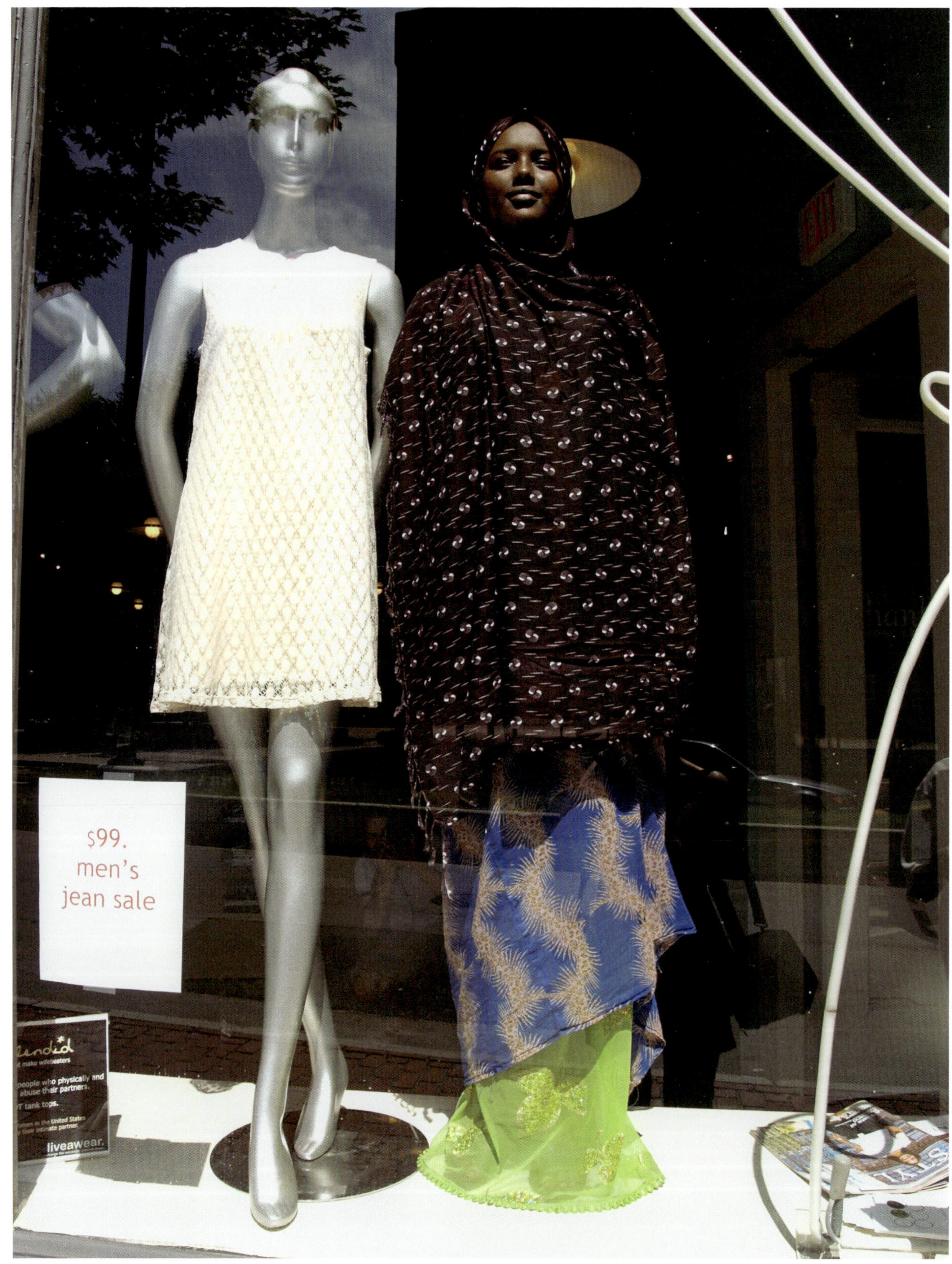
$99.
men's
jean sale
people who physically and
abuse their partners.
tank tops.
liveawear.

"Home is a fond memory. Separation means an ending and a scar.

Our story is American. Struggle, strength, and pride sprinkled with parades, pools, and secrets, all pushed under the rug."

—LIZETTE ARIAS, WASHINGTON, D.C., U.S.A., MASTER CLASS 2019

MARYAN OKASH / MAINE, U.S.A. 2007

Māori Pride
Te Aho Jordan

TE AHO JORDAN WAS ONCE sharply critical of her Māori looks, Māori hair, and Māori identity.

Now, Te Aho's pride in her Indigenous New Zealand roots forms the core of who she is. Her embrace of her background goes beyond family history; she also hearkens to the strengths of the Māori living culture, as well as her mother's Samoan culture.

Today, Te Aho studies public policy at a Māori institution of higher learning online while working at the Hawke's Bay District Health Board as a youth adviser serving the Māori community. But in 2019, at Photo Camp in the New Zealand town of Murupara, she was less settled. "Photo Camp brought me to a place of acceptance," she said. But she says that through observing Māori youth at work and in the community, she feels they are "constantly searching for who they are. [They have] no solid place to start their journey."

Today, she chronicles her family's history by taking pictures—so much so that her sister jokes that her camera has become her extra arm and extra eye.

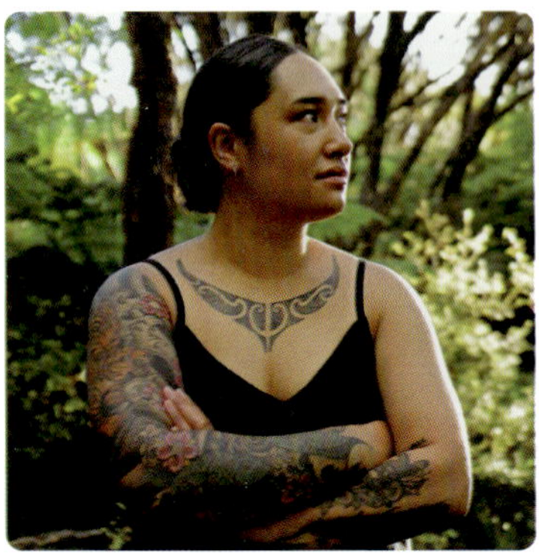

Te Aho Jordan is a visual storyteller of Māori and Samoan heritage. She is pursuing a bachelor of humanities with a focus on public policy.

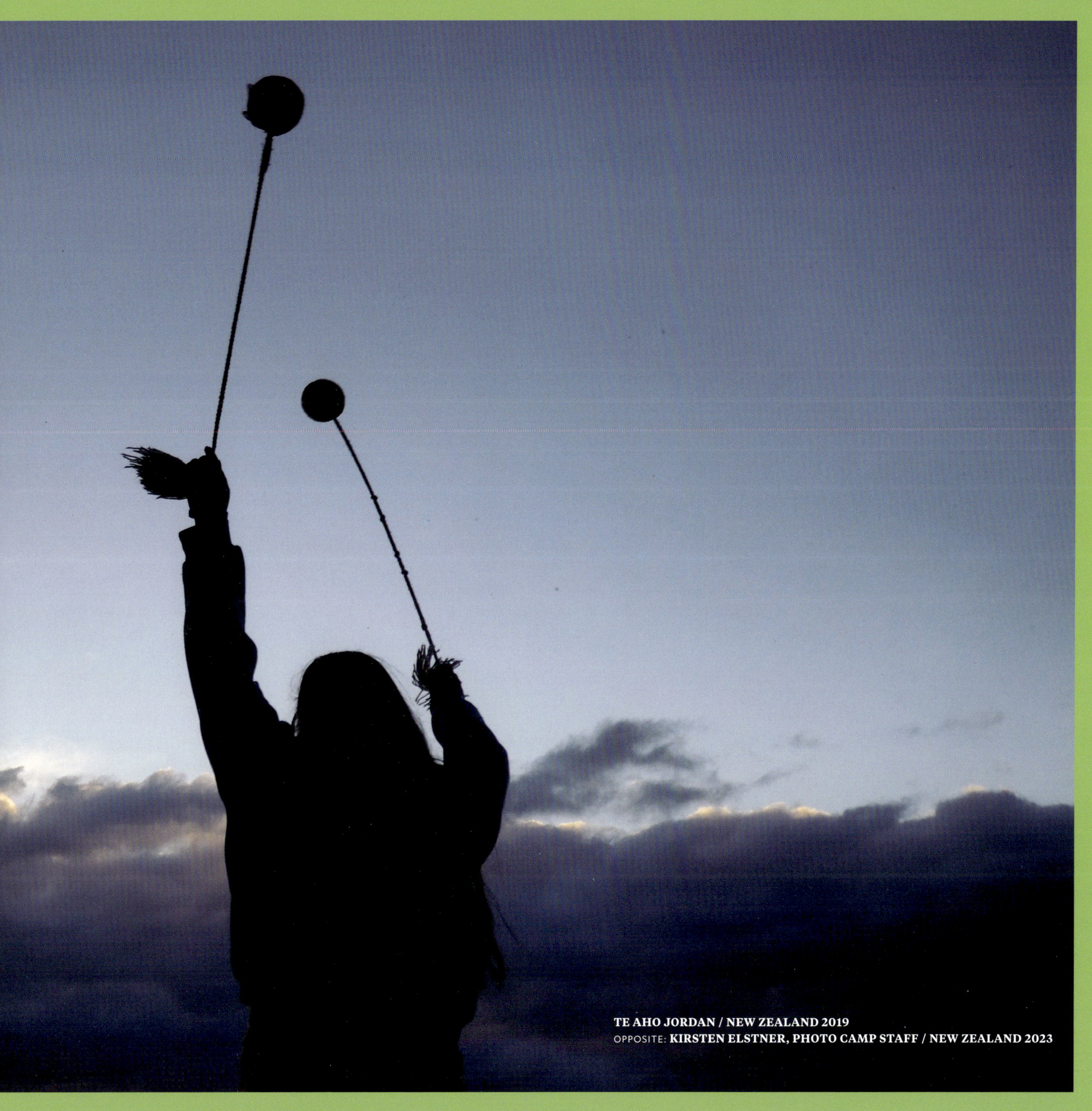

TE AHO JORDAN / NEW ZEALAND 2019
OPPOSITE: KIRSTEN ELSTNER, PHOTO CAMP STAFF / NEW ZEALAND 2023

CHAPTER 4

Inspiration

"Being able to express myself through an art form was never something I have been able to do. That was, until a camera was placed in my hands."

—ILEY MICKAN, NEW ZEALAND 2023

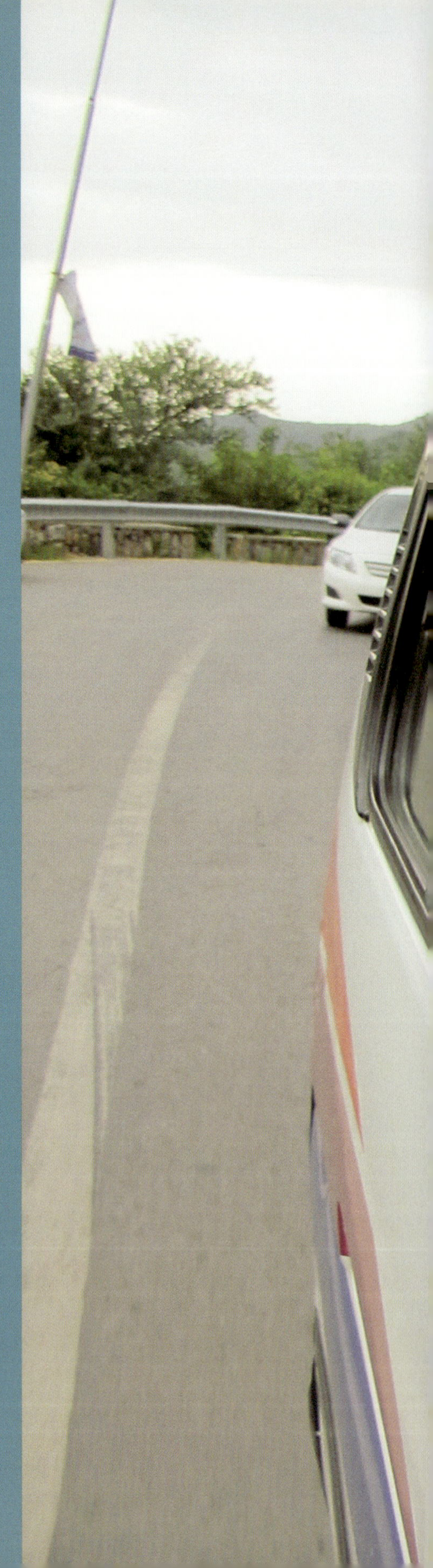

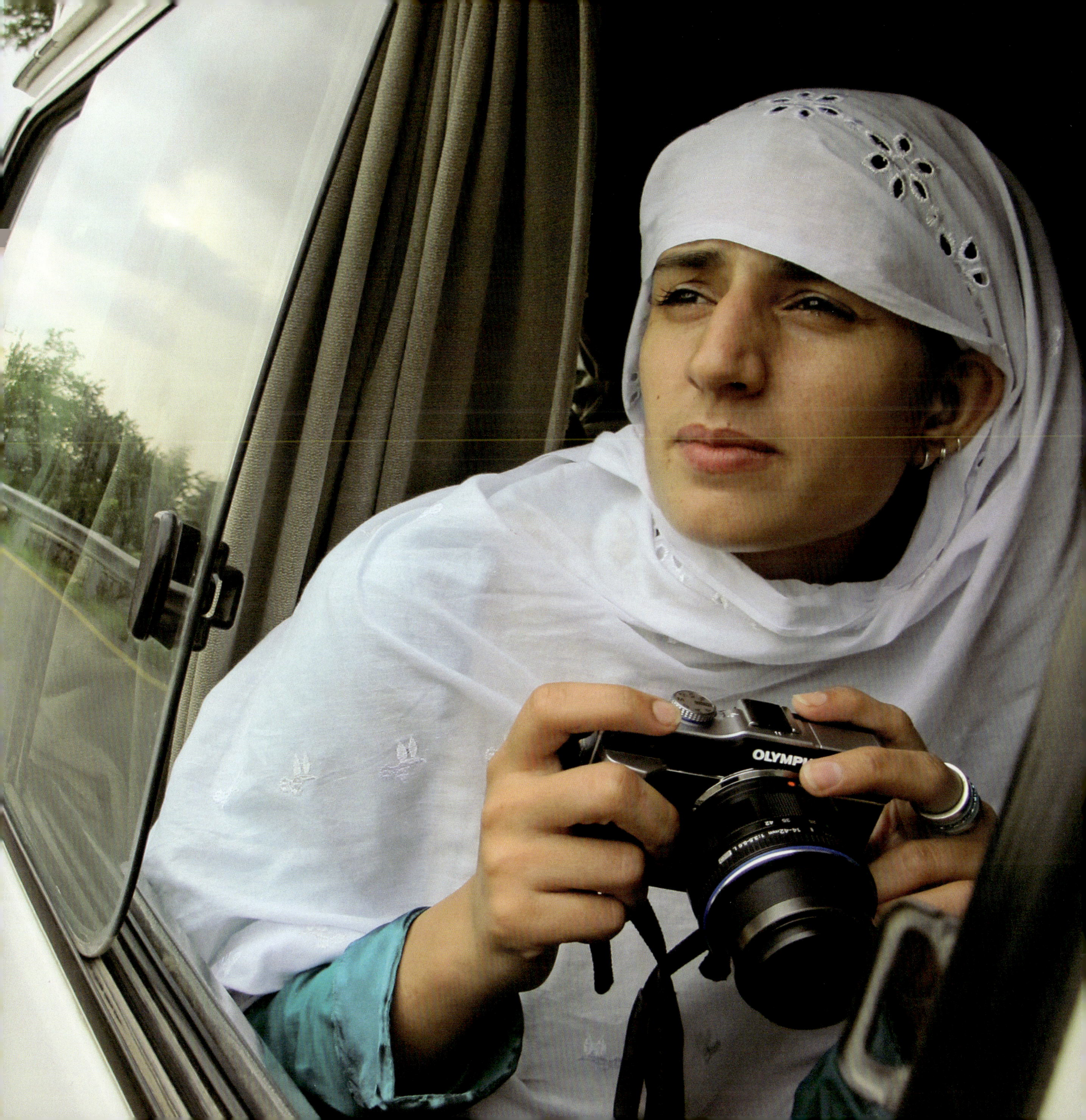

Beneath the Surface

ANKITA DAS, 21, WAS STRUGGLING with the story she wanted to tell. She had set her sights on photographing rickshaw-wallahs, the drivers of hand-pulled carts—the last to be found anywhere in the world—in her hometown of Kolkata, India. But she wasn't getting what she wanted. Looking for guidance, she turned to photographer Matthieu Paley and writer Paul Salopek, her mentors at a 2018 Photo Camp, held in Kolkata. They urged her to think hard about the lives of the drivers. Storytelling, they explained, is about trying to understand someone's life.

Inspired by the feedback, Ankita returned to the place where the drivers congregate. She kicked off her shoes and started to run alongside them: her first step in getting to understand the men. Word spread around that Ankita's new batch of images at the camp were something special.

Photo Camp students often turn to their mentors, and mentors are eager to impart what they know. Mentors also understand that to inspire their students, they need to treat them all as individuals, and to respond to their work honestly but not judgmentally. "We'll say, 'What were you looking for? What attracted you to that situation?'" photographer and mentor Tyrone Turner explained.

Sometimes, the mentorship extended to a student has transformative power. At the final show of student work at a 2023 Photo Camp in New Zealand, a photo was presented that caught everyone's attention. It was a simple composition showing two arms, one of them bearing a long scar resulting from a 21-stitch wound. The student, Ayla Brockes, kept the scar—the result of a recent attempt to take her own life—hidden out of embarrassment. She always covered it with an elastic sleeve. But on the last day of camp, working with director Kirsten Elstner, Ayla decided she would photograph it; she had received so much compassion that she wasn't afraid of a bad reaction. "No one was disgusted," she said. Off came the sleeve. At the photo review, Ayla explained that her left arm with the scar represented the past; her right arm symbolized a new reality free of shame.

PHOTO CAMP STAFF LIKE NOTHING BETTER THAN channeling student enthusiasm. That was the case when Elstner met with Jasiah Jennings to discuss a poem he had written. It sparked a cascade of connections that would eventually put the Samoan-Tokelauan youth in contact with a photographer in Peru.

Jasiah, broad-shouldered and sporting a hibiscus tattoo ("like my family crest," he explained, laughing) attended a Photo Camp in Auckland, New Zealand, in early 2023. As part of a writing assignment, he composed a poem imagining his recently deceased grandfather as a star in the night sky. Sitting in a cozy room with a bank of windows looking out to the South Pacific Ocean, the 20-year-old

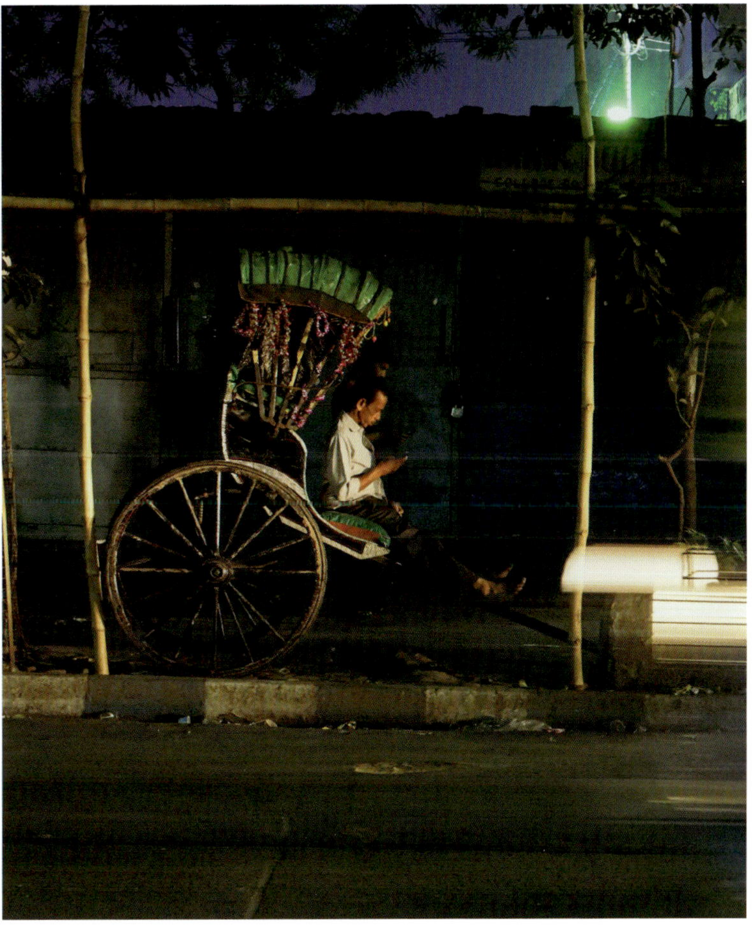

ABOVE: **ANKITA DAS / INDIA 2018**
PREVIOUS PAGES: **SUSAN POULTON, PHOTO CAMP STAFF / PAKISTAN 2012**

asked Elstner if and how it might be possible to transfer the feelings expressed in his poem into his photography work.

Photographer Citlali Fábian, who was working close by on her laptop, called Jasiah over. As they talked about how he might take photos of stars at night, she pulled up photos by her colleague Victor Zea, who depicts night skies employing an unusual technique called solarigraphy, which captures the journey of the sun across the sky.

Then Fábian went a step further, contacting Zea and asking him to explain the method to Jasiah. Now Zea and Jasiah communicate via Instagram. The young man, who had never taken a picture before Photo Camp, has managed to set up an internship with another company to continue to develop his skills with a camera.

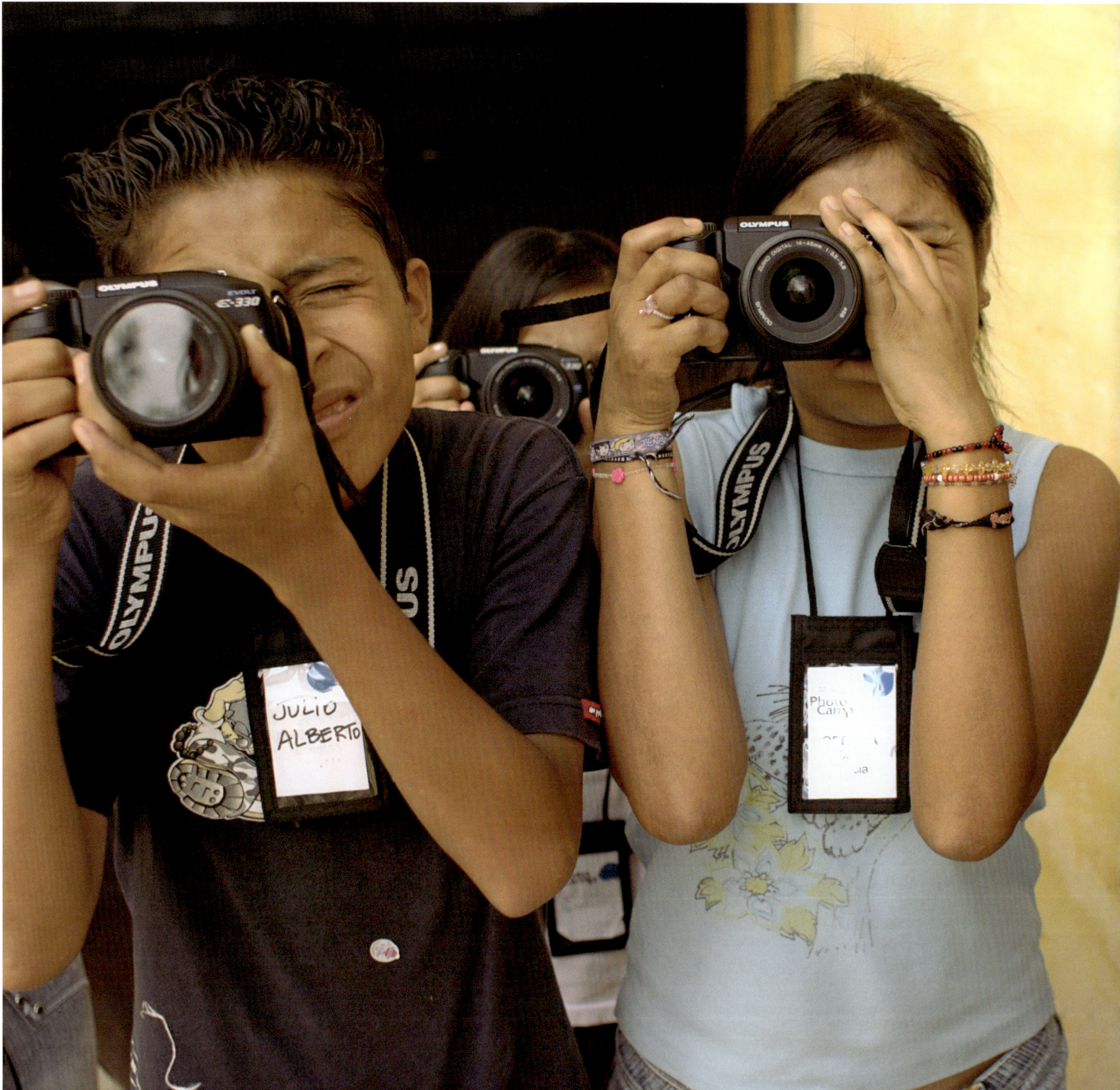
OLYMPUS
E-330
OLYMPUS
OLYMPUS
JULIO
ALBERTO
Photo
Camp

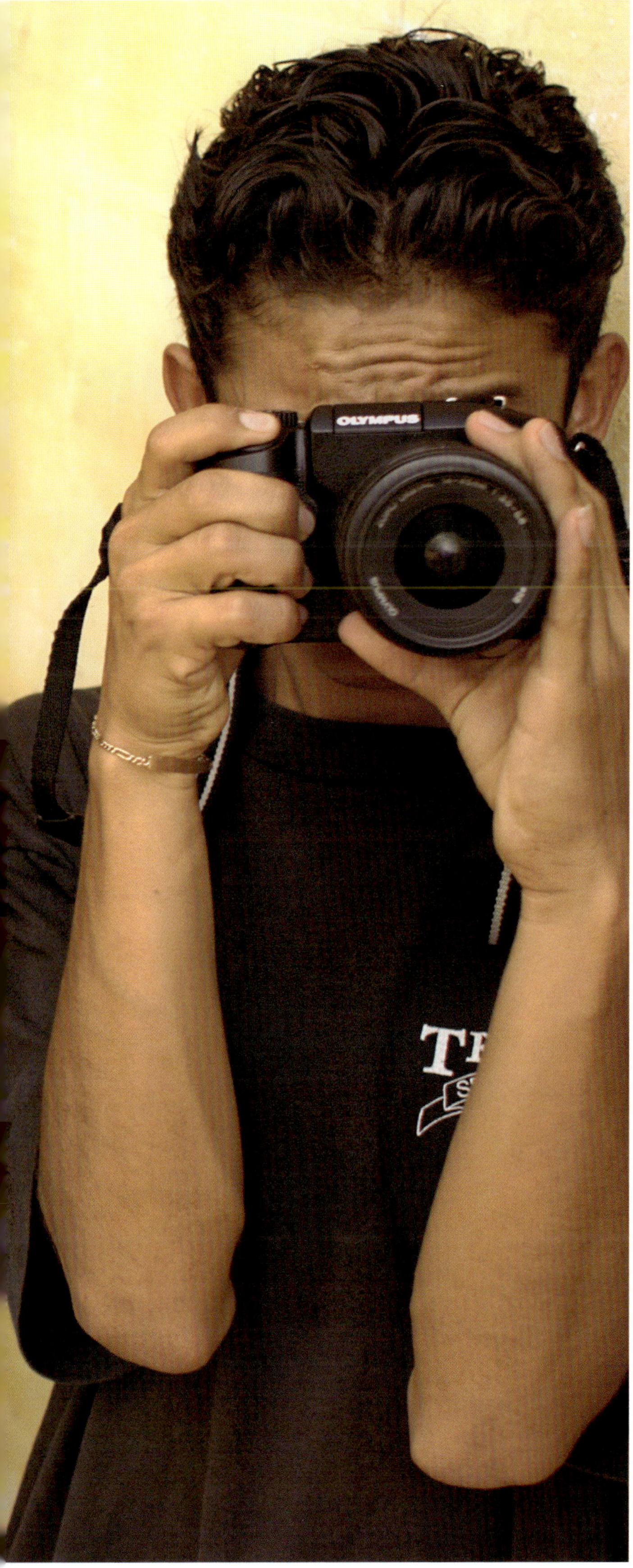

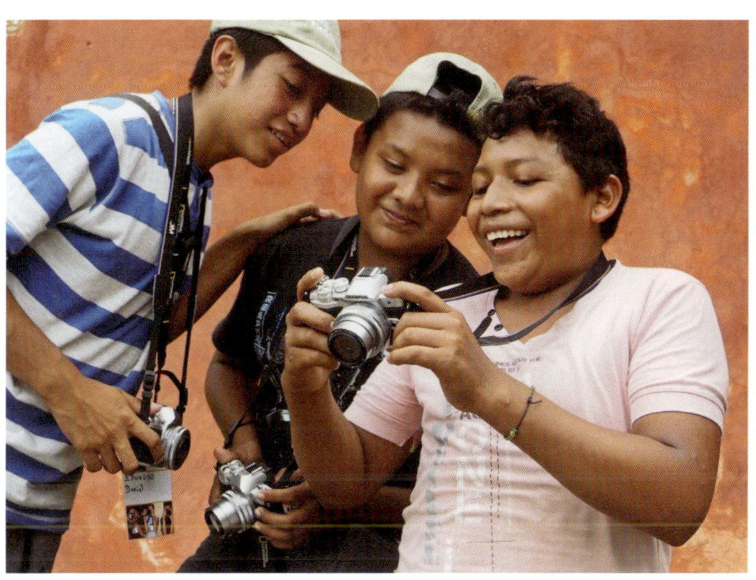

ABOVE: **KIRSTEN ELSTNER, PHOTO CAMP STAFF / MEXICO 2019**
LEFT: **JIM WEBB, PHOTO CAMP STAFF / MEXICO 2007**

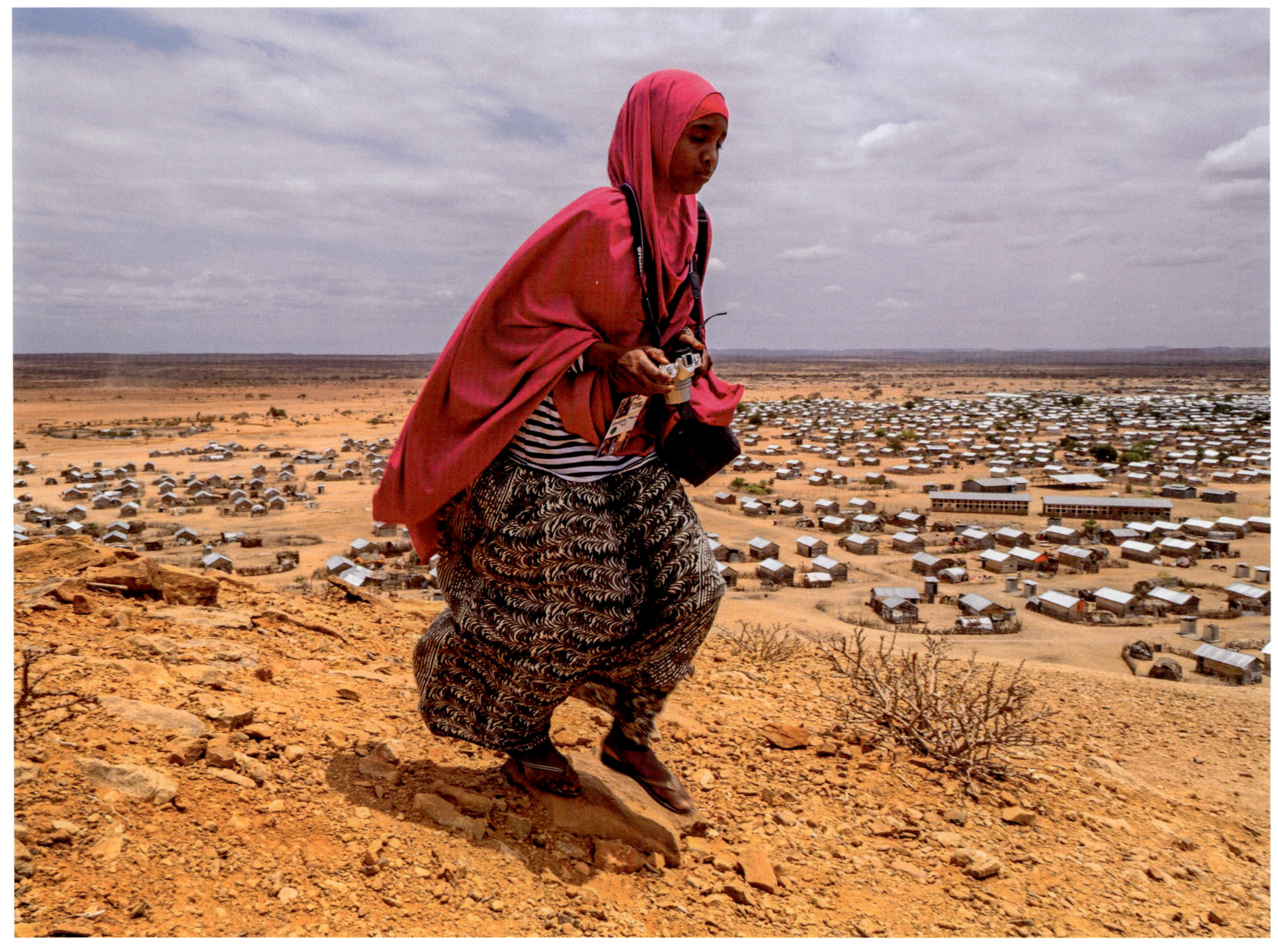

ABOVE: **ERIKA LARSEN, PHOTO CAMP STAFF / ETHIOPIA 2019** OPPOSITE TOP: **HASAN ADAN / ETHIOPIA 2019** OPPOSITE BOTTOM: **SOWDA OMAR / ETHIOPIA 2019**

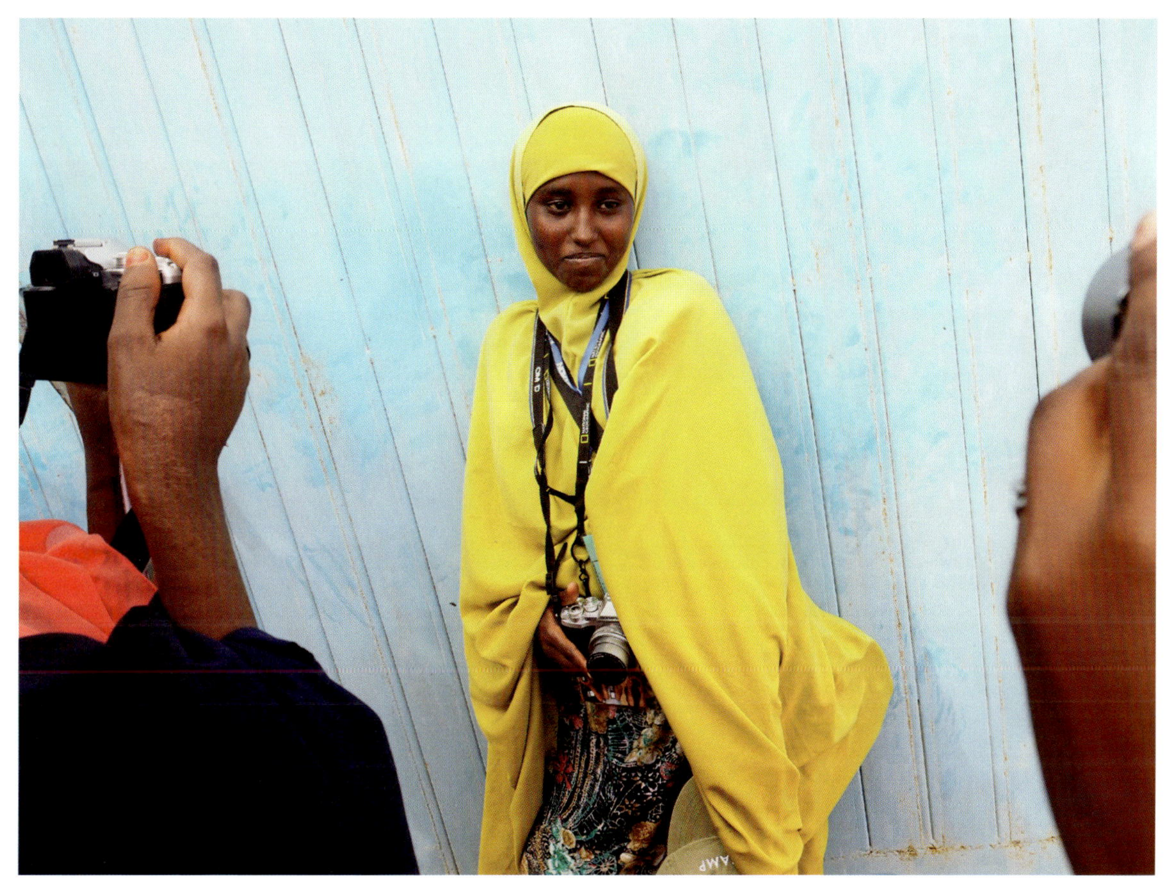

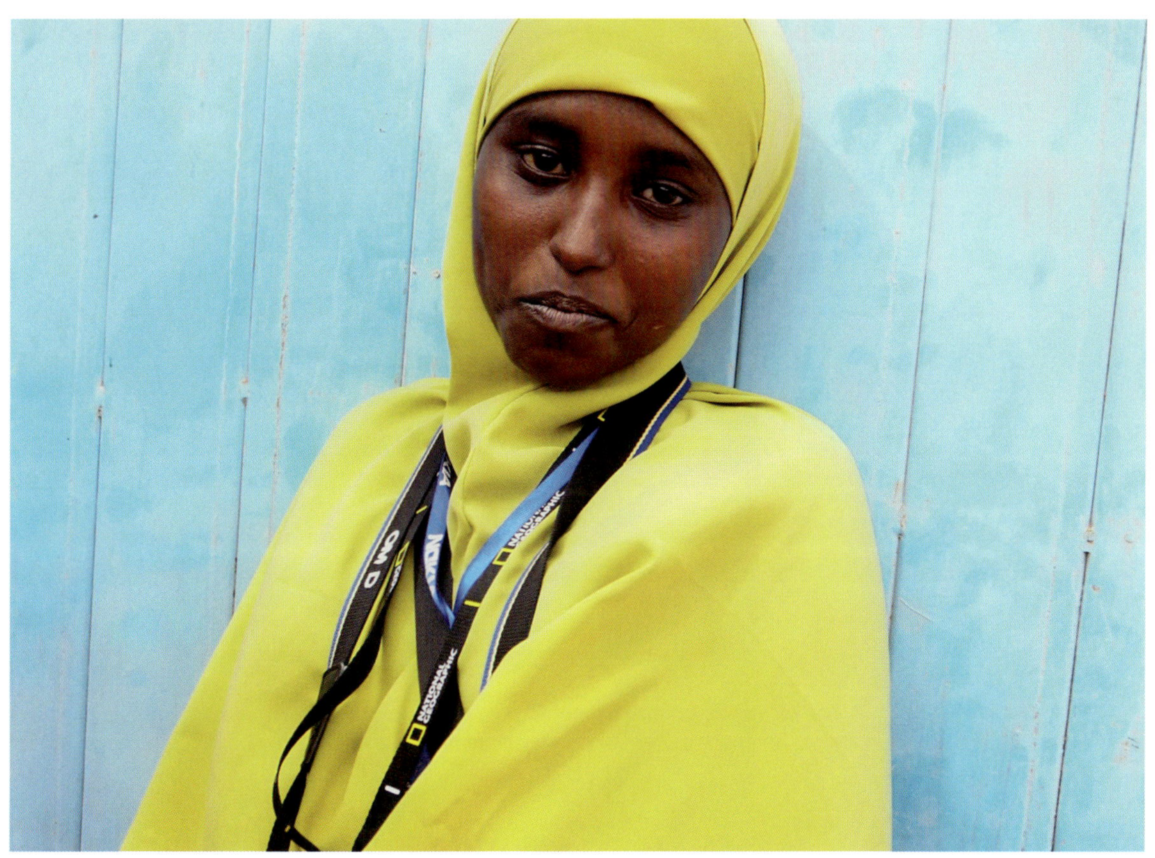

> ***"If heaven was on earth, I think the Okavango Delta would be the place."***
>
> —WELLINGTON MUTASA, BOTSWANA 2022

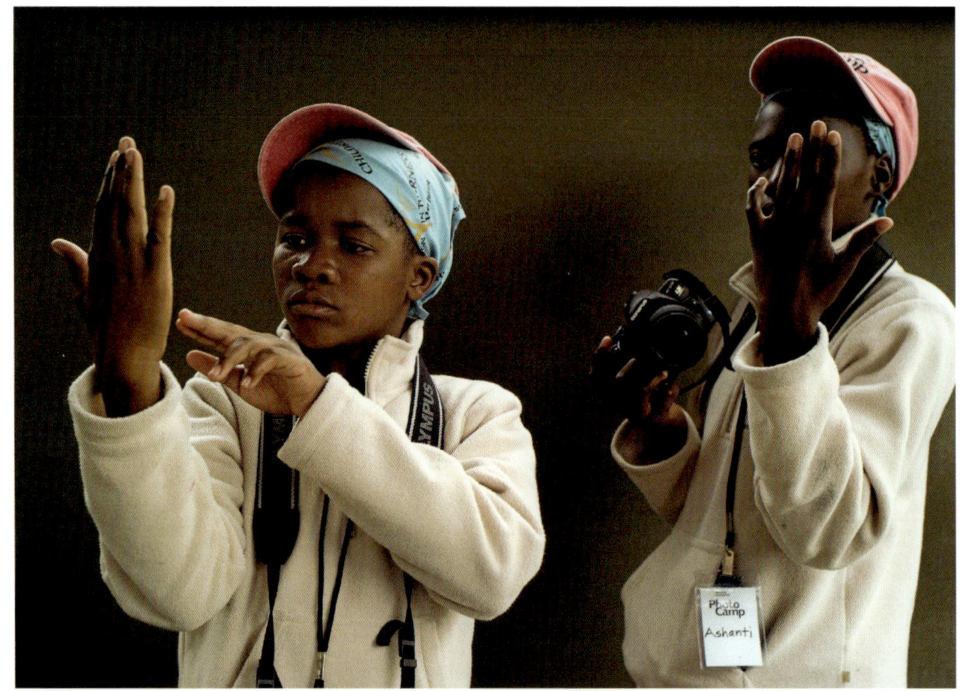

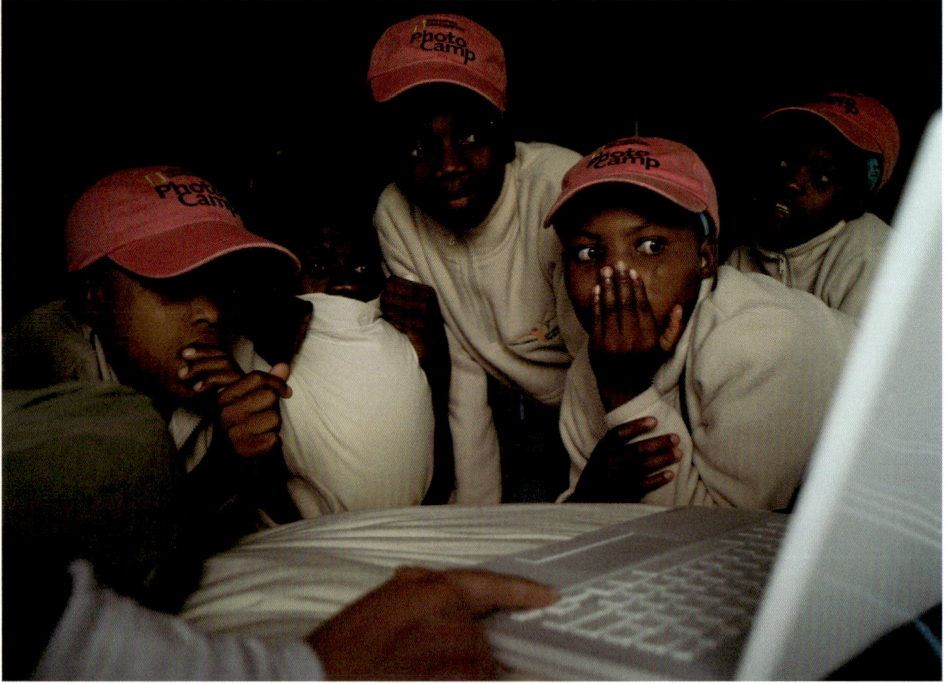

TOP: **LYNN JOHNSON, PHOTO CAMP STAFF / BOTSWANA 2009** ABOVE: **LYNN JOHNSON, PHOTO CAMP STAFF / BOTSWANA 2009** OPPOSITE: **KESETSELEMANG MOLAO / BOTSWANA 2009**

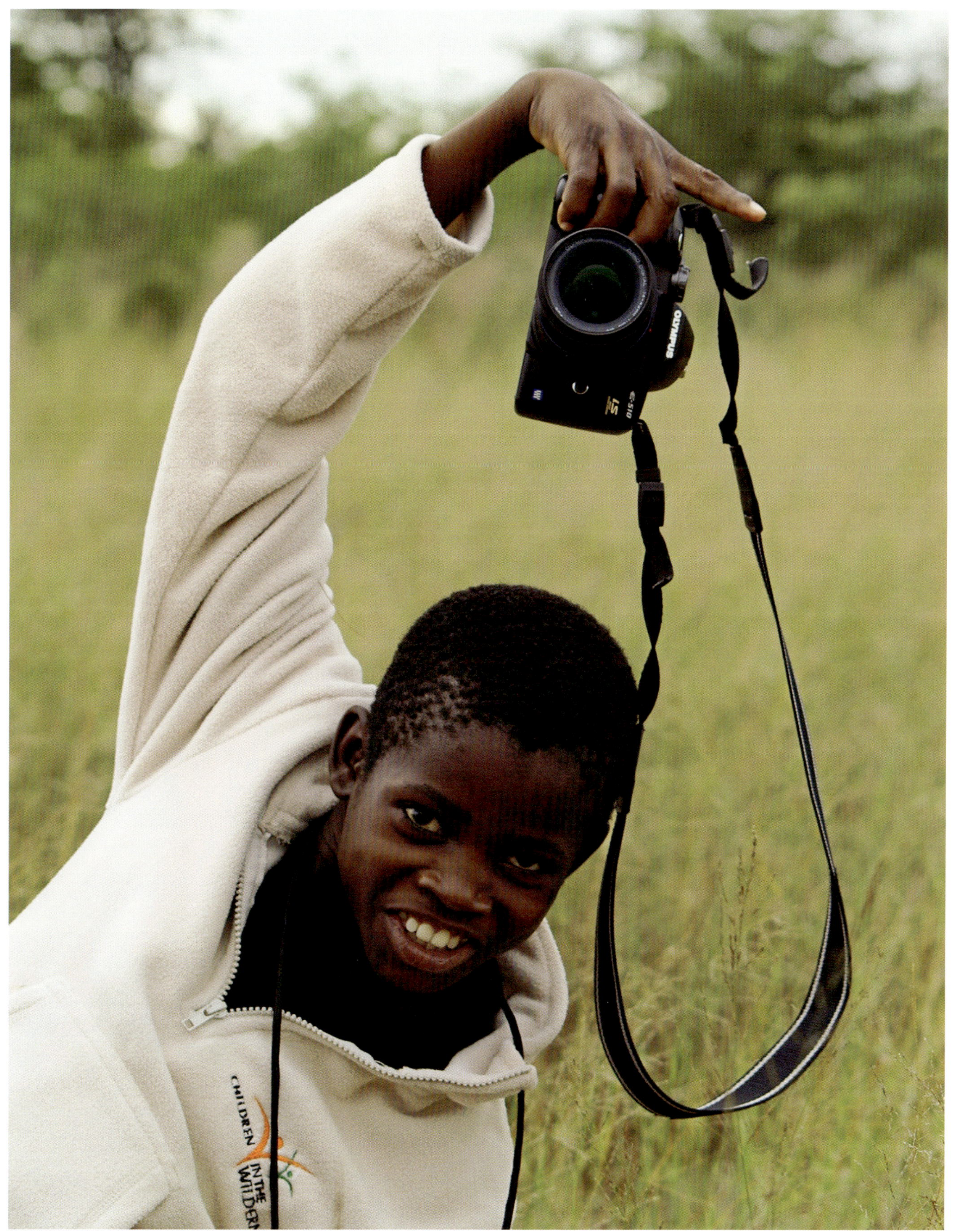
OLYMPUS

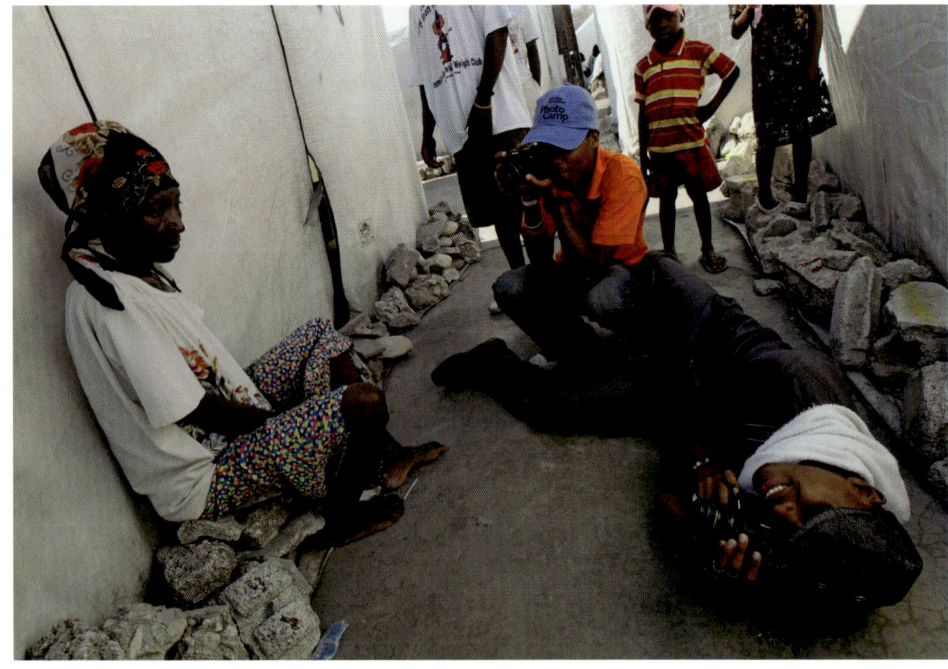

ABOVE: **LYNN JOHNSON, PHOTO CAMP STAFF / HAITI 2012** RIGHT: **SAMUEL LAMERY / HAITI 2012**

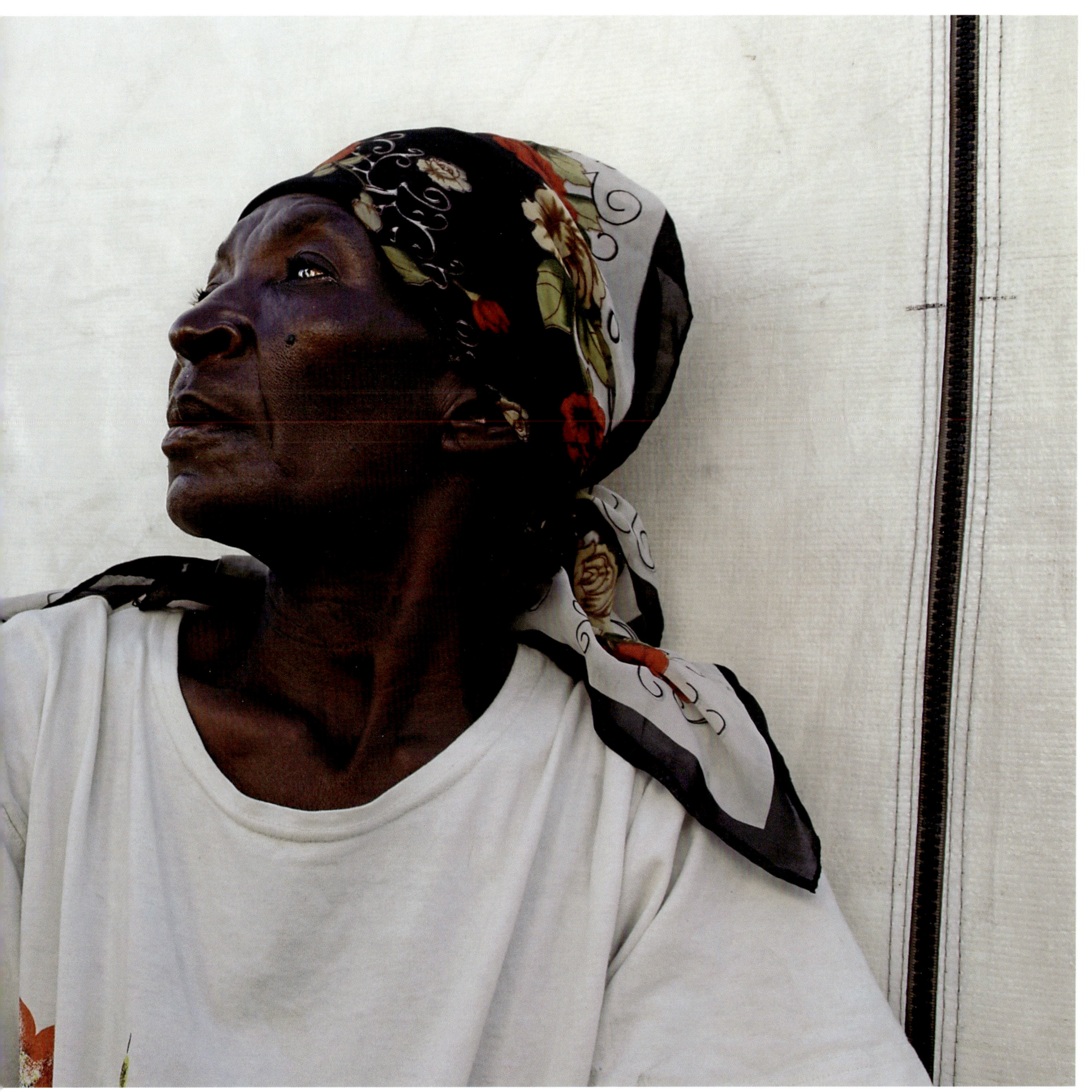

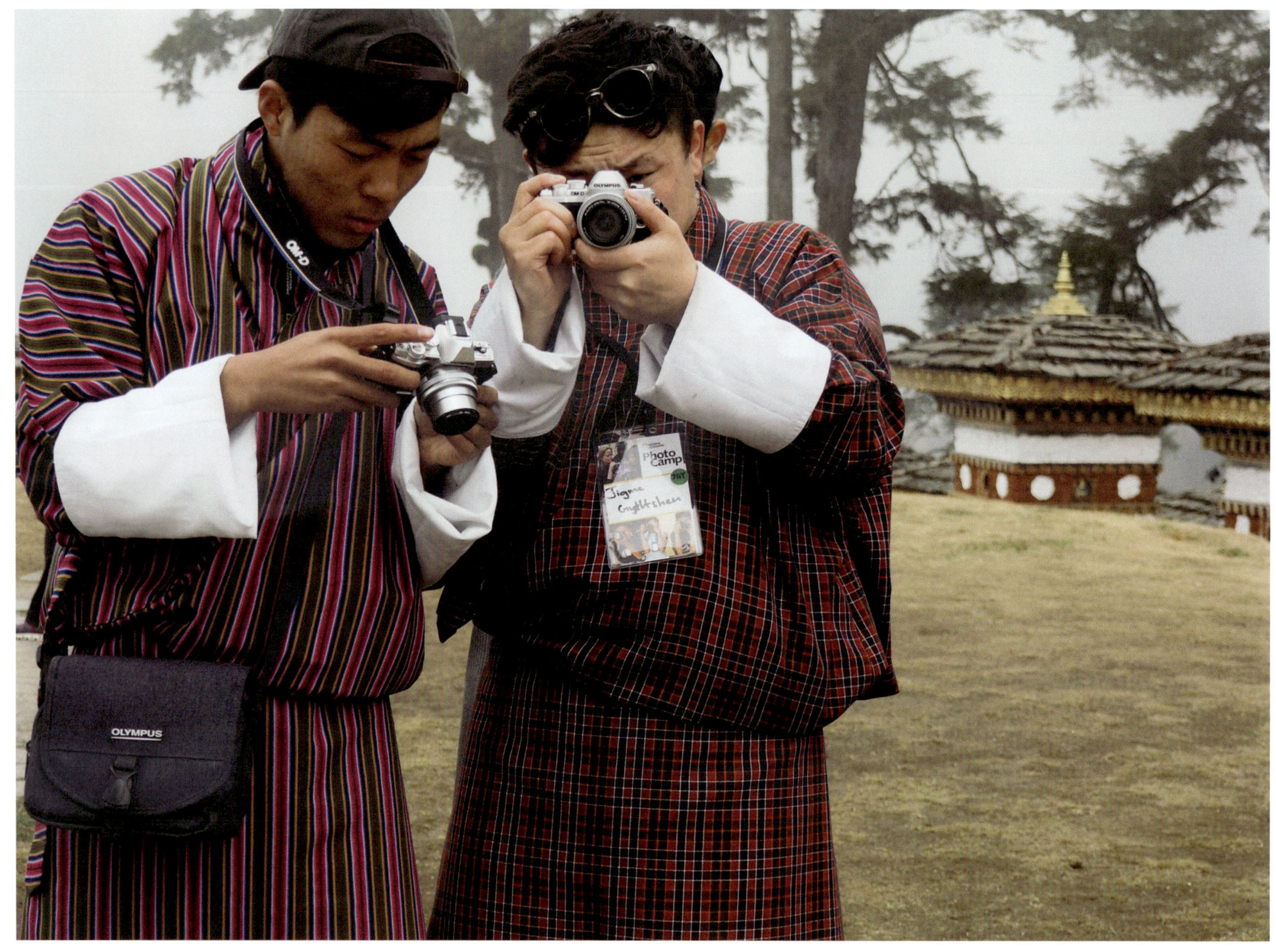

KIRSTEN ELSTNER, PHOTO CAMP STAFF / BHUTAN 2019

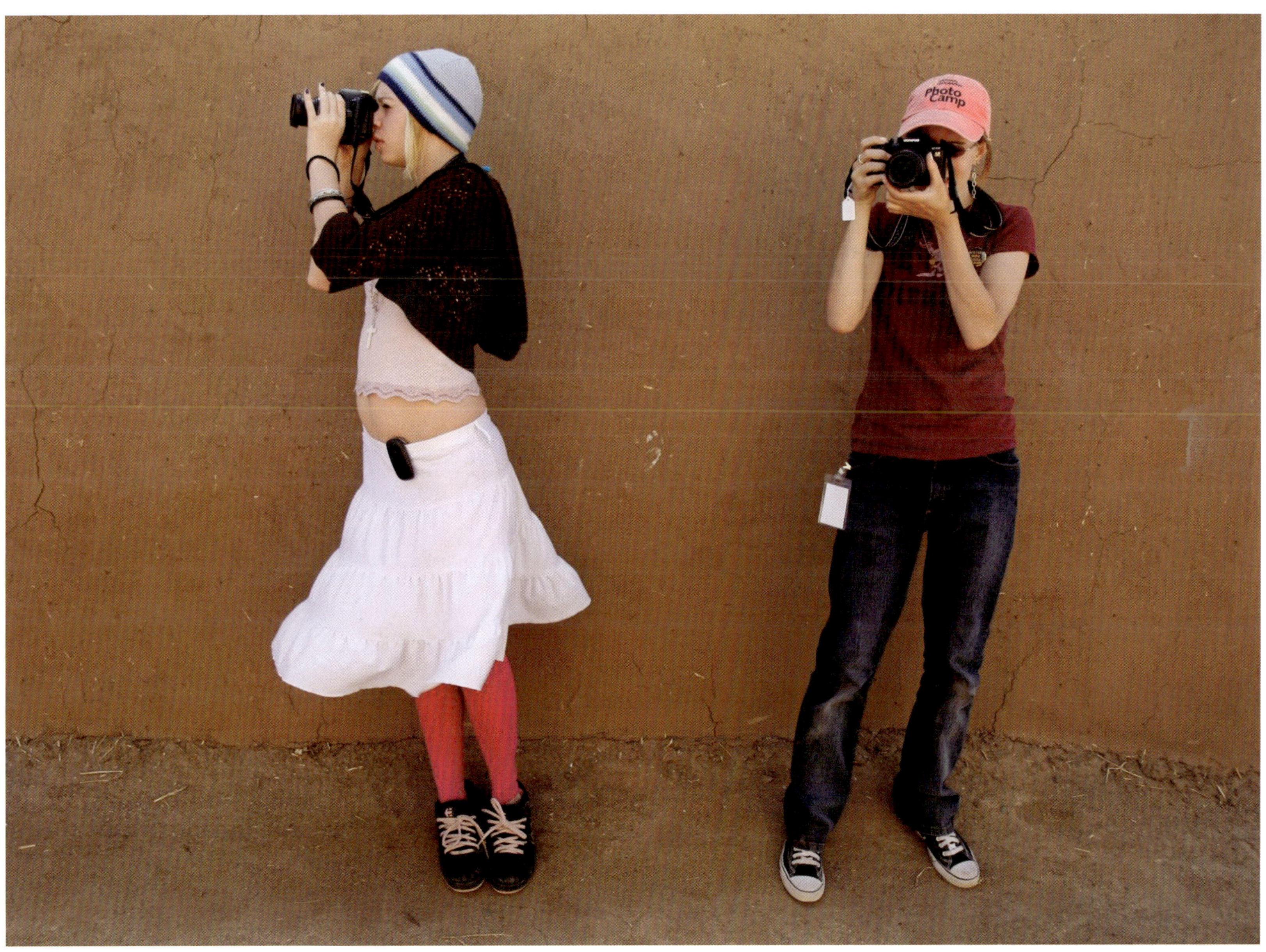

JIM WEBB, PHOTO CAMP STAFF / NEW MEXICO, U.S.A. 2008

"Photographs are important because they give us the opportunity to engage humanely with people we don't know, from different religions or ethnicities. Every picture that I take is important to show what [my country] has been through, what happened in my country. Many times, she has been burned to ashes and has always risen from the ashes."

—HAMZA AVDIC, BOSNIA AND HERZEGOVINA 2015

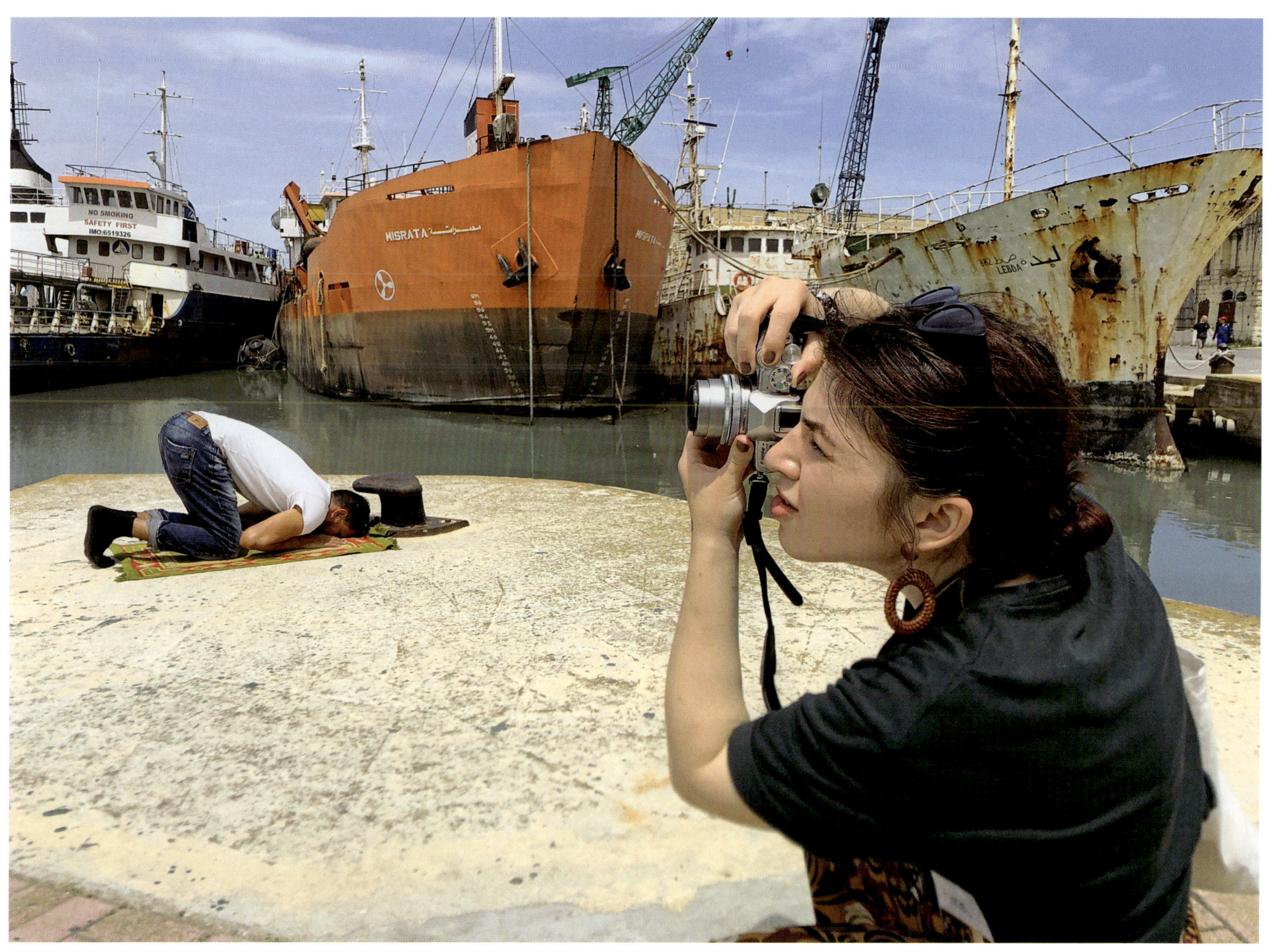

BRAHIM HIMI / MALTA 2019

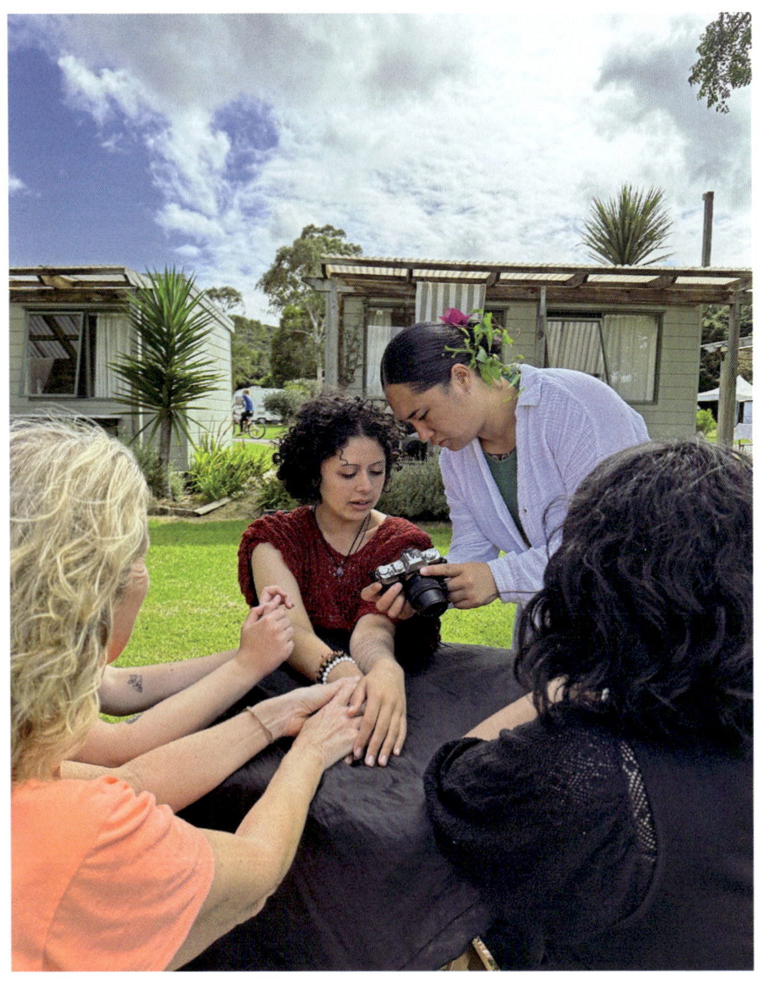

ABOVE: **PJ SHEPHERD, PHOTO CAMP STAFF / NEW ZEALAND 2023**
RIGHT: **AYLA BROCKES / NEW ZEALAND 2023**

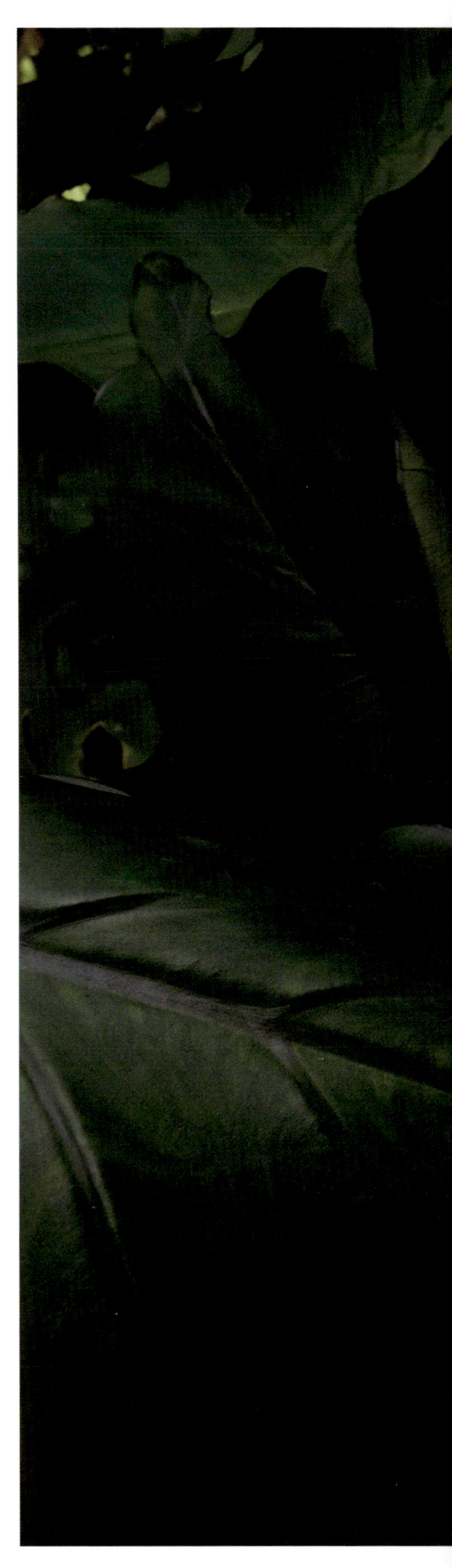

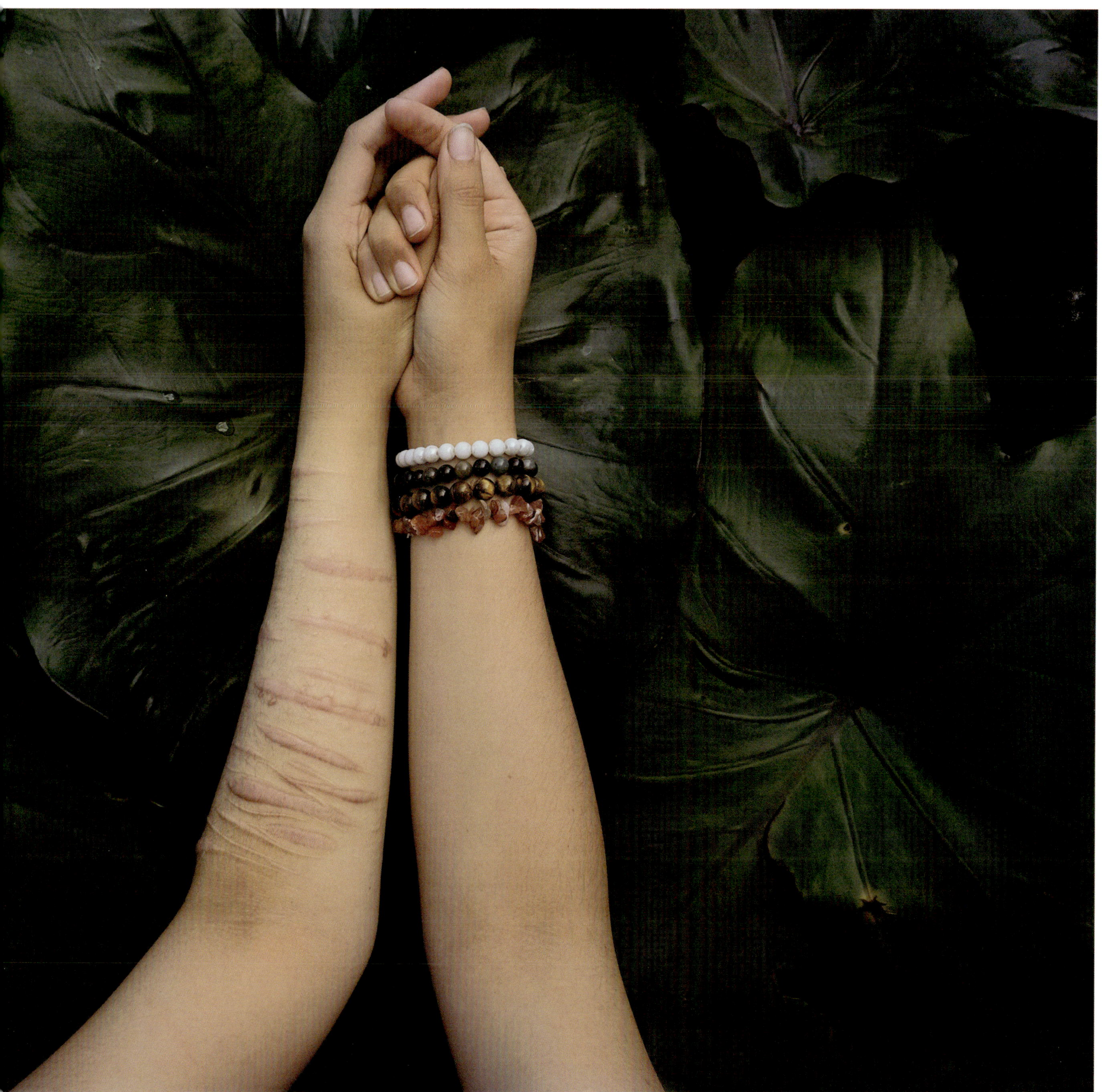

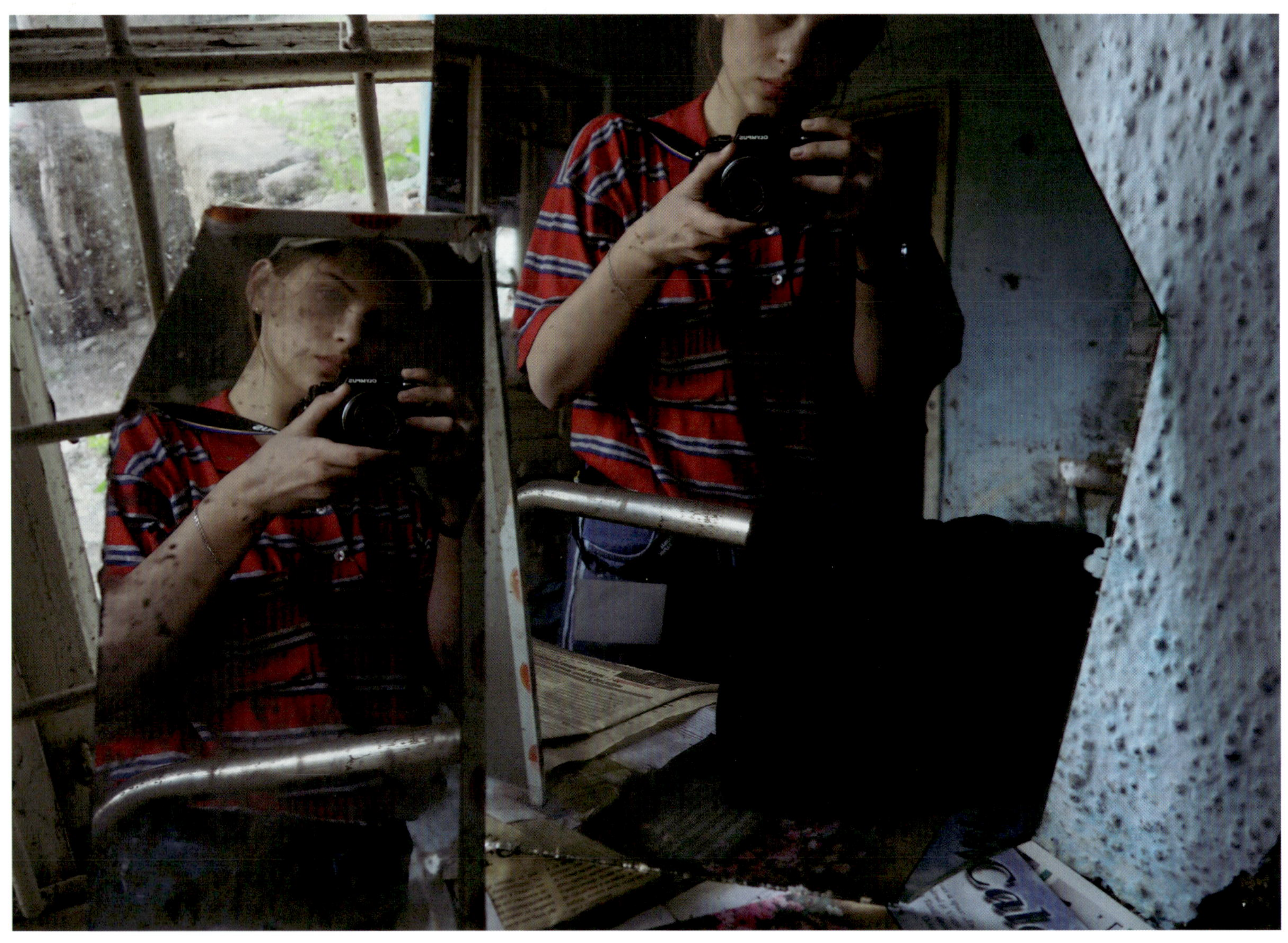

ABOVE: **LIUBOVI TABUNȘCIC / MOLDOVA 2018** OPPOSITE: **JIM WEBB, PHOTO CAMP STAFF / JORDAN 2009**

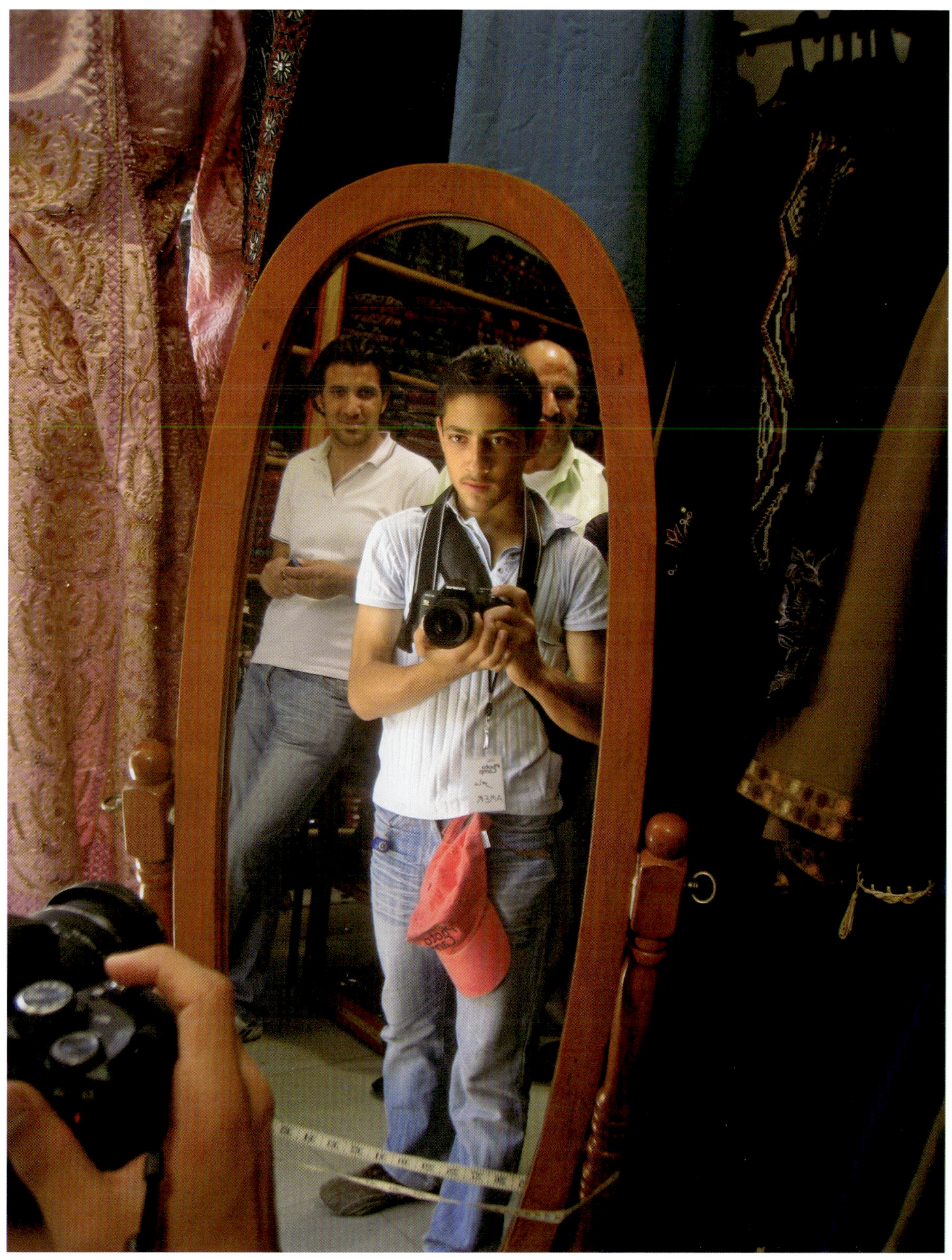

Camp Profile
Cuba 2016

PHOTO CAMP WENT TO CUBA in the fall of 2016. Following the renewal of diplomatic relations with the United States, the Cuban government began investing millions in tourism; communications with the outside world were improving.

Meeting in a room at Havana University, the 21 attending students were animated about the changes in society. In the photos they would create around the city, they showed an unabashed love for their home; in their writing, they expressed fear that sudden change would rob the country of its uniqueness. And they were frank about the contrasts between touristic Havana and the rest of the city. "One is bright and splendid, full of life and movement. The other, sad and gray, hit by time," wrote Ernesto Herrera Pelegrino.

At that time, no one could predict what was coming: the ravages of COVID-19; the cutting off of crucial oil supplies from Venezuela, which Cuba depends on for power generation; and the crackdowns that followed the 2021 protests, which were triggered by frustration over lack of freedoms and an economic crisis that included widespread power outages. This reality is worlds away from the kinds of innovation the students anticipated. Some of the revelations of the workshop week now strike a somber note. "Cuba needs the change that is happening now," Jennifer Albin wrote during that simpler time. "I don't want to live in another country to make my dreams come true."

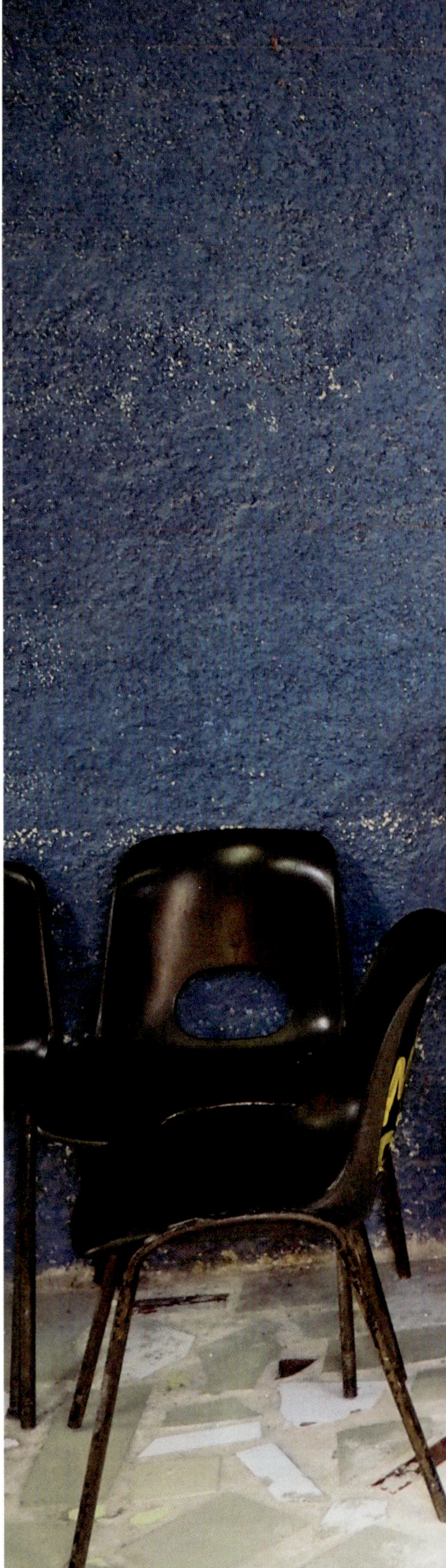

JONATHAN LOPEZ AVILA / CUBA 2016

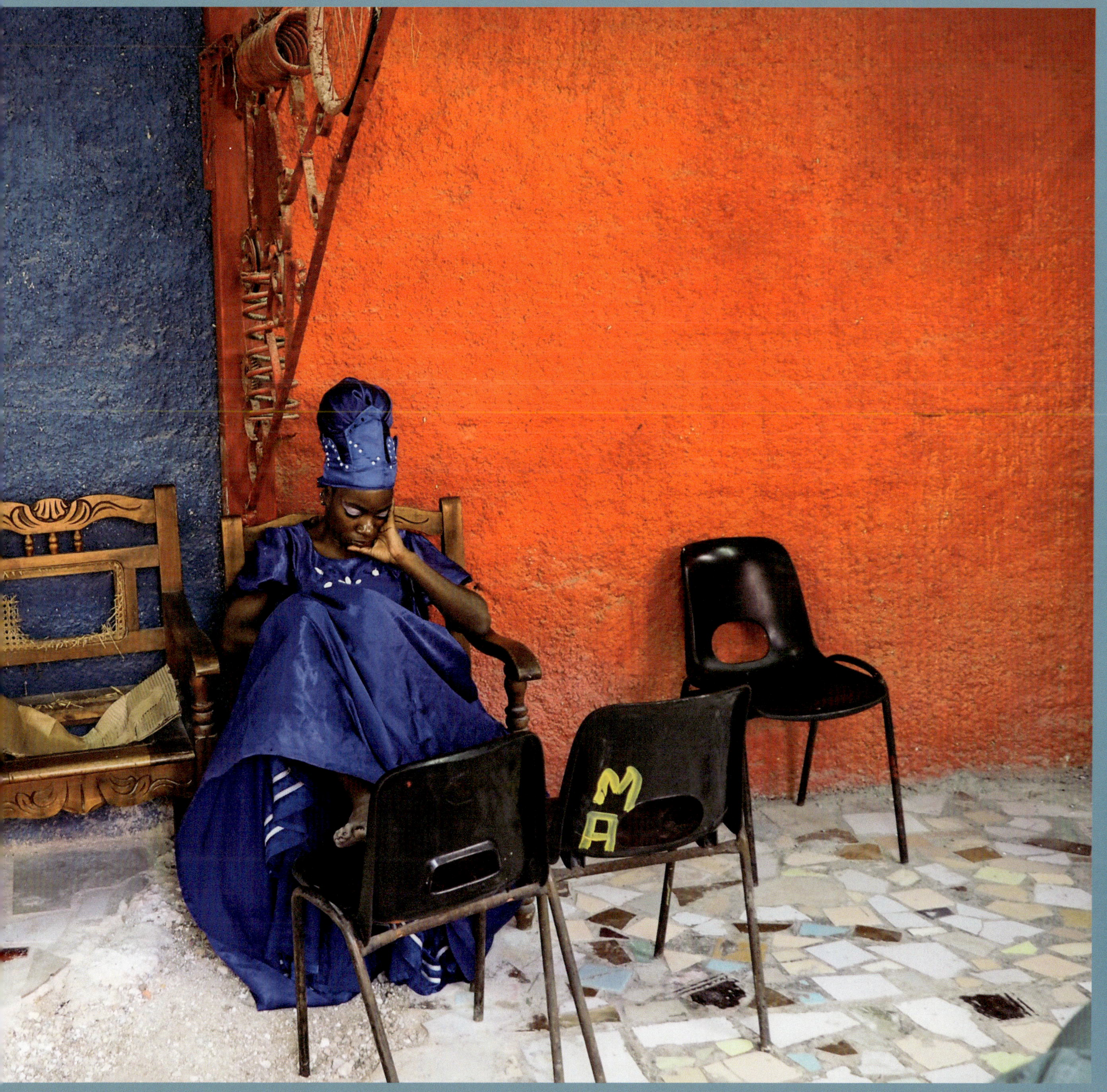
MA

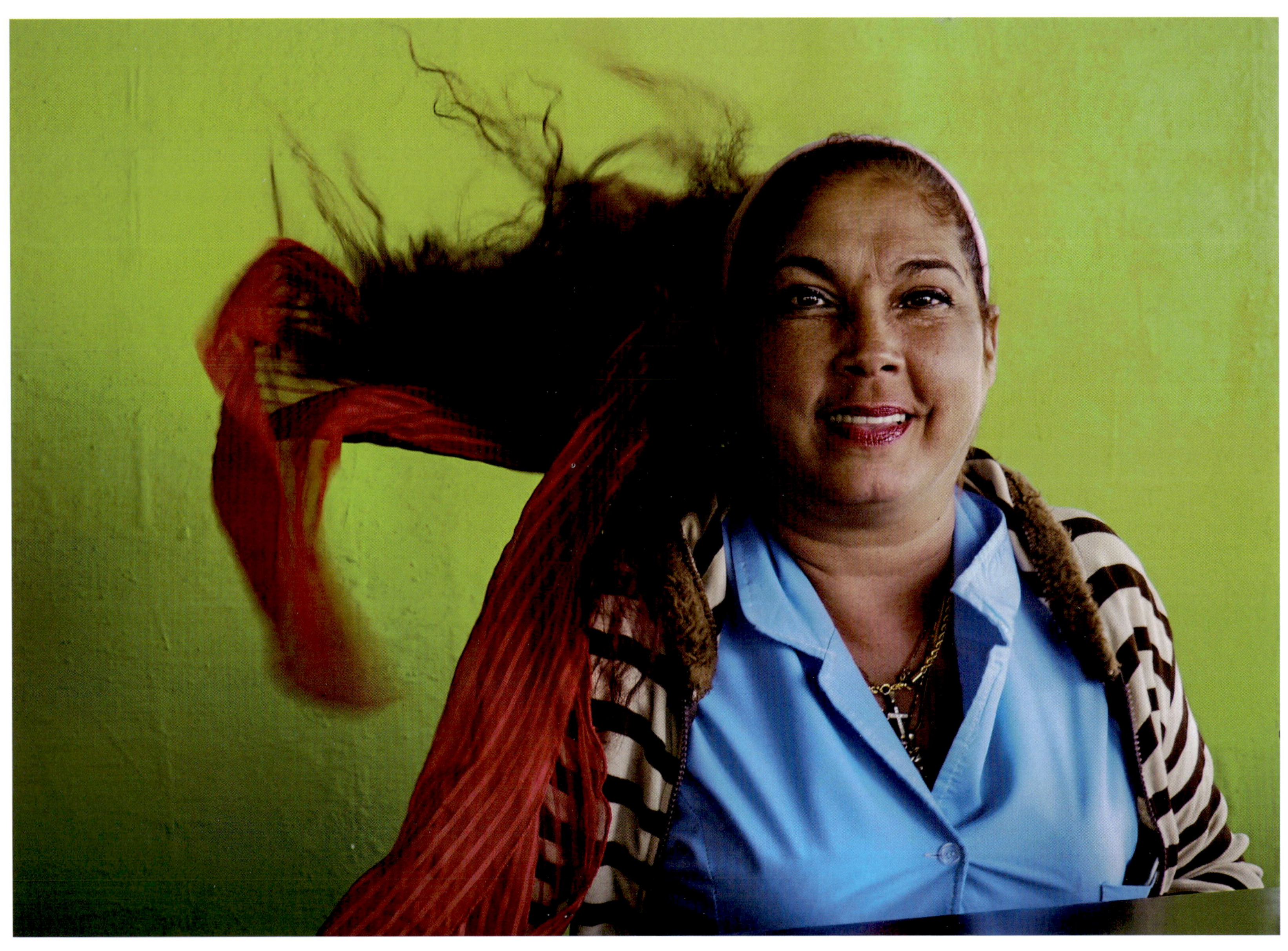

ODALYS EMILIA OROZCO ACOSTA / CUBA 2016

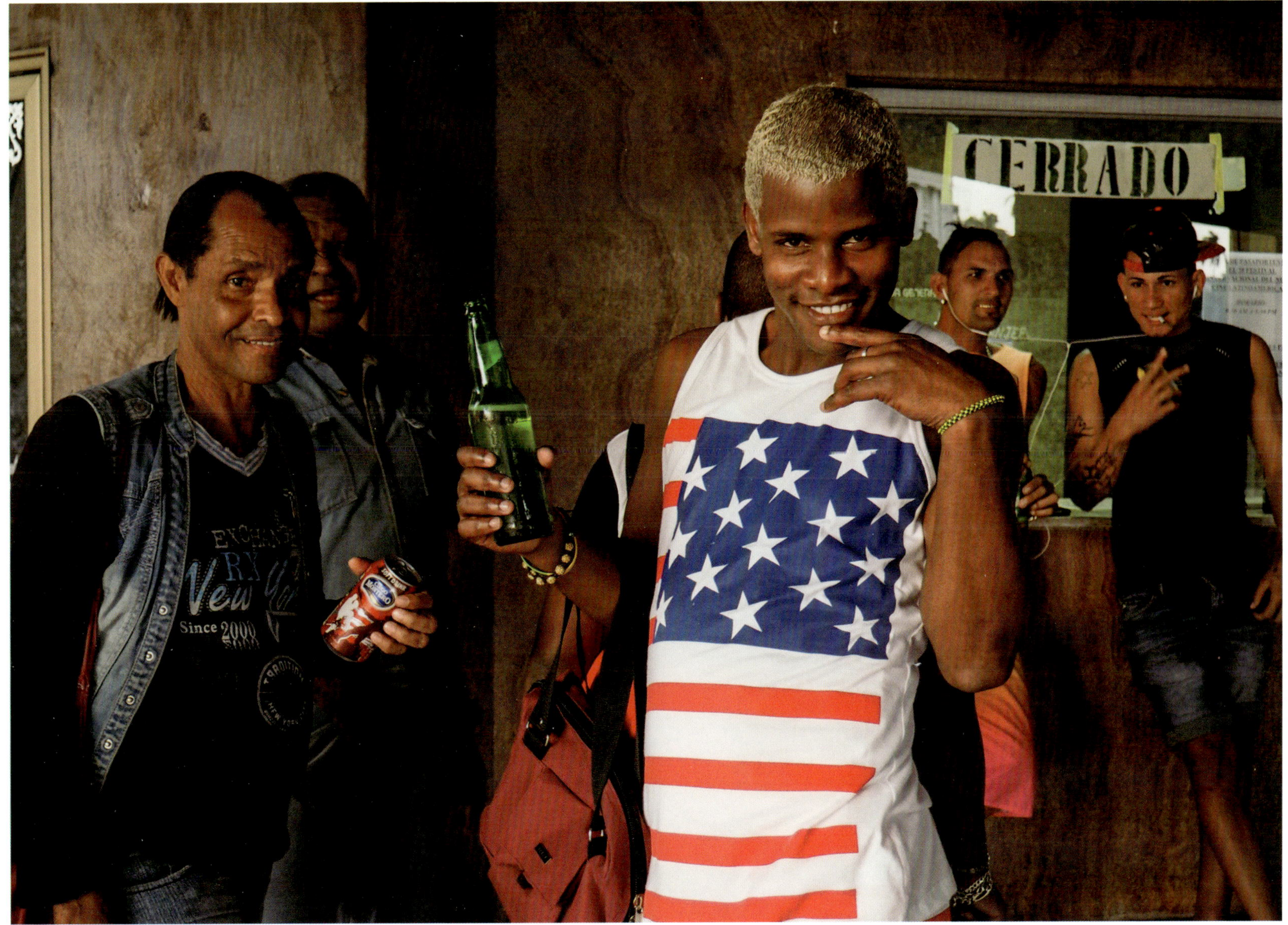

ODALYS EMILIA OROZCO ACOSTA / CUBA 2016

"It's late afternoon in Havana. The sun, nostalgic, hides himself behind the sea and fades away like the dreams of a generation. Tomorrow, when the sun comes up, young people will continue weaving dreams in the sea."

—ERNESTO HERRERA PELEGRINO, CUBA 2016

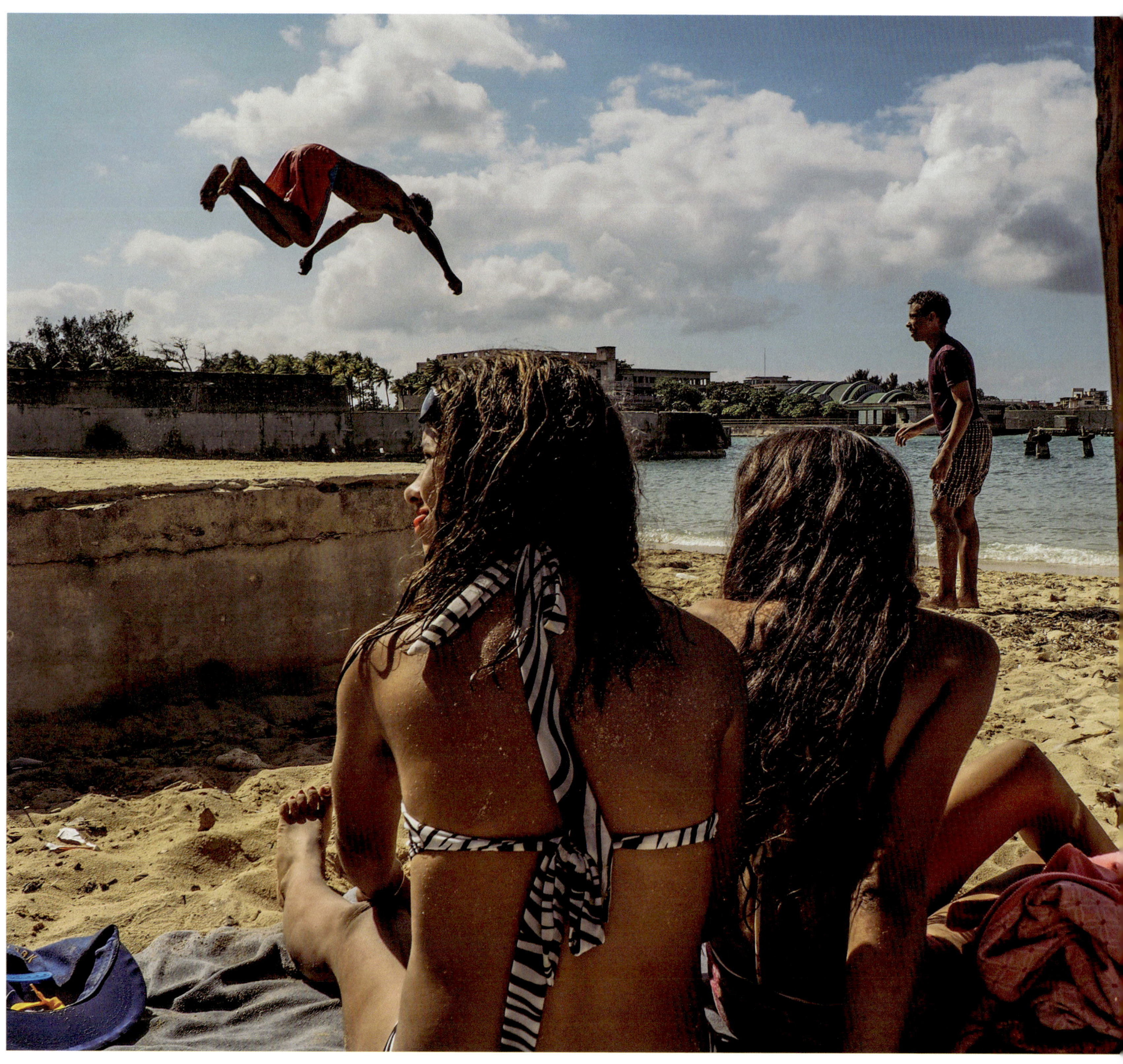

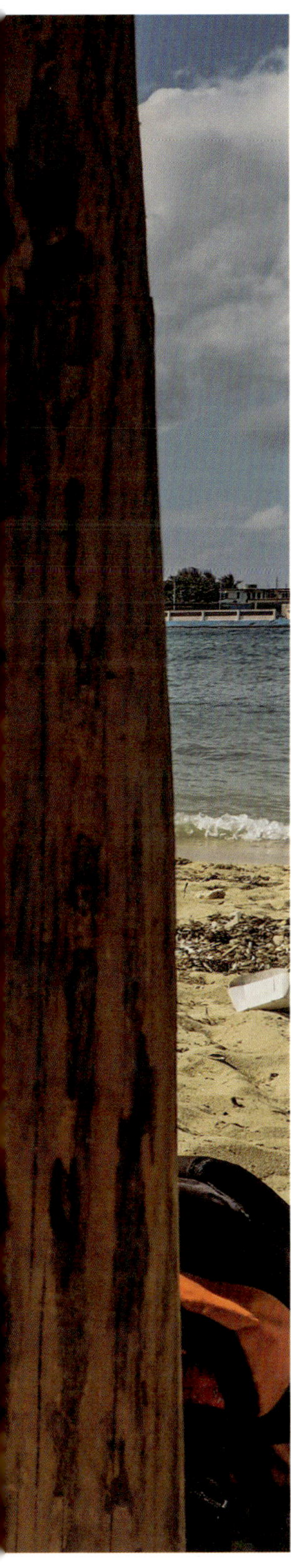

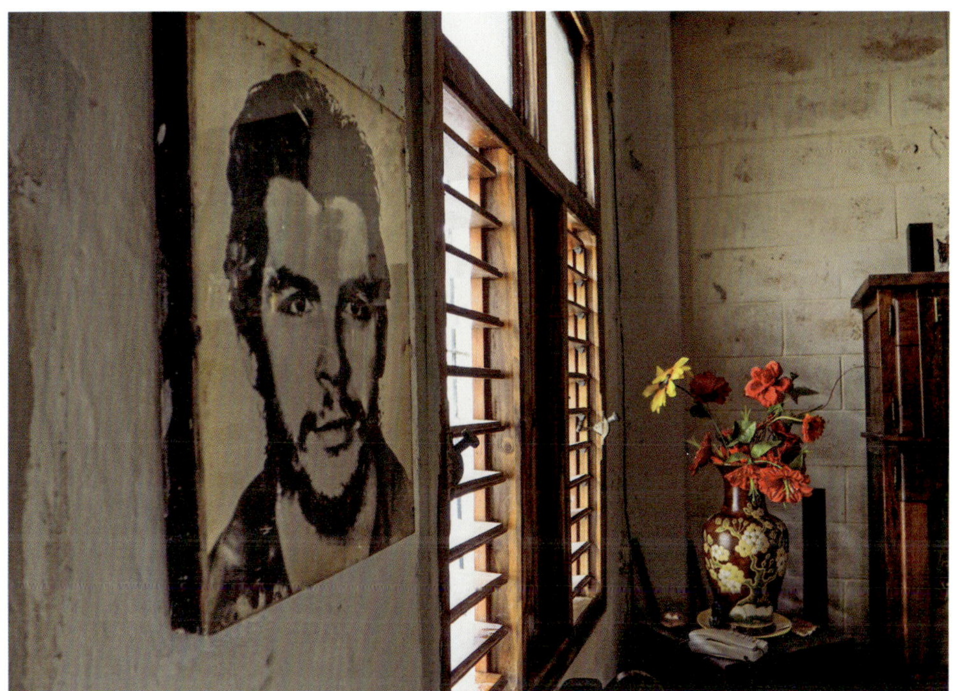

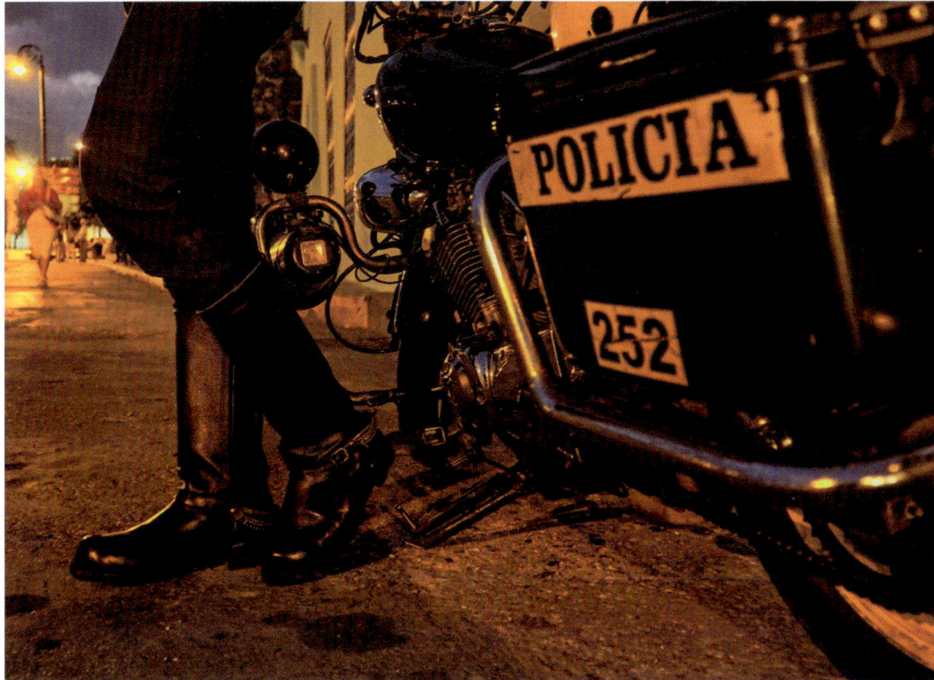

TOP: **CRISTOBAL ECHEVARRIA GARCIA / CUBA 2016** ABOVE: **AMALIA CASTILLO SILES / CUBA 2016**
LEFT: **ODALYS EMILIA OROZCO ACOSTA / CUBA 2016**

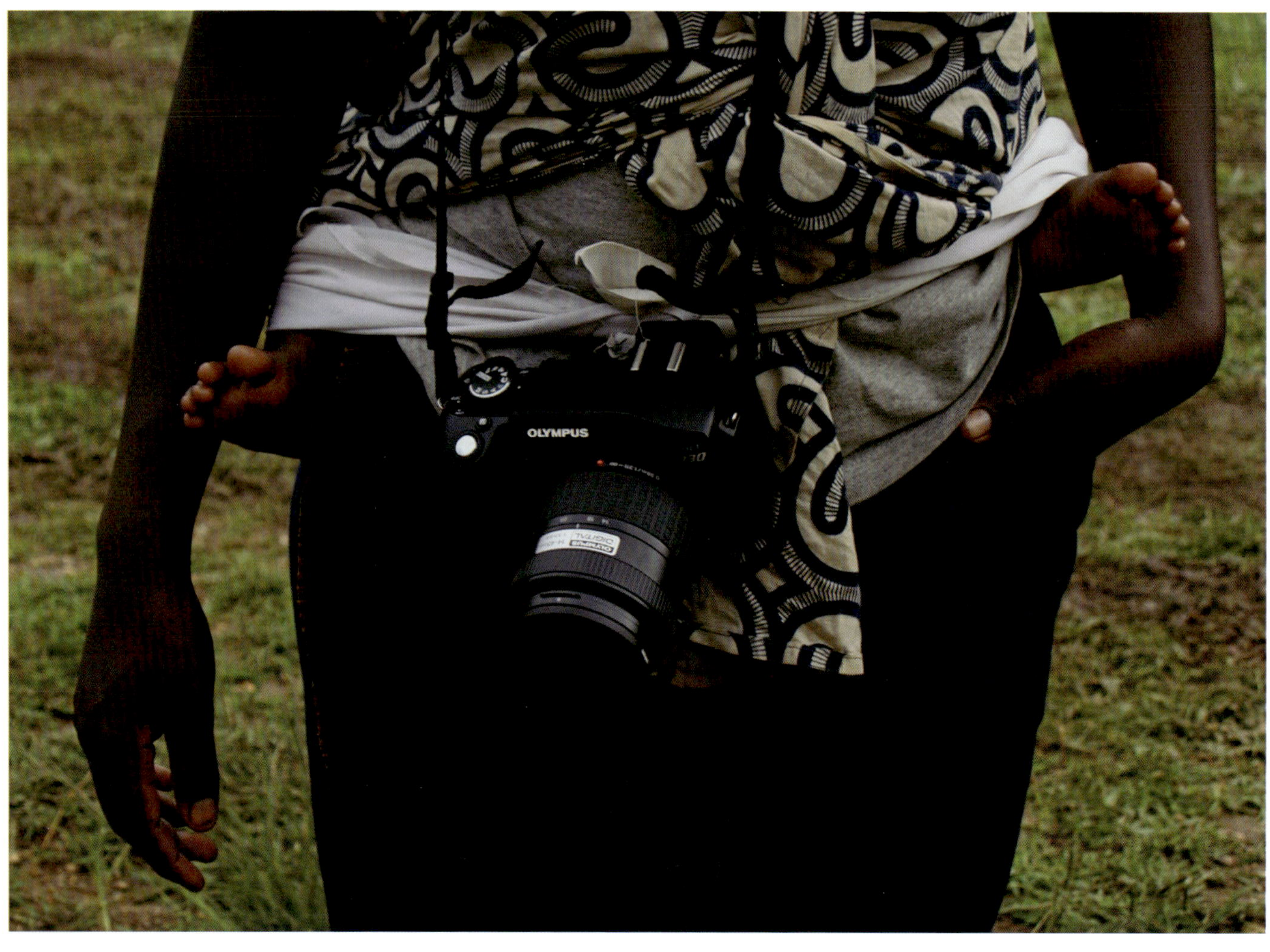

ABOVE: **REZA DEGHATI, PHOTO CAMP STAFF / UGANDA 2006** OPPOSITE: **LYNN JOHNSON, PHOTO CAMP STAFF / KENYA 2014**

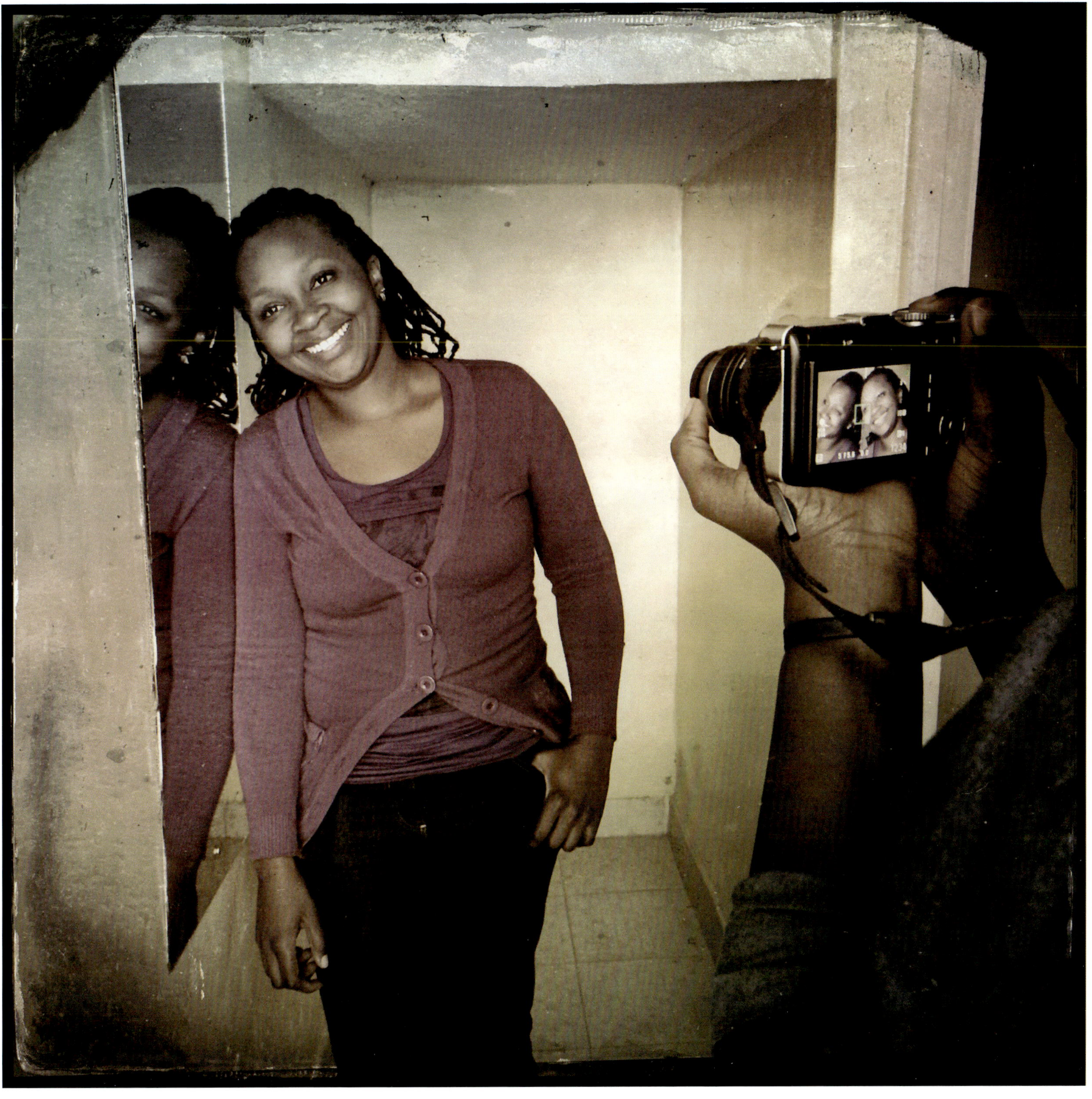

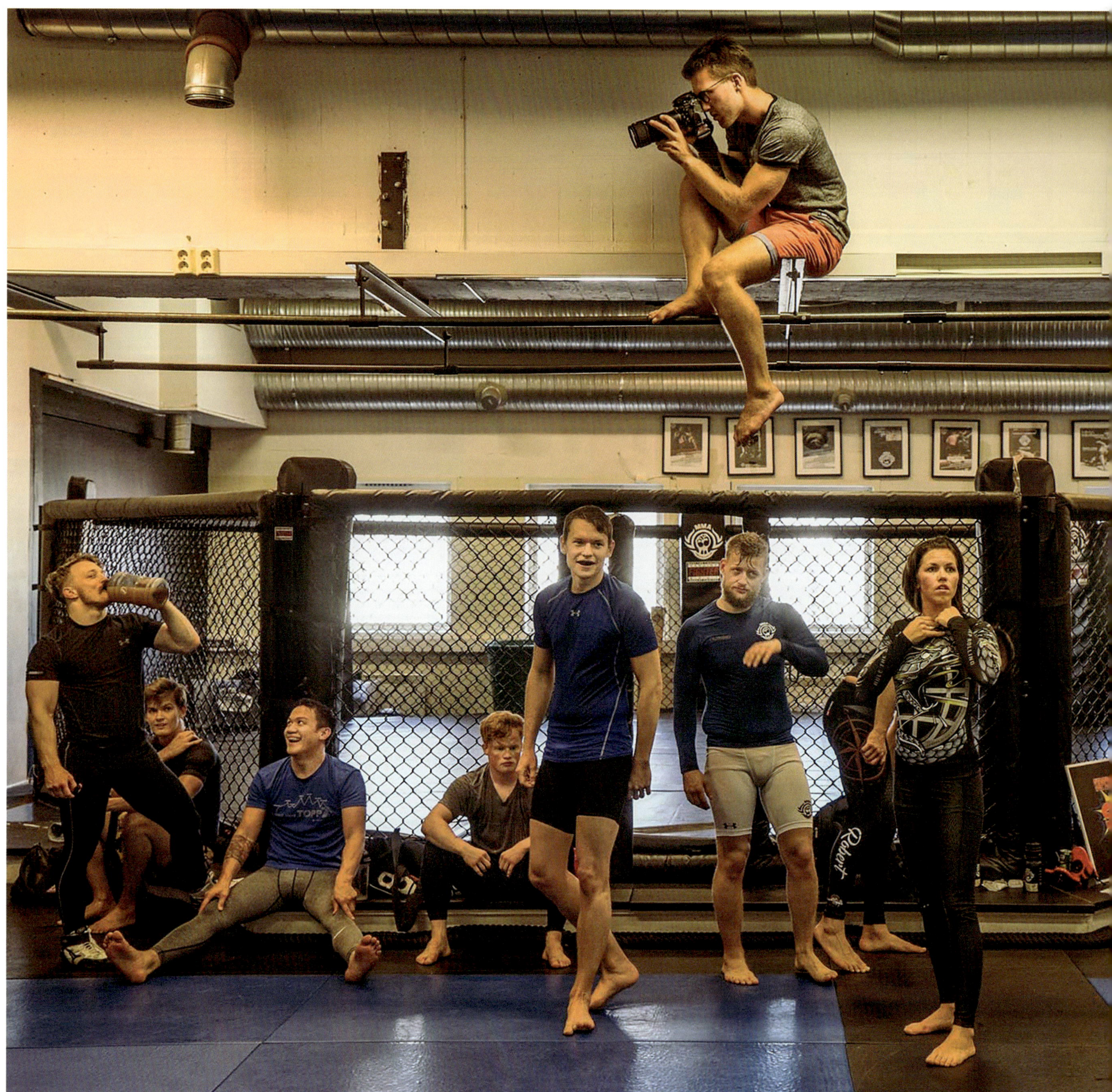
MMA
TOPP
Robert

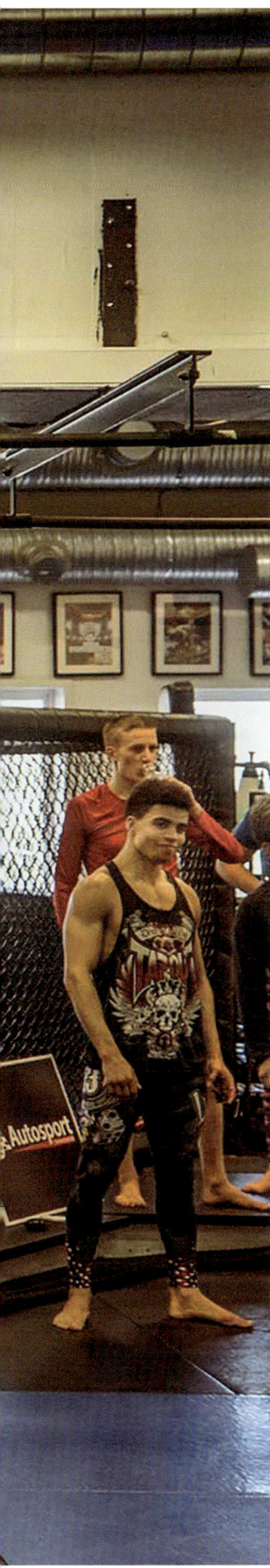

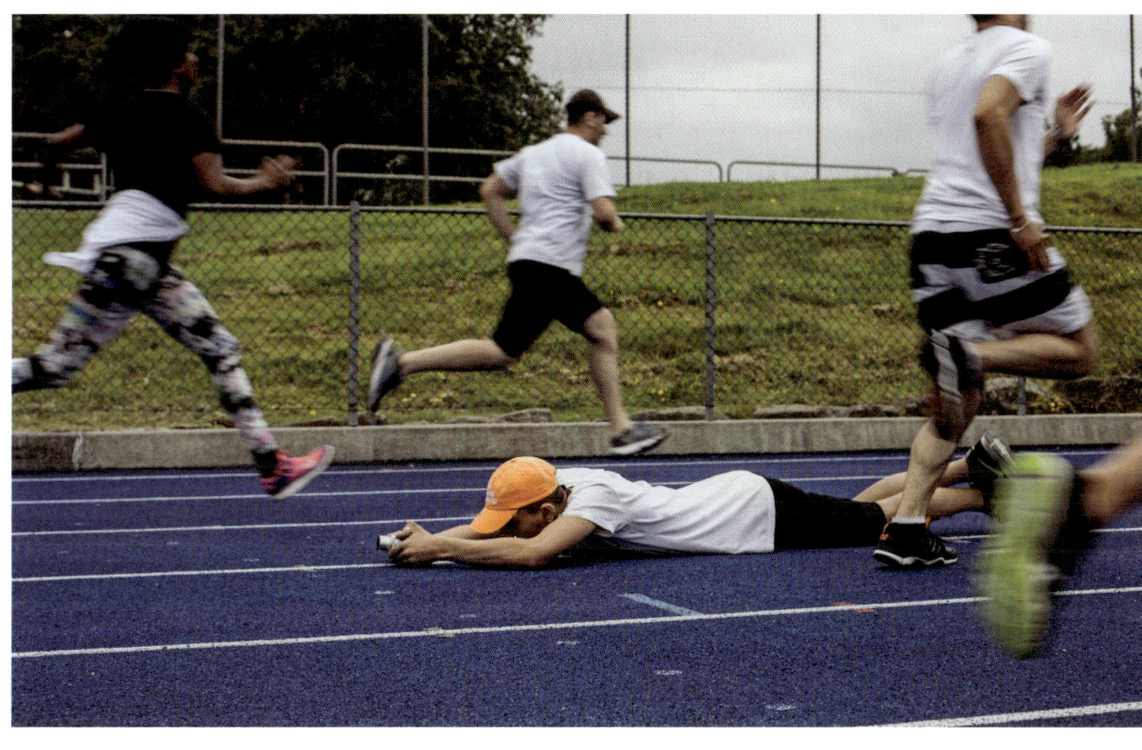

ABOVE: **LISA VICTORIA, PHOTO CAMP STAFF / NORWAY 2017** LEFT: **PETE MULLER, PHOTO CAMP STAFF / NORWAY 2017**

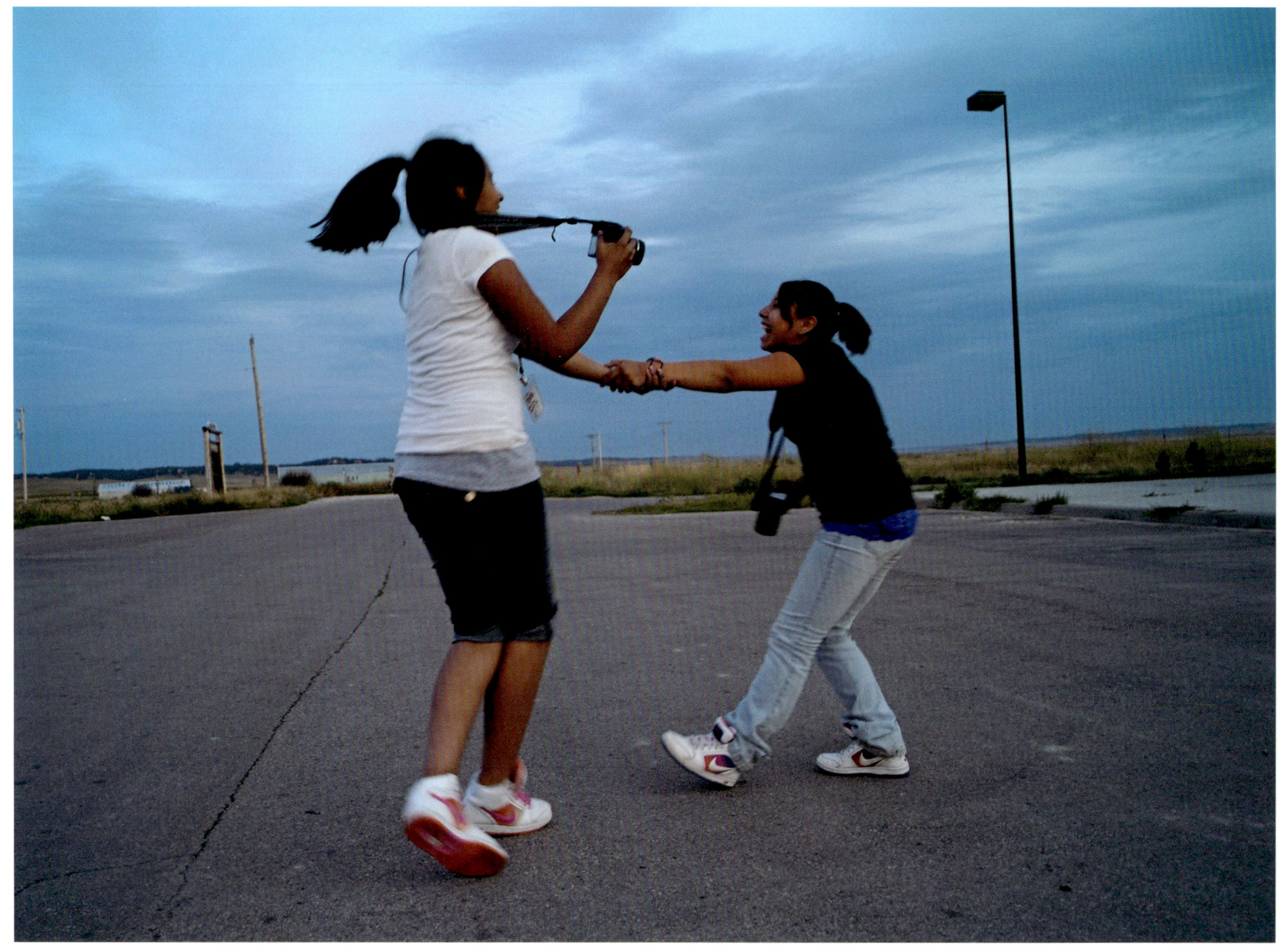

ABOVE: **LYNN JOHNSON, PHOTO CAMP STAFF / SOUTH DAKOTA, U.S.A. 2009** OPPOSITE TOP: **LYNN JOHNSON, PHOTO CAMP STAFF / SOUTH DAKOTA, U.S.A. 2009** OPPOSITE BOTTOM: **DEMCIE MESTETH / SOUTH DAKOTA, U.S.A. 2009**

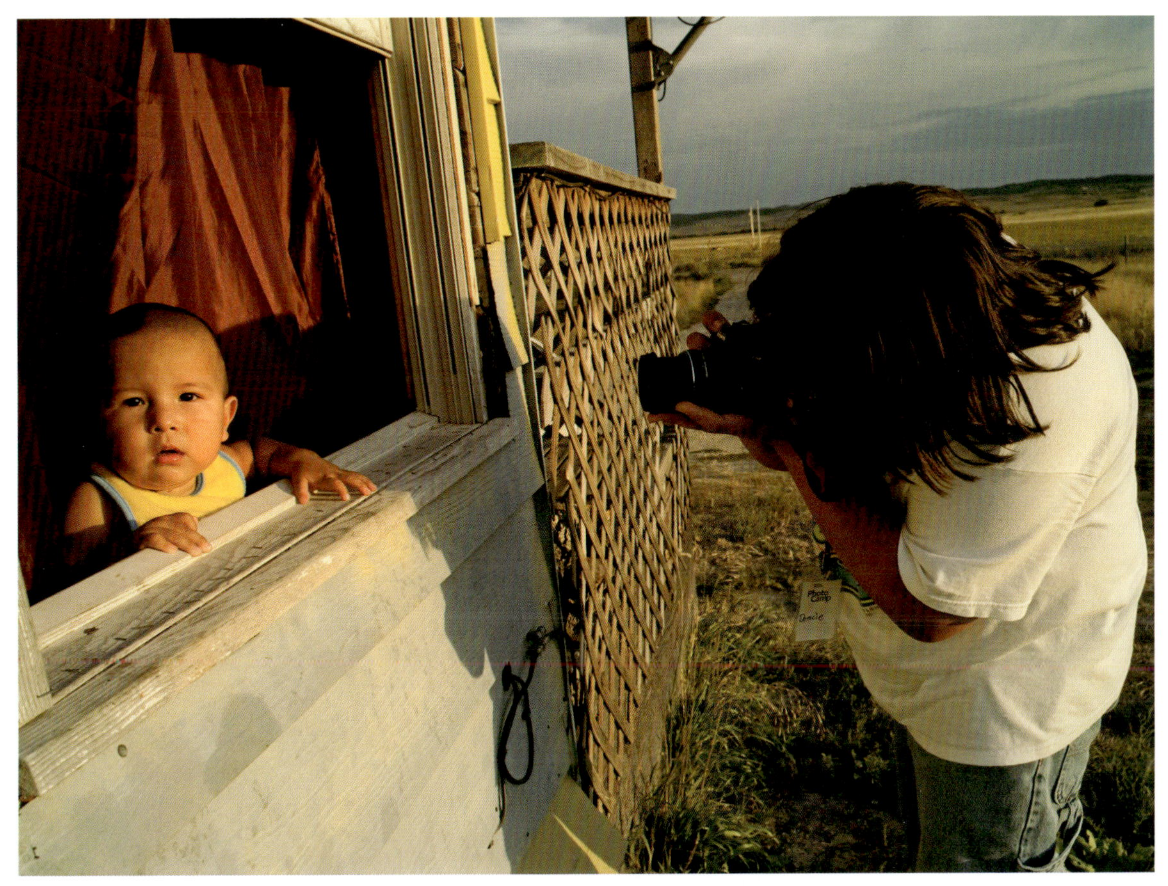

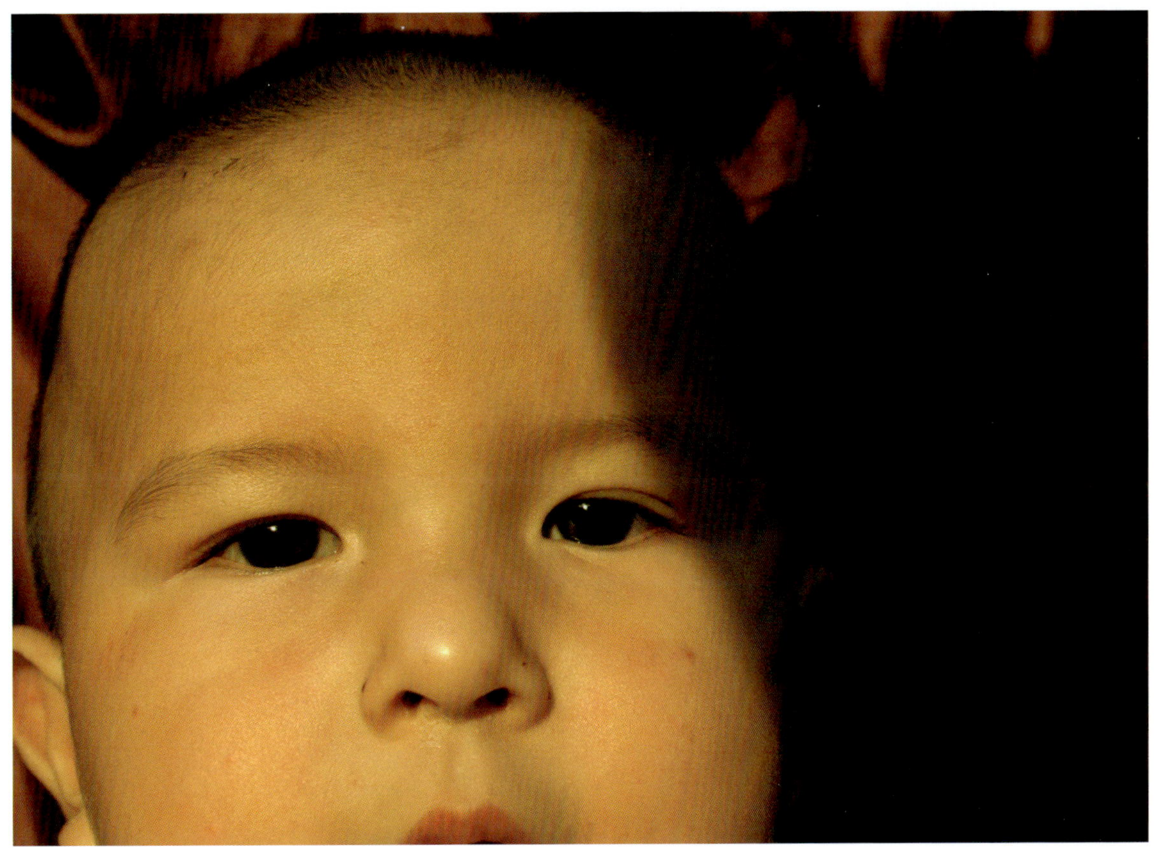

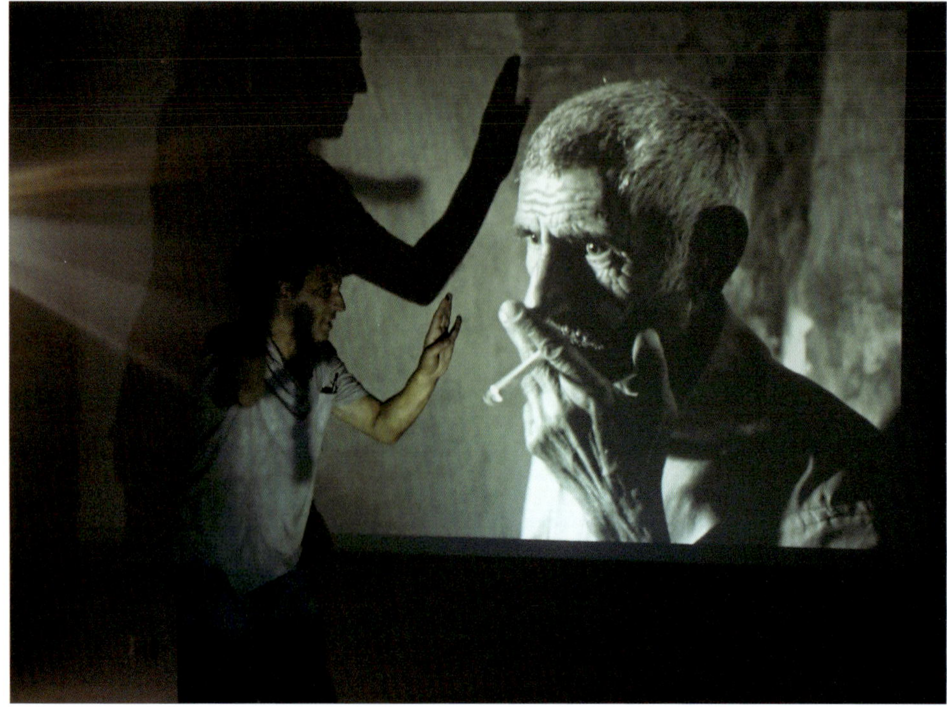

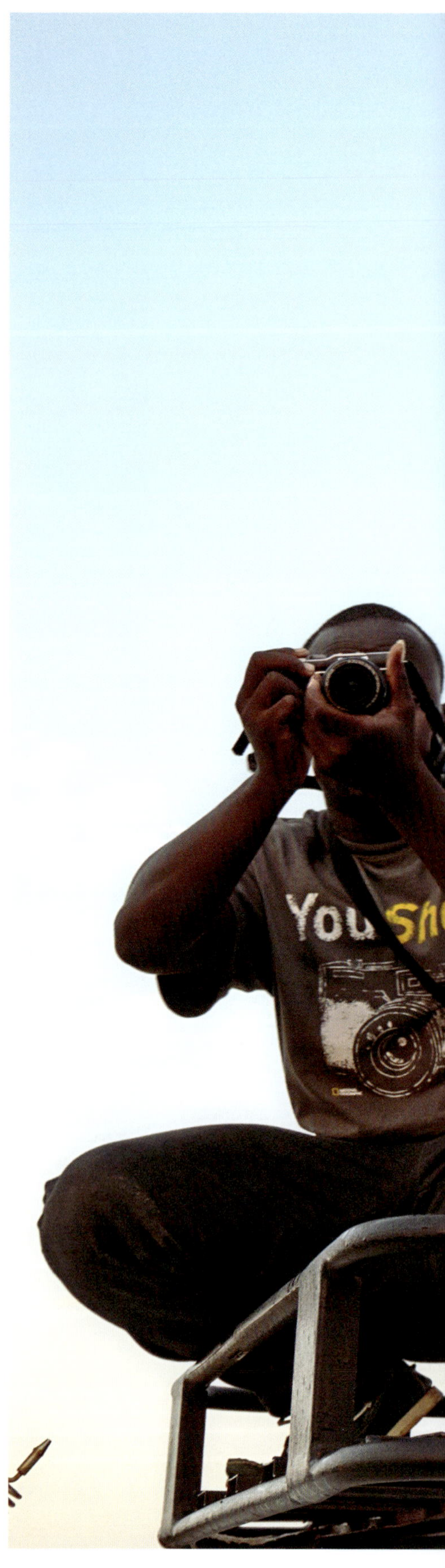

ABOVE: **LISOK JAMES MOSES / SOUTH SUDAN 2014**
RIGHT: **ED KASHI, PHOTO CAMP STAFF / SOUTH SUDAN 2014**

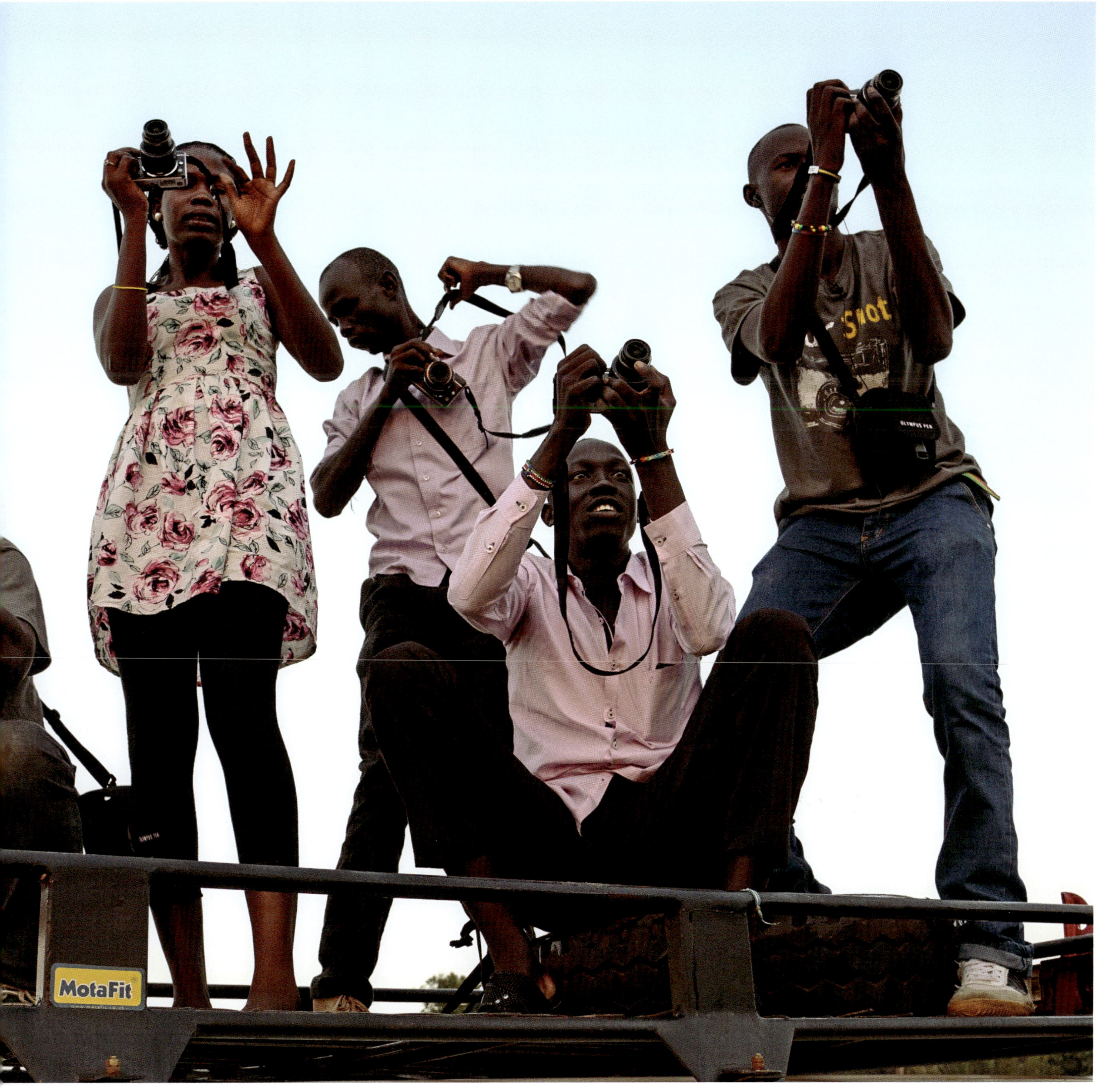
MotaFit

"This is the same land that was called 'unlivable'—land where my people thrived and still are thriving.

This is the same land that my family has lived on for seven generations.
This is the same land that Ahkeknaaknooshe gifted us in times of need.

This land holds a special place in my heart.
I believe I was destined to protect it with all my might.
For my people
For my culture
For my animals
For the plants and trees.

I want people to know that this land is vital not just for my people
But for every single living being.

I grew up in a village,
Raised by my mother, grandmother, great grandparents, aunts, uncles.
I grew up in the Everglades.

Everything really is put here on this Earth for a reason."

—MAE'ANNA OSCEOLA, EVERGLADES, FLORIDA, U.S.A. 2022

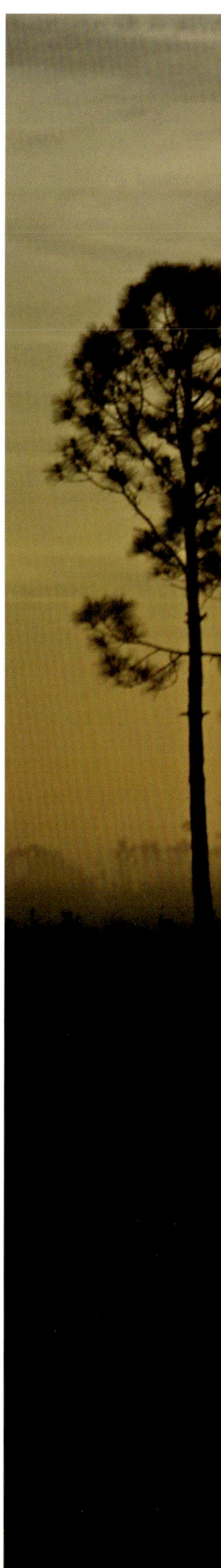

CARMELLO SHENANDOAH / FLORIDA, U.S.A. 2022

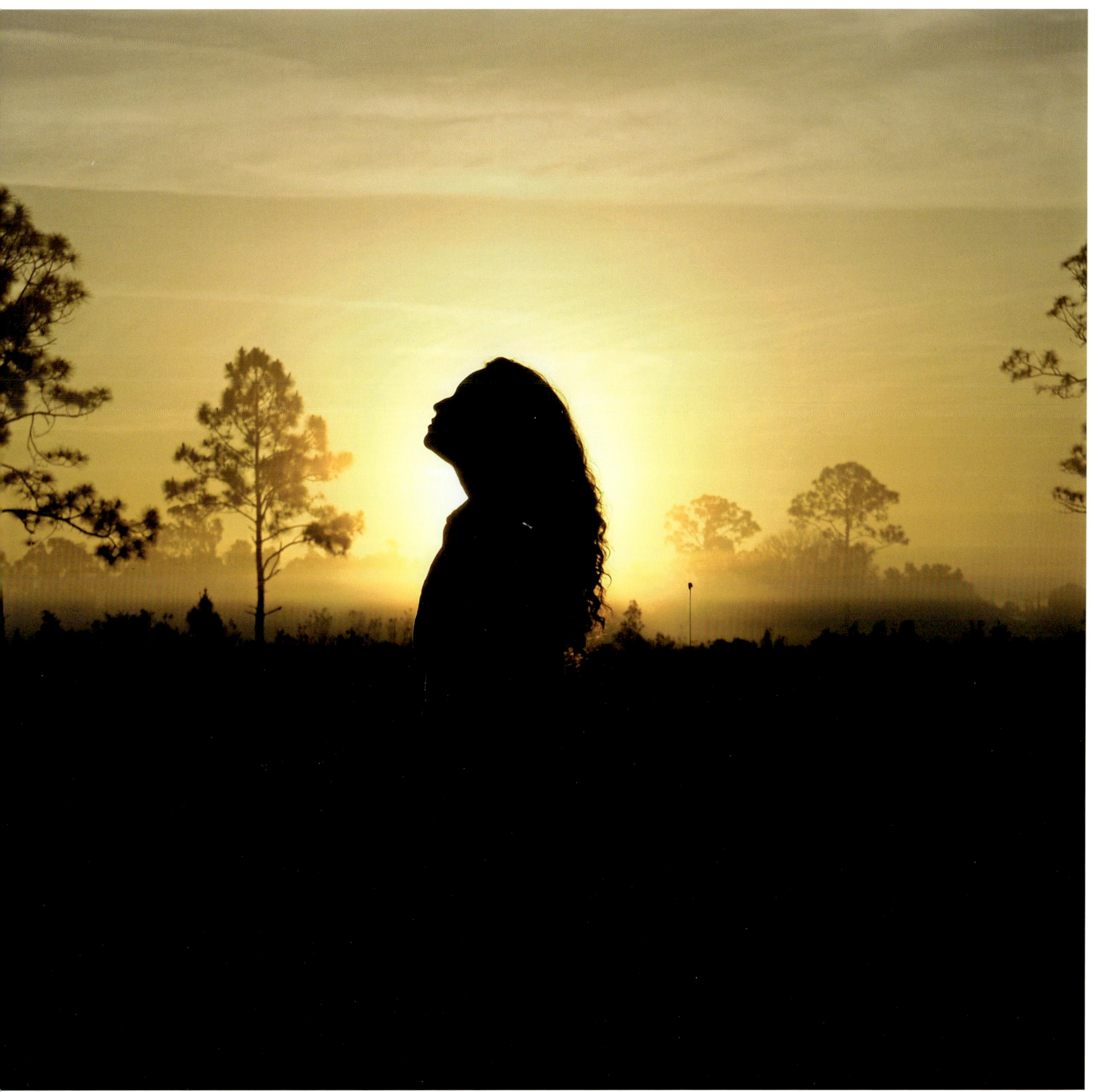

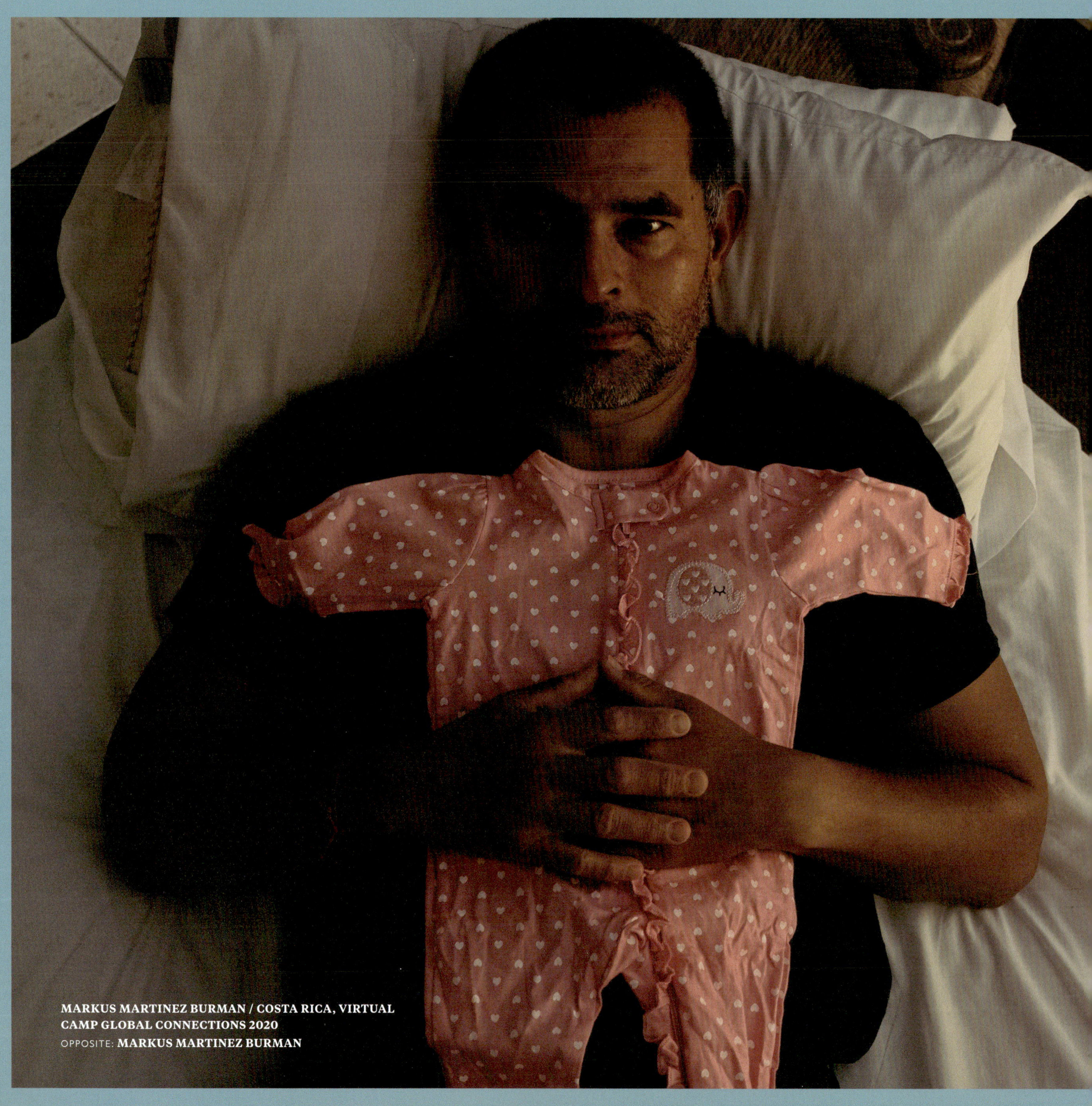

MARKUS MARTINEZ BURMAN / COSTA RICA, VIRTUAL CAMP GLOBAL CONNECTIONS 2020
OPPOSITE: MARKUS MARTINEZ BURMAN

Finding His Roots
Markus Martinez Burman

PHOTO CAMP WAS A TURNING POINT for Markus Martinez Burman. Midway through his university studies, doing fieldwork on Costa Rica's Osa Peninsula, he was tapped in 2020 to help run a Photo Camp planned nearby. "If the Photo Camp hadn't happened, I would have probably gone back to my university, gotten my master's in tropical ecology and conservation, and probably pursued work with bats because I love them," he said.

But the program's focus on storytelling through photography captured his imagination. The following year, he participated in a virtual Photo Camp during the COVID-19 pandemic. "Being able to focus on [my own] story was a relief," he says.

Markus had a "happy, comfortable" childhood in Mexico, where his father is from. But when he was 14, his parents divorced, and he moved with his Swedish mother to her homeland—a drastic change. The camera became his companion as he walked the streets of Stockholm alone.

Now, Markus has returned to research, but this time it's of a highly personal kind. He is delving into the life and times of his grandfather—a journalist from Juchitán, Mexico, who was driven from his region for promoting the Indigenous Zapotec language and culture—and learning to speak the Zapotec dialect. In 2022, driven to connect with other Indigenous cultures and using Photo Camp as a model, Markus created a program in the Bolivian lowlands to engage the youth of the Monkoxi Nation in storytelling and photography. For three months, he lived and worked in the region, creating, as he put it, "that personal and safe space for youth to tell their story." What's more, he observed, his kinship with the Monkoxi gave him a deeper appreciation for his own Indigenous identity.

■ Markus Martinez Burman is an environmental scientist, educator, and documentary photographer. He was born and raised in Mexico and is of Indigenous Oaxacan and Swedish descent.

At left is a portrait Markus made of his father, whose wife was expecting a child at the time, during Virtual Photo Camp Global Connections in 2020.

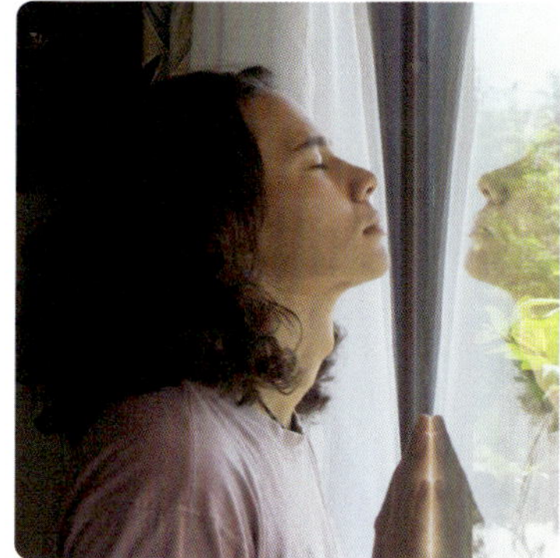

CHAPTER 5

Hope

"The strangest thing is that it is exactly during this excruciating and helpless time of 'displacement' that you feel tremendous power rising in you like never before."

—ANTON ALEKSAKHA, UKRAINE 2015

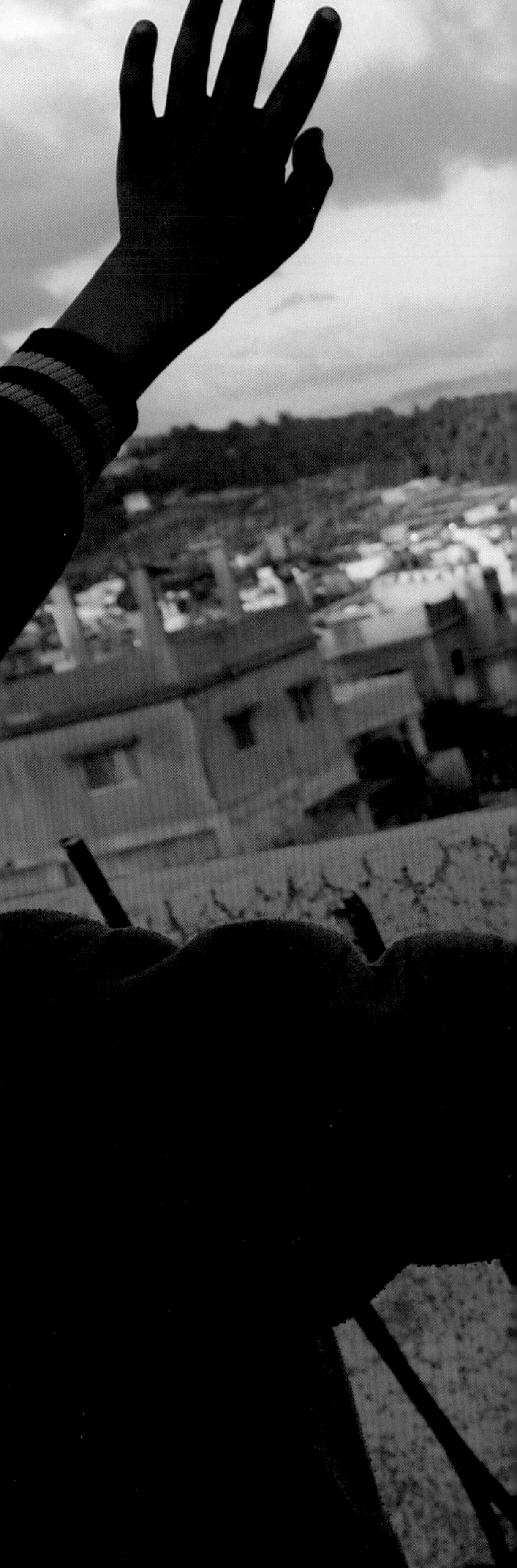

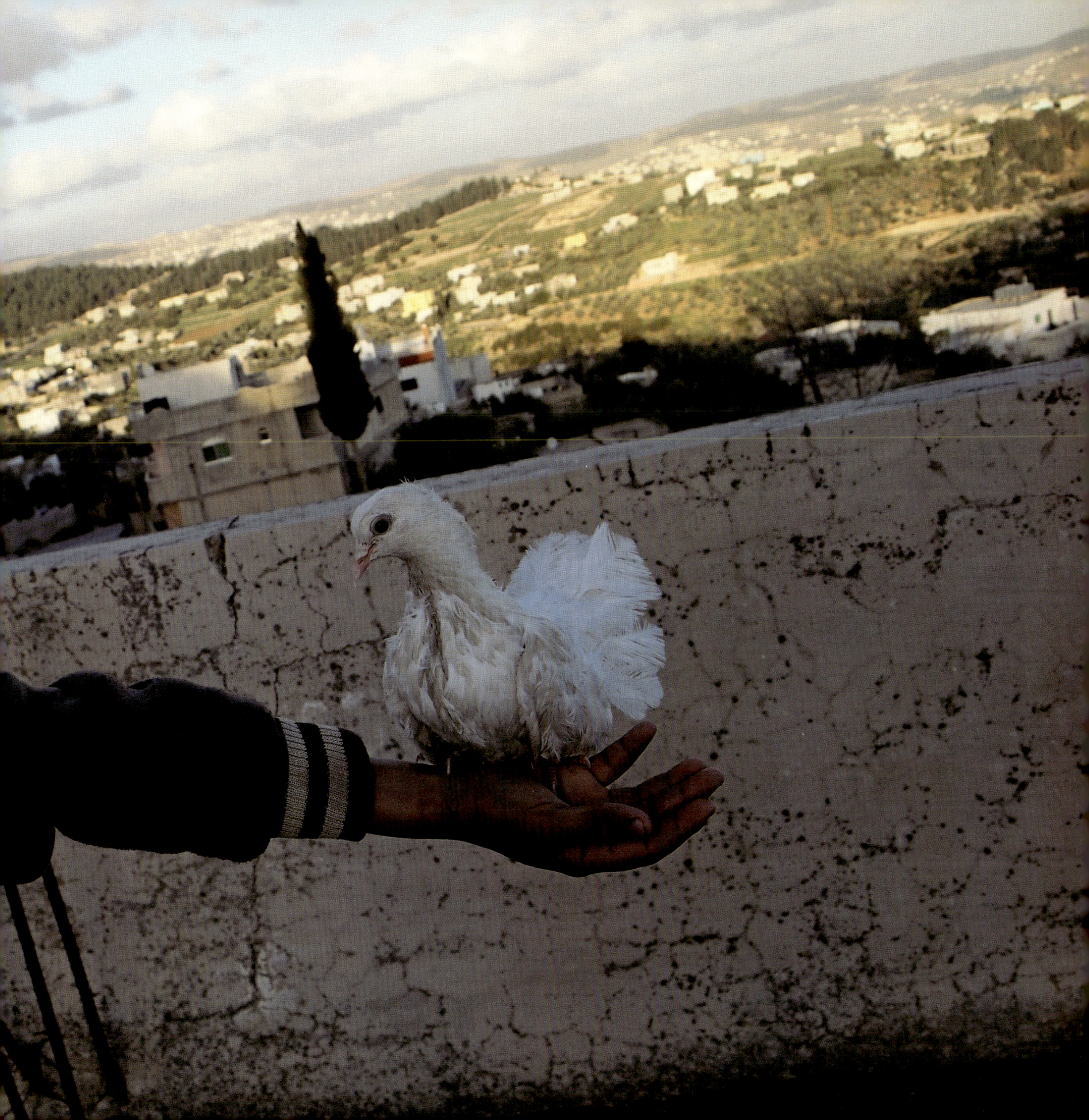

Power Rising

I REMEMBER THE NOISE OF KATRINA—the singing of the wind made you stay awake to listen to her.

The next day, people were walking through water with anything and everything they could carry. No one knew what to believe. When we looked outside, a lot of people had taken mattresses and placed the kids on them and let the taller ones hang on the edges and guide the mattresses through the water ... I was one of the walkers. The water reached my chin.

I remember the hours when walking through five feet of water was better than twelve. Walking to nowhere through nothing that made any sense ... but it was survival.

As we walked, someone on the outside would see strangers acting in unity. We were all walking to the same place: Interstate 10. Thousands of people were already there.

JANNAE ASHLEY PACK DESCRIBED THIS SCENE for a 2006 Photo Camp writing assignment. The workshop took place just a year after Hurricane Katrina, which ravaged her hometown of New Orleans, Louisiana. But despite the trauma, Jannae and her fellow students refused to wallow. "We are this city's future, and we have to believe in it and bring it back to life," her classmate Bayley Crow observed at the time. "There's no point in giving up when we can make a difference and make it better for ourselves."

Many Photo Camp mentors note that sentiments like these are often expressed at workshops around the world. The students' optimism, they say, is contagious and dispels cynicism—fitting, since many students feel they have a message to impart.

And those messages are profound. Students from Ukraine and Syria try to imagine peace in their homelands and what they will do to rebuild them. Anton Aleksakha spoke with pain and strength about leaving his home in Crimea. "The strangest thing is that it is exactly during this excruciating and helpless time of 'displacement' that you feel tremendous power rising in you like never before," he said. Young people from Syria hold out hope that they can return. At a 2015 Photo Camp in Jordan, Waleed Ashreef spelled out his dream: for Syria to be "a peaceful country, and that ... we will go back and free its land and rebuild it. We want to ... reconstruct our future."

The Photo Camp program has worked extensively with Indigenous youth, including the Maya in Mexico's Yucatán and the Oglala Lakota in Pine Ridge, South Dakota. These students use their time together as a forum to express pride and consider ways they can strengthen their tribes. "Our community is like a treasure," said Māori student Aliah Semmens, who attended a Photo Camp in Murupara,

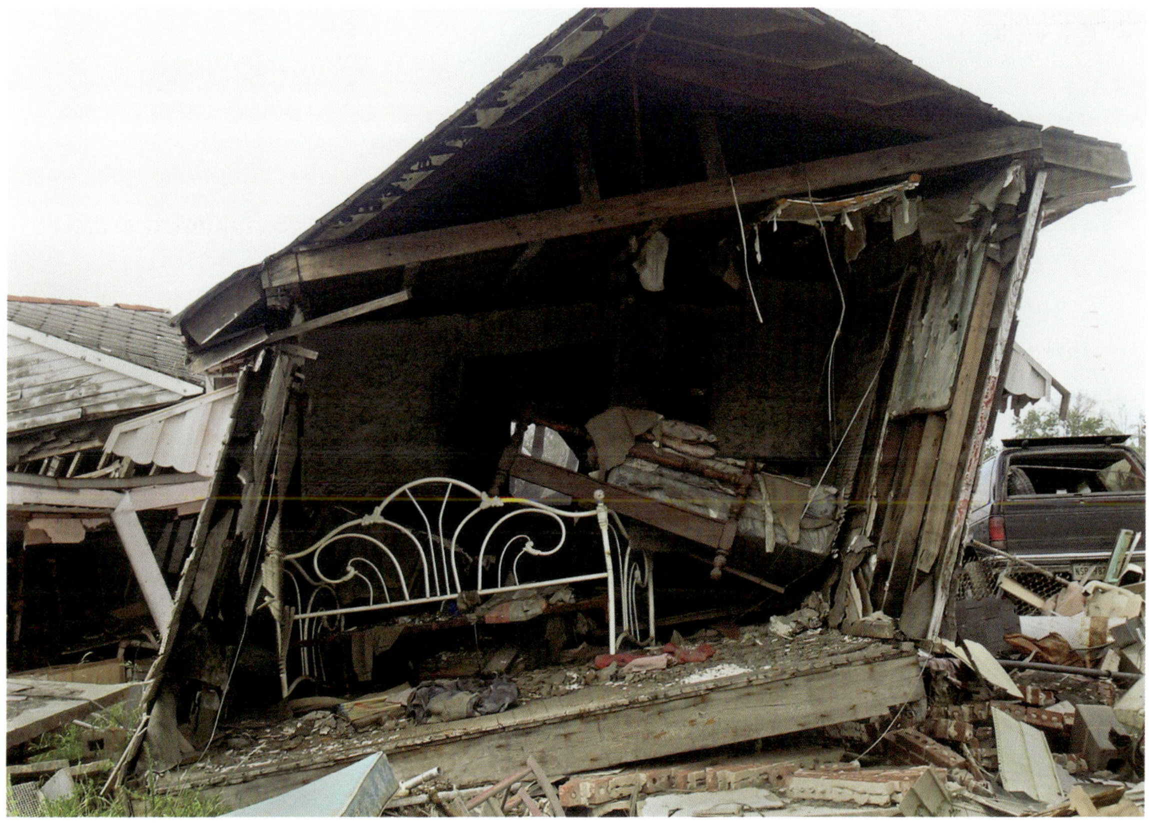

ABOVE: **HANNAH DEFELICE / LOUISIANA, U.S.A. 2006** PREVIOUS PAGES: **MOHAMMED MAHMOUD / JORDAN 2015**

New Zealand, in 2019. "We all treat each other like family, and we take care of each other. Every individual has their story to tell, their own *tikanga* [tradition]. But together, we all share the same love and compassion."

Nevertheless, some Photo Camp participants emphasize their efforts to keep their traditional ways and avoid being swallowed whole by mainstream culture. "With fierce love and immense joy, we have lived for time immemorial on the land," said Jordynn Paz, a member of the Apsáalooke Tribe at the Crow Reservation in Montana. Tehatsistahawi Kennedy, an Anishnaabe, Onyota'aka man who participated in a virtual Photo Camp in 2020, uses a series of photographs to portray his personal growth and hopes for self-realization. "I can't say I fully know myself anymore," he wrote. "Now is a time to rebuild, heal, and carry myself in the direction I wish to grow in the future."

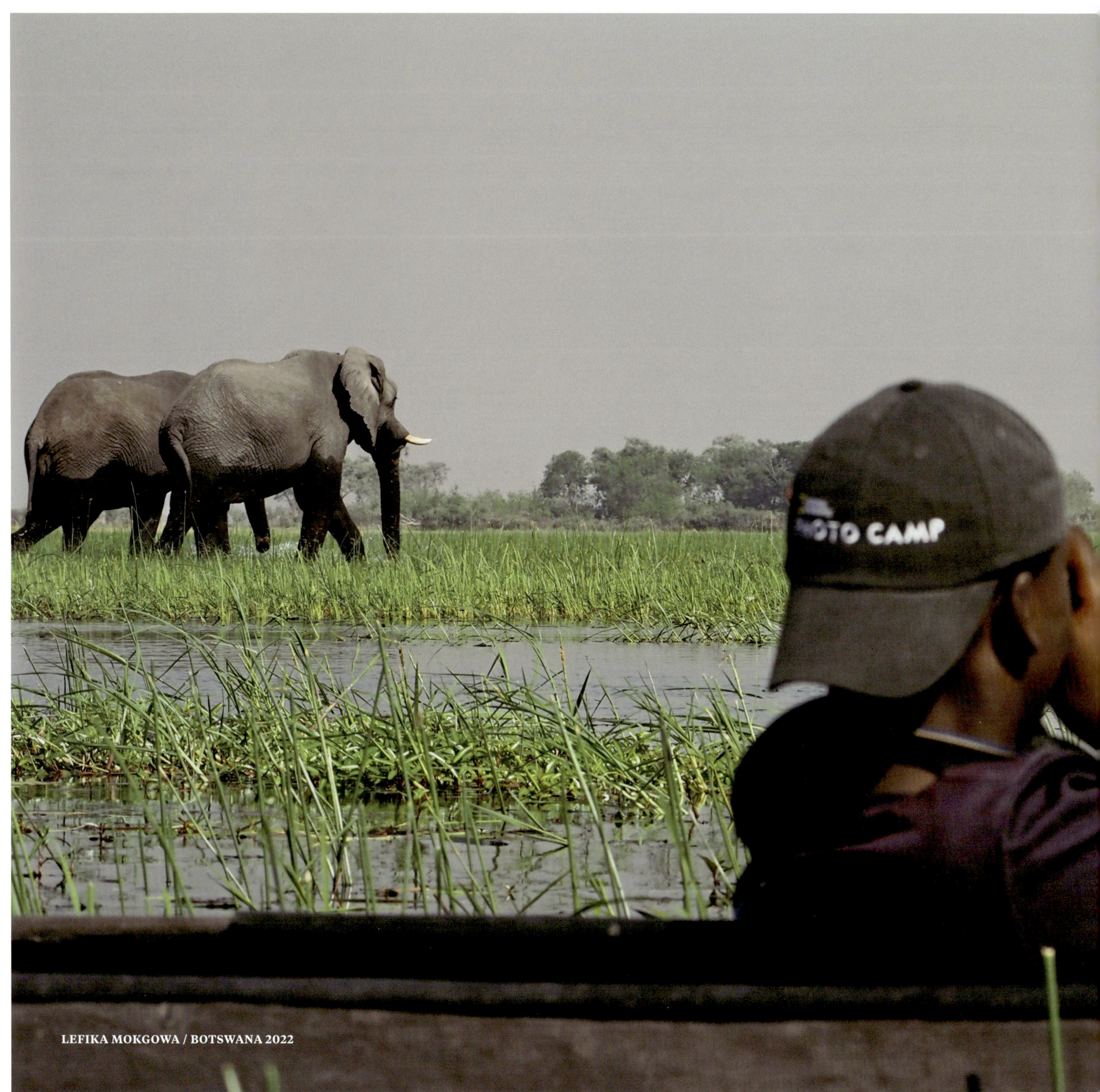

LEFIKA MOKGOWA / BOTSWANA 2022

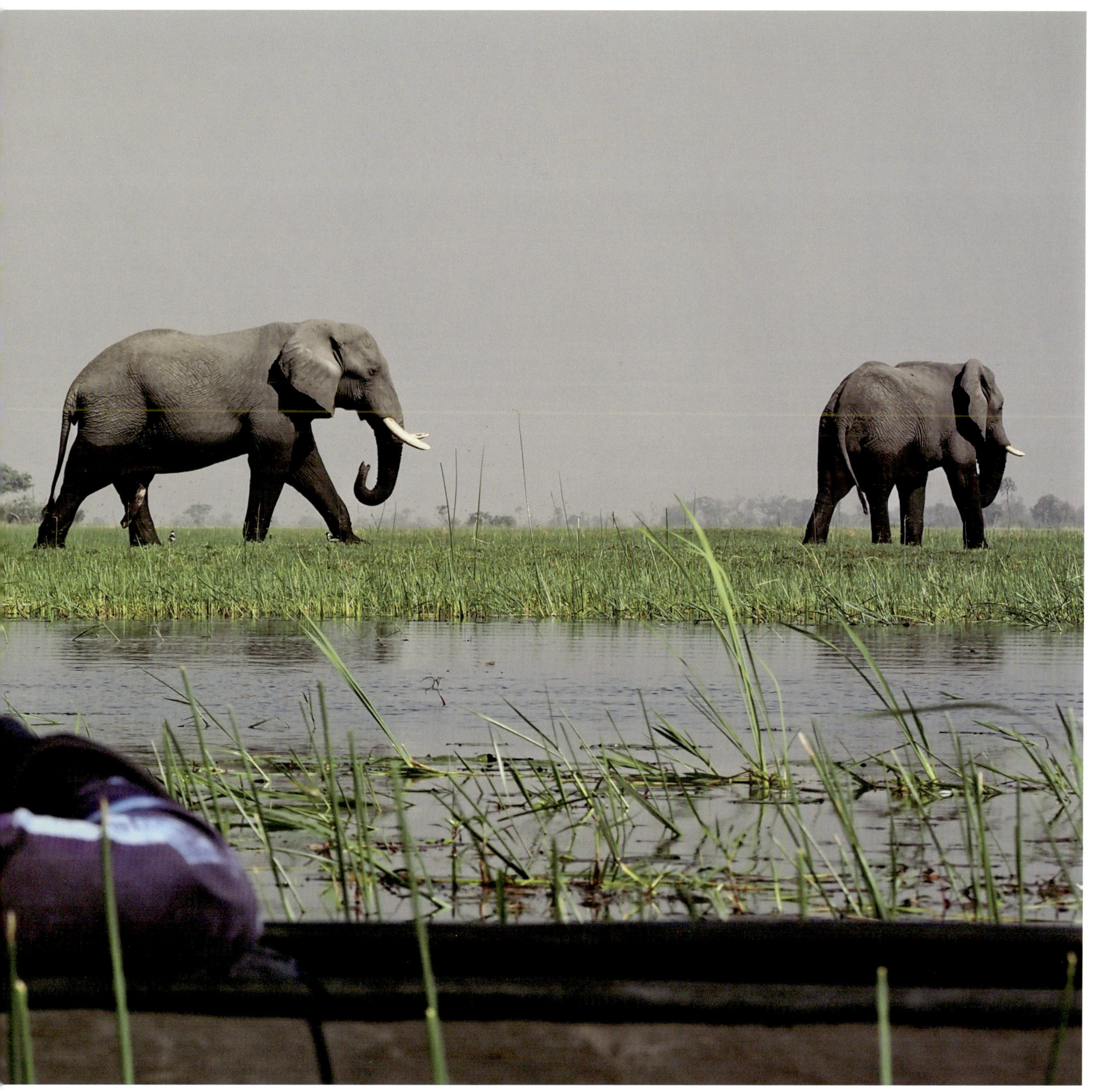

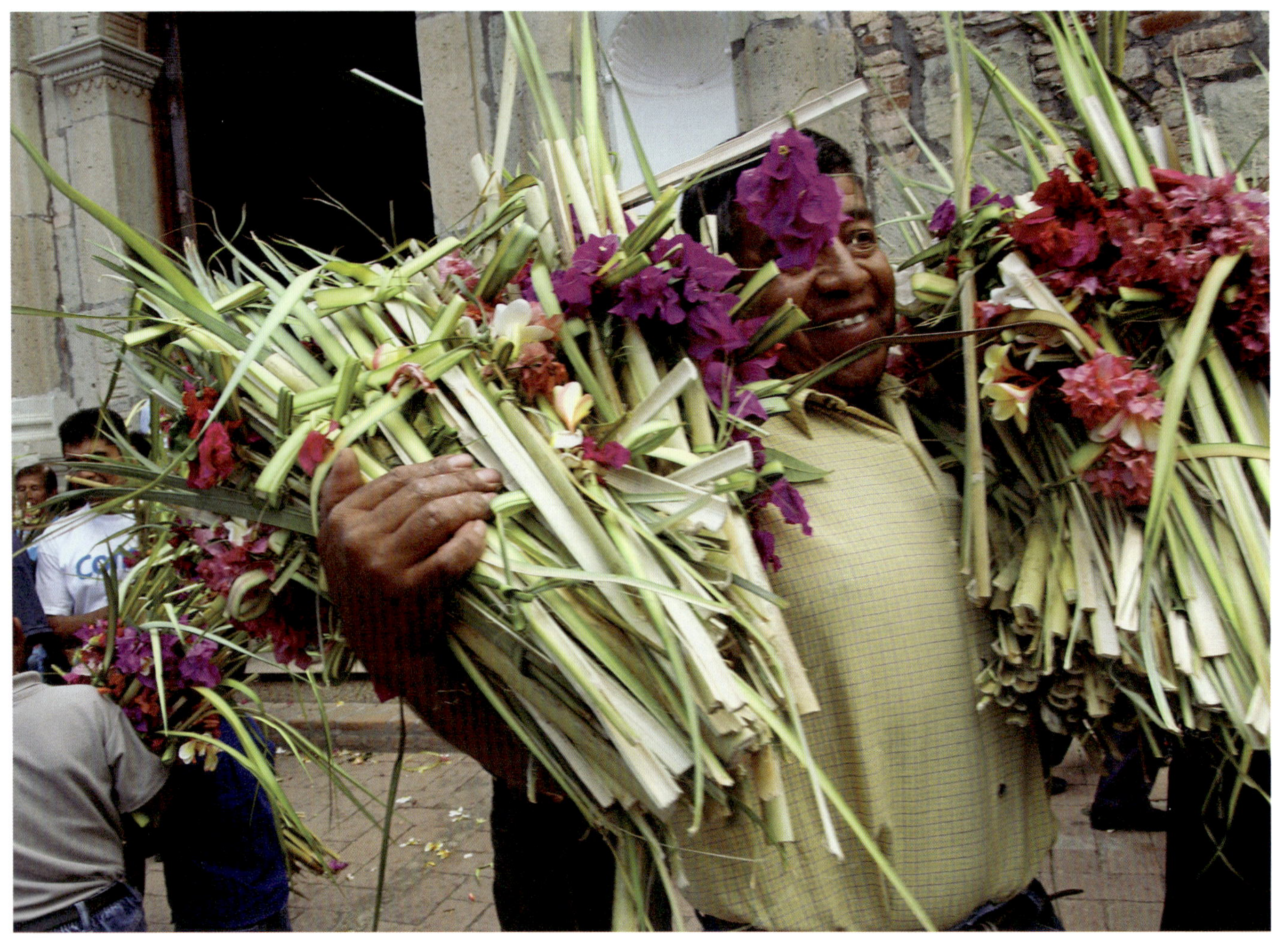

ABOVE: **ANA DIAZ CISNEROS / MEXICO 2007** OPPOSITE: **DIANA LESCAS LUNA / MEXICO 2007**

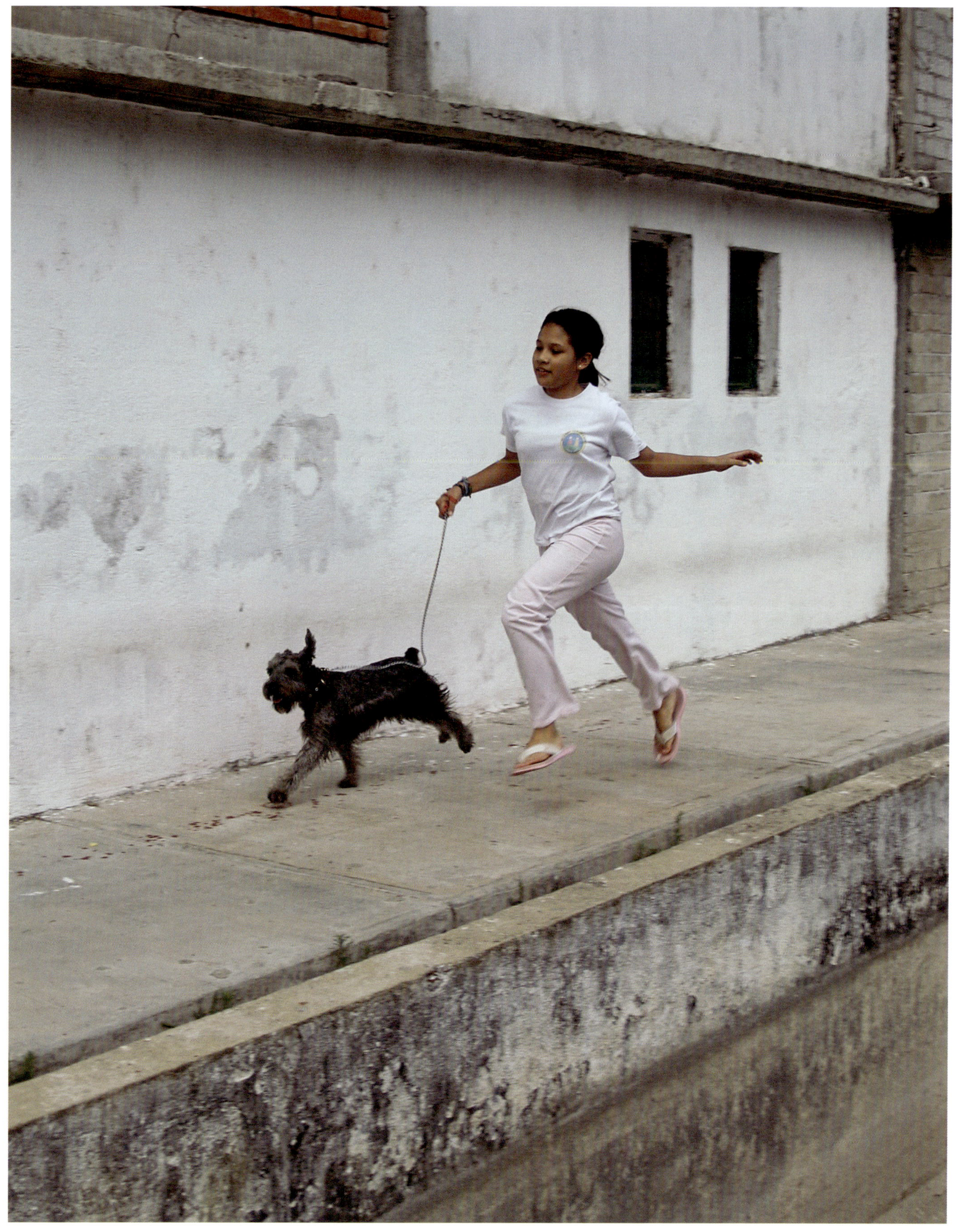

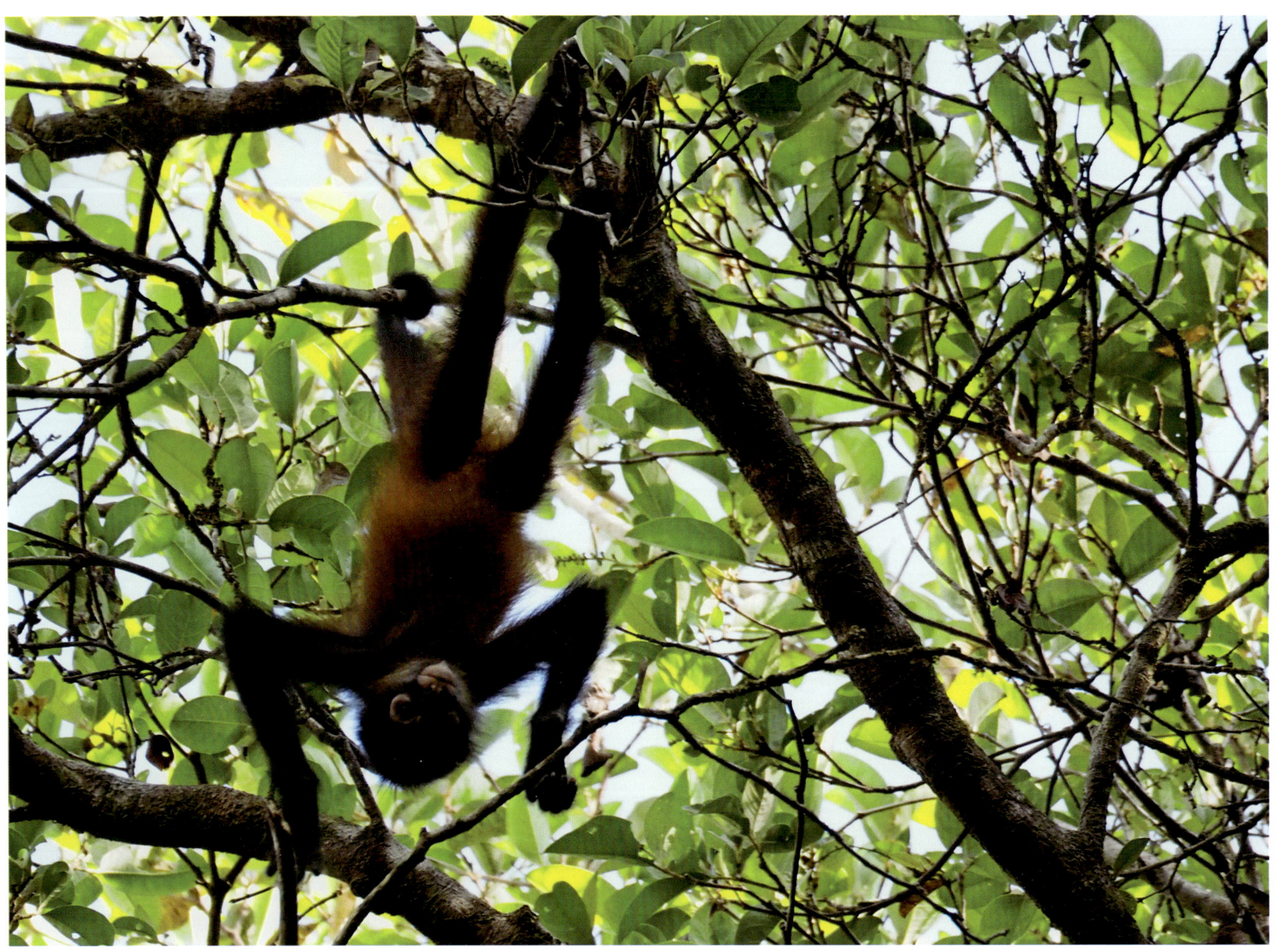

BRAYAN CASTRO GRANADOS / COSTA RICA 2020

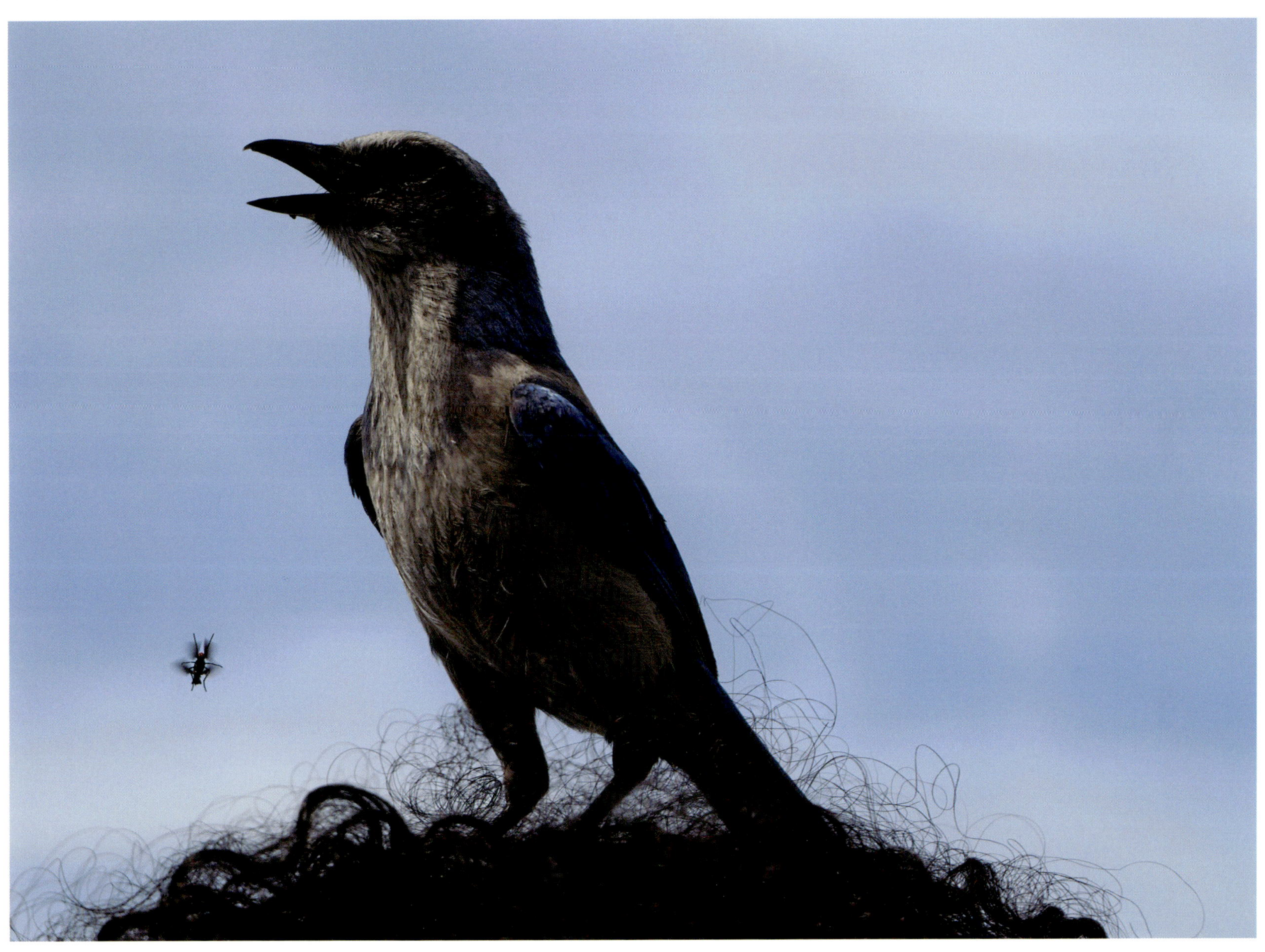

ISABEL GUERRA / FLORIDA, U.S.A. 2022

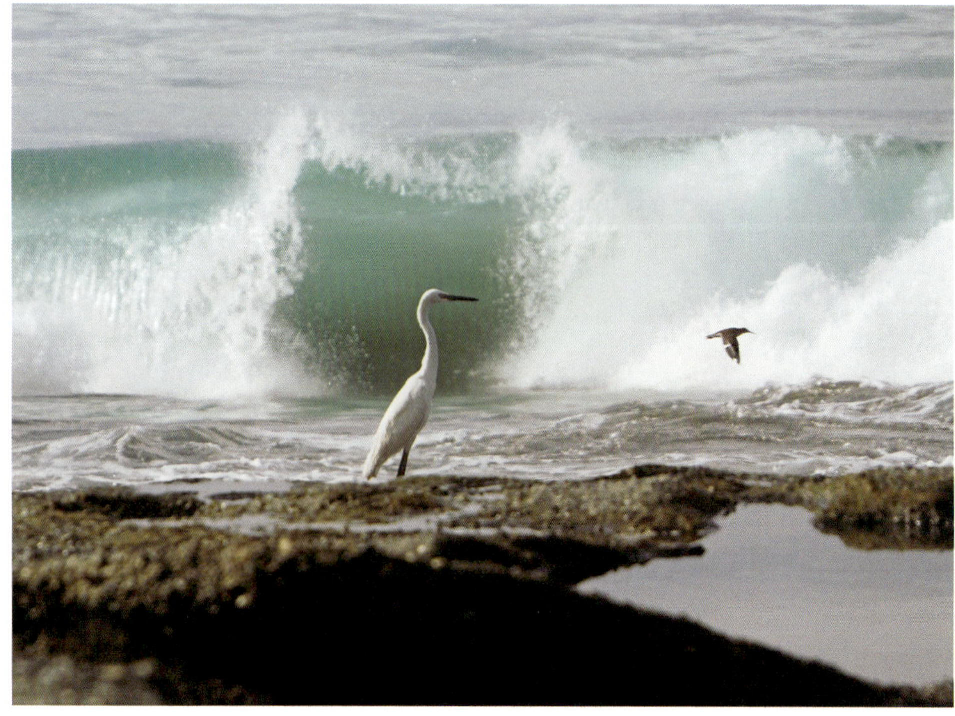

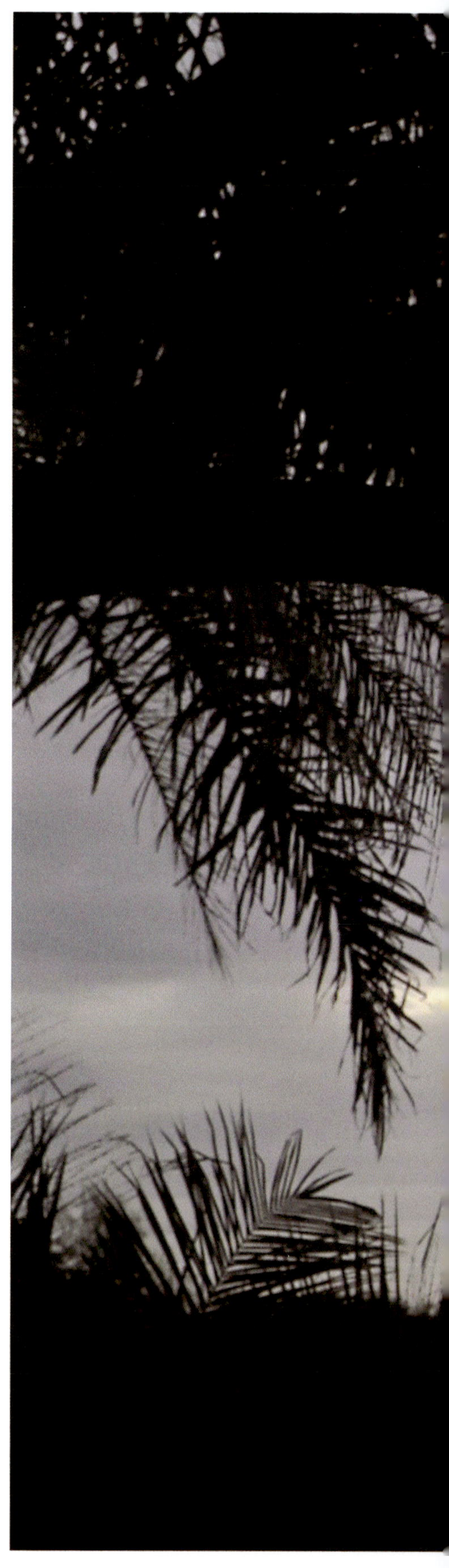

ABOVE: **ALISSON CARRILLO CHAVARRIA / COSTA RICA 2020**
RIGHT: **MARIA JOSE ARBUROLA / COSTA RICA 2020**

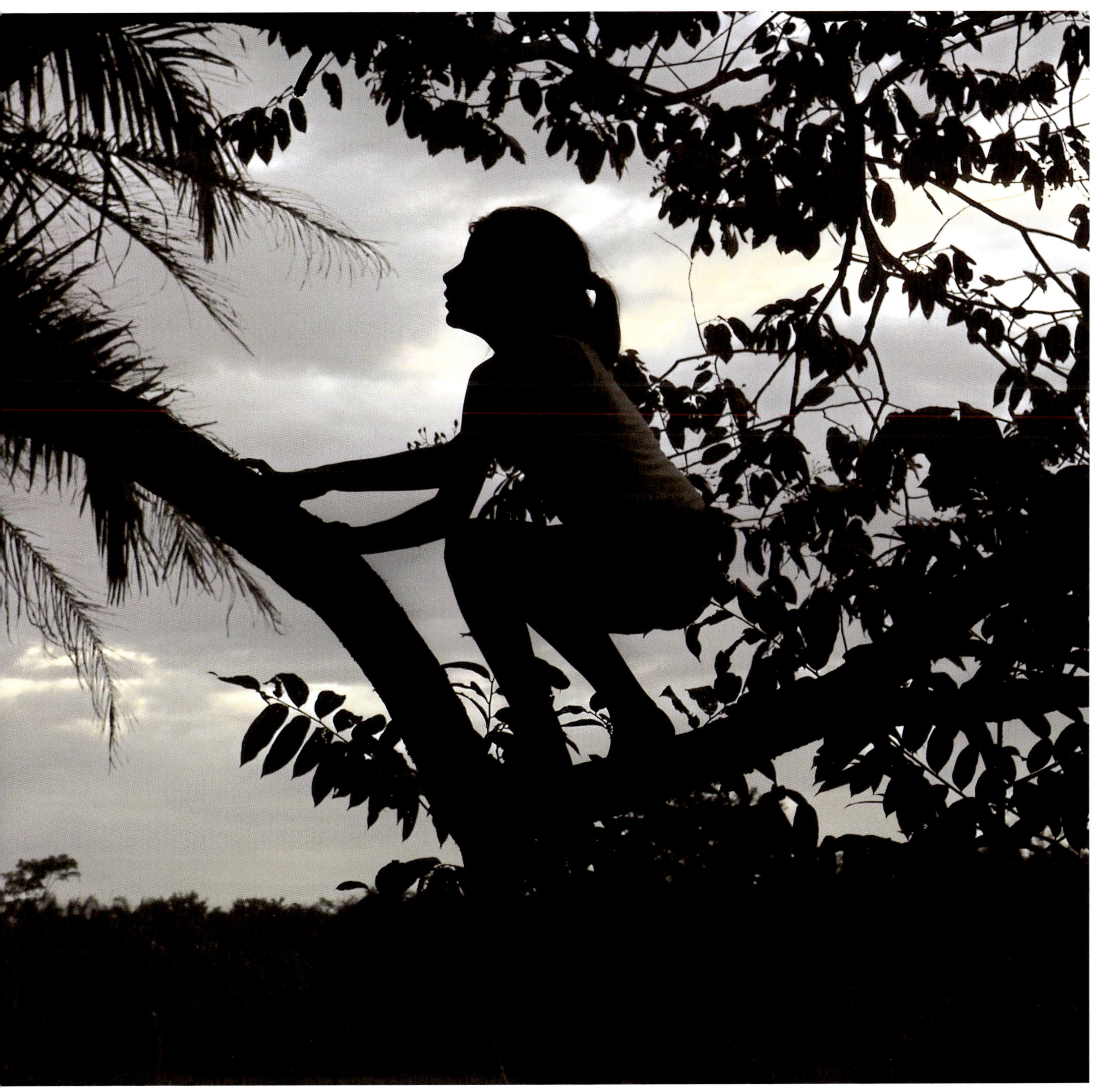

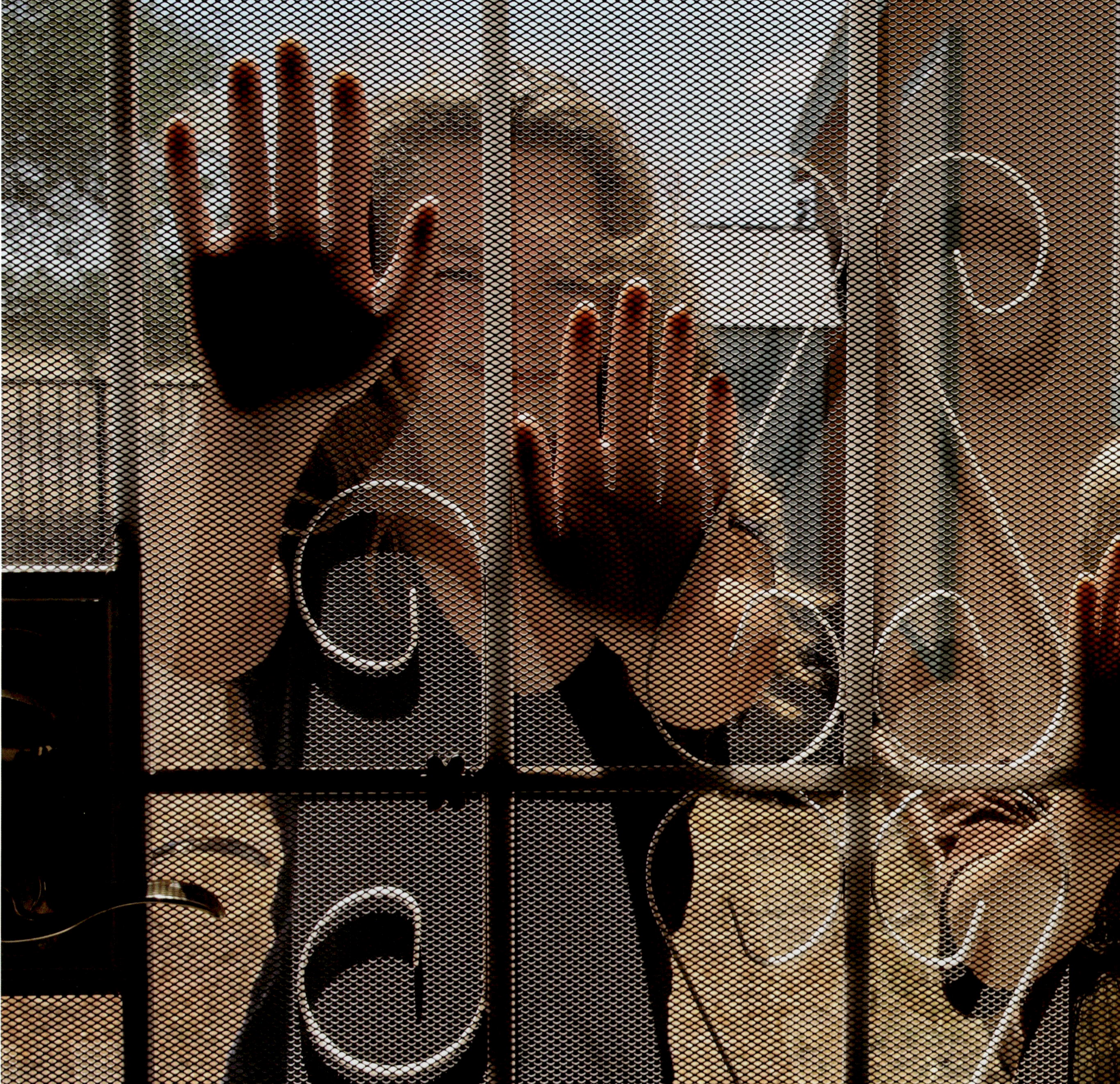

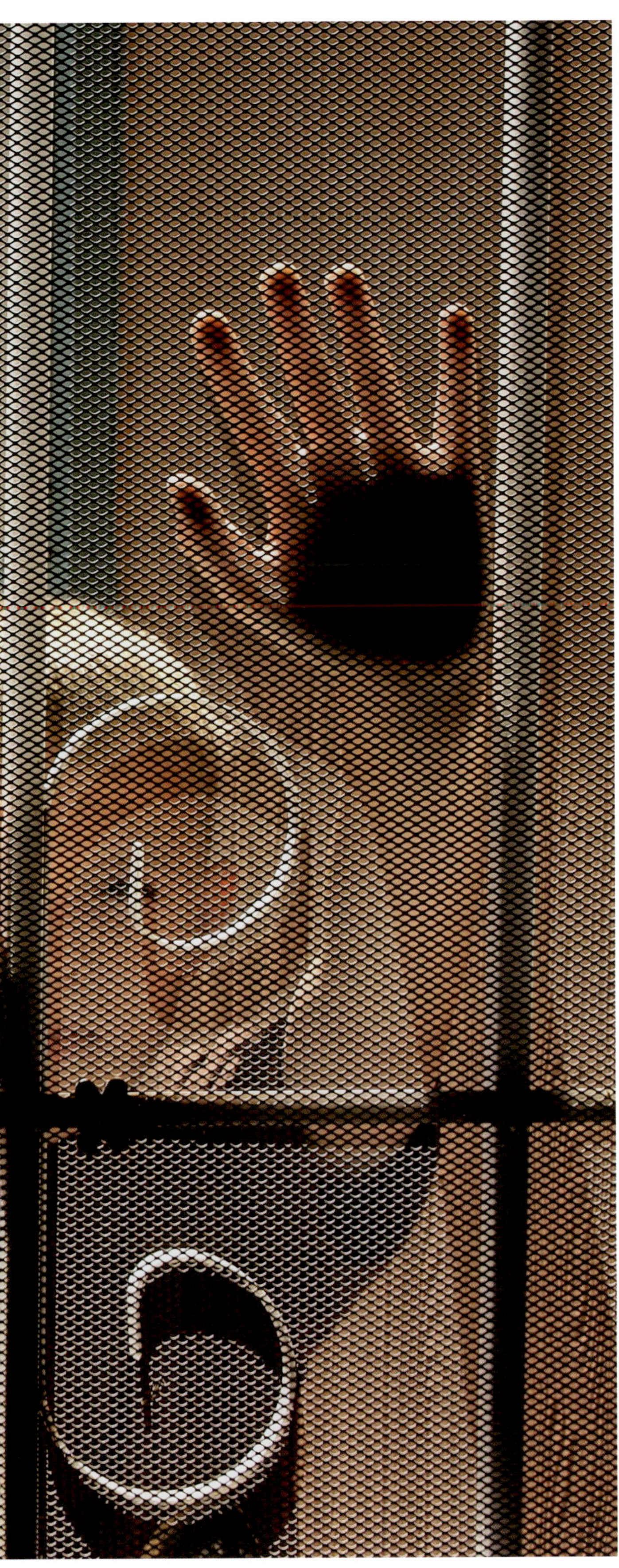

> ***"People don't do well [behind] closed walls ... The body and heart need to be free in order to achieve happiness. And isn't happiness everyone's main goal?"***
>
> —ALEXANDRA PANAGIOTOU, GREECE 2017

LANEY JUAN / ARIZONA, U.S.A. 2014

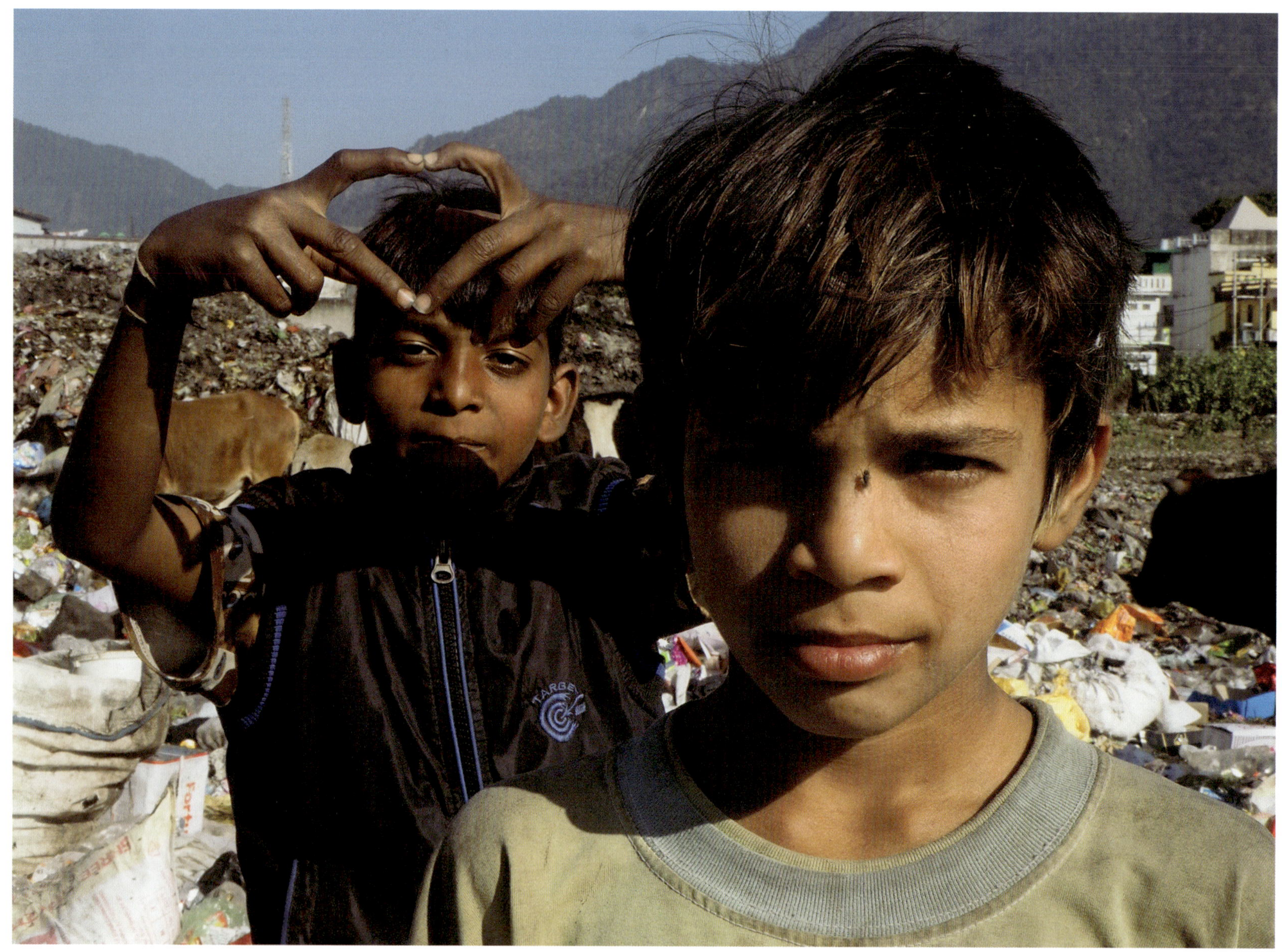

GAGAN SINGH / INDIA 2019

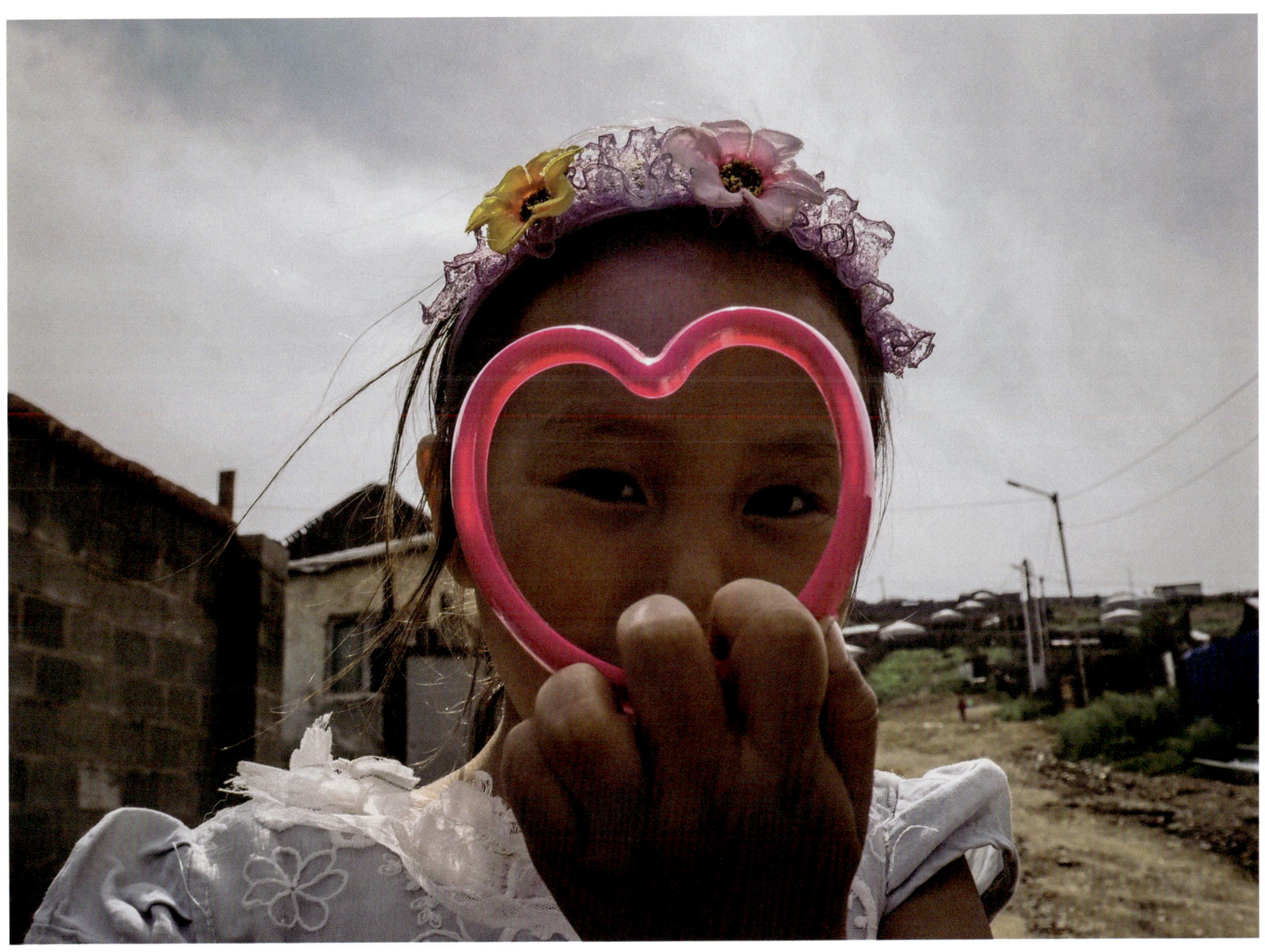

L. MISHEEL / MONGOLIA 2019

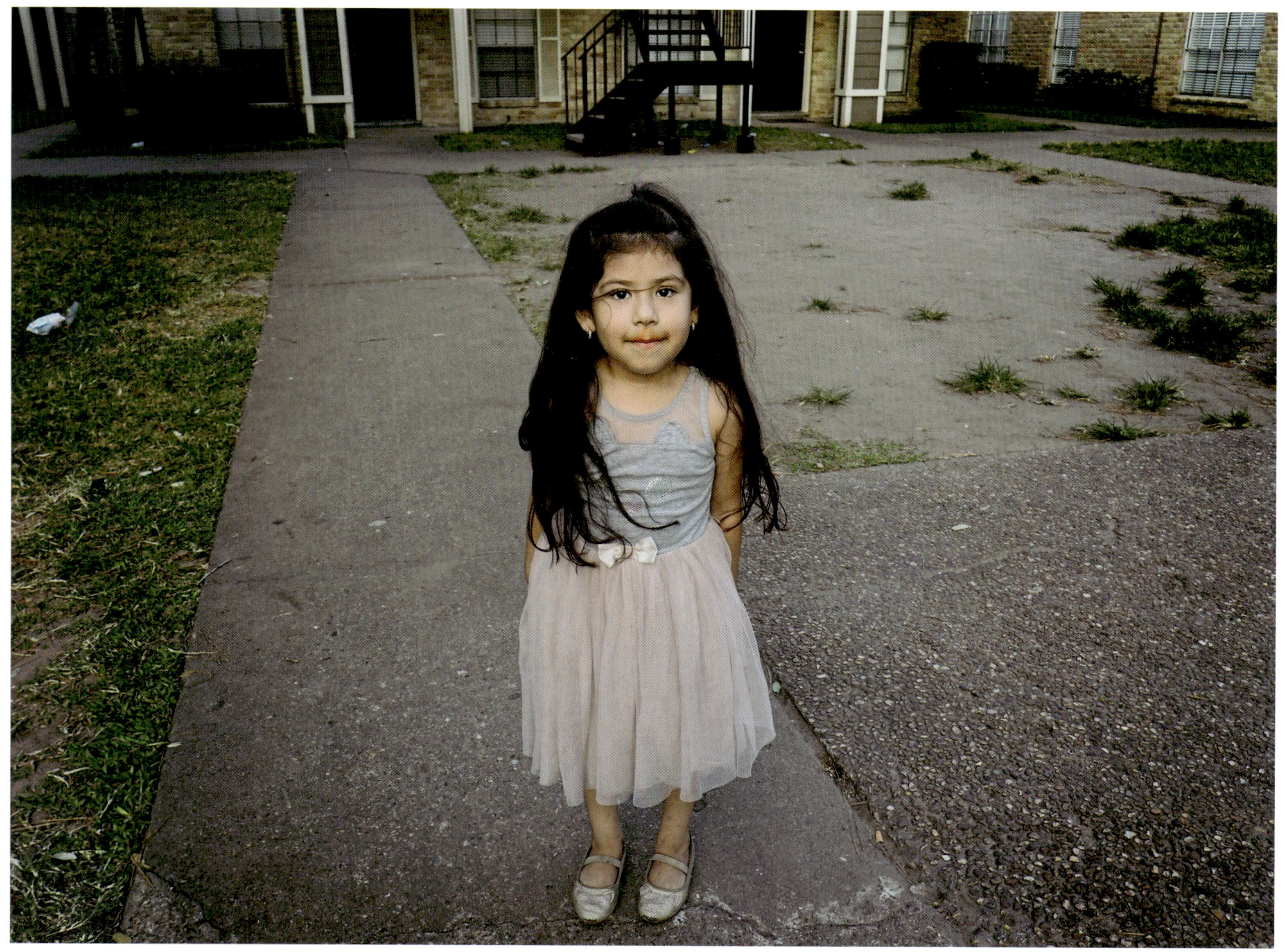

VIVIANA MEDINA / TEXAS, U.S.A. 2018

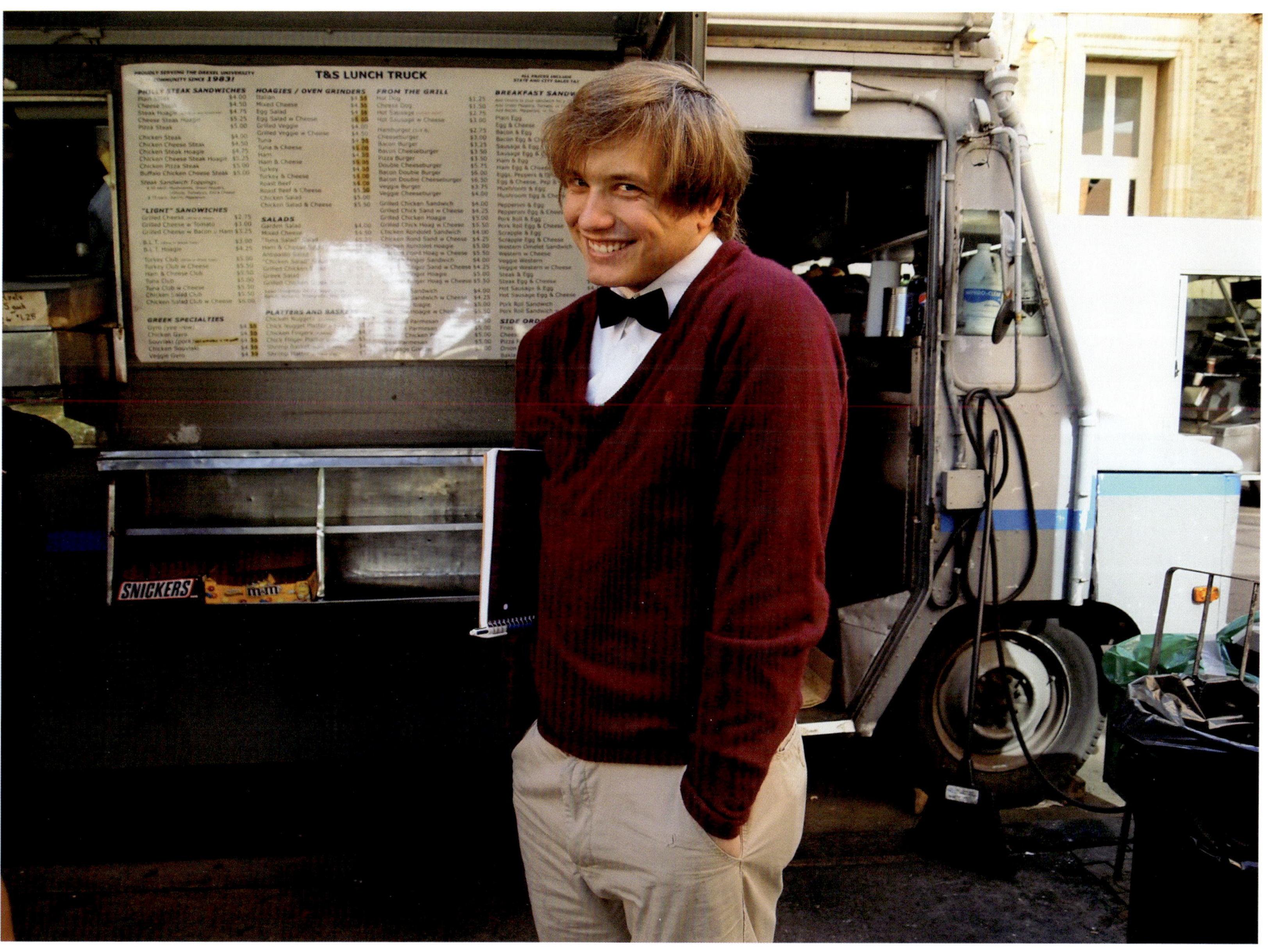

MALEIKA OGILVIE / PENNSYLVANIA, U.S.A. 2011

Camp Profile
Ukraine 2015

TWENTY STUDENTS CAME TOGETHER in Kharkiv, Ukraine, to attend a Photo Camp in September 2015. All were forced from their homes in Crimea, Donetsk, and other parts of eastern Ukraine by the threat of invasion. They became wanderers in their own land. "It's the moment jet fighters start flying over your head and the streets are suddenly full of armed people dressed in camouflage when this world stops making any sense to you," wrote Yelena Pemyakova during the week-long camp.

The work of the Photo Camp attendees poignantly captures the plight of the refugee families living in their midst—especially those of young children. Their essays and images reflect worlds turned upside down: empty playgrounds, abandoned homes.

Just before she arrived at camp, student Olena Bilous had quit her job as a purchasing manager to pursue photography. The atmosphere, she recalled, was so charged with emotion that she rarely slept. Photo Camp became her springboard to full-time work as a visual chronicler of wartime. Her most recent project, titled "The Inseparables," follows families waiting for their loved ones to return from the front lines. "I want to create memories for future generations," she said. "I want my creativity to help draw people's attention to what they don't want to see."

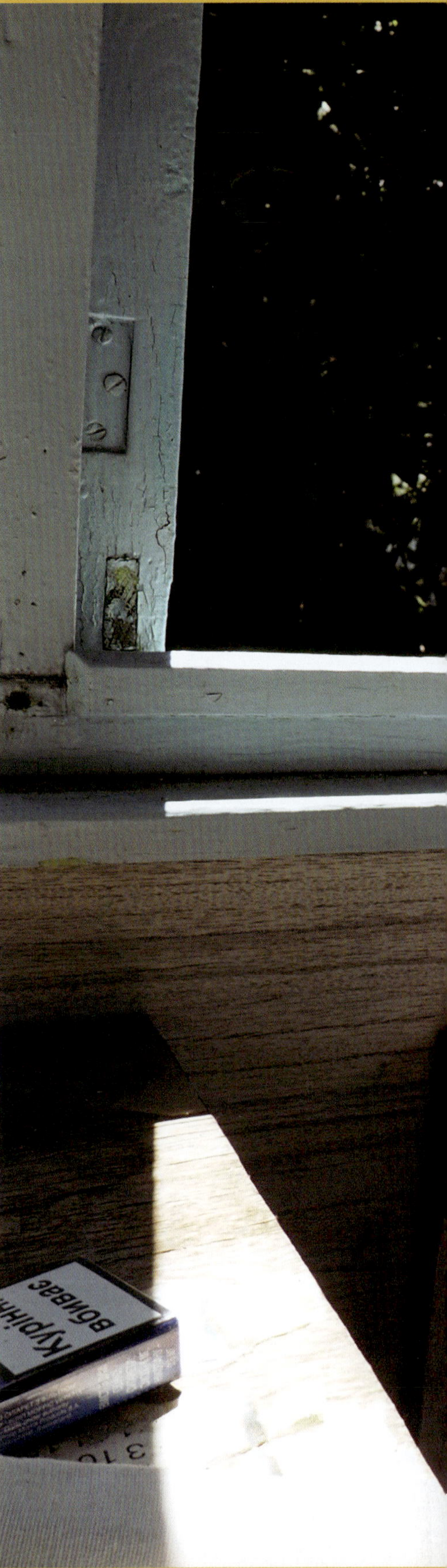

RODION UZBEK / UKRAINE 2015

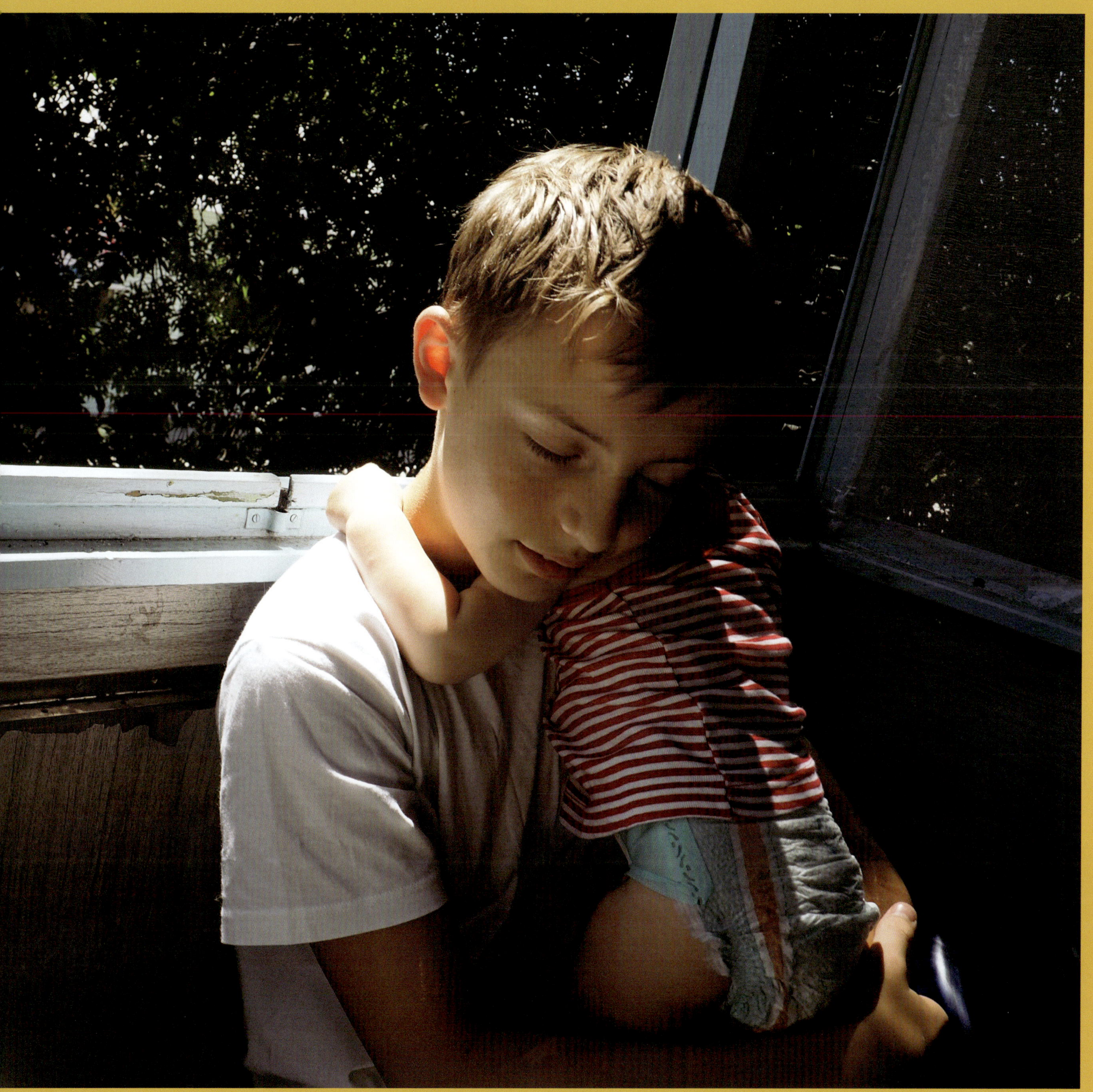

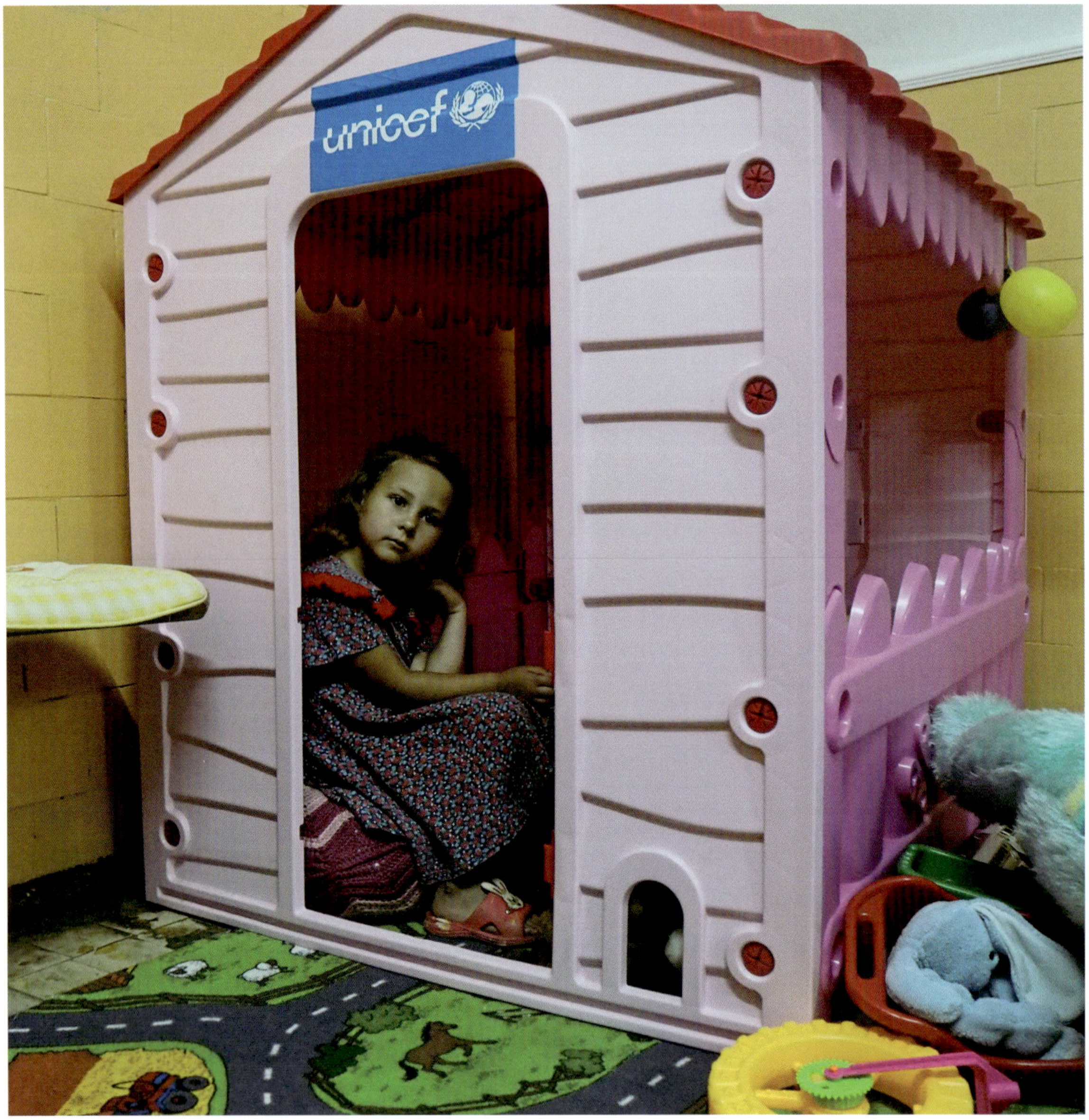

YELENA PERMYAKOVA / UKRAINE 2015

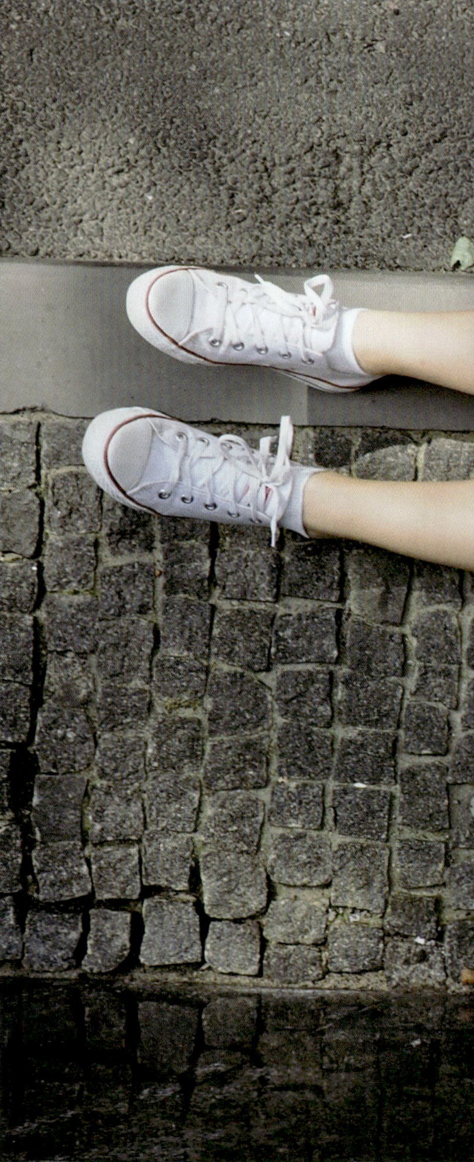

ANTON ALEKSACHA / UKRAINE 2015

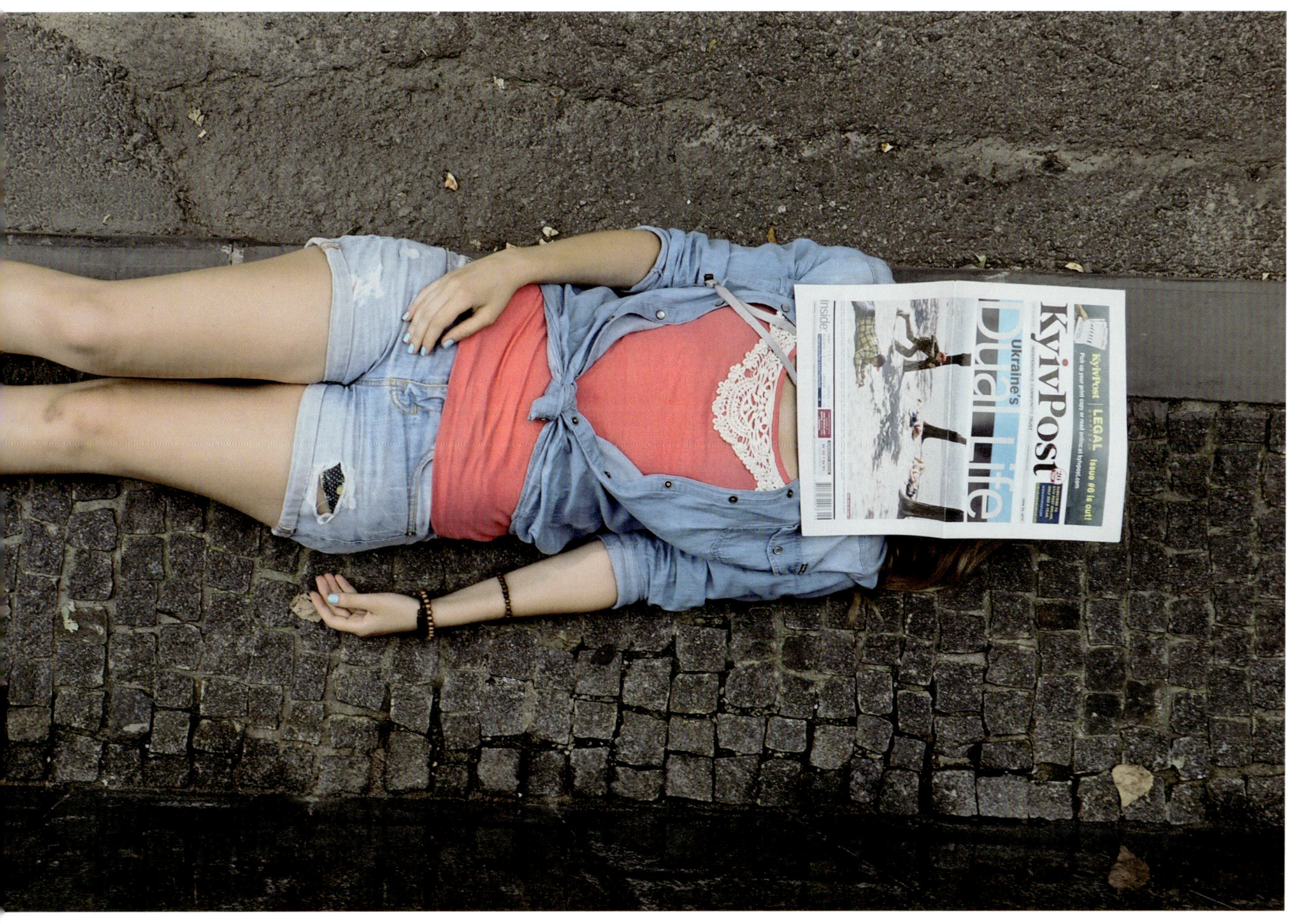

"To Ukraine and the whole globe I wish peace. I wish us open minds and open souls. To know that humans are not enemies of each other."

—MYKYTA NEKH, UKRAINE 2015

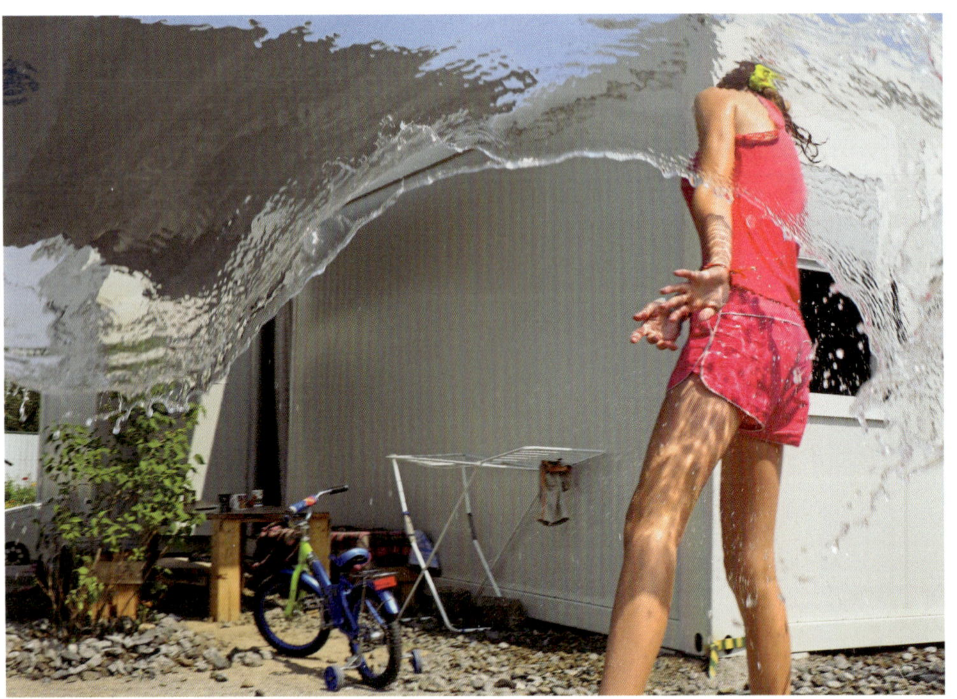

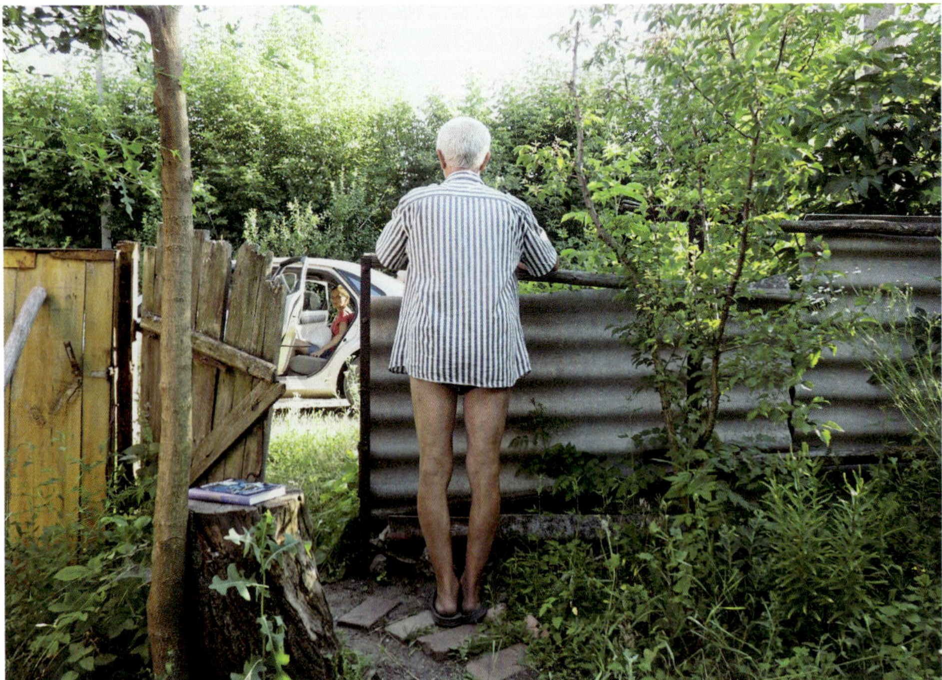

TOP: **MARIYA ZMYSLA / UKRAINE 2015** ABOVE: **ANTON ALEKSACHA / UKRAINE 2015**
RIGHT: **OLENA BILOUS / UKRAINE 2015**

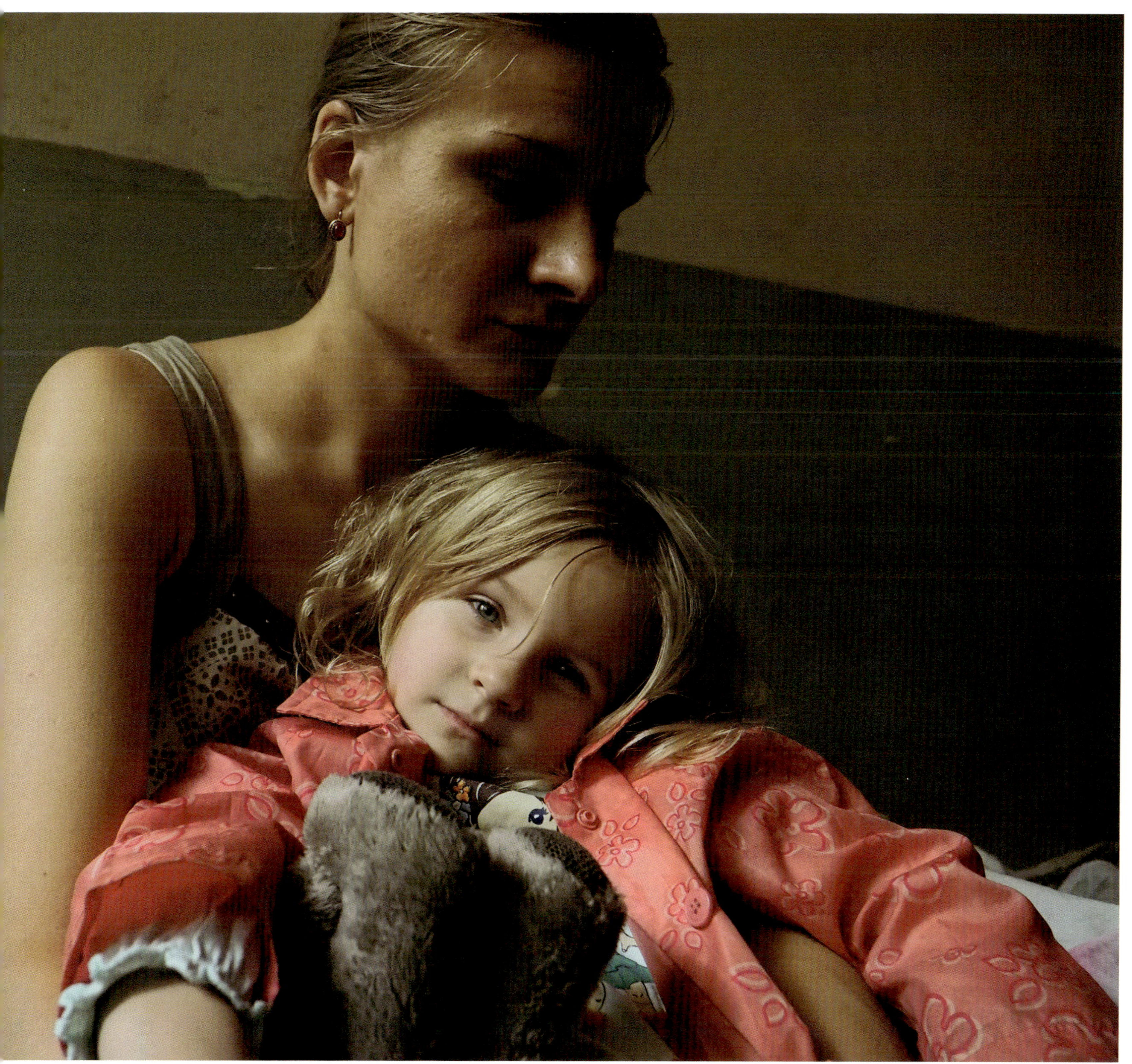

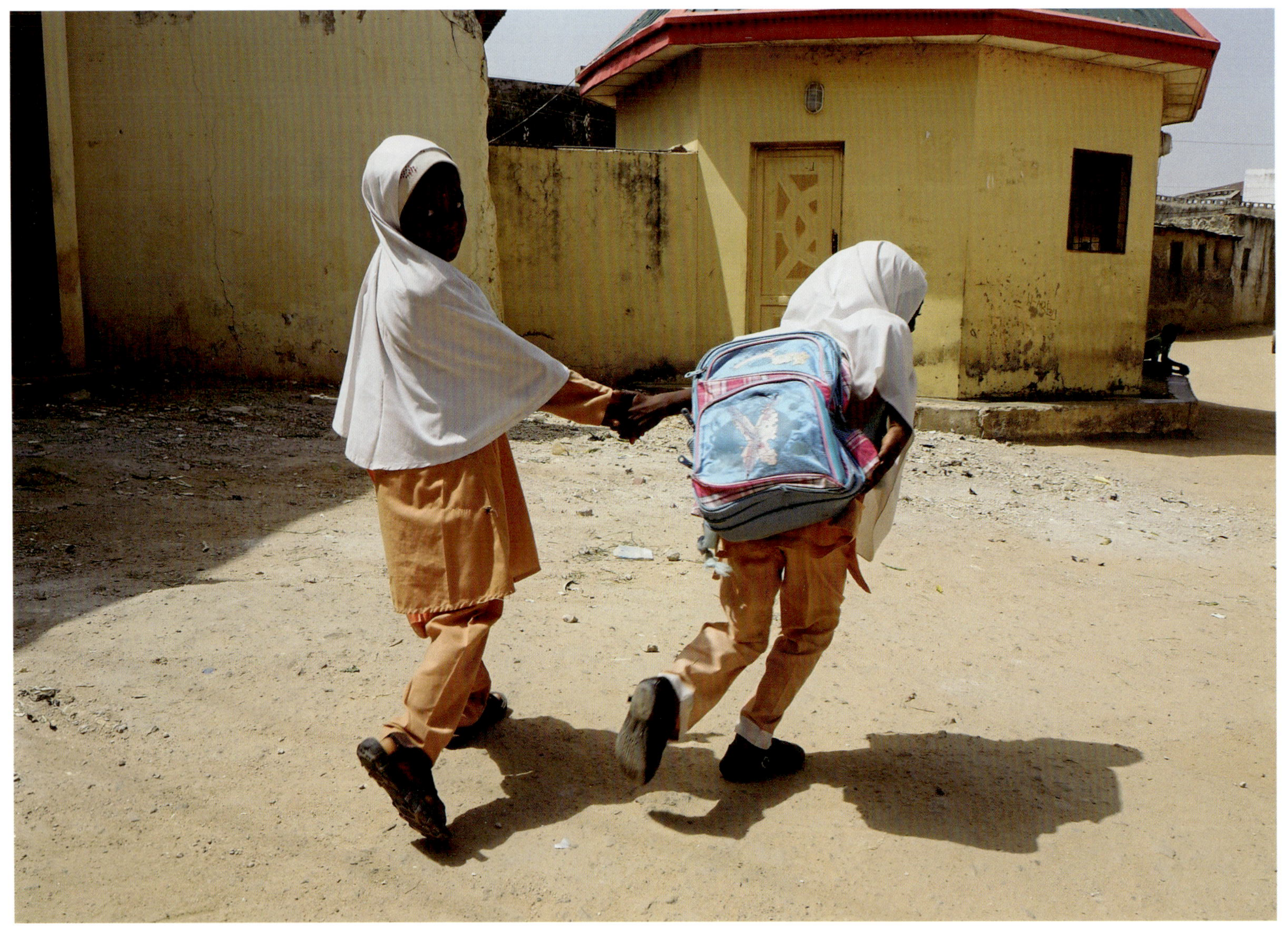

ABOVE: **SIMON PETER / NIGERIA 2019** OPPOSITE: **MANISH GURUNG / INDIA 2019**

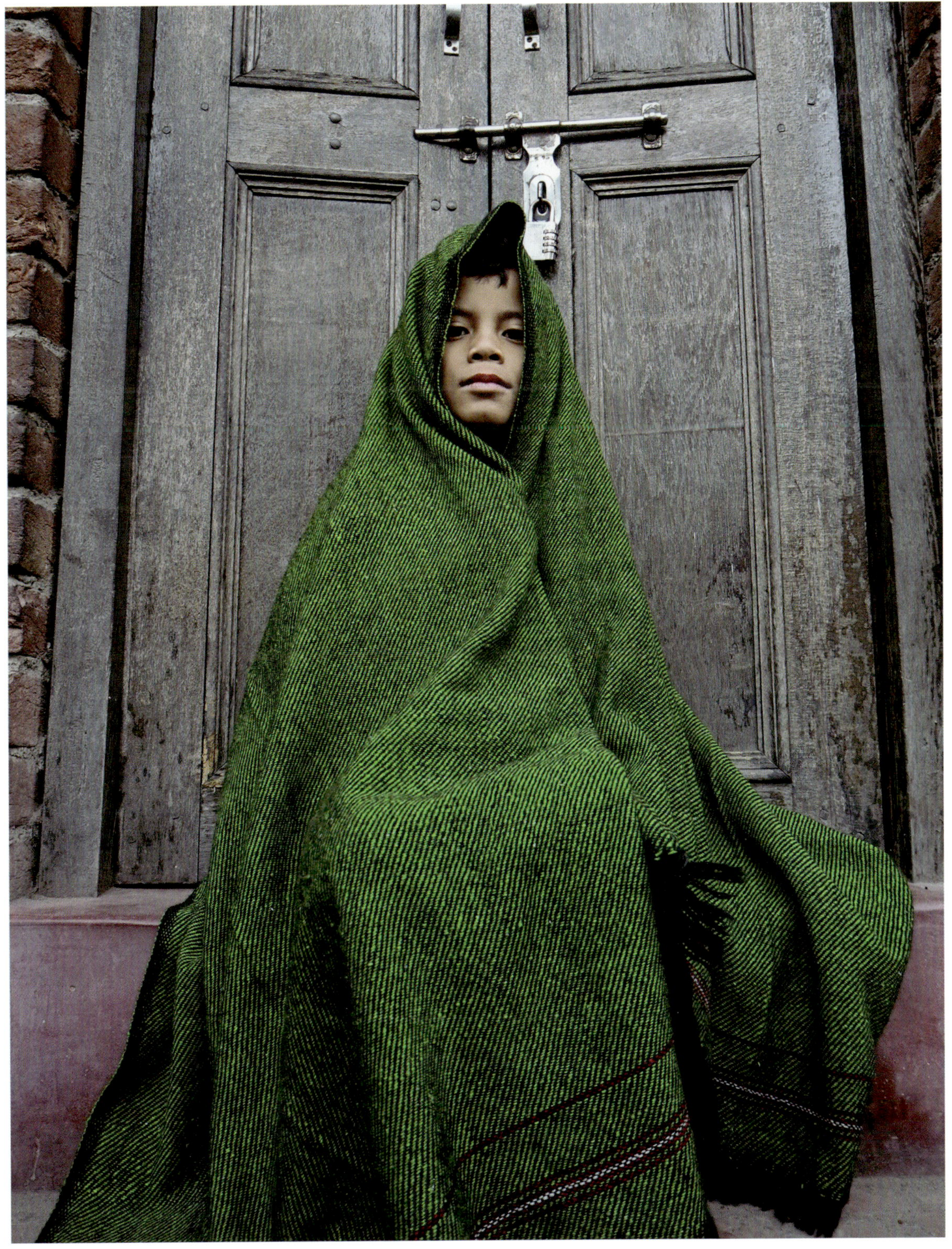

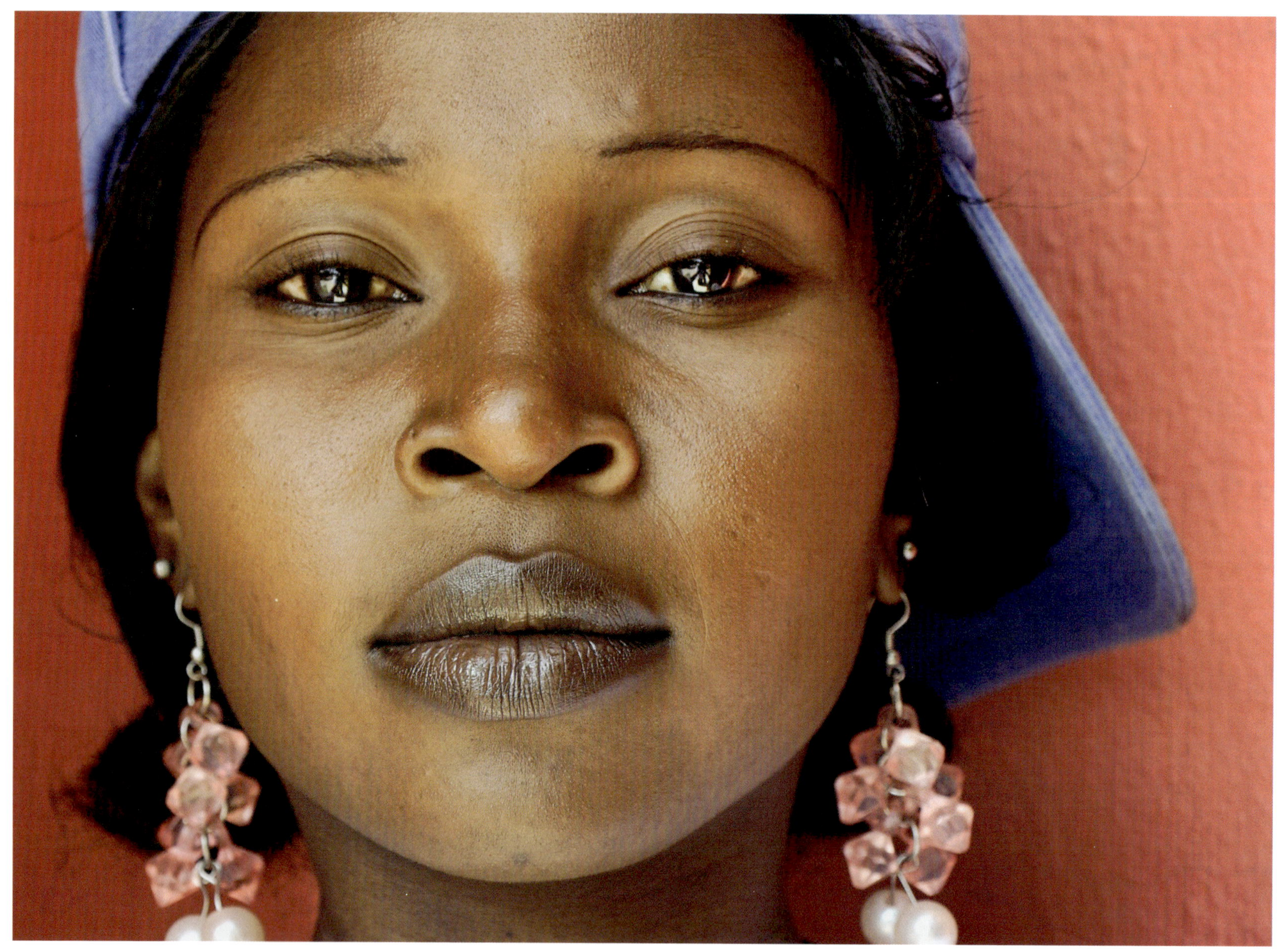

MAINBE DJENONSSEM GISLAINE / CHAD 2010

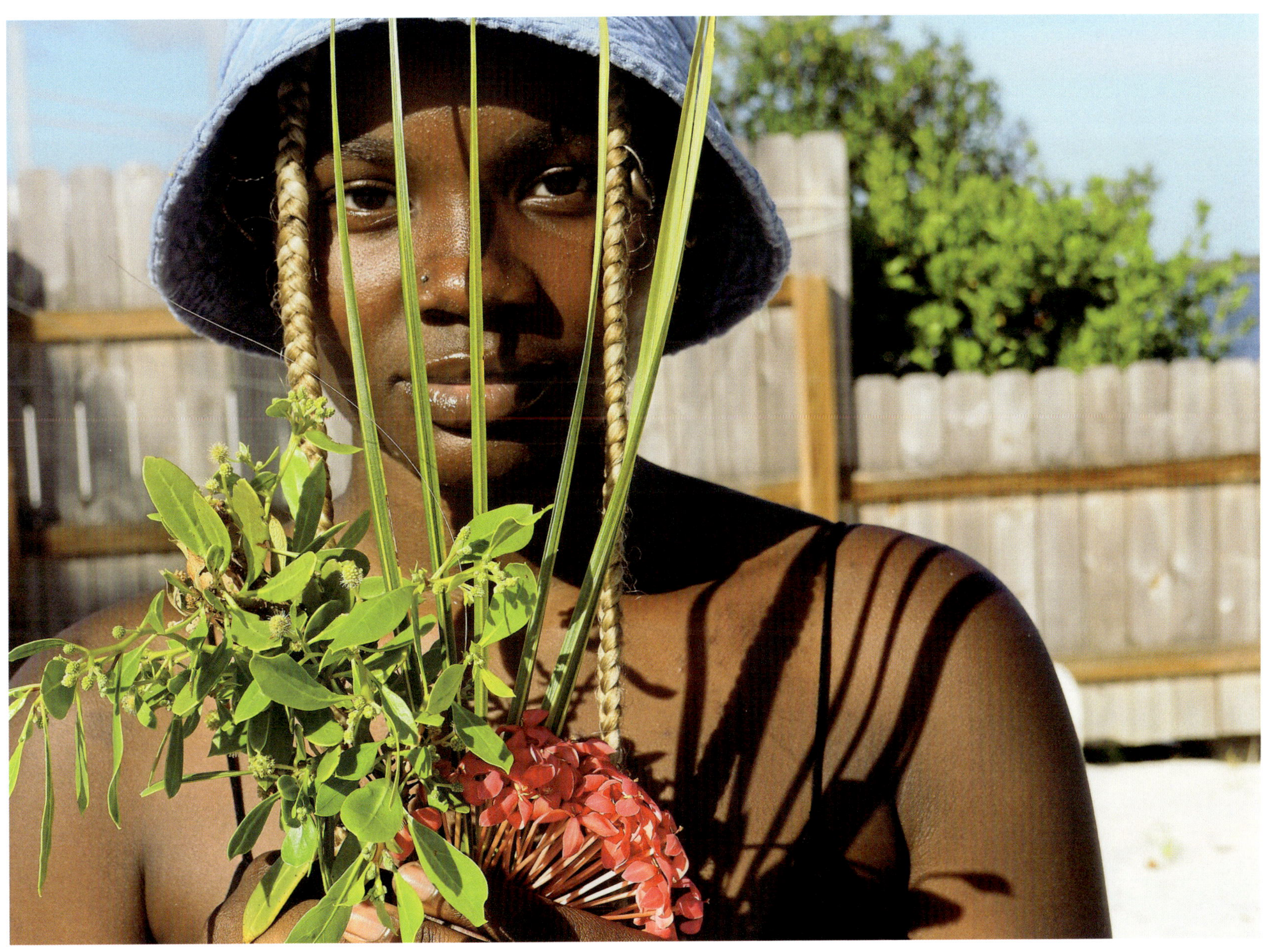

CHRISTEN MURPHY / FLORIDA, U.S.A. 2022

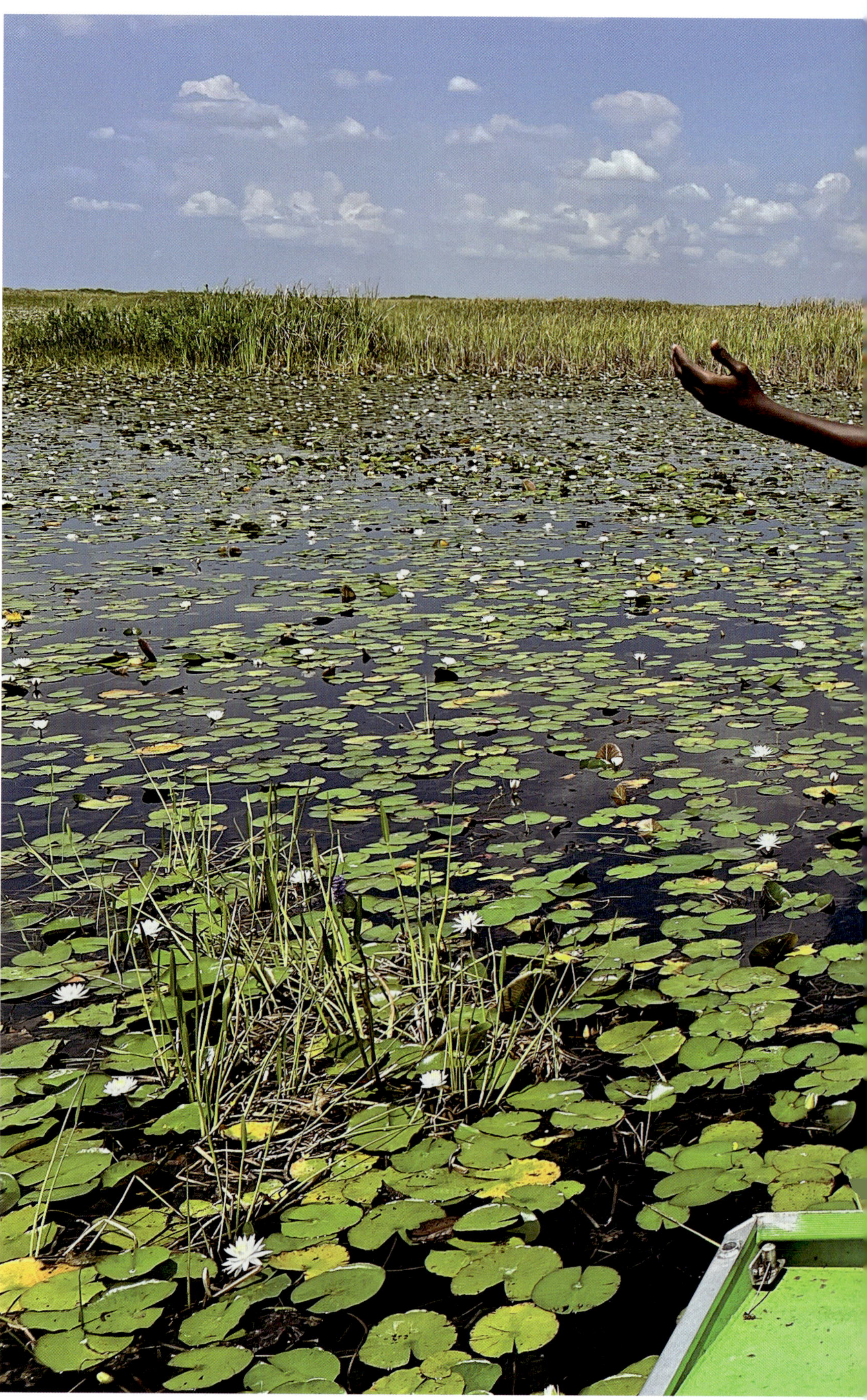

ERIKA LARSEN, PHOTO CAMP STAFF / FLORIDA, U.S.A. 2022

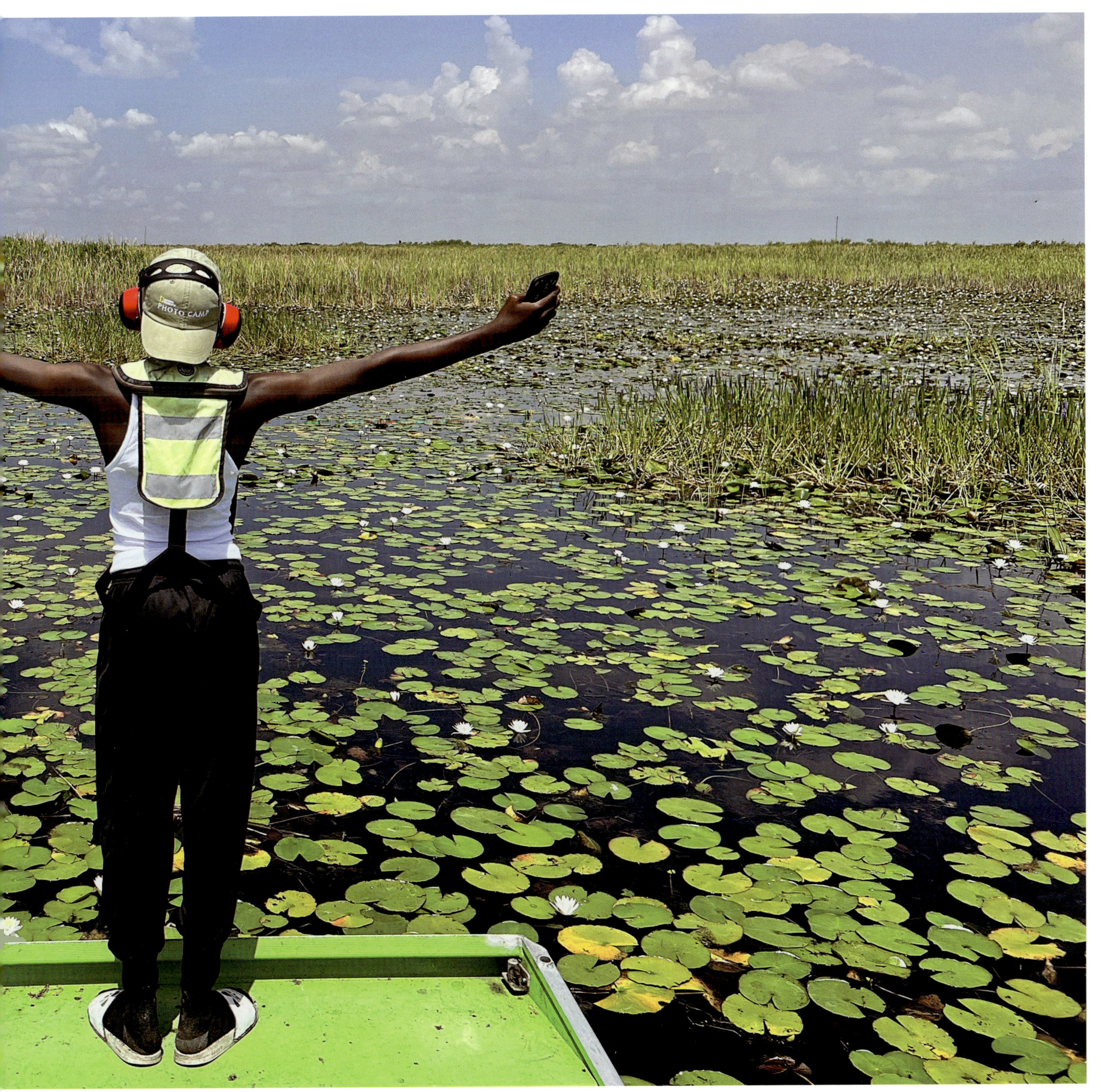
PHOTO CAMP

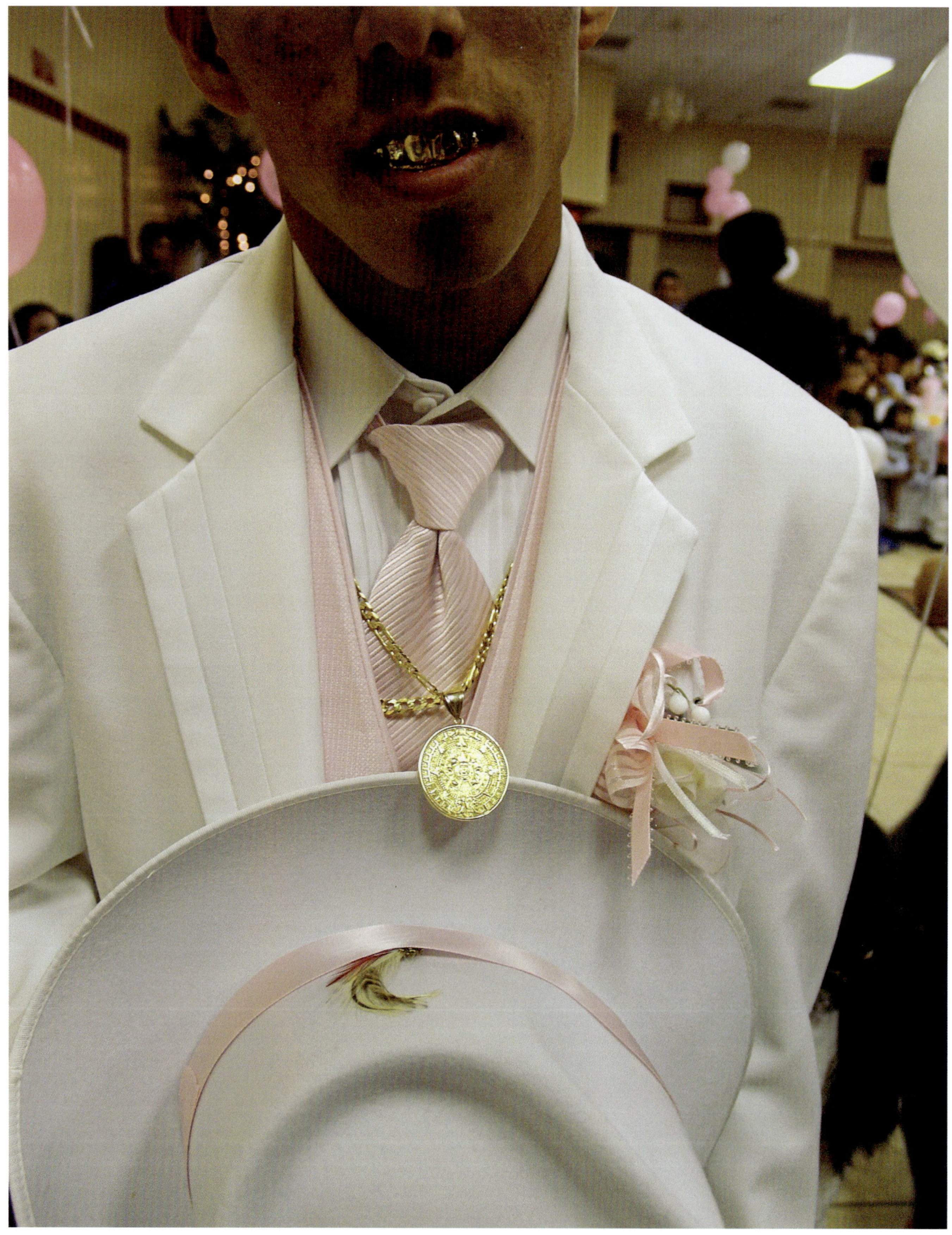

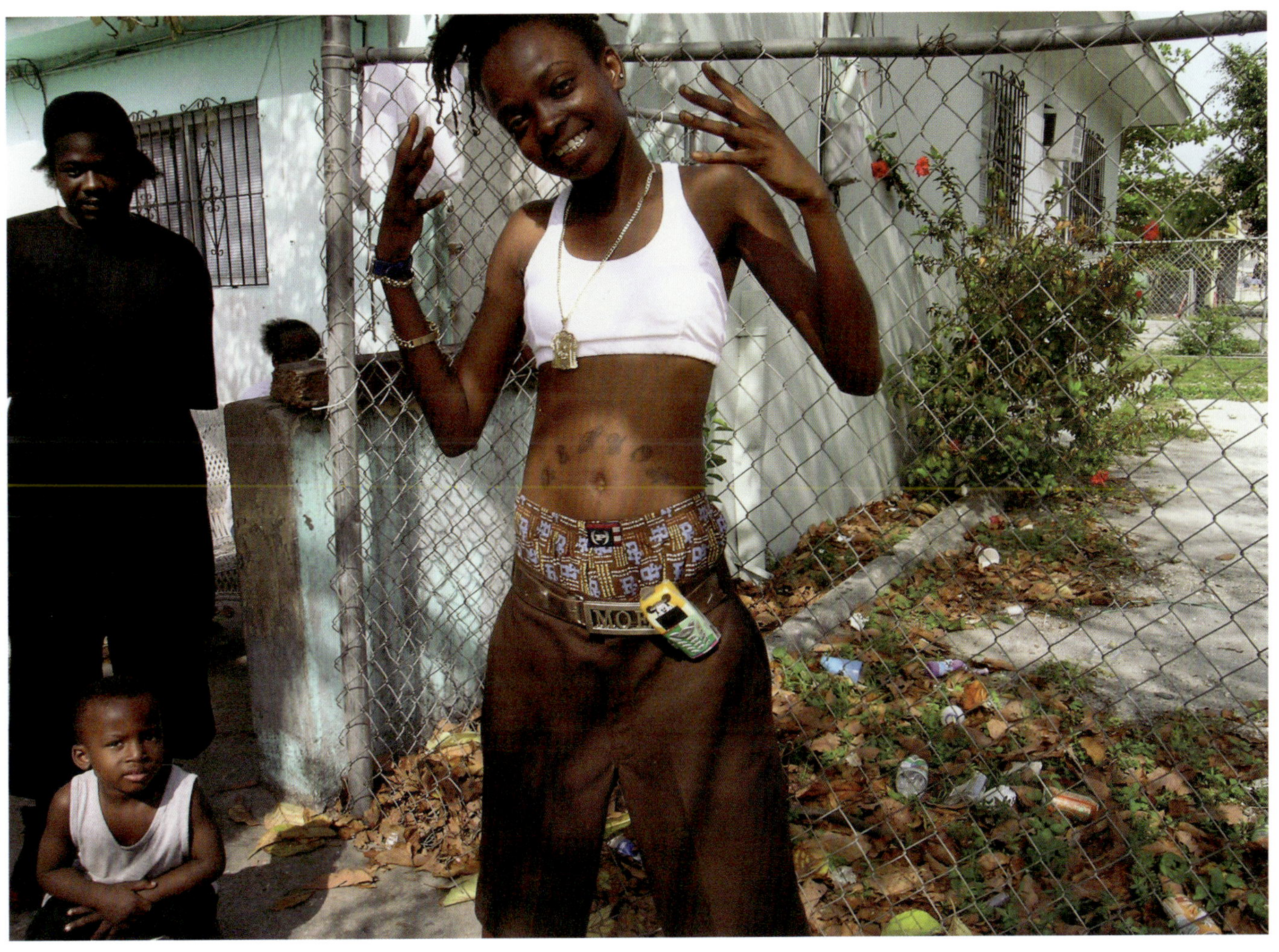

ABOVE: **LINDA THERVE / FLORIDA, U.S.A. 2005** OPPOSITE: **ILIANA GUTIERREZ / FLORIDA, U.S.A. 2006**

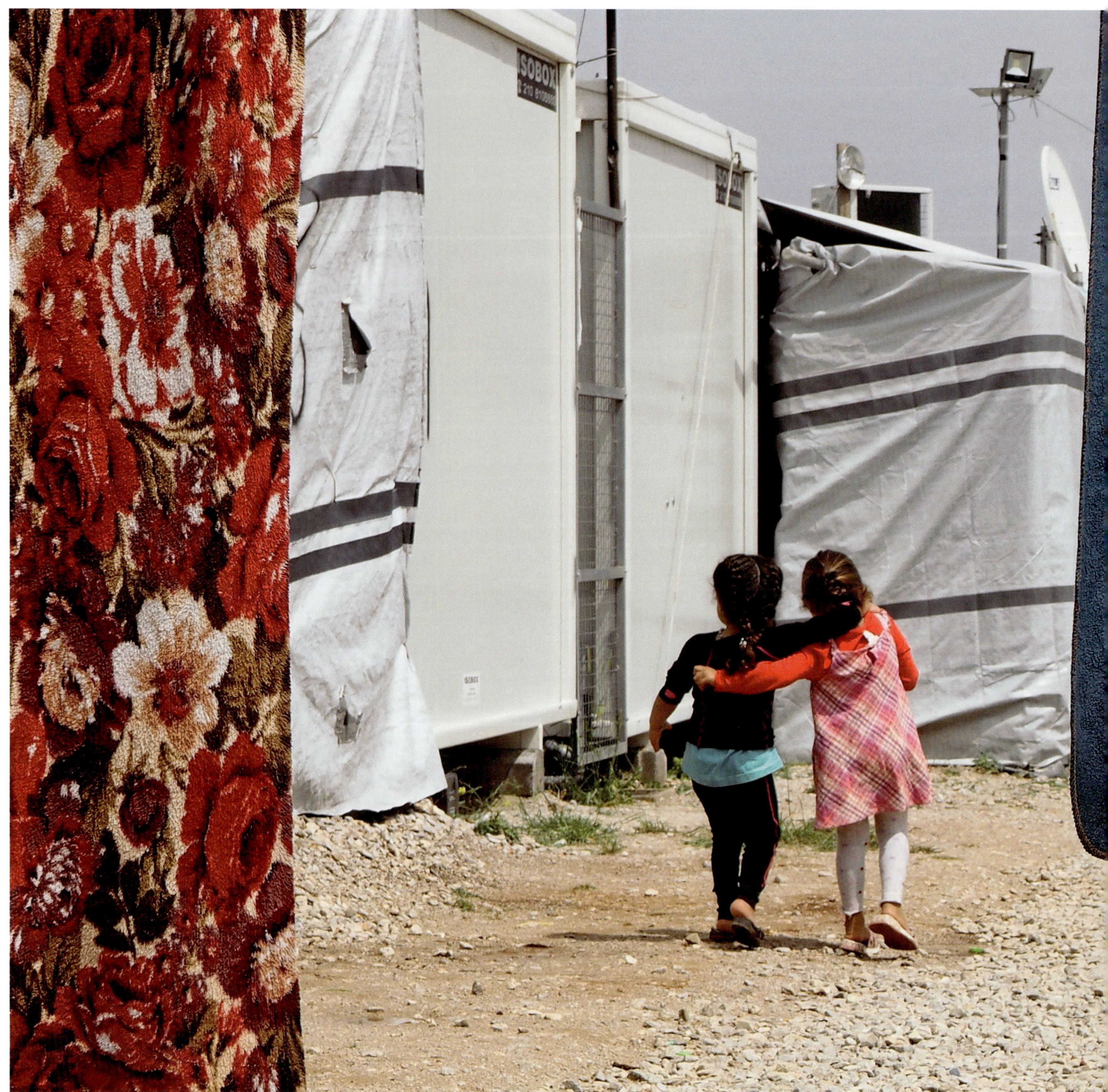
SOBOX

OMID AHMADI / GREECE 2017

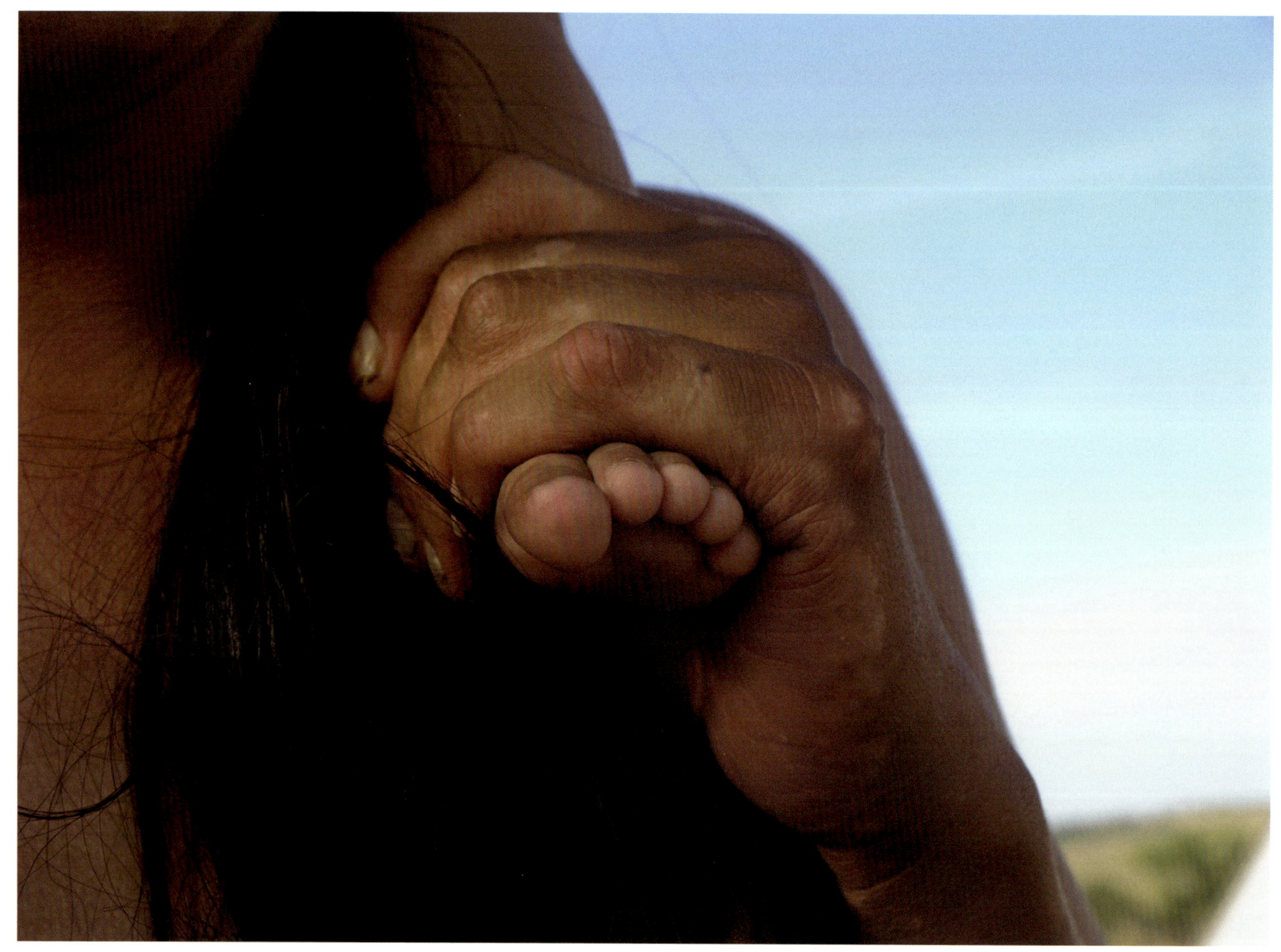

JASON TWO BULLS / SOUTH DAKOTA, U.S.A. 2009

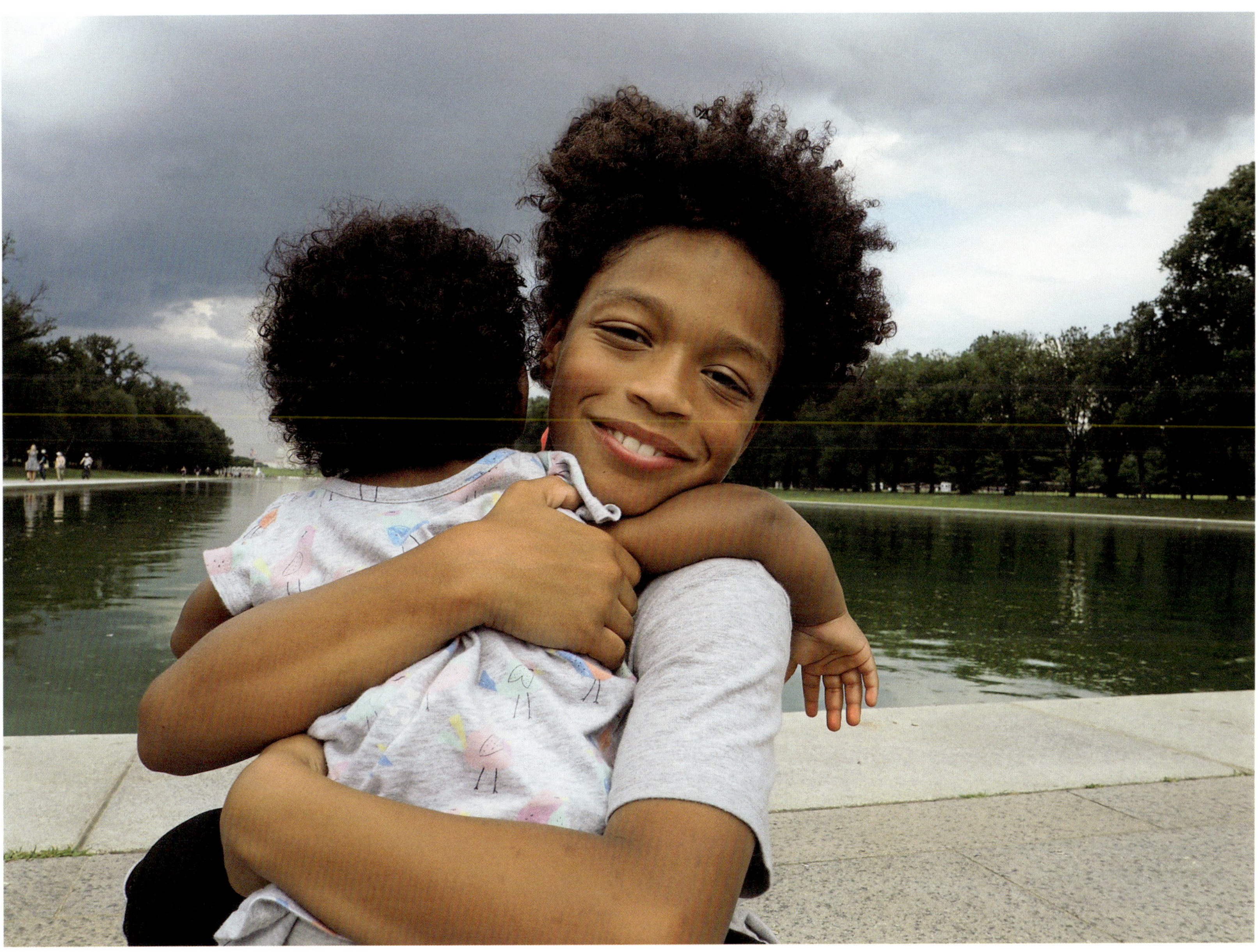

NAUM KHAN LUN / WASHINGTON, D.C., U.S.A., MASTER CLASS 2019

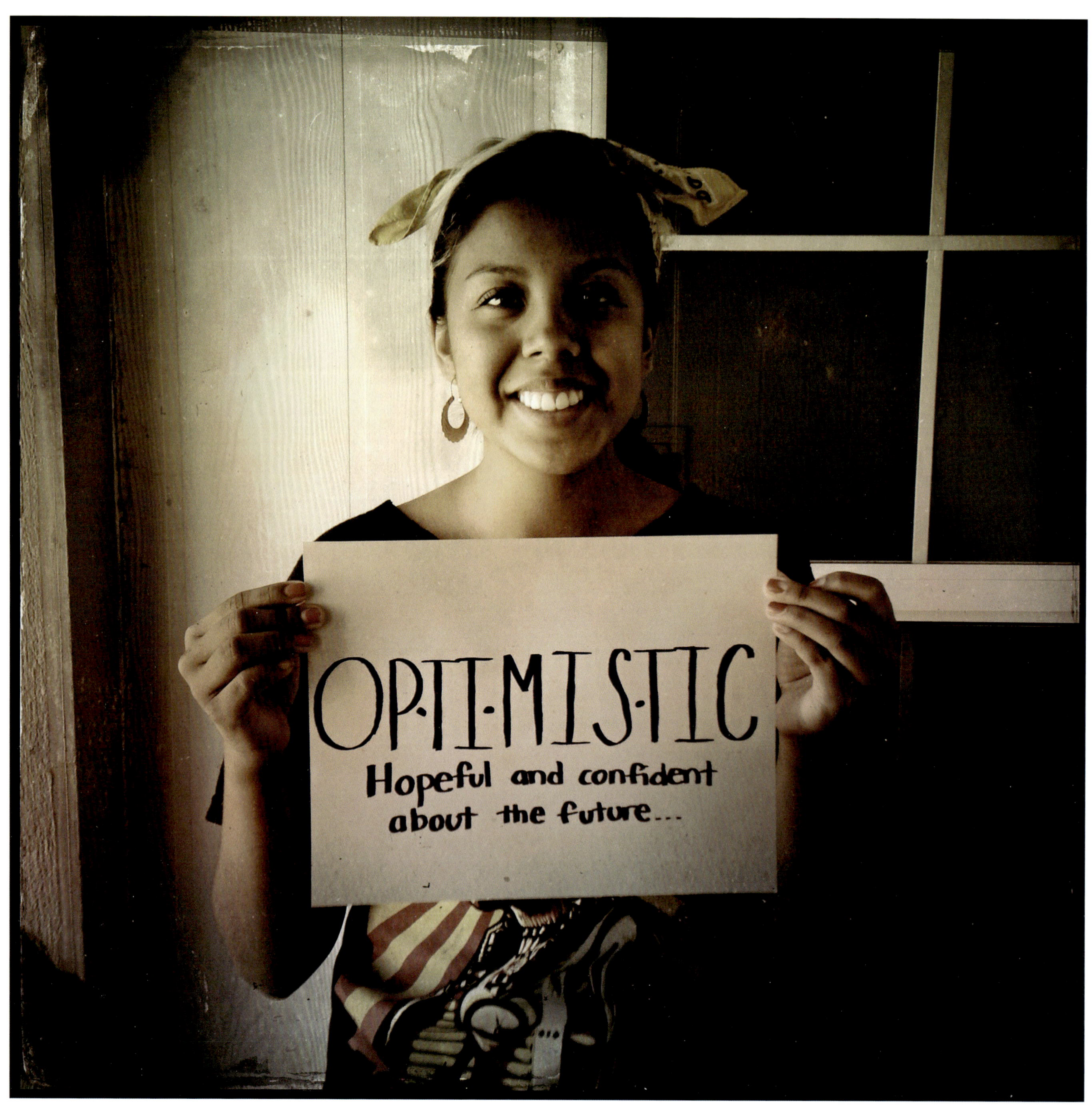
OP·TI·MIS·TIC
Hopeful and confident
about the future...

"My gift to the world? Optimism."

—PACHYNNE IGNACIO, ARIVACA, ARIZONA, U.S.A. 2014

PACHYNNE IGNACIO / ARIZONA, U.S.A. 2014

The Solace of Photography
Ranita Roy

IT WASN'T A STRAIGHT OR EASY PATH that brought Ranita Roy to central India to take photographs on a prestigious Magnum Foundation fellowship. This achievement might never have happened but for encouraging words from the right person when she was full of self-doubt.

Ranita attended a Photo Camp in 2018 in Kolkata, India. On the second day, when the students' photos were reviewed for the group on a large screen, National Geographic photographer Evgenia Arbugaeva deemed her a pro.

Arbugaeva has remained a mentor to Ranita, who is now a full-time photographer and filmmaker. She produced a story about sex workers for her Magnum Foundation project; other assignments have taken her to the Western Ghats mountain range to photograph wildlife. Ranita finds solace in the way photography allows her to live in the moment and takes her away from her cares. This has been true since she first tried using a small point-and-shoot camera back in 2015. She was suffering from depression then, and photography lifted her mood. Now it provides equilibrium when she worries about her financial responsibilities. Since her father had a debilitating stroke in 2018, Ranita has been the breadwinner in her family. "My whole family is on me," she said. "Sometimes I cry because there is no one to help me with this. But I try to keep a balance."

And she keeps following her dream.

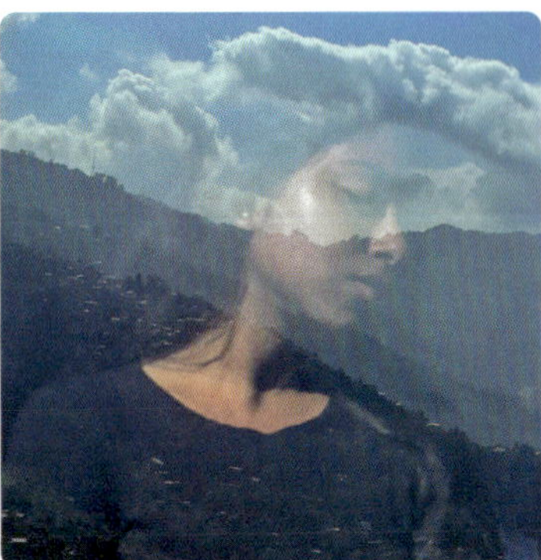

Ranita Roy was born in Andul, a small town near Kolkata, India. A documentary photographer and filmmaker, she describes photography as "a kind of meditation for me."

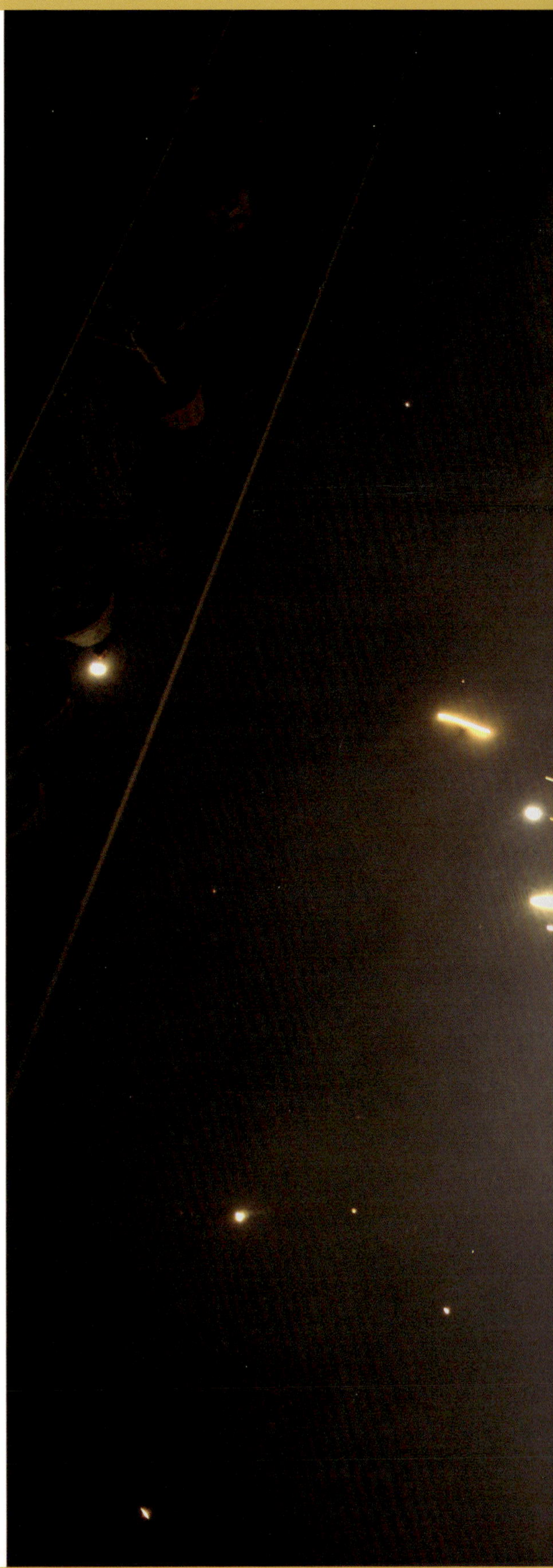

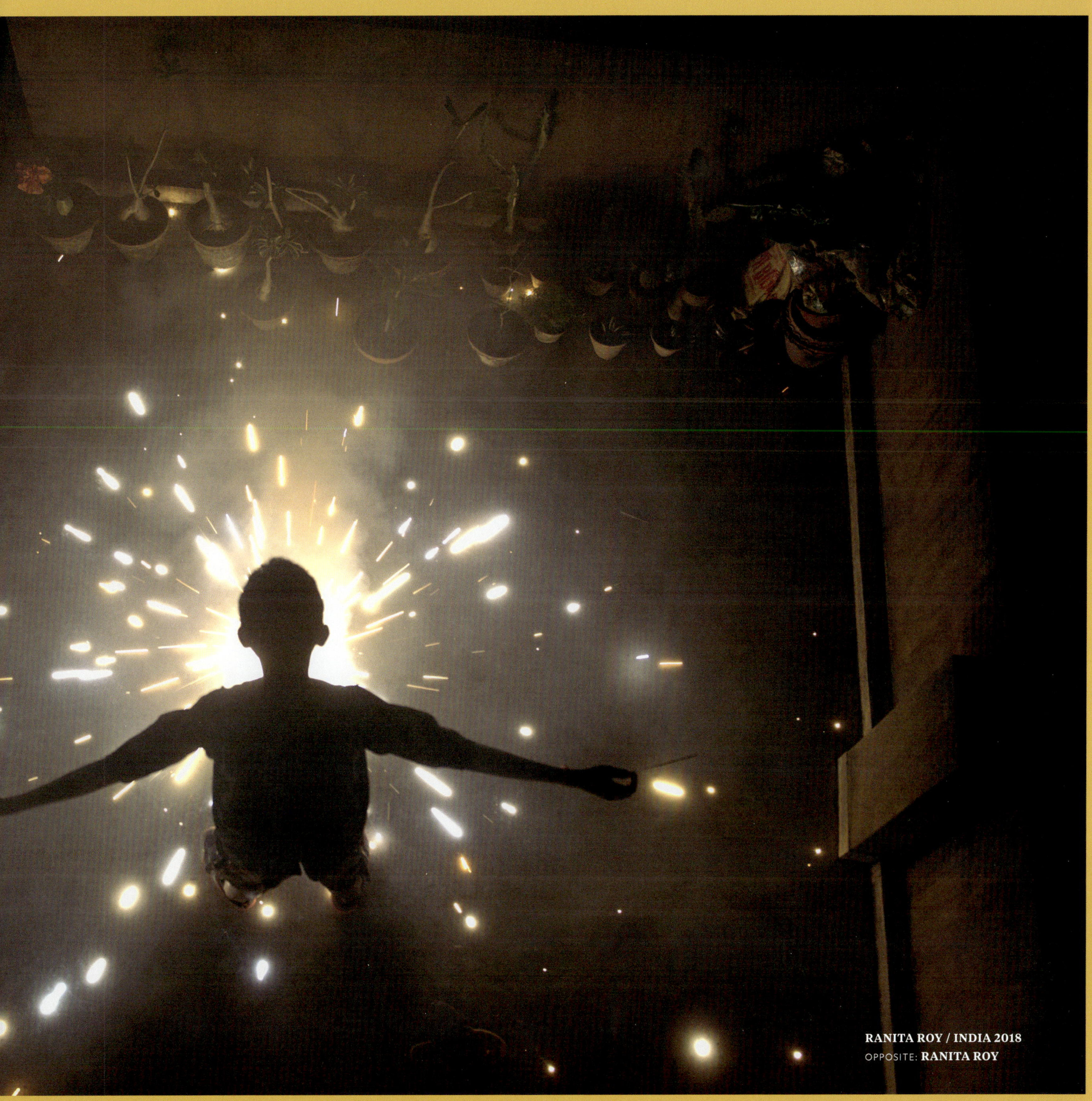

RANITA ROY / INDIA 2018
OPPOSITE: **RANITA ROY**

The Art of Truly Seeing

The image I have carried over the years is of two slender hands. There is tenderness in the way one supports the other; in the presence of a small callus near the thumb. The palm is both notepad and talisman. Written there in blue ink are simple facts that photographers know as fundamental to making an image, whether intimate or universal. These are words for beginners—ways of categorizing and simplifying the complexity of everything from the nuances of nature to the conflict within us: Portrait, Detail, Overall, Action. Choose one and begin.

The hands belonged to Naledi Kgoba, a youth in northern Botswana who was then becoming the man of his family after the death of his father. He had also suffered the loss of his mother and was being raised by his grandmother. Could Photo Camp provide the building blocks to facilitate Naledi's first steps into adulthood?

Yes, it's that serious, this Photo Camp culture: five days of looking, creating, and forming community. Whether in Botswana, Moldova, the Pine Ridge Reservation in South Dakota, Haiti, or New Zealand, and regardless of language, gender identity, or religious beliefs, all those who pass through these photography workshops grow and change in fundamental ways.

That first day of camp in 2009, Naledi shared this: "I don't have house. I still sleep with my brother. His name is Willson, and when I am at home I like to play football and read many kinds of book such as wildness books, English poetry books and Setswana story books."

Each camp begins with a handful of photographers welcoming children or young adults. Surely we all remember that feeling: anxious and vibrating with restless energy at the beginning of the unknown.

Together, we will not just examine but also practice the art of storytelling. And beyond that, we will strive to practice the act of truly seeing, observing patiently—ideally without judgment. Each skill is different and critical to photography. Each process is essential to understanding self and the world in which we survive—and hopefully, celebrate.

Both groups carry trauma; this is the baseline of what staff and students share, though it is rarely discussed. The youth that Photo Camps collaborate with are often displaced in some way. The professional photographers who teach and learn from them also carry trauma, having spent years documenting not just quotidian life but also conflict, cruelty, loss. We may be different in age and culture, but these chasms can be crossed. The bridge that we offer is the language of photography—a creative practice that can help reveal meaning and purpose in all that we have seen and will experience.

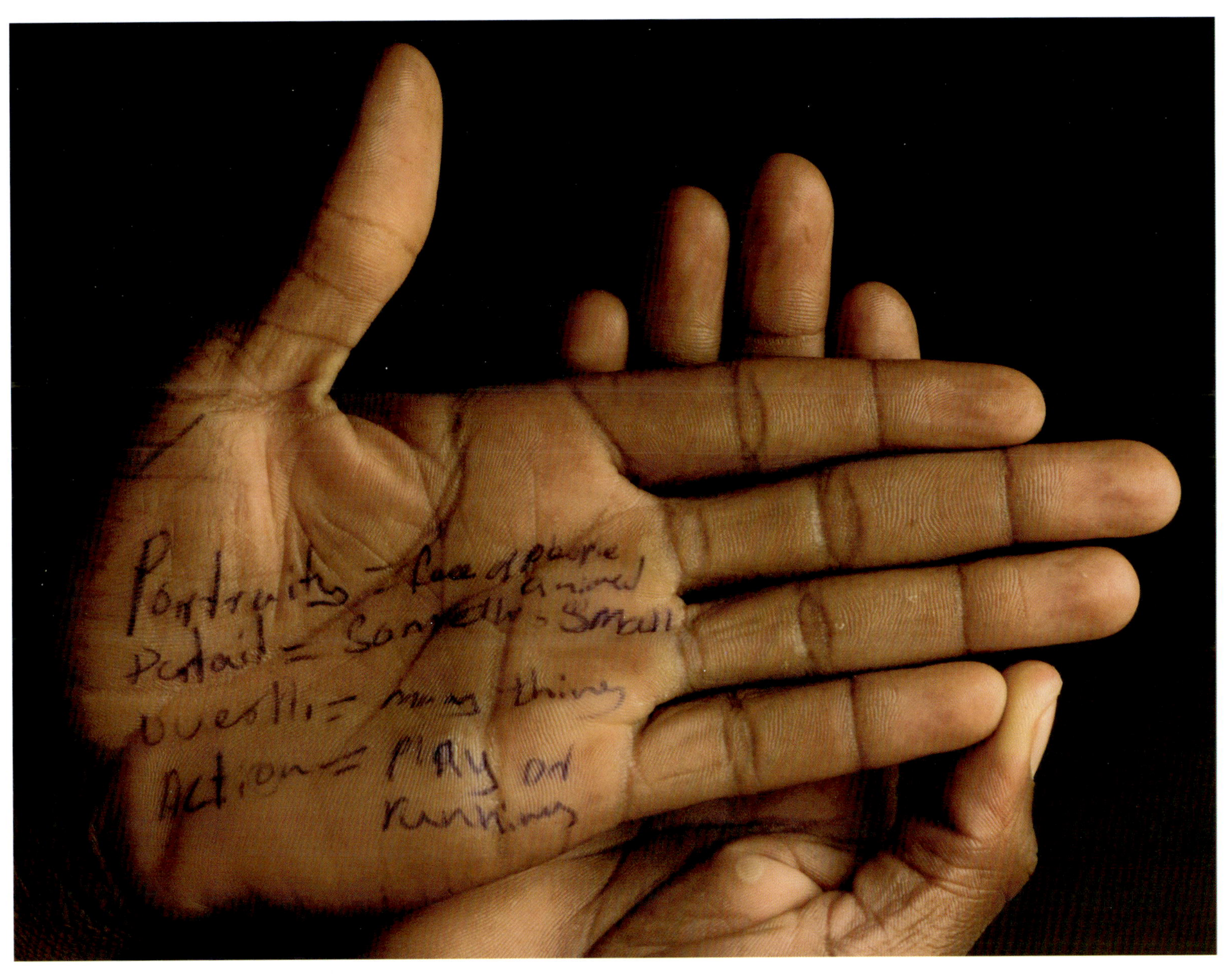

LYNN JOHNSON, PHOTO CAMP STAFF / BOTSWANA 2009

And now there is a camera in your hands and a stranger asking you to tell your story. The world shifts. Each image is a clue as to how life could be different, lighter, deeper, more joyful. And we are all listening.

Every camp begins as a circle of strangers. Then, at warp speed, a family is formed through the passing of ideas, stories, cameras, moments ... back and forth, hand to eye. This is the essence of Photo Camp: sharing the true self. In the end, we are all liberated by the trust that comes from taking time to truly know another person and, for an instant, see through their eyes.

My personal photographs from the Botswana camp show an arc of shared experience, from children in look-alike ponchos huddled in an open-air safari vehicle to staff and children crying as they cling to each other in goodbye. The single-engine plane waits on the tarmac, still empty. Last embraces, then liftoff. As a rule, I do not cry; I'm steeled by a lifetime of leaving. But now, in the quiet of my home, revisiting these memories, I'm crying as I type. Is it possible that I'm still learning from those children I met in Botswana 13 years ago?

In between welcome and farewell were moments of dancing, lying on the ground to get the lizard's-eye view, riding through grasslands searching for elephant dung, flinging cameras in the air to capture a chance frame, and singing. I remember the ride back to base camp: It was as if the students' innocent voices and unchecked exuberance were powering the truck forward.

The goal of this camp was to challenge the children's learned perspective that nature is the enemy. For five days the students climbed anthills that dwarfed them and wandered across the savanna, amber in the evening light. They were a world away from their villages. Naledi's last writings about his experience reflect this transformation: "This program, it has changed my mind [about] protecting our environment."

When each program ends, it feels that we always depart too soon and never leave enough behind—cameras, support, ideas—to change the direction of the children's lives. But Photo Camp is an offering, a means to squint into the future. I believe photography can be a way of life, and the camera a tool to help negotiate that balance between self and other.

Photo Camp is not an unselfish mission; we professionals gain as much from the exchange as the students, if not more. They remind us why we have chosen this profession. We are jaded; they have fresh eyes. We offer wisdom, but they inspire.

Remembering now how Naledi and the entire Botswana Photo Camp family grew together, I wonder if this vital program just might have the power to tilt this world toward joy.

—**LYNN JOHNSON,** NATIONAL GEOGRAPHIC PHOTOGRAPHER

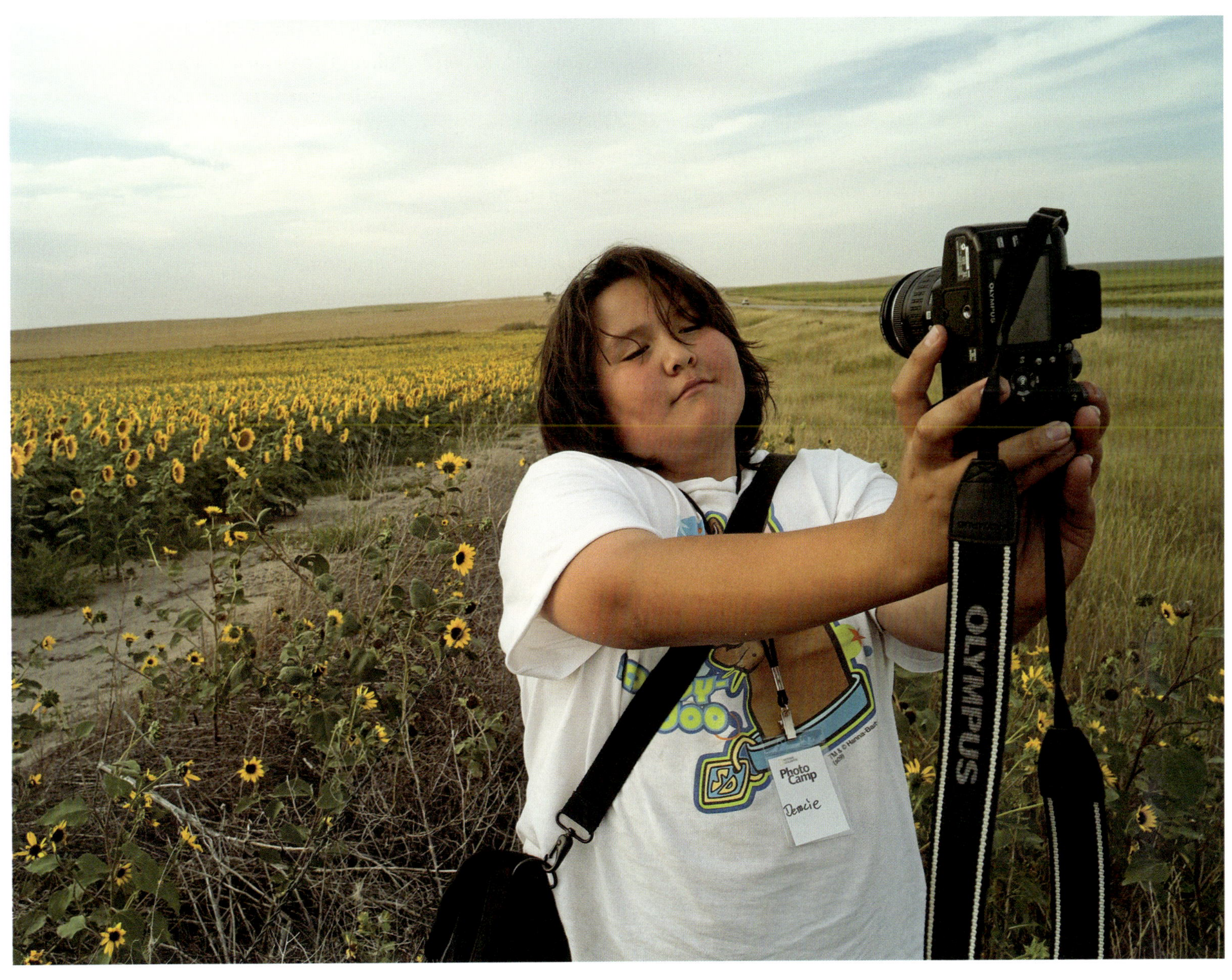

LYNN JOHNSON, PHOTO CAMP STAFF / SOUTH DAKOTA, U.S.A. 2009

Acknowledgments

COLLABORATION IS AT THE CORE of any Photo Camp project, and this book is the culmination of 20 years spent building what we refer to as the Photo Camp family. This family consists of the many mentors, staff, and partners who supported this seed of an idea in 2003, and who understood that young people's stories can connect us to our hopes for the future.

We're grateful to the partners who have made it possible for Photo Camp to work in so many locations around the world. Without your connections to students and their families, we would not have been able to build the trust and relationships that were crucial to our ability to understand our students' backgrounds and communities.

The last decade of the Photo Camp journey has been transformed by the vision of Kaitlin Yarnall, Rachael Strecher, and other leaders at the National Geographic Society. Thank you for believing in me. The program wouldn't be possible without the tireless efforts of the Photo Camp team: Jess Elfadl, Will Thompson, Dani Cales, Paul Nwulu, Maryam Shuja, and Ally Moreo.

I've had the honor of working beside an incredible team of photographers and Photo Camp staff who have given so much of their energy and creativity to our students: late-night edits, long days in the field, sincere concern and care for these precious stories and lives. To name just a few: Sam Abell, Luján Agusti, Evgenia Arbugaeva, Tony Ayigah, Jahawi Bertolli, Dominic Bracco, Jon Brack, Andrea Bruce, Stephen Crowley, William Daniels, Meghan Dhaliwal, Ronan Donovan, Stacy Gold, David Guttenfelder, Sara Hylton, Tailyr Irvine, Lynn Johnson, Ed Kashi, Erika Larsen, John Marshall, Matt Moyer, Matthieu Paley, Federico Pardo, Susan Poulton, Sadie Quarrier, Susan Reeve, Tara Roberts, Paul Salopek, Clifton Shipway, Amy Toensing, Tyrone Turner, Malaika Vaz, Jim Webb. I'm thankful for all of you. There are many others who are integral parts of the Photo Camp team, and it would take pages and pages to list you all.

Many thanks to the talented book team of Victoria Pope, Hilary Black, Gabriela Capasso, Elisa Gibson, and Adrian Coakley, who created a book that brings the spirit of Photo Camp to life.

But the heart of this family is, of course, the many young people we've had the privilege of knowing, working with, and mostly learning from over all these years. Ankita, Saba, Bullen, Raouf, Cathy, Latamai, Camden, Ayla, Choki, Te Aho, Zazu, Sartre: I remember what you have taught me. I'm grateful that we've remained connected, and that you've continued to share your stories with me. Your names listed here represent the thousands of young people who have touched my heart since the beginning of this journey. You have all showed me the beauty of your communities and the power of each of your individual gifts to the world.

You are our letter to the future.

THANK YOU ALL, ***Kirsten Elstner***

Photo Camp Faculty, 2003–23

Sam Abell
Luján Agusti
Karine Aigner
Evgenia Arbugaeva
Shin Arunrugstichai
Tomas Ayuso
Anush Babajanyan
Ahmed Badr
Jahawi Bertolli
Marcus Bleasdale
Dominic Bracco II
Jon Brack
Andrea Bruce
Mel Burford
David Burnett
Kitra Cahana
Thalefang Charles
Adrian Coakley
Stephen Crowley
William Daniels
Reza Deghati
Meghan Dhaliwal
Jay Dickman
Ronan Donovan
David Doubilet
Kirsten Elstner
Citlali Fabián
Melissa Farlow
Bert Fox
Stacy Gold
Annie Griffiths
David Guttenfelder
Robin Hammond
Dave Harp
David Alan Harvey
Sebastián Hidalgo
Sara Hylton
Tailyr Irvine
Todd James
Lynn Johnson
Whitney Johnson
Te Aho Jordan
Ed Kashi
Karen Kasmauski
Alexa Keefe
Carol King Woodward
Jonathan Kingston
Elizabeth Krist
Emory Kristof
Arati Kumar-Rao
Laura Lakeway
Erika Larsen
Kirsten Luce
Markus Martinez Burman
Esther Ruth Mbabazi
Jeanne Modderman
Koketso Mookodi
Rosem Morton
Matt Moyer
Pete Muller
Kurt Mutchler
Ashima Narain
Randy Olson
Maurice Oniango
Matthieu Paley
Jorge Panchoaga
Oksana Parafeniuk
Federico Pardo
Susan Poulton
Sadie Quarrier
Chris Rainier
Eli Reed
Susan Reeve
Hannah Reyes Morales
Tara Roberts
Paul Salopek
Joel Sartore
Stephanie Sinclair
John Stanmeyer
Gena Steffens
Asha Stuart
Anastasia Taylor-Lind
Mark Thiessen
Amy Toensing
Raul Touzon
Tyrone Turner
Ivan Valencia
Anand Varma
Malaika Vaz
Pau Villanueva
Danielle Villasana
Carlton Ward
Susan Welchman
Jessie Wender
Dan Westergren
Julie Winokur
Prasenjeet Yadav
Kiliii Yuyan
Victor Zea

Photo Camp Partner Organizations, 2003–23

Academy for Educational Development
Air New Zealand
America's Cup Healthy Oceans Project
Appalachian Trail Conservancy
Asian College of Journalism
Bayfront Maritime
Bhutan Centre for Media and Democracy
Blacks of the Chesapeake
Blackstone Ranch Institute
Boys and Girls Clubs of Philadelphia
Boys and Girls Clubs of San Francisco
Centro Fotográfico Manuel Álvarez Bravo and Centro de las Artes de San Agustín
Chesapeake Bay Foundation
Dian Fossey Gorilla Fund International
Dream Project of Virginia
Drexel University
EARTH University, Costa Rica
Equal Access International
Finish
Good Shepherd Agricultural Mission
Government of Hong Kong
Houston Grand Opera
International Center of Photography
International Medical Corps
Internews
Island Institute
John F. Kennedy Center for the Performing Arts
Knight Foundation
La Vaca Independiente
Latin American Youth Center
Lenfest Institute for Journalism
Lowlander Center
Loyola University New Orleans
Mercy Corps
Miami Herald
Minnesota State University
Mohawk Valley Resource Center for Refugees
National Oceanic and Atmospheric Administration (NOAA)
Native Village of Quinhagak
NatureBridge
New York Times
Newcomers High School, Queens
Nobel Peace Center
Norwegian Red Cross
Office of the United Nations High Commissioner for Refugees
Okavango Wilderness Project and Wild Bird Trust
Osa Conservation
Out of Eden Walk
PopTech
Project Amal ou Salam
Project CETI
Project Rhino
Qatar Foundation International
Ramana's Garden
Refugee Youth Project of Baltimore City Community College
Restore the Delta
SALT Institute for Documentary Studies
San Francisco Chronicle
Sandro Demaio Foundation
Sanjhi NGO
School of Leadership, Afghanistan
Selinda Preserve and Children in the Wilderness
SuAnne Big Crow Boys and Girls Club
Talking Eyes Media
Times-Picayune (New Orleans)
University of Miami
University of Texas Rio Grande Valley
U.S. Embassy Barbados
U.S. Embassy Bosnia
USAID
Walter Anderson Museum of Art
Youth Diving With a Purpose

About the National Geographic Society

The National Geographic Society is a global nonprofit that uses the power of science, exploration, education, and storytelling to illuminate and protect the wonder of our world.

Since 1888, the National Geographic Society has driven impact by identifying and investing in a global community of Explorers: leading changemakers in science, education, storytelling, conservation, and technology. National Geographic Explorers help bring our mission to life by defining some of the most critical challenges of our time, uncovering new knowledge, advancing new solutions, and inspiring transformative change in our world.

To learn more about the Explorers we invest in and the efforts we support, visit *natgeo.com/impact*.

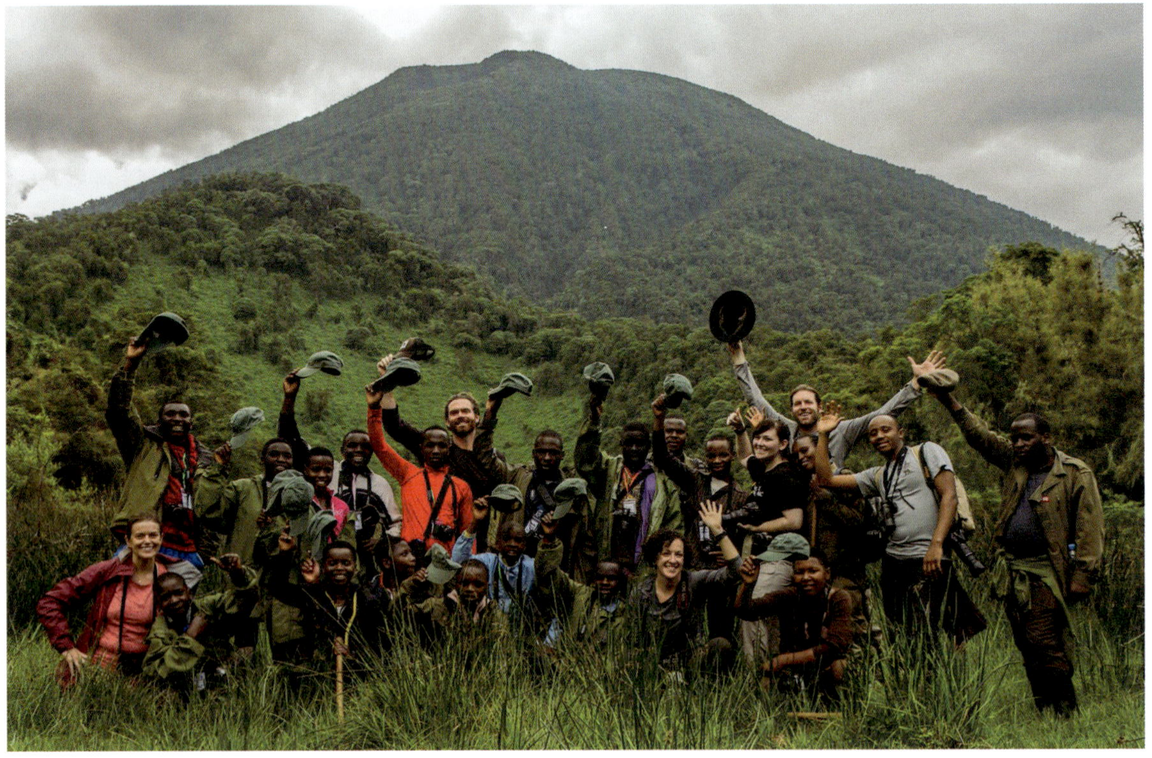

RONAN DONOVAN, PHOTO CAMP STAFF / RWANDA 2016

Illustrations Credits

All images courtesy of the National Geographic Society.

Cover photo: Aye May Zan, Myanmar 2018

Back cover photo: Shalia Pohaikealohaikapilimakamae Henderson, Hawaii, U.S.A. 2021

Page 9 (L to R): Becky Hale, Photo Camp Staff, Washington, D.C., U.S.A. 2003 | Branden Wilkinson, Georgia, U.S.A. 2004 | Willy Zhang, California, U.S.A. 2005

Page 10 (L to R): Susan Reeve, Photo Camp Staff, Uganda 2006 | Diana Lescas Luna, Mexico 2007 | Lois Raimonda, Photo Camp Staff, South Dakota, U.S.A. 2008

Page 11 (L to R): Kesetselemang Molao, Botswana 2009 | Ahmat Mahamat Bilal, Chad 2010 | Cori Granger, Virginia, U.S.A. 2011

Page 12 (L to R): Hina Gul, Pakistan 2012 | Hanif Ullah, Washington, D.C., U.S.A. 2013 | Stacy Gold, Photo Camp Staff, Arizona, U.S.A. 2014

Page 13 (L to R): Omar Al Zoubi, Jordan 2015 | Odalys Emilia Orozco Acosta, Cuba 2016 | Alexandra Panagiotou, Greece 2017

Page 14 (L to R): Isaac Nelly, Uganda 2018 | Jigme Namgyal, Bhutan 2019 | Nastasia Caole, Alaska, U.S.A. 2020

Page 15 (L to R): Nazarene Winston, Dominica 2021 | Esther Ruth Mbabazi, Botswana 2022 | Erika Larsen, New Zealand 2023

Since 1888, the National Geographic Society has funded more than 14,000 research, conservation, education, and storytelling projects around the world. National Geographic Partners distributes a portion of the funds it receives from your purchase to National Geographic Society to support programs including the conservation of animals and their habitats.

National Geographic Partners, LLC
1145 17th Street NW
Washington, DC 20036-4688 USA

Get closer to National Geographic Explorers and photographers, and connect with our global community. Join us today at nationalgeographic.org/joinus

For rights or permissions inquiries, please contact National Geographic Books Subsidiary Rights: bookrights@natgeo.com

Financially supported by the National Geographic Society.

Library of Congress Cataloging-in-Publication Data
Names: National Geographic Photo Camp, author. | Yarnall, Kaitlin, writer of foreword. | Elstner, Kirsten, writer of introduction. | National Geographic Society (U.S.), editor.
Title: Photo Camp stories : our world through the lens of young photographers / National Geographic ; foreword by Kaitlin Yarnall ; introduction by Kirsten Elstner.
Description: Washington, D.C. : National Geographic, [2023] | Summary: "This lush coffee table book celebrates 20 years of National Geographic's legendary photo camp program"-- Provided by publisher.
Identifiers: LCCN 2023016520 | ISBN 9781426223679 (hardback)
Subjects: LCSH: Photography, Artistic. | Photography--Study and teaching--Activity programs.
Classification: LCC TR655 .N383 2023 | DDC 770.76--dc23/eng/20230510
LC record available at https://lccn.loc.gov/20

ISBN: 978-1-4262-2367-9

Printed in Canada

23/FC/1

TO YOU WHO'S READING

I DON'T KNOW IF
YOU're SHY OR NOT
BUT IF YOU ARE
TRY TO SPEAK UP
WITH THESE PEOPLE.
THEY WILL DEFINITELY
LISTEN TO YOU.
ALSO, TAKE GOOD
CARE OF THE CAMERA.

■ Students tuck notes into their camera bags to be passed on to the person who will receive it at the next Photo Camp. This note was written by a young photographer in Botswana and later opened by a student in New Zealand, part of a continuous stream of connection throughout the Photo Camp community around the world.